W9-BWF-884

Taxing Ourselves,
5th edition

Taxing Ourselves, 5th edition

A Citizen's Guide to the Debate over Taxes

Joel Slemrod and Jon Bakija

The MIT Press
Cambridge, Massachusetts
London, England

This book was set in Palatino LT Std by Toppan Best-set Premedia Limited. Printed and bound in the United States of America.

Library of Congress Cataloging-in-Publication Data is available.

ISBN: 978-0-262-03567-5

10   9   8   7   6   5   4   3   2   1

Contents

Preface

Albert Einstein is reputed to have said that "the hardest thing in the world to understand is the income tax."[1] But understand it we must because it is a critical part of how government affects the lives of Americans. Unfortunately, though, when tax policy enters the political arena, the subtleties of the key issues are usually lost in self-serving arguments and misleading simplifications. Academic treatments of the subject are of little help to the vast majority of citizens who are unfamiliar with the jargon and methods of economics.

This book is an attempt to bridge the gap between sound bites and treatises. It lays out what is known and not known about how taxes affect the economy, offers guidelines for evaluating tax systems, and provides enough information to evaluate both the current income tax system and the leading proposals to replace or reform it. We have attempted to present this information in a clear, nontechnical way and to avoid misleading the reader by oversimplifying. We do not conclude with our own pet plan for improving the U.S. tax system, which would require applying not only our professional expertise about the economics of taxation but also our values about such issues as what constitutes a fair system, as well. This book does, however, provide readers with enough background to make informed judgments about how we should tax ourselves.

We have been gratified by the positive response from readers of the first four editions of *Taxing Ourselves*, especially those who have used this book as a textbook or a supplementary reading in economics, accounting, and law courses. The positive e-mails we've received from citizens who have learned from this citizen's guide have also been encouraging. At the MIT Press, first Terry Vaughn, then John Covell, and most recently Emily Taber have been helpful throughout the development process and supportive of our desire to update the book with new editions. This fifth edition has been extensively revised to incorporate the latest data, empirical evidence, and tax law through late 2015, along with selected coverage of new developments through September 2016. It offers new coverage of many different topics, such as recently developed tax reform packages, the proposals of the 2016 presidential candidates, expanded coverage of international tax issues, and recent enforcement initiatives. We have been fortunate to have at our disposal the resources of the Office of Tax Policy Research (OTPR) at the University of Michigan, where Joel is a professor at the Stephen M. Ross School of Business and in the economics department and Jon was a graduate student during the writing of the first edition. Jon has since moved to the economics department at Williams College, where he is a professor of economics. We owe a special debt to those colleagues who read and made extensive comments on an early draft of the book—Gerard Brannon, Leonard Burman, Don Fullerton, Louis Kaplow, and three anonymous reviewers. We also benefited from the insightful comments and suggestions of three anonymous reviewers of the fifth edition. Mary Ceccanese, research process coordinator at OTPR, reviewed the entire manuscript (five times!) and has provided encouragement and advice from start to finish. Julie Skelton, Brent Smith, and Monica Young helped to track down information and citations for the first edition, and Varsha Venkatesh at OTPR was instrumental in updating the second and third editions. Chris Lyddy of the Brookings Institution provided invaluable research assistance on the third edition, as did Marcus Choudhary and Alexander Gribov on the fourth edition. Garrett Anstreicher, Patrick Aquino, Melissa Caplen, Tiffany Chang, Regina Im, Marissa Kimsey, Josephat Koima, James Pappas, and Brian McGrail provided outstanding research assistance for the fifth edition. Finally, Joel would like to thank Ava, Annie, and Jonny for providing support, love, and challenging questions about the relationship between individuals and the government. Jon would like to thank Rebeccah, Miriam, Jude, and his parents for their love, support, and understanding.

1   Introduction

As it has for the last three and a half decades, taxation continues to play a central role in the debate over economic policy in the United States. This is not surprising, because no other economic issue (and perhaps no issue at all) more clearly defines the differences between the two major political parties. The modern tax policy era began with the presidency of Ronald Reagan, who made large tax cuts a linchpin of his campaign and then presided over a historically large tax cut in 1981, followed in his second term by perhaps the most ambitious income tax reform in American history—the Tax Reform Act of 1986—which significantly broadened the tax base by removing many deductions and loopholes in exchange for lower tax rates. Tax changes in 1990 and 1993 raised rates on upper-income taxpayers in an effort to reduce budget deficits. In the mid-1990s, many politicians and experts were calling for a fundamental overhaul—even complete abolition—of the income tax and the Internal Revenue Service. Proposals to replace the income tax with a "flat tax" or a national sales tax began to appear in Congress and in the platforms of presidential hopefuls.[1]

The presidency of George W. Bush took Reagan's first-term approach a step further by enacting in 2001 large phased-in cuts in both the income tax and estate tax. This was followed in 2003 by reductions in the taxation of dividends and capital gains and an accelerated implementation of the tax cuts enacted in 2001.

The financial crisis of 2008 and subsequent "great recession" drastically changed the terms of tax policy debates. Tax cuts figured prominently in the stimulus packages of 2008 and 2009, where the policy criteria shifted to what kind of tax cuts would produce the biggest "bang per buck," generated by getting people to spend, rather than save, the extra income from the tax cuts. The combination of the recession and the revenue cost of the financial sector bail-outs and stimulus packages led to massive fiscal deficits, adding to already worrisome long-term fiscal imbalances.

Barack Obama was elected president in the midst of the financial crisis and an economy in free-fall. He helped craft the stimulus-driven tax cuts, but then had to confront the fact that all of the Bush-era tax cuts were scheduled to expire in 2011. He had campaigned on extending all of these tax cuts except for those that applied to taxpayers with income over about $250,000, but tax increases of any kind were difficult to justify in such a fragile economy. As the extension of the Bush tax cuts grew near, the political environment had changed as well, because the 2010 mid-term elections brought a Republican majority to the House of Representatives, with many of the newly elected members adamantly opposed to any tax increases. Finally, in December 2010 all the tax cuts were extended for just two more years, assuring that a future Congress would soon have to revisit which of these changes to accept and which to reverse.

Looking ahead, an aging population and rising medical costs imply that promised spending on Social Security and Medicare will greatly exceed currently scheduled taxes for those programs, meaning that some combination of massive tax increases and substantial cutbacks in promised benefits will likely be required eventually. In January of 2010, President Obama appointed a bipartisan advisory commission to make recommendations about addressing the tax system and long-term fiscal imbalance. The commission came up with a proposal to cut $4 trillion from the deficit over a ten-year horizon. However, the commission failed to receive enough votes from its own members for it to be forwarded to Congress, and its tax reform proposals, which included lowering income tax rates while eliminating many tax loopholes, abolishing the alternative minimum tax, a radical revamping of the mortgage interest deduction, and an increase of 15 cents per gallon in the federal gas tax, faded into obscurity.

Although it is clear that conservative Republicans favor low, and lower, tax collections, what kind of tax reform they favor is much less clear. In 2008, one prominent House Republican, Paul Ryan (R-WI), proposed as part of his Roadmap for America a stunningly radical tax plan that would allow individuals to choose between an income tax system similar to the current one or another plan with lower rates and virtually no deductions or credits; it would also have replaced the corporate income tax with an 8.5 percent value-added tax (albeit with a different name), the tax staple of most of the rest of the world. Once in control of the House, though, Ryan, the new chair of the House Budget Committee, championed a very different tax plan as part of the Path to Prosperity. It dropped both of the two key aspects of the Blueprint and instead featured an income tax with a top rate of 25 percent, compared to the existing 35 percent rate, while eliminating most deductions and credits.[2]

In the election of 2012 Paul Ryan was Mitt Romney's running mate, and by then he had substantially modified his ideas for tax reform. The Romney-Ryan ticket proposed to make the Bush tax cuts permanent and then to cut income tax rates by 20 percent beyond that, repeal the estate tax and the alternative minimum tax, and eliminate income taxes on dividends and interest for families earning below $200,000 annually ($100,000 for single filers), offsetting the revenue loss by eliminating unspecified deductions and credits. President Obama proposed to extend most of the tax cuts that had been enacted during 2001 through 2011 permanently for most people, but advocated elimination of most such tax cuts that applied to high-income people.

On January 1, 2013, after the election and just as the extension of the Bush tax cuts was set to expire, Congress passed the American Taxpayer Relief Act of 2012, which accepted most of the reduced rates passed under President Bush, but brought back the higher tax rates on upper income groups that pre-dated the Bush tax cuts. The top marginal tax rate on ordinary income reverted to 39.6 percent (up from 35 percent), and the top rate on capital gains and dividends rose to 20 percent, up from 15 percent. The top rate on estates was set at 40 percent, up from 35 percent. A linchpin of the last stimulus program, a cut in payroll taxes of 2 percent in 2011 and 2012, was not extended. After that, little new tax legislation was enacted until December 2015's Protecting Americans from Tax Hikes Act, which extended or made permanent a large number of expiring provisions in the tax code.

Debates over taxation heated up again in early 2016, as all of the leading candidates in the 2016 Republican presidential primaries proposed sweeping changes to the way we tax ourselves. Each candidate's tax plan involved a package of reforms, including cuts in tax rates and measures to broaden the tax base, but they also left many details to be spelled out. Here are just a few of the most striking elements of some of the plans that were proposed by candidates who lasted deep into the primary season. Donald Trump, the eventual nominee and president-elect, proposed a plan that would cut the top personal income tax rate from 39.6 percent to 25 percent, and cut the corporate income tax rate from 35 percent to 15 percent. Ted Cruz proposed abolishing the corporate income tax and the payroll tax, replacing them with a value-added tax (under a different name) at a rate of 16 percent, and adopting a flat 10 percent personal income tax. Marco Rubio's plan would have cut the top personal income tax rate to 35 percent and the corporate tax rate to 25 percent, integrated the corporate and personal income tax systems to remove double-taxation of corporate income, allowed businesses to "expense" (immediately deduct) the full cost of their investments, and created a $2,500 tax credit per child. All three of the candidates mentioned above proposed eliminating the estate tax.

The Urban-Brookings Tax Policy Center estimated that without accounting for any effects on economic growth, the revenue loss between 2016 and 2026 that would result from adopting these tax plans would amount to 4.0 percent of GDP for Trump, 3.6 percent of GDP for Cruz, and 2.6 percent of GDP for Rubio (GDP is a measure of the total income of the nation).[3] To put that in perspective, as of early 2016 (before any tax changes proposed by the 2016 presidential candidates had been enacted) federal tax revenues were projected to average 18.1 percent of GDP over the next ten years.[4] The Republican candidates' promises in 2016 essentially amounted to doubling down on the tax-cutting strategy of the most recent successful Republican presidential candidate, George W. Bush, who during the 2000 campaign proposed tax cuts which at the time were projected to reduce tax revenues by about 1.0 percent of GDP over the following ten years.[5]

In June of 2016, the House Republicans released a new tax reform proposal that would, among other things, lower the top personal income tax rate to 33 percent, reduce the corporate income tax rate to 20 percent, exclude half of all dividend, interest, and capital gains income from personal income taxation, allow expensing of business investment, limit deductions for interest paid by businesses on new loans to be no more than their interest income, increase the standard deduction and the Child Tax Credit in exchange for eliminating personal exemptions, and eliminate all personal itemized deductions aside from those for charitable donations and mortgage interest. The Urban-Brookings Tax Policy Center estimates suggested that, before accounting for any effects of the tax reform on the economy, the new House plan would reduce federal revenue by 1.0 percent of GDP over the next ten years, and that by 2025, when the plan would be fully phased in, people in the top 1 percent of the income distribution would get 99.6

percent of the benefits from the tax cut. Trump revised his tax plan in August and again in September, moving it closer to the recently released House plan. Some of Trump's revisions included a smaller cut in the top personal income tax rate (to 33 percent), new tax provisions for child care expenses (including both a deduction and a credit), and the introduction of expensing for business investment. Estimates from the Tax Foundation suggested the ten-year revenue loss from the September 2016 version of Trump's plan would be between 2.0 percent and 2.6 percent of GDP, before taking into account any effects of the plan on the economy.[6]

During the 2016 Democratic presidential primaries, eventual nominee Hillary Clinton proposed a package of tax changes that the Urban-Brookings Tax Policy Center projected would increase federal tax revenues by a total of about 0.5 percent of GDP between 2016 and 2026. Clinton's proposals included limiting the tax savings upper-income households could obtain from certain deductions and exclusions, introducing a 4 percent surcharge on the portion of adjusted gross income above $5 million, increasing tax rates on capital gains from assets held for less than six years, an estate tax increase, and a variety of reforms intended to reduce tax avoidance by multinational corporations. She had also promised a package of tax cuts for low- and middle-income people but had not yet spelled them out in any detail.[7]

By contrast, Bernie Sanders, Clinton's main challenger for the 2016 Democratic presidential nomination, proposed tax changes that the Urban-Brookings Tax Policy Center estimated would increase federal tax revenues by 6.4 percent of GDP between 2016 and 2026. This was intended to pay for ambitious expansions of government such as "Medicare for All" (which would extend a Medicare-like single-payer health insurance program to the entire population) and free public college education. Major components of Sanders' tax plan included a new 6.2 percent payroll tax, substantially increased tax rates on upper-income taxpayers, taxing capital gains and dividends at the same tax rates as ordinary income, extending the Social Security payroll tax to cover earnings above $250,000, adopting a carbon tax, increasing the estate tax, and reforming the taxation of multinational corporations.[8]

Why the tax system attracts all this attention is no mystery. It is the aspect of government that directly affects more people than any other, and in the long run we can't have more government spending without raising sufficient taxes to pay for it. Taxes at all levels of government take slightly less than one-third of people's income. Although tax cuts and tax reform are appealing to many people, Americans also have a right to be apprehensive about big changes in the tax system. Some are concerned that tax cuts just create big budget deficits and trade better times now for much higher taxes, or even a financial crisis, later. Others are concerned that fundamental tax reform would trade the deductions and credits they rely on for lower tax rates and that rates would soon afterward climb back up to where they were, leaving them worse off. In both cases, some people worry that big changes in the distribution of the tax burden will eventually shift more of it their way, or lead to cuts in government spending programs that would otherwise benefit them. Despite these concerns, there's plenty of frustration with the existing tax system and little doubt that we ought to be able to do better.

Complaints about the Current Tax System

The most common complaint about taxes is straightforward enough: they are too high. To some degree, this complaint just reflects self-interest; no one likes to owe taxes, just as no one enjoys paying utility bills. We all benefit in some way, however, from the government activities that those taxes finance. As U.S. Supreme Court Chief Justice Oliver Wendell Holmes, Jr., once noted, "Taxes are what we pay for civilized society."[9]

Some people's dissatisfaction with the overall level of taxes arises from a deep-seated opposition to allowing government to play an active role in society or from a belief that the government is wasting money. Many voters want to see a smaller government, with a correspondingly smaller tax bill.[10] Such questions are naturally controversial and difficult to resolve. But even agreement on how big government should be would not resolve *how* the taxes that are necessary to fund government expenditures should be designed. Similarly, people who disagree vehemently about the proper size of government might well find agreement on how our tax system ought to be designed. The *design* of the tax system sometimes gets short shrift in a political debate dominated by differences over the *level* of taxes, but it is a crucially important issue.

It Is Too Complicated

Another common grievance with the U.S. tax system is that it is too complicated. For many, complying with our labyrinthine tax regulations is frustrating, costly, and intrusive. Literally billions of hours are spent every year in the United States on fundamentally unproductive tax-related activities such as recordkeeping, wading through instructions, hunting for deductions and credits, and arranging personal and business financial affairs to avoid unnecessary tax payments and to take advantage of tax breaks.

The cost of this complexity is staggering. In total, individual taxpayers spend as much as 1.8 *billion* hours of their own time on tax matters, or about 12.5 hours per taxpayer on average.[11] That is the equivalent of over 900,000 full-time (but hidden and unpaid) IRS employees![12] Many buy books or computer software programs such as TurboTax to help them through tax season. On top of that, well over one-half of all individual taxpayers purchase professional assistance from an accountant, a lawyer, or another adviser to help prepare their tax returns.[13] Businesses also face a heavy compliance burden, with a typical Fortune 500 firm spending almost $5.5 million per year on tax matters. The total cost of collecting income taxes, including the value of those billions of hours that taxpayers could have put to better use, was about $170 billion in 2010, which amounted to more than 15 cents for every dollar of federal income tax revenue raised in that year.[14]

Of course, the taxpaying process is not difficult for everyone. Millions of low-income households need not submit a return at all. Of the 148 million taxpayers who filed an individual return in 2013, 16 percent were able to use the very simple Form 1040EZ, and 27 percent used the fairly straightforward Form 1040A.[15] In fiscal year 2014, about 84 percent of returns, or 125 million, were filed electronically, of which 77 million were filed by a tax practitioner.[16] Among individual taxpayers, the average number of hours per year spent complying with taxes declined from 27.4 in 1989 to 12.5 in 2010, which largely reflects the increasing use of tax preparation software.[17] But for businesses and individuals with more complicated finances, the burden of compliance can be onerous indeed.

It Is Difficult and Sometimes Intrusive to Enforce

The IRS budget for 2014 was $11.6 billion.[18] In fiscal year 2014, the IRS processed over 240 million returns, including 147 million individual returns. It audited or "examined" about 1.4 million tax returns and additionally sent 3.8 million computer-generated notices to taxpayers who were suspected of having reported incorrect tax liabilities. The IRS compared data from 2.3 billion documents—such as information reports from banks, stockbrokers, and mortgage lenders—to the numbers that taxpayers report on their returns.[19]

Despite the significant expenditures on IRS enforcement, the massive compliance costs borne by the public, and the miseries suffered by those who are investigated by the IRS, a great deal of cheating on taxes apparently still occurs. Such things are hard to measure accurately, but the most recent estimate by the IRS, for the years 2008 through 2010, suggests that about 18 percent of what should be paid in federal taxes, amounting to $458 billion per year, was not paid and that $406 billion of this will never be collected.[20] Other things being equal, this means higher tax rates and a heavier burden for the many people who are honest or who have few opportunities to cheat.

The flip side of tax evasion is that the IRS has sometimes been accused of using heavy-handed tactics to enforce the tax law. Televised congressional hearings in the late 1990s highlighted cases where the IRS appeared to overstep its bounds and led to new legislation that set up an oversight board for the IRS and shifted the burden of proof in a tax court case to the IRS, among other changes. In 2013, a scandal erupted over whether conservative nonprofit organizations were singled out for scrutiny by the IRS. In recent years, the IRS made progress in modernizing its operations, improving taxpayer service, and burnishing its public image, but its budget stagnated and then was cut significantly. Abundant evidence shows that the budget cuts have been accompanied by erosion of this progress in service, and by a dramatic decline in the amount of auditing and enforcement activity undertaken by the IRS, raising concerns of a major adverse impact on taxpayer service tax compliance.[21]

It Is Bad for the Economy
Political debates often revolve around how taxes affect the economy. Proponents of tax reforms or tax cuts almost always trumpet the economic benefits that they expect to result from their proposals, and opponents argue that these claims are greatly exaggerated. During recessions, the focus turns to whether tax cuts will jumpstart the sluggish economy. Other times, the focus is on how the design of the tax system affects long-term economic prosperity.

The sheer size of taxes—in 2014, federal taxes were $3.1 trillion, or 18.1 percent of the gross domestic product, while state and local taxes took up another 8.9 percent—suggests that they can have an important effect on the way the U.S. economy operates.[22] But beyond the magnitude of tax collections, taxes affect the terms of almost every economic decision that an individual or a company makes. Taxes affect, and for the most part reduce, the rewards obtained from saving, working hard, taking a second job, and investing in education or training. The income tax reduces also how much it costs to contribute to charity, buy a home, or put children in day care. Business decisions such as how many workers to hire, whether and how much to invest in a new technology, or whether to locate a factory in the United States or India can hinge on the tax consequences of the action. Because it alters the *incentives* associated with all these and scores of other decisions, the tax system can affect the *actions* people and businesses take. And the sum of all these actions comprises the economy.

Some critics of the current income tax charge that high tax rates on the wealthy discourage the hard work, innovation, and entrepreneurship necessary for a vibrant economy. Others stress that the tax system inordinately penalizes saving and investment, which are essential for maintaining and improving the country's long-run standard of living, and that it is at least partly responsible for a U.S. national saving rate that is low by both international and historical standards. Another criticism is that the preferences and penalties that are littered throughout the individual and corporate income tax codes can significantly distort economic choices. By capriciously changing the relative costs and benefits of various activities and investments from what they would be in the free market, goes this argument, the tax system induces us to channel our resources to the wrong places, hampering the efficiency of the economy and shackling long-term growth prospects.

It Is Unfair

Americans are divided in their opinions on the fairness of the tax system. In a 2015 poll, 56 percent of Americans said they regarded the amount of income tax they paid as fair, while 40 percent said it is not fair.[23]

What is it about taxes that people think is either fair or unfair? For one thing, people disagree about how the burden should be shared across families of different levels of affluence. The current personal income tax is designed to be "progressive," meaning that higher-income people typically pay a larger percentage of their incomes in taxes than do those with lower incomes. For some, a "fair" tax system means maintaining this progressivity and perhaps increasing the burden on those with high incomes. But others dismiss this as "soaking the rich" or "class warfare" and would prefer a less progressive system. Not surprisingly, people's views about whether the tax system is fair are strongly influenced by how hard the tax system hits their own families.

Even among families with the same income, the tax burden can differ widely depending on whether family members are married, how many dependent children they have, how much they give to charity, whether they own or rent housing, and whether their income is mostly from wages or salaries or from capital gains. Whether these and other characteristics and choices *should* affect one's tax burden is a contentious and often divisive issue that raises fundamental questions about the role of government in favoring or penalizing particular types of people and choices.

Finally, many believe that those individuals and corporations with good lobbyists, lawyers, and accountants are able to manipulate the tax code and take advantage of numerous loopholes to avoid paying their "fair share" of the tax burden. Such beliefs may lead to support for a streamlined tax system that eliminates opportunities for tax avoidance or for a more effective system of enforcement that prevents the tax burden from being shifted onto those taxpayers who do not have the influence, opportunity, or inclination to escape them.

A Different Way to Tax

One way to deal with these problems is to start over. Indeed, several congressional leaders, some Republican presidential candidates, a talk-show host or two, as well as some prominent economists, have advocated *abolishing* the existing personal and corporate income tax systems and replacing them with something quite different. A former chair of the House Ways and Means Committee once said: "We've got to tear the income-tax system out by its roots. We have to remove the Internal Revenue Service from the lives of Americans totally."[24] According to the one-time Republican presidential hopeful Steve Forbes: "With a beast like this, the only thing to do is kill it."[25]

Many of those dissatisfied with the current income tax system want to replace the personal and corporate income taxes entirely with some form of tax on consumption—that is, on that part of income that people spend rather than save. Most attention has focused on three forms of consumption tax—a national retail sales tax, a value-added tax, and a so-called flat tax. The retail sales tax is the most familiar to Americans, as it is already used by all but five states.

The value-added tax, or VAT as it is commonly known, is used by over 160 countries, and is a way of collecting a consumption tax not only from retailers, but from all businesses in the production and distribution chain. The least familiar is the "flat tax" developed by Robert Hall of Stanford University and Alvin Rabushka of the Hoover Institution. Steve Forbes championed a 17 percent flat tax in his run at the Republican presidential sweepstakes in early 1996 and 2000. Under the flat tax, the personal tax base would subject wages, salaries, and pension benefits, but not capital income such as interest, dividends, and capital gains above an exempt level, to a single, "flat" rate of tax, and allow no itemized deductions or other special preferences of any kind—no deductions for mortgage interest, charitable contributions, or child care and no credits for higher education. Proponents emphasize that, as a result of this clean tax base, the flat-tax return for individuals could fit on a postcard.

Objections to Radical Reform

Although almost everyone criticizes some aspects of the U.S. tax system, not everyone favors a complete overhaul. Nearly 90 percent of the members of the National Tax Association, the leading professional group of tax experts from academia, government, and business, favor retaining a personal income tax with rates that rise with income.[26] The most commonly expressed objection to radical reform proposals is that the average taxpayer would end up with the short end of the stick. Robert McIntyre of Citizens for Tax Justice says, "There is little or no disagreement among serious analysts that replacing the current, progressive income tax with a flat-rate tax would dramatically shift the tax burden away from the wealthy—and onto the middle class and the poor."[27] Unless a national sales tax is accompanied by some difficult-to-implement form of rebate scheme, it could shift even more of the tax burden toward low-income families.

Are we willing to accept a big change in who bears the tax burden in exchange for the promised benefits of the reforms? The public appears to be ambivalent. Surveys consistently find that solid majorities of the public want taxes on upper-income people to go up instead of down. On the other hand, polls generally find that support for a flat tax is close to that for a progressive income tax and that the poll results can depend on precisely how the question is asked. A crucial factor is that many Americans apparently believe (incorrectly) that the current distribution of income tax burdens is not progressive (i.e., the rich do not owe a higher fraction of their income in taxes than others), perhaps because they think loopholes for the rich are pervasive. Survey evidence also makes clear that most people know relatively little about the current tax system or proposals for reform, so in the event of a serious reform effort, public opinion may change as people learn more about the details.

A second common critique of the radical reform proposals is that their promised economic and simplification benefits are overstated. Although proponents have touted their potential for improving long-run economic growth and simplifying the taxpaying process, the degree to which they would accomplish these goals is subject to much debate among economists. There is much more uncertainty about the positive economic consequences of tax reform than advocates let on.

Even most skeptics admit that a flat tax could be significantly simpler than the current system. But much of the simplification that the flat tax promises comes at the cost of forgoing progressivity and the kind of personalized tax system that many Americans appear to favor. And while a national retail sales tax may appear simple on its surface, many experts are concerned that it would be impossible to administer equitably at the rates necessary to replace the revenues now generated by the income tax—rates probably in excess of 30 percent, far higher than the current level of any combined state and local sales tax rate.

Finally, some skeptics are afraid that we're opening quite a can of worms. A free-for-all over tax policy, with special interests thrown into the mix, could conceivably end up producing legislation that is even more of a mess than what we have now. Similarly, some critics and advocates of reform are united by the concern that once we overhaul the system it will inevitably and gradually get messed up again. They argue that any one-time tax change ought to be accompanied by reforms in the policy process itself to prevent a gradual drift back to complexity, inefficiency, and unfairness.

Changes in the Context of the Current System

Don't hold your breath waiting for the Congress to dump the income tax and start over from scratch. In the meantime, big—if not radical—changes in the tax system are being debated and enacted all the time. Politicians are constantly fighting over and changing things like income tax rates, saving incentives, the tax treatment of capital gains, and special deductions and credits for all manner of politically favored items. These debates may not capture the imagination in the same way that throwing the whole system out and starting over might, but the resulting changes in the tax code can have important implications for the economy and for the fairness and complexity of the tax system. Indeed, it should be possible to reform the income tax in a way that makes it significantly simpler, better for the economy, and arguably fairer without running afoul of the objections to more radical reforms raised above and without necessarily throwing the existing system out altogether.

The Need for Objective Analysis

Sorting out the claims and counterclaims made for tax-cut, tax-increase, or tax-reform proposals is a difficult task even for the most informed and interested citizens, who must wade through a sea of self-serving arguments. Those groups that have the most to gain or lose from a particular tax reform produce arguments that buttress their point of view. They don't trumpet the money that they (or their constituencies) stand to make but emphasize growth, productivity, and achieving the American dream. The potential losers seldom say they are opposing a policy simply because it skins their own hides, but instead couch their argument in terms of how the national interest is hurt, how many jobs will be lost, and how unfair it is.

Making an intelligent judgment about tax policy requires seeing through the self-serving arguments to a clear understanding of the issues involved. Unfortunately, judgments and policy decisions must be made without the luxury of having definitive answers to many of the critical questions. For example, whether cutting taxes by 10 percent will cause the gross domestic product to rise by 2 percent, fall by 2 percent, or have no effect at all will never be definitely known, although economists can shed light on such questions and rule out certain outlandish claims. Some issues, such as what is "fair," ultimately rely on individual value judgments.

What's in This Citizen's Guide?

This book offers a guide to the always contentious debate over tax policy, and is designed to help the concerned citizen come to informed judgments. Our goal is to cut through the academic jargon, the "Washingtonspeak," and the self-serving arguments to explore the fundamental choices and questions inherent in tax policymaking. We have no tax plan of our own to push.

Chapter 2 offers some historical and international perspectives on taxation in the United States and a concise description of the current federal tax system. Chapters 3 through 5 examine the basic criteria by which tax policy should be judged—how fairly it assigns tax burdens, whether it promotes or inhibits growth and prosperity, and whether it is simple and enforceable. As we lay out the basic principles underlying these criteria, we also explore the controversies and difficulties that arise and examine evidence on crucial questions, such as how the burden of our tax system is distributed and what is known about the economic effects of taxation. Such evidence is critical for evaluating the claims of various policy proposals and for weighing the inevitable trade-offs among criteria in any tax system. Chapter 6 goes over the key elements of many proposals for fundamental tax reform—a clean base (removal of all the deductions and exceptions of the current code), a single rate, and a consumption rather than an income base. Although reform proposals often contain more than one of these elements, they are indeed separable issues; in principle, we could adopt any combination of these elements without accepting the whole package. Chapter 7 provides a thorough examination of specific proposals to replace the income tax with a consumption tax. Chapter 8 addresses a variety of major policy changes that would stay within the general framework of the current tax system. Chapter 9 closes with a brief voter's guide to tax policy that summarizes some essential points to keep in mind when considering the debate over how we should tax ourselves.

2   An Overview of the U.S. Tax System

Before addressing how we *should* tax ourselves, it will be useful to consider the history and basic features of the system we already have. First, we take a glance at the overall tax picture for the United States, surveying how much revenue governments at all levels take in, what kinds of taxes they use, how our tax system compares to those in other countries, and how U.S. tax rates and revenues have evolved over the long run of history. Next, we provide a more detailed picture of how the major taxes used by the federal government currently work, with a particular emphasis on income taxes. Finally, we discuss recent changes and the outlook for tax policy in the near future.

How Governments in the United States Get Their Money

Table 2.1 lists the major taxes used by federal, state, and local governments in the United States, illustrating the relative importance of each. Altogether, governments in our country raised $4.7 *trillion* in taxes during 2014. One way to put such a huge number in perspective is to compare it with the size of the economy, which is usually measured by the gross domestic product (GDP). GDP is a measure of the total dollar value of all goods and services produced within the United States in a single year. In 2014, total federal, state, and local government taxes amounted to 27.0 percent of our $17.3 trillion GDP. Federal taxes were 18.1 percent of GDP, while state and local revenues accounted for 8.9 percent of GDP.

The biggest source of revenue for the federal government is the personal income tax. It raised $1.397 trillion in 2014, accounting for 44.5 percent of all federal revenues. Corporate income taxes took in another $418 billion (13.3 percent of federal revenues). Together, the personal

Table 2.1
Sources of tax revenue for U.S. governments, 2014

	Billions of 2014 dollars	Percentage of taxes at that level of government	Percentage of GDP
Total federal tax revenues	$3,138	100.0%	18.1%
Personal income tax	1,397	44.5	8.1
Contributions for social insurance	1,145	36.5	6.6
Corporate income tax	418	13.3	2.4
Excise taxes and customs duties	138	4.4	0.8
Estate and gift taxes	19	0.6	0.1
Other federal tax revenues	22	0.7	0.1
Total state and local tax revenues	$1,541	100.0%	8.9%
Sales taxes	525	34.1	3.0
Property taxes	456	29.6	2.6
Personal income taxes	350	22.7	2.0
Corporate income taxes	58	3.8	0.3
Contributions for social insurance	19	1.2	0.1
Estate and gift taxes	5	0.3	0.0
Other state and local tax revenues	129	8.4	0.7
Total federal, state, and local tax revenues	$4,680	100.0%	27.0

Source: Authors' calculations based on data from U.S. Bureau of Economic Analysis (2015).

and corporate income taxes accounted for 57.8 percent of all federal revenues in 2014.

The other major source of federal revenue, accounting for 36.5 percent of the total, is "contributions for social insurance." Taxes for Social Security and Medicare, which finance cash benefits and hospital insurance for the elderly and disabled, account for 88 percent of this total.[1] Taxes for unemployment insurance and a few other smaller programs make up the rest.

A handful of other federal taxes also collect revenue. Excise taxes on commodities such as cigarettes, alcohol, and gasoline, together with customs duties on imported goods, provided 4.4 percent of federal revenues in 2014. Estate and gift taxation generated another 0.6 percent of federal revenues in 2014.

State and local governments rely heavily on two kinds of taxes not levied by the federal government—retail sales taxes and property taxes. In 2014, retail sales taxes accounted for 34.1 percent of state and local tax revenues, while property taxes provided another 29.6 percent. Income taxation plays a smaller role for state and local governments; 22.7 percent of their tax revenues came from personal income taxes, while just 3.8 percent came from corporate income taxes.

International Comparisons

The claim that Americans are "overtaxed" is often heard in tax policy debates. Assessing this claim is difficult, and mostly deferred to later chapters, but we can gain some perspective by comparing the U.S. tax system to the tax systems of other similar countries. Table 2.2 shows that, relative to the size of our economy, the United States has a lower tax burden than most comparable countries. In 2013, the United States had the third-lowest tax-to-GDP ratio among the 34 countries in the Organisation for Economic Co-operation and Development (OECD), a group of industrialized nations from North and South America, Europe, Asia, and the Pacific; only Chile, Mexico, and South Korea were lower. On average, OECD countries raised taxes equal to 34.2 percent of their GDPs in 2013, compared to 25.4 percent for the United States (this is lower than the 27.0 percent figure shown in table 2.1 because the OECD uses a slightly narrower definition of "tax," and because it is from one year earlier).[2] Among rich countries, only Switzerland, Australia, and Ireland, are close to the low U.S. level, with taxes equal to 26.9, 27.5, and 29.0 percent of GDP, respectively. At the high end, Denmark had taxes amounting to a whopping 47.6 percent of GDP, with France and Belgium close behind at 45.0 and 44.7 percent, respectively.

It is not our reliance on income taxes or social insurance taxes that sets the United States apart from most other advanced nations; for these two types of tax, our tax-to-GDP ratio is not that far from the average among OECD countries. Rather, the big difference is how much less we collect from consumption taxes—just 3.7 percent of GDP compared to the 10.3 percent OECD average. This is due mostly to the fact that the United States is the only OECD country not to have a value-added tax (VAT), a close cousin of both the retail sales tax and flat tax discussed at length in chapter 7. The VAT is the most common variety of consumption tax in the rest of the world and is now used in over 160 countries.[3] On average, the OECD countries raise 6.3 percent of GDP from value-added taxes, while the United States collects nothing at all. In contrast, retail sales taxes, the kind

Table 2.2
International comparison of taxes as a percentage of GDP, 2013

	United States	OECD average (a)	Japan	United Kingdom	Canada	Germany	Sweden
Total taxes	**25.4**	**34.2**	**30.3**	**32.9**	**30.5**	**36.5**	**42.8**
Income taxes	**12.0**	**11.5**	**9.8**	**11.7**	**14.5**	**11.3**	**14.8**
Personal income taxes	9.8	8.8	5.8	9.1	11.2	9.5	12.2
Corporate income taxes	2.2	2.9	4.0	2.5	3.0	1.8	2.6
Consumption taxes (b)	**3.7**	**10.3**	**4.8**	**10.4**	**6.9**	**9.8**	**11.8**
Value-added taxes	–	6.3	2.8	6.9	4.0	7.0	8.9
Sales taxes	2.0	0.1	–	–	0.3	–	–
Social insurance taxes	**6.1**	**9.1**	**12.4**	**6.2**	**4.8**	**13.9**	**10.0**
Other taxes	**3.6**	**3.3**	**3.3**	**4.6**	**4.3**	**1.5**	**6.2**

Source: Authors' calculations based on data from Organisation for Economic Co-operation and Development (2015c).
Notes: Dash (–) indicates tax not used by country in question. Includes taxes at all levels of government. (a) Unweighted average of all 34 nations in the OECD. (b) Includes value-added taxes, sales taxes, excise taxes, import and customs duties, and other consumption taxes.

of general consumption tax used by the states, are rare outside the United States.

Completely replacing the U.S. personal and corporate income taxes with a consumption tax, as some advocate, would be an unprecedented move among major industrialized nations. All of the OECD countries have significant income taxes *in addition to* their value-added taxes. However, the amount of revenue relative to GDP that would be required to replace income taxation in the United States would not be that much larger than what is raised by value-added taxes already used in some other countries. Retail sales taxes of that scope, though, have never been attempted in any of these nations; we discuss why in chapter 7.

Historical Perspectives on the U.S. Tax System

The Overall Level of Taxes

Figure 2.1 illustrates how U.S. tax revenues, measured relative to the size of the economy, have changed since 1900. Most striking is the tremendous growth in the role of the federal government in the first half of the twentieth century. From 1900 to 1943, the federal tax-to-GDP ratio rose sevenfold, from 2.8 percent of GDP to 19.1 percent. World War II was clearly the critical juncture, although the New Deal years of the 1930s were also important. Not only did federal revenues grow significantly relative to GDP during the 1930s, but many programs that would require high taxes in later years, such as the Social Security system, were enacted in this period and expanded since.

Equally striking is just how little the ratio of federal taxes to GDP has changed since the mid-twentieth century. Since 1950, federal taxes have averaged 17.4 percent of GDP and seldom strayed far from that level. For all the contentious debate about the expanding federal government and attempts to downsize it, federal taxes as a share of the

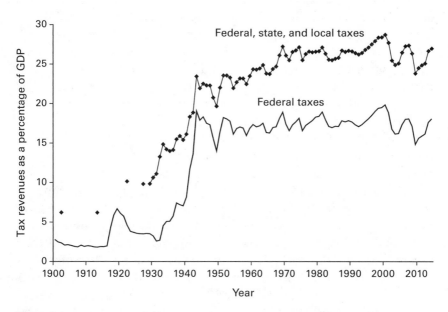

Figure 2.1
Tax revenues in the United States as a percentage of GDP, 1900–2014.
Note: Before 1929, data on state and local revenues are available only for selected years.
Sources: Carter et al. (2006); U.S. Bureau of Economic Analysis (2015).

economy have not changed greatly for more than sixty years. There have been some recent blips, though. Beginning in the late 1990s, there was a largely unexpected, and apparently temporary, surge in federal income tax revenues, caused more by economic conditions than by any changes in tax law, and federal tax revenues peaked at an all-time high of 19.8 percent of GDP in 2000. Two large tax cuts and a recession dropped that back down to 16.2 percent of GDP by 2003. After a brief rebound, the financial crisis, recession, and stimulus-motivated tax cuts pushed federal tax revenues down to just 14.9 percent of GDP by 2009, its lowest level in sixty years. In the same year federal government expenditures totaled 25.9 percent of GDP, and the federal budget deficit, which is the gap between federal government expenditures and federal government receipts (which include taxes and also a small amount of non-tax revenues) was $1.5 trillion, or 10.2 percent of GDP, the highest deficit relative to GDP since World War II.[4] By 2014, federal taxes and overall revenues were back up to 18.1 percent and 18.9 percent of GDP, respectively, and federal outlays were down to 22.9 percent of GDP, decreasing the budget deficit to 3.9 percent of GDP. This largely reflected the economic recovery and the expiration of temporary federal economic stimulus measures, together with the 2013 enactment of an increase in federal income tax rates on high-income people. Immediately following some federal tax cuts and spending increases enacted in December 2015, Congressional Budget Office estimates suggested that the federal budget deficit would shrink to 2.6 percent of GDP by fiscal year 2017, but would then increase to a deficit of 3.9 percent of GDP by 2025.[5]

State and local taxes have followed a somewhat more complicated pattern. In the early part of the twentieth century, state and local governments together actually raised more money than the federal government. At their peak in 1932, they were collecting almost four times as much tax revenue as the federal government—10.6 percent of GDP versus only 2.7 percent. But then, as the federal role in the economy expanded due in large part to New Deal programs, state and local revenues shrank dramatically relative to GDP, hitting a low of just 4.1 percent by 1944. They then rebounded throughout the 1950s and 1960s and reached 9.2 percent of GDP by 1972. Since then, they have consistently remained in the 8 to 10 percent range, and stood at 8.9 percent of GDP as of 2014.

Considering all levels of government, taxes rose enormously from 6.2 percent of GDP in 1900 to 23.4 percent by the middle of World War

II. After the war they continued growing at a slower pace to 27.2 percent of GDP by 1969. They experienced relatively little net change throughout the 1970s and 1980s, increased a bit during the 1990s, and then fluctuated significantly after 2000. By 2014, overall federal, state, and local taxes stood at 27.0 percent of GDP. The bottom line is that, despite a massive increase in taxes over the last century as a whole, there have been only relatively modest changes in the share of national income that goes to taxes at all levels of government for about the last forty-five years. Of course, the somewhat smaller share of GDP collected in taxes today can buy a great deal more in real terms than the larger share of GDP that was collected forty-five years ago, due to the growth of the economy. For instance, total tax revenues including all levels of government were 3.4 times as high in inflation-adjusted dollars in 2014 as they were in 1969.[6]

History of U.S. Personal Income Tax Rates and Revenues
Our nation's first income tax was a temporary emergency measure enacted during the Civil War; it was first levied in 1861 and expired in 1872.[7] Beginning in the late 1800s, popular opposition mounted against what were then the major sources of federal revenues—tariffs, excise taxes, and property taxes—on the grounds that they were unfairly burdensome to working-class Americans. Many critics of the existing tax structure viewed a personal income tax—and especially a graduated income tax that exempted some amount of income—as an appealing alternative because it could be made progressive, imposing a heavier proportional burden on the rich than on the poor. Congress enacted an income tax in 1894, but one year later the U.S. Supreme Court declared it in violation of the clause in article I, section 9, of the Constitution, which states: "No capitation, or other direct, tax shall be laid, unless in proportion to the census or enumeration herein before directed to be taken."[8] This obstacle to an income tax was eliminated by the Sixteenth Amendment to the U.S. Constitution, which was ratified in February 1913. The amendment reads as follows: "The Congress shall have power to lay and collect taxes on incomes, from whatever source derived, without apportionment among the several States, and without regard to any census or enumeration." President Woodrow Wilson signed the modern personal income tax into law shortly thereafter, in October 1913.[9]

The 1913 personal income tax had graduated rates, like the current system, but they ranged from only 1 to 7 percent. Even at those rates, tiny in comparison to today's, opponents were outraged. Senator Henry Cabot Lodge of Massachusetts remarked that graduated tax rates levied on income above an exemption level would "set a class apart and say they are to be pillaged, their property is to be confiscated."[10] Many of today's most important deductions and exclusions were already there in 1913, including the deductions for home mortgage interest, the deduction for tax payments to state and local governments, and the exclusion of interest on state and local bonds. A deduction for charitable contributions was soon added, in 1917.[11] One big difference between the 1913 income tax and today's was that personal exemptions were so large relative to typical incomes of the day that only those with extremely high incomes had owed any income tax at all—only about 1 percent of households were required to file a tax return at the tax's inception in 1913.[12]

Figure 2.2 illustrates how several aspects of the U.S. personal income tax—revenues as a percentage of GDP, the percentage of households filing tax returns, and marginal tax rates—have changed since 1913. The "marginal" tax rate is the tax rate applied to the next, or last, dollar of income that a person receives. Since its beginning, the U.S. personal income tax has had "graduated" tax rates, meaning that there are multiple tax brackets, with successively higher marginal tax rates applying to the portions of taxable income falling into successively higher tax brackets (further explanation of this is provided later in the chapter). Marginal tax rates get a lot of attention from economists because they are the tax rates that affect the incentive to engage in more or less income-earning economic activity. The bottom panel of figure 2.2 shows the marginal tax rate in the top bracket from 1913 through 2014. For 1958 through 2012, it also shows the marginal tax rates at the 99th percentile of the distribution of marginal tax rates among all tax returns (that is, 1 percent of households filing returns faced a marginal tax rate higher than that, and 99 percent faced that rate or lower), and at the median of that distribution (half of filers faced higher marginal tax rates, and half faced that rate or lower), which were originally computed by Dan Baneman and Jim Nunns of the Urban-Brookings Tax Policy Center and were updated by us.[13]

Until World War II, personal income tax receipts were quite small, staying well below 2.0 percent of GDP, despite the fact that the marginal tax rate in the top tax bracket was very high, in some years exceeding 70 percent. This occurred because the income tax applied to only a very small number of high-income people, and because only a

(a)

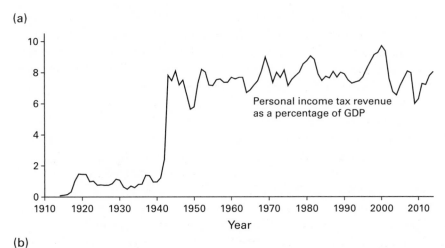

(b)

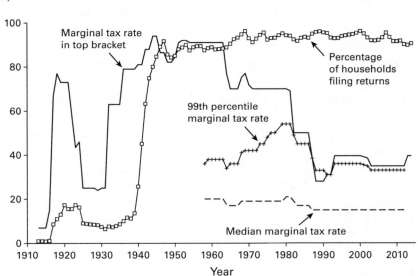

Figure 2.2
The U.S. personal income tax: (a) revenues as a percentage of GDP, 1913–2014, and
(b) marginal tax rates and percentage of households filing returns, 1913–2014.
Sources: Author's calculations based on data from Carter et al. (2006), U.S. Bureau of
Economic Analysis (2015), Internal Revenue Service (2016a), Baneman and Nunns (2012),
2010–2012 editions of *Internal Revenue Service Statistics of Income—Individual Income Tax
Returns*, Publication 1304, and Piketty and Saez (2003, updated 2016).

small subset of those people had any income taxed at a rate anywhere near the top rate. Between 1913 and 1939, the number of personal income tax returns filed never exceeded 18 percent of households. Christina and David Romer of the University of California, Berkeley have estimated that between 1918 and 1939, 95 percent of all personal income taxes were owed by people in the top 0.2 percent of the income distribution.[14]

Because of the need for a lot of revenue fast, personal income taxation was expanded dramatically during World War II. The exempt level of income was reduced greatly, transforming what had been a "class tax" into a "mass tax." In the five years between 1939 and 1944 alone, personal income tax revenues surged from 1 percent to 8 percent of GDP, and the number of returns filed rose sharply from 14 percent to 80 percent of households. To facilitate the collection of taxes from this many people, employer withholding and remitting of income taxes on wages and salaries were introduced to the income tax in 1943.[15]

After World War II, the personal income tax remained a "mass tax." Even though revenue needs tailed off sharply, the exemption level was not raised to its pre-war level. The percentage of households filing returns rose gradually to exceed 90 by 1965, and then stayed around or above that level (in 2014 it was 90.6 percent). After rising to 8 percent of GDP during World War II, personal income tax revenues stayed near that level most of the time, but recently experienced significant fluctuations. Federal income tax revenues surged during the 1990s, and peaked at 9.7 percent of GDP in 2000. Legislated hikes in federal income tax rates on high-income taxpayers in 1991 and 1993 played some role in this increase, but the surge was driven largely by the booming economy and stock market and especially by a tremendous jump in the taxable incomes of the most affluent families. When the share of the nation's income that goes to people who are already in high-income tax brackets increases, tax revenues rise relative to GDP. Tax cuts enacted in 2001 and 2003, together with a recession, caused personal income tax revenues to plunge to 6.5 percent of GDP by 2004. With economic recovery they rebounded to 8.1 percent of GDP in 2007, before falling further to 6.0 percent of GDP in 2009, due to severe economic weakness, the continued impact of the 2001 and 2003 tax cuts, and additional temporary tax cuts intended as stimulus measures. In 2009 and 2010, personal income tax revenues were lower as a percentage of GDP than they had been in any year since 1950. By 2014 they were back up to 8.1 percent of GDP, due to economic recovery and tax rate increases on upper-income taxpayers enacted in 2013.

One striking feature of figure 2.2 is the dramatic rise and then decline of top tax rates. The marginal tax rate in the top bracket hit a peak of 94 percent in 1944 and 1945, stayed at 91 percent or higher from 1951 until the Kennedy-Johnson tax cut of 1964, and remained as high as 70 percent until 1980, when it began to tumble dramatically. Due to Reagan-era tax cuts enacted in 1981 and 1986, by 1988 the top rate had fallen all the way to 28 percent. After increasing to 31 percent in 1991 and 39.6 percent in 1993, the top rate was gradually cut from 39.6 percent to 35 percent between 2001 and 2003, and stayed there until being raised again in 2013 back to 39.6 percent, a rate that is still low by historical standards.

While the top tax rate is attention-grabbing, it is important to recognize that when it was above 50 percent, it affected only a small fraction of 1 percent of households, and even most people within the top 1 percent of the income distribution typically faced marginal tax rates that were much lower than the top rate. For example, figure 2.2 shows that in 1960, when the marginal tax rate in the top bracket was 91 percent, 99 percent of all tax return filers actually had marginal tax rates of 38 percent or below, and half of all filers had marginal tax rates of 20 percent or below. The higher rates did apply to a select few, though. In 1960, 0.1 percent of taxpayers faced marginal tax rates of 62 percent or above.[16] The marginal tax rate at the 99th percentile of the rate distribution did rise during the 1970s, and reached a peak of 54 percent in 1979, but it still remained well below the marginal rate in the top tax bracket until 1982, when the top rate was cut to 50 percent. Those two rates have been quite close ever since. Meanwhile, the median marginal income tax rate has hovered in the narrow range of 15 to 21 percent since 1958, and has been at 15 percent each year since 1987.

The decline in marginal tax rates at the top of the income distribution has coincided with dramatic changes in the income tax *base*—the portion of income that is subject to tax, after exclusions, deductions, and exemptions have been applied. The Tax Reform Act of 1986 (TRA86), which we will discuss in detail in chapter 8, cut the marginal tax rate in the top bracket from 50 percent to 28 percent, but also made significant changes to the individual and corporation tax bases, broadening them by enough to keep revenues roughly unchanged. Among other changes, TRA86 increased the portion of capital gains included in taxable income from 40 percent to 100 percent, and eliminated or curtailed various deductions that were used disproportionately by high-income people.

The juxtaposition of the large changes in the top tax rate with modest changes in personal income tax revenue as a percentage of GDP, apparent in figure 2.2, is sometimes cited as evidence that changes in tax rates on the rich have little effect on aggregate revenue.[17] But the historical relationship is partly explained by the fact that when the top rate was above 50 percent, only a tiny fraction of 1 percent of taxpayers faced marginal tax rates close to the top rate (which is much less true today), and also by the fact that the biggest cut in the top rate (due to TRA86) was intentionally accompanied by extensive legislated base broadening. The other major confounding factor is the dramatic increase in the share of the nation's pre-tax income received by the top 1 percent of the income distribution since the late 1970s (see chapter 3). This phenomenon offset the decline in revenues that otherwise would have resulted from cutting top tax rates, because an increasing share of the nation's income was subject to the highest tax rates. It also means that the revenue consequences of tax rates on the rich are correspondingly larger than they used to be. Whether the rise in pre-tax income inequality was partly *caused* by the cuts in marginal tax rates is an important issue we'll explore in upcoming chapters.

History of U.S. Corporate Income Tax Rates and Revenues
As with the personal income tax, the first special tax on corporations in the United States was a temporary emergency levy enacted during the Civil War. Corporate income taxation was first adopted on a permanent basis in 1909. As with the personal income tax, its support arose from opposition to the prevailing taxes of the day and a belief that its burden would fall disproportionately on the wealthy. In addition, many thought it would facilitate the regulation of corporations in an era of loose financial reporting. Unlike the personal tax, however, the corporate tax was able to escape constitutional problems because Congress packaged it as an "excise" tax.[18]

Federal corporate income tax revenues followed a pattern similar to that of the personal income tax up through World War II (see figure 2.3). Revenues increased sharply from 1.4 percent of GDP in 1939 to a peak of 6.7 percent in 1942. In contrast to the personal income tax, however, between 1951 and the early 1980s, corporate tax revenues declined sharply relative to GDP, falling to just 1.5 percent of GDP by

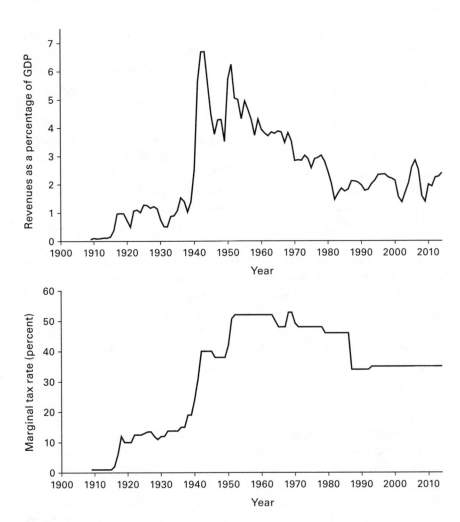

Figure 2.3
The U.S. corporate income tax: (a) revenues as a percentage of GDP, 1909–2014, and
(b) marginal tax rate on the largest corporations, 1909–2014.
Sources: Authors' calculations based on data from Carter et al. (2006), U.S. Bureau
of Economic Analysis (2015), Internal Revenue Service (2012c, 2013e, 2014g), and Joint
Committee on Taxation (2013b, 2014).

1982. Since then, because of fluctuating taxable profits, corporate tax revenues have bounced up and down with the business cycle, ranging between 1.4 percent and 2.9 percent of GDP. In 2014 corporate income tax revenues were 2.4 percent of GDP, higher than the average of 2.0 percent since 1980.

The statutory marginal tax rate on the largest corporations peaked at 52.8 percent in 1968–1969, and has declined since then, dropping to 34 percent after the Tax Reform Act of 1986. Since 1993, this rate has been 35 percent. The long-term decline in corporate tax revenue relative to GDP was much greater than the decline in statutory tax rates, because profits subject to corporate taxation declined relative to GDP. We'll consider some reasons why this may have occurred later in the book.

Now that we have provided some context, we turn to explanations of how the major components of the federal tax system—the personal income tax, corporate income tax, payroll tax for Social Security and Medicare, estate and gift taxes, and excise taxes—currently work. We then close with a discussion of recent and scheduled future changes in federal tax law, and consider the outlook for U.S. tax policy.

Income Taxation

What Is Income? The Economist's Definition

On the road to understanding what an income tax is and how it works, a necessary first step is to understand precisely what is meant by *income*. This may, at first glance, seem easy, and certainly for some taxpayers calculating taxable income is very straightforward. But in many situations determining income turns out to be rather tricky.

To start, let's put aside how taxable income is calculated for U.S. tax purposes and instead ponder what income means. Economists have a standard definition of income, which is called *Haig–Simons* income after the two people who first developed it. It is the increase in an individual's ability to consume during a given period of time.[19] In other words, your annual income is the value of the goods and services you consume during a year, plus the net change in your wealth (saving) that occurs in that year—income equals consumption plus saving. The saving comprises that part of annual income that you choose not to spend this year but, because you've saved it, increases your ability to consume goods and services in the future. This concept of income is a reasonable, but not perfect, measure of an individual's or family's potential standard of living during a particular time period.

Clearly, receiving cash wages and salaries increases one's ability to consume (or save), so these are part of Haig–Simons income. A noncash benefit that your employer provides to you, such as health insurance, is also a part of income by this definition. Most people probably don't think of employer-provided health insurance as income, but it certainly does increase their ability to consume services—in this case, services provided by doctors and hospitals. Someone whose health insurance is provided by an employer is clearly better off than someone with the same cash income but no insurance. Similarly, benefits provided by the government—such as Social Security, Medicare, or unemployment insurance benefits—also increase a person's ability to consume and are considered part of the economist's definition of income.

The return to the ownership of capital (wealth), or *capital income*, adds to your ability to consume as well and thus counts as income. Common examples of capital income would be interest and dividends that you accumulate on your savings or rent received on a building you own. A royalty (generally a license fee for the use of intellectual property, paid, for example, to an author or an inventor) usually represents some combination of returns to capital and labor.

An important example of capital income is a capital gain, which is the increase in value of an asset you own, such as a house or shares in a corporation. Symmetrically, capital losses would be subtracted from income. According to the Haig–Simons concept of income, whether you sell the asset does not matter because an increase in the value of assets you own increases your purchasing *power*. Ideally, only *real* capital income and losses, as opposed to those due to inflation, would be counted. For example, if you earn interest of 4 percent this year but inflation is also 4 percent, the dollars of interest you've received overstate the increase in your purchasing power because they have just compensated for the decline in purchasing power of your wealth due to inflation.

The costs of earning income reduce the ability to consume and so would be subtracted from the Haig–Simons definition of income. For example, if a farmer earns $50,000 from selling crops but pays $20,000 for seeds, fertilizer, and so forth, then net income is only $30,000. On the other hand, the cost of purchasing capital goods (durable business inputs), such as a tractor or a barn, would not be deducted in full right away. Capital goods still have value at the end of the year, so subtracting their full purchase price immediately would cause an understatement of the change in the ability to consume that year. Rather, to calculate income one would subtract only a measure of how much *depreciation* had occurred—the amount by which the capital goods had declined in value because they had worn out or become obsolete. Finally, if you had to borrow money to purchase the materials and equipment necessary to earn your income, the interest payments on that borrowing would be subtracted.

Most consumer durable goods, such as a home or a car, provide consumption services to their owners over multiple years, and the value of these services is part of income according to the economist's definition. For example, buying a home is an investment, and a major part of the return on that investment is the shelter it provides to its owner every year, a service equal in value to the amount of rent that could be charged on that home and need not be paid to a landlord. Just as dividends are a form of capital income that represent part of the return to investing in corporate stocks, the rental value of a home is capital income representing part of the return to investing in a house. Thus, according to the economist's conception, this rental value counts as income because owning the house certainly reflects a greater ability to consume housing services. Depreciation and interest payments would be subtracted to obtain the net income associated with owning the house.

The Haig–Simons definition of income refers to people, so that all net income earned by businesses must be assigned in some way to individuals whether the income is paid out to owners of the firm or reinvested back into the company. In the former case, it is fairly clear that the money paid out is income to the business owners, including shareholders. What is less clear—but equally true—is that the earnings retained in the firm also represent income for the owners of the firm to the extent that they increase the value of the firm.

In some situations, often involving the timing of when income is earned, the Haig–Simons definition of income does not provide a clear answer. As an example, consider the case of lottery winners. It will seem that the increase in the "ability to consume" of a multi-million-dollar winner occurs at the moment her lucky number is drawn out of the bin. In most state lotteries, the advertised prize consists of a series of payments over a period of time, twenty-nine years in the case of Powerball. The winner can opt for an immediate one-time payment, but this is considerably lower than the simple sum of the annual payments. For example, when Florida resident Gloria MacKenzie and her son won the Powerball jackpot in 2013, they were given the choice of either receiving $185 million (before taxes) up front each, or receiving about $10.2 million a year each for the next twenty-nine years; because of the ability to earn interest on the lump-sum payment, it comes out to be worth about the same as the twenty-nine installments.[20]

Here's the question. If the winner opts for annual payments, has her annual income gone up by $10.2 million for each of the next twenty-nine years? Or was her income $185 million in the year she won and zero thereafter? The Haig–Simons concept suggests the latter, but this might not seem natural to most people, and the winner would understandably object to having to pay tax on $185 million of income in a year she received much less in cash.

Things get trickier when you consider an inventor who one day conceives of a brilliant idea that will certainly bring astounding future returns. Taking the Haig–Simons concept literally suggests that her income went up that year, even though it will likely take many years before the invention actually starts to bring in money. These kinds of timing issues come up often in the accounting for corporations' income and are resolved by a set of guidelines. The tax system has to deal with the same kind of issues, and the conceptual definition of income does not always provide clear and intuitive answers.

Taxable Income versus Haig–Simons Income

Readers somewhat familiar with the U.S. income tax system were likely a bit put off by the Haig–Simons definition of income because of the many ways it differs from income as defined for tax purposes. The design of the U.S., and indeed, every country's income tax, reflects to some degree the Haig–Simons income concept, but no country's income tax system follows it precisely, nor even really aspires to do so. In the United States, the process of filling out one's personal income tax return begins with reporting amounts of potentially taxable income in a variety of different categories, and then adding up the total, which is called *gross* income. But as we'll see, gross income already leaves out many parts of income, which are collectively known as *exclusions*. Taxpayers are then allowed to subtract various *deductions* and *exemptions* from gross income in order to compute *taxable income*, which is the measure of income to which tax rates are applied to determine ordinary tax liability (further adjustments to tax liability, such as addition of alternative minimum tax and subtraction of tax credits, follow). In the following sections, we discuss how the U.S. personal income tax system defines gross income and taxable income, and highlight the major divergences from the conceptual benchmark of Haig–Simons income.

By laying out a conceptual definition of economic income above, and comparing it to taxable income below, we do not mean to imply that Haig–Simons income is necessarily the "correct" basis for taxation. Indeed, later in the book we carefully examine the case for replacing the income tax with a tax based on consumption. Much of the difference between Haig–Simons income and taxable income arises from a reluctance to fully tax the return to saving—capital income—and, as we'll see in chapter 6, a consumption tax would completely eliminate the tax system's negative effect on the incentive to save, an approach advocated by many tax experts. Nor do we mean to imply that a real-life income tax is necessarily better the closer its working definition of taxable income is to Haig–Simons income. For example, some types of Haig–Simons income are quite difficult to measure, and thus including them in taxable income may contribute to the capriciousness of the distribution of the tax burden and/or increase the costs of collection. In some cases exclusions or deductions may be motivated by a desire to incentivize certain behaviors, such as purchasing health insurance or donating to charity, and there are reasonable arguments both for and against these provisions.

Despite these caveats, as long as we are operating an income tax, it is important to understand how the tax system's definition of income compares to a reasonable conceptual measure of income. Taxing some forms of income and not taxing others creates incentives for taxpayers to alter their actions so that they earn (or appear to earn) less of the kind of income that gets counted and more of the kind that does not, and requires higher marginal tax rates to raise a given amount of revenue, because of the narrower base. Such a system may also create arbitrary differences in tax burdens across otherwise similar taxpayers. Many of the problems with the income tax—including complexity, distortions of economic decision making, and arguably some unfairness—arise from differences between Haig–Simons income and the tax system's measure of income. Thus, the choice of what to include and what not to include in taxable income involves some difficult trade-offs. Whether any particular deviation from "true" income is justified must be evaluated on a case-by-case basis, and we explore many of them in more detail in later chapters. For now, we summarize the basic similarities and differences between Haig–Simons and taxable income, starting with employee compensation, moving on to capital and business income, and then considering deductions and exemptions.

Income Tax Treatment of Employee Compensation

Employee compensation is the single most important category of income in the U.S. economy, accounting for $8.8 trillion, or 61 percent of national income, in 2013. About 81 percent of that employee compensation was wage and salary income, which is generally subject to personal income taxation in a straightforward fashion. In 2013, 93 percent of the $7.1 trillion of wages and salaries in the U.S. economy was included in gross income on personal tax returns. Those payments were deductible from the taxable incomes of the employers, because employee compensation is a cost of earning income for the employers. Most of the excluded 6.9 percent of wages and salaries accrued to people with incomes too low to be required to file tax returns, while a small portion reflected tax evasion. While wage and salary income largely represents standard payments in exchange for services, in both the national accounts and the personal income tax it also includes less obvious things, such as the value (upon exercise) of most executive stock options.[21]

Employer-provided insurance has for a long time been the most significant example of nontaxable employee compensation. Employers' contributions to private insurance plans for their employees are excluded from gross income reported on employees' personal tax returns, but are still deductible from employers' taxable income just as any other employee compensation is. Such contributions amounted to $703 billion, or 8 percent of total employee compensation, in 2013. Contributions to employer-provided health insurance plans accounted for $624 billion of this. The exclusion for employer-provided health insurance dates back to an IRS ruling in 1943, and was officially enacted into law by Congress in 1954.[22] It creates a strong incentive to provide more generous health insurance benefits in lieu of wages and salaries at the margin. The "Patient Protection and Affordable Care Act" (ACA), which is the major health care reform law enacted during the Obama administration in 2010, involves a provision intended to reduce that incentive: insurance companies would, starting in 2020, be subject to a

40 percent excise tax (colloquially known as the "Cadillac Tax") on the portions of the costs of employer-provided health insurance for individuals and families that exceed very high threshold amounts. We'll explore this and other aspects of tax policy toward health insurance in greater detail in chapter 6. The remaining $80 billion of excluded employer-provided insurance premiums consisted of contributions to group life insurance and worker's compensation plans.[23]

Employer contributions to pension and profit-sharing plans, and the employer portions of payroll taxes for government social insurance programs such as Social Security and Medicare, each accounted for 6 percent of employee compensation in 2013.[24] These are deductible for the employer and excludable for the employee, but the cash retirement or disability benefits arising from them can be subject to tax when they are disbursed. We defer fuller explanations of income taxation of pensions and Social Security to later in the chapter.

Many other miscellaneous employee compensation issues are addressed in detail by U.S. income tax laws and regulations.[25] For example, employer reimbursement of employee expenses for things such as moving costs, day care, and tuition are all deductible from taxable income for employers, and are excludable from employees' taxable income with some limitations. One might argue that these, to varying degrees, represent costs of earning income, which would be excluded from Haig–Simons income, but there's room for debate. Employer-provided lodging and meals are examples of compensation that can pose tricky questions. For instance, if a hotel provides free lodging to its manager on the premises, and requires the manager to live there as a condition of the job, should the full market rental value of the hotel accommodations be included in the manager's taxable income? What if the manager would have preferred to live elsewhere, perhaps at a much lower rent? As an imperfect compromise, U.S. tax law has settled on the principle that if lodging and meals at work are provided "for the convenience of the employer," they will be entirely excluded from employees' taxable income, and otherwise they generally will not. Employers are allowed to deduct their costs either way. Exclusion of employer-provided lodging and meals is estimated to cost about one-fifth of 1 percent of personal income tax revenue, while exclusions for employer reimbursement of educational expenses and child care, for example, cost far less than that.[26] Aside from insurance and pensions, the aggregate revenue cost of other excluded forms of employee compensation in the United States is not large, but that is in a context where detailed laws and regulations have been developed and enforced to help keep tax avoidance under control.

Introduction to the Tax Treatment of Capital Income

Real net income from interest, dividends, capital gains, rents, and royalties, together with business income (which often represents a mix of capital income and labor income) not already counted in one of these other categories, averaged about $3.6 trillion per year between 1987 and 2013 in the United States. This is one-half of the annual average of $7.2 trillion of employee compensation over this period (both are measured in constant year 2013 dollars).[27] Differences between taxable income and Haig–Simons income are especially pronounced for these items of capital and business income.

One issue is that capital income, to the extent that it is included in taxable income at all, is included at its *nominal* value rather than at its *real* (inflation-adjusted) value. This is true both for income received and for deductions, such as those for capital losses, interest paid, and depreciation. To measure Haig–Simons income accurately, the portion representing compensation for inflation would be taken out of all of these items. The U.S. income tax makes no such adjustments, nor do the income taxes of most other countries. One reason is that such an adjustment could be very complicated, and would therefore increase administrative and compliance burdens, for example because it would require taxpayers to measure and report the values of assets and debts on an annual basis, an issue we consider in chapter 6. As measured by the consumer price index, the inflation rate in the United States in the twelve months leading up to August 1, 2016 was only 1.1 percent, and as of August 2016, the Federal Reserve Bank of Cleveland forecast an average annual inflation rate over the next ten years of just 1.64 percent, based on information about peoples' expectations that can be inferred from financial market asset prices, among other things.[28] When inflation is so low, the failure of a tax system to account for it when measuring taxable capital income is not an especially pressing problem, but when inflation is higher, the failure to do so can cause major economic problems, an issue we'll also return to in future chapters.

Another issue is that capital gains are counted as taxable income only when they are *realized*, which is generally when the asset is sold, whereas the Haig–Simons definition would include capital gains in income each year as they accrue. The difference between the proceeds from selling an asset and the cost of the asset when originally purchased (also known as its "basis") is counted as taxable income at the time of sale (for purposes of this calculation, the basis is sometimes adjusted—for example, by adding the cost of subsequent home improvements to the original purchase cost of a home). This tax treatment is partly a concession to measurement difficulties. For some assets, such as a small business or a house, the only time reasonably accurate information on market value is available is when the asset is sold. Taxing accrued gains would also raise some concerns about "liquidity"—in some cases it could be difficult for the owner to come up with the cash to remit the tax on a capital gain without selling the asset.

Postponing tax on an accrued gain until an asset is sold is more financially advantageous to the taxpayer, compared to remitting the tax in the year the gain accrues, because interest can be earned on the funds that otherwise would have been used to remit the tax. For example, if a $100 tax payment is deferred for twenty years, and saved (or used to pay off debt) at an annual interest rate of 3 percent in the meantime, the taxpayer earns (or saves) an extra $81 of interest compared to what would have happened if the tax had to be remitted immediately.[29] This deferral of tax until sale of the asset makes the personal tax burden on capital gains lighter, in real economic terms, than that on other types of income such as interest or dividends that are taxed on accrual. Moreover, capital gains on assets that are held until the owner's death are completely absolved from personal income taxation.[30]

Taxing capital gains upon realization instead of accrual creates tax avoidance opportunities, and efforts to limit these through tax law lead to further differences between Haig–Simons and taxable income. For example, suppose realized capital losses and interest were always subtracted in full from taxable income, and then consider the following portfolio strategy: sell assets that decline in value, hold on to assets that increase in value (so-called "cherry-picking"), and borrow against the appreciating assets if one needs cash on hand (deducting the interest on the loans all the while). This strategy could reduce one's income tax liability substantially, without changing one's pre-tax economic income at all. Indeed, this basic strategy is such a fundamental part of tax avoidance strategy that tax experts often refer to it as "Tax Planning 101."[31] To address this, the personal income tax limits deductions for capital losses to just $3,000 beyond the amount of realized capital gains in any one year, although the unused portion may be carried forward into future years. In addition, the tax law limits deductions for interest on loans related to financial investments to no more than the amount of investment income included in taxable income. But there are ways to get around this, such as borrowing more against one's home instead.

A large portion of the income from capital gains, interest, and dividends in the United States is excluded from personal income taxation because the assets that generate these returns are held in pensions and individual retirement accounts, which we will discuss in greater detail in the next section. In 2014, 41 percent of financial assets (and 28 percent of all assets) owned by households and nonprofit institutions were in such accounts.[32]

Nonprofit institutions, such as churches and most universities, account for roughly 7 percent of the combined assets of the households and nonprofits, and capital income earned on their assets is also generally exempt from personal income tax.[33] One rationale for this is to subsidize the charitable activities that such institutions are supposed to be engaged in. Interest on state and local government bonds is also exempt from federal income taxation, which effectively serves as a federal subsidy to the debt-financed activities of state and local governments because it reduces the interest rates they have to pay.

For many people, the most valuable asset they own is their home, but the returns to investment in owner-occupied housing are largely excluded from taxable income as well. As noted above, the rental value (less depreciation and expenses) of owner-occupied housing is part of Haig–Simons income. But this is excluded from the income tax base, in part because it would be difficult to measure, and in part because most people would resist the unfamiliar idea that the rent they save by buying a house represents income that should be taxed. Capital gains realized on sales of owner-occupied housing, up to a limit of $500,000 for a married couple (or $250,000 for a single person), are also excluded from personal income taxation, and capital losses on a home are not deductible. The personal income tax allows deductions for some expenses of owning a home, such as mortgage interest and property taxes. Haig–Simons income would allow such deductions, but the case for doing so is less clear when the implicit income from investing in a home is excluded, an issue we'll consider in chapter 6. Nonbusiness real estate owned by households accounted for 21 percent of the value of assets of households and nonprofit institutions in 2014.[34] So, considering retirement accounts, nonprofits, and homes together, the portion of household and nonprofit assets earning returns that are almost entirely excluded from personal income taxation exceeds one-half.

A few other examples of "imputed" capital income are also excluded from personal taxation. For example, the difference between the market interest rate and the interest rate that financial institutions actually pay to depositors and savers is an implicit form of economic income that is used to purchase financial services (such as the convenience and security provided by a checking account). It would probably be impractical to attempt to tax this, and the U.S. tax system makes no attempt to do so. As noted earlier, the annual value of services flowing from consumer durable goods, less their depreciation, also technically belongs in Haig–Simons income, but the personal income tax neither includes the value of the service flow nor allows deductions for the depreciation.

Introduction to the Tax Treatment of Business Income

Much income in the economy derives from ownership of businesses. The Haig–Simons definition of income would allocate all business income to the owners of the business in the year the income is earned. The actual tax treatment of business income differs from this principle to varying degrees, depending upon how the business is classified for tax purposes. Table 2.3 presents summary information on the major tax classifications of businesses.

In 2012, "pass-through entities" accounted for 95 percent of all businesses, and 60 percent of all business income, in the United States.[35] Pass-through entities are so named because the tax system treats all of their income as having been "passed through" directly to the owners. U.S. tax law specifies three major categories of pass-through entity—sole proprietorships, partnerships, and "S corporations"—with different qualifying rules for each. All income realized by a pass-through entity in a given year is divided up among the owners and included on their personal income tax returns in that year, regardless of whether the income is actually distributed to the owners or reinvested in the firm.[36] Pass-through entity income is not subject to any separate entity-level tax—e.g., there is no separate tax on partnerships. Income from the other 5 percent of businesses is subject to the corporate income tax, and that income might then be subject to taxation a second time on shareholders' personal tax returns if it is distributed as a dividend, or if it is realized as a capital gain. Pass-through entities avoid

Table 2.3
Tax classification of businesses in the United States

Tax classification of businesses	Subject to corporate income tax?	Key restrictions	Percentage of businesses, 2012	Percentage of business income, 2012
Sole proprietorship	No	Owned by individual or married couple	73	11
Partnership	No	Not publicly traded (with exceptions)	10	30
S corporation	No	No more than 100 owners	12	18
C corporation	Yes	None	5	40

Sources: Authors' calculations based on data from IRS Statistics of Income Tax Stats website <http://www.irs.gov/taxstats/>.
Notes: Includes both nonfarm and farm sole proprietorships. LLCs are included in the categories they choose for tax purposes (usually partnership). Excludes real estate investment trusts and regulated investment companies. The last column is calculated based on net income (less deficit) reported to the IRS.

such "double taxation," but the tax law only permits businesses with certain ownership structures to qualify for pass-through status. The first three rows of table 2.3 present information on each type of pass-through entity.

As of 2012, 73 percent of all businesses in the United States were sole proprietorships, that is, businesses owned by just one person (or under certain conditions, by a married couple).[37] Because on average they are small (and tend to underreport income—see chapter 5), sole proprietorships accounted for just 11 percent of all business income reported to the IRS in the United States in 2012.

Another 10 percent of businesses in 2012, accounting for 30 percent of reported business income, were partnerships. To qualify as a partnership for tax purposes, a business can have any number of owners, but shares of ownership cannot be publicly traded on a stock market or otherwise easily transferred, unless at least 90 percent of income received by the business is "qualifying" passive income such as interest, dividends, capital gains, and rents. A limited liability company (LLC) is an increasingly popular form of business. Owners of LLCs can choose to have them treated either as partnerships or S corporations for tax purposes, and in almost all cases they choose partnership status. LLCs are included in the categories elected by their owners in table 2.3. In 2012, 65 percent of all partnerships were LLCs, compared to just 1 percent in 1993.[38] LLCs cannot be publicly traded. The "limited liability" aspect of an LLC means that an owner's potential for financial loss due to the actions of the firm is limited to his or her investment in the firm, and the owner cannot personally be held legally liable for the actions of other owners. Sole proprietorships and some other kinds of partnership lack this feature that all corporations have.

The third category of pass-through entity is an "S corporation," named for Subchapter S of the Internal Revenue Code. These accounted for 12 percent of businesses and 18 percent of reported business income in 2012. An S corporation benefits from limited liability, but is not allowed to have more than 100 separate owners.[39]

In the United States, "C corporations" (named for Subchapter C of the Internal Revenue Code) are the only kind of business subject to the federal corporate income tax, an entity level tax with graduated marginal tax rates topping out at 35 percent for the largest corporations. Most of the well-known, big publicly traded corporations in the United States, such as Wal-Mart, General Electric, and Ford Motor Company, are C corporations.[40] Although just 5 percent of U.S. businesses were C corporations in 2012, they accounted for 40 percent of all reported business income in that year.[41]

The design of the U.S. personal income tax has been influenced by efforts to ameliorate the degree of "double taxation" of C corporation income—taxation first on the corporation's profits, and then again on the shareholders if and when they receive the benefits of those profits via dividends or realized capital gains. One provision that reduces the degree to which such profits are double-taxed is that both "qualified" dividends (mainly dividend payments that originated in C corporations), and long-term capital gains (defined as gains on assets held for longer than one year) in excess of capital losses, are taxed at lower rates than "ordinary income" (which is basically any other type of taxable income). In 2015, these net capital gains and qualified dividends were subject to a 20 percent marginal tax rate for the highest-income people who were in the top income tax bracket (where the marginal tax rate on ordinary income was 39.6 percent), were exempt from tax for the lowest-income taxpayers who are in the bottom two tax brackets (where the marginal tax rates on ordinary income are 10 percent and 15 percent), and were subject to a 15 percent marginal tax rate in the tax brackets in between (where marginal tax rates on ordinary income range from 25 percent to 35 percent). Notably, though, the reduced capital gains tax rates applied not just to gains on C corporation stock, where the double tax argument applies, but to gains on many other types of assets as well.

While the measures mentioned above reduce double taxation of C corporation income, pass-through entities avoid it altogether, which raises the question of why any firm would choose to be a C corporation. The major attraction for some firms is that shares of ownership in C corporations can be publicly traded without restrictions on the types of income they receive.[42] This makes C corporation status a no-brainer for such companies as Apple or ExxonMobil. But less than 1 percent of C corporations are publicly traded.[43] C corporations benefit from limited liability, but so too do certain types of pass-through entities. One important consideration is that personal income tax on income from a C corporation can be deferred for as long as the income is retained in the business, and this can be an advantage relative to pass-through status under certain circumstances, such as when personal income tax rates are higher than corporate tax rates at the margin (which is the case today for owners of some small C corporations). Another issue is that certain regulations restricting the ownership structure of S corporations, and more generally the fact that pass-through entities must pass income through to owners in the year it is earned, make businesses that choose pass-through entity status an unattractive or impractical target for investment by venture capital firms.[44] In any event, the percentage of businesses choosing C corporation status used to be much higher—for example, 14 percent in 1980—and has declined precipitously since then.[45] Top personal tax rates have fallen significantly since 1980, and requirements to qualify for partnership and S corporation status have been relaxed, both of which undoubtedly have influenced the trend away from C corporations.

Regardless of how a business is classified for tax purposes, there are many commonalities in how the tax system measures business income. In general, net income of a business is computed by beginning with receipts and subtracting the costs of doing business, including wages and salaries paid to employees and allowances for the depreciation of capital goods and interest payments. Some parts of this calculation, such as depreciation deductions, deviate significantly from Haig–Simons income. Later in the chapter we'll discuss such details and also further explain how the corporate income tax works.

Issues in Classifying Business Income

Business income can show up in a variety of different guises on personal income tax returns. How such income is classified can have important consequences; for example, classification can affect the applicable tax rate. As noted above, income from shares of ownership in a C corporation is usually classified as a qualified dividend or a capital gain and subject to reduced tax rates on personal returns. For pass-through entities, the character of the income received at the business level is retained at the owner level. On personal returns, ordinary income received by a nonfarm sole proprietorship is reported on Schedule C and called "business income" (we use that term more broadly to refer to the incomes of *all* types of businesses) and ordinary farm sole proprietorship income is reported on Schedule F and called "farm income." Ordinary partnership and S corporation income is reported under these names using Schedule E on the personal tax return. When a pass-through entity receives qualified dividends, or realizes capital gains on assets that it sells, those are counted as qualified dividends or capital gains on the personal returns of the owners. In 2007, 40 percent of net capital gains (less losses) on personal income tax returns were of this sort. When a person sells an ownership stake in a pass-through entity, the difference between the sales proceeds and the amount the person invested in the firm over the years (either directly or through retained earnings) is included as a capital gain on the owner's personal tax return. That accounted for another 5 percent of capital gains (less losses) on personal tax returns in 2007.[46]

Business income generally comprises some mixture of capital income and labor compensation for owners who work for the firm, and in cases where it is necessary to separate the two, the results are likely to be very inaccurate. Corporations are required by the tax law to pay "reasonable" wages or salaries to shareholders who are officers of the firm, and these are reported as such on personal returns and are deducted from business income.[47] "Reasonable" is obviously a difficult concept to define and enforce, and changing the allocation of an owner's income between salary and dividends, or between salary and S corporation income, can have consequences for tax liability, for example due to double taxation, deferral, and low dividend and capital gains tax rates in the case of C corporations, or because S corporation income is not subject to the payroll taxes for Social Security and Medicare. In the case of sole proprietorships and partnerships, the law specifies that compensation of owners cannot be treated as wage and salary income for tax purposes.[48] As a result, a large portion of sole proprietorship and partnership income is probably best thought of as compensation for the owners' labor. This usually does not affect tax liability, because ordinary income from sole proprietorships and partnerships is treated similarly to wage and salary income by both the income tax and the payroll tax for Social Security and Medicare. However, if income flowing through a proprietorship or partnership can be classified as qualified dividend or capital gain on the owners' returns, it matters, because those are subject to lower personal income tax rates than ordinary income and are exempt from payroll tax. In certain circumstances, that income might actually represent compensation for labor.

An issue that has gotten a lot of recent attention in the media and politics is the controversy over the taxation of "carried interest." Private equity funds and hedge funds have grown enormously in importance, with the value of assets in such funds exceeding $2 trillion in recent years.[49] Such funds are usually organized as partnerships for tax purposes. Typically, investors in the funds (often nonprofits, pension funds, or wealthy individuals) put up most of the capital, but play no role in managing the fund, and so are called "limited partners." The investment managers are called "general partners," and put in a small portion of the capital but do all the work identifying investments and managing the firms. Investment managers of these funds are usually paid an annual "management fee" that is a fixed percentage of the value of assets under management, plus a percentage of the profits of the partnership, which is called the "carried interest." So, for example, a private equity fund might buy a struggling publicly traded corporation, take it private and restructure it, and then sell it for a profit later; the fund managers would typically be paid an annual management fee of 2 percent of asset value, plus a carried interest of 20 percent of the realized capital gain upon sale of the assets. The management fee is taxed as ordinary income, but the carried interest is treated as a capital gain on the managers' personal tax returns, because the character of the income earned by a partnership is passed through to the partners. Thus, the investment managers can benefit from deferral (the carried interest is not taxed until the underlying asset is sold), but, more importantly, the carried interest is subject to the relatively low (no more than 20 percent) personal income tax rates on capital gains as long as they are long-term gains. Controversy arises because carried interest looks a lot like compensation for the investment managers' labor effort, and so arguably should be taxed at ordinary income tax rates (up to 39.6 percent in 2015), perhaps without deferral.

The carried interest issue is further complicated because the tax savings from treating it as a capital gain instead of as ordinary income might be exactly offset by lower deductions for, and therefore higher taxes on, the fund clients (the limited partners). For example, if the investment managers were paid in ordinary salary instead of in capital gains, that would raise the tax bill of the investment managers because they pay a higher tax rate on ordinary income than capital gains, but it could also reduce the tax bill of the limited partners by the same amount because they'd get to deduct the wage and salary payment, reducing their ordinary income, in exchange for realizing more capital gains that are taxed at a lower rate.[50] In practice, however, a large portion of the money invested in such funds comes from tax-exempt entities such as pensions or nonprofits, so the tax classification of the general partners' income has no offsetting effect on the limited partners' (nonexistent) tax liability, and treating the carried interest as capital gain instead of ordinary income definitely reduces taxes overall.[51]

Classification of income for tax purposes was also an important consideration in Donald Trump's tax proposals, and in the tax plan proposed by House Republicans in June 2016. Trump's initial tax plan would have reduced the personal income tax rate on all pass-through entity income to 15 percent, while taxing ordinary personal income at rates up to 25 percent. This one aspect of his tax plan was expected to cost roughly $1.5 trillion of revenue over ten years, and would create strong incentives for people to form pass-through entity businesses and then reclassify their ordinary income (such as labor income) as pass-through entity income in order to benefit from the lower tax rate, which could lead to further revenue losses. When the Trump campaign revised its tax proposal in September 2016, it sent mixed signals about whether this provision would be retained. Meanwhile, the House Republicans proposed a tax plan in June 2016 that would cap the tax rate on pass-through entity income at 25 percent, while taxing ordinary personal income at rates of up to 33 percent.[52]

Most Capital and Business Income Is Excluded from Personal Income Taxation

Table 2.4 provides an overall picture of how much capital and business income is excluded from personal income taxation. It compares, for the period 1987–2013, the average annual capital and business income

Table 2.4
Capital income and business income: amount in the U.S. economy compared to amount on personal income tax returns, 1987–2013

	Average annual amount, 1987–2013, in billions of constant year 2013 dollars		
	(a) Total in U.S. economy	(b) Included on personal income tax returns	(b) as a percentage of (a)
Capital gains less losses	$1,947	$436	22%
Interest, dividends, S-corporation, partnership, sole proprietorship, rental, royalty, estate, and trust income	2,790	967	35
Imputed rental value of owner-occupied housing, less expenses other than taxes and interest	638	0	0
Property taxes on nonbusiness real estate (-)	-122	-129	106
Interest payments by persons (-)	-613	-387	63
Adjustment for erosion of real value of net worth by inflation (-)	-1,066	0	0
Total capital and business income	3,575	888	25

Sources: Authors' calculations based on data from Board of Governors of the Federal Reserve System (2015), U.S. Bureau of Economic Analysis (2015), *IRS Statistics of Income—Individual Income Tax Returns, Complete Report,* Publication 1304 (various years), and Parisi (2015).
Note: In the row for property taxes on nonbusiness real estate, column (a) only includes property taxes on owner-occupied homes, whereas column (b) also includes a small amount of property tax on other types of nonbusiness real estate.

in the economy, measured approximately according to Haig-Simons principles (in column a), with the average annual amount of such income on personal income tax returns (in column b), both measured in billions of constant year 2013 dollars.[53] We use a multi-year average in order to smooth out large year-to-year fluctuations in capital and business incomes (especially capital gains) that can make data from any particular year atypical and misleading, and we start in 1987 because the structure of the income tax was very different before then compared to today. The calculations in the table suggest that over this period only about 25 percent of the real net economic value of capital and business income showed up on personal income tax returns. This occurred for all the reasons outlined above—retirement savings accounts, taxing capital gains on realization, differences between economic and tax measures of depreciation, etc.—plus additional factors such as tax evasion (which we'll cover in chapter 5) and a small amount of capital or business income accruing to those with incomes too low to file tax returns.[54]

Realized capital gains (less deductible losses) included in gross income on personal tax returns averaged $436 billion annually during 1987–2013, which was 22 percent of the $1.947 trillion annual average of accrued capital gains (less losses) in the economy during this period. Dividends, interest income, ordinary income from pass-through entities, market rent, and royalties averaged $2.790 trillion annually during 1987–2013, and of this, an average of $967 billion, or 35 percent, was included in gross income on personal income tax returns (either directly, or indirectly as income from an estate or trust). As of 2004, only 28 percent of interest income and 42 percent of dividend income in the U.S. economy were included in gross income on personal tax returns (data to make such comparisons for these narrower categories of income are unavailable after 2004).[55] The imputed rental value of homes (less depreciation, but before subtracting interest and property taxes) averaged $638 billion annually, and was excluded from personal income taxation altogether. An average of $129 billion of property taxes on nonbusiness real estate were deducted in the calculation of personal taxable income each year, which was actually slightly larger than the closest available U.S. Bureau of Economic Analysis estimate of the value of such taxes in the economy. (A small discrepancy arises here because the estimate in column (a) only includes property taxes on owner-occupied homes, leaving out property taxes on some other kinds of nonbusiness real estate that are deductible on personal tax returns and so are included in column (b)). On average, $387 billion of interest payments made by persons were deducted annually on personal income tax returns, which represented about 63 percent of the amount of such personal interest payments in the economy. Finally, the real value of net worth was eroded by inflation by an average of $1.066 trillion per year, and no adjustment was made for this in the income tax.[56] All in all there was on average $3.575 trillion of real net Haig–Simons capital and business income in the economy during 1987–2013, but only $888 billion (25 percent) of such income was included on personal tax returns.

This estimate actually overstates the degree to which capital and business income is subject to personal income taxation, because it does not account for the interest savings to taxpayers from deferring tax on capital gains, or for the reduced personal tax rates on capital gains and qualified dividends. On the other hand, some of the capital gains and dividend income shown in table 2.4 had already been subjected to the corporate income tax. Average annual C corporation income subject to tax during 1987–2012 was $882 billion per year in constant year 2013 dollars, or 27 percent of average annual net real economic capital and business income during that period.[57] Thus, roughly 54 percent of the real net economic value of capital and business income was included in some combination of the personal and corporate income tax bases in the period from 1987 to 2012.[58] Some of that 54 percent represents double-counting of the same income, so more than 46 percent was not subject to income taxation at all.

This discussion of excluded capital and business income highlights that our existing income tax is in fact an awkward hybrid between an income tax that taxes both labor and capital income, and a piecemeal kind of consumption tax (which would exempt from tax the portion of capital income that represents the return to saving). A policy choice that contributes greatly to this hybrid status is the decision to exclude from taxation the capital income accruing in pensions and several other types of saving plans. We turn to these next.

Tax-Favored Saving Plans
The U.S. income tax system contains a wide array of features that exempt from tax the returns to saving, and these features account for much of the excluded capital income discussed above. Most tax-sheltered saving for retirement takes place in two basic types of employer-provided pension plans—*defined-benefit* plans and *defined-contribution* plans. In defined-benefit plans, employees are promised a fixed level of benefits in retirement that may, for example, be set at some percentage of the average wage and salary income that he or she received from the firm in some period of years preceding retirement. The employer makes regular contributions to a pooled fund for the whole firm, which are invested in financial assets to accumulate enough to pay out the benefits. In defined-contribution plans, by contrast, the employer and usually also the employee make regular contributions to a specific account for that particular employee. The worker generally has some choice of how the funds are invested, and the amount of money that is available on retirement depends on the value of the worker's particular accounts by the time he or she retires. Some

examples of defined-contribution pensions are 401(k) plans (used in the for-profit sector) and 403(b) plans (used in the nonprofit and public sectors), named after the sections of the tax code that detail their special status.

Generally, employer contributions to pension plans are deductible in the calculation of the employer's business taxable income in the same way as wages and salary payments are, but these contributions are not included in the gross income of the employees. Limits have been placed on the amount of income that can receive this favorable tax treatment, however. For defined-contribution plans, there is an annual limit (adjusted for inflation every year) on the combined employer and employee contribution that can be made to any particular individual's account, which was set at $53,000 in 2015. For a defined-benefit plan, the amount of tax saving is effectively limited by setting a maximum annual *benefit* that may be paid out in retirement (also adjusted for inflation), set at $210,000 in 2015.[59] In either type of plan, when benefits are eventually received in retirement, any portion that was not subject to income tax previously is then included in gross income and taxed under the personal income tax. Thus, the retirement benefit part of worker compensation is not completely exempt from tax, but rather the taxation is deferred until retirement.

If the marginal tax rate that applies to the disbursements from the plan during retirement was about the same as the marginal tax rate that applied when the contributions were made, taxing the payments that pension plans make to retirees would roughly offset the benefits of excluding from tax the contributions into the pension plans in the first place. But for most people the marginal tax rate is lower during retirement than during their working years. The more consequential deviation from Haig–Simons income measurement is that the interest, dividends, and capital gains that accumulate in the pension plans are excluded from taxation while they accumulate, thereby exempting the returns to saving from personal income taxation altogether.

Individual retirement accounts (IRAs) provide another method of sheltering capital income from taxation. As of 2015, each individual could contribute up to $5,500 ($6,500 for those of age 50 or over) to an IRA, with the limits to be adjusted for inflation in subsequent years.[60] There are now three general classes of IRAs. In all three cases, interest, dividends, and capital gains that accumulate in the account are excluded from taxation from the time of contribution until the time of withdrawal. The three approaches differ with regard to the tax treatment of contributions and withdrawals from the IRA. In a "traditional" IRA, the income used to make the contribution to the account is excluded from tax, and all withdrawals from the account are subject to tax. If an individual or his or her spouse is covered by an employer-provided pension, eligibility for traditional IRAs is phased out above certain levels of income. In a "Roth" IRA, no deduction is allowed for contributions, but returns and withdrawals are excluded from tax. Eligibility for these is also phased out at higher levels of income. Those who are ineligible for either of the other two types of IRAs can contribute to "nondeductible" IRAs, where the income used for the contribution cannot be excluded from tax, and the withdrawals of any funds above and beyond what was contributed are also subject to tax. In all cases, penalties are imposed if withdrawals are made before age 59½, unless the funds are used for certain approved purposes such as first-time home purchases and some education and medical expenditures.

The above discussion only scratches the surface in terms of the array of tax-favored savings options available and their complex rules. For example, recent years have seen the introduction of a number of tax-favored savings plans for education, including education IRAs. The salient point for now is simply that these plans are a major reason that our "income tax" is in some ways not a tax on income after all, and is especially generous toward capital income accumulating in retirement savings vehicles.

From Gross Income to Personal Income Tax Liability

Table 2.5 displays, for the year 2013, the total amount of gross income reported on personal income tax returns, its major components, the deductions and exemptions that are subtracted from gross income to get to taxable income, and then the additional steps involved in calculating personal tax liability or refund, along with their dollar values and percentages of gross income. Going step by step through the list of items that get us from gross income to tax liability provides a helpful overview of the most basic features of our personal income tax code.

Components of Gross Income

After the various exclusions discussed above, the amount of gross income reported on personal income tax returns totaled $9.24 trillion in 2013. The major constituents of gross income, shown in panel A of

Table 2.5
From gross income to tax liability in the U.S. personal income tax, 2013

	Billions of dollars	Percentage of gross income
A. Gross income reported on personal income tax returns	**9,244**	**100.0**
A1. Wages and salaries	6,627	71.7
A2. S-corporation, partnership, and sole proprietorship income	873	9.4
A3. Capital gains less losses	416	4.5
A4. Dividends	191	2.1
A5. Taxable interest	79	0.9
A6. Taxable pension, annuity, and IRA distributions	866	9.4
A7. Taxable Social Security benefits	245	2.7
A8. Other components of gross income (net)	−52	−0.6
B. Above-the-line deductions (adjustments)	**133**	**1.4**
C. Adjusted Gross Income (A−B)	**9,111**	**98.6**
D. Itemized Deductions	**1,135**	**12.3**
D1. Taxes paid	486	5.3
D2. Interest paid	308	3.3
D3. Charitable contributions	179	1.9
D4. Medical and dental expenses	82	0.9
D5. Other itemized deductions	80	0.9
E. Standard deductions & personal exemptions (less unused deductions and exemptions)	**1,566**	**16.9**
F. Taxable income (C−D−E)	**6,410**	**69.3**
G. Ordinary income tax	**1,271**	**13.8**
H. Alternative minimum tax	**23**	**0.2**
I. Income tax before credits (G+H)	**1,294**	**14.0**
J. Tax credits (including portions that offset other taxes and refundable portions)	**173**	**1.9**
J1. Earned Income Tax Credit	69	0.8
J2. Child Tax Credit	56	0.6
J3. Other credits	48	0.5
K. Income tax minus credits (I−J)	**1,121**	**12.1**

Source: Authors' calculations based on preliminary data from Parisi (2015).
Note: Line A2 is net income less loss, and includes both nonfarm and farm businesses.

table 2.5, are wage and salary income (71.7 percent of the total), income from pass-through entities (9.4 percent), capital gains less losses (4.5 percent), dividends (2.1 percent), interest (0.9 percent), pension, annuity, and IRA distributions (9.4 percent) and Social Security benefits (2.7 percent).

Deductions and Exemptions in the Personal Income Tax

After adding up the components of gross income, the next step in the tax calculation process is to compute and then subtract a variety of deductions and exemptions. A total of $2.834 trillion of such deductions and exemptions (the sum of items B, D, and E in table 2.5) were subtracted from gross income in 2013, leaving taxable income of $6.410 trillion, or about 69.3 percent of gross income (see panel F of table 2.5).

The first set of deductions are "above-the-line deductions" (also known as "adjustments"), which totaled $133 billion, or 1.4 percent of gross income, in 2013. A few examples of above-the-line deductions include contributions to IRAs, unreimbursed expenses of moving to a new job, health insurance costs of self-employed people, interest on student loans (tax-deductible for people with incomes below a certain level), and fees for higher education (deductible up to $4,000 in 2014 for households with incomes below certain levels—a provision that is scheduled to expire after 2016, but could be extended).[61] Gross income minus above-the-line deductions yields "adjusted gross income" (AGI), which was $9.111 trillion in 2013.

Next, taxpayers have the choice of claiming the larger of two options: *itemized deductions,* or a *standard deduction* that differs depending on one's filing status—single, head-of-household (single parent), or married filing jointly. The higher their income, the more likely it is that taxpayers' itemized deductions exceed the standard deduction. In 2013, only 21 percent of those with AGI below $100,000 chose to itemize, while 83 percent of those with AGI above $100,000 did.[62] Altogether, itemized deductions reduced the tax base by $1.135 trillion, or 12.3 percent of gross income, in 2013 (see panel D of table 2.5).

The largest itemized deduction, for state and local taxes, amounted to $486 billion, or 5.3 percent of gross income, in 2013. State and local income taxes and property taxes are deductible. Since 2004, taxpayers have been able to take a deduction for the *larger* of their state and local sales taxes or their state and local income taxes (but not both), a provision that was scheduled to expire and then extended multiple times before being made permanent in 2015.[63] The next largest itemized deduction, for interest payments, totaled $308 billion in 2013, or 3.3 percent of gross income, $293 billion of which was home mortgage interest. A taxpayer can deduct interest on up to two homes with a total value of up to $1 million. One can also deduct up to $100,000 in interest on home equity loans (second mortgages), the money from which can be used for any purpose.[64] Interest payments on credit cards and other consumer debt, such as automobile loans, however, are not deductible. Interest used to finance investments can be deducted but only to the extent that it offsets investment income.

Contributions to qualifying charitable organizations are the next largest deduction, amounting to $179 billion, or 1.9 percent of gross income, in 2013. Medical and dental expenses are deductible to the extent that they exceed 10.0 percent of AGI (or 7.5 percent of AGI for those aged 65 or above until 2017).[65] In 2013 the deductible portion amounted to $82 billion, or 0.9 percent of gross income. An array of minor itemized deductions comprised another $80 billion, or 0.9 percent of gross income. These included, among other things, unreimbursed employee expenses (such as travel costs), casualty and theft losses, gambling losses, and tax-preparation fees. For taxpayers with AGI above certain thresholds ($250,000 for singles, $275,000 for heads of household, and $300,000 for married couples filing jointly in 2013, with thresholds indexed for inflation in subsequent years), some itemized deductions are subject to a limitation provision. Under this provision earning more income reduces the amount of deductions one can take, which in most cases amounts to a tax on AGI above the threshold. A provision roughly like this, but with lower income thresholds, existed from 1991 through 2009, was eliminated during 2010 through 2012, and then restored with higher income thresholds starting in 2013.

Those who do not itemize deductions can take a standard deduction, which as shown in table 2.6 in tax year 2015 was $12,600 for married taxpayers filing joint returns, $9,250 for a single-parent head of household, and $6,300 for a single person. These deduction levels are somewhat higher if the taxpayer is elderly or blind. In addition, a personal exemption—equal to $4,000 in 2015—is allowed for each member of the taxpayer's family. The standard deduction and personal exemption are automatically increased at the rate of inflation each year to keep their values constant in real terms. Because of personal exemptions and standard deductions, a certain amount of income

Table 2.6
Dollar values of personal exemptions and standard deductions, 2015

	Single Person	Head of household with 2 children	Married couple with 2 children
Total value of personal exemptions	$4,000	$12,000	$16,000
Standard deduction	6,300	9,250	12,600
Sum of personal exemptions and standard deduction	$10,300	$21,250	$28,600

Source: Internal Revenue Service (2014a).

can be received before any tax is owed, as if there were an extra tax bracket at the bottom of the income scale, within which the tax rate is zero. For example, for a married couple with two children, the first $28,600 (the standard deduction of $12,600 plus four exemptions of $4,000 each) of income is exempt from income taxation. This effectively eliminates any positive income tax liability for low-income families and also contributes to the graduated nature of tax rates for those who do pay taxes, which we discuss next. In 2013 and later years, the benefits of personal exemptions are gradually phased out for taxpayers with AGI above the same thresholds used for the itemized deduction limitation discussed above.

Personal Income Tax Rate Structure
Once you've gone through all the hoops to get to taxable income, the next step of calculating tax liability (before tax credits) is usually pretty straightforward. Tax software calculates it automatically. People who don't use software look up how much they owe based on a table in the instruction booklet. The tax rate schedule applies successively higher tax rates to the portions of taxable income that fall into higher and higher tax brackets (which, as noted above, is sometimes called a "graduated" tax rate structure). The 2015 tax rate structure is shown in table 2.7. Note that there are separate rate structures depending on the tax return's filing status. Almost every return falls into one of three filing statuses: married filing jointly, single, or "head of household" (the last of which generally applies to single parents). In most cases, a married couple filing jointly will pay less tax on the same taxable income than a single taxpayer, with a head of household filer being somewhere in between.[66]

Table 2.7
Brackets and statutory marginal rates in the personal income tax, 2015

Taxable income range, by filing status

Single	Head of household	Married couple, joint return	Marginal tax rate
0–9,225	0–13,150	0–18,450	10.0%
9,225–37,450	13,150–50,200	18,450–74,900	15.0%
37,450–90,750	50,200–129,600	74,900–151,200	25.0%
90,750–189,300	129,600–209,850	151,200–230,450	28.0%
189,300–411,500	209,850–411,500	230,450–411,500	33.0%
411,500–413,200	411,500–439,000	411,500–464,850	35.0%
above 413,200	above 439,000	above 464,850	39.6%

Source: Internal Revenue Service (2014a).

In 2015, the seven official tax brackets for each filing status shown in table 2.7 featured rates that started at 10 percent on the first dollars of taxable income and gradually rose all the way up to 39.6 percent at higher levels of taxable income; recall, though, that personal exemptions and the standard deduction effectively created another bracket (shown in table 2.6) with a zero tax rate on the first dollars of AGI, before we even got to taxable income. The dollar amounts that form the dividing point between each tax bracket are increased each year by the rate of inflation to prevent inflation from pushing people into higher tax brackets over time (bracket creep).

To illustrate how the tax calculation works, consider the example of a married couple that takes the standard deduction, has two children, has no above-the-line deductions, and has a gross income of $100,000 in 2015. First, $28,600 (the sum of personal exemptions and the standard deduction) is subtracted off (see table 2.6), leaving a taxable income of $71,400. Although, as the third column of table 2.7 shows, this family is "in" the 15 percent bracket, their tax liability is much less than 15 percent of their income. Rather, they pay no tax at all on their first $28,600 of income, 10 percent on their next $18,450 of income (which is the first $18,450 of taxable income) and 15 percent on taxable income between $18,450 and $71,400, for a total tax bill of $1,845 + $7,942.50 = $9,787.50.

This example illustrates a critically important conceptual issue—the distinction between an *average* tax rate and a *marginal* tax rate. The *marginal* tax rate is defined as the tax rate that would apply to the next few dollars of income you could earn, given the income you already have. In the case of the family in this example, it is 15 percent; if their taxable income increased by $100 from $71,400 to $71,500, their tax liability would increase by $15. This is the tax rate that should affect any marginal decisions that change taxable income; for example, working an extra hour at $12 an hour before tax only yields $12 x (1–0.15) = $10.20 after tax.

The *average* tax rate is defined as total tax liability expressed as a percentage of some measure of total income. As a share of gross income, this family's average tax rate is (9,787.50/100,000), or about 9.8 percent, significantly lower than the 15 percent marginal tax rate. The graduated rate structure, together with the personal exemptions and standard deductions, make our income tax *progressive*, meaning that average tax rates are generally higher for people with higher incomes. For example, repeating the above example for the same family with $200,000 of gross income would yield a tax liability of $35,043.50. This is considerably more than twice the tax liability on $100,000 of gross income and amounts to an average tax rate of 17.5 percent.[67]

A common misconception about the tax-rate schedule is that moving to the next (higher) bracket can trigger so much extra tax that after-tax income actually declines, and that it is therefore especially important to avoid crossing into the next bracket so as to escape this extra tax liability. In fact this is not how things work, because the marginal tax rates apply only to the income within that bracket. For example, a married couple with $74,900 of taxable income is at the top end of the 15 percent bracket. Earning one more dollar pushes that couple into the 25 percent bracket but increases tax liability by only 25 cents; earning that extra dollar thus *increases* after-tax income by 75 cents. Thus there is no particular reason to avoid decisions that push you into a higher tax bracket.

The true structure of marginal tax rates is actually a bit more complicated than is implied by the "statutory" rates shown in table 2.7. One reason is that myriad provisions "phase out" the benefits of various exemptions, deductions, exclusions, and credits as income increases over certain ranges of income. In most cases, the impact of these phaseouts is more or less identical to what would happen if we just increased marginal tax rates by a bit over those same income ranges. For example, in 2015, phaseouts of personal exemptions and itemized deductions typically raised the effective marginal tax rate on a married couple with two children and $380,000 of AGI from 33 percent to 38.2 percent.[68]

Other examples of provisions that are phased out for people with higher incomes include certain exclusions (such as one for Social Security benefits) and deductions (such as those for IRA contributions and student loan interest), as well as various credits discussed below.[69] In addition, the returns of taxpayers who have capital gains income or qualified dividends are subject to some additional complicated calculations at the stage of computing tax liability, in order to apply special reduced marginal tax rates to those two types of income.

Applying tax rates to taxable income in the manner described above, and adjusting for special tax rates on capital gains and dividends, yields "ordinary" income tax liability, which in 2013 totaled $1.271 trillion, or about 13.8 percent of gross income (see panel G of table 2.5). For many people, however, the process of computing income tax does not end here. Additional steps, including computation of the alternative minimum tax and various tax credits, have become increasingly important in recent years.

The Personal Alternative Minimum Tax

The alternative minimum tax (AMT) is essentially a second, parallel income tax that requires many taxpayers to calculate (or have their tax software calculate) an alternative definition of taxable income, subtract an AMT-specific exemption, and then apply a separate AMT tax rate schedule. AMT taxable income disallows all personal exemptions, the standard deduction, the itemized deduction for state and local taxes, a portion of the medical and dental expense deduction, and miscellaneous deductions. It also requires recalculating business income using different rules for things such as depreciation, and treats income from the exercise of stock options differently than the regular tax system, among other things.

The AMT tax bracket structure provides an exemption that depends on marital status (which is phased out at higher income levels), and then imposes a tax rate of 26 percent on the first $185,400 of AMT taxable income above the exemption and 28 percent on amounts beyond that in 2015 (indexed for inflation in subsequent years). In 2015, the AMT exemption amounts were $83,400 for a married couple filing a joint return and $53,600 for an unmarried filer (indexed for inflation). The AMT exemption is gradually phased out for those with AMT taxable income (before subtracting the exemption) above thresholds of $158,900 (for joint returns) or $119,200 (for unmarried taxpayers); these thresholds are also indexed for inflation.[70] This exemption phaseout effectively raises the AMT marginal tax rate to 32.5 percent or 35 percent over certain income ranges.[71] The calculation of AMT is adjusted to preserve the same reduced marginal tax rates on capital gains and qualified dividends that apply in the ordinary income tax. If the AMT tax liability thus calculated is larger than a taxpayer's "ordinary" tax liability calculated as described above, the difference is added to the tax bill. Effectively, each taxpayer must pay the greater of either the tax liability under the AMT or the regular income tax. In 2013, about 4 million taxpayers were subject to the AMT, which represented 2.7 percent of all returns filed, and it raised about $23 billion in tax revenue.[72]

Credits in the Personal Income Tax

For many people, the next step in the process of computing personal income tax is to calculate and apply tax *credits*. Recall that exemptions, deductions, and exclusions all decrease taxable income, which lowers tax liability only by the amount of the reduction in taxable income times the marginal tax rate. For example, when taxable income falls by $100, tax liability for someone in the 25 percent tax bracket declines by $25. In contrast, a tax credit directly reduces tax liability dollar for dollar, so its value does not depend on the marginal tax rate.

In recent years credits have proliferated dramatically in the tax code. In 2013, the total value of personal income tax credits was $173 billion, which reduced net personal income tax revenue from 14.0 percent to 12.1 percent of gross income (see panels I, J, and K of table 2.5). The largest of all credits is the *Earned Income Tax Credit* (EITC), which is a program intended to improve the work incentives and well-being of the working poor. The basic idea of the EITC is to subsidize earnings from work (in part offsetting disincentives to work caused by payroll taxes and some other government programs) by offering a tax credit for every dollar earned up to a certain level. To limit the benefits to low-income households, the EITC phases out after a certain income threshold is reached.

Unlike almost all of the other credits in the personal tax system, the EITC is "refundable," meaning that if it is larger than your total tax bill, you get a check for the difference. In 2013, the total dollar value of the EITC was $69 billion (see panel J of table 2.5). Of that, only about $1.3 billion was used to offset income taxes, $7.9 billion was used to offset other taxes reported on the personal income tax form (such as Social Security and Medicare tax on self-employment and tip income), and $60.3 billion was refundable.[73] Although technically part of the tax system, the EITC as of 2009 paid out more in benefits, and removed more children from poverty, than any other single government cash- or nutrition-based assistance program targeted to the poor. On the other hand, in that year the EITC still cost considerably less than Medicaid (the federal-state health care program for the poor) or unemployment insurance (which is not targeted specifically to the poor).[74]

The EITC is relatively small for childless taxpayers, and increases in value for each "qualifying" child that a taxpayer has, up to three. To be a qualifying child for purposes of the EITC, a child must: live more than half the year with the taxpayer; be under age nineteen, or under age twenty-four but a student who is younger than the taxpayer, or permanently and totally disabled; meet a relationship test; and not file a joint tax return unless it is solely to claim a refund.[75] In 2015, a married couple with three qualifying children received 45 cents of Earned Income Tax Credit for every dollar earned from work over the range of annual work income between $1 and $13,870. Between $13,870 and $23,630 of work income, the family received the maximum available credit of $6,242. The credit was then phased out gradually at a rate of 21.06 cents per additional dollar earned between $23,630 and $53,267.[76] In the phase-in range of up to $13,870 of income, the EITC provided a 45 percent subsidy to working. But in the phaseout range, the credit declined by 21.06 cents for each dollar earned, so that the EITC *added* 21.06 percent to the effective marginal tax rate on working. Thus, some taxpayers in the 10 percent statutory tax bracket actually faced a 31.06 percent marginal income tax rate because every additional dollar earned generated both an additional 10 cents of tax liability and also a cutback of 21.06 cents in the EITC. Because the credit is always positive, it always makes working more attractive relative to not working at all. But because for some people in the phaseout range it increases their marginal tax rate, it can actually have negative effects on incentives regarding *how much* to work.

Also of note is the *Child Tax Credit*, which was introduced in 1997. In 2015, this credit reduced a family's tax liability by $1,000 for each qualifying dependent child under age seventeen. Child Tax Credits are gradually phased out at higher income levels (starting at $110,000 for married couples). For those with incomes too low to face any tax liability, the Child Tax Credits are refundable to the extent of 15 percent of the amount by which earned income exceeds $3,000. Child Tax Credits were worth $56 billion in reduced tax liability and refunds in 2013 (see panel J of table 2.5).

The EITC and Child Tax Credit, together with personal exemptions and the standard deduction, contribute greatly to the progressivity of the tax system. Considering all four of these provisions together, in 2015 a married couple did not have a positive income tax liability until family income reached $49,187 if they had two qualifying children under seventeen, or $58,750 if they had three such children. Largely because of the EITC, many of the lowest-income families effectively face *negative* average income tax rates—they get money from the government.

The long and growing list of other tax credits in effect as of 2015 included a credit for a portion of certain expenditures on care for a child or other dependent, such as payments to a day care center. This applied to children under age thirteen and sometimes to other family members who are unable to care for themselves. The American Opportunity Tax Credit, which was enacted in 2009 as a temporary measure and then made permanent in 2015, provided a partially refundable credit of up to $2,500 per eligible student per year for educational expenditures on the first four years of post-secondary education, and the Lifetime Learning Credit provided a nonrefundable credit of up to $2,000 per return for post-secondary educational expenses as of 2015. They could not be claimed in the same year for the same student, and eligibility was phased out at higher income levels. The Saver's Credit provided up to 50 cents of tax credit for every dollar, capped at $1,000, contributed to an IRA for relatively low-income households, as of 2015. These and other credits not already mentioned above amounted to another $48 billion in combined reduced tax liability and refunds in 2013 (see panel J of table 2.5).

More on Taxation of Business Income and the Corporate Income Tax

In our introduction to income taxation of capital and business income earlier in the chapter, we noted that as of 2012, 95 percent of businesses in the United States were pass-through entities, where all income is allocated directly to owners and included on their personal income tax returns, while 5 percent of businesses were C corporations subject to the corporate income tax (see table 2.3). In this section, we discuss the details of how taxable income is measured for both types of businesses, and lay out the basic features of the corporate income tax.

Defining the Business Tax Base

Broadly speaking, the net income for tax purposes of a business is the proceeds from its sales minus the costs of doing business. The costs of many inputs to production are deductible in the year of purchase or when the items they produce are sold. These include wages, salaries, and benefits for employees; the costs of material inputs; taxes paid to state and local governments; employer contributions to Social Security; costs of repairs; advertising costs; and many other miscellaneous expenses. The tax treatment of the costs of investment in capital goods—durable equipment and buildings—is, however, a bit more complicated.

Depreciation Allowances

The costs of investing in capital assets, such as productive machinery and buildings, are generally *not* deducted in full at the time of purchase, although in recent years some notable exceptions to this rule have been enacted, which we will explain later. Usually, in accordance with the economist's concept of income described earlier, a depreciation deduction is allowed instead. Recall that in principle depreciation is the decline in value of an asset, such as a factory building or a machine, that occurs as the asset wears out or becomes obsolete. In practice a firm can deduct a portion of the capital asset's purchase price every year for several years until eventually the full purchase price has been deducted. Spreading the deduction out over time is generally less favorable to the firm than allowing a full deduction at the time of purchase because the tax savings from an immediate deduction can be invested and accumulate interest: it's better to have the tax saving sooner rather than later.

Accurately measuring the depreciation of a capital good—its decline in value—is difficult and would be feasible only in cases where active markets for used capital goods exist. In this case, a business would deduct the difference in the market price between, say, a two-year-old combine and a three-year-old one.[77] The depreciation allowances provided in the tax code are rough approximations of the average changes in value for broad categories of capital equipment and structures. For instance, all equipment is assigned to one of six categories of useful life—three, five, seven, ten, fifteen, or twenty years. In addition, Congress periodically enacts provisions that intentionally accelerate depreciation schedules to encourage investment.

As an example of how the depreciation rules usually work, consider a large corporation that in 2007 (the most recent year without any special temporary accelerated depreciation incentives) paid $1,000 for a photocopier. Tax law assigns a five-year life to a photocopier. Using a convention that a capital asset is placed in service in the middle of the first year, the firm is allowed to deduct $200 in the first year (2007 in this example), and in subsequent years can deduct $320, $192, $115.20, $115.20, and $57.60.

Tax laws enacted in response to the past two recessions made dramatic but supposedly temporary increases to the portion of the cost of investment that could be deducted in its first year of use, an approach known as "bonus depreciation." For example, a law enacted in 2010 allowed the entire cost of investment to be deducted immediately (an approach known as "expensing"), applying to investment purchased and put into service after September 8, 2010, and before January 1, 2012. It also allowed 50 percent of the cost of investment taking place in 2012 to be deducted in the first year, with the remaining 50 percent deducted according to the normal depreciation deduction schedules like those discussed in the previous paragraph. A law enacted at the beginning of 2013 extended the 50 percent first-year bonus depreciation to investments made through the end of 2013, a 2014 law extended it again to the end of 2014, and a law enacted in December 2015 extended it through the end of 2019, or 2020 for certain narrow classes of long-lived and transportation-related assets. Most, but not all, types of business investment were eligible for bonus depreciation, including among other things tangible business property with a life of 20 years or less.[78]

Small businesses (technically, businesses that do not make large amounts of investment) have long been eligible to expense the cost of a limited amount of investment, and this amount was increased dramatically, but supposedly temporarily, in recent efforts to fight recessions. A law enacted in December 2015 made permanent the most recently enacted increase in generosity of expensing provisions for small businesses, which had previously been scheduled to expire. In 2015, businesses could expense up to $500,000, reduced by the amount that investment exceeded $2 million, and both of those figures will automatically be adjusted in future years to keep up with the rate of inflation.[79]

Deductibility of Interest and Double Taxation

If a business raises money by borrowing, the interest payments it pays to the lenders—the providers of capital—are generally deductible as a cost of business from its taxable income in the year they are made. So business proceeds that are paid out in the form of interest escape taxation at the business level. Interest receipts may be taxable income to the recipient under the individual income tax, although as noted above, the vast majority of interest income is excluded from personal income taxation through various means (such as pensions).

In contrast, when a C corporation raises money by issuing shares, the returns to the providers of capital (i.e., the shareholders)—in the form of dividends and capital gains—are *not* deductible from the corporate tax base. Thus, for C corporations there is a stark difference between the tax treatment of the two basic ways that firms raise money. One implication is that C corporation income that is distributed as dividends or retained within the firm (which presumably pushes up stock prices) may be subject to tax at two levels—once at the corporate level and then again at the personal level when distributed to shareholders as dividends or realized in the form of a capital gain. Recall, though, that only a small portion of capital gains and dividends is taxed under the personal income tax, and then they are generally taxed at a rate capped at 20 percent. As noted above, pass-through entities avoid so-called double taxation of business income altogether.

To the extent that it occurs, the double taxation of income from C corporations has several troublesome consequences. It can produce a very high combined marginal tax rate on saving and investment done in C corporations, it creates economically inefficient, uneven taxation of investment done in C corporations versus other types of businesses, it distorts decisions about which organizational form of businesses to adopt, and it creates an incentive to finance investment through debt (the selling of bonds) rather than equity (the selling of shares), as double taxation potentially applies only to the returns to the latter. We'll explore these problems and possible solutions to them in chapter 6.

Corporate Tax Rate Structure and the Size Distribution of C Corporations

The U.S. corporate income tax applies the tax rate structure shown in table 2.8 to a measure of taxable income. Unlike the personal tax rate

Table 2.8
Brackets and marginal tax rates in the corporate income tax,
2015

Taxable income range ($)	Marginal tax rate
0–50,000	15%
50,000–75,000	25%
75,000–100,000	34%
100,000–335,000	39%
335,000–10,000,000	34%
10,000,000–15,000,000	35%
15,000,000–18,333,333	38%
above 18,333,333	35%

Source: Internal Revenue Service (2015n) and Joint Committee on Taxation (2015a).

schedule, there is no exempt level of income. The marginal tax rate is 15 percent for any taxable income below $50,000, 25 percent for taxable income between $50,000 and $75,000, 34 percent for taxable income between $75,000 and $100,000, and 35 percent for taxable income above $18,333,333. There is a complicated pattern of marginal tax rates, ranging between 34 and 39 percent, for taxable incomes between $100,000 and $18,333,333, which mainly reflects the fact that the benefits of low tax rates in the lower brackets are phased out over certain income ranges so that for corporations with income in the top bracket, both the average and marginal tax rate on taxable income is 35 percent.

Most C corporations are relatively small, but a tiny minority of very large C corporations account for almost all of the taxable income and tax revenue of the corporate income tax. In 2012, 41 percent of C corporations had business receipts of less than $100,000, and 66 percent had business receipts of less than $500,000. Just 1.2 percent of C corporations had business receipts of $50 million or more, but they accounted for 94 percent of income subject to corporate tax and 92 percent of corporate income tax liability after credits. In 2012, 94 percent of all C corporations had corporate income tax liability after credits of less than $15,000, and the vast majority of those faced statutory marginal tax rates of 0, 15, or 25 percent.[80] All of the remaining 6 percent of C corporations faced statutory marginal tax rates of 34 percent or above, and these firms accounted for 97 percent of income subject to corporate tax, and 99.6 percent of corporate income tax after credits. Thus it is true that, while most C corporations face marginal tax rates of 25 percent or less, most C corporation *income* is subject to a marginal tax rate of 34 percent or more.[81]

Business Tax Credits

The income tax code allows a wide variety of business tax credits, most of which can be used by both C corporations and pass-through entities (in the case of S corporations and partnerships, the credits are computed at the business level and then allocated among the owners). An important example is the tax credit for certain expenditures on research and experimentation (R&E). The basic credit is 20 percent of the amount by which qualified research expenditures exceed an average base level for that firm, although two other alternative methods of computing the credit are also available. The R&E credit was for a long time technically a temporary provision, but since its original enactment in 1981 it had been "temporarily" extended sixteen times.[82] A law passed in December 2015 finally made the R&E credit permanent.[83] Investment tax credits have been in effect numerous times since 1962, although the latest version was repealed in 1986. These credits reduced tax liability by a certain percentage for every dollar of new investment spending on capital equipment, and in their time were used to stimulate investment during economic downturns, much as accelerated, or bonus, depreciation has been used in more recent years. There are over twenty-five other, relatively minor, business tax credits, such as for investment in low-income housing and testing expenses for orphan drugs.[84]

Corporate Alternative Minimum Tax and Treatment of Losses

Like the similarly named tax that applies to individuals, the corporate tax system has its own alternative minimum tax (AMT), which is intended to prevent apparently profitable corporations from reducing their taxes "too much." The AMT applies a lower tax rate (20 percent) to a broader definition of net income, involving less generous depreciation and accounting rules. Firms then pay the larger of the AMT or the regular tax. In 2011, this provision affected only 0.7 percent of C corporation tax returns and raised just $3 billion in revenue, which amounted to 1.6 percent of total corporate income tax after credits.[85]

If, after subtracting out all the deductions and allowances, a corporation has a net loss, the company does not automatically receive a refund check from the IRS. Instead, it can carry that loss either forward or backward to a limited number of other years to offset positive taxable income earned in those years.

Treatment of International Income of Corporations

In principle, a corporation based in the United States owes U.S. tax on all of its income, regardless of where in the world it earns its income. However, because other countries will also levy tax on income earned within their borders, to avoid a punitive second layer of tax the U.S. tax system allows U.S. corporations a limited credit for income taxes paid to foreign governments, called the *foreign tax credit*.

The mechanics of the foreign tax credit are as follows. If a corporation based in the United States has operations in foreign countries, it pays corporate tax on the profits earned abroad directly to the foreign governments. If the sum of all these tax payments is less than the U.S. tax liability that would have been owed on those profits, the corporation pays the difference to the United States. In effect, the company pays the total U.S. tax due on the income earned abroad and then subtracts the credit for foreign taxes already paid on that income. If, on the other hand, the sum of tax payments to foreign governments is greater than what the U.S. tax liability would have been on those profits, the corporation's foreign tax credit is capped at what the U.S. tax liability would have been. So if a firm invested mostly in low-tax countries, it would pay (in total to foreign countries and the United States combined) the U.S. tax rate, but if it invested mostly in high-tax countries, it could pay more than the U.S. rate.

There's a catch, though, to this story, and it turns out that U.S. corporations can reduce their tax burdens by investing in low-tax countries after all. First, if a company based in the United States owns a subsidiary in a foreign country, no U.S. tax is paid on the subsidiary's profits until those profits are sent back to the U.S. parent company as dividend payments. Thus, the parent company can defer paying the difference between the U.S. rate and a low-tax country's rate indefinitely by having the subsidiary keep reinvesting its profits within the foreign country. Moreover, complicated accounting devices can be used to make the profits of the subsidiary in the low-tax country look larger than they really are and make the profits of the U.S. parent company look smaller. For example, the subsidiary located in a low-tax country could sell items to the parent company at an inflated price. The IRS has rules designed to minimize such practices, but they are hard to enforce, especially when the transactions between related corporations involve difficult-to-value intangible commodities, such as patents. We consider this issue and its consequences in greater depth in chapter 5.

Social Security and Medicare Taxes

Social Security and Medicare taxes together represent the second most important source of revenue for the U.S. federal government after the personal income tax, raising revenue equal to 5.8 percent of GDP in 2014 (compared to 8.1 percent of GDP for the personal income tax).[86] The payroll tax for Old Age, Survivors, and Disability Insurance (OASDI, the official name for the Social Security cash benefit program) is 12.4 percent of the total of wages, salaries, and self-employment income below a "maximum taxable earnings level" (equal to $118,500 in 2015 and adjusted by the average rate of wage growth each year), with no tax above that level.[87] The payroll tax for the Medicare Hospital Insurance (HI) program consists of two parts. First, there is a tax of 2.9 percent of all wages, salaries, and self-employment income, with no cap. Second, as of 2013 there is a tax of 0.9 percent of combined wage and salary and self-employment income that exceeds $250,000 for a married couple filing a joint income tax return or $200,000 for an unmarried taxpayer, which was enacted as part of the Affordable Care and Patient Protection Act of 2010 (ACA), popularly known as "Obama-care." The 12.4 percent OASDI and 2.9 percent HI taxes are nominally split half and half between employer and employee (although for most employees the employer remits both portions to the IRS), while self-employed people are responsible for remitting the entire tax themselves. Employees and the self-employed are responsible for the new 0.9 percent HI tax themselves, but in the former case the extra tax will usually be withheld and remitted by the employer as well.[88]

The ACA also introduced, for the first time, a 3.8 percent Medicare HI tax on the amount of "net investment income" that is included in gross income on personal income tax returns. This new tax only applies to people with income exceeding thresholds of $250,000 (for married couples filing jointly) or $200,000 (for unmarried taxpayers). "Net investment income" includes most forms of capital income included on the personal income tax return, such as capital gains, dividends, royalties, and rents, as well as business income from pass-through entities when the business is a "passive activity" of the taxpayer (that is, the taxpayer does not materially participate in the conduct of the business).[89] Together with the provisions of the American Taxpayer Relief Act of 2012 (the deal to avert the "fiscal cliff" which was enacted at the beginning of 2013), this increased the top federal marginal tax rate on capital gains and qualified dividends, considering both personal income tax and Medicare tax, from 15 percent (the rate that prevailed from 2003 through 2012) to 23.8 percent in 2013 and later years.

Although the personal income tax raises more revenue for the federal government than do taxes for Social Security and Medicare, the Urban-Brookings Tax Policy Center has estimated that in 2014, about 79 percent of households who owed any Social Security tax, Medicare tax, or income tax at all owed more in Social Security and Medicare taxes (counting both employee and employer portions) than in income taxes.[90]

A unique characteristic of Social Security payroll taxes is that the cash benefits that people receive after retirement or disability are related by an explicit formula to the amount of taxes, or contributions, remitted (or more precisely, to the amount of earnings on which such taxes were levied) over one's working years. People who contribute large amounts of taxes into Social Security over their lifetimes typically receive larger retirement benefits from the system than those who contribute less, although the relationship is far from proportional (lower-income people get back a higher percentage of their earnings). This of course differs from other taxes, such as income taxes, where a higher tax liability does not entitle one to more of what the federal government provides, whether it be VIP treatment at national parks or personalized national defense. Indeed, if each individual received back in retirement exactly what they contributed, plus interest, it wouldn't really be a tax at all, but rather just forced saving.

The income tax and the payroll taxes for Social Security and Medicare interact in some notable ways. For instance, the employer portion of the payroll tax is excluded from income taxation, but the employee portion is subject to personal income tax. In addition, a portion of Social Security benefit payments is subject to personal income taxation for people with incomes above a certain threshold.

Intense controversy surrounds whether and how to reform the Social Security and Medicare systems. As we'll see in chapter 4, the long-run financial outlook for Medicare is dire, and the long-run situation for Social Security is less severe but still out of balance. This suggests that something eventually will have to be done. Analysis of specific proposals for reforming Social Security and Medicare are outside of the scope of this book, but we will consider the implications of the long-run fiscal imbalance for tax policy in general in later chapters.

Estate and Gift Taxes

The modern federal estate tax was adopted in 1916, and for much of its history it was a little-noticed part of federal tax policy, but it has attracted much more attention and debate in recent times. The estate tax is a tax on the wealth that very rich individuals leave to their heirs at death, and so it is a tax on the *transfer* of wealth rather than wealth itself. For those dying in 2015, the first $5.43 million of an estate was effectively exempted from tax, and a 40 percent tax rate was imposed on wealth above that level.[91] Bequests to a spouse or to a charity are deductible from the taxable estate. The Urban-Brookings Tax Policy Center has estimated that in 2011, when the exemption level was $5 million, only slightly more than 3,000 estates (representing the richest 0.13 percent of all adult decedents in the United States) would be subject to the estate tax.[92]

To limit opportunities for tax avoidance, the estate tax is integrated with a tax on lifetime gifts. In 2015, each individual was allowed to give any number of recipients up to $14,000 (adjusted for inflation in subsequent years), plus any gifts for educational or medical purposes, completely tax-free.[93] The portion of any gifts beyond that began to count against the $5.43 million exemption mentioned above. If the total of these gifts in excess of the $14,000 annual exemption reach $5.43 million, the donor is required to start remitting gift taxes while still alive. Otherwise, the excess gifts just reduce the amount of the exemption that is available to the estate at death.

Recent Changes in Tax Law and the Outlook for Tax Policy in the United States

Starting in 2001, U.S. tax policy went through a period of pronounced instability and unpredictability, as Congress enacted an array of tax cuts that were scheduled to expire at various dates in the future. When their expiration dates approached, they were frequently extended, temporarily, often at the last minute, and usually following much uncertainty about what would happen. The American Taxpayer Relief Act (ATRA) of 2012, enacted at the very beginning of January 2013, and the Protecting Americans from Tax Hikes Act of 2015, both restored some degree of stability and predictability to tax policy, by making "permanent" many aspects of tax law that had recently gone through these cycles of scheduled expiration and last-minute extension. Here and throughout the rest of the chapter, we mean "permanent" in the very limited sense that these provisions will remain in effect until any future legislative action changes them instead of expiring automatically at some future date.

The apparent return of stability and predictability in tax law may well turn out to be short-lived, however. Projections that federal tax revenues will fall far short of promised federal government spending in the long-run future, a problem driven largely by rapid growth in health care costs combined with an aging population, but also exacerbated by the tax cuts of the 2000s, most of which have now been made "permanent," have become increasingly salient as we get closer to that future. These budgetary pressures, together with dissatisfaction over the ever-increasing complexity of the tax code and the idea that a redesigned tax system could be better for the economy, have sporadically led to renewed interest in tax reform. But the budgetary pressures have also arguably made compromise between the political parties more difficult. The looming imbalance between revenue and spending, together with increasing political polarization, makes it harder to separate discussion of tax reform (or indeed, practically any other issue) from fundamental disagreements between the parties about the desirable size and scope of government. As a result, tax policy in the United States is currently at a crossroads, with the two political parties wanting to take different roads leading to very different destinations. In what follows in the rest of this chapter, we review the recent history of tax policy in the United States, and briefly summarize the outlook for tax policy in the future, which will provide useful context for the discussion of the debate over how we ought to tax ourselves that constitutes the rest of this book.

2000–2012: Tax Cuts with Expiration Dates, Repeated Temporary Extensions, and the Threat of the "Fiscal Cliff"

It may be hard to imagine this now, but in the late 1990s the federal government briefly ran a budget surplus, and by the turn of the millennium, budget projections looked so good that government offi-cials, including then Chairman of the Federal Reserve Alan Greenspan, were seriously contemplating the prospect that the federal govern-ment's entire debt might be completely paid off, perhaps as soon as 2012.[94] As of 2000, the Internet bubble was beginning to deflate, and that, combined with an emerging recession, began to make prospects for the budget look less rosy, but initially only by a bit. Even so, it was well understood that in the longer-run future, we faced a major short-fall of government revenues relative to promised federal government spending. These issues played starring roles in the 2000 Presidential election contest. Republican candidate George W. Bush proposed a major across-the-board cut in income taxes and repeal of the estate tax. Democratic candidate Al Gore proposed a much smaller package of tax cuts mostly targeted at low- and middle-income people (including provisions such as increases in the EITC and the Child Tax Credit, expanded tax breaks for education, and an increased standard deduc-tion for married couples). Gore's expressed goal was to maintain sufficient tax revenue to continue running surpluses in the overall government budget, in order to save up for the future costs of Social Security and Medicare—an idea he memorably referred to as putting Social Security and Medicare in a "lockbox." Bush's arguments for his tax cut started out by emphasizing that the budget surplus was "your money," and later shifted to emphasizing the idea that tax cuts would help stimulate a flagging economy.[95]

George W. Bush became president in January 2001 after an election that was still in dispute until the Supreme Court's *Bush v. Gore* decision, announced on December 12, 2000. The Economic Growth and Tax Relief Reconciliation Act (EGTRRA), a slightly modified version of Bush's campaign tax proposal, was enacted soon after, in May 2001. EGTRRA scheduled a gradual reduction of the marginal tax rates in the top four tax brackets of the personal income tax from Clinton-era levels of 39.6, 36, 31, and 28 percent, down to new lower rates of 35, 33, 28, and 25 percent. It also split the existing bottom 15 percent tax bracket into two brackets, with a 10 percent rate in the lower bracket and a 15 percent rate in the upper bracket. Standard deductions and the size of tax brackets for married couples were increased in order to reduce "marriage penalties." The Child Tax Credit was to be increased gradually from $500 to $1,000 per qualifying child and made partly refundable, and the credit for child care expenses was also increased. Contribution limits for various tax-favored savings vehicles were increased, a deduction for higher-education expenses was introduced, and limitations on the above-the-line deduction for student loan interest were relaxed. EGTRRA also scheduled the gradual elimination over time of provisions that phased out personal exemptions and a portion of itemized deductions for high-income taxpayers, which had effectively served as hidden increases in marginal income tax rates over certain income ranges. The exemption levels for the estate and gift taxes were set to increase over time, and their tax rates were set to slowly decline until 2010, when the estate tax would be eliminated altogether. Most of the key provisions were designed to be phased in gradually over the subsequent decade. Strikingly, all of the provisions of EGTRRA were scheduled to "sunset" (expire) at the end of 2010, at which time the tax law would, absent new legislation, revert to what it had been prior to the 2001 enactment of the new law.[96]

A 2002 act for the first time introduced "bonus depreciation," allowing an extra 30 percent of the cost of business investment to be deducted in the first year of the investment, for investment taking place through late 2004.[97] In 2003, another major tax cut, the Jobs and Growth Tax Relief Reconciliation Act of 2003 (JGTRRA) accelerated some tax-cut provisions that under EGTRRA were to be phased in later but, more importantly, reduced the top personal income tax rates on dividends and capital gains to 15 percent. Historically, capital gains have often been subject to lower tax rates than ordinary income. For example, the effective top marginal tax rate on long-term capital gains (ignoring minor effects of phaseouts) was 20 percent from 1982 to 1986, 28 percent from 1987 to 1996, and 20 percent again from 1997 to 2002.[98] Only briefly, during 1988–1990, did the top effective marginal tax rate on capital gains match the statutory marginal tax rate on ordinary income in the top tax bracket. But 15 percent was the lowest top tax rate on capital gains since World War II. This was the first time since 1935 that dividends were subject to a special lower rate of personal income tax, although there had been limited dividend exclusions from 1954 through 1986 (e.g., dividends up to $100, or $200 if married, were excluded during 1964 to 1986). JGTRRA also increased the amount of small business investment that could be expensed, and increased first year "bonus depreciation" to 50 percent of the cost of investment, with both scheduled to expire in 2005. As with EGTRRA, all of the provisions of JGTRRA were scheduled to "sunset" at various dates on or before the end of 2010. A tax bill passed in 2004 extended some expiring provisions of EGTRRA and JGTRRA, and a 2005 bill extended through

2010 the reduced capital gains and dividend tax rates enacted in 2003, and extended increased small business expensing limits through 2009, among other things.[99]

By late 2007, it appeared that the economy was beginning to slip into another recession. The tax policy debate turned to the appropriate role of tax in a stimulus package, and a flurry of tax legislation ensued. In February 2008, President George W. Bush signed the Economic Stimulus Act of 2008 into law. It included a temporary tax credit of up to $600 (or $1,200 for a joint return) plus $300 for each qualifying child. The credit was partly refundable for households that met certain conditions relating to size of income and income tax liability (but not for the lowest-income households), and was phased out for returns with high incomes. To get stimulus into the economy quickly, checks equal to the estimated credit amount were distributed to households during the middle of 2008. The act reintroduced bonus depreciation, allowing an extra 50 percent of the cost of business investment taking place in 2008 to be deducted immediately, and increased limits on small business expensing for 2008. In July 2008, further stimulus was enacted, involving among other things the introduction of a temporary first-time homebuyer tax credit and a temporary property tax deduction for non-itemizers.

In September 2008, the collapse of Lehman Brothers signaled the beginning of a massive global financial crisis, and it soon became clear that we were in for a much more severe economic downturn than had previously been anticipated. In October of 2008, yet more tax legislation was enacted, which among other things extended various expiring tax cut provisions through the end of 2009.[100]

Meanwhile, in 2008 Barack Obama had campaigned for president on a platform that called for new or expanded credits and deductions targeted to low- and middle-income people, making the 2001 and 2003 tax cuts permanent for those with AGI below $250,000 (for married couples) or $200,000 (for singles), and ending the 2001 and 2003 tax cuts ahead of schedule for those with incomes higher than that.[101] By the time Obama took office in January 2009, any tax increase seemed ill-timed due to the severe recession, and the focus was instead on further economic stimulus.

Major stimulus came in the form of the American Recovery and Reinvestment Act (ARRA), enacted in February of 2009, which included about $540 billion of increased government expenditures and $300 billion of temporary tax cuts.[102] ARRA introduced a refundable "making work pay" credit, equal to the smaller of 6.2 percent of earned income and $800 (if married) or $400 (if unmarried), which was gradually phased out for taxpayers with AGI above $150,000 (if married) or $75,000 (if unmarried). It was delivered to most taxpayers in advance, a little at a time, by automatically adjusting tax withholding rates. The act also increased the EITC phase-in rate from 40 percent to 45 percent for those with three or more qualifying children, increased the income level at which the EITC begins to phase out for married couples, and expanded the refundable portion of the Child Tax Credit. It intro-duced the refundable American Opportunity Tax Credit (described above) to replace a less generous, nonrefundable "Hope Scholarship Tax Credit" for higher education expenses. All of the ARRA tax provi-sions described so far were scheduled to apply in 2009 and 2010 only. A much more generous version of the first-time homebuyer credit was also introduced, applying to home purchases in 2009 only. Fifty percent bonus depreciation and higher limits on small business expensing were extended to apply to investment taking place through the end of 2009. Further legislation enacted in November 2009 extended the first-time homebuyer credit to apply to closing dates through the end of June 2010.[103]

In March 2010, the Patient Protection and Affordable Care Act (ACA), the major health care reform law informally known as "Obama-care," was enacted. This included numerous significant tax provisions relating to health insurance and health care, scheduled to begin in 2013 or later years, including the new 0.9 percent HI payroll tax and 3.8 percent HI tax on the net investment income received by high-income people, discussed above in the section on Social Security and Medicare taxes. Tax credits to help low- and moderate-income people afford insurance were scheduled to begin in 2014, and many other significant tax provisions were scheduled to kick in at various times between 2013 and 2018. Its fate remained in doubt for some time, due to court challenges and Republicans' vows to repeal it. But Supreme Court decisions in June 2012 and again in 2015 upheld almost all of the law.[104] Together with President Obama's re-election and Democrats retaining control of the Senate in November 2012, this meant that the health care law would survive long enough for most of its major provi-sions to take effect. We defer detailed discussion of these provisions to chapter 6.

By 2010, the emergence of the "Tea Party" movement and public disappointment with the pace of economic recovery re-energized

Republicans, helping them take control of the House and gain some seats in the Senate in the November 2010 mid-term election. In December 2010, a compromise agreement led to enactment of yet another tax bill, which extended the 2001 and 2003 income tax cuts (which had been due to expire at the end of 2010) through the end of 2012, regardless of the income level of the taxpayer. Some components of the ARRA, such as the increased EITC, expansion of the refundable portion of the Child Tax Credits, and the American Opportunity Tax Credit, were also extended through the end of 2012. Investment incentives such as bonus depreciation and small business expensing were temporarily increased and extended, and the payroll tax rate was temporarily reduced for 2011 (this payroll tax cut was subsequently extended through the end of 2012 by a law enacted in March 2012).[105]

One particularly important development during the 2001 to 2012 period that we have so far skipped over was the transformation of the personal alternative minimum tax (AMT) from an obscure provision affecting few people, into an issue with major implications for the federal budget, personal tax liabilities, and compliance burdens, inspiring nearly annual legislative action. Congress established an early, rather different version of the AMT (then called the "minimum tax") in 1969 to minimize the number of high-income taxpayers with unusually large exclusions and deductions who escape taxation entirely. In 1970 it applied to less than 0.3 percent of all taxpayers, and until 1998 the minimum tax or its successor the AMT always affected less than 1 percent of taxpayers.[106] The subsequent growth of the AMT had two main causes. First, between 1993 and 2012, the "permanent" long-run AMT exemption level established in the Internal Revenue Code had been set at $45,000 for a joint return and $33,750 for a single or head of household return. Unlike in most of the rest of the tax code, the exemption levels and brackets for the AMT were not indexed for inflation. Second, the 2001 and 2003 tax acts, by reducing marginal tax rates and increasing deductions and credits, reduced ordinary tax liability below AMT liability for many taxpayers, thereby exposing them to the AMT. These factors combined to create a situation where vast numbers of taxpayers would gradually become subject to the AMT over time absent further legislative action. Between 2001 and 2010, Congress responded by enacting, every year or two, "patches" that temporarily increased the AMT exemption and also prevented certain tax credits from pushing people onto the AMT. This kept the exemption from returning to its low "permanent" level. The percentage of returns paying AMT grew over time, to 2.9 percent by 2011,[107] but by much less than it would have otherwise because of the patches.

Another legacy of the 2001 tax cut (EGTRRA) was a rather curious pattern of changes over time for the estate tax. Recall that the 2001 act gradually phased out the estate tax, scheduling full elimination for 2010. Due to EGTRRA's sunset, the estate tax was then scheduled to return, in pre-EGTRRA form, starting in 2011. In addition, unrealized capital gains held until death are usually absolved from income taxation forever, but under EGTRRA, heirs of 2010 decedents who subsequently sold any of the inherited assets would owe income tax (at capital gains tax rates) on the difference between the proceeds of the sale and the cost of the asset when the decedent had originally purchased it, less a prorated share of exemptions of $1.3 million per estate and $3 million for assets bequeathed to a spouse. Most observers at the time expected that the one-year elimination of the estate tax and associated capital gains provision would not come to pass, but they did, with one qualification. A law enacted in December 2010 gave the executors of the estates of 2010 decedents a choice: either have the estate treated as EGTRRA had specified (no estate tax would be imposed, but the associated capital gains provision would apply), or pay an estate tax with a $5 million exemption and a flat 35 percent tax rate and avoid the special capital gains provision. The latter would usually be the less attractive of the two options. As a result of the 2010 law, for 2011 and 2012, all estates would be subject to a tax with a $5 million exemption (indexed for inflation in 2012) and a 35 percent rate (with no option to pay tax on unrealized capital gains instead), after which the EGTRRA sunset was scheduled to kick in, at which point the estate tax would revert to its pre-EGTRRA form, with a $1 million exemption and graduated rates topping out at 55 percent.

The anticipated temporary elimination of the estate tax in 2010, its *ex post* optional nature in that year, and the widespread (and realized) expectation that the tax would be reinstated in 2011, together created some macabre incentives regarding the timing of death.[108] The changes to the estate tax that actually took place also ended up saving heirs of some very wealthy individuals a great deal of money. For example, George Steinbrenner, owner of the New York Yankees, died in July of 2010, with a net worth of about $1.1 billion. The tax due on his estate was probably hundreds of millions of dollars below what would have been due had he died in 2009 or 2011. On the other hand, his heirs will eventually be subject to income tax on capital gains should they sell the inherited assets. Steinbrenner originally purchased his share of the Yankees in 1973 for $10 million, and as of 2012 that stake was worth just over $1 billion. If his heirs had sold their stake in the Yankees in 2012, they would have owed tax on the difference between $1 billion and $10 million, less $4.5 million in exemptions, resulting in around $150 million in capital gains taxes.[109] Because they did not sell in 2012, they will be able to defer the tax on those capital gains until they do sell. By contrast, had Steinbrenner died in any other year, heirs selling assets inherited from him only would have owed capital gains tax on the appreciation since the date of his death in 2010.

All this raises the question of why federal tax law became so unstable. Some of it had to do with efforts to provide temporary economic stimulus during an especially severe and long-lasting recession, without worsening budget deficits in the longer-term future too much. And sometimes the rationale for setting expiration dates for tax provisions was to force Congress to re-evaluate and vote on these provisions periodically, instead of letting inertia exert undue influence over tax policy. But much of the proliferation of expiring provisions was rooted in the political strategies followed by Republicans to facilitate adoption of EGTRRA and JGTRRA, combined with the inability or unwillingness of Republicans and Democrats to reach lasting compromises in an increasingly polarized political atmosphere. Both EGTRRA and JGTRRA were scheduled to "sunset" within ten years to circumvent the "Byrd Rule" in the Senate, which would have required sixty votes instead of fifty to pass the bill if it had increased the budget deficit more than ten years after the year it was enacted.[110]

Sunsets, gradual phase-ins, and temporary extensions also served to hide the true long-run revenue costs of the bills, which was politically useful (assuming the stealth went unnoticed) given concerns about budget deficits. At the time they were adopted, the revenue costs of EGTRRA and JGTRRA during 2001–2011 were projected to be approximately $1.35 trillion and $350 billion, respectively, for a total of $1.7 trillion, not including the costs of increased interest on the debt.[111] These were the numbers that got the most attention in the media.[112] But those estimates unrealistically assumed that the temporary AMT patches adopted in EGTRRA and JGTRRA (that lasted only through 2004) and other expiring provisions would be allowed to expire, issues that were recognized and emphasized by tax experts at the time.[113] Once the cost of the subsequent AMT patches, extension of expiring provisions, and additional interest on the debt are taken into account, the true revenue loss from those two tax cuts over 2001–2011 turned out to be almost double the initial "headline" estimates, at about $3 trillion, or 2.2 percent of total GDP during that period.[114]

That brings us to the "fiscal cliff." Almost all of the tax cuts enacted during the administrations of George W. Bush and Barack Obama were scheduled to expire on December 31, 2012. Some other tax-cutting provisions, such the AMT patch and the R&E credit, had already expired a year before, and December 31, 2012 was close to the last chance to enact extensions before the printing of forms and instructions for taxes on income earned in 2012 (the returns for which would be filed in 2013). At the same time, major spending cuts were scheduled to kick in as a result of the Budget Control Act of 2011, a deal enacted in August 2011 in response to threats by congressional Republicans to vote down an increase in the federal debt ceiling (which would have caused the U.S. federal government to default on its debt, creating economic tumult). Because negotiators were not able to reach an agreement on an alternative way to reduce the budget deficit by a November 2011 deadline, that act was scheduled to impose substantial automatic cuts in federal government spending starting January 1, 2013, including dollar caps on various categories of government expenditure and a "sequester" imposing across-the-board reductions in broad categories of spending relative to a baseline that allowed past spending to grow at the rate of inflation, which would push spending well below the caps.[115] If sustained over ten years, these spending cuts would result in a cumulative reduction in federal deficits of $1.9 trillion, or about 0.9 percent of GDP over that period.[116]

The U.S. economy at the time was still operating well below capacity, with weak demand despite interest rates pushed as low about as they could go, and there was legitimate fear that large and sudden tax increases and government expenditure cuts at this point would weaken the economy severely. In May of 2012, the Congressional Budget Office estimated that in the absence of further legislative action, tax increases and government spending cuts would reduce the budget deficit by 5.1 percent of GDP in 2013 compared to 2012, before taking into account feedback effects caused by any resultant weakening of the economy.[117] Neither political party wanted all of the tax cuts to expire, but there was no prospect of compromise between the parties until after the 2012 election contests had been decided.

Tax Policy in the 2012 Presidential Campaign

Both Barack Obama and Mitt Romney campaigned in 2012 on platforms that would have permanently extended numerous expiring tax cut provisions. But aside from that, their plans involved very different visions for future tax policy.

During the 2012 election campaign, President Obama once again proposed making "permanent" all of the 2001 and 2003 tax cuts that applied to taxpayers with AGI below $250,000 (if married) or $200,000 (if unmarried), and allowing the expiration, starting in 2013, of the portions of the 2001 and 2003 tax cuts applying to taxpayers with AGI above those levels. He also proposed making numerous other tax provisions permanent, including the increased AMT exemption (which would also be indexed for inflation), the 2009 version of the estate tax, and certain ARRA provisions applying to low- and moderate-income people (including, for example, the American Opportunity Tax Credit and changes to the EITC and Child Tax Credit). Obama advocated limiting itemized deductions and certain exclusions for high-income taxpayers, and taxing carried interest as ordinary income. He also proposed to cut the corporate tax rate from 35 percent to 28 percent (25 percent for manufacturing firms), and to offset the revenue loss from that by broadening the corporate tax base, without committing to any particular base-broadening measures.[118]

Mitt Romney's 2012 presidential campaign tax proposals promised to make *all* of the 2001 and 2003 tax cuts permanent, and to add more. He proposed to cut marginal tax rates in the personal income tax across the board by 20 percent relative to those specified by EGTRRA. Long-term capital gains and dividends would be made completely exempt from personal taxation for those with incomes below $200,000 (if married) or $100,000 (if single), and taxed at a 15 percent rate for those with higher incomes. Romney proposed to completely repeal the AMT, the estate tax, and all of the tax provisions included in the Obama health care reform. His tax plan would also allow the expiration of many temporary provisions of the ARRA that benefited low-income households, such as an increase in the EITC, expanded refundability of the Child Tax Credit, and the American Opportunity Tax Credit. Romney also proposed to cut the top corporate tax rate from 35 percent to 25 percent.[119]

In addition to the specifics noted above, Romney promised: "I'm not looking to cut ... taxes and to reduce ... the revenues going to the government ... my number-one principle is, there will be no tax cut that adds to the deficit."[120] To make this possible, he promised: "I will place some curbs on personal tax deductions, exemptions and credits, and I will also broaden the corporate tax base. Higher-income Americans who receive the greatest benefit from rate cuts will see the most significant limits. Middle-income Americans will continue to enjoy tax benefits that favor important priorities such as home ownership, charitable giving, health care, and savings."[121] Romney also promised: "I am not going to have people at the high end pay less than they're paying now. The top 5 percent of taxpayers will continue to pay 60 percent of the income tax the nation collects. So that'll stay the same. Middle-income people are going to get a tax break."[122] Romney never offered specifics regarding which tax deductions, exemptions, or credits might be curtailed, but during the second presidential debate he suggested that capping income tax deductions at $25,000 per return was one possibility.[123]

The candidates' competing tax proposals played a big role in the presidential election campaign, receiving considerable attention during all three debates, with much of the discussion focusing on impacts on the budget deficit and the distributional effects. President Obama repeatedly referred to Romney's plan as a "$5 trillion tax cut."[124] This was a rough estimate of the ten-year revenue loss from the tax cuts that had been specified in the Romney plan relative to a "current policy" baseline (which assumed all of the expiring tax cuts except for the payroll tax cut would be extended permanently), extrapolated from an Urban-Brookings Tax Policy Center analysis of the effects in 2015.[125] That estimate did not include the offsetting effects of the unspecified base-broadening measures Romney had promised. In the absence of such measures, the tax cut would increase budget deficits by a total of about 2.5 percent of GDP over ten years.[126] Obama acknowledged that Romney had promised offsetting base-broadening measures, but expressed skepticism that much base broadening could be achieved if Romney was unwilling to specify what he planned to do in advance. The President also alluded to an Urban-Brookings Tax Policy Center analysis suggesting that it was mathematically impossible for Romney to achieve all of the promised goals of his tax plan at the same time. That analysis found that even if Romney succeeded in eliminating all credits, deductions, and exemptions benefiting high-income people (aside from savings incentives, which Romney promised to keep), the plan would still cut taxes on people in the top 5 percent of the income distribution substantially. As a result, for the personal income tax to raise the same revenue as "current policy" would require increasing taxes on people outside the top 5 percent by an average of 1.1 percent of their incomes. Or, if the promise to cut taxes on the middle class were kept instead, it would entail a loss of revenue of more than 0.5 percent of GDP, not counting the effects of the proposed corporate tax rate cuts.[127] A subsequent analysis by the Urban-Brookings Tax Policy Center suggested that capping itemized deductions at $25,000 would only offset about $1.3 trillion of the $5 trillion gross revenue lost from the Romney tax plan over ten years.[128]

The main response to these analyses offered by the Romney campaign was that they underestimated the extra tax revenues that would arise from improved economic growth caused by the tax plan.[129] Whether and how much tax cuts would stimulate growth is taken up in chapter 4. Romney also emphasized that if elected, he would cut government spending, starting with repeal of the Affordable Care Act, while Obama countered that Romney had promised to increase military spending by $2 trillion over the next ten years.[130]

The American Taxpayer Relief Act of 2012

In November 2012, President Obama won re-election, Democrats retained control of the Senate, and Republicans retained control of the House. Negotiations soon began on a deal to avert the "fiscal cliff." A compromise deal, the American Taxpayer Relief Act of 2012 (ATRA 2012), was finally reached at the very last minute. It passed in the Senate, by a vote of 89 to 8, two hours before midnight on New Year's Eve 2012. It then passed in the House by a closer 257 to 167 vote (with 151 Republicans and 16 Democrats voting against it) on New Year's Day, and was signed into law by President Obama on January 2, 2013.[131]

ATRA 2012 made permanent essentially all of the 2001 and 2003 individual income tax cuts applying to people with taxable incomes below $450,000 (if married), $425,000 (if head of household), or $400,000 (if single), with those thresholds indexed for inflation after 2013. Above those income levels, the marginal income tax rate on ordinary income was raised from 35 percent to 39.6 percent, and the marginal income tax rates on capital gains and qualified dividends were increased from 15 percent to 20 percent. A limitation on itemized deductions and phaseout of personal exemptions that EGTRRA had temporarily eliminated were restored, but only for people with AGI above $300,000 (if married), $275,000 (if head of household), or $250,000 (if single), indexed for inflation after 2013. The AMT exemption was permanently increased to a new higher level similar to the one that had applied in recent AMT "patches," and would now be indexed for inflation annually. The estate tax, which had been scheduled to revert to a $1 million exemption and 55 percent rate in 2013, was set permanently with a $5.25 million exemption (indexed for inflation in subsequent years) and 40 percent rate. Some provisions from ARRA 2009, including the American Opportunity Tax Credit and increases in the EITC and Child Tax Credit, were extended temporarily. In addition, a variety of other expiring provisions such as the R&E tax credit and bonus depreciation were extended through the end of 2013 (and later through 2014 as well). The temporary payroll tax cut that had applied in 2011 and 2012 was allowed to expire.

Budget Politics after 2012 and the Protecting Taxpayers from Tax Hikes Act of 2015

While a large portion of the tax increase threatened by the "fiscal cliff" was averted, the government spending part of the fiscal cliff was not. ATRA 2012 delayed the implementation of "sequester" required by the Budget Control Act of 2011 by just two months, to the beginning of March 2013, and reduced the first year's cuts slightly. But the cuts did indeed go into effect starting in March. The sequester imposed 8 percent cuts in defense spending and 5 percent cuts in nondefense discretionary spending, along with some small cuts in Medicare. Most "mandatory" nondefense spending, including programs such as Social Security, Medicaid, and food stamps, was exempt from the cuts. The cuts within the affected categories of spending were across the board, applying to all activities in these categories indiscriminately, and allowing little flexibility on how to allocate the cuts.[132] Soon, government employees were being forced to take unpaid furloughs, scientific research grants that had already been awarded were being cut, housing assistance and preschool programs for low-income families were being scaled back, and so forth.[133]

In 2013, the federal budget deficit was shrinking rapidly due to the aforementioned tax increases and spending cuts, together with the effects of continued but slow economic recovery in the wake of the financial crisis. Nonetheless, policy discussion in Washington was still very much focused on addressing our projected longer-term budget problems. Democrats preferred an approach that mixed revenue increases with spending cuts, while Republicans wanted deeper spending cuts and were adamantly opposed to any further tax increases, especially after ATRA 2012. Members of both political parties were unhappy with the indiscriminate nature of the spending cuts required by the sequester.[134]

Because Republicans did not control the Presidency or the Senate, they were unable to get their desired policies enacted through normal legislative means, so in 2013 they once again turned to the strategy of demanding concessions from Democrats, including a one-year delay in the implementation of the Affordable Care Act, in exchange for a vote to increase the debt ceiling. This time, Democrats refused to give in. The resulting delay in approving a debt-ceiling increase led to a sixteen-day shutdown of the federal government in October 2013, and brought the nation to the brink of defaulting on the federal debt, which threatened catastrophic economic consequences. The shutdown was extremely unpopular, and congressional Republicans in particular were hurt by it in public opinion polls. On October 16, a plan to increase the debt ceiling and temporarily fund the government—without exacting significant concessions from Democrats—garnered support from a large enough minority of House Republicans that it was able to pass in both the House and Senate, ending the shutdown.[135]

In December 2013, negotiations led by Democratic Senator Patty Murray and House Republican Paul Ryan produced agreement on a two-year budget deal that would slightly loosen the constraints of the sequester, allowing an additional $63 billion in spending in exchange for other offsetting cuts in spending and increases in various user fees.[136] This was followed in January 2014 by an agreement on a detailed budget that would fund the federal government through September 2014. Both agreements were opposed by significant numbers of congressional Republicans, but had the support of the Republican leadership.[137] A higher debt limit was passed in February 2014, which would eventually extend the government's ability to cover its debts through the fall of 2015. The measure passed with support from Speaker John A. Boehner but few other Republicans, as it was presented without any attached federal spending cuts.[138] This suggested that perhaps at least a brief respite from the war over the federal budget was at hand.

In September 2015, as the most conservative faction of congressional Republicans continued to advocate using threats of government shutdown and default on the federal debt to extract further concessions on federal government spending, John Boehner announced that he would soon be resigning from Congress.[139] This was followed in late October by one of Boehner's last acts as Speaker, helping to broker a two-year bipartisan budget deal in the face of opposition from many congressional Republicans. The deal averted yet another government shutdown, increased federal spending by $80 billion over previously imposed caps across the next two years, and raised the federal debt ceiling by enough to last through early 2017.[140]

Eventually, Paul Ryan emerged as the next Speaker of the House. This was soon followed by a December 2015 deal between the more moderate factions of the congressional Republicans and Democrats to enact the Protecting Americans from Tax Hikes Act of 2015, which was projected to reduce government revenues by $620 billion over the next ten years, together with a package of government spending increases totaling $1.15 trillion over ten years.[141] The tax act made a number of expiring tax provisions permanent, including, for example, the research and experimentation tax credit, increased limits on expensing for small businesses, the income tax deduction for state and local taxes, a reduced refundability threshold for the Child Tax Credit, the American Opportunity Tax Credit, and the expansions of the EITC that had originally been enacted in 2009. Several other provisions, including bonus depreciation, were extended for up to five years (through 2019).[142]

The Outlook for Tax Policy
In this highly contentious political environment, presidential candidates, members of Congress, various appointed commissions, and numerous outside groups have, to varying degrees, continued to push for further big changes to the tax code, with different actors motivated by different, sometimes conflicting goals such as improving economic performance, enhancing fairness, simplifying taxes, helping to close the long-run budget gap, or shrinking the government. In chapters 6 through 8, we will consider the major competing approaches to reforming the tax system, including some of the most notable plans that have been put forward in recent years.

Conclusion

The basic background information presented in these first two chapters should be helpful as an introduction to the debate over taxes. Chapter 1 looked at the complaints about the current system, outlined the suggested replacements, and laid out some of the key issues in the debate over the future of the income tax. Chapter 2 explained the essentials of how the major federal taxes work, placed them in their historical and international contexts, and summarized the recent changes and outlook for the future that have set the stage for the current debate over taxes. Along the way, we've addressed many of the aspects of the system that bother would-be reformers. To provide a foundation for evaluating different approaches to tax reform that we'll consider in chapters 6 through 8, the next three chapters explore what principles ought to guide any tax system, and address to what extent our current system adheres to these principles.

3   Fairness

The worst riots seen in London for decades occurred on March 31, 1990. More than 400 demonstrators and police officers were injured, and 341 people were arrested for assault, looting, and arson. Rioters set fire to parked Porsches and Jaguars, smashed restaurant and store windows, and demolished a Renault showroom. The reason? A new tax proposed by the government led by Prime Minister Margaret Thatcher was scheduled to take effect the next day. The new tax, called a *community charge* or *poll tax*, was a standard amount levied on all adults living in a jurisdiction—the same amount for rich and poor alike—and replaced a system of real estate taxes based on property value. The public outcry, which included not only civil unrest but also widespread nonviolent protest and noncompliance, is widely credited as the principal reason for the challenge to Thatcher's Conservative Party leadership and her eventual replacement as party leader. The government soon after abandoned the poll tax.[1]

Fast forward twenty years, when in the fall of 2010 protesters in England and Scotland staged sit-ins and forced the closing of several stores of the British telecommunications company Vodafone, alleging multi-billion dollar tax avoidance at the same time that large expenditure cuts were proposed by the Conservative-Liberal Democrat coalition government.[2]

In both cases the public outcry was exceedingly mild compared to the previous time a poll tax was attempted by a British government, more than half a millennium earlier, in 1381. In that year, mobs roamed from town to town, beheading several prominent citizens and tax officials and sacking their houses. One unfortunate soul dispatched to collect taxes was not only "tortured and wounded so that he was half killed, [but] the miscreants then turned to his horse, cut off its tail and ears and affixed them to the pillory there to be subjected to public opprobrium and derision."[3]

The overriding reason for the outcry over the modern poll tax was that people thought it was unfair. The poll tax was to replace a property tax that resulted in tax payments that varied with the value of the property. Under the poll tax, every adult in a given local jurisdiction paid the same annual tax, *period*. The duke with his estate paid the same tax as the butcher in his three-room flat. That the affluent should owe more tax than everyone else struck many in the United Kingdom as a first principle of fair taxation, one that was violated by the poll tax.

Although in the United States it has been a long time since controversy over fair taxation has erupted into such violence, our nation's very origin has roots in colonial indignation over the taxes imposed by England. Indeed, the Boston Tea Party was a protest of British tax policies. An excise tax on distilled spirits spurred the Whiskey Rebellion of 1794, which caused several deaths and much property damage; to quell the rebellion, President Washington nationalized 13,000 militiamen, an army three times as large as the one he commanded at Valley Forge during the Revolution.[4]

In recent years, there have emerged in the United States two passionate, influential, and for the most part peaceful mass protest movements with sharply contrasting views on tax fairness. In 2009, a new "Tea Party" began demonstrating on behalf of conservative or sometimes libertarian principles, opposing bailouts, fiscal stimulus, and what many protesters saw as a federal government that was overstepping its Constitutional bounds. While taxation was just one among many targets of the Tea Party's ire, it was a central one (consider the name of the organization), and in 2010, Tea Party activists helped elect numerous members of Congress, many of whom advocated replacing progressive income taxation with a flat tax or national retail sales tax.[5] In September 2011, the "Occupy Wall Street" movement began in Zuccotti Park in Manhattan, and adopted the slogan "we are the 99 percent," alluding to their opposition to what they saw as the growing concentration of income and power in the top 1 percent of the income distribution and to policies favoring them. Encampments and protest marches soon arose in many places around the country; eventually, there were thousands of arrests (mostly for trespassing or disorderly conduct) and occasional clashes with the police, including notorious pepper-spraying incidents. While the grievances and aims of the Occupy movement were diverse, a major practical goal of many in it was "to see steps taken to ensure that the rich pay a fairer share of their income in taxes," as the *New York Times* put it.[6]

While violence over the fairness of taxation has largely subsided in the United States, the rhetoric in tax debates still evokes images of war. Accusations of "class warfare" have become a standard response to the arguments that inequality is too high, or that taxes on upper-income people are too low (or should not be cut further). For example, in October 2011, Mitt Romney, campaigning in the Republican presidential primaries, replied to a question about the Occupy Wall Street protests by saying: "I think it's dangerous, this class warfare."[7] When asked in 2011 about President Obama's "Buffett Rule" proposal to raise taxes on millionaires, Congressman Paul Ryan, chairman of the House Budget Committee (who became the Republican vice presidential candidate in 2012 and Speaker of the House in 2015), responded: "Class warfare may make for really good politics, but it makes for rotten economics."[8] Meanwhile, advocates of higher taxes on the rich have not been shy about turning similar rhetoric on their opponents. For example, in 2006, billionaire investor Warren Buffett (inspiration for the "Buffett Rule") said: "There's class warfare, all right, but it's my class, the rich class, that's making war, and we're winning."[9]

Usually the first question anyone asks about a new tax proposal is "Who pays?" and about a tax cut is "Who benefits?" For tax bills discussed in Congress, government agencies and independent organizations will publish *distributional tables* that purport to show how the burden or benefits of the proposed tax change will be distributed, or shared, across various income groups. In recent years, the distributional tables have themselves become political footballs as the economic assumptions underlying the assignment of tax burden to income classes have been challenged. Whether the burden of taxes is shared fairly is not only a matter of the distribution across income groups. In addition, the distribution of tax burdens by region becomes an issue when, for example, residents of the Northeast complain about a tax increase on heating oil or when Westerners object if a gasoline tax increase is considered. One might consider the distribution of burdens by age or generation (for instance, in a debate over further taxing Social Security benefits) or by some other characteristic (such as being a smoker, if cigarette taxes are the issue).[10]

The prominence of fairness in tax policy debates makes it essential that the issues it raises are clearly understood. But fairness also deserves close scrutiny because of the costs that achieving it may exact. Much of the bewildering complexity of the tax law is justified in the name of fairness. After all, the poll tax is arguably the simplest tax system of all, and evidently most everyone rejects it precisely because they think it's unfair. Even that system is expensive to administer if it engenders widespread resistance. Slightly more complicated systems (but still much simpler than our current system)—such as the flat tax—do not allow the tax burden to be fine-tuned for personal circumstances and also permit limited flexibility in assigning the tax burden across income groups. Before we resign ourselves to accepting so much complexity as the price of achieving fairness, we should think carefully about what we mean by fairness and about how much we are willing to sacrifice to achieve it.

There is one other potentially important cost of tax fairness. Attempting to achieve a very progressive distribution of tax burdens (i.e., skewed toward high-income households) inevitably generates disincentives to earn income, which may inhibit economic growth. How much of this economic cost we tolerate depends on how much we value the reduced inequality that more progressivity achieves. The more we value reducing inequality, the more economic cost from progressivity should be accepted as a trade-off.

Vertical Equity and Tax Progressivity

There are two distinct aspects to the fairness of a tax system. The first, called *vertical equity* by economists, concerns the appropriate tax burden on households of different levels of well-being. If we measure well-being by income, vertical equity is about how much of the burden tax should be shouldered by a family with $200,000 of income versus a family with $50,000 of income versus a family with $10,000 of income, and so on.

A tax system can be evaluated against another standard of fairness— to what extent families of about the *same* level of well-being end up bearing the same tax burden. Or to put it another way, under what, if any, circumstances is it acceptable that two equally well-off households bear a different tax burden? We will address this issue, called *horizontal equity* by economists, a bit later.

First, we deal with the divisive issues of vertical equity and *tax progressivity*. Recall that a tax structure is called *progressive* if a family's total tax liability as a fraction of income rises with income.[11] If, for example, total taxes for a family with an income of $50,000 are 20 percent of income, taxes for a family with an income of $100,000 are 30 percent of income, and so on, then the tax structure is progressive. If, on the other hand, everyone pays the same percentage of income in tax, regardless of income, then the tax structure is called *proportional*. Finally, a tax that takes a smaller percentage of income from those with higher incomes is called *regressive*.

Loosely speaking, one tax structure is more progressive than another if the average tax rate (tax liability as a percentage of income) rises more rapidly with income.[12] Using this terminology, the question of vertical equity usually boils down to whether the tax burden ought to be distributed in a progressive fashion and, if so, how progressive it should be.

Before plunging in, we must make a frank admission: fairness is not in the end a question of economics. Neither an A+ in Economics 101, nor a PhD in mathematical economics, nor a lifetime of study of the theory of political economy will reveal the one true answer. Fairness in taxation, like fairness of just about anything, involves ethical issues and value judgments that, by their nature, cannot be decisively resolved—certainly not by economic reasoning—and about which reasonable people will disagree.

The elusiveness of the concept of fairness has not stopped people from simply asserting, with absolute confidence, what is fair and what is not. In his 1992 presidential campaign, Bill Clinton advocated making an already progressive U.S. income tax system more progressive to achieve "an America in which the wealthiest, those making over $200,000 a year, are asked to pay their fair share."[13] Once in office, he joined with Congress to raise income tax rates on those very people. William Safire, the late columnist, journalist, and well-known stickler for precise language, expressed a not dissimilar view of the meaning of tax fairness when he said "most of us accept as 'fair' this principle: The poor should pay nothing, the middlers something, and the rich the highest percentage."[14] Safire apparently thought that a progressive tax distribution is fair.

In contrast, others argue that it is fair to impose the same (i.e., a "flat") tax rate on everyone's income, perhaps after exempting a certain amount of income from tax. Robert Hall and Alvin Rabushka, inventors of the flat tax, once took this stand, saying that "the meanings of *even, just,* and *equal*, in keeping with rules and logic, better fit a flat rate of taxation than any multiple-rate system that discriminates among different classes of taxpayers."[15]

Some favor more extreme, and more regressive, interpretations of the meaning of tax fairness. A letter to the editors of *The Wall Street Journal* asserted that a fair tax would feature "the same amount charged to each citizen—much as each member pays a fixed dues to a club, irrespective of assets," which is essentially a poll tax.[16] The *Parade* magazine columnist Marilyn vos Savant, who has been listed in the *Guinness Book of World Records* under "Highest IQ," agrees, saying that it is "clearly unfair" to require some persons to pay more taxes than others, just as it is unfair to ask one person to pay more for a hamburger than another.[17] Note that the same absolute level of tax for all people implies that high-income households face a much lower average tax rate (tax liability divided by income) than low-income households. Another letter to the editor of *The Wall Street Journal* contends that a fair tax "is never possible, any more than anyone can ever commit a fair murder or a fair rape; for taxation is, without an exception, theft."[18]

Clearly, opinions vary widely about what makes for a fair sharing of the tax burden. Economists add to the dissonance, often proclaiming at congressional hearings and in the press that one tax system is superior to another, and disagreeing with one another about which system is best. To make such a judgment, the economist is implicitly introducing his or her own values into the choice, values that Congress or the majority of Americans may not share. For this reason, in principle, any panel of economists offering their opinions on the best tax system should be followed by a panel of philosophers or ethicists who offer their views on tax equity. In practice, of course, we do not convene such a panel every time an adjustment in the pattern of tax liabilities is considered, and we rely on the political system to make these kinds of choices. Careful economic analysis can clarify the issues involved and can identify the trade-offs that arise when tax fairness questions are at issue. Economic reasoning, however, cannot be decisive in the choice about replacing one tax system with another, whenever there are winners and losers from the switch.

The Benefit Principle versus the Ability-to-Pay Principle

Economists have proposed two principles for determining the fair distribution of tax burden across income classes. Unfortunately, neither of these principles provides a definitive answer to the question of exactly how the burden of taxes should be distributed, but considering them does help to clarify thinking about tax fairness. The first is the *benefit principle,* which states that each individual's (or household's) tax burden ought to be commensurate to the benefits he or she receives from the government. The second is the *ability-to-pay principle,* which states that the tax burden ought to be related to the taxpayer's level of economic well-being.

The Benefit Principle

When we buy ordinary goods and services in the free market, we generally consider it fair to "get what we pay for." The benefit principle of taxation would apply this same reasoning to the financing of government-provided goods and services. In some cases, applying this principle is easy and familiar. For example, one must purchase postage to use the U.S. mail, and many local governments charge households for their use of water and sewage facilities. These *user charges* can be an effective policy when it is easy to determine how much of a government-provided good or service each person is using. Such a levy is not only arguably fair (because of the correspondence between the amount consumed and the amount paid), but it is also economically efficient because it induces people to consume the good or service only when it is worth more to them than it costs (if the price approximately reflects the cost of providing it).

This may work for postage stamps or water, but for many important government services, such as national defense or the justice system, determining exactly how much each citizen benefits is difficult to say the least, and often impossible. In these cases, user charges are impracticable, and so implementing the benefit principle would require levying a tax based on a rough estimate of the benefits each person receives.

This is the first place where the benefit principle runs into trouble. You certainly can't just ask people what government activities like national defense are worth to them. Imagine how you would respond if you received a survey from the IRS in the mail, asking you to estimate how much the Department of Defense is worth to you each year. If you suspected that your tax bill would depend on your answer, you would have a strong temptation to lowball your estimate. (It's not as if the government could threaten not to defend those who claimed not to value the armed forces.) Those who answered honestly would be caught holding the bill. If the government could credibly promise not to assess taxes based on your survey response (e.g., by promising to use the information only to get a sense of the average benefit by income class), then people might respond more honestly. But even with no incentive to lie, many households would undoubtedly find it difficult to provide a sensible answer to such a question. Because there is no reliable way to estimate the value of most of what the government provides to each household or even to estimate the average benefit received by each income group, the benefit principle fails to offer practically implementable guidelines about how the tax burden should be distributed.

The benefit principle does, though, suggest that because households with higher income and wealth have more to lose from the lack of security and anarchy that would prevail if the government withdrew from providing defense, a justice system, police, and so on, those households should therefore carry a higher tax burden. (Still, the benefit principle doesn't tell us *how much* higher that tax bill should be.) In 1776, Adam Smith, the father of free-market economics, argued on these grounds in favor of proportional taxation (the same percentage tax rate on everyone), which would indeed put a larger tax burden in absolute terms on people with higher incomes.[19] More recently, William Gates, Sr. (father of Microsoft cofounder Bill Gates) defended progressive taxation (particularly the estate tax) on the grounds that rich people in the United States owe a great deal to their country because they would not have been able to achieve such wealth in the many other countries of the world that are poorly or corruptly governed, lack effective institutions and infrastructure, and underfund scientific research, technological innovation, and education.[20] Philosophers Liam Murphy and Thomas Nagel of New York University provide a spirited and controversial defense of a similar perspective in their 2002 book *The Myth of Ownership*.

Given these disparate considerations, it is by no means obvious what the benefit principle implies about the appropriate distribution of tax burdens. Clearly, though, if the benefit principle supports a progressive tax system, it does so not to ameliorate income inequality but instead to "charge" correctly for the progressive benefits of government programs. To see this, imagine for a moment that somehow each household's true benefit from government could be determined and that their tax liability was set at exactly that value so that, on net, everyone comes out "even." There would be no way to go easy on low-income people by assigning them low or no taxes; everyone would owe an amount of tax that equaled their individual benefit from national defense, police protection, roads, and so on. Nor would there be any scope to supplement the incomes of the very poor by providing benefits such as the supplemental nutrition assistance program (SNAP, also known as food stamps), because the value of SNAP would have to be exactly offset by a corresponding tax liability. Children who grew up in disadvantaged families could not be provided education free of charge. Social Security could not guarantee that virtually all workers receive at least some minimal survival level of retirement support, as it does now; retirees would get back exactly what they had contributed during their lifetimes, even if it meant that many elderly people would be impoverished. Thus, a strict application of the benefit principle has radical implications for both how the government raises money and how it spends it: taxes should be set to reflect benefits received and not to redistribute income from one group or household to another.

Some people argue that restricting the government in this way would be just, because as long as the economic system that determines (pre-tax) incomes in society is just (for example, the income did not result from theft), then the outcomes are just: people have a right to keep what they earn. This might be termed a *libertarian* view of justice, elucidated by philosopher Robert Nozick in his 1974 book *Anarchy, State and Utopia*. Writing in 2010, economist Greg Mankiw of Harvard University appealed to Nozick's principle in arguing that the distribution of tax burdens should be guided exclusively by something like the benefit principle, while acknowledging (for reasons similar to Adam Smith's) that this might imply a progressive distribution of burdens.[21] Nozick, at least initially, made a much farther-reaching assertion—that government should be limited to a minimal role, providing only services, such as criminal justice and national defense, necessary to prevent people from violating each other's rights and to avoid chaos and anarchy, which would impoverish everyone. Once that was achieved, according to Nozick, justice required relying as much as possible on voluntary consent, and as little as possible on the government coercion that would be necessary to enforce enough taxation to finance a bigger government. Many who are sympathetic to these views—including Milton Friedman, Friedrich Hayek, Mankiw, and even Nozick himself later in life—do allow for a larger role for government, although they would prefer a smaller role than in the United States today.[22]

The Ability-to-Pay Principle

Most people, though certainly not all, would reject strict adherence to the benefit principle's implicit limitation on the appropriate role of government. Instead, they would allow that one's tax burden should be related to how well-off one is. In this view, affluent people can more easily *afford* to pay taxes, and this should influence how the burden of taxes is shared. This is usually called the *ability-to-pay principle* for determining the appropriate assignment of tax burden.

According to the ability-to-pay principle, tax burdens should be related not to what a family receives from government but rather to its ability to bear the sacrifice of material well-being that a tax burden entails. Reasoning from the plausible idea that giving up a dollar via tax is a lot less of a sacrifice for a billionaire than for a single mother struggling to make ends meet, an equal sacrifice requires higher tax payments from a well-to-do family. After all, $100 more in taxes may require an affluent family to cut back on magazine subscriptions, but it may force a poor family to eat less. It makes sense that a rich family would need to forgo a whole lot of magazine subscriptions before its sacrifice is as great as the one undergone by the poor family.

Although this is a sensible and even compelling proposition, it is also one that is impossible to prove and quantify. We have no way to reliably compare across individuals the sacrifice caused by having less money, just as it is impossible to compare the relative pain suffered by two people from a pinprick. We do know, though, that people place a relatively low value on increments to their own income when their income is relatively high. For instance, people routinely buy insurance that pays off when they would otherwise be impoverished by some unlucky event such as a health crisis or a house fire, even though on average they will lose money on the deal (due to the need to pay for the administrative costs and profits of the insurance company). In buying insurance they reveal that they value a dollar more when they are poor than when they are rich. Indeed, some social scientists have argued that risk aversion provides a justification for redistribution through the tax system: it provides a kind of insurance against bad economic outcomes that people might value but for which no private market exists.[23]

Even if one accepts both that the tax system should impose equal sacrifices on all taxpayers and that a dollar of tax payment is a greater sacrifice for a poor family than for a rich family, the ability-to-pay principle does not indicate what should be the precise relationship between income and tax burden because there is no objective way to measure and compare the degree of sacrifice across people. A proportionate tax, whereby everyone owes the same percentage of income, would take more dollars from a rich family than from a poor family. Indeed, even a regressive tax—for example, a tax of 25 percent on the first $20,000 of income and 10 percent on all additional income—would take more dollars from a rich family than from a poor family. Whether one of these two schedules, or some other, assigns an equal amount of sacrifice across families is impossible to know.

Furthermore, why should everyone make an equal sacrifice? Why not require a greater sacrifice from the affluent than from the poor? For example, utilitarian philosophers argue that it is ethically right to seek to maximize the sum total of human well-being, or happiness, in society.[24] Achieving that principle, taking into account both the relative values of dollars to the rich and to the poor in terms of happiness, and any dollars lost when people respond to the changed incentives caused by taxes (for example by working less), could suggest a more progressive distribution of taxes and transfers than does the equal sacrifice principle. Moreover, while a utilitarian would oppose a further increase in tax progressivity if it reduced the happiness of the rich more than it raised that of the poor, philosopher John Rawls in his seminal 1971 work *A Theory of Justice* argues that we should continue making taxes and transfers more progressive as long as it makes the worst-off members of society better off.[25] Accepting the premise that policy ought to take into account differences across individuals in the sacrifice associated with giving up a dollar thus involves two separate layers of indeterminacy—how to measure the amount of sacrifice, and how to determine the appropriate level of sacrifice at different levels of well-being. Neither of these questions is the sort that can be answered analytically.

We conclude that the ability-to-pay principle is really just an intuitively appealing defense of the notion that an individual's tax liability should be linked to some measure of his or her well-being, rather than to an estimate of the benefits from government activities. However, on the compelling questions of the day—such as whether millionaires should owe 70 percent, 50 percent, or 30 percent of their income in tax, or whether poor families should bear any tax burden at all—the ability-to-pay principle has nothing concrete to offer.

Equality of Opportunity and Luck Egalitarianism

"Equality of opportunity" is another ethical principle commonly invoked in the debate over the appropriate role for government, although not everyone agrees on what it means or implies for policy. To some influential thinkers, such as late philosopher Ronald Dworkin and Yale University economist and political scientist John Roemer, equality of opportunity requires designing government policy to compensate as fully as possible for differences in well-being that are due to luck (or more generally, factors beyond individuals' control), and to compensate as little as possible for differences in well-being that are due to effort and voluntary choice. The idea (also known as "luck egalitarianism") is that individuals have a stronger moral claim to income arising from effort than from luck, and a stronger moral claim on help from society to the extent their bad fortune arises through no fault of their own.[26]

The difficulty of disentangling the parts of one's circumstance that are caused by one's own effort and choices from the parts due to factors beyond one's control makes it infeasible to implement this principle precisely. But some practical government policy measures, such as improving access to high-quality education among children born to low-income parents, or helping those with medical problems arising from genetic bad luck to afford health care, seem consistent with this principle. Moreover, it implies that even if we can't practically disentangle the role of effort from the role of luck for any particular individual, the ethically desirable degree of tax progressivity ought to be greater when luck accounts for a larger portion of income variation in general. The idea does seem to capture an important element of popular thinking on inequality—as Google chief economist and former Berkeley and University of Michigan professor Hal Varian says, "if you want to determine whether someone is a Republican or a Democrat, just ask that person whether differences in income come mostly from luck ..."[27]

Progressivity and Economic Incentives

Most economists have given up on seeking operational guidance regarding the "right" degree of progressivity (i.e., what is vertically equitable) from first principles of fair taxation. Instead, they have concentrated on understanding the economic consequences, or *costs*, of different levels of tax progressivity that arise because of the disincentive effects of taxation.

To see why progressive tax systems reduce the incentive, or reward, to earning income, consider the least progressive of all tax structures, a "lump-sum" tax, where tax liability is the same for everyone regardless of their income. If tax liability were the same amount for rich and poor alike, the tax system would place no penalty whatsoever on all the efforts people undertake to better themselves—working hard, getting an education, starting a new business, and so on. In contrast, a proportional income tax system levied at a constant 20 percent rate puts a 20 percent penalty on the reward from all such efforts. Tax systems that are progressive place an even higher penalty on getting ahead, relative to the revenue they raise. Conversely, efforts to limit the penalties that taxation imposes on productive economic activity often entail reducing the tax burden on the affluent. As Paul Krugman put it in his 2001 book *Fuzzy Math*, "When your goal is to increase the incentive to *become* rich, it's very hard to avoid also giving benefits to those who already *are* rich."[28]

If the tax penalty on getting ahead causes some people to shy away from working hard, getting an education, and so on, then there is a hidden economic cost to the tax system that is not reflected directly in the amount of tax paid. This extra cost arises because some activities, for which the benefits otherwise exceed the costs, are forgone purely for tax reasons. When taxes on labor income reduce hours worked, the value of the goods and services no longer produced exceeds the value of the time no longer spent working. When a (hypothetical, thankfully) tax on cell phones reduces the supply of cell phones, the forgone value of the cell phones that would otherwise have been produced is greater than the value to consumers of what other goods and services the freed-up resources will produce instead.

Measuring this cost allows us to pose the critical trade-off that must be faced in resolving the vertical equity question—how to balance the potential social benefits of a more equal distribution of well-being against the economic damage imposed by highly progressive taxes. As Henry Simons of the University of Chicago stated so elegantly in his influential 1938 book *Personal Income Taxation*, "Both progress and justice are costly luxuries—costly, above all, in terms of each other."[29] How the trade-off between progress (read economic growth) and justice is resolved depends in part on the value society places on a more equal distribution of well-being and in part on the bread-and-butter concern of economists—how people and businesses respond to incentives. The magnitude of the behavioral response, which determines the

economic cost of progressive tax systems, is addressed in the next
chapter.

Just How Unequal Is the Distribution of Economic Well-Being?

If everyone in our society were equally well off, we would have little
reason to worry about tax progressivity. But we don't live in that world.
In the United States, there is an enormous gap between the standard
of living of the best off and the worst off, as well as a big difference
between the best off and the middle class. Moreover, government statistics provide abundant evidence that, after declining significantly
from the 1920s through the 1970s, the degree of income inequality in
the United States has grown sharply thereafter, returning to levels not
seen since just before the onset of the Great Depression in 1929. Figure
3.1 tells the story.

The gray line in the top panel of the figure depicts, for the years
1913 through 2015, the percentage of total pre-tax market income in
the United States going to households in the top 1 percent of the
income distribution, calculated by Thomas Piketty of the Paris School
of Economics and Emmanuel Saez of the University of California,
Berkeley. This gray line represents the top 1 percent's share of the
following: gross income reported on personal income tax returns
(including realized capital gains), plus an estimate of what that would
be for those not filing tax returns, less any government transfers
included in gross income such as Social Security or unemployment
insurance. By this measure, the minimum and average incomes of
households in the top 1 percent in 2015 were $442,900 and $1.36
million, respectively.[30]

The top 1 percent's share of income has followed a U-shaped pattern
since the early 20th century. It fell from a peak of 24 percent in 1928 to
about 10 percent by the mid-1950s, and stayed around this level through
the mid-1970s, when it briefly fell below 9 percent. It then began to rise
dramatically, eventually reaching about 24 percent again by 2007,
dipped temporarily to 18 percent during the recession year of 2009, but
had rebounded to about 22 percent by 2015.

The dashed line in the top panel of figure 3.1 shows an alternative
estimate of the top 1 percent's income share, based on the Congressional Budget Office (CBO) measure of pre-tax market income. This is
similar to Piketty and Saez's measure (including realized capital gains),
but accounts for some additional kinds of market income, the most
important being employer-provided health insurance and pension

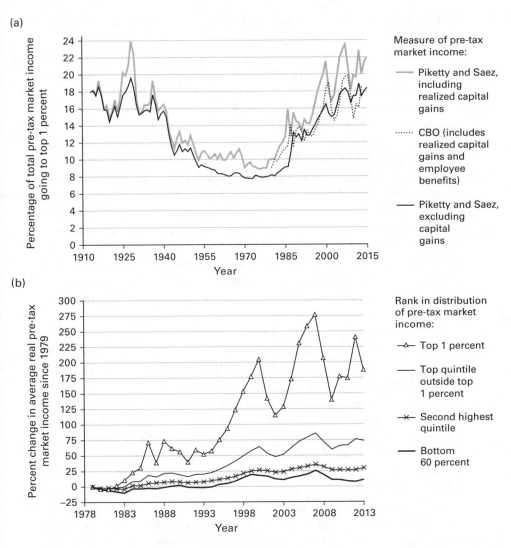

Figure 3.1
Growing income inequality in the United States: (a) percentage of total pre-tax market income going to top 1 percent of income distribution, 1913–2015, and (b) percentage change in average real pre-tax market income per household since 1979 in different parts of the income distribution, 1979–2013.
Source: Authors' calculations based on data from Piketty and Saez (2003, updated 2016) and Congressional Budget Office (2016b).

contributions. CBO's data suggest a roughly similar degree of inequality and a similar pattern of changes over time, at least since 1979 when the CBO data start. The CBO dashed line is a bit lower than the gray line from Piketty and Saez, especially in recent years, because compared to other market income, employee benefits are less concentrated in the top 1 percent and growing faster over time. But this does not change the overall picture very much.[31]

The solid black line in the top panel of figure 3.1 shows the top 1 percent's share of the Piketty-Saez measure of income *excluding* capital gains. Comparing this to the gray line demonstrates that almost all of the recent volatility in the top 1 percent's income share has been due to fluctuations in realized capital gains, mostly reflecting the wild swings in the stock market. Excluding capital gains, there is evidence of an even steadier upward trend in the share of pre-tax market income going to the top 1 percent since the 1970s, which thus far shows little sign of abating. The top 1 percent's share of this measure of income rose from less than 8 percent in the late 1970s to 18.4 percent in 2015.[32]

The bottom panel of figure 3.1 demonstrates that since 1979, average real (inflation-adjusted) pre-tax market income per household, as measured by CBO, has grown much faster the higher one goes in the income distribution.[33] In the top 1 percent of the income distribution, it grew by 277 percent between 1979 and 2007. Despite recent fluctuations due to recession and volatile capital gains realizations, it was still 188 percent higher in 2013 than it was in 1979. In the rest of the top quintile (or fifth) of the income distribution, income growth was strong but less dramatic, at 86 percent from 1979 to 2007 and 74 percent from 1979 through 2013. In the second highest quintile, average real pre-tax market income grew by 35 percent between 1979 and 2007, and by 2013 was still 30 percent higher than in 1979. For the bottom 60 percent of the income distribution, the comparable figures were 25 percent and 11 percent, respectively.

Table 3.1, also based on CBO data, presents additional indicators of U.S. income inequality and its growth over time, and depicts the direct effects of government policy on these indicators.[34] In table 3.1, households are now ranked by pre-tax income including both market income and federal and state government transfers through such programs as Social Security, Medicare, Medicaid, SNAP (food stamps), Temporary Assistance to Needy Families (TANF, a program of time-limited cash welfare benefits with work requirements), and

Table 3.1
The distribution of income before and after government transfers and federal taxes, and real growth of income after transfers and federal taxes in different parts of the income distribution in the United States.

Rank in the distribution of pre-tax income (including transfers)	Average per household, 2011–2013, in thousands of constant year 2013 dollars		Percentage of total pre-tax market income		Percentage of income after government transfers and federal taxes		Percentage growth in average real income per household, after transfers and federal taxes, 1979–2013
	Pre-tax market income	Income after government transfers and federal taxes	Average, 2011–2013	Change 1979–1981 to 2011–2013	Average 2011–2013	Change 1979–1981 to 2011–2013	
	(1)	(2)	(3)	(4)	(5)	(6)	(7)
Top 1 percent	1,632	1,142	17.9	8.0	13.2	5.4	192
Rest of top 5 percent	309	239	14.1	1.9	11.6	1.0	90
Bottom half of top decile	185	154	10.7	0.3	9.4	0.1	72
Bottom half of top quintile	133	117	15.2	-0.9	14.1	-0.6	57
Second highest quintile	87	86	19.7	-3.2	20.5	-1.5	46
Middle quintile	52	61	12.0	-3.8	14.8	-1.6	35
Second lowest quintile	31	43	7.0	-2.6	10.5	-1.6	37
Lowest quintile	16	25	3.7	0.2	6.0	-1.2	46
Top quintile	253	200	57.7	9.4	48.2	5.9	88
Bottom 60 percent	33	43	22.6	-6.2	31.3	-4.4	41

Source: Authors' calculations based on data from Congressional Budget Office (2016b). *Note:* "Government transfers" includes transfers from both federal and state governments.

unemployment insurance benefits. To smooth out fluctuations arising from the business cycle and to provide a better sense of longer-run trends, for some statistics we compute and compare three-year averages (1979–1981 and 2011–2013) from CBO's annual data.[35]

The first two columns of table 3.1 illustrate vast differences in incomes of people at different points in the income distribution. For example, in the top 1 percent of the income distribution, from 2011 to 2013 average annual pre-tax market income per household was $1.6 million, and average annual income after federal and state government transfers and federal taxes was $1.1 million (both in 2013 dollars). The comparable figures for the middle quintile were about $52,000 and $61,000, respectively.

The inequality of income is smaller when government transfers and federal taxes are taken into account. On average, in each of the three lowest income quintiles, income is higher after transfers and federal taxes than before them. This statement must be interpreted with caution, however. As we demonstrate later in the chapter, this is overwhelmingly due to transfers, such as Social Security and Medicare, that benefit the minority of people in each quintile who are elderly or disabled, making it unrepresentative of the typical household in each quintile (at least on an annual basis; on a lifetime basis, it might be closer to representative, as—luckily—most people eventually reach old age). Also note that these figures include the effects of state government transfers, but not state taxes. Average income after transfers and federal taxes is lower than market income by an increasingly wide margin for households in successively higher slices of the income distribution above the bottom three quintiles. As we will see later in the chapter, this is mostly due to federal taxes.

Columns (3) and (4) of table 3.1 show shares of pre-tax market income going to each part of the income distribution and how they have changed over time. The share of pre-tax market income going to the top 1 percent was 17.9 percent on average during 2011–2013, an increase of 8.0 percentage points relative to the 1979–1984 average. The shares of pre-tax market income going to all parts of the income distribution below the top 10 percent, except for the bottom quintile, shrank over time. The small gain in pre-tax market incomes for the bottom quintile reflects the fact that working-age people, who tend to have higher market incomes relative to the elderly, became increasingly concentrated in the bottom quintile over time. Elderly childless households made up 36 percent of the bottom quintile in 1979 but only 16 percent of that group in 2013.[36] This compositional change was driven mainly by the rising value of Medicare benefits pushing elderly people into higher quintiles, and stagnant wages for low-wage workers pushing more of them into the bottom quintile. Thus, when looking at table 3.1, all of the comparisons over time for the bottom quintile in particular should be interpreted with caution, due to the dramatic change in that group's composition.

Columns (5) and (6) of table 3.1 show the shares of income, after transfers and federal taxes, going to each part of the income distribution, and how those have changed over time. On average during 2011–2013, government transfers and federal taxes reduced the percentage of income going to the top quintile from 57.7 percent to 48.2 percent, and reduced the percentage of income going to the top 1 percent from 17.9 percent to 13.2 percent, while raising the share of income going to each of the bottom four quintiles. Transfers and federal taxes also mitigated the rise in income inequality over time, but not by much. Comparing the 2011–2013 average with the 1979–1981 average, the percentage of income going to the top 1 percent of the income distribution increased by 8.0 percentage points before transfers and federal taxes, and by 5.4 percentage points after them. Thus, while transfers and federal taxes clearly played an important role in reducing income inequality, they do not change substantially the bottom line about the degree of income inequality and its growth over time.

Column (7) of table 3.1 shows the percentage growth in real income after transfers and federal taxes, on average, for households in each part of the income distribution between 1979 and 2013. Once again, the top 1 percent experienced by far the fastest real growth in average income, at 192 percent between 1979 and 2013. That was actually slightly larger than the 188 percent growth in their pre-tax market incomes over this period, shown in figure 3.1. This mainly reflected a modest reduction in this group's average federal tax rate (shown later in figure 3.2). Average income after transfers and federal taxes in the rest of the top 5 percent grew 90 percent. Rates of real income growth after transfers and federal taxes were more modest, but still positive, at all lower points in the distribution.

Figure 3.1 showed that average real pre-tax market income was only 11 percent higher in 2013 than in 1979 among households in the bottom 60 percent of the income distribution. When one takes transfers and federal taxes into account in table 3.1, by contrast, the bottom 60 percent of the income distribution experienced a 41 percent increase in real

incomes, on average, between 1979 and 2013. Thus, government policies helped low- and middle-income people share in the benefits of
long-term economic growth to a greater degree than they would have
otherwise. But government policies did not come close to undoing the
growth in inequality since the 1970s.

All of the income inequality data discussed above are based on
single-year snapshots of income, and re-rank individuals each year, so
which people are in a given segment of the distribution, such as the
top 1 percent of income earners, can change from year to year. As a
result, these data do not necessarily provide an accurate picture of
inequality in longer-run averages of income across individuals, because
some of the apparent inequality in a single-year snapshot represents
temporary fluctuations, such as a business owner having an exceptionally profitable year or a young person who is still in school but will
one day earn a high income. If we could look at *lifetime* incomes, the
distribution would not appear quite as unequal as it does in figure 3.1
and table 3.1. In principle, there could be substantial inequality in
annual incomes even if everyone ended up earning the same total
income over a lifetime!

That is not how the world works, though. The best available evidence shows that the distribution of long-term income is only a bit less
unequal than the distribution of single-year income. U.S. Treasury
Department data that follows a large sample of individual taxpayers
over the ten years 1987 through 1996 indicates that when individual
taxpayers are ranked by ten-year averages of income (closer to, but not
the same as, lifetime income), the top 1 percent received 12 percent of
income, exactly the same share received by the richest 1 percent using
a one-year snapshot from 1987. The share of ten-year average income
received by the top 20 percent of taxpayers was 48.7 percent, only
slightly less than the 49.4 percent in the one-year snapshot from 1987.[37]
Furthermore, income is no less concentrated among taxpayers within
many age groups than it is for all taxpayers.[38] If most of the observed
inequality at a point in time was due to the life-cycle pattern of earnings, we would expect to see much less inequality of incomes among
people of the same age, but we do not.

If income mobility were increasing over time—that is, if people were
now moving up and down the income ranks farther and/or more frequently than in the past—then rising annual income inequality need
not necessarily imply rising lifetime inequality. In that case, the effects
of increased annual income dispersion on individuals' longer-term

average income could be offset by increased probability of low-income individuals moving up and high-income individuals moving down the income scale over time. To test whether this is the case, Wojciech Kopczuk of Columbia University, Emmanuel Saez, and Jae Song of the Social Security Administration examined earnings records from 1937 through 2004, collected for purposes of administering the Social Security payroll tax, which allowed them to follow the earnings of an enormous number of individual (but unidentifiable) workers over many consecutive years. They conclude that income mobility has been remarkably stable in the United States since the 1950s, which implies that the increases in annual earnings inequality since the 1970s have been matched by increases in lifetime inequality. Consistent with this, they show that the increase in the degree of inequality of labor income in recent decades has been substantial, and roughly similar whether they use single-year data, 5-year averages, or 11-year averages of such income for particular individuals followed over time.[39]

Researchers have also examined the inequality of consumption, as measured by annual household expenditures on goods and services reported in surveys. In principle, accurate information on annual consumption could be a better indicator of households' long-term level of well-being than annual income, for example because people tend to save when income is temporarily high and run down their savings or borrow when income is temporarily low, keeping consumption in line with their notion of what economists call "permanent" income. Unfortunately, the Consumer Expenditure Survey, which contains the best available data on the consumption of individual households in the United States, surveys only a very small sample of households, with many fewer high-income people than are in the combination of income tax return data and Census data used to construct the CBO income inequality figures cited above.[40] Thus there is simply no reliable information at all about what has been happening to consumption in the upper reaches of the distribution (i.e., the top 1 percent, or even the top 10 percent), which is where all of the dramatic changes in income inequality have occurred.

Consumption data is probably more insightful for lower-income groups. Bruce Meyer of the University of Chicago and James X. Sullivan of the University of Notre Dame argue that at the bottom of the distribution consumption seems to be better measured than income, and show that between 1980 and 2009 consumption increased in real terms by about 54 percent at the tenth percentile (top of the bottom 10 percent) of the consumption distribution, and by about 50 percent at the median. These data on consumption growth for the bottom and middle of the distribution are actually fairly consistent with the CBO data on growth in income after transfers and federal taxes, shown in table 3.1, with the consumption data suggesting only slightly better improvement in well-being over time. None of this evidence comes close to changing the conclusion that the inequality of financial well-being has been increasing dramatically over time, particularly due to the extraordinary income growth at the top of the distribution. But it is relevant to questions such as whether the poor and middle class have benefited from economic growth over time after taking into account the effects of transfers and taxes (which will be reflected in consumption), and whether policy changes such as expansion of the Earned Income Tax Credit have been successful at raising the well-being of the poor (Meyer and Sullivan would answer yes to both).[41]

Wealth is distributed in an even more unequal fashion than income or consumption, and it too appears to have grown most dramatically at the very top in recent decades. Estimates based on the Survey of Consumer Finances (SCF), a survey that asks a sample of several thousand households directly about their wealth, suggest that the share of wealth held by the richest 10 percent of households increased from 67 percent in 1989 to 76 percent by 2013.[42] Emmanuel Saez and Gabriel Zucman, both of the University of California, Berkeley, have recently estimated the share of U.S. wealth held by households at the top of the wealth distribution in each year since 1913, by cobbling together indirect evidence from a variety of sources, relying most importantly on inferences based on the distribution of capital income reported on individual income tax returns. They conclude that the share of wealth held by the top 1 percent of the wealth distribution gradually declined from a peak of 51 percent in 1928 to a low of 23 percent by 1978, and then rose to 28 percent by 1989 and to 42 percent by 2012.[43] Their ambitious data work is quite an achievement, but there is significant room for error in their inference techniques and assumptions, and their estimates suggest a higher level and faster rate of growth of wealth concentration in recent decades than are implied by other data sources (which have their own limitations).

Jesse Bricker, Alice Henriques, and John Sabelhaus of the Federal Reserve, together with Jacob Krimmel of the University of Pennsylvania—relying primarily on data from the SCF, supplemented by information from the Forbes 400 list of the wealthiest Americans—estimate that the share of wealth held by the richest 1 percent of households increased from 27 percent in 1989 to 33 percent in 2013.[44] Like Saez and Zucman, these authors make some compelling arguments for the superiority of their estimates. Some uncertainty inevitably arises because reasonable people can differ about the best ways to deal with various imperfections in the available data. Our impression is that the best answer is probably closer to the estimates by Bricker and co-authors, but time will tell as more and better data gradually become available to resolve some of the uncertainties.

Why inequality has been growing sharply in recent decades is a controversial subject. As shown above, inequality in income before taxes and transfers has grown faster than inequality after them, so changes in government policy cannot be *directly* responsible for the trend toward greater inequality. Some economists, however, have argued that cuts since 1980 in the tax rates that apply to high-income households may be *indirectly* responsible for some of the surge in reported incomes at the very top of the income distribution. Lower marginal tax rates, they argue, increased the incentive for the well-to-do to work harder and to invest more, and reduced their incentive to hide income from the IRS. This is just one of the many plausible explanations for rising inequality that we examine closely in the next chapter. Other explanations that we consider there, such as the effects of technological progress and globalization—which have raised demand for the services of highly skilled American professionals and reduced demand for lower-skilled workers—or developments in financial markets and changing executive compensation practices, have very different implications for the economic costs of progressive taxation.

If the rich are getting richer and the incomes of the poor and middle class are growing slowly because of market forces such as globalization and technological change, then there is a compelling case that some of the increased inequality ought to be offset by a more progressive tax system—and certainly should not be exacerbated by *reducing* the progressivity of the income tax. This policy response to increasing inequality is sensible not because higher incomes for those in high-skill professions are bad per se. Instead, the idea is to take advantage of the surging incomes of the already affluent to rearrange tax burdens in such a way that makes many people better off without making the rich much worse off in terms of "happiness sacrificed." Moreover, to the extent that the inequality is driven by factors beyond one's control, the moral justification for that inequality may be weaker, as discussed in the "equality of opportunity" section above; from the point of view of the less skilled, globalization was bad luck, and not due to their own decisions.

If, on the other hand, the incomes of the affluent surged because cuts in top tax rates beginning in the early 1980s unleashed a torrent of income-producing activity in response to improved incentives, we should take seriously the economic benefits of reducing tax progressivity and view progressive taxation more skeptically. If the cuts in top tax rates caused a reduction in tax evasion and tax avoidance, that too might weaken the case for progressive taxes, because evasion and avoidance activities are economically costly, and because it would suggest that some of the increase in inequality over time that is apparent in personal income tax return data is not real. But in that case, the implied policy response might be to reform the tax code in order to reduce opportunities for avoidance and evasion, and to improve enforcement, instead of reducing progressivity.

Regardless of the primary cause of the increased inequality, the degree of progressivity that people prefer must depend partly on value judgments. But for any given set of values about fairness, the appropriate degree of progressivity is lower if the economic cost of achieving it is higher.

What Americans Think Is Fair
Any first principles of fairness leave plenty of room for disagreement over the appropriate distribution of the tax burden. Why not forget about first principles and trade-offs between fairness and growth, and instead just ask Americans what they think is fair based on their own values and principles? In fact, public opinion surveys generally reveal widespread support for progressivity in taxation. But the survey responses are sometimes internally inconsistent or are difficult to interpret, can differ greatly depending on how the question is framed, and in some cases seem to indicate considerable public confusion about how the U.S. tax system works.

An April 2015 Gallup poll found that 62 percent of people felt that "upper-income people" paid "too little" in taxes. While previous iterations of the same poll have shown strong support for this proposition, support did decline gradually from 77 percent in 1992 to a low of 55 percent in 2010, before rebounding more recently.[45] ABC / *Washington Post* polls conducted in 2012 found that 72 percent of respondents supported increasing taxes on millionaires, and 60 percent supported increasing taxes on people who make more than $250,000 per year.[46] Recall that an increased marginal tax rate applying to those with incomes above $400,000 was enacted immediately following the re-election of President Obama.

Because the federal tax system is already quite progressive, on the surface these polls seem to suggest public support for a substantial degree of progressivity. It is not clear, however, whether Americans believe that the existing tax system actually is progressive. For instance, in a 2003 survey, 51 percent said that "middle-income people" pay "the highest percentage of their income in federal income taxes," while only 26 percent said that "high-income people" do.[47] As we demonstrate later in this chapter, this impression is probably way off, as the best available estimates suggest that higher-income people do owe a much higher share of their incomes in income taxes than others, on average. A stark illustration of this apparently pervasive misperception comes from a 1989 survey that found, on average, people believed that 45 percent of millionaires paid *no income tax at all*; IRS statistics showed the actual figure was less than 2 percent.[48]

Occasionally, more detailed surveys have asked people to report what they think "fair" average tax rates would be at various income levels. Surveys of nationally representative samples of adults carried out in the 1990s found that the majority of respondents picked "fair" average tax rates at various income levels that were consistent with a progressive distribution of tax liabilities, and the median and mean preferred patterns of average tax rates by income were reasonably similar to the actual pattern of average tax rates at the time. A more recent (2007) survey of college students corroborates this finding, although it is unclear whether the students' views are representative of the views of the broader adult population. The general similarity between the actual and desired distributions suggests one or both of two things. It may mean that we manage to get the sharing of tax burdens about where Americans, on average, want it to be. Alternatively, it may mean that, when people are asked their preferences, their answers tend to mirror the system currently in place.[49]

A large number of surveys have asked questions about "flat" taxes, which tend to reduce tax progressivity by eliminating graduated tax rates, and the responses might, in principle, shed some light on these issues. But the survey results vary widely, seem to depend greatly on the wording of the question, and tend to reveal that many people do not have enough information either about the current system or the flat tax to form a strong opinion. For example, in a November 2011 CBS News poll, when asked about replacing "the current income tax system [which] taxes higher income people at higher rates and lower income people at lower rates" with "a flat tax which would tax people at all income levels at one flat tax rate," 32 percent said it was a good idea, 36 percent said it was a bad idea, and 28 percent said they "don't know enough to say." In another November 2011 poll, conducted by NBC News and *The Wall Street Journal*, respondents were a bit more willing to venture an opinion—56 percent said they preferred "a graduated income tax system, in which people with higher incomes pay a higher tax rate," while 40 percent preferred a "flat tax system in which every-one pays the same rate regardless of income."[50] In several surveys, large percentages of respondents say they believe that high-income people would pay *more* under the flat tax than they do now, a belief that we demonstrate later to be almost surely factually incorrect.[51] Evidence from a 2003 survey suggests that holding this belief significantly increases the probability that someone supports the flat tax.[52] Thus, what support there is for the flat tax might weaken if people were better informed.

An intriguing 2015 study by economists Ilyana Kuziemko of Princeton University, Michael Norton and Stefanie Stantcheva of Harvard University, and Emmanuel Saez investigates how certain types of information influence opinions about inequality and taxation. They surveyed about five thousand U.S. residents in 2011 and 2012, and randomly assigned respondents into control and treatment groups. Members of the control group were asked a series of questions about their attitudes toward inequality and tax policy, while members of the treatment group were asked the same set of questions, but only after going through an interactive online presentation intended to make them better informed about relevant facts. This online presentation included information about the degree of income inequality in the United States and how it has been changing over time, the fact that the federal estate tax at the time only affected people with wealth above $5 million at death, and the fact that the periods of U.S. history when marginal income tax rates on people at the top of the income distribution were highest were also the times when economic growth was highest. The online presentation viewed by the treatment group explicitly interpreted that last fact to mean that "increasing the federal income tax rate and the estate tax rate on very high incomes can raise tax revenue without hurting economic growth."

When members of the control group were asked what the average (not marginal) federal personal income tax rate on people in the top 1 percent of the income distribution should be, the average response was 30 percent; even among self-described conservatives, the average response was 24 percent.[53] (Note that the actual average federal income tax rate on the top 1 percent at the time was 23 percent.)[54] These results are consistent with other survey evidence at the time suggesting support for raising taxes on upper-income people, and indicate that support was not entirely driven by popular misperceptions that the rich pay less in tax than they actually do.

A comparison of survey responses across the treatment and control groups in the Kuziemko, Norton, Saez, and Stantcheva study suggests that the information provided to the survey respondents about inequality and the statement about the economic costs of taxation had only modest impacts on desired tax progressivity. However, the more accurate information about who is subject to the estate tax had a large impact on support for this tax. The information treatment did change some peoples' minds about income inequality—people in the treatment group were more likely to agree that income inequality had increased over time in the United States (86 percent, versus 74 percent in the control group), and were more likely to agree that inequality was "a very serious problem" (39 percent, versus 29 percent in the control group). But in spite of these at least temporarily changed attitudes, the preferred average income tax rate on those in the top 1 percent of the income distribution was only 1 percentage point higher in the treatment group compared to the control group. The information treatment caused support for increasing tax rates on millionaires to go up a bit, from 74 percent in the control group to 79 percent in the treatment group, but caused support for increasing the estate tax to go up a lot, from 17 percent in the control group to 53 percent in the treatment group. While the study leaves open many interesting questions about the impact of information on attitudes toward taxation, it's an interesting start.[55]

Tax Incidence: Who Bears the Burden of a Tax?
Determining who bears the burden of taxation in the United States is a much more difficult task than it might first appear. This is because the most straightforward approach—adding up how much money people send to the IRS each year and tabulating these figures by, say,

income group—doesn't produce the right answer. Instead it will often provide a very misleading answer because the burden often is shifted off of the person who sends the check to the IRS onto someone else, via changes in market prices caused by the tax system. For example, if the owner of a business can respond to a particular tax levy by raising prices, then even though he or she is the one sending a check to the IRS, the firm's customers are bearing part of the burden of the tax. Moreover, the straightforward totaling up of money remitted is not at all helpful for tracing the ultimate burden of corporation income taxes. To understand who bears the burden of taxes and whether that burden is shared fairly, it is necessary to look beyond who writes the checks to the government.

If "paying" taxes means writing checks to the IRS, most wage and salary earners have no right to complain about income taxes—because they pay no tax at all! Of course, all this means is that taxes on wages and salaries are "withheld" from their paychecks by their employers and forwarded by the employers to the IRS. By April 15 (or the extended filing deadline), employees owe to the IRS the difference between their tax liability and what has already been remitted on their behalf by their employers.[56] Because for about three-quarters of taxpayers what has been withheld exceeds their tax liability, they qualify for a refund. Thus, if *paying* means writing a check to the IRS, not only do most Americans never "pay" any income taxes, they *receive* money. American workers are familiar enough with employer withholding to know instinctively that they can, and do, bear the burden of income taxes without ever writing a check to the government. Some conservative commentators apparently disagree that taxpayers are so clear-sighted, arguing that employer withholding obscures the true burden of taxes and should be eliminated so that employees "feel the pain" of taxpaying by remitting all the tax themselves.

What a tax is *called* is also usually irrelevant to who bears the burden of taxes. Imagine if all taxes levied on wages and salaries became the sole legal responsibility of the business employing the labor and were renamed labor *usage* taxes rather than labor *income* taxes; what was a tax "on" workers' income now becomes a tax "on" business, while what triggers the tax and the rate of tax stay exactly the same. Although the wording on the pay stubs would change, there would be no change in take-home pay and no change in who really bears the burden of the taxation. A weekly stub that used to show $600 in wages, $200 in federal income taxes withheld, and $400 in take-home pay might instead show simply $400 in wages because the employer would remit the $200 "labor usage tax" separately. The bottom line is that the worker takes home $400 either way. Changing the name of the tax won't suddenly make an employer more generous; firms will still try to pay as little as they can to maintain a workforce of the size and quality they desire. Whether the legal liability to remit taxes resides with the buyer of labor services (the firm) or the seller of labor services (the worker), the same result is attained in the end. That who remits tax is generally irrelevant to who bears the tax burden is a critically important, but often misunderstood, concept that recurs in much of the analysis that follows.

To be sure, there are some exceptions to the general rule that where the legal responsibility for remitting taxes lies doesn't affect who bears the burden of those taxes. For example, suppose employer withholding were abolished and the IRS had to collect all income taxes from employees. If this opened up new avoidance and evasion opportunities, this would affect the supply and demand for workers and therefore the equilibrium terms—the wage rate—of employment contracts. The remittance system matters in this case because it affects the incentives of the workers and employers to comply with the tax law. But this qualification does not contradict the important concept that one must look beyond who remits the tax to understand the ultimate consequences of a tax.

So far, we have explained how *not* to measure the burden of taxes— by identifying who remits taxes or is legally responsible for remitting money to the IRS—but we have yet to explain how to do it right. Does a tax on labor income make workers worse off by lowering their take-home pay, or does it make employers worse off by increasing the cost of labor? Or some of both? Do taxes on cigarettes burden smokers, the owners of cigarette companies, the people who work for these companies, or tobacco farmers?

The phenomenon that taxes ostensibly levied on one group of people may end up being borne by others is known as *tax shifting*. The ultimate distribution of tax burdens across people after this tax shifting occurs is called *tax incidence*. For any given tax, the true incidence is difficult to determine precisely, and for some taxes there is still substantial disagreement among economists about what the truth is.

The burden of a tax can be shifted when the tax changes the pre-tax prices of the goods and services that people buy and sell. As an example, consider the effect of a 20 percent income tax on someone making $10 an hour. How much worse off the tax makes the worker depends on whether levying the tax causes the worker's pre-tax wage to rise and by how much. If the pre-tax wage rose to $12.50 an hour, the after-tax wage ($12.50 × (1–0.2)) would still be $10, and the burden of the tax would have been shifted entirely off the worker. If the pre-tax wage rose to $11, some, but not all, of the burden would have been shifted.

Why would the pre-tax wage rate rise when the tax is imposed? More generally, what determines whether shifting occurs? A good rule of thumb is that the better the alternatives to what is taxed, the less likely one is to bear a burden.[57] Some examples may help to illustrate this idea. Will a tax of 5 cents per can of Coca-Cola cause its price to rise and thus be borne by Coke consumers? The answer is no if most consumers can't tell the difference between Coke and Pepsi—that is, if they have good alternatives to the taxed good.[58] If one is as good as the other (that is, they are close substitutes, in economists' language), the market simply will not support Coke selling for $1.05 a can, tax included, while Pepsi sells for $1.00: no one would buy Coke at those prices. In that case, Coke would sell for $1.00, and the people involved in producing Coke would bear the burden of the tax; if their net-of-tax receipts no longer covered their costs, they might have to shut down production entirely. If, on the other hand, neither Pepsi nor any other drink is viewed as a good substitute for Coke, the market price of Coke is likely to rise toward $1.05, so that the burden of the tax is borne by consumers of Coke.

The alternatives to supplying the taxed good are equally important. Consider the incidence of a surprise tax of 10 cents per tomato imposed on farmers as they arrive in the morning at your local farmers' market. Because the tomatoes will soon start to rot, the farmers have no alternative but to sell them at this market on this day. In that case, the likely scenario is that the market price will be not much more than what would have prevailed in the absence of the tax, and the farmers will lose out by receiving a lower net-of-tax price than otherwise. If, however, the tomato tax had been announced months in advance, the farmers would have had the option of growing other crops or, if announced days in advance, of taking their tomatoes to be sold elsewhere. With fewer tomatoes to be sold, the price at the farmers' market would be bid up, causing the tax burden to shift away from the farmers toward the people who favor shopping at that market and will find that tomatoes cost more than otherwise. Note that these lovers of fresh tomatoes bear a burden from the tax even though they remit no money to the tax authority—the burden of the tax levied on tomato farmers is "passed through" to them in the form of a higher price.

The same logic applies to taxes on labor income. As already discussed, a tax on wages and salaries will be shifted off workers to the extent that the tax causes pre-tax wage rates to rise. It will be completely shifted if wages rise enough so that after-tax wages are no lower than they would have been absent taxes. How does the rule of thumb about shifting apply to this case? It says that shifting will tend to occur if on average workers have better alternatives to working than employers have to hiring workers. For workers, the alternative to paid work is leisure or unpaid work at home; for employers, the alternative to hiring labor is to economize on workers by moving to more capital-intensive, or automated, modes of production.

As we discuss in chapter 4, most evidence suggests that aggregate labor supply is not highly responsive to the after-tax wage, suggesting that on average people do not perceive they have any alternative but to work. On average, businesses are more flexible in their ability to find alternatives to labor. The relative flexibility of businesses compared to workers implies that very little of the income tax is shifted off workers by forcing up pre-tax wage payments and that the tax is borne largely by the workers themselves in the form of lower after-tax wages. Note that this reasoning applies to any tax that is triggered by labor income, whether it is called a business tax on labor usage or a tax on individuals' labor income and whether it must be remitted to the tax authority by the business or by the employee.

In some cases, a tax will exact a burden on the consumers or producers of *untaxed* goods or services that are related in some way to the taxed good. For example, if a tax on butter causes people to substitute margarine on their toast and in their cooking, this will probably drive up the price of margarine. In this way, part of the tax burden is shifted onto margarine consumers. Another important example applies to state and local government bonds. Interest on these bonds is excluded from federal taxation, while the returns on federal and corporate bonds are fully taxable. Because of this tax advantage, there is greater demand for state and local bonds. The increased demand pushes up the bonds' price or, in other words, lowers the interest rate they offer. Because of the tax on other investments, holders of state and local bonds—who remit no tax at all—pay an *implicit tax* equal to the difference between the interest rate they receive and the higher rate they would receive on a taxed bond of similar maturity and riskiness.

Corporations Don't Pay Taxes, People Do

The controversial bumper sticker inspired by the National Rifle Association—"Guns don't kill people, people do"—may seem like a semantic fine point, but at first blush the tax version of the NRA slogan seems just plain wrong. Corporations certainly do remit a great deal of taxes. By one estimate, in 1999 corporate and noncorporate businesses remitted 84 percent of all federal, state, and local government taxes. This included $231 billion of corporate income taxes, $1.7 trillion of withheld personal income tax and payroll tax payments, as well as numerous other taxes.[59] Moreover, many people favor higher taxes on corporations in the hope that this means that they or their constituents will avoid bearing any burden. For instance, in an April 2015 Gallup poll, 69 percent of respondents said corporations pay less than their "fair share" of tax.[60]

Nevertheless, corporations do not "pay" tax in the sense of bearing the burden of it. The fact that Alcoa's treasurer signs checks made out to the IRS tells us nothing about which Americans bear the burden of taxation. Certainly, the treasurer does not bear the burden of his employer's corporation income taxes, but who exactly does bear it? Is it Alcoa's stockholders, its employees, or perhaps its customers? What-ever the answer to this question, it is not informative to say that the legal entity that is Alcoa Inc. will be worse off because of the corpora-tion income tax. Rather, we need to identify precisely which *people* end up bearing the burden of a tax. This point became a major news item in 2011 when, at a Mitt Romney campaign event, protesters called for increasing taxes on corporations instead of on people. Romney famously replied "corporations are people, my friend ...," subsequently clarifying that he meant that "everything corporations earn ultimately goes to people."[61]

Which people bear the burden of the corporate income tax? To answer this question, imagine that a corporate tax is enacted, without prior warning, in an economy that previously had no such tax and that contains many businesses that are corporations and many that are not. In the short run, the holders of corporate stock—the owners of the corporation—suffer as a result of imposing this tax, as share prices will tumble in anticipation of lower after-tax earnings. This is not the end of the story, though, because new investments by corporations subject to the tax are now less attractive compared to alternative investments, such as those in businesses not subject to the tax (pass-through entities), foreign investments, real estate, etc. Corporate investment declines, while noncorporate investment expands. But more people seeking non-corporate investments will inevitably drive down the pre-tax return in these sectors, as the most profitable opportunities are used up and less profitable ones are pursued. The reduced profitability of noncorporate business, due to more competition, shifts some of the burden of the tax to the owners, and possibly consumers, of these other forms of business. In the long run, the after-tax, risk-adjusted return on investment will be the same for corporate investments as it is for noncorporate investments, and the burden will be shared among all owners of business capital.

Because this is a difficult bit of economic reasoning, the following analogy may be helpful. Imagine there are two highways leading from a suburb to the central city. The two highways get commuters to work in about the same amount of time, and almost everyone has settled into the habit of regularly taking one road or the other. Now imagine that a tollbooth is constructed on one of the roads. Who will be worse off? At first, the losers will be those who are accustomed to taking the newly taxed route to work. Over time, though, more and more commuters will switch to the untaxed alternate highway to avoid the toll, making it more congested and increasing the commuting time. In this way, the burden of the toll imposed on taking one road is shifted to those people who usually had taken the other. Once the dust has settled, all commuters will probably be about equally burdened by the toll. (If not, people will continue to change their commuting habits.) By analogy, a tax on the income from corporations will be spread to the recipients of all types of capital income as funds that otherwise would have been invested in corporations flow into the noncorporate sector.[62]

Do Workers Bear Taxes on Capital?

Some economists argue that the shifting story does not end here and that part of the burden of a corporation income tax—or of any tax levied on the return to capital investment—will be shifted from wealth owners to wage earners. Their argument goes as follows. Taxes on capital income (including, but not restricted to, corporation income taxes) reduce the rate of return to saving, which in turn reduces how much people save. Because saving finances capital investment, a decline in saving over time means that the economy is less capital-intensive and therefore labor is less productive. By this reasoning, workers ultimately bear some of the burden of taxes on capital income because their wages are reduced when they are less productive.

This argument is highly controversial because it depends on a couple of hotly debated presumptions about how the U.S. economy works. First, it requires that individual saving behavior be responsive to changes in the after-tax return a person receives. The experience of the 1980s and 1990s, when the after-tax rates of return to saving surged but the savings rate gradually declined, has cast doubt on that proposition.

Second, the argument requires that domestic investment must decline if U.S. saving declines. The global economy reduces the impact of a decline in domestic saving on domestic investment because that investment need not be financed entirely by U.S. residents' savings. If a tax on the capital income of U.S. citizens, a budget deficit, or anything else is causing a reduction in our nation's saving, foreign savers have proven only too happy to pick up some of the slack and finance some of our investment.[63] In this case, the link between the future productivity of American workers and the return to our own investments is weakened, and more of the burden of taxes on the return to saving will be borne by American savers—that is, American wealth owners. Evidence that rates of domestic saving across countries are highly correlated with rates of domestic investment suggests, however, that declines in domestic saving are probably only partly offset by inflows of saving from abroad.[64]

We have argued that the possibility that foreigners will invest in the United States makes it less likely that a tax on U.S. residents' savings will be shifted onto U.S. workers. The possibility that U.S. citizens will invest abroad, though, makes it more likely that taxing U.S. domestic *investment* will in fact be somewhat shifted onto American workers. Investment abroad is an alternative to domestic investment, which limits the degree to which investors will accept a lower return to investing in the United States. Thus, an attempt to tax the income from U.S.-located investment to some extent drives investment offshore, leaving U.S. workers with less productive work opportunities and putting downward pressure on their wages.

The lesson of the global marketplace is that it is difficult for a country to impose a tax burden on individuals whose income-earning opportunities are mobile across borders. Capital currently is more mobile than labor, implying that taxes on the income from capital in a particular location will tend to be shifted onto those workers who reside in that location. Evidence suggests, however, that capital is still far from perfectly mobile across borders for a large country such as the United States, so even in this case capital owners are likely to bear a substantial part of the tax burden.[65]

The 19th-century French pamphleteer and leader of the free-trade movement, Frédéric Bastiat, wrote that there is only one difference between a bad economist and a good economist: a good economist considers both policy effects that can be seen and those that cannot be seen, while a bad economist considers only what can be easily seen.[66] Because individuals and businesses can respond to taxes by changing their behavior, the true burden of taxes can be shifted in ways that are unanticipated and unintended by policymakers—and unseen, if one looks only at who the tax law asserts that the tax is "on." We have discussed how taxes on capital income can, in principle, be shifted to workers, but this is only one among many examples of tax shifting. For instance, taxes on the profits from innovation can, in principle, be shifted to those consumers who would have enjoyed the innovative products that the tax discouraged from reaching market. Although it is impossible to know for sure how much tax shifting occurs, good economists provide answers based on what they know about the critical factors and, ideally, provide a range of possible consequences based on alternative sets of reasonable presumptions.

Who Bears the Burden of U.S. Federal Taxes?

So who does bear the burden of federal taxes in the United States? In recent years, the most thorough analyses of this question have been provided by the Urban-Brookings Tax Policy Center and the Congressional Budget Office (CBO). Both use roughly similar methodologies and come to similar conclusions.

In table 3.2, we present the Urban-Brookings Tax Policy Center's estimates of the distribution of federal taxes in 2015. As we just discussed, coming up with such estimates requires making assumptions about the *incidence* of the various federal taxes. The Urban-Brookings Tax Policy Center's estimates assume that the entire burden of the individual income tax falls on those families that have the legal liability, with no shifting at all of tax levied on either labor or capital income. This assumption would be consistent with a situation where neither labor supply nor saving is responsive to its after-tax return.

Table 3.2
Urban-Brookings Tax Policy Center Estimates of the Distribution of Federal Taxes, 2015

Rank in distribution of cash income	Minimum pre-tax income to qualify, thousands of 2015 dollars	Average tax rate as a percentage of cash income				Percentage of total	
		All federal taxes	Personal income tax	Corporate income tax		Pre-tax income	Federal taxes
	(1)	(2)	(3)	(4)		(5)	(6)
Overall	0	19.8	9.5	2.4		100.0	100.0
Top 1 percent	709	33.4	25.1	5.1		16.5	27.9
Rest of top 5 percent	290	25.2	15.2	3.0		12.5	15.9
Bottom half of top decile	204	21.8	10.6	2.5		9.9	10.8
Bottom half of top quintile	138	19.9	8.4	2.1		14.2	14.3
Second highest quintile	78	17.0	6.1	1.8		20.3	17.5
Middle quintile	45	13.1	2.9	1.4		13.8	9.2
Second lowest quintile	23	7.8	-1.9	1.1		8.5	3.4
Lowest quintile	0	3.6	-5.0	0.8		4.3	0.8

Source: Urban-Brookings Tax Policy Center (2015a, 2015b, and 2015c).

Regarding the corporate income tax, they assume that 60 percent of the burden falls on shareholders of corporations, 20 percent falls on owners of capital in general, and 20 percent falls on labor. These assumptions are consistent with some mobility of investment across the corporate and noncorporate sectors, and allow for some negative effect of the corporate tax on U.S. investment, which in turn reduces wage rates. The burden of payroll taxes is attributed to families according to their income from wages or self-employment, whether the tax payments are denoted as employee or employer contributions; thus, the assignment of legal liability between firm and individual (as well as who remits the money to the IRS) is ignored. Each taxpayer is assigned an expected estate tax burden, equal to the estimated estate tax that would be due if the person died in that year, times the probability that the person will die in that year. Federal excise taxes are assumed to be completely passed through as higher prices to consumers of the taxed goods.[67]

The Urban-Brookings Tax Policy Center's estimates of average tax rates (tax burdens divided by income) shown in columns 2 through 4 of table 3.2, use as the denominator a concept they call "pre-tax expanded cash income," which is essentially gross income as reported on the federal income tax form (or an estimate of what that would be for those who do not file returns) plus the nontaxable portions of interest income, government cash transfers, employee benefits (including employer-provided health insurance), retirement income, and a few other items.[68]

Column 2 of table 3.2 indicates that the distribution of federal taxes as a whole is quite progressive, with average tax rates rising from 3.6 percent for people in the lowest fifth of the income distribution, to 13.1 percent in the middle fifth, and then to 33.4 percent in the top percentile. An older analysis by the Urban-Brookings Tax Policy Center demonstrated that as of 2006 (when the top marginal federal income tax rate was 35 percent, as opposed to 39.6 percent in 2013), the pattern of federal average tax rates was still quite progressive even when a more comprehensive measure of "economic income" (close to the Haig–Simons income measure discussed in chapter 2) was used. The average federal tax rates in the bottom quintile, middle quintile, and top 1 percent of the distribution were 3.5 percent, 14.3 percent, and 30.7 percent, respectively, when using cash income, and 2.2 percent, 13.4 percent, and 24.7 percent when using economic income.[69] Thus, it is far from the truth that upper-income people—by taking advantage of loopholes, tax shelters, and the like—have a tax burden that is a smaller share of their income than it is for everyone else.

The estimates in the third column of table 3.2 indicate that the federal personal income tax in particular is highly progressive. Average income tax rates range from -5.0 percent in the bottom quintile, to 2.9 percent in the middle quintile, to 25.1 percent in the top percentile. The negative average tax rate figures for the bottom two quintiles are due to the refundable portions of the Earned Income Tax Credit as well as the Child Tax Credit. Many people in these income groups on net receive payments *from* the federal government through the personal income tax. A comparison of the estimates for overall federal taxes (in column 2) and personal income taxes (in column 3) makes clear that income taxation accounts for nearly all of the progressivity of the federal tax system; most other federal taxes are either proportional or regressive.

Estimates of the distribution of corporate taxes are shown in column 4 of table 3.2. Under the incidence assumptions described above, the implicit tax burden is estimated to be quite progressive; for instance, it amounts to just 1.4 percent of income for people in the middle quintile but 5.1 percent of income for those in the highest percentile. As noted earlier, however, the question of who actually bears the burden of the corporate income tax is particularly controversial. Reasonable alternative assumptions about its incidence could make the overall federal tax system look somewhat less progressive, but under most reasonable assumptions it would still be progressive. For example, if we were to assume that the burden of the corporate tax were proportional to total pre-tax expanded cash income (implying that the vast majority of the burden of the tax falls on labor), then total federal taxes would be 14.1 percent of income for people in the middle income quintile and 30.8 percent for people in the top income percentile.

Columns 5 and 6 of table 3.2 show the Urban-Brookings Tax Policy Center's projection of the percentage of total pre-tax expanded cash income that people in each part of the income distribution will receive in 2015, and their estimates of the percentage of the total federal tax burden that is borne by people in each part of the income distribution. The share of taxes is higher than the share of income throughout the top quintile, and lower than the share of income below the top quintile, another indicator of tax progressivity. The top 1 percent is estimated to bear 27.9 percent of the overall federal tax burden, which is the combined effect of progressive taxes and receiving such a large share (16.5 percent) of all pre-tax income.

Recently, the fact that *some* very high-income people appear to pay low average tax rates has become a high-profile political issue. In 2012, Warren Buffett helped make the issue salient with an op-ed revealing that he had a lower average tax rate than anyone in his office, including his secretary—he reported that his personal income tax and combined employer-employee payroll tax amounted to 17.4 percent of his taxable income in 2010.[70] Mitt Romney's revelation that he owed only 13.9 percent of his adjusted gross income (AGI) in personal income tax in 2010, together with his refusal to release returns from earlier years, became a lightning-rod issue in the 2012 presidential campaign.[71]

As table 3.2 shows, *on average* people in the top 1 percent of the income distribution owe significantly higher average federal tax rates than do people lower down in the distribution. But there is indeed quite a bit of diversity in tax burdens among high-income households. The U.S. Department of the Treasury estimated that in 2012, average federal tax rates (including personal income tax, payroll tax, and corporate income tax, and expressed as a percentage of "cash income") were 8.7 percent or less for 10 percent of the households in the top 1 percent of the income distribution, 21.2 percent or less for a quarter of households in the top 1 percent, and 32.3 percent or more for another quarter of households in the top 1 percent.[72] Much of the variation arose from the fact that, in 2012, the maximum personal tax rate on long-term capital gains (including those arising from "carried interest," discussed in chapter 2) and qualified dividends was only 15 percent, while that on ordinary income was 35 percent (these rates were increased to 20 percent and 39.6 percent, respectively, in 2013); differences in the fraction of income subject to these lower rates explains much of the variation of average tax rates. Variations in the amount of deductions claimed (e.g., for charitable contributions) also explain some of the diversity in average tax rates. The heterogeneous use of sophisticated tax shelters could explain some of the diversity as well, although tax shelters will sometimes reduce the apparent income in addition to reducing tax, in which case their effects might not show up in the estimates of average tax rates.

Partly in response to these issues, the Obama administration in 2011 proposed a "Buffett Rule" that would impose a minimum average tax rate (including personal income taxes and a portion of Social Security and Medicare taxes) of 30 percent of income for those with income above $2 million (to be gradually phased in for those with incomes between $1 million and $2 million, and with "income" defined as AGI less a modified measure of charitable contributions).[73] The proposal had no hope of making it through Congress, but the debate over this issue touches on many interesting questions. How progressive should the tax system be? Should different kinds of income be taxed at different rates? Should deductions and loopholes be scaled back? Are minimum taxes a good way to compensate for the effects of deductions, loopholes, and low tax rates on tax progressivity? We will take up these questions in various parts of the book, and revisit the Buffett Rule in particular in chapter 5.

For some historical perspective on the distribution of tax burdens, figure 3.2 illustrates how average federal tax rates changed between 1979 and 2013 for people at different points in the income distribution. This is based on the same CBO data used in table 3.1, and follows a similar but not identical approach to the Urban-Brookings Tax Policy Center's study just discussed. Figure 3.2 expresses average tax rates as a percentage of CBO's measure of "pre-tax income" (including transfers), which is roughly similar to the Urban-Brookings Tax Policy Center's "expanded cash income" measure, but with some differences (e.g., CBO includes the value of Medicare and Medicaid while the Urban-Brookings Tax Policy Center does not). CBO's incidence assumptions are similar to the Urban-Brookings Tax Policy Center's, except that CBO assigns one-quarter of the burden of the corporate income tax to workers, and three-quarters to recipients of capital income. CBO also excludes estates and gift taxes, which the Urban-Brookings Tax Policy Center includes.

The most dramatic changes in average federal tax rates since 1979 occurred at the top of the income distribution. The average federal tax rate in the top income percentile fell from 35.1 percent in 1979 to a low of 24.6 percent in 1986 as a result of the Reagan-era tax cuts, rebounded to 35.3 percent in 1995 after an increase in the top tax rate during the Clinton administration, fell a bit to 32.4 percent by 2000 partly due to a 1997 cut in the capital gains tax rate, and then dropped more significantly to 29 percent by 2011 mainly because of tax cuts enacted during the George W. Bush administration. The increase in the top federal income tax rate enacted at the beginning of 2013 restored the average federal tax rate on the top 1 percent to 34 percent in 2013.

In the rest of the income distribution, federal average tax rates changed relatively modestly between 1979 and 2000, then declined

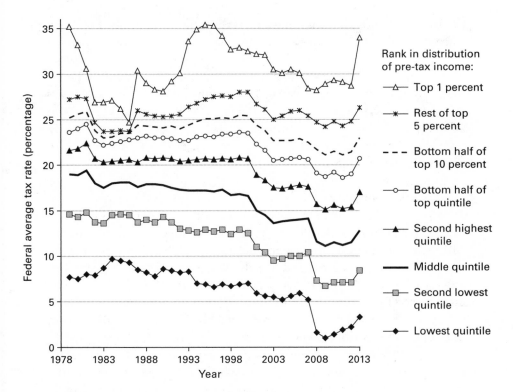

Figure 3.2
Average federal tax rates on households at different points in the income distribution, 1979–2013.
Source: Congressional Budget Office (2016b). *Note:* Depicts all federal taxes (except for estate and gift taxes) as a percentage of the Congressional Budget Office's measure of "before tax market income plus government transfers" (households are also ranked by that definition of income).

substantially between 2000 and 2012, but rebounded a bit in 2013. In the bottom quintile, the average federal tax rate fell from 7.7 percent in 1979 to 7 percent in 2000, then plummeted to a low of just 1 percent in 2009, subsequently rising to 3.3 percent by 2013. In the middle quintile, the average federal tax rate fell from 19 percent in 1979 to 16.6 percent in 2000, then dropped to just 11.1 percent by 2010, before rising to 12.8 percent by 2013. For the top 5 percent outside of the top 1 percent, the average federal tax rate was 27.2 percent in 1979 and 28 percent in 2000, dipped to a low of 24.3 percent by 2011, and rebounded to 26.3 percent in 2013. Average federal tax rates in the middle and bottom of the income distribution were unusually low during 2008 through 2012 partly because of temporary stimulus measures that have since expired, such as the refundable "Making Work Pay" tax credit that applied in 2009 and 2010, and a temporary payroll tax cut applying in 2011 and 2012. While average federal tax rates had rebounded a bit in the middle and bottom of the distribution by 2013, they were still generally a few percentage points lower in 2013 compared to 2000 in all parts of the income distribution outside the top 1 percent, mainly reflecting the fact that most of the George W. Bush–era tax cuts were made permanent starting in 2013 for all but the highest-income taxpayers.

As is often pointed out, even though taxes were a lower percentage of income for high-income people in recent years compared to, say, 1979, the share of total taxes they owed increased. For example, the CBO analysis suggests that people in the top 1 percent of the income distribution owed 14.2 percent of federal taxes in 1979, 24.1 percent of federal taxes in 2011, and 25.4 percent of federal taxes in 2013.[74] The main reason for this is simple: as figure 3.1 and table 3.1 show, the share of before-tax income received by the rich increased dramatically during this same time period. Somewhat lower average tax rates applied to much higher incomes brought in more tax revenue. This surge in incomes also moderated the degree to which cuts in statutory marginal tax rates caused average tax rates to decline for upper-income people, as shown in figure 3.2, because it pushed a larger share of their income into the highest tax brackets.

Research by Thomas Piketty and Emmanuel Saez suggests that changes in average federal tax rates at the very top of the income distribution over the longer run of history have been much more dramatic than anything shown in figure 3.2. They estimate that for households in the top 0.1 percent of the income distribution (those with incomes above $2 million in 2015), the average federal tax rate was typically close to *60 percent* of pre-tax market income throughout the 1960s and early-to-mid-1970s, and fell dramatically thereafter, to 34 percent by 2004. This drop was partly due to cuts in personal income tax rates applying to high-income people, but actually had more to do with large declines over time in the amounts of revenue raised by the corporate income tax and the estate tax relative to incomes, combined with Piketty and Saez's incidence assumption that the burdens of both of these taxes fall disproportionately on high-income people.[75]

Whenever changes in tax policy are contemplated, advocates on different sides of the debate attempt to frame the distributional consequences of the potential tax changes in a way that favors their side. So, for example, in debates over proposed tax cuts that were enacted during the administration of George W. Bush, critics of the proposals emphasized that they would reduce average tax rates by more, and would reduce tax liability per household by *much* more, for people at the top of the income distribution than for others. Supporters of the proposals emphasized that large numbers of people would get tax cuts, and that the tax cuts would represent a larger percentage of federal tax liability for moderate-income people than for upper-income people, which could be true at the same time as the claims of their opponents were true, because upper-income people owed much more tax than moderate-income people to begin with.[76]

Another important issue in the framing of debates over the distributional effects of tax changes is that focusing only on how tax burdens change for current taxpayers ignores inevitable effects on future taxes and government spending. For example, figure 3.2 suggests that, while the tax cuts enacted during the George W. Bush administration did reduce average federal tax rates the most for people at the top of the income distribution, people in most of the rest of the income distribution saw their average tax rates decline significantly too, which might suggest that the tax cuts made almost everyone better off. But this provides an incomplete picture of the winners and losers from the tax cuts. Tax cuts do not come for free, and the extra borrowing that the tax cuts require will have to be paid off at some time in the future. Ultimately, either government spending will have to be lower than it otherwise would have been, future taxes will have to be higher than they otherwise would have been, or some combination of the two will have to occur. Those who argued that the 2001 and 2003 tax cuts were unfair believed that they disproportionately benefited upper-income taxpayers at the time, at the expense of future taxpayers and the people who lose out from whatever government spending cuts may occur as a result.

If tax changes eventually lead to changes in federal government expenditures on transfer programs, then a complete picture of the distributional consequences must also address the impact on transfers. The overwhelming majority of such transfers go to the elderly and disabled. Social Security and Medicare, federal programs which go exclusively to the elderly, disabled, and dependent survivors of deceased workers, accounted for 71 percent of the value of all federal and state government transfers in 2013.[77] Medicaid, the federal-state program that provides health insurance for low-income people, comprised another 15 percent of transfers, and this program in particular is now a major point of contention between the political parties. The elderly and disabled accounted for about two-thirds of Medicaid expenditures in 2009, even though they only represented a quarter of the people covered by Medicaid.[78] A major reason is that Medicare does not cover long-term care (such as an extended stay in a nursing home), which is often so expensive that it pushes elderly and disabled people who need it into poverty, qualifying them for Medicaid. The Medicaid program also provides health insurance to large numbers of children—in 2014, about one-third of all children in the United States were enrolled in Medicaid, up from one-quarter in 2007, with the recent increase due to the ACA and to the recession.[79] All other transfers, including unemployment insurance benefits, SNAP (food stamps), TANF, and many other programs, accounted for just 14 percent of federal and state government transfers in 2013. This figure was higher than usual because of a sluggish recovery from a massive recession and the associated temporary reduction in employment rates, leading to a temporary increase in the share of people receiving unemployment benefits, SNAP, etc.

The Congressional Budget Office estimates the values of federal and state government transfers received at different points of the income distribution separately for elderly childless households and for others, and table 3.3 summarizes the key lessons from that data for 2013.

The average dollar value of transfers received by elderly childless households was $34,200, accounting for 38 percent of their pre-tax incomes, compared to $7,500, or 7 percent of pre-tax income, for all other households. Among elderly childless households, 93 percent of transfers came from Social Security and Medicare, and as table 3.3 shows, the absolute dollar values of government transfers tended to be *larger* for higher-income people. That distributional pattern is not surprising once one recognizes that elderly people at all income levels are eligible for both Social Security and Medicare, and that Social Security benefits are an increasing function of lifetime earnings.

Among "all other households," Social Security and Medicare still accounted for 41 percent of the value of transfers, because this group includes the disabled, survivors, and elderly households with children, many of whom are eligible for such benefits. For households other than elderly childless, Social Security and Medicare receipt was most common in the middle and lower parts of the income distribution, but

Table 3.3
Federal and state government transfers in different parts of the U.S. income distribution in 2013

Rank in distribution of pre-tax income (including transfers) among all households	Elderly childless households				All other households			
	Average transfer per household in thousands of dollars			Total transfers as a percentage of pre-tax income	Average transfer per household in thousands of dollars			Total transfers as a percentage of pre-tax income
	Social Security and Medicare	Medicaid	All other transfers		Social Security and Medicare	Medicaid	All other transfers	
All income levels	31.7	0.9	1.6	38	3.1	2.4	2.0	7
Top 1 percent	38.2	0.2	0.9	3	1.0	0.8	1.0	0
Rest of top 5 percent	36.5	0.3	1.2	13	1.7	0.4	0.7	1
Bottom half of top decile	37.1	0.5	1.4	22	1.9	0.4	1.1	2
Bottom half of top quintile	35.9	0.5	2.0	30	2.4	0.7	1.2	3
Second highest quintile	36.3	0.8	2.3	44	3.3	1.3	1.4	6
Middle quintile	33.1	1.4	1.8	62	4.2	2.9	2.3	13
Second lowest quintile	28.5	1.2	1.3	83	4.1	4.3	2.9	22
Lowest quintile	19.5	0.4	1.1	97	2.0	3.0	2.4	28

Source: Authors' calculations based on data from Congressional Budget Office (2016b).

was still spread widely throughout the distribution. Among house-holds other than elderly childless, average dollar amounts of transfers other than Social Security and Medicare did tend to be larger for lower-income people, but were not very large for any income group. In the bottom quintile of the income distribution, households other than elderly childless received $3,000 of Medicaid benefits and $2,400 of other transfers (aside from Social Security and Medicare) on average in 2013—and keep in mind that these figures were atypically high in 2013 due to the lingering effects of the recession.[80]

Overall, taking all government transfers together, the average dollar values of transfers per household are not dramatically different across the income distribution, and, if anything, tend to be smaller for lower-income people. But transfers are a much larger percentage of pre-tax income in the lower parts of the income distribution. Transfers accounted for 97 percent of pre-tax income for elderly childless house-holds in the bottom quintile, and 28 percent of pre-tax income for all other bottom quintile households. Thus, transfers are relatively much more important to the well-being of lower-income households.

To illustrate this issue, consider a 2008 study by Doug Elmendorf, Jason Furman, Bill Gale, and Ben Harris (who were all then at the Brookings Institution). The study calculated the distributional implica-tions of the 2001 and 2003 tax cuts, assuming they would ultimately be paid for in a way that cost each household an equal dollar amount—for example, through reductions in government expenditures. Given the distribution of transfers shown in table 3.3, this is a plausible descrip-tion of what might happen if the tax cuts eventually result in an across-the-board reduction in government transfers, relative to what those transfers would have been without the tax cuts. The analysis incorpo-rates a moderate increase in pre-tax income (3 percent) to account for the possibility that people respond to the improved incentives caused by lower marginal tax rates. Under this scenario, the 2001 and 2003 tax cuts would ultimately make 78 percent of all households, including almost everyone in the bottom three quintiles, *worse off*, because the reduced benefits received down the road would more than offset the value of the tax cuts received starting in 2001 and 2003. By contrast, 90 percent of households in the top quintile would ultimately come out ahead, as their tax cuts exceed the value of lost government benefits.[81] Thus, a strikingly different conclusion about who gains and who loses from deficit-causing tax cuts can emerge when one considers the long-term impacts on government spending.

Questions about the distributional impact of changes to taxation and government spending programs will undoubtedly continue to play a big role in political debates in the United States in the years to come. In spring of 2016, all of the leading candidates in the Republican presidential primaries had proposed substantial tax cuts, with much of the benefit accruing to people at the top of the income distribution. On the Democratic side, Hillary Clinton was proposing tax increases mainly affecting upper-income people in order to preserve existing government programs, and Bernie Sanders was proposing much larger tax increases to finance major expansions of government in areas such as health care, education, and infrastructure. The proposals left some important details unspecified, so even setting aside uncertainty about the economic impacts of the tax plans, estimates of their revenue and distributional impacts could also vary depending on the assumptions analysts made about how details might be filled in later.

With that important caveat, it's worth considering estimates of the revenue and distributional consequences of tax plans proposed by 2016 presidential candidates. Urban-Brookings Tax Policy Center analysts estimated that the tax plans proposed during the primaries would have the following impacts on federal tax revenues as a percentage of GDP during 2016–2026, not including any feedback effects from induced changes in economic growth: −4.0 for Trump, −3.6 for Cruz, −2.6 for Rubio, +0.5 for Clinton, and +6.4 for Sanders. The share of the benefits of the tax cut going to people in the top 1 percent of the income distribution would be 44 percent for Cruz, 35 percent for Trump, and 34 percent for Rubio. By contrast, the share of the total proposed tax increase that would be imposed on people in the top 1 percent of the income distribution was 78 percent for Clinton and 38 percent for Sanders. At opposite ends of the spectrum, Cruz's proposals would cut the average federal tax rate on people in the top 1 percent of the income distribution by 17.4 percentage points, while Sanders' plan would increase that average tax rate on people in the top 1 percent by 22.5 percentage points. The difference in the proposed size of government between the most right-wing and most left-wing candidates garnering significant electoral support in 2016 was in the vicinity of 10 percent of GDP or more, and the difference in proposed taxes on incomes of people in the top 1 percent of the distribution was close to 40 percent of income, both of which were surely all-time records for major candidates in a single U.S. presidential primary season. In August and then again in September of 2016, Donald Trump revised his tax plan. The Tax Foundation estimated that if the September version of the Trump plan were to keep the tax rate on income from pass-through entities the same as that for ordinary personal income, the ten-year static revenue loss would be 2 percent of GDP, and the tax cut as a percent of after-tax income would be 10.2 percent for people in the top 1 percent of the income distribution but only 1.3 percent for people in the middle quintile of the income distribution. If pass-through entity income were taxed at 15 percent, the revenue loss would increase to 2.6 percent, and the tax cut for people in the top 1 percent of the income distribution would rise to 16 percent of after-tax income.[82]

The Republican presidential candidates promised to offset some of the impact of their proposed tax cuts on the budget deficit through cuts to government spending programs. None had yet spelled out their spending plans in much detail, but Paul Ryan's 2014 House Budget Committee budget proposal may provide hints as to what might be on the table if Republicans were to achieve undivided control of the federal government. That plan proposed cuts to federal nondefense government spending totaling $4.8 trillion over 10 years, which would amount to 2.2 percent of ten-year GDP, and which would be partly offset by a $0.4 trillion increase in defense spending. Richard Kogan and Joel Friedman of the Center for Budget and Policy Priorities estimated that 69 percent of those spending cuts would come from programs that are targeted at low- and moderate-income people, such as Medicaid, Affordable Care Act subsidies for the purchase of health insurance, Pell Grants (financial aid for college students from low-income families), and SNAP (food stamps).[83] Given that the Urban-Brookings Tax Policy Center projected the revenue losses from the original Trump and Cruz plans to be significantly larger than 2.2 percent of GDP over the next ten years, the spending cuts needed to offset those tax plans would need to be that much deeper.[84]

The Democratic presidential candidates promised to raise enough revenue to preserve spending on existing federal programs, and in the case of Sanders, to significantly expand the role of government through universal government-provided health insurance and tuition-free public higher education, among other things. A 2016 analysis by Gordon Mermin, Len Burman, and Frank Sammartino of the Urban-Brookings Tax Policy Center estimated that under the Sanders plan, the increase in government transfers received would exceed the increase in tax burdens, on average, for households in each of the bottom four quintiles of the income distribution, and even for households in the top quintile outside of the top 5 percent. Households in the bottom income quintile were estimated to come out ahead by an average of about $10,100 each in calendar year 2017, and households in the middle income quintile were estimated to gain an average of about $8,700 in the same year. But the estimates also suggested that households in the top 5 percent of the income distribution would on average experience a tax increase that exceeded the increase in transfers received by about 17 percent of adjusted gross income.

Another consideration is that the revenue and distributional consequences of the presidential candidates' tax and spending plans discussed above are based on "static" estimates that do not account for any changes in economic growth that might be induced by the proposed modifications to tax policy and government spending. Potential impacts on economic growth are worth taking seriously, and any such effects would in turn alter the revenue and distributional effects described above. We address this issue in general terms in chapter 4. Some analysts did undertake ambitious efforts to simulate the economic impacts of the 2016 presidential candidates' plans using complex models of the economy. For reasons we discuss in chapter 4, estimates based on such simulations are only as good as the empirical evidence behind the assumptions built into the models. There is uncertainty about both the evidence and the models, and reason for skepticism that the economic effects of any of these tax plans will be large.

Horizontal Equity: Equal Treatment of Equals

Special Privileges for Everyone

In Garrison Keillor's fictional town of Lake Wobegon, all the children are above average. A similar paradox applies to the U.S. income tax system: everyone gets special privileges. You get a special tax break if you have children, if you are elderly, if you give money to your favorite charity, if you set up an IRA, if you receive fringe benefits from your employer, and the list goes on and on.

Of course, it is no more possible for everyone to get above-average tax breaks than it is possible for all children to be above average. Remember, *we are taxing ourselves*. To raise a given amount of revenue, the long list of special tax privileges requires higher tax rates. Allowing large families to take additional dependent exemption allowances lowers their taxes but inescapably increases taxes on smaller families.

The fact that mortgage interest payments are deductible certainly lowers taxes for those folks who have borrowed to buy their homes but inevitably raises taxes on those who rent housing. A family benefits from the whole system of tax breaks only if it receives more of them than other families at the same income level receive. Otherwise, what it saves in tax preferences is just offset by the higher-than-otherwise tax rates. But some people benefit and others lose. In fact, Alvin Rabushka of flat-tax fame has called the tax code "the most discriminatory body of law in a country that has tried to exterminate discrimination everywhere else in society."[85]

To expose the Wobegonish nature of our income tax system, allow us to reconfigure the tax system a bit. Gone is the current system of first calculating your adjusted gross income, subtracting off the deductions, and taking the credits that are your special privileges. The new system features a radical reduction in all tax rates, but—and there must be a "but"—now there are special tax *penalties* rather than special tax *privileges* for particular characteristics and activities. For example, there is a tax penalty for being *under* 65 years of age, for giving *less* than 1 percent of your income to a charity, for *not* setting up an IRA, and for receiving labor compensation in cash rather than in fringe benefits. In other words, there are penalties for not engaging in favored activities rather than tax breaks for engaging in them. If this tax redesign were done carefully enough, it could come pretty close to replicating the current pattern of tax liabilities, so that everyone would be right back to where they are now. It could also replicate the existing pattern of rewards and subsidies: the charitable would pay less tax than the uncharitable, the elderly would pay less than the non-elderly, and so on.

We're not suggesting that we go through the hassle of converting our tax system with high tax rates and special privileges for all to one with much lower tax rates and special penalties for all. The point is that we are all in the tax game together, and what is a privilege to one group of people ends up being a penalty to everyone else through higher tax rates.

Is there any justification for imposing special tax penalties—the inevitable consequences of granting special privileges—on some families? Or do these penalties imply a failure to achieve what economists call *horizontal equity*, when tax liability is the same for any two families with the same level of well-being—equal treatment of equals?

Certainly, we could probably all agree it would be inappropriate to base tax liability on some characteristics—such as race or religion. Although your race or religion won't lead to higher taxes today in the United States, many other personal characteristics and choices will. Which, if any, of these are justifiable reasons to penalize some people and reward others?

Let's start with spending patterns. Would it be fair that the Hatfields have a higher tax burden than the McCoys just because they like to go to the movies while the McCoys prefer to watch television? Would it be fair to tax the Astors more than the Vanderbilts because the Astors prefer yachts while the Vanderbilts favor private trains? Such distinctions based on one's "tastes" for consumption appear arbitrary and without a place in the tax system. But hold on a second. If you agree with that, then income tax penalties or preferences based on spending patterns are inappropriate, and moreover, excise taxes on particular goods and services are inappropriate because both discriminate against people that have a penchant for those kinds of expenditure. Taxes on movies discriminate against movie lovers, taxes on yachts discriminate against yacht lovers, and so on.[86] Note that taxing some goods but not others would not be a major problem for horizontal equity if the taxed goods represented the same share of total income for most people. If, for example, *all* families spent 20 percent of their income on food, then a 5 percent excise tax on food sales would be no more horizontally inequitable than a 1 percent income tax. If most, but not all, families spent 20 percent of their income on food, then the food tax would be almost as equitable but not quite. The fact that tastes *vary* renders horizontally inequitable a policy that relates tax burden to tastes.

Many aspects of the U.S. income tax system can be viewed as discriminating against certain people simply because of their tastes. For example, the home mortgage interest deduction penalizes those who prefer to rent housing rather than own housing. The charitable contribution deduction penalizes those who are not charitable. The deduction for state and local taxes penalizes people who prefer to live in places with low levels of public services, and therefore have a lower state and local tax bill. And the dependent exemption effectively penalizes families that prefer to have a small number of children.

Is there a more positive way to look at those tax features we've characterized as discriminating against certain activities? Yes, if the activity directly benefits other Americans in a particular way—what economists call positive *externalities*—special tax treatment can serve a legitimate social purpose by, in essence, subsidizing taxpayers for the benefits they provide to others. This argument does not contradict that special tax treatments are horizontally inequitable, though. Instead, the horizontal inequity is *tolerated* to achieve a more efficient economic system. The next chapter explores how to evaluate such arguments.

Tax preferences or penalties may also be justified on the grounds that income is an imperfect measure of a family's level of well-being and certain adjustments to income are required to make it a better measure. According to this argument, these tax features *improve* the horizontal equity of the tax system. This argument certainly applies to the existing deduction for extraordinary medical expenses. Comparing two families with the same income, one that incurs $10,000 in involuntary medical expenses is clearly not as well off as one that doesn't and may justifiably be liable for less tax. What makes this case different than the Hatfields and McCoys is that medical expenses are mainly not a matter of taste: you don't choose to get a serious illness.[87] Allowing a deduction for medical expenses helps out families singled out by circumstance, not by taste, and thus is unlikely to be a source of horizontal inequity. Even in this case, however, some discrimination by taste creeps in. Those who prefer to buy the best medical care they can find, instead of economizing, will receive an extra tax benefit.

Misleading Inequity

In some cases of apparent horizontal inequity, it is tricky to tell whether circumstances or tastes are involved. Consider the deductibility of casualty losses due to earthquake damages. If earthquakes were truly a random event, not at all predictable by location, then this deduction makes sense as a way to adjust tax liability to reflect the reduced ability to pay of earthquake victims: they are victims of circumstance. In fact, though, earthquakes are much more likely to occur in certain areas, such as California. Living on a fault line is a choice that is to some degree compensated by lower-than-otherwise housing prices. In this situation, allowing the casualty loss deduction provides a tax break to people who are willing to take the risk of an earthquake for some gain, which is certainly a matter of taste, and it penalizes everyone else through the higher tax rates needed to make up for the lost revenue. The argument gets even murkier when private earthquake insurance is available. In this case, the deduction rewards those who choose to live in a risky place and also choose not to insure themselves against a catastrophe. In this example, lower housing prices already provide partial compensation to people bearing earthquake risk, weakening the argument for a tax break.

In many other cases, the fact that tax liabilities differ across people does not reflect inequity because the market prices of the tax-favored activities offset all or some of the tax benefits. As discussed earlier, investors owe no tax on the interest they receive from state and local bonds, but this does not necessarily cause horizontal inequity because the market interest rate on these bonds is lower than the interest rate on taxable bonds because of their federal tax exemption. People with jobs in which a large part of their compensation is tax-exempt fringe benefits are not better off than other workers if their total pre-tax compensation is lower than otherwise. In both of these examples, the tax preference makes the activity (buying tax-exempt bonds or working at a job with fringe benefits) more attractive than otherwise, and the added attractiveness tends to drive up its market price. The price of tax-exempt bonds rises because of the tax exemption, lowering the market interest rate; the market wage for high-fringe-benefit jobs falls because more people want to have these jobs, other things equal.

Offsetting changes in market prices are more likely to happen if the tax-preferred activity is available widely. When it is restricted to only certain people, the benefit is less likely to be offset by price changes. Tax-exempt bonds surely fall into the former category.[88] A tax privilege granted to one company, sometimes called a *rifle-shot* provision, is certainly in the latter category. A legislator who wants to favor an important campaign contributor or some particular company based in his or her district occasionally succeeds in writing such a provision into the law, sometimes by sneaking provisions into a larger bill shortly before it is voted on when few are paying attention to the details.

Who Are Equals: Families or Individuals?

If horizontal equity requires "equal treatment of equals," who exactly should be considered equals—individuals or families? This question inevitably raises some tricky and controversial policy issues, ranging from the so-called marriage tax to the proper role of government in family-size decisions.

The U.S. income tax system uses the family as the unit of taxation but compromises between treating equal individuals equally and treating equal families equally. To see how this works out, consider how the number of children in a family affects tax liability. Under the current system, a family's tax bill declines with each additional child because each dependent qualifies the family for an additional exemption allowance, which amounted to a $4,000 deduction from taxable income in tax year 2015. In addition, each child under age 17 can qualify the taxpayer for a tax credit of up to $1,000, and those with incomes low enough to qualify for the Earned Income Tax Credit get larger benefits if they have children. The rationale here appears to be that in families with, say, $50,000 of gross income, each member will not be as well-off if the family has six people compared to a family that has three people. So our tax system treats the larger family more generously on ability-to-pay grounds and imposes a lower tax liability.

This argument sounds reasonable because a dollar has to stretch further in a big family.[89] But the other issue here is that it is not at all clear that *parents* are made worse off by each additional child they have. Having children is largely a voluntary choice and may even be viewed as a matter of personal consumption preference, or "taste," from the point of view of the parents. Some adults prefer to save their money and spend it on an annual (money-losing!) trip to Las Vegas, while others prefer the joy that children provide, the attendant costs of food, diapers, video games, and possibly college notwithstanding. Is it fair to reward adults who prefer to have more children with lower taxes at the expense of adults who prefer other ways of spending their money?[90]

Undoubtedly, some people would object to lumping together child rearing and carousing in Las Vegas as two comparable ways to spend money, and perhaps even consider the former as a sacred duty rather than a choice. Whether something is a choice or a duty is not an issue that economics can resolve. Moreover, the choice of how many children will be in the family is not voluntary from the children's point of view. So a child in a six-person family may indeed be materially worse off than a child in a three-person family with the same income.

Common sense suggests that a system that rewards families for having children would also reward—or at least not penalize—marriage. Common sense would be wrong for the U.S. tax system. Sometimes, getting married can increase a couple's total tax bill. This increase in tax liability is often called the *marriage penalty* or *marriage tax*. It arises not because any politician wants to dissuade people from getting married. Rather it happens because we insist on two requirements for our income tax system—that the tax system be progressive (i.e., average tax rates generally rise with income) and that tax liability be based on total family income and not on how that income is divided between spouses. It turns out that these two requirements are incompatible with *marriage neutrality*—the principle that getting married should have no tax consequences.

An example illustrates why this is true. Barbie and Ken are considering tying the knot but are practical people who are worried about the tax consequences of this decision. Each now makes $30,000. For this example, assume that the average tax rate on $30,000 of income is 15 percent and the average tax rate for $60,000 of income is 20 percent; the tax system is therefore progressive. Thus, Ken and Barbie now each pay $4,500 as singles, for a total of $9,000. As a married couple, however, they would pay $12,000 (20 percent of $60,000), amounting to a marriage penalty of $3,000. Note that there would be no marriage penalty at all if Barbie earned all the money or, for that matter, if Ken did; in that event, their combined tax liability would be $12,000 single or married.

In this example, the marriage tax happens not because anyone thinks it is good policy but rather as an unintended consequence of progressivity and family-based taxes. Some argue that a marriage tax is appropriate on ability-to-pay grounds because it reflects savings in the cost of living that marriage provides—sharing a kitchen, a washing machine, and so on. These savings could, though, be achieved largely by having a roommate rather than a spouse, and no one is suggesting that tax liability should depend on how many roommates you have.

If these are not convincing arguments for a marriage penalty, what can be done to alleviate it? One way to address the problem is to have separate tax tables for single taxpayers and for married couples, as we do in the United States. Each schedule can be progressive on its own terms so that the fraction of income owed in tax rises with income for single taxpayers and also for married taxpayers. If the tax due on the same income is lower for a married couple compared to a single taxpayer, then the marriage tax can be reduced or erased completely. Let's go back to Barbie and Ken and see how this would work. For single taxpayers, let the average tax rate still be 15 percent for $30,000 income and 20 percent for $60,000 income; this is progressive. For married taxpayers, let the tax rate be 10 percent on $30,000 and 15 percent on $60,000; this is progressive, too (at least when considering only taxpayers of a particular marital status). This scheme eliminates the marriage tax on Barbie and Ken because they pay $4,500 each as singles and $9,000 as a married couple.

Some important consequences arise, though, when we try to get rid of the marriage tax in this way. First of all, it imposes a penalty for being single because under this system a single taxpayer earning $60,000 pays $12,000 in tax, while a married couple with exactly the same family income owes only $9,000. This situation provides what is usually called a *marriage bonus* of $3,000, but it just as well could be called a penalty for being single.

As long as we desire a progressive tax system based on family income, there is no way to make it also marriage-neutral. Any tax schedule will feature either a marriage bonus (single penalty), a marriage penalty (single bonus), or some combination of both bonus and penalty, depending on the tax schedules and circumstances of the people involved.

In the United States, we have opted for a compromise among the approaches. Historically, a two-earner couple has typically faced a tax penalty for getting married, although the penalty is not as large as it would be if all families and individuals were taxed under the same schedule. A single-earner couple has typically received a tax bonus for getting married. There is a single penalty, as well, because a single person pays more tax than a single-earner married couple with the same income. Under current policy, marriage penalties for two-earner couples tend to be larger and more common near the bottom and the top of the income distribution. Lower-income households with two wage earners can face large marriage penalties because marriage causes the Earned Income Tax Credit they qualify for to shrink, among other reasons. This occurs because the maximum Earned Income Tax Credit, and the income level at which the credit starts to phase out, is substantially less than twice as large for married couples as it is for single individuals or unmarried heads of household.

Adam Carasso and Eugene Steuerle of the Urban Institute have calculated that, as of 2004, a man and a woman with two children and a combined income of $30,000 typically faced a marriage penalty of around $2,000 if each of them earned close to half of the combined income.[91] This marriage penalty has since been slightly reduced by a 2009 increase in the level of income at which the Earned Income Tax Credit begins to phase out for married couples. In the middle of the income distribution, marriage penalties for two-earner couples tend to be smaller and rarer, and marriage bonuses for single-earner couples larger and more common, because the standard deduction and the 10 percent and 15 percent tax brackets are now twice as large for married couples as for single taxpayers. In the upper ranges of the income distribution, marriage penalties become more common again, as tax brackets higher than 15 percent are less than twice as large for married couples as for singles.

We could achieve marriage neutrality if each person's tax liability was based solely on their own income, regardless of their marital status, as is the case in several European countries and as was the case in the United States in the early days of the income tax.[92] Under this system, marriage can have no tax consequences at all. But note that, under this system, a married couple's total tax liability depends on who earns what. A couple whose total income is divided up equally will owe less than another couple with exactly the same total income but with one primary earner. This system of basing tax liability on individual, rather than family, income also creates the incentive to shift income from the higher-earning family member to the lower-earning member. Couples can manipulate which spouse receives capital income and incurs deductible expenses, and which participant in a family business reports what fraction of the business's income; all of these practices would be difficult for the IRS to monitor, and if not monitored would reward those who engage in them, at the expense of everyone else.[93]

Lifetime and Generational Perspectives on Equity

Imagine the following hypothetical two-year tax-and-transfer program. In the program's first year, half of all taxpayers are subject to a new tax of $1,000, while the other half each receive a special $1,000 grant. In the next year everyone switches places: those who were taxed get the grant, and those who got the grant face the tax levy. It would be clear that (ignoring interest) over a two-year horizon everyone's net benefit comes to exactly zero, even though a one-year analysis would reveal apparently capricious horizontal inequity: some receive money, and some remit money. More seriously, when comparing two tax systems that differ in the timing of tax liabilities but that add up to the same burden over a longer horizon, it is important not to be misled by an annual analysis to conclude that there is inequity. For example, special credits to the elderly don't have significant equity consequences if everyone eventually is elderly. The fact that, over a lifetime, income taxes are levied during the working years and sales tax payments are apparently spread out more evenly over one's lifetime, including retirement, is not in itself relevant for horizontal inequity, even though in any one year the tax payments of two individuals with the same income will appear to differ depending on their ages. We return to this issue in chapters 6 and 7, where we discuss the relative merits of income and consumption tax systems, because the apparently different timing of tax liability between those types of taxes is a major issue in that discussion.

Some tax policy issues require us to look beyond even a lifetime perspective to a multigenerational perspective. This perspective is essential for discussing deficit financing of government expenditures because borrowing puts off specifying who will bear the burden of taxes and tends to impose that burden on future generations. This issue also enters the debate over whether to replace the income tax with a consumption tax because, depending on how the transition is handled, that could shift a substantial tax burden onto the elderly and decrease the tax burden on future generations.

Transitional Equity

Whenever the tax system changes, inevitably some people lose and others benefit. This is true regardless of whether the change ultimately makes the tax system fairer. The losers lose in part because they have entered into some long-term commitments that made sense only because of the old tax system. They may have bought houses counting on the mortgage interest deduction, and will be worse off if it is abolished. They may have taken jobs far from their homes, counting on cheap gasoline for commuting, and will lose if gasoline taxes are increased. They may have invested in state and local bonds, counting on the benefit of tax-free interest, and will see the value of these bonds fall if marginal tax rates are reduced or plummet if the tax exemption is removed entirely.

Others will reap windfall benefits when the tax law changes. These are people who happen to be in the right place at the right time. For example, individuals who own stock in companies that pay dividends (or, more precisely, that are likely to pay them in the future) will see their shares rise in value if the tax on dividends is eliminated, as President Bush proposed in early 2003, or if the tax on dividends is reduced, as the 2003 tax law did. People in the ethanol business will undoubtedly benefit if gasoline taxes are raised, and the owners of Mom and

Pop grocery stores (Mom and Pop, hopefully) would prosper if the government enacted special taxes on chain stores, as several states did in the 1930s.

Of course, the political pressure against change always comes from those who stand to lose from a tax change, not from those who stand to win. What should be done about the losers? Some would say "tough beans" and leave it at that, arguing that there are constantly ups and downs in the economic environment and everyone has to expect to lose out from time to time. This argument is especially compelling when talk of tax changes has been in the air for a while. In that case, the possibility of windfall losses is probably already reflected in the price of the activity or asset. For example, serious congressional consideration of lower tax rates can drive down the price of tax-exempt securities, increasing their yield. The bargain price and high interest rate reflect the possibility that tax rates might go down. If lower tax rates materialize, fully compensating the holders of the bonds wouldn't make sense. They took a gamble when they bought the bonds, fully aware of the possibility of a tax reduction, and they've already been partly compensated for this risk by earning a higher return on their investment. This recalls our earlier discussion of earthquake risk.

Sometimes, though, there is simply no way that the tax change could have been anticipated. A family that took out a home mortgage five years ago, counting on the interest deduction, could not have reasonably anticipated that the deduction would be eliminated. If the mortgage deduction were to be eliminated, what can be done to prevent this family from being hurt? The usual fix is to "grandfather" existing mortgages so that interest on them remains deductible, even as interest on new mortgages is no longer deductible. Although this seems reasonable, grandfathering arrangements and other transition rules can easily become quite complicated. They require two parallel sets of rules—one to apply to decisions taken under the old tax law and one to apply to decisions taken since; the dividing line requires monitoring to prevent abuse. These arrangements also cost the Treasury revenue and thus require higher tax rates than otherwise, at least for a while.

The point is that even if we could all agree that another tax system is fairer and simpler, getting from here to there might be unfair to many people. If, though, we try to devise rules to compensate losers, the transition can become extremely complicated. Moreover, if only those potential losers who are politically powerful get compensated, the transition can end up becoming both extremely complicated *and* unfair.

Conclusion

What's fair in taxation plays a crucial role in the debate about tax reform because many reform proposals effect a radical reshuffling of the tax burden. Some proposals collapse the graduated rate structure to a single rate, substantially lessening the tax system's progressivity. Other proposals cut back on the special provisions in the tax law that are justified on the grounds that they fine-tune the sharing of the tax burden or reward socially beneficial activities. Fine-tuning tax liability and ensuring progressivity inevitably complicate the tax process, and abandoning these goals can allow significant simplification. Moreover, the effort to use the tax system to redistribute incomes and single out particular activities for reward may inhibit economic growth. How much is the subject of the next chapter.

4   Taxes and Economic Prosperity

The question of how taxes affect the economy has long been at the heart of the American political debate. At one end of the spectrum are those who argue that our tax system is a serious drag on the economy and that radical changes could unleash a new era of unbridled growth and prosperity. Ronald Reagan made this a central theme of his presidential campaigns and rode to landslide victories as he promised and delivered lower income tax rates, with dramatic reductions concentrated at the top. The Republican presidential candidate in every general election from 1996 through 2012 ran on a platform that advocated either significant across-the-board cuts in income tax rates, or making all of the expiring 2001 and 2003 tax cuts permanent, arguing each time that this would greatly benefit the economy. Throughout his presidency, George W. Bush argued that low taxes are critical for prosperity, stating that "countries with low taxes, limited regulation, and open trade grow faster, create more jobs, and enjoy higher standards of living than countries with bigger, more centralized governments and higher taxes."[1]

In 2016, several Republican presidential primary candidates promoted tax reform plans that would reduce income tax rates, or replace the income tax with a flat tax or a national sales tax, and touted the economic benefits of doing so.[2] For example, Ted Cruz claimed his tax plan would cause GDP to increase by an extra 13.9 percent over ten years.[3] Donald Trump responded to a question about how much economic growth would result from his tax plan by saying: "we are looking at 3 percent but we think it could be 5 [percent] or even 6 [percent]. We are going to have growth that will be tremendous."[4] A growth rate of 5 or 6 percent per year would be quite a large improvement relative to the 2.7 percent average real GDP growth rate of the past 40 years, to say the least.[5] Trump further claimed that the economic benefits of his tax and trade plans would be so great as to enable the U.S. to pay off the $19 trillion federal debt within eight years—despite estimates that the tax cut he was proposing at the time would lose revenue amounting to about $9.5 trillion through 2026 before accounting for any induced economic effects, and despite promises to avoid cutting Social Security and to refrain from making any significant changes to Medicare, aside from attacking "waste, fraud, and abuse" and negotiating lower drug prices.[6]

In recent years, leading Democratic politicians' predictions about the economic benefits of their own plans for taxation and government spending programs have tended to be a bit more circumspect, or at least less specific—but not always. For example, in 2016, the campaign manager for Bernie Sanders (technically an Independent, but running in the Democratic presidential primary) defended a study by economist Gerald Friedman of the University of Massachusetts at Amherst, which projected that Sanders' plan would boost the U.S. real economic growth rate to about 5 percent per year through 2026.[7] Several economists who had previously chaired the Council of Economic Advisers under Democratic presidents criticized Friedman's claims as wildly optimistic and highly inconsistent with the best available evidence, and expressed concern that such claims would squander what they saw as Democrats' hard-won credibility on claims about economic evidence.[8]

More generally, Democratic politicians tend to be dismissive of the notions that shrinking the size of government or making taxes less progressive are necessary to achieve strong economic growth. They point to the sustained period of robust economic growth following the increase in tax rates on high-income people enacted in 1993 under President Bill Clinton, or the steady continued pace of economic recovery following a similar tax increase for high-income people under the Obama administration in 2013. Democratic politicians argue that the government programs that taxes fund, in areas such as education, infrastructure, and scientific research, will enhance economic productivity and growth, and they emphasize how government programs and progressive taxation promote security, fairness, and shared prosperity. They also claim that tax changes proposed by Republicans will in practice lose revenue and increase government budget deficits, which in turn will harm long-run economic growth. Hillary Clinton expressed a common Democratic sentiment in a July 2015 speech, when she said: "For 35 years, Republicans have argued that if we give more wealth to those at the top by cutting their taxes … it will trickle down to everyone else. Yet every time they have a chance to try that approach, it explodes the national debt, concentrates wealth even more and does practically nothing to help hard-working Americans."[9]

While political advocates' claims about the economic effects of tax changes they tout obviously need to be taken with a grain of salt, the empirical question of how taxes affect economic prosperity still ought to be taken seriously. Understanding how the tax system affects the economy and how to evaluate partisan claims about those effects is critically important to assessing what tax policy we should have. For one thing, if certain features of our tax code hinder the economy without good reason, most of us could agree that we should change those features. Often, however, changes to the tax code that could improve economic performance conflict with other valued goals or require cuts in popular expenditure programs. In these cases, there is a trade-off or balance to be struck, and the terms of that trade-off depend crucially on how large the economic benefits arising from the tax change would be.

This chapter explores how taxes affect the economy. Our main concern is how the *design* of the tax system—as opposed to the level of tax revenues—influences economic prosperity in the long run. We examine the specific ways that taxes affect economic behavior, and the evidence on the magnitude of those effects. Before we begin this task, though, we address some important issues that are in principle separate from how the design of the tax system affects long-run prosperity, but often get mingled or confused with that question, and sometimes end up dominating the political debate.

Short-Run Economic Fluctuations

As is painfully obvious after the severe recession that began in 2008, the economy does not proceed steadily along a long-run trend, but instead experiences temporary ups and downs known as the *business cycle*. The downs—periods when the economy is sluggish and stuck significantly below its capacity—are known as *recessions*. Unemployment rates rise above their normal levels, and industrial plant and equipment go underutilized.

When the economy falls into a recession, tax revenues tend to drop automatically both in absolute dollar terms and as a percentage of GDP, for example because people's incomes fall, thus putting them in lower tax brackets. In addition, politicians often enact tax cuts during recessions in an effort to boost the economy. The recession is inevitably followed, eventually, by a recovery, which is usually—but not always—a period of rapid economic growth, as we make up lost ground and more fully utilize the capital and labor that are already available. This kind of growth is fundamentally different from the kind of sustainable long-run growth that involves an expansion of the economy's capacity or potential—more and better capital and technology and more and better-skilled labor. Regardless of whether the association between low taxes at the bottom of recession and subsequent recovery from recession is coincidental or causal, it is not particularly informative about how taxes affect long-run economic prosperity. The association might tell us something about the effect of taxes on how quickly the economy returns to its long-run trend after a shock but, even if it does, that could be consistent with any possible effect of taxes on the long-run trend itself, including no effect at all.

To clarify the issues involved, we need to take a momentary detour from our discussion of tax policy to talk about the economics of recessions. But it will soon become clear how the two interact.

Why Recessions Happen
The explanation for recessions that we outline below has been the conventional economic explanation for them since at least World War II, in the sense that it is consistent with what is in most undergraduate textbooks in macroeconomics, and is typical of the thinking of most economists working for central banks such as the U.S. Federal Reserve. It owes a lot to the writings of economist John Maynard Keynes during the Great Depression (his views were anything but conventional at the time), but is actually also fairly consistent with the thinking of economist and libertarian hero Milton Friedman.[10]

The now-conventional economic explanation for recessions is fundamentally about an imbalance between the supply of saving and the demand for investment in an economy, whereby "investment" we mean purchases of new capital (e.g., factories, productive machinery, and office buildings) by firms, and purchases of newly constructed homes by individuals and families. Normally, this is not a problem, because interest rates can adjust to maintain balance between saving and investment. If the supply of saving increases or the demand for investment drops, that sets in motion natural market forces that push down interest rates. Lower interest rates make borrowing less expensive, which makes firms more willing to borrow to finance investment, and makes households more willing to borrow to invest in new homes. When increased saving is converted into increased investment in this manner, it maintains aggregate spending in the economy and keeps the economy humming along at capacity. This is also good for long-run economic prosperity, as it means we are investing more in capital that will increase our future wealth and productivity.

A critical problem is that under certain circumstances, *money*, by which economists mean cash and checking accounts, can throw a monkey wrench into the natural adjustment process of interest rates. The relevant distinguishing characteristics of money here are that it is a safe way to store your wealth, that it pays little or no interest, and that its supply is controlled by the nation's central bank, which in the United States is called the Federal Reserve (or "The Fed"). Our economic difficulties since 2008 provide an apt illustration of how money can mess up the economy's adjustment to shocks and how it can contribute to causing a prolonged economic slump.

In the fall of 2008, enormous housing bubbles in the United States and parts of Europe burst, and a massive global financial crisis ensued. Prices of homes and stocks dropped sharply, and consumer and business confidence plunged. Consumers cut back on spending due to shrinking wealth, fears about losing their jobs, and the need to tighten belts to pay back debts, all of which increased the supply of savings. At the same time, firms and households reduced their demand for investment in business capital and new housing. Businesses had little incentive to invest in new productive capacity as demand for their products was falling. Demand for new homes plummeted, as households were now having trouble qualifying for mortgages, and the prospect of further declines in home prices made housing look like a very risky investment. In that context, we would need a very large drop in interest rates to get firms and households to turn all the extra saving that was being supplied into investment.

The hitch is that when things turn bad in the economy, households and businesses typically want to hold a larger share of their wealth in the form of safe money, and want to sell off risky assets that on average pay higher rates of return, such as bonds and stocks. If they try to do this, but the supply of both money and other assets is fixed in the short run, then natural market forces are going to push interest rates on bonds *up* in order to induce people to hold interest-bearing bonds instead of noninterest-bearing money. Similarly, expected rates of return on stocks (expected future dividends and capital gains as a percentage of the price of the stock), will also surge up, as stock prices fall, which makes it more expensive for businesses to finance invest- ment by issuing new shares. Thus, if the supply of money were held fixed, there would be a natural tendency for bad economic times to push interest rates and the costs to businesses of financing investment *up* exactly when the economy needs these to go *down* to boost con- sumption and investment to prevent a recession. So for example, the average interest rate on Baa-rated corporate bonds jumped from 7.15 percent to 9.21 percent between August and November 2008, just as the collapse of Lehman Brothers and the ensuing financial crisis dealt a harsh blow to demand for consumption and investment.[11]

If, during bad economic times such as 2008, interest rates do not fall far enough and fast enough to turn the nation's saving into investment, then consumption and investment decline simultaneously. If no other form of spending (such as government spending or exports) picks up the slack, then aggregate spending falls. That is a big problem, because everyone's income comes from others' spending. The drop in spending in turn causes incomes to shrink and people to lose their jobs. That then causes further drops in spending, and so forth in a vicious cycle that plunges the economy into recession. Saving and investment are ulti- mately equalized, but only because national income drops below what it would have been if the economy were operating at capacity, which makes saving (which is a function of income) shrink enough to match the now-lower demand for investment.

Monetary Policy

The most important jobs of a central bank such as the Federal Reserve are to manage monetary policy so as to prevent, or quickly correct, the kind of slump just described, and to maintain a low, but stable and positive, rate of inflation. If the Fed observes that demand for consumption or investment is dropping, it can print money and use it to purchase government bonds and other interest-bearing assets on the open market. This increased supply of money, and reduced supply of bonds, pushes down the interest rate that is required to make people willing to hold the now smaller available quantity of bonds. The reduced interest rates in turn stimulate household and business demand for consumption and investment, which helps the economy recover.

To combat the unusually deep recession that began in 2008, the Fed initiated purchases of government bonds and other assets totaling $800 billion starting in November 2008, another $300 billion in March 2009, and yet another $600 billion starting in November 2010.[12] These actions allowed interest rates on very short-term, low-risk loans to fall to near zero, where they stayed continuously from late 2009 through at least the summer of 2016. This also helped reduce nominal interest rates on riskier longer-term assets such as home mortgages and Baa corporate bonds to around 5 percent or less over much of this period, which was very low by historical standards.[13]

Other times, when the economy is booming, the Fed takes action to sell bonds in the open market in order to push up interest rates, which in turn restrains spending and prevents inflation from rising. When high rates of inflation became the norm in the late 1970s and early 1980s, the Fed went even further and took extreme action to push inflation back down. In 1981, the Fed hiked short-term interest rates up to nearly 20 percent, which eventually succeeded in bringing the inflation rate down from 11 percent to around 4 percent, but at the cost of inducing what was, at the time, the most severe recession since the Great Depression, with an unemployment rate peaking at nearly 11 percent.[14]

Unfortunately, there's another way that money can throw a monkey wrench into the process by which interest rate adjustments keep the economy operating at its capacity, which is that money prevents nominal interest rates from dropping below zero. Money reliably pays a nominal interest rate of zero. It is not possible to push nominal interest rates on interest-bearing assets such as bonds substantially below zero, because then there would be no reason to hold such assets in lieu of money, and the drop in demand for such assets would push their interest rates back up to induce people to be willing to hold them.[15] Moreover, even if short-term interest rates are pushed all the way to zero, interest rates on longer-term and riskier assets will typically stay at least a few percentage points above zero, to compensate for their greater illiquidity and risk—otherwise, everyone would want to hold the short-term safe assets, and the flight from the longer-term riskier assets would push their yields back up.

In a depressed economy, this "zero lower bound" on nominal interest rates can be a big problem, because when demand for consumption and investment drops sharply enough, the nominal interest rate that would keep the economy operating at capacity could in principle be well below that lower bound, in negative territory. In that case, there would be no way for interest rates to drop far enough to induce recovery from the recession. This problem is especially likely when inflation rates are very low, as they have been in the United States, Japan, and Europe in recent years. The interest rate that should matter for saving and investment decisions is the *real* interest rate, which is the nominal interest rate minus the expected inflation rate. If the nominal interest rate is stuck at zero and the real interest rate that is required to get the economy back to potential is a very negative number, the only way to get there would be to have a high rate of expected inflation. As of August 2016, differences in the yield between inflation-indexed government bonds and non-indexed bonds and surveys of economists suggest that expected inflation rates over the next ten years in the United States were well below 2 percent per year.[16]

Cases where the zero lower bound on nominal interest rates is a constraint that prevents the economy from operating at full capacity are historically rare, but consequential. Arguably, parts of the Great Depression, sluggish growth in Japan since the 1990s, and the slow recovery of Europe and the United States from the recession that began in 2008 all owe a lot to the combination of the zero lower bound on interest rates and very low or negative rates of inflation.[17]

Fiscal Policy

When interest rates cannot fall far enough or fast enough to prevent or quickly cure a recession, *expansionary fiscal policy* can act as a supplement to monetary policy, and this is where taxes potentially come into play. Expansionary fiscal policy involves deficit-financed increases in government spending and/or tax cuts. If the problem that gets a recession rolling is that the supply of saving exceeds the demand for investment at the going interest rate, expansionary fiscal policy offers a potential solution, by having the government borrow some of the excess saving and turn it into spending, either directly (for example through government spending to build or repair infrastructure, or to hire more teachers), or indirectly (through tax cuts that might boost households' consumption).

There is greater controversy among economists about whether activist fiscal policy should be used to fight recessions than there is about using monetary policy for the same purpose. Skepticism about fiscal policy as a recession-fighting measure is most pronounced when the economy is *not* at risk of being constrained by the zero lower bound on interest rates. Paul Krugman, who became a leading advocate for expansionary fiscal policy in response to the recession that began in 2008, wrote in 2001 (when the economy was suffering from a relatively mild recession and the Fed had much more room to reduce interest rates): "Monetary policy and fiscal policy are like aspirin and morphine. Both are painkillers, but when you feel a headache coming on you reach for the aspirin first."[18] By this, Krugman meant that, in most cases, monetary policy should be the first line of defense, whereas fiscal policy tends to be addictive (that is, hard to reverse) and should be used to fight a recession only in special circumstances when nothing else works. Enacting tax cuts or new spending programs that make sense only in a recession can cause problems later on when they stick around long after the recession is over. Among these problems would be larger long-term budget deficits, the negative economic consequences of which we discuss later. Thus, fighting a recession with larger budget deficits might mean short-term gain but long-term pain.

This problem is compounded by the fact that by the time the government recognizes a recession and enacts a tax cut or spending increase, the economy has often begun to rebound on its own, making the policy unnecessary at best and inflationary at worst. The increased demand caused by either a tax cut or a government spending increase is helpful if the economy is operating below its capacity, but problematic otherwise. If the economy is already at or near capacity, as it normally is, the increase in demand caused by tax cuts or increased government spending can't be met by a big increase in output, so the result instead will be higher inflation, higher interest rates which lead to lower investment and a bigger trade deficit, or some combination of these.

The case for expansionary fiscal policy is much stronger when the Fed has pushed short-term nominal interest rates all the way down to zero, yet that's still not enough to get the economy to fully recover. In that case, expansionary fiscal policy could be the only effective way to avoid a very prolonged slump.[19] Moreover, when we're at the zero lower bound, the fiscal costs of deficit-financed government spending and tax cuts are relatively small because interest rates are so low, and the usual problem that budget deficits crowd out private investment by soaking up some of the supply of saving, thereby pushing up interest rates, is no longer operative. In this case the Fed can keep interest rates at zero despite the increased government borrowing with little risk of inflation, because the interest rate needed to get the economy back to potential and boost demand enough to get inflation to rise is still below zero. This explains why Krugman and many other leading economists changed their tune and started calling for aggressive expansionary fiscal policy in response to the recession that began in 2008.

Even at the zero lower bound, expansionary fiscal policy involves some risks. It tends to increase government debt, and if the debt gets too large, it could lead to worries that the government might fail to repay the debt, or that after the economy recovers the government might eventually become tempted to print money to pay back the debt, which could cause inflation and erode the debt's real value. If this were a problem, we should see it reflected in rising interest rates on government debt, which savers would demand in order to be compensated for the higher perceived risk. In the United States, federal government debt held by the public (i.e., excluding debt held by government agencies) increased from 35 percent of GDP in fiscal year 2007 to 74 percent of GDP in fiscal year 2014.[20] Yet interest rates on U.S. government bonds remained extremely low throughout this period, and by 2015 the rate on a ten-year U.S. government bond was still only around 2 percent.[21] This suggests financial market participants were not yet particularly worried about the ability of the United States to repay its debt.

In the United States, there have been many examples since the 1960s of tax cuts and spending increases enacted with the intention of boosting demand in a recession, ranging from the 1964 Kennedy-Johnson tax cuts to stimulus packages enacted toward the end of George W. Bush's second term. In early 2009, a Democratic-controlled Congress enacted, on a party-line vote, a particularly dramatic example of expansionary fiscal policy, the American Recovery and Reinvestment Act (ARRA). As mentioned in chapter 2, it included about $540 billion of temporary increases in government spending and $300 billion of temporary tax cuts. Recovery from the deep 2008 recession was quite slow, but that tells us little or nothing about whether the ARRA stimulus plan helped the economy or not. To answer that question, we'd need to know what would have happened to the economy if the ARRA had not been enacted, and given the way things were going at the time, it looked like the alternative could have been another Great Depression.

A drawback of tax cuts in particular as a recession-fighting measure is that the extra disposable income may be mostly saved rather than spent, in which case it will be largely ineffective at achieving the needed boost in demand. Theoretically, this should be especially true of a temporary tax cut. If people know that their taxes are temporarily low today and will go up again in the future, they may want to save most of today's tax cut to smooth their consumption over time instead of living a "feast or famine" lifestyle. If this is true, then when monetary policy can't do the job on its own, it is probably the case that deficit-financed government spending is a more effective measure for fighting recessions than a tax cut.

Some survey evidence suggests that recent tax cuts intended as recession-fighting stimulus measures were mostly saved rather than spent. Consider taxpayers' response to the 2001 and 2008 tax cuts. To make the tax cuts more vivid to taxpayers, parts of these cuts came in the form of rebate checks mailed to their homes or, in 2008, made through an electronic funds transfer. Surveys of taxpayers taken at the time suggested that less than a quarter of those who got the checks planned to mostly spend them, even though in 2001 these checks were "down payments" on a very large ten-year tax cut.[22] Tax cuts enacted as part of the 2009 stimulus package were delivered through a reduction in employer withholding, and an even lower fraction of households indicated that this would mostly lead to their spending more.[23]

Economists have tried many other strategies to get credible evidence on the effectiveness of expansionary fiscal policy as a recession-fighting tool, but the challenges are great. One important problem is that we should expect expansionary fiscal policy to be much more effective when the economy is constrained by the zero lower bound on interest rates than when it is not, because in those cases interest rates won't rise to offset the expansionary effects. But such episodes are historically rare, making it difficult to estimate effects under those conditions with much statistical confidence. Another challenge is a pervasive reverse-causality problem—a more severe recession will tend to cause the political system to adopt more aggressive expansionary fiscal policies, which makes it difficult to identify the causal effect of the fiscal policy on the economy, the classic chicken-and-egg problem. When we look back at history, we find that expansionary fiscal policy tended to happen when the economy was sluggish. Does that mean the policy doesn't work, or does it mean that politicians only choose to enact the policy when recessionary forces are buffeting the economy?

One strategy to get around these problems has been to take advantage of the fact that after 2008, some U.S. states got more fiscal stimulus funding from the federal government than other states for relatively random reasons that had nothing to do with the condition of the state's economy, and investigate whether those states recovered more quickly. Studies taking this approach have typically found that government fiscal stimulus spending was indeed effective at hastening the pace of economic recovery relative to what would have happened otherwise.[24]

A number of other studies have used aggregate national-level time-series data, or panel data that follows multiple countries over time, to attempt to identify the short-run response of economic growth to legislated changes in taxes or government spending that were plausibly *not* enacted in response to economic conditions, so as to get around the reverse-causality problem. Examples of this kind of change in government spending or taxes might include, for example, an increase in military expenditures driven by a war, or a tax cut that was motivated by something other than current economic conditions. The rapid recovery from the Great Depression that occurred when the United States started to engage in massive deficit-financed military spending just before and during World War II is a particularly compelling example of this, and is probably the single best piece of evidence for the effectiveness of expansionary fiscal policy. Aside from the striking example of World War II, there are questions about how well econometric studies exploiting this general strategy really identify the causal effects of changes in taxes or government spending on the economy. For example, the 1981 tax cut is sometimes used as an example of expansionary fiscal policy not caused by economic conditions, because it was not sold politically as a response to a recession. But it happened to coincide with big changes in monetary policy that caused a very deep recession and then a rapid recovery, and it is difficult to credibly disentangle the independent effects of each. There are also questions about whether studies that estimate the average effects of many different fiscal shocks over a long span of history might understate what the effects are when there is a lot of slack in the economy, or when the economy is constrained by the zero lower bound on interest rates. In any event, most such studies do suggest that increases in government spending and tax cuts can help get the economy out of a recession more quickly, but there is substantial variation in the estimated size of the effect.[25]

By July 2016, the U.S. unemployment rate had declined to 4.9 percent, down from a peak of 10.0 percent in October 2009.[26] This might suggest the economy was almost fully recovered from the recession. Assuming that the economy was nearing capacity, in late 2015, the Fed took action to raise short-term interest rates slightly, in an effort to forestall any potential rise in inflation.[27] On the other hand, there were conflicting signs suggesting the economy might still be operating with excess capacity. As of July 2016, the share of the population aged 25–54 that was employed was still 2.3 percentage points below where it had been in January 2007, and 3.9 percentage points below where it had been in April 2000.[28] This partly reflected discouraged workers who had lost their jobs in the recession and had given up looking for work, so that they were no longer counted in the unemployment statistics. In addition, short-term nominal interest rates were still very close to zero, inflation was still well below 2 percent and showed no convincing signs of increasing, and there were concerns that economic problems in China and Europe might spill over into the United States (for example by reducing demand for our exports).

As late as 2016, Larry Summers, the Harvard economist and former Treasury Secretary, was arguing that further fiscal stimulus and a sustained period of near-zero interest rates were still needed to get the economy back to its potential, and to get inflation high enough that the Fed would have sufficient room to reduce real interest rates to fight the next recession that comes along. Summers warned of the potential for a prolonged period of "secular stagnation," similar to what Japan has experienced since the 1990s, where the economy limps along with subpar growth and very low inflation because a zero nominal interest rate is still not low enough for the economy to reach its potential.[29] While there is hope that the economy has mostly returned to normal, so that the longer-run concerns addressed in the rest of this chapter should return to center stage, there's also some reason for caution.

Our main point here is not to pass judgment on the wisdom of using tax cuts, or fiscal policy more generally, as a countercyclical policy. What we do want to emphasize is that these issues are conceptually separate from the question of how our tax system should be designed over the long run. Indeed, what might work to counter a recession (stimulating private consumption through tax cuts) might be exactly the opposite of a common goal of many fundamental tax reform proposals—to increase the national saving rate—and exactly the opposite of what many feel should be part of a comprehensive plan to address the long-term fiscal imbalance (some tax increases). This tension in tax and budgetary policy is especially important in 2016. When should we replace the priority of expansionary fiscal policy with attention to the deficit and debt, and can we manage the transition without endangering a fragile economic recovery? This leads us naturally to the next issue—budget deficits and surpluses.

Budget Deficits and Surpluses

The *budget deficit* or *surplus*—that is, the difference between tax collections and government spending—is a second important issue that, in principle, is separate from the question of how our tax system should be designed. If tax rates are set appropriately, many different systems could raise enough revenue to cover spending, so that there is neither a deficit nor a surplus. Moreover, people on all sides of the tax reform issue tend to agree, at least publicly, that persistently large budget deficits should be avoided when we are not in a recession.

Conversations about tax reform and budget deficits do, though, overlap. Tax reform plans put forward in Congress and by candidates for president often have implications for budget deficits, and many of the recently designed proposals to address our country's long-run fiscal imbalance prominently involve plans for fundamental tax reforms. Advocates of these plans sometimes argue that tax rates can safely be set much lower than what is conventionally considered *revenue neutral*, on the grounds that the induced economic growth will expand the tax base and thereby make up the apparent revenue shortfall. They also often promise reductions in government spending, and broadening of the tax base by limiting or eliminating deductions and "tax loopholes," but often are a bit vague about how this will be done. We need to understand the economics of deficits to know what is at risk if the advocates of these plans turn out to have been too optimistic about the economic growth consequences of cutting tax rates, or if the politically popular tax rate cuts happen but some of the politically unpopular reductions in government expenditures and tax deductions don't. Given the way politics and political advocacy work, these have to be taken as rather probable outcomes.

First, as noted above, running a budget deficit during a recession can be a good thing, because the lower taxes and higher government spending that this implies can boost aggregate demand for goods and services and get the economy to put its existing productive capacity back to work. In that case, the benefits of deficit-financed expansionary fiscal policy include the extra GDP we get for a time, because we've moved the economy closer to its potential. In a deep recession, these benefits can easily outweigh any costs of the deficits. This is especially true when we're up against the zero lower bound on interest rates, in which case there may not be any effective alternatives for achieving this goal. Eventually, however, the economy will return to operating at full capacity. Once that happens, the costs of budget deficits become a major concern again, and the offsetting benefit from putting unused capacity back to work no longer applies.

Often public debate about the budget deficit overlooks some basic economic reasoning. First of all, cutting taxes and increasing the deficit doesn't reduce the cost of government expenditure; it merely puts off the reckoning of who bears the cost of that expenditure. One legacy of past deficits is that, despite historically low interest rates, interest on the federal debt remains a significant component of federal government expenditures, accounting for 6.5 percent of the total in 2014, and this burden is expected to grow in the future, especially if interest rates go up.[30] This expense is unavoidable; not paying it would precipitate financial catastrophe because the government would lose credibility and have great difficulty ever borrowing again. Paying this interest requires some combination of higher taxes and lower spending on government programs, and the more the debt grows, the higher these interest payments become. Repaying the debt itself, and not just the interest on the debt, would require even higher taxes or deeper spending cuts, although this could be avoided by rolling over the debt, which is sustainable only as long as the debt doesn't grow too large relative to the size of the economy.

One way that budget deficits can push the cost of today's government onto future taxpayers is by reducing the size of the future economy relative to what it would otherwise be. Budget deficits do this by eroding *national saving*—that is, private saving minus government borrowing—which reduces the funds available for private investment in such things as machinery, technology, and factories. When the government runs a budget deficit, it borrows from the public by selling bonds. This causes people to put their savings into government bonds instead of, say, corporate bonds or stocks that would be used to finance productive investments in the private sector. The reduced supply of saving available for private investment pushes up the interest rate, making borrowing more costly for firms that need to finance investments and thereby depressing the rate of investment. A decline in investment reduces the productivity and long-run growth potential of our economy because it results in less machinery, factories, and technology, and therefore less productive workers. When interest rates are as low as they were as of 2016, this story is not so applicable—reducing our budget deficit isn't going to boost investment by reducing interest rates, because interest rates are already as low as they can possibly go. But this unusual situation won't last forever.

Deficits need not reduce national saving dollar for dollar. If taxpayers correctly perceive that deficits imply higher taxes or lower government transfers (for themselves or their children) in the future and correspondingly increase their own saving and bequests to make up for the consequences of the deficit, this private saving would somewhat offset the increase in government dissaving. Deficits might not reduce national investment if foreigners are induced to increase their holdings of U.S. government bonds and other U.S. investments. This has, in fact, occurred to some extent in the United States since the 1980s. Foreign investment is of only limited help to us, however, because foreigners will also end up reaping most of the rewards of that extra investment and interest payments will flow out of the country.

If tax cuts are not accompanied by cuts in government spending programs, then today's borrowing means that future taxes eventually must be *higher* than they otherwise would have been. When that time comes, the higher taxes will harm incentives and depress the economy. If low taxes now are accepted as a boon to the economy, then the higher taxes that must come in the future must be accepted as a large liability. This discussion raises two crucial questions that are explored later in this chapter: how responsive is economic behavior to incentives, and do deficit-financed tax cuts change the behavior of politicians toward the level of government spending?

In February 2003, Federal Reserve Board chair Alan Greenspan bluntly challenged the idea that big budget deficits pose little danger or that the government can largely offset them through faster economic growth. Greenspan told the Senate Banking Committee that "faster economic growth, doubtless, would make deficits easier to contain" but added that "faster economic growth alone is not likely to be the full solution to the currently projected long-term deficits."[31] Greenspan's successor, Ben Bernanke, made the same point, arguing that "unless we as a nation demonstrate a strong commitment to fiscal responsibility, in the longer run we will have neither financial stability nor healthy economic growth."[32] For these reasons, once the economy recovers, further increases in future budget deficits are likely to make us worse off in the long run.[33] Deficit-financed tax cuts have a cost, even though many claims about the economic impact of taxation conveniently ignore this fact of life. People making such claims often predict that a general reduction in taxes will have a beneficial impact on economic activity because it unleashes demand and reduces the disincentives that taxes create. This prediction may be true to a degree, but it ignores the very real negative consequences generated by the increased deficit.

How Much Should Government Do?

Another issue that is often confounded with tax reform is the question of how big the government should be. Some proponents of fundamental tax reform plans are also strong advocates of big tax cuts and sharply reduced federal government spending. For example, the House Republican budget introduced in 2015 promised to enact comprehensive tax reform that would lower tax rates and broaden the tax base, but also promised to cut government spending by $5.5 trillion over the next ten years.[34] Crucially, though, people who disagree on the proper size of government needn't necessarily disagree on what's the best way to finance whatever level of government activity we choose.

This is not a book about how big the government should be—how much should it do, what it should do, and what it should not do. Rather, it is about how the tax system ought to be designed, given whatever level of government spending is chosen. We limit the scope in this way not because we believe that today's level and composition of government expenditures are exactly right, but because comparing the consequences of two different tax policies that raise different amounts of revenue involves questions of both tax design and questions of whether the extra government spending is worthwhile. Each government activity needs to be evaluated on its merits, and this is not the place to do that. For example, whether an additional aircraft carrier should be purchased is in the end a question of whether the benefits it provides by increasing national security exceed its cost. As in many cases, the benefits are difficult to quantify, and the ultimate resolution must come through the political system.

Nevertheless, some important connections can be drawn between the economic impact of taxation and the appropriate size of government. Most importantly, how big the government should be depends in part on how costly it is to raise taxes. The cost to the economy of raising one dollar in taxes is generally more than one dollar, both because taxes reduce the incentive to undertake income-earning activities and because of the administrative and compliance costs of collection (a point addressed in the next chapter). So when the government decides to spend a dollar on something like military hardware or a roads project, it had better produce social benefits worth *more* than a dollar.

The economic costs of taxation must also be taken into account in decisions about how much the government should do to address economic inequality. In his 1975 book *Equality and Efficiency: The Big Tradeoff*, Brookings Institution economist Arthur Okun famously compared public policies intended to address economic inequality to carrying water in a "leaky bucket." When the government imposes taxes on higher-income people in order to transfer funds to lower-income people, the taxpayers are made worse off by more than the transfer recipients are made better off, when measured in dollars. The difference reflects the economic costs that arise because taxpayers respond to the change in incentives caused by taxes (e.g., they work less), and because of the administrative and compliance costs of taxation. These are the leaks in the bucket. So, for example, hypothetically suppose that, for these reasons, to get an additional dollar of government spending, we have to make taxpayers worse off by $1.50. If we are to use the dollar to address economic inequality, for example by transferring resources to the poor, then it had better be the case that the value to society of an additional dollar to the poor person is at least 1.5 times as large as the value to society of that dollar to the upper-income taxpayers who financed the transfer.[35] If you believe the economic and collection costs of taxes are very large, you may be less willing to accept extensive government efforts to address economic inequality.

Second, the distinction between tax policy and government expenditure programs is sometimes not as clear-cut as the official language

suggests. Much of the federal government is a check-writing operation. In particular, many of these checks are written to pay for retirement benefits and health care for the elderly. Whether these payments
are called "spending," "transfers," "negative taxes," or "entitlements
earned through contributions made earlier in life" is somewhat arbitrary. The justifications for such payments are often no different than
those offered in chapter 3 for tax progressivity: they derive from an
attempt to achieve an equitable distribution of economic well-being.
Moreover, certain ways of limiting government spending can have
exactly the same kind of negative economic consequences that high
marginal income tax rates have. For example, suppose we were to cut
spending by "phasing out" 50 cents of Medicare benefits for every
dollar of income or savings that an elderly person has. For those
people, the result would be similar to a 50 percent marginal tax rate
on the rewards to working and saving, and it would be a big disincentive to do either. We can find many examples of this in our current
government spending programs. For example, "phaseouts" of the
Earned Income Tax Credit, SNAP (food stamps), Affordable Care Act
(ACA) subsidies for health insurance, and other programs, when combined with other tax rates, can produce very high marginal tax rates
for some low-income households. In 2016, among households with
AGI below 450 percent of the federal poverty line (about $109,350
for a family of four in that year), the effective marginal tax rate
on labor income, taking into account federal and state income and
payroll taxes and phaseouts of SNAP and ACA subsidies, averages
31 percent, and exceeds 60 percent for about 4.2 percent of such
households.[36]

Some people argue that the tax system and government spending
are linked because some tax systems facilitate government spending
more than others do. In particular, they favor taxes that are as "visible"
as possible, so that people will be reminded of the true cost of government. Otherwise, they contend, government will tend to expand
beyond what the citizens would prefer if they were better informed.
In this sense, visibility might help reduce the economic costs of government. The argument may have some merit, although it depends on
the empirical question of whether citizens are more likely to get the
government they want when taxes are more visible. This is an unset-
tled proposition, but some recent studies suggest that there may be
some truth to it in at least some cases. One such study showed that
the introduction of the EZ-Pass system of automatic electronic toll

collection was followed by faster toll increases than otherwise, presumably because although the system made it quicker and easier to pay for tolls, the less intrusive method of collection weakened public opposition to toll increases.[37] However, another study demonstrated that the introduction of employer withholding for income taxes—a bête noire of conservatives who argue that it reduces the visibility of the tax burden—did not significantly increase the size of state government.[38]

Some take the argument one step further, arguing that the taxpaying process should *purposely* be made burdensome precisely to restrain growth in government.[39] We see little justification for this view, and this book adopts a diametrically opposed perspective. This book seeks to find ways to streamline the tax system and to make it as efficient and unintrusive as possible. If institutional flaws bias the political system toward overspending, these flaws should be addressed, but not by shackling American taxpayers with a needlessly costly and obtrusive tax system.

Tax Cuts to Force Spending Cuts versus Surpluses to Prepare for an Aging Population

Some who favor tax cuts do so in part because they hope that the lower revenue, and the deficits that accompany it, will put pressure on Congress to restrain its spending. Milton Friedman, the Nobel Prize-winning economist, advocated this approach, saying that "deficits will be an effective—I would go so far as to say, the only effective—restraint on the spending propensities of the executive branch and the legislature."[40] This political strategy is usually called *starve the beast*, where the beast is the government itself.

Creating large budget deficits could plausibly change the terms of the political debate, eventually making it more difficult to propose new spending programs and creating pressures to slash existing ones. If the strategy turns out to be effective, then whether it is a good idea depends on the costs of running large budget deficits until the goal of reduced spending is met and critically on whether the forgone spending is worth the taxpayers' money. There's no guarantee that the most wasteful kinds of spending will be cut.

But does it work? After all, whether tax cuts will actually effectively restrain government spending later is ultimately an empirical question.[41] There are reasons to believe that it may not succeed, so that the results will instead be persistently large budget deficits that will eventually lead to higher taxes.

Figure 4.1 depicts historical data on federal government spending and taxes as a percentage of gross domestic product since 1965, along with projections of future spending and taxes through 2059 from the Government Accountability Office. The first thing to note is that the large tax cuts enacted in the first year of the Reagan administration in 1981 were not obviously successful, at least in the short run, at

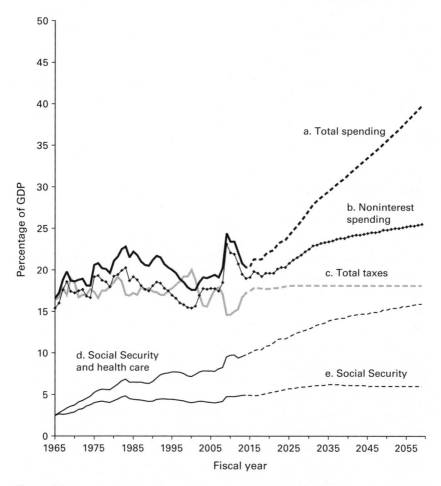

Figure 4.1
U.S. federal government spending and taxes as a percentage of GDP, 1965–2059. *Note:*
Data after 2014 are Government Accountability Office projections.
Sources: Office of Management and Budget (2015) and Government Accountability Office (2015a, 2015b).

restraining government spending and that large budget deficits ensued. For instance, between 1980 and 1985, taxes were cut from 18.5 percent of GDP to 17.2 percent, yet spending increased from 21.1 percent of GDP to 22.2 percent. Still, spending did start to come down eventually, and it's possible that this might not have happened without the pressure created by the deficits of the 1980s. But the big decline in spending relative to GDP actually occurred in the 1990s at the same time that tax revenues were increasing. Between 1990 and 2000, taxes rose from 17.4 percent of GDP to 20.0 percent, yet spending still fell from 21.2 percent of GDP to 17.6 percent. Then, from 2000 to 2014, taxes were cut from 20.0 percent of GDP to 17.5 percent, yet spending rose from 17.6 percent to 20.3 percent of GDP, and the enactment of a Medicare prescription drug plan and a major health care reform committed the government to higher future expenditures as well. Between 2007 and 2014, federal spending experienced a big temporary increase that soon reversed itself, while federal taxes dipped sharply and then rebounded. These were temporary consequences of a deep recession and the economic stimulus measures intended to cure it, and so are not particularly informative about the "starve-the-beast" hypothesis.

If anything, recent history seems to suggest the opposite of "starve the beast"—that is, tax cuts seem to be associated with *increased* spending and tax increases associated with spending cuts. Of course, many factors influence government spending and taxes, and maybe spending would have risen even more than it did since 2000 without the tax cuts. But some economists, including the late William Niskanen, former chairman of the libertarian Cato Institute, have argued that the apparent inverse correlation between taxes and spending in recent history is no accident. Maybe, he suggests, tax cuts encourage loose fiscal discipline on both tax and spending sides of the budget, or perhaps financing government through budget deficits reduces the perceived cost of government to voters, making them more willing to support higher spending.[42]

The second essential fact illustrated by figure 4.1 is that a large portion of federal government spending is for health insurance and retirement benefits for the elderly. Social Security, Medicare, and Medicaid alone accounted for 47 percent of federal spending in 2014.[43] All of Social Security and Medicare and most of Medicaid spending go to the elderly and disabled.[44] All of this spending will automatically increase by a great deal in the future as the elderly become a much larger share of our population and health care costs continue to climb.

The "health insurance" category in figure 4.1 also includes spending on low-income younger people, but this is a small fraction of the total, partly because younger people are on average much less expensive to cover—for example, the Children's Health Insurance Program (CHIP) and the refundable portion of the Affordable Care Act's tax credits to subsidize purchase of private health insurance amounted to only 2.7 percent of federal spending on health insurance in 2014.[45]

The Government Accountability Office projections in figure 4.1 are based on reasonable assumptions about the future implications of current government practices and promises, but there's considerable uncertainty, especially about health care costs. Between 1970 and 2013, the growth rate of Medicare cost per beneficiary was 1.9 percentage points higher than the rate of growth in per capita GDP, and the analogous figure for Medicaid was 1.5 percent.[46] If those rates of growth were to continue, figure 4.1 would look much, much worse. However, growth rates in health care costs have slowed more recently, and this has helped convince analysts to revise projected long-run future health care cost growth downward in recent years. The GAO projections, perhaps optimistically, assume that the growth rate in health care costs per beneficiary will be considerably lower in the future than it was on average since 1970.[47] Federal spending aside from Social Security, health insurance programs, and interest is assumed to stabilize at 9.6 percent of GDP in the long run, which is meant to approximate the average over the past twenty years. On the revenue side, figure 4.1 assumes all expiring tax cuts are made permanent and that federal revenues eventually stabilize at 18.1 percent of GDP after 2024, which is approximately the post-1945 historical average.

Figure 4.1 shows that by 2059, Social Security and federal health care spending are projected to be 15.9 percent of GDP, or 88 percent of projected tax revenues. In that year, the projections suggest noninterest outlays will exceed receipts by 7.4 percent of GDP, and exploding interest payments on the debt would lead to total outlays exceeding receipts by a whopping 21.7 percent of GDP.

Economists Alan Auerbach of Berkeley and William Gale of the Brookings Institution provide another way of quantifying the imbalance between projected government spending and taxes. Based on assumptions similar to those in figure 4.1 but involving somewhat less projected future government spending outside of Social Security and health care, they estimate that to keep the ratio of federal government debt to GDP from ever rising above its 2013 level, we would need to immediately enact permanent tax increases and spending reductions, relative to currently projected levels, of about 6.8 percent of GDP.[48] Acting in this manner to address the fiscal gap would involve running budget surpluses today to prepare for the known future expenses of an aging population and rising costs of government health care programs. The longer the delay in addressing the problem, the larger the necessary tax increases and spending cuts would be.

As the late economist Herb Stein (former Chairman of the Council of Economic Advisers and father of actor and writer Ben Stein) once said, "If something cannot go on forever, it will stop."[49] Some combination of spending cuts and tax increases (relative to expectations) will have to occur before the projected outcomes in figure 4.1 come to pass. But addressing the imbalance mostly through reductions in promised spending will be difficult, partly because so much of the growth in spending benefits the elderly. The elderly understandably receive public sympathy, and they have great political power in their own right that will probably grow over time. In the case of Social Security and Medicare, in particular, people have been promised benefits on the basis of having been subject to payroll taxes, or *contributions*, all their lives to support previous generations' benefits. Polls consistently show overwhelming opposition to cutting these programs. In a 2013 survey, a large majority of respondents said they would prefer to "increase" or "keep spending the same for" Social Security (87 percent) and Medicare (82 percent).[50] And these are by no means the only kinds of spending that are popular (and therefore difficult to cut) or unavoidable. If, for example, we add national defense, veterans' benefits, administration of justice, and interest on the national debt to spending on Social Security, Medicare, and Medicaid, we are already up to 77 percent of 2014 federal outlays.[51]

How Taxes Affect Long-Run Economic Prosperity: A First Cut at the Evidence

Having addressed the role of taxes in fighting recessions, the long-term deficit, and the appropriate level of government spending, we now turn to the central issue of this chapter—the impact of tax design on long-run economic prosperity. To what extent does our current tax system impose costs that reduce our well-being, and could a better designed tax system avoid some of these costs? Before getting into the details, we first take a look at the big picture—the relationship between the level of taxation and economic performance from historical and international perspectives.

Economic Growth, Tax Levels, and Tax Rates in U.S. History

Figure 4.2 offers a very long-run perspective on the relationship between growth in real gross domestic product (GDP) per person and tax rates in the United States, covering the period from 1870 through 2014. As a measure of the total value of goods and services produced in a country in a year, as well as the total income produced in the country in a year, GDP is a reasonable but imperfect indicator of economic prosperity. It is imperfect because it ignores the value of leisure, environmental amenities, and numerous other influences

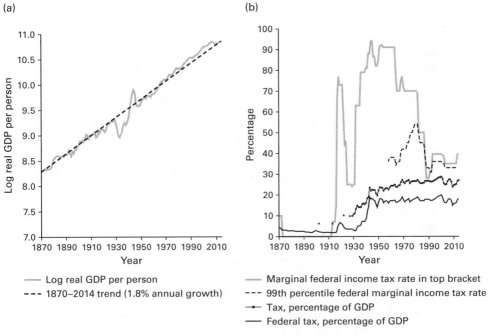

Figure 4.2
History of economic growth and tax rates in the United States: (a) log of real GDP per person in the United States, 1870–2014, and (b) tax rates in the United States, 1870–2014. *Note:* Real GDP per person is measured in constant year 2014 dollars.
Sources: Authors' calculations based on data from the Maddison Project (2013), Bolt and van Zanden (2014), U.S. Bureau of Economic Analysis (2015), Carter et al. (2006), Internal Revenue Service (2016a), Baneman and Nunns (2012), 2010–2012 editions of Internal Revenue Service *Statistics of Income—Individual Income Tax Returns*, Publication 1304, and Fox (1986).

on the quality of life that are hard to measure. But it has the important advantage that it is the only indicator of economic prosperity that can be measured on a consistent basis over a very long period of time and across many countries, which is essential if our goal is to understand the truly *long-run* relationship between taxation and economic prosperity.

The gray line in the left panel of figure 4.2 illustrates the natural logarithm of real GDP per person in each year from 1870 through 2014. The advantage of depicting this in log form is that then the slope indicates the growth rate. The straight dashed line shows the trend from 1870 through 2014, which represents a constant annual compound growth rate of 1.8 percent. As the diagram shows, log real GDP per person (the gray line) did experience temporary fluctuations around its long-run trend, most notably during the Great Depression. But the graph also seems quite consistent with the conclusion that the economy has always tended to return to a fairly stable long-run trend, with no apparent change in the long-run trend itself.

The remarkable stability of long-run growth rates in the left panel of figure 4.2 is juxtaposed against dramatic changes in tax rates shown in the right panel of figure 4.2. From 1870 through 1935, federal taxes were just 3 percent of GDP on average, and were always below 7 percent of GDP. Federal taxes soon jumped to near 20 percent of GDP during World War II and remained near that level ever since, averaging 17 percent of GDP from 1940 through 2014. Total federal, state, and local government tax revenues were similarly a much larger percentage of GDP in the second half of the time period shown in the graph than in the first half. Marginal federal personal income tax rates at the top of the income distribution rose dramatically and then fell. Yet the long-run trend in log real GDP per person remained remarkably stable. Indeed, the average annual growth rate in real GDP per person was 1.8 percent per year from 1870 to 1929, and also 1.8 percent per year from 1929 through 2014, despite dramatically different tax rates during the two periods. Similar patterns hold for other rich countries for which data is available dating back to the late 1800s, despite the fact that they generally had even larger increases in the size of government. If anything, those other countries tended to see real GDP per capita rise above its previous long-run trend for a time after World War II (and during the era of big government), as countries that started below U.S. income levels started to catch up with the United States.[52]

The evidence in figure 4.2 seems consistent with the notion that large and persistent changes in tax rates have not had much effect on economic growth rates in the long run. By itself, this evidence is not decisive. For example, perhaps an accelerating pace of technological innovation (something we can't measure well) would have caused the long-run trend in log real GDP per person to grow steeper during the latter half of this period if the size of government had not increased so much. But figure 4.2 has to cast some doubt on the idea that permanent changes in tax rates affect economic growth rates in a permanent way, or even that they cause real income per person to permanently diverge from its long-run trend.

Table 4.1 zooms in to examine growth rates in real GDP per person over shorter time periods since 1947, and also shows rates of growth in *productivity*, defined as real GDP produced in the private business sector divided by the total number of hours worked in that sector. Real GDP per person has the drawback that part of its growth over this time period is due to rising labor-force participation rates, particularly among women. As such, it overstates the degree to which Americans have become better off because some of the growth has come at the expense of time spent on nonmarket activities such as child rearing, which is of indisputable benefit but whose value is not captured in

Table 4.1
U.S. economic growth since 1947

Years	Average annual rate of real growth (percent)	
	GDP per person	Productivity
1947–1973	2.5%	3.2%
1973–2014	1.6	1.9
1950–1960	1.8	2.8
1960–1970	3.0	3.1
1970–1980	2.1	1.8
1980–1990	2.4	1.8
1990–2000	2.2	2.2
2000–2014	0.8	2.0

Sources: U.S. Bureau of Economic Analysis (2015), and U.S. Bureau of Labor Statistics (2015, series PRS84006093).
Note: Productivity is measured here as GDP produced in the private business sector in constant chained 2009 dollars, per hour worked in that sector.

GDP. In addition, when growth is measured using real GDP per person, the rapid rate of population growth during the post-war baby-boom years obscures an unusually fast rate of growth in the productivity of the working-age population that occurred during that same time (all the new babies were adding to population but obviously not adding to the production of anything except joy). Productivity is a valuable indicator of changes in living standards that is closely connected to growth in hourly wages and compensation. Note, though, that neither of these measures accounts for changes in aspects of well-being unrelated to output, wages, or private consumption, such as the quality of the environment. Nevertheless, these are the most reliable measures of prosperity and its underlying determinants that are available over long periods of time.

As measured by the growth of productivity, the U.S. economy grew at a much faster pace in the 1950s and 1960s than it did before or after.[53] Productivity grew at an annual rate of 3.2 percent between 1947 and 1973 but at only 1.9 percent per year from 1973 to 2014. When this diminished growth is combined with the increasing income inequality discussed in chapter 3, it implies that the economic well-being of many low- and middle-income people has stagnated for the past three decades. The growth rate of productivity during the 1970s and 1980s was much lower than the "golden era" of the 1950s and 1960s. Productivity growth in the 1990s as a whole was slightly higher than in the 1970s or the 1980s, at 2.2 percent per year versus 1.8 percent. From 2000 to 2014, productivity growth was on average 2.0 percent per year, which was still a bit better than both the 1970s and 1980s. Growth in real GDP per person during the 2000–2014 period was a very low 0.8 percent, however, which largely reflects the employment effects of the Great Recession and an aging population.

Advocates of lower taxes sometimes give the impression that our taxes were much lower during the "golden age" of economic growth in the 1950s and 1960s and that many of our current economic problems, including the slowdown of productivity growth since 1973, are caused by the strangling influence of big government and high taxes. By implication, all we need to do to return to the halcyon days of yesteryear is to lift this burden.

One problem with this argument is that, as figure 4.2 shows, the overall federal tax burden was not that different between the period of fast growth and the period of slow growth. Federal taxes averaged 17.2 percent of GDP from 1950 to 1973, and 17.6 percent of GDP from 1974 to 2014![54] Total taxes, including those of state and local governments, rose modestly—they averaged 24.3 percent of GDP from 1950 to 1973 and 26.4 percent from 1974 to 2014.[55] Yet as figure 4.2 shows, total federal, state, and local taxes were much higher during the 1950s and 1960s than they had been from the late 1870s through 1929, yet compared to that period, growth rates of real GDP per person in the 1950s and 1960s were a bit higher, and productivity growth rates picked up substantially.

What is detrimental to a vibrant economy may be not the overall level of taxes, but rather particular aspects of the tax system. Some argue that steep marginal tax rates on high-income people are particularly destructive because they discourage the most highly talented and entrepreneurial members of society from pursuing the activities they do best and hiring others to help them do it. The emphasis on the economic consequences of taxing high-income households has been dubbed *trickle-down economics* by its detractors. We discuss this idea in more detail later, but for now, take a look at figure 4.3, which shows the top tax rate on individuals and the rate of productivity growth for certain periods. Rather than telling a trickle-down story, the graph suggests the opposite. The strongest productivity growth period was when the top tax rates were the *highest*.

We're certainly not arguing that levying high marginal tax rates on the rich *causes* faster economic growth.[56] On the contrary, most economists agree that top marginal rates as high as the United States had in the 1950s and 1960s—in the vicinity of 90 percent—are too high to do any good for anyone. Our point is that no simple relationship or single graph can establish how the tax system affects economic prosperity or growth. The many dimensions of the tax system—rates on individuals, the corporation income tax rate, the tax rate on capital gains, the definition of the tax base, and so on—all matter. Furthermore, many factors unrelated to taxation probably have a much more profound influence on the economy. For example, the unusually fast growth of the 1950s and 1960s partly resulted from the adoption of many important technological advances that had been developed over previous decades but that, because of the Great Depression and World War II, had not yet been fully utilized to the benefit of consumers. The huge jump in the price of oil in 1973 caused major economic disruptions and contributed, at least temporarily, to slower growth in the United States and throughout the world. For these reasons, identifying precisely what role a slightly increasing overall tax burden and

(a)

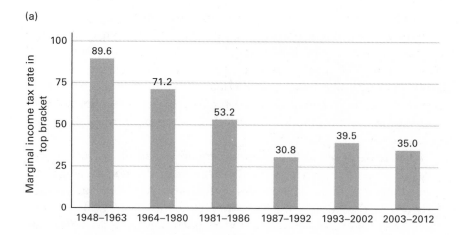

(b)

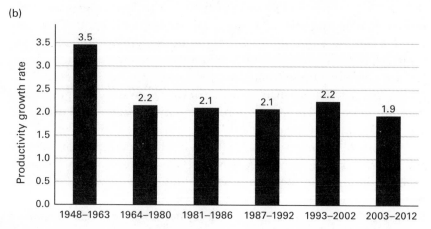

Figure 4.3
(a) Marginal income tax rate in top bracket, average over period, and (b) annual percentage growth rate in productivity, average over period. *Notes:* Bottom panel shows annual percentage growth in real GDP produced in the private business sector per hour worked in that sector, fourth quarter over fourth quarter of end of previous period.
Sources: Internal Revenue Service (2016a) and U.S. Bureau of Labor Statistics (2015, series PRS84006093).

changing features of the tax system have played in the slowdown is exceedingly difficult. One potentially more promising approach is to look at the evidence across countries. Have low-tax countries flourished and high-tax countries floundered?

International Evidence on Economic Prosperity and the Level of Taxes

Figure 4.4 plots for the thirty-four industrialized OECD countries the relationship between GDP per capita and the ratio of total tax to income. If a high level of taxes is the kiss of death for prosperity, we would expect to see the points in figure 4.4 clustering along a line with a negative slope: higher taxes would go hand in hand with a lower standard of living. But no such pattern emerges from figure 4.4. Some of the world's most prosperous countries, such as the United States and Japan, do have relatively low tax ratios. But other countries, particularly in Scandinavia, have done quite well, thank you, with far higher tax ratios. That Sweden could maintain a 2012 GDP per capita of $43,869—18 percent above the OECD average, in the face of a whopping 42.3 percent tax-to-income ratio, more than two-thirds higher than in the United States—challenges the hypothesis that high taxes are a sure cause of economic decline.

Our disclaimer about figure 4.3 also applies to figure 4.4: no simple scatter plot can possibly settle such a complicated issue as this one. It might be, after all, that the Scandinavian countries would be even more prosperous than they are now if they lowered their tax burdens. The pattern of points in figure 4.4 might be telling us that history, geography, culture, and demography have enabled some countries to be more prosperous than others and those countries so favored have chosen to spend relatively more of their bounty on the services provided by government and to tax themselves more to provide these services. Alternatively, because richer countries also tend to have a higher literacy rate and to be more urbanized, they might be more suited to take advantage of relatively efficient ways to raise revenue. Under any of these scenarios, comparing the relative levels of prosperity to total tax burdens will not reveal the economic impact of taxation, positive or negative. Indeed, if one looked at a graph like figure 4.4 that included all countries, not just the most affluent countries, the scatter plot would suggest a clear *positive* relationship between tax ratios and GDP per capita, in large part because poorer nations lack

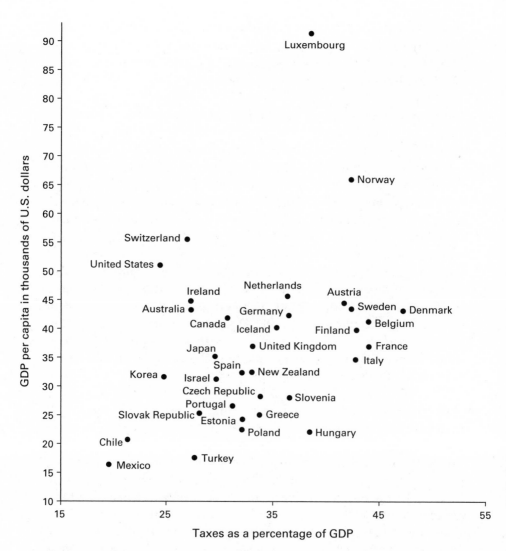

Figure 4.4
Economic prosperity and the level of taxes in OECD countries, 2012.
Sources: Organisation for Economic Co-operation and Development (2014a, 2015a). GDP per capita is converted to 2012 U.S. dollars and is adjusted for purchasing-power parity.

the administrative capacity to collect as much in taxes as developed countries do.[57]

One might also look to see whether any relationship exists between tax ratios and the *growth rate* of countries' economies. Analyzing the rate of growth over a given time period frees us from having to explain why some countries were more prosperous than others at the start of the period and allows us to focus on what has enabled them to better themselves.

Figure 4.5 does just this. For the period 1970 to 2012, it plots the average tax ratio of twenty-four of the OECD countries against their real growth rate.[58] Yes, some low-tax countries such as South Korea did exceptionally well over this period, and high-tax countries such as Sweden did relatively poorly. But some high-tax countries did well, and some low-tax countries (like the United States) performed below average. Again, no clear relationship emerges. Moreover, there is no significant correlation between which rich countries had the biggest increases in the size of government relative to GDP between the 1960s and today, and which countries had the fastest rates of economic growth during that period.[59] More sophisticated statistical analyses of the relationship between the level of taxation and economic growth, which attempt to hold constant the impact of other determinants of growth to isolate the tax effect, have come to no consensus.[60]

Our point is *not* that taxes do not affect the economy. On the contrary, in certain situations taxes might have a major impact. The effect of taxes on economic performance is, however, subtle and cannot be established by any one simple graph—not by the figures presented here and not by other ones that purport to demonstrate the damaging effects of high taxes. Understanding how taxes affect the economy requires looking behind data on overall economic performance and examining the kinds of choices that taxes affect and the ways that taxes influence these choices.

How Taxes Affect Economic Prosperity: The Specifics

Owing taxes means having to change your behavior. For every dollar remitted to the government, taxpayers have one less dollar to spend or save. Belts must be tightened. This is as true for a lump-sum tax as it is for an income tax or a sales tax. But a lump-sum tax is different in one important way from all other taxes: by definition, there is nothing you can do to change your tax liability. That sounds ominous for the

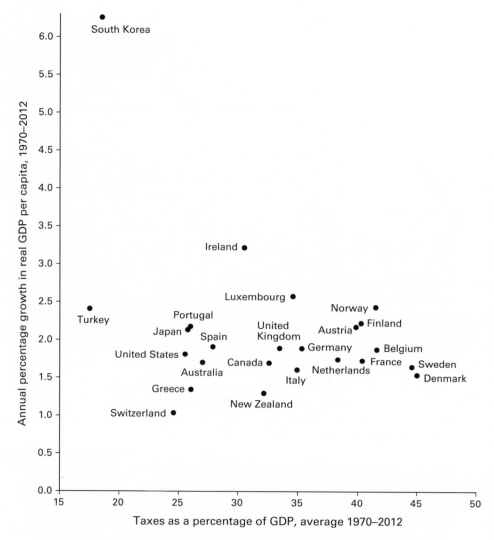

Figure 4.5
Economic growth rates and tax levels in OECD countries, 1970–2012. *Notes:* Data for South Korea is for 1972–2012. Excludes OECD countries with missing data for parts of 1972–2012.
Sources: Authors' calculations based on Organisation for Economic Co-operation and Development (2014a, 2015a).

family whose income barely exceeds the lump-sum tax due: nothing can be done to reduce this burden. But reversing the emphasis reveals the unique characteristic of the lump-sum tax that is intriguing to economists: nothing you do *increases* your tax bill, either. In particular, nothing you do to better your lot—going to night school for an MBA, getting a second job so you can afford a new house or car, successfully starting your own business—increases your taxes. If all taxes were lump-sum in nature, any decision you can think of can be made without a moment's consideration to the tax consequences.

This is quite a contrast to the current situation where taxes change the terms of just about any decision that a taxpayer faces. A spouse contemplating returning to work must (or ought to) consider that taxes (federal and state income plus payroll) will possibly take 50 percent of any earnings, while many expenses incurred will not be deductible. A wealthy alumna contemplating a gift of $1 million to her alma mater will be gently reminded that the donation could save her hundreds of thousands of dollars in taxes. The CEO of Hewlett-Packard may be tempted to open another research lab by the knowledge that, because of the research and experimentation tax credit, 20 percent of its cost may be creditable against corporate income tax liability.

The belt tightening that taxation forces is an inevitable consequence of taxation, but taxation does more than force people to tighten their belts. It also changes the cost and reward of most economic decisions, and it distorts these choices away from what would otherwise be chosen. What is the cost to the economy when the tax system changes the terms of—and therefore distorts—economic choices?

Economists agree that, except in certain situations discussed below, the baseline for measuring the economic cost of taxation is how the economy would operate in the absence of any taxes other than lump-sum taxes.[61] The idea is that participants in a free market will voluntarily produce and consume all goods and services for which the benefit (measured as the maximum amount a consumer would be willing to pay for something) exceeds the costs of production, and will not produce or consume any goods or services for which the costs exceed the benefits. As Adam Smith observed over 200 years ago, prices in an unfettered free-market economy act as signals of benefits and costs, spontaneously guiding the economy (as with an "invisible hand," in Smith's words) to make *efficient* use of the country's physical and human resources.

Taxes interfere with efficiency by creating a "wedge" between the price paid by the consumer and the price received by the producer. The higher price paid by consumers discourages them from buying the item, and the lower price received by producers discourages them from producing it. As a result, when a tax distorts prices, we forgo some consumption and production for which the benefits exceed the costs and thus reduce efficiency. Firms and individuals are induced to shun taxed activities in favor of relatively untaxed ones that they would otherwise value less. We thus do not get as much value from the economy's resources as we could, and in a sense are wasting the resources we have by putting them to use inefficiently.

There are exceptions to this story, referred to as cases of *market failure*. When the difficulty of obtaining necessary information, the presence of activities with spillover effects, or monopoly—all cases where the invisible hand fails—leads markets to function inefficiently, taxes do not necessarily detract from efficiency. On the contrary, in these cases judicious tax policy might correct an inefficiency. For example, a tax on pollution might correct a market failure and lead to a more efficient use of resources rather than cause a misallocation of resources.

The problem of market failure figures prominently in our subsequent discussion of a number of key tax-policy issues. For now, though, we leave market failures aside and examine several specific areas of economic behavior where taxes do have a distorting effect. Because one of the goals of most tax reform plans is to mitigate these distortions, understanding these issues is crucial for evaluating the potential benefits of reform.

Labor Supply: Theory

Labor income in the form of wages, salaries, and benefits constituted 61 percent of national income in 2014.[62] Therefore, any story about how taxes affect the economy must come to terms with how they affect the incentive people have to work and the incentive businesses have to hire workers. If the tax system makes it unattractive to work hard or work at all, or to employ labor, then it cannot be contributing to a vibrant economy. Many tax reform plans seek to change the tax system so that work is rewarded more generously.

Taxes have two countervailing influences on the decision to work. First of all, most taxes, including income and consumption taxes, reduce the marginal reward for working. Work becomes less attractive because working that extra hour or taking on a second job buys fewer consumption goods and services; an economist would say that the tax reduces the *real wage rate*. Put differently, leisure and other nonmarket activities become more attractive because the alternative of working becomes less remunerative. The reduced after-tax return to working provides an incentive to substitute more leisure and nonmarket endeavors for less work and less consumption of goods and services. Economists call this impact of taxes the *substitution effect* or sometimes the *incentive effect*.

Besides changing the marginal reward to working, most taxes make you poorer, and when people are poorer, they tend to cut back at least a bit on all the things they value, including leisure. Economists refer to this as the *income effect* of taxes. Because the belt tightening of taxes causes people to cut back on leisure, it causes people to work *more* than otherwise. Thus, the substitution effect of taxes reduces labor supply, but the income effect tends to increase labor supply. Because of the countervailing effects of the substitution and income effects, it is not clear a priori whether taxes make people work more than they otherwise would, or less.

Note that the decision whether to work a few extra hours or to choose a harder job that pays a little better is affected only by one's marginal tax rate—that is, the tax rate on the next few dollars of income. What is relevant for the "income effect," however, is the total tax burden or, expressed as a fraction of income, the average tax rate.

The relationships between average tax rates, marginal tax rates, and total taxes collected are crucial characteristics of any tax system and are inextricably linked to how progressive the tax burden is. A lump-sum tax system could, in principle, raise a trillion dollars a year while imposing a zero tax at the margin for everyone's work decisions. Under a purely proportional tax system in which tax liability is the same fraction of income for everyone regardless of what their income is, the marginal tax rate equals the average tax rate. The more progressive the distribution of the tax burden is, the higher the marginal tax rates will be, and therefore the greater will be the overall marginal disincentive to work per dollar raised.

Note also that the correct marginal tax rate for measuring the disincentive effect is not necessarily the statutory marginal income tax rate. For example, a 20 percent statutory marginal rate levied on labor income excluding fringe benefits is not, in terms of its incentive effect on labor supply, materially different from a 16 percent statutory marginal tax rate levied on labor income including fringe benefits, if fringe benefits constitute about one-fifth of total labor compensation for everyone.[63] In principle, such a policy change does not in itself provide a significantly increased incentive to work. This is an important point to keep in mind when we later discuss proposals that broaden the tax base and use the revenue so collected to lower marginal tax rates.

It is also true that a consumption tax such as a retail sales tax has the same kind of effects on the incentive to work as an income tax because it reduces the purchasing power that an additional hour of work provides—the real wage. With an income tax, the reduction in one's real wage is salient because one's paycheck is cut, while with a retail sales tax the reduction is salient because prices are higher so one's paycheck doesn't buy as much—but the ultimate effect is the same. This equivalence must be kept in mind when we address moving from an income tax to a consumption tax.

An example can help illustrate the economic cost of the incentive effect. Consider the case of Roger Brown, who works forty hours a week on construction sites. Roger is also a talented carpenter and can earn $20 an hour working at night and on weekends; he can find ten hours a week of such work. Roger has plenty of hobbies and enjoys spending time with his family, so it goes without saying that he won't work for nothing. In fact, he won't work those extra ten hours unless he can earn at least $15 an hour; in economics jargon, that is the *opportunity cost* of his time—what his leisure time is worth to him.

In the absence of any taxes, Roger will clearly decide to moonlight. The $200 he earns for the ten hours of extra work exceeds the $150 he requires as compensation for the reduced leisure time. Everyone is better off from this decision. Roger's carpentry customers are better off, or else they wouldn't have been willing to pay him the $200. Roger is better off. We can even put a dollar measure on how much everyone is better off—$50. This represents the difference between $200, which is the value put on Roger's carpentry by his customers, and $150, which is Roger's own evaluation of the next best use of this time.[64]

Alas, there is taxation, and on an extra $200 per week of income Roger's tax bill turns out to be $60, or 30 percent. He is a dutiful citizen, so he does not consider simply not reporting his outside income to the IRS. Given his 30 percent rate of tax, he concludes that his after-tax compensation for carpentry, $14 per hour ($20 minus 30 percent of $20), is not high enough to justify giving up the extra leisure. This is an example of the disincentive to work caused by the tax system; it has changed the reward to working and in this case changed the decision of how much to work.

What is the economic cost of the altered decision? You might jump to an answer of $200, Roger's forgone wages. But that is not correct because although Roger has decided to forgo the $200 in income, by so doing he has ten more hours per week to pursue his other interests—ten more hours he values at $150. The loss to Roger, and to the economy, is the difference between $200 and $150, or $50. Because of the tax system, a transaction that should have been made was not; from society's perspective (but not from his own perspective), Roger consumes "too much" leisure and works "too little."[65]

Per dollar of revenue raised, the economic cost of taxing labor income depends on how responsive labor supply is to changes in the after-tax return to working. More precisely, the economic cost depends only on the substitution effect of taxes, and not the income effect. The change in behavior due to the income effect is inevitable regardless of how a given amount of revenue is raised, and applies even when a lump-sum tax is used, so it is not relevant to a comparison of the economic cost of alternative ways of raising that revenue. If there is no substitution effect, then the fact that taxes lower the return to working does not translate into significant economic costs because people are not dissuaded from working by the fact that tax liability gets larger when more labor income is earned. The more that people are willing to substitute leisure (i.e., not working) for working when tax rates go up, the larger are the economic costs—per dollar raised—of imposing taxes that reduce the reward to working.

Labor Supply: Evidence
Economic researchers have tried a variety of strategies to estimate how much labor supply responds to incentives. In our opinion the best available evidence suggests that, at marginal tax rates like those prevailing in the United States today, a further increase in marginal tax rates probably would cause some reduction in aggregate labor supply, but the effect would not be large. For certain subgroups of the population, such as single mothers with children, decisions about whether to participate in the labor force do seem to be fairly responsive to incentives, but they do not account for a large enough share of labor income to change the conclusion about the responsiveness of labor supply in aggregate. With that said, the evidence does not all speak with one voice, so there's some room for disagreement. In what follows, we'll

describe the different strategies economic researchers have used to get evidence on these questions, summarize the lessons from that research, and explain the reasons for disagreement.

The most common strategy for estimating the responsiveness of labor supply to incentives has involved cross-sectional comparisons of how self-reported annual hours of work differ across people with different after-tax wages and different levels of nonlabor income (e.g., interest, dividends, and government benefits). A recent review of the labor supply literature that focuses mainly on the kind of cross-sectional comparisons described above, conducted in 2012 by Rob McClelland and Shannon Mok of the Congressional Budget Office, attempts to summarize the evidence for the United States.[66] McClelland and Mok conclude that, taking into account both the effects on hours worked for those who are working and the effects on decisions whether to work at all, a 10 percent increase in the after-tax wage is associated with a 1 to 3 percent increase in hours worked due to the substitution effect, and about a 1 percent decrease in hours worked due to the income effect. They also conclude that the substitution effect is somewhat smaller than average for men and single women, and somewhat larger than average for married women. There is also evidence that the substitution effect for married women has declined dramatically over the past few decades in the United States, as women have become more attached to the labor force, so that the responsiveness of their labor supply to after-tax wages seems to be gradually converging to that of married men.[67]

If McClelland and Mok's summary of the evidence is correct, it would imply that at current levels of taxation, the economic costs of distorting labor supply decisions through taxation are relatively modest. Research by Soren Blomquist and Laurent Simula of Uppsala University in Sweden suggests that if the substitution effect of a 10 percent increase in after-tax wage is to increase hours worked by 2 percent, then an across-the-board increase in marginal tax rates on labor income in the United States in 2006 would have involved $0.13 of economic costs (from substituting less-valuable leisure for more-valuable market consumption) for each additional $1 of tax revenue raised.

There are a number of reasons for caution in interpreting cross-sectional evidence on the responsiveness of labor supply to incentives. One concern is that the positive correlation between after-tax wages and hours worked might actually be driven by a third factor—

differences across people in the taste for work. Being naturally inclined to hard work, or having a stronger preference for market consumption compared to leisure, may well lead someone to work harder in school and choose a more lucrative occupation, leading to a higher wage, and may independently cause someone to work long hours. Thus harder-working people have a higher net-of tax wage rate, but not because higher wage rates *cause* more work effort. This would tend to bias estimates of the causal substitution effect upward, so that we'd over-state the economic costs of higher tax rates. Another problem is that people who work long hours are likely to have other traits (higher earnings, greater patience and discipline) that cause higher saving and thus higher nonlabor income, which biases estimates of the income effect upward.

One strategy to get more convincing evidence about the effect of income on labor supply has been to examine cases where people were randomly awarded additional income. Studies of lottery winners in Massachusetts and Sweden, and winners of a housing voucher lottery in the United States, all suggest that a 10 percent increase in income, holding the incentive to work constant, is associated with about a 1 percent decline in labor supply, consistent with the conclusion of the McClelland and Mok review noted above.[68]

Another strategy for estimating the incentive effect of changes in after-tax wages is to look for "quasi-experiments"—in this case, situations where the after-tax wage changed in different ways over time for different people for some reason that was plausibly unrelated to their tastes for work—and then compare the relative changes over time in the different groups' hours worked and labor force participation decisions. The main advantage of this approach is that, by studying changes in the behavior over time of the same individuals (or the same types of individuals—e.g., people with a given level of educational attainment), the researcher can statistically control for any factors that differ across the groups but are constant over time for a given group (such as, perhaps, tastes for work), and control for any factors that are changing similarly over time for the different groups (e.g., the business cycle).

Consider the following example of this methodology. During the 1980s and 1990s in the United States, reforms to the Earned Income Tax Credit (EITC) improved the incentive to work for low-income single mothers relative to single women without children and middle-income married women; much research has demonstrated that labor force

participation rates went up more over time for the women who benefited most from increases in the EITC, compared to women whose
incentives were not affected by changes in the EITC.[69] Another example
is that in the United Kingdom during the 1980s, after-tax wages went
up more over time for people with higher educational attainment, due
to both rising before-tax wage inequality and the disparate effects of
income tax reforms across the income distribution. Richard Blundell of
University College London, Alan Duncan of Curtin University, and
Costas Meghir of Yale University found that men and women in the
educational groups that experienced larger increases in after-tax wages
experienced modestly larger increases in labor supply.[70]

Raj Chetty of Stanford University and co-authors reviewed 16 especially high-quality empirical studies of labor supply in the United
States and other rich countries, most of which took advantage of quasi-
experimental variation in incentives to work of the sort noted above.
On average, these studies implied that a 10 percent increase in the
after-tax wage is associated with about a 4 percent increase in aggregate
hours worked, including both the participation decision and the decision about how much to work.[71] The somewhat larger responsiveness
relative to McClelland and Mok might reflect better research designs
that reduce bias, but it could also reflect the fact that 11 of the 16 studies
considered by Chetty and colleagues focus on women (in many cases
low-income women with children), who we'd expect to have higher
responsiveness.

Starting from a tax rate of 30 percent, an increase in the after-tax
wage of 10 percent requires a 23 percent reduction (from 30 percent to
23 percent) in the tax rate. So this evidence implies that a very large
tax cut would have a relatively modest positive impact on aggregate
hours worked. If labor supply is indeed as responsive to incentives as
Chetty and colleagues conclude, then the Blomquist and Simula analysis noted earlier implies that if we were to enact an across-the-board
increase in marginal tax rates on labor income in the United States, each
additional dollar of tax revenue raised would impose $0.31 of economic
harm from distorting labor supply decisions.

In 2010, Costas Meghir and David Phillips of the Institute of Fiscal
Studies reviewed a much broader selection of the labor supply literature and provided new estimates of labor supply responses to reforms
of the tax-and-transfer system in the United Kingdom from 1994
through 2004.[72] They largely concur with the conclusions of Chetty and
co-authors, but shed more light on variation in responsiveness across

groups of people. Meghir and Phillips conclude that "hours of work do not respond particularly strongly to the financial incentives created by tax changes for men, but they are a little more responsive for married women and lone mothers. On the other hand, the decision whether or not to take paid work at all is quite sensitive to taxation and benefits for women and mothers in particular."[73] Particularly relevant to the question of how "leaky the bucket" is when we increase tax rates on people at the top of the income distribution is their conclusion that "[f] or highly educated individuals the sensitivity of both hours of work and participation to work incentives are almost zero."[74]

Evidence from the United States from the 1980s, when marginal tax rates were cut sharply for high-income people relative to everyone else, corroborates the conclusion that decisions about how many hours to work are probably not very responsive to incentives at the top of the income distribution, at least within the range of tax rates we've experienced in recent decades. Robert Moffitt of Johns Hopkins University and Mark Wilhelm of Indiana University–Purdue University at Indianapolis examined data that followed the same group of people between 1983 and 1989, and they found no evidence of a significant labor supply response to lower marginal tax rates, even among those in the high-income group who saw their marginal tax rate fall from 50 percent to 28 percent.[75] Nada Eissa of Georgetown University concluded that wives of very high-income husbands increased their hours of work relative to wives of middle-income husbands after 1986, but a subsequent analysis of panel data from 1981 through 1999 by Jeff Liebman of Harvard and Emmanuel Saez found no compelling evidence of increased labor supply for wives of high-earning men when household marginal income tax rates were cut.[76]

In a 2011 review of the labor supply literature, Michael Keane of Oxford University offers some dissent to the seeming consensus that the responsiveness of labor supply to incentives is on the whole rather modest.[77] On the one hand, he reports that among the large number of studies he reviewed, the average implication was that a 10 percent increase in after-tax wage was associated with a 3 percent increase in hours worked among males, when isolating the substitution effect. This is not particularly at odds with the conclusion of Chetty and colleagues. But Keane goes on to emphasize the diversity of the estimates, suggesting a lack of consensus, and further argues that this average estimate may be biased downward by a failure to take into account that harder work while young might improve one's skills, leading to an increase in wages later in life. In this way a tax cut has an amplified effect on incentives for the young, because to the extent that it causes the young to work longer hours, it may lead to higher wages later in life that increase the incentive to work even more. This could imply larger efficiency costs from taxation than otherwise. While the theoretical point is sound, efforts to infer whether and how much this might matter from available data require some heroic assumptions, so the existing evidence on this point is at the moment somewhat speculative.[78]

Raj Chetty emphasizes another reason why the estimates of the responsiveness of labor supply to incentives summarized above could be biased downward, if our goal is to determine the long-run effect of a big tax change. He argues that many frictions stand in the way of adjusting one's labor supply in response to a change in incentives. For one thing, people may not understand or pay attention to subtle changes in incentives caused by tax reforms, which would tend to attenuate estimates based on policy-driven quasi-experiments within countries. In addition, many employees do not have much control over how many hours they work at their job, as employers often expect their workers to work a standard work week of 40 hours or so. It may be difficult for an individual employee to deviate from the social norm of the standard work week, for fear of being labeled a slacker, and achieving the flexibility to reduce work hours might require switching jobs, which can be costly. Thus, if workers wish to reduce work hours in response to a big tax increase, the full response may only play out gradually over a long period of time, as social norms and institutions (such as the standard length of the work week) may need to adjust first. Therefore, comparisons across countries that have had very large differences in tax rates for long periods of time might be especially informative about the long-run responsiveness of labor supply to incentives, as such evidence would be less likely to be attenuated by the kinds of frictions discussed above.[79]

Comparisons of hours worked per adult and tax rates across selected rich countries, using data from the 1970s through the 1990s, did seem to suggest greater responsiveness of labor supply to incentives than the quasi-experimental studies of micro data we just discussed.[80] This was one factor that led Chetty to conclude that in the long run, the effect of a 10 percent increase in after-tax wage rates would be closer to a 5 or 6 percent increase in aggregate hours worked. However, using more recent data on a larger number of countries weakens the relationship between hours worked and taxes.[81] For example, a cross-sectional comparison of taxes as a percentage of GDP and average hours worked per person aged 15 to 64 across 23 rich countries, using averages from the decade spanning 2004 through 2013, implies that a 10 percent increase in the after-tax wage would be associated with a 4 percent decline in hours worked, although the relationship is not tight enough to merit much statistical confidence.[82] The cross-country relationship now seems rather consistent with the conclusion of Chetty and co-authors based on their review of within-country micro data studies.

A potential problem with this sort of cross-country comparison is that there are many other factors that differ across countries, such as cultural tastes for leisure and labor market institutions, which might explain differences in hours worked. To the extent that these other differences are fairly persistent over time, one can get around this problem by examining whether countries that had relatively larger tax increases over time experienced correspondingly larger declines over time in average hours worked per working-age adult. Research of this nature by Nobel-laureate economist Edward Prescott of Arizona State University compared changes in tax rates and changes in hours worked across the United States and a small number of other rich countries such as France and Germany between 1970 and the mid-1990s. The findings suggested that, indeed, countries with larger increases in tax rates had experienced larger declines in hours worked per working-age adult (with a particularly striking difference in the amount of vacation).[83]

Prescott's claim sparked much controversy. For example, Alberto Alesina and Edward Glaeser of Harvard and Bruce Sacerdote of Dartmouth responded by arguing that it is impossible to empirically distinguish the effects of differentially rising taxes on changes in hours worked from the effects of unions, which grew in power and changed their strategies in Europe relative to the United States at the same time as taxes were going up in Europe. Unions in many continental European countries have pushed hard for mandatory vacation time and mandatory restrictions on the maximum number of hours an individual can work in a week (achieving, for example, a thirty-five-hour work week in France) under the slogan "work less, work all," on the (apparently misguided) theory that reducing hours worked for each worker would open up more jobs. Alesina and co-authors further hypothesized that restrictions on hours worked in Europe might have been partly motivated by the plausible notion that leisure time is more valuable to each individual when there are more other people to share it with, a coordination problem that might be ameliorated by regulations mandating vacation time, for instance. Many other long-standing non-tax policies and institutions in Europe—such as generous public pension rules and unemployment insurance, as well as relatively high minimum wages—also discourage work or hiring, further weakening the case that taxes alone were to blame for the pattern identified by Prescott.[84]

In figure 4.6, we present updated evidence on relative changes in tax rates and hours worked over time across countries since the 1960s, for a larger number of countries than the studies noted above. The figure plots, for twenty-three rich countries, the change in hours worked per person aged 15–64 against the change in general government tax revenue as a percentage of GDP, comparing decadal averages for 1960–1969 with 2004–2013.[85] If collecting more revenue in taxes depresses labor supply, we should observe a scatter plot with a

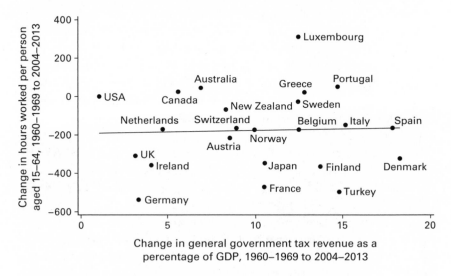

Figure 4.6
Change in hours worked per person aged 15–64 versus change in general government tax revenue as a percentage of GDP, 1960–1969 to 2004–2013, among twenty-three rich countries.
Sources: Data on hours worked are from The Conference Board (2015). Data on population aged 15–64 are from World Development Indicators (World Bank, 2015). Data on general government tax revenue as a percentage of GDP are from Tanzi (2011) and Organisation for Economic Co-operation and Development (2014a, 2015b). Data for Greece, Luxembourg, and Turkey for the earlier period are for 1965–1974.

downward-sloping tendency: a larger increase in tax rates over time would be associated with a larger decline in labor supply over time. But we see nothing of the kind. The relationship is, if anything, slightly upward-sloping.[86] We conclude that the evidence relating changes in hours worked over time to changes in taxes across countries does not provide compelling evidence that tax increases significantly depress labor supply. Earlier studies such as Prescott's reached a different conclusion partly because they examined a smaller number of countries for which the correlation between taxes and hours worked was stronger, and partly because the cross-country relationship between taxes and hours worked has become weaker in more recent data than it was in the mid-1990s.[87]

Henrik Kleven of the London School of Economics offers one explanation for the non-finding illustrated in figure 4.6. He demonstrates that some high-tax countries, including the Nordic nations, provide very high "participation subsidies" due to public spending on the provision of child care, preschool, and elder care; these policies effectively subsidize labor supply, by lowering the prices of goods that are complementary to working. From this perspective, the kind of cross-country correlations we have been discussing must be reinterpreted, because the tax-financed public support for preschool, child care, and elder care supports, rather than discourages, employment.[88] This matters, because it implies that a country may be able to mitigate economic inequality, as the Nordic nations do, without necessarily imposing large costs in terms of economic efficiency, by adopting compensatory policies that help offset the negative effects of taxes and transfers on the incentive to work.

Taxes and Saving

A second critical choice affected by taxes is the one that people make about how much to consume now versus how much to save for future years' consumption or for bequests. An income tax affects the terms of this choice because, by taxing interest and other returns to capital, it reduces the rate of return that can be earned on savings and increases how much must be put aside today to finance any given amount of consumption later. Many would-be tax reformers support a switch to a consumption tax, which would effectively eliminate the negative influence of taxes on the incentive to save. Chapter 6 explains how consumption taxes accomplish this. For now, we focus on how our current system affects the incentive to save and how saving behavior is influenced by such incentives.

It's easy to see how a tax of, say, 20 percent on interest income reduces the reward to saving that income. If the before-tax interest rate is 10 percent, you get only an 8 percent return after tax. Another feature of our tax system can exacerbate this distortion: it fails to adjust the measurement of capital income for inflation. Suppose that in the example above, inflation was 5 percent. In that case, half of the 10 percent nominal interest rate you receive is just making up for the 5 percent decline in the real purchasing power of your savings. So in this case, the 20 percent tax rate on the nominal interest rate turns out to be a 40 percent tax on *real* interest because the 5 percent real (inflation-adjusted) return turns into a 3 percent return after tax. With inflation as low as it has been recently, this is a relatively minor concern, but it has been a major consideration in earlier periods of our history such as the 1970s.

Income taxes can also reduce the reward to saving indirectly by taxing the returns to business investment. Leaving aside international capital flows, savings and investment are two sides of the same coin. The saving of individuals—often funneled through a financial intermediary such as a bank, a savings and loan, or an insurance company—eventually is used by businesses to finance the purchase of physical capital goods such as factories, equipment, and inventories and intangible capital such as "know-how." Through this process, individual saving adds to the productive capacity of the country and increases the productivity of the workforce.

Although the connection is not always apparent to the saver, the return to saving is governed by the return to the productive investment that the saving finances. If the return to investment is taxed at the business level, then the amount that can be paid out to those who financed it—by lending money or buying shares in the corporations that make the investments—must fall. As explained in chapter 2, certain forms of corporate income, such as dividends and some capital gains, can be "double taxed"—once under the corporate tax and again at the personal level. The extent of this taxation depends not only on the tax rate levied on net business income but also on the depreciation schedules, the generosity of any investment tax credits, and the preferential treatment now accorded to both capital gains and dividend income in the personal tax.

Together, taxes on the returns to saving and business investment distort the choices of individuals, because by making future spending relatively more expensive they encourage people to consume more today and save less for the future than they otherwise would. One negative consequence is that people may end up with too little savings when they retire. In the likely event that myopia and temptation cause people to save too little for their own and their children's futures even in the absence of taxes, reductions in saving caused by taxes would be even more harmful. A progressive income tax puts the highest disincentive to save on a small group of people who account for a very large portion of national saving—the rich. Recall, though, from chapter 2, that there are a host of tax-preferred savings vehicles that mute the disincentive to save that an income tax would otherwise cause.

If the tax law does in fact reduce national saving and investment, our future national economic prosperity will be lower than it otherwise could be. Part of the appeal of the consumption tax reform plans—including the flat tax and the national retail sales tax—is that they would eliminate all tax on the normal return to saving and investment.[89] To the extent that this boosts saving and investment to more efficient levels, we would be better off.

If empirical evidence showed a strong positive relationship between saving and its after-tax rate of return, the economic costs of our income tax and the economic benefits of switching to a consumption tax could be quite large. However, the available evidence does not readily reveal any such relationship. Figure 4.7, which is derived from a study done by Jane Gravelle of the Congressional Research Service and then updated by us, plots the net private saving rate and a measure of the real after-tax return to saving.[90] The net private saving rate includes saving by households plus saving by corporations in the form of retained earnings, but does not reflect government "dissaving" through budget deficits. The incentive to save is represented by the average real interest rate on Baa-rated corporate bonds, plus a fixed equity risk premium, reduced by the average marginal income tax rate on interest income. Note that this measure of the incentive to save remains positive in recent years, despite the fact that interest rates on short-term low-risk assets have fallen toward zero, because the rate of return shown in the figure includes premiums for bearing risk and sacrificing liquidity (by holding a longer-term asset).

If anything, figure 4.7 suggests a *negative* relationship between saving and the incentive to save. Saving as a fraction of disposable

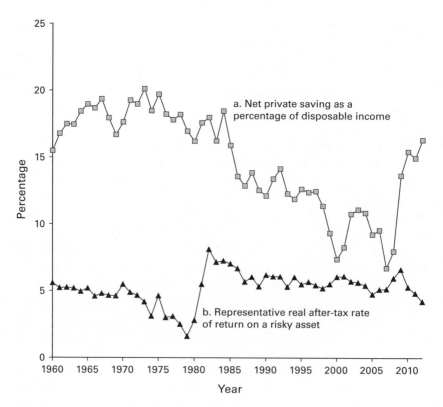

Figure 4.7
Percentage of income saved versus the incentive to save in the United States, 1960–2012.
Sources: (a) net private saving as a percent of disposable income (where disposable income is GNP less private consumption of fixed capital and government receipts), from U.S. Bureau of Economic Analysis (2015); (b) interest rate on Baa corporate bonds plus a fixed-equity premium, adjusted for expected inflation and the average marginal tax rate on personal interest income, calculated by authors following Gravelle (1994). See endnote 90 of chapter 4 for further details.

income was relatively high in the 1960s and 1970s, when the return to saving was relatively low, and then declined dramatically after about 1980 at the same time that the incentive to save went up significantly. Net private saving rates continued to drop for a long time after that, reaching an historic low of just 6.7 percent by 2007, despite long-term real after-tax interest rates that were persistently high by historical standards. In the time since the 2008 financial crisis and Great Recession struck, private saving rates have increased dramatically, at the same time that the incentive to save has fallen.

Of course, as we've now said several times, no simple graph can decisively disprove or prove that saving is or is not responsive to incentives. One obvious problem with interpreting figure 4.7 is that the causality runs both ways. If people decide to reduce their saving for a reason unrelated to interest rates, this will reduce the supply of saving and push up interest rates, producing a negative correlation between saving and interest rates unrelated to the effect of interest rates on saving. A second problem is that the definition of saving used here does not include capital gains arising from sources other than reinvestment of corporate profits (for example, it excludes capital gains arising from changing optimism about future profits or altered tolerance of risk).[91] Therefore, this measure of saving does not fully reflect the effects of a booming, or collapsing, stock market, nor does it reflect the impact of the ups and downs of house prices on household wealth. For the purposes of measuring the amount of resources that are being set aside and made available for private investment, this is perfectly appropriate. But factors such as the stock market boom of the 1990s and its collapse and then recovery since 2008, and the boom in housing prices during the early 2000s followed by a sharp decline beginning around 2006, might help explain the three-decade decline in saving and its recent turnaround, as increased wealth first led people to feel less need to save for retirement, and collapsing wealth later convinced people that they needed to save more. To be sure, many other factors have influenced aggregate saving behavior over time—such as business cycles, demographic changes, or changes in cultural attitudes—and these are hard to distinguish from the effects of the after-tax return to saving. Some of these factors, though, suggest that saving should have gone up since 1980. For instance, the 1990s and early 2000s represent prime saving years for the large baby-boom cohort.

Given the problems with inferring the causal effects of incentives on saving behavior from aggregate time-series data, recent studies have instead focused on other kinds of evidence These studies analyze micro data in settings where tax policies and other retirement savings policies changed in different ways over time for different people, for reasons that were plausibly unrelated to changes in other factors that also influence saving behavior. One such study by Raj Chetty and co-authors examines the effects of retirement savings policies on saving in Denmark, a country that, unlike the United States, has fairly comprehensive data on wealth linked to tax and employment records for nearly the full population.[92] The authors take advantage of two kinds of quasi-experiments—one where the Danish rate of tax subsidy for contributions to a retirement savings account was reduced for upper-income people but left unchanged for others, and another where the employer's "default" contribution rate to retirement savings accounts for a given worker changed because the worker moved from one firm to another.

Evidence from the first quasi-experiment suggested that tax subsidies for retirement accounts, which rely on individuals to take an action to raise savings, had no effect on saving behavior at all for the vast majority of people, because they responded passively and did not change their contribution rates to the retirement savings accounts. Among the few who did change their contribution rates in response to the reduction in the tax subsidy, the main effect was to shift assets from the retirement account with the reduced tax subsidy to other forms of retirement saving, with practically no effect on overall net saving. The authors concluded that each additional dollar of tax subsidies for retirement savings increased total private saving by only 1 cent (which implies that if the dollar of tax subsidy is not offset by an equal reduction in government spending, it actually *reduces* national saving by 99 cents).

In contrast, evidence from the second quasi-experiment suggested that policies that raise retirement contributions if individuals take no action—such as automatic employer contributions to retirement accounts—do seem to increase saving substantially. The vast majority of people who switched from lower to higher employer contribution rates to their retirement savings accounts because they switched jobs did not take actions in their personal consumption or other accounts to undo the extra saving that resulted.

Alex Gelber of the University of California, Berkeley studied what happens to the saving in 401(k) plans of individuals who become eligible after working for one year, comparing the change in their saving from the first year to the second year relative to the change in saving of a control group whose 401(k) eligibility does not change over the same period of time.[93] He finds that the initiation of 401(k) eligibility raises saving in 401(k) accounts substantially. That could be a result of improved incentives to save, or it could be due to other features of a 401(k) that encourage saving, such as the fact that deducting a bit from your paycheck each week and contributing it to a saving account acts as a kind of commitment device that helps you resist the temptation to spend immediately. The study does not find evidence that the value of other financial assets fell or that debt rose to offset the increase in 401(k) saving. This would seem to suggest that 401(k) eligibility led to an increase in overall saving, but there's enough statistical noise that the author cannot rule out the possibility that people might have offset the 401(k) contributions with reductions in other saving.

Other recent research also suggests that people make saving and retirement decisions in a way that standard economic theory would not predict: for example, they are influenced by default rules, being more likely to join an employer pension plan if they must opt out rather than opt in. The evidence from Denmark noted above is quite consistent with this notion. This is an area where "behavioral economics," which looks beyond standard theory to confront the fact that many people systematically make apparently irrational decisions, has provided a major contribution. We return to this point and its implications for policy in chapter 6.

Taxes and Investment

As we have discussed, many aspects of the tax code might affect the amount and nature of business investment: the business tax rate (corporate or pass-through), the personal tax treatment of corporate business income (the tax rate on dividends and capital gains), and the depreciation schedule. With some assumptions, all these factors can be captured in one number, called by economists the *marginal effective tax rate on investment*. This is one factor that influences the *user cost of capital*, which summarizes the cost (including taxes) of buying or renting capital. Other things equal, the user cost of capital will be higher when the marginal effective tax rate on investment is higher, and when real interest rates are higher. A higher user cost of capital means a higher cost, and therefore a lower incentive, to invest in physical capital.

The empirical literature provides suggestive evidence that business investment does respond to the user cost of capital, but the evidence is also imperfect and subject to multiple interpretations. A common strategy is to take advantage of situations where a change in the corporate tax rate, or a change in the schedule of allowable tax deductions for depreciation, caused different changes in marginal effective tax rates on investment across firms across time. For example, a tax reform might accelerate depreciation deductions more for some types of investment than for others (e.g., shorter-lived equipment such as computers versus longer-lived structures such as buildings), and that will reduce marginal effective tax rates on investment more in firms or industries that for technological reasons tend to use the relatively favored type of capital more. One can then investigate whether investment increased by more over time in the firms that had larger declines in the user cost of capital, relative to firms for which the user cost of capital did not change as much.

Most studies that attempt to identify a long-run response of investment to incentives using strategies like those described above find that the effect of a 10 percent increase in the user cost of capital is associated with somewhere between a 2.5 percent and 10 percent increase in the amount of investment that businesses undertake.[94] With that said, this kind of research involves many challenges that suggest it should be taken with a big grain of salt. One problem is that in many studies of this nature part of the variation in the user cost of capital that contributes to the estimates is driven by economy-wide changes in interest rates, which once again raises a reverse-causality problem. For example, if demand for investment is changing for some reason unrelated to changes in the user cost of capital (e.g., business cycle fluctuations), that will cause interest rates to change, and may also cause politicians to enact changes in tax laws that affect incentives to invest. Another issue is that it can be difficult to disentangle re-timing of investment in response to temporary changes in the user cost of capital from the response of long-run changes in investment to persistent changes in the user cost of capital. The former is relevant to the question of whether temporary tax incentives might help us get out of a recession more quickly, but not so relevant to deciding what the long-run design of the tax system should be, whereas the latter has the opposite characteristics. Some studies do a better job of dealing with these challenges than others, but none completely solves them, and just focusing on the best-done studies doesn't narrow the range of estimates much.

Economists have performed simulations to illustrate what the estimates at each end of the range noted above would imply about what would happen to investment in the United States if we were to replace our existing income tax system circa the mid-1990s with a Hall-Rabushka flat tax, which (for reasons we discuss in chapter 6) would eliminate the negative effect of the tax system on the incentive to invest by allowing "expensing" (immediate deduction) of the full cost of investment. The lower end of the range of estimates implies that such a reform would boost the U.S. capital stock by about 3.5 percent and GDP by about 1.1 percent in the long run, whereas the upper end of that range implies that the reform would lead to a long-term boost to GDP of about 8.4 percent.[95] In the 2000s, depreciation deductions in the United States were accelerated significantly for many types of investment. These provisions were supposedly "temporary," but many ended up being extended repeatedly. A reform such as adopting a Hall-Rabushka flat tax would have a smaller effect on investment than the simulations described above imply, when compared to the U.S. tax system that applied through most of the 2000s.

Two recent research studies, one by Chris House and Matthew Shapiro of the University of Michigan and the other by Erick Zwick of the University of Chicago and James Mahon of Harvard University, used especially convincing research designs to study how temporary accelerated depreciation provisions enacted in the United States in the early 2000s affected investment.[96] Their evidence suggests that these provisions substantially increased investment in those assets to which they applied, and implies responsiveness even greater than that implied in the studies summarized earlier. Given the temporary nature of the incentives, though, it seems especially likely that this response largely reflects retiming of investment, as businesses moved forward some investment they would otherwise have done later.[97] This is exactly the result one would hope for when such policies are enacted as a recession-fighting measure, but is not very informative about the long-run costs and benefits of investment incentives in the tax system.

While most of the research above emphasized the effects of corporate income tax changes on investment, in principle personal taxation of capital income ought to matter for investment decisions too. Danny Yagan of the University of California, Berkeley has demonstrated that the 2003 reduction in the personal income tax rates on dividends from as much as 35 percent to a maximum of 15 percent—one of the largest changes ever to a U.S. capital income tax rate—had no detectable near-term impact on investment.[98] The analysis compares the change in investment of C corporations affected by the dividend cuts to S corporations that were not. Recall that S corporations are pass-through entities. As such, they are not subject to corporation tax, and their incomes are passed through directly to their owners and taxed at ordinary personal income tax rates instead of the reduced dividend tax rates. Before 2003, the C corporation and S corporation investment series trended similarly. After the 2003 dividend tax cut improved investment incentives for C corporations but not S corporations, there was no divergence in the investment rates of C corporations relative to S corporations. That evidence is inconsistent with the idea that the dividend cut stimulated corporate investment. This null result could be consistent with a small or zero responsiveness of investment to the cost of capital (as dividend tax cuts do reduce that), but it could instead be consistent with a world in which marginal investments are funded out of retained earnings and riskless debt rather than out of newly issued equity or risky debt, in which case it would not necessarily imply that corporate tax reforms would have no effect on investment.

Yagan's study does find that the dividend tax cut (and associated capital gains tax cut) led C corporations to increase distributions to shareholders through dividend payouts and share buy-backs. In principle, it is at least possible that in the long run, increased distributions to shareholders would eventually deplete corporations' retained earnings enough so that the dividend tax cut might start to induce increased investment, although even then it might have no effect if the marginal source of funds is riskless debt. In any event, this study does call into question the effectiveness of dividend tax cuts if the goal is to increase business investment.

Another way that taxes can influence the quantity of business investment in a country is by affecting the location of investment. For example, high corporate tax rates in the United States might, in principle, cause domestic saving to flow overseas in order to invest in more lightly taxed enterprises there, and reduce inflows of saving to the United States to finance investment here. A number of studies have found correlations across countries between higher effective corporate income tax rates and lower investment, but it is difficult to convincingly disentangle the effects of corporate tax rates from the effects of other factors that differ across countries and affect investment. For example, Simeon Djankov of the New Economic School of Moscow and co-authors, including Andrei Shleifer of Harvard University, construct comparable measures of marginal effective tax rates on investment for a small firm in 85 countries, and investigate the correlation between those tax rates and business investment as a share of GDP. Such a correlation could in principle shed light on how taxes affect both domestic and foreign decisions about investment into a particular country. When they control for a few other factors that differ across countries and that might be expected to affect investment, they find that a 10 percentage point increase in the effective tax rate is associated with a decline in investment of about 2.5 percent of GDP. However, when they control for enough other variables that differ across countries and that might affect investment, the estimated effect on investment becomes smaller and one can no longer conclude that it is different from zero with statistical confidence.[99]

A number of other studies find evidence from cross-country comparisons suggesting that flows of foreign direct investment are sensitive to effective corporate tax rates. But many of these studies suggest that artificial shifting of profits across countries to avoid taxes (for example by manipulating the prices that different parts of the same firm located in different countries pay to each other) is far more sensitive to tax rates than is the location of real economic activity (a point we return to in chapter 5).[100]

Another strategy for estimating how corporate income taxes affect both real economic activity and tax avoidance activity has been to use cross-country data to estimate how changes in corporate tax rates affect corporate tax revenue. In principle, as corporate tax rates get higher and higher, eventually we'd reach a point where any further increases in the rate would cause real corporate economic activity to decrease so much, or artificial corporate tax avoidance efforts to increase so much, that corporate tax revenues would actually go down. Research by Laura Kawano of the U.S. Department of the Treasury and Joel Slemrod finds that once we adjust for the fact that cuts in statutory corporate tax rates are often associated with reforms that broaden the tax base, OECD countries that reduce their statutory corporate tax rates by more over time do experience reductions in corporate tax revenues over time. Their evidence suggests that the revenue-maximizing statutory corporate tax rate is probably well above the combined federal and state corporate rates applying currently in the United States, which implies that cutting the statutory corporate tax rate, by itself, would not be a free lunch—it would involve some cost in terms of government revenue.[101]

A number of economic studies have also attempted to infer the economic effects of distorting investment decisions through taxation by estimating how relative changes in corporate tax rates across countries are associated with relative changes in the level of real GDP per person. Some of these studies have found evidence of a negative effect of higher corporate tax rates on the level or growth rate of GDP per person, but there are big questions about whether these studies are actually picking up a long-run effect of the corporate tax on GDP, or just a co-movement of taxes and GDP over the business cycle that does not necessarily tell us anything about the causal effect of the tax on the long-run trend of GDP itself.[102]

Neutrality

A major goal of tax reform is to make our tax system more "neutral" so that it minimally distorts economic choices. As mentioned earlier, it is almost always beneficial when people and businesses make decisions based on the underlying merits of the alternatives rather than on their tax consequences. Minimizing the influence of taxes on the incentives to work, save, and invest is an important example of this principle.

But there's a problem with this objective. The only tax system that is perfectly "neutral" is a lump-sum tax, because in this case *no* decision anyone makes impacts their tax bill and therefore such a tax causes no disincentive effects. The kind of neutrality that income tax reformers strive for is less ambitious but still important—making sure that tax rates do not differ arbitrarily across various types of consumption and investment. Note that even if this kind of neutrality is achieved, distortion is still introduced by the tax system because the return to working and to saving is reduced. Avoiding arbitrary differences in tax rates across different types of consumption and investment, however, helps to reduce wasteful distortions of decisions about what to consume and how to produce it and thus makes us better off.

Our current tax system is a far cry from this kind of neutrality. The many deductions, special preferences, and compromises in the measurement of capital income mean that different types of consumption and investment are taxed at widely different rates. Cleaning up the tax base to eliminate such distorting features is a major goal of most tax reform plans.

Before discussing how our tax system fails to achieve such neutrality, a couple of qualifications are in order about its economic advantages. First of all, *uniform* taxation of different kinds of consumption does not necessarily minimize the economic cost of raising a given amount of revenue. Other things being equal, it is desirable to tax more heavily those goods for which demand (and supply) is relatively price-insensitive. Taxing these goods will change behavior less for any given amount of revenue raised compared to taxing price-sensitive goods: it effectively makes the tax system more like a lump-sum tax. Moreover, singling out for taxation recreational goods such as skis and amusement parks (goods that are *complementary* to leisure) could offset to some extent the inevitable disincentive to labor that income and consumption taxes create. Among economists the idea that certain deviations from uniform taxation of consumption might actually reduce the economic cost of raising revenue is known as the *optimal commodity tax principle.*

Although it is impossible to identify when a particular country's tax policy was inspired by optimal tax reasoning, it has been argued that Scandinavian countries are following the optimal commodity tax principle by subsidizing complements to work such as child care, preschool, and paid family leave, all policies that make it easier to stay attached to the labor force and therefore reduce the distortion of too little labor supply.[103]

While there's a reasonable economic case to be made for some applications of the optimal commodity tax principle, such as the Scandinavian approach to subsidizing services that are obviously complementary to labor supply, when we go much beyond that, the principle runs into practical problems that make it less useful as a guide to policy. First, identifying which goods and services are more or less responsive to taxation (or more or less complementary to leisure) is difficult. Second, even if economists could measure such things accurately, differentiating taxes according to this approach often conflicts with both equity and simplicity. Whenever some goods are taxed at higher rates than others, taxpayers whose tastes happen to favor those goods are penalized; this is horizontally inequitable. Moreover, the price-insensitive goods taxed most heavily under this principle would probably be necessities (for example, the demand for food is relatively inelastic), placing a disproportionate burden on the poor. It is also more costly to operate a tax system that differentially treats goods because it requires setting and monitoring which goods fall on which side of the tax-rate lines. Finally, politicians are unlikely to distinguish among goods based solely on their price sensitivity. Particularly in the face of uncertainty about which goods have relatively price-elastic demand, the pleadings of special interests would almost certainly carry the day. For all these reasons, uniform taxation—either in the form of a broad-based income tax with limited deductions for specific expenditures or a consumption tax with limited exemptions—is still a very good rule of thumb. It is likely to cause much less economic distortion (i.e., overconsumption of untaxed goods and services) than any other feasible approach, and it allows lower rates of tax because of the broader base it covers.

One more qualification deserves serious consideration. In some special cases, the free market does not lead to efficient outcomes. The most important case is when an activity has a direct impact on other people in a way that is not reflected in the price paid or received for the activity. Economists refer to this as an *externality*. A classic example of a *negative* externality is pollution; businesses that pollute impose a cost on their neighbors by reducing the quality of air they breathe or the water they drink; more controversially, some kinds of pollution accelerate global warming and potentially devastating climate change. If these costs are not reflected in the prices faced by the owners of these businesses, too much pollution will be generated. In such a case, taxes can be used to alter incentives and therefore to mitigate the problem. Ideally, such a tax would be set at a rate that equals the marginal social cost the taxed activity creates. Then, when people and businesses make decisions, they are induced to take into account the costs they impose on others. Supporters of higher gasoline taxes, or taxes on all carbon-based fuels, rely on this rationale. A leading alternative to such taxes, the cap-and-trade system, follows the same principle. Once "permits" to pollute are traded on a market, regardless of whether they were initially auctioned off or handed out, businesses have the incentive to economize on their use by polluting less just as they would in the presence of a tax.

The U.S. tax system more often nominally subsidizes activities rather than penalizes them. By requiring higher tax rates, though, these subsidies cause all other activities to be penalized. But such subsidies may be justified if they encourage activities with *positive* externalities. A fairly clear-cut example is research and development (R&D). Engaging in R&D is costly, and when it leads to a good idea, the benefits almost never accrue entirely to the researcher or to his or her employer, especially when it is fundamental research. Although the patent system is designed to ensure that inventors are amply rewarded for their ideas, people other than the inventor inevitably will capitalize on and profit from the idea. This means that there are some R&D projects that are not worth doing from a private individual's, or firm's, perspective, but are worth doing from society's point of view. In an attempt to alleviate this problem, our income tax system grants preferential tax treatment to R&D expenses.[104] Unlike other types of long-lived investment, these expenses can be deducted immediately and, in addition, qualify for a 20 percent tax credit to the extent that they exceed a base amount meant to approximate the "normal" level of expenditures for that firm. It is hard to tell whether this is the appropriate level of subsidy (is the marginal social external benefit 20 percent of the private cost?), but most economists would agree that at least some subsidy is justified.

The externality argument should be a high hurdle for justifying preferential treatment of particular goods or activities. For example, the vague but ubiquitous argument that an activity is "good for the economy" is certainly inadequate. Yet our tax system violates the principle of neutrality, usually due to subsidizing rather than penalizing, over and over again, often for no good economic reason. The Treasury Department recently identified over 100 specific deviations from a uniform, comprehensive income tax base, which in the aggregate cost hundreds of billions of dollars in revenue.[105] Next, we introduce some of the most important examples of non-neutrality and discuss some of the consequences.

Let's look first at the taxation of capital income and the returns to investment. Different types of investments face vastly different tax treatment under our current system. Because of double taxation at the corporate and personal levels, investments in a corporation are often taxed more heavily than noncorporate business investments; this has been less pronounced since the maximum personal tax rate on dividends was reduced to 15 percent starting in 2003 (it was subsequently increased to 20 percent starting in 2013). Both forms of business income are taxed more heavily than investments in owner-occupied houses, whose owners can claim a mortgage interest deduction but need not report as taxable income the value of the services the houses provide.

The Congressional Budget Office estimates that under fully phased-in 2014 law (assuming that all provisions that were then scheduled to expire, such as bonus depreciation and the research and experimentation credit, had expired), the effective marginal tax rate on investment, including the effects of both personal and corporate income taxation, would average 31 percent for C corporations, 27 percent for pass-through entities, and −2 percent for owner-occupied housing.[106] The result of such disparities is that much more money has flowed into housing and pass-through entity investments—and less to C corporation investment—than would have occurred otherwise, leading to a less productive economy.[107]

Among C corporation investments, those that are financed by debt are taxed less heavily than those that are financed by equity (selling shares of stock), which has no good economic rationale. Depreciation schedules are only rough approximations of true economic depreciation, so the effective tax rate on new investments varies capriciously across types of capital assets, causing certain types of equipment or structures to be favored over others and causing certain industries to receive more generous treatment while others are penalized.[108]

Many features of our tax code provide special preferences for particular types of consumption spending; most of these arise from deductions, exclusions, and credits in the personal income tax. Some of the most important preferences are for housing and health care. A few of these exceptions may be justified, but there is broad agreement among economists that eliminating many of these features would provide significant benefits by rationalizing the allocation of resources. The potential economic gains from making the tax system more neutral are hard to quantify precisely, but they may well be as important as the benefits that could be derived from reducing the tax-induced disincentive to work and save.

Risk-Taking and Entrepreneurship

Some people argue that the tax system is particularly punitive for small, risky start-up firms that embody the ideas and energies of those entrepreneurs who are an important engine of growth for the U.S. economy. Another common complaint is that our tax system is biased against risky investments in general.

What truth is there to these criticisms? First of all, treating entrepreneurial or risky activities *more* favorably than other kinds of activities, except to the extent that they embody R&D or innovation that spills over to benefit others who do not pay for it, has little economic rationale. Nor would precisely singling out "entrepreneurial" income for favorable tax treatment be feasible, as we have no meaningful way to define it precisely. On the other hand, *penalizing* such activities relative to others has no good economic rationale, either, and some argue that the current tax code does in fact penalize such activities in a number of ways.

The most frequent complaint concerns capital gains taxes. The owners of risky ventures often receive their return in the form of large capital gains when they sell all or part of the company; however, they also risk the possibility of a capital loss. The U.S. tax code imposes a (preferential) tax on the gains but allows only a small amount of net capital loss to be deducted against other income in a given year (although the losses can be carried forward to be deducted from taxable income in future years). This tax treatment has a practical rationale because unlimited deductibility of losses would open up opportunities for some sophisticated and troublesome tax avoidance schemes; people could "cherry-pick" and sell only assets with losses, continually generating losses for tax purposes, and letting the appreciating assets ride. However, the loss limitation discourages risk-taking because the system taxes away some of the rewards if the venture is successful but doesn't provide symmetrical insurance against a loss.

Taxation of capital gains is also blamed for a *lock-in* effect in which individuals are deterred from selling stocks because they pay tax only at the time of sale. The fact that capital gains are taxed only when the appreciated asset is sold—and are not taxed at all if held until death—creates such an incentive. Critics contend that investment funds are kept locked up in the stocks of older, established firms at the expense of newer entrepreneurial ventures that might offer a higher return. Any lock-in effect probably affects mainly *who* owns particular stocks rather than which companies receive investment funds.

Although these arguments may have some merit, one popular solution, a further cut in capital gains tax rates, has many problems of its own. For one thing, it is a very blunt instrument for addressing this set of issues because innovative entrepreneurial ventures are the source of only a tiny fraction of the total value of capital gains.[109] Thus, only a small fraction of the revenues lost from preferential taxes on capital gains is going toward improved incentives for entrepreneurship.

Some people point to the graduated nature of income tax rates as discouraging entrepreneurship and risk-taking. In many cases, the incentive to engage in such activities depends on a small possibility of a very large return, and progressive tax rates take their largest hit from just such returns. In addition, the returns to entrepreneurship represent largely the product of hard work, so this is to some extent an argument about how marginal tax rates affect labor supply.

Another argument points out that, because of imperfections in capital markets and lack of collateral, small start-up firms often have trouble obtaining loans and have to rely heavily on equity financing provided directly by the entrepreneur and his or her family.[110] This suggests that, even in the absence of taxes, a less than efficient amount of entrepreneurial activity might occur. Highly progressive income taxes and heavy taxes on capital gains might then make the problem worse. Moreover, to the extent that these firms become C corporations, the double taxation of corporate equity would be particularly harmful to entrepreneurs, and corporate entrepreneurial ventures are penalized relative to other investments that have access to more tax-favored debt.

Entrepreneurship is hard to define and measure, and partly for that reason, little evidence can be found to contradict the claims that are made about the deleterious effects of the tax system in this area. Such claims should not necessarily be discounted, and the fact that tax reform might help improve incentives in this area (for example, by eliminating double taxation) should be viewed as a plus. Yet there is also no hard evidence demonstrating that the potential economic benefits in this area are large. Some have suggested that a burgeoning of entrepreneurial efforts, in response to lower marginal tax rates, was partly responsible for the surge in the incomes of the affluent since the 1980s. This question is addressed in more detail at the end of this chapter.

International Competitiveness and International Aspects of Taxation

Another claim sometimes made about tax reform is that it would somehow improve America's "international competitiveness." We put quotation marks around that term because what it really means is unclear. Are there circumstances under which we should forego policies that would increase national income—i.e., people's well-being—to increase something called international competitiveness? We and nearly all other economists think not.

The United States is not in competition with other countries in the same sense that the Chicago Bulls are in competition with the Golden State Warriors, in which one side wins and the other side loses each game between them. IBM rightly views Toshiba as a competitor in this sense, but the United States should not view China, Japan, or Germany in this way. For at least two centuries, a broad consensus among economists has held that the opposite is true—that unfettered commercial relationships benefit all participating countries (although not necessarily all people in all countries) because they allow nations to concentrate their resources on what they do best.[111] This is the venerable theory of *comparative advantage*. In general, looking for ways to boost our standard of living *at the expense* of other countries is not a useful pursuit.

Our standard of living ultimately depends on our own productivity, resources, and efficiency in using these resources. This is where we should focus our efforts.

With that said, a number of interesting and controversial issues do arise in connection with taxation in a global economy. For instance, how should we tax foreign investment done by U.S. companies and U.S. investment done by foreign companies? Should the tax system actively discourage U.S. companies from moving operations abroad, or should it strive to be neutral toward such locational choices?

In most situations, a good rule of thumb is that the tax system should be neutral with respect to the location of investment. Applying that rule to foreign investment implies that the tax system certainly shouldn't encourage U.S.-based multinational corporations to invest offshore when they otherwise wouldn't, but neither should it offer tax breaks to these companies to induce them to invest in the United States when investments abroad would be more profitable. From a *global* point of view, if all countries follow this practice, firms are induced to make investment decisions undistorted by differences in countries' tax systems, which leads to an efficient allocation of investment. This approach tends to maximize worldwide income.

Each individual nation, however, may be able to gain at the expense of others by lowering its tax rate to attract some extra investment away from other countries. To the extent that investment moves to particular locations for favorable tax treatment rather than in pursuit of productive investment opportunities, it is inefficient and worldwide income is reduced. But the income of the country that attracts the extra investment may increase. If *all* countries try to lower tax rates to attract investment from each other, they may end up worse off than if they had agreed to refrain from competing in this manner. Investment ultimately goes where it would have gone anyway, but each country ends up with lower tax revenues and therefore less ability to provide programs that their residents value.

Some economists are concerned that as capital becomes increasingly mobile across countries, a "race to the bottom" in taxation of capital income might be triggered as countries compete to reduce their tax rates to attract more foreign investment. This sometimes leads to proposals for *harmonization* of tax rates across countries—a mutual agreement to conform to a single tax rate or within a band of tax rates, which would eliminate much of the incentive that firms now have to reduce their taxes by relocating, at least among the countries that are party to the agreement.[112]

Opinions on whether tax competition is really a problem and whether harmonization would be a good idea vary greatly. Dani Rodrik of Harvard University contends that "it is generally accepted that integration into the world economy reduces the ability of governments to undertake redistributive taxation or implement generous social programs" because countries that attempt to do this will end up driving capital abroad.[113] Others argue that tax competition is actually beneficial—for instance, because they believe that any taxation of capital income is inefficient (and so any downward pressure is welcome) or because such competition might induce governments to provide services more efficiently to attract more capital.

While there is no doubt that in setting their tax policy countries need to be aware of what other countries' tax policies are, some people see opportunities to use the tax code to benefit their own country at the expense of other nations where no such opportunity actually exists. The most obvious example is a *tariff* (a tax on imports). This is a particularly inefficient tax from the perspective of the country that imposes it because it induces its residents to buy domestically produced goods that could be obtained more cheaply by importing. At first blush, it may look like a tariff protects domestic jobs, but in the long run it just ends up affecting the *kinds* of jobs, diverting domestic resources away from their relatively most productive uses.

Misunderstanding about taxes and international competitiveness also confuses the debate over whether the United States should adopt the type of consumption tax called a value-added tax (VAT). Some American business people and politicians look with envy at a particular feature of European VATs: the tax is levied on imports, while all tax that had been collected on goods for export is rebated to the exporters, making exports effectively tax free. Although at first glance this might seem like an ingenious export promotion scheme, it is nothing of the sort.[114] In fact, all it does is reproduce how a retail sales tax works. After all, states that have sales taxes levy them on goods sold to their residents, regardless of where they were produced, and don't charge sales taxes on goods produced at home but consumed out-of-state. This treatment doesn't give domestically produced goods any special edge. Suppose the United States were to implement a 20 percent VAT that increased the price of everything we buy. Charging a 20 percent VAT on imported goods purchased here would simply mean they are treated equally to domestically produced goods, just as they are now. The same story holds true for our exports: we wouldn't charge foreigners any VAT on the goods they imported from us, but their home countries would, just as they do for any other goods sold to their residents.

More fundamentally, even if we could figure out some way to give a temporary edge to our domestically produced goods through the tax system, it would soon be dissipated by adjustments in exchange rates. Any apparent advantage to exports would be offset by a combination of a strengthening of the U.S. dollar, which makes dollar-priced exports less attractive to foreigners, and domestic price level increases, which make U.S. markets more attractive to both foreign exporters and U.S. manufacturers. If the exchange rate strengthening and domestic price increases did not occur, the trade surplus stimulated by the demand for U.S.-produced goods would drive up the value of the dollar, dissipating the temporary advantage obtained.

Jobs, Jobs, Jobs

Politicians love to promise more and better jobs for voters, and so do advocates of tax reform. Moreover, whenever any kind of tax increase or elimination of tax preference is threatened, those who perceive they would be made worse off immediately generate and publicize a study purporting to show how many jobs it will cost. And vice versa. For example, during the debate over the Tax Reform Act of 1986, when eliminating the deductibility of business lunches was being considered, the restaurant industry association warned that thousands of jobs would be lost in the restaurant business. In support of the Bush administration's 2003 tax cut proposal, his economic advisers claimed it would create 2.1 million jobs over the following three years.[115] In 2015, the Tax Foundation estimated that Jeb Bush's tax plan would "create" 2.7 million new jobs.[116]

Aside from the natural and understandable tendency of interested parties to exaggerate, do such claims about jobs have any economic content? In a word (okay, two words), not much. Standard economic reasoning suggests that if the economy is functioning normally, there is nothing about taxes that would cause people who are willing to work at the going wage rate to be unable to find jobs.[117] To be sure, jobs in tax-favored sectors may be lost as a result of eliminating preferences, but that doesn't mean that the total quantity of jobs in the economy is reduced. Rather, demand shifts away from the formerly tax-preferred sectors toward the production of other goods and services in the economy, and as a result new jobs will be created in these sectors. Shifting jobs from one sector to another can be a jarring, painful process, but it happens all the time for reasons unrelated to taxes and is a key to keeping the economy running efficiently. The transitional costs should not be dismissed, but they are likely to be outweighed by the economic benefits that arise if eliminating an unwarranted preference shifts resources into a more productive area; the latter gain persists long after the transitional disruption is past.

As we discussed earlier in this chapter, tax policy can certainly help the economy and generate more employment in the short term if it increases demand and if the economy is operating below capacity because of a recession. Even in this case, though, the effect is only to restore the number of jobs to their normal level more quickly, not to increase the number of jobs in the long run. Not coincidentally, liberal economists tend to think that the best countercyclical policy is either tax cuts for low-income households or social spending directed to the same folks. And conservative economists generally think that the best stimulus is a tax cut designed to generate more business investment. It is a troubling fact for the aspiration of economics to be a hard science that economists' values about equity end up being so correlated with their beliefs about what kind of fiscal, or tax, policy works best for the economy. The underlying and generally unspoken concern is that these alternative stimulus plans benefit different people and have different implications for the long-term level and nature of government involvement in the economy. These things matter, to be sure, but they have nothing to do with which policy is the most effective short-term economic stimulus.

The truth is that, for reasons discussed earlier, many economists of widely varying political inclinations are not very enamored of any kind of short-term fiscal policy—whether tax credits targeted to the poor, tax cuts aimed at the affluent, or expenditure increases, except in the unusual case where the economy is up against the zero lower bound on interest rates. In spite of this, the ubiquity of such policies continues. We suspect that there are at least two reasons for this. First, when the economy is going well, governments are quick to claim credit, whether or not their policies had anything to do with the good times. Then, when bad times roll around, voters naturally look to government for another dose of the apparently effective fiscal medicine, and no administration wants to be seen as uninterested in the economy. The doctor may or may not have effective medicine, but something must be prescribed. Second, a recession provides a convenient marketing opportunity for politicians who support tax cuts to achieve other objectives, such as shrinking the size of government or improving incentives.

Another important point is that the number of jobs or the amount of employment should not be relied on as the sole indicator of economic health. To see why, consider the following sure-fire way to generate millions of new jobs: pass and enforce a law requiring that every able-bodied adult work at least sixty hours per week. This law would "create" millions of new jobs and cause GDP to soar. But it would not make us better off because we value our leisure time and have for the most part chosen how we will allocate our time between working for pay and using our time in other ways we value.

Although claims about the effects of tax cuts on the number of jobs are suspect, at least when the economy is operating normally, the idea that tax reform could lead to *better* jobs makes more sense. This could happen if tax reform caused a more efficient allocation of resources by shifting them from less productive but tax-preferred sectors to more inherently productive uses. But for the most part, this claim depends on the idea that reduced tax rates on high-income people, combined with greater incentives for saving and investment, will lead to a larger and higher-quality capital stock. In turn, workers would have more capital—better "tools"—to work with, increasing their productivity and raising their wages. This is the essence of how tax changes that are targeted mainly at high-income people are supposed to help the rest of the population. This is essentially the same thing as saying that part of the burden of taxes on capital income is currently falling on workers. Democrats have often derided this thinking as "trickle-down economics," while Republicans have made it one of their central themes. Although the logic of the argument is sound, the crucial question is the magnitude of the effect; as discussed above, the evidence is highly uncertain.

Human Capital: Education and Training

A more direct way to increase worker productivity and generate better, if not more, jobs is to encourage people to acquire more education and skills. Economists refer to the stock of productive skills that people possess as *human capital*. Just as investing in better physical plant and equipment adds to labor productivity, so does investing in skills. Many economists contend that human capital and research and development are the most important elements of long-run economic growth. Although putting a dollar value on such things is difficult, the aggregate value of human capital is probably at least as large as that of physical capital in our country.[118] Tax policy is not a central part of education policy, but at a minimum the two should not work at loggerheads.

Acquiring human capital requires an investment. Some of this investment takes the form of tuition and other direct outlays, which can be substantial. The other important cost, to the student and to society, is whatever the student could have earned but passed up to acquire the skills—their "forgone" earnings. For some college students, forgone earnings are undoubtedly lower than the cost of tuition, although they are many times higher than tuition for some MBA and law students who leave lucrative jobs to obtain professional degrees.

How our tax system treats investments in human capital depends on the nature of the investment. The investment of time spent at school rather than at work is treated more generously than most investments in physical capital. Although you pay tax on the return to your investment in skills (higher wages), you save any taxes you would have paid on the earnings you pass up while at school. In essence, you get an immediate write-off for your lost wages. In contrast, the cost of an investment in long-lived physical capital would typically be depreciated over many years rather than immediately deducted.

Until recently, human capital investment in the form of direct costs such as tuition was treated less generously by the tax system than physical capital because it generated no tax deductions whatsoever, yet the return to the investment (in the form of higher earnings) was fully taxed. The Taxpayer Relief Act of 1997 altered this comparison by introducing the Hope Scholarship Credit and Lifetime Learning Credit (which allow nonrefundable credits for qualified tuition and related expenses) and a new limited deduction for interest on qualified education loans. Furthermore, you can deduct interest on a home equity loan used for education, the government pays the interest on some student loans while the student is in school, and scholarships used for tuition are tax-free. The 2001 tax cut introduced a limited deduction for higher-education expenses, expanded the deductibility of student loan interest, and expanded opportunities to save for education in tax-preferred accounts. The American Opportunity Tax Credit, which was enacted temporarily in 2009 and then made permanent in 2015, expanded the Hope Scholarship Credit to cover four years of higher education. It is not clear whether the tax system now favors human or physical capital investment more, but the balance seems to be tilting toward the former.

An argument can be made that the tax code ought to treat human capital more generously than physical capital. Because people can't pledge their future labor earnings as collateral for a loan, private capital markets on their own often fail to offer loans even to students who are "good investments." However, government-guaranteed loan programs already exist to address this problem. In addition, some external benefits produced by education (such as creating better citizenship and passing on knowledge) might spill over to others, which would suggest that some degree of subsidy would be justified on externality grounds. While a case can be made for providing tax incentives for education, the hodgepodge of current provisions is unlikely to be the most efficient approach. First, the code's considerable duplication and complexity seem to suggest that some consolidation and simplification are in order. Second, low-income people, whose decisions about pursuing higher education are most likely to be influenced by financial considerations, often receive little or no benefit from these provisions because they have no tax liability (the American Opportunity Tax Credit addresses this to some extent because it is partly refundable). Third, many of the benefits of the tax provisions serve simply as windfalls to students who decide how much education to pursue regardless of tax considerations.

Recently, many economists have taken seriously policies such as income-contingent student loans, where the repayment depends (positively) on one's post-schooling income. This type of plan has the advantage of providing insurance against uncertain future incomes. Australia and New Zealand have the most extensive programs of this kind.[119]

Avoidance and Evasion

Our current tax code provides many opportunities for individuals and firms to reduce their taxes without making any significant changes in how much they work, save, or invest. For example, workers may choose to receive much of their compensation in the form of tax-exempt fringe benefits. Many self-employed people underreport—or do not report at all—their net income.

These types of responses—called *tax avoidance* when the methods are legal and *tax evasion* when they're not—are key to understanding how taxes affect the economy. First of all, they are symptoms of the economic cost of taxation in the same way that tax-induced alterations in "real" behavior (such as labor supply or investment) are.[120] Although real behavioral responses to taxation might appear to be more important than the others, this reasoning is faulty. On all the margins of choice, taxpayers will undertake behavior that reduces tax liability up to the point that the marginal cost equals the marginal tax saving. In the real-behavior case, the cost is that people's consumption patterns or business investment plans are not what they would, absent taxes, prefer. With avoidance, the cost may be expenditures on professional assistance. With evasion, the cost may be exposure to the uncertainty of an audit and any attendant penalties for detected evasion, or banking in the Cayman Islands rather than on Main Street. Most of these costs represent a deadweight loss to the economy.

The relationship among avoidance, evasion, and decisions such as labor supply is particularly subtle. The avoidance responses may mitigate the extent to which real economic decisions are affected by taxation. In response to taxes, you'd almost always prefer to relabel your compensation as an untaxed fringe benefit than to cut back on your hours worked. In addition, avoidance responses can cloud the evidence about how taxes are affecting real economic decisions. For example, if the taxable incomes of the rich go down significantly when their tax rates go up, they might have cut back on their labor supply, or they might be reporting less of their income and taking greater advantage of avoidance opportunities. Distinguishing among these kinds of responses may be important because they can have very different policy implications. In the example just mentioned, if we care about progressivity, then the appropriate policy response might be to limit opportunities for avoidance and evasion rather than to abandon a progressive tax structure because of the apparently large disincentive effects it causes.

Past experience has shown that individuals and firms are very willing to take advantage of opportunities for tax avoidance when they present themselves. One notable example of such a response occurred when the 1986 tax act reduced the top marginal tax rate in the personal income tax below that of the corporate income tax for the first time in decades. This, combined with the promise of avoiding double taxation of business income, made it much more attractive to organize a business as an S corporation or a partnership, which are taxed solely under the personal code, instead of as a traditional C corporation, which is taxed under the corporate code. The response was swift and dramatic. The number of S corporations, which had been rising at a 7.7 percent annual pace from 1965 to 1986, jumped by 17.5 percent a year from 1986 to 1990. The number of C corporations, which had been growing by an average of 3.5 percent per year from 1965 to 1986, dropped by 4.8 percent per year between 1986 and 1990; the biggest decline was among small C corporations, the ones that can more easily switch to S status.[121]

The vast amount of evidence produced by past tax changes suggests a hierarchy of behavioral responses to taxation. At the top of the hierarchy—the most clearly responsive to tax incentives—is the timing of certain economic transactions, of which the pattern of capital gains realizations before and after the 1986 tax reform is the best example. In the second tier of the hierarchy are financial and accounting responses, best exemplified by the shift from C to S corporations after 1986 and by the large post-1986 shift away from newly nondeductible personal loans into still-deductible mortgage debt. On the bottom of the hierarchy, where the least response is evident, are the real economic decisions of individuals and firms concerning labor supply, savings, and investment. The consensus among economists is that the evidence shows that aggregate labor supply responds little to its after-tax return, that the evidence is not clear on whether saving responds to its after-tax return, and that the evidence regarding investment is somewhat mixed.

How Do Very High-Income People Respond to Tax Cuts?

The hierarchy of behavioral responses provides a useful perspective for evaluating one of the most dramatic impacts of a tax change in history. Right after the Tax Reform Act of 1986, which reduced the top marginal tax rate from 50 percent to 28 percent, the reported taxable income of affluent Americans increased strikingly. Between 1984 and 1990, the total inflation-adjusted gross income of the most affluent 1 percent of taxpayers rose by 68 percent, and their *share* of total AGI increased by more than a third, from 9.9 percent to 13.4 percent.[122] Data that follow the same taxpayers over time reveals the same pattern: those high-income households for which the 1986 tax reform provided the biggest reductions in marginal tax rates experienced the biggest increases in reported income.[123]

But did the reduced marginal tax rates of the 1980s *cause* the large increase in reported incomes of the affluent? Or was the timing of the high-income surge just a coincidence? After all, income inequality, led by an explosion in the incomes at the top of the income distribution, had been steadily increasing since about 1970, and many explanations for this trend have nothing to do with tax changes. For example, the demand for the services of a select few highly skilled "superstars" in various fields appears to have been increasing over time, and the ability to deliver their services to a worldwide audience has increased with technological advances in telecommunications.[124] The share of income received by the highest earners undoubtedly would have increased during this period even without any tax changes. But the sharpness of the increase right around 1986 suggests that the tax cut was a major factor in the increase.

A closer look at the anatomy of the high-income behavioral response suggests that it had little if anything to do with increased hours worked.[125] Some of the increased income was accounted for by the shift in the legal organization of small- and medium-sized businesses from being C corporations, whose income shows up on corporation tax returns, to S corporations, whose income shows up on individual tax returns. Such a shift does not reflect the creation of new income or an increase in total tax revenues: although income reported by individuals went up, the taxable income of C corporations showed a mirror-image decline. Another part of the explanation is that the 1986 tax reform sharply reduced the advantages of using partnerships as tax shelters. To the extent that these tax losses stopped showing up after 1987 on the tax returns of high-income taxpayers, their incomes appear to have risen, but any such increase reflects only the tightening up of the rules governing tax shelters. In sum, not all of the post-1986 increase in reported income of the affluent reflected improved incentives to earn income due to the cut in tax rates.

This issue became critical in the debate over the impact of the increases in the top marginal rate enacted in 1990 and especially in 1993. Bill Clinton was elected in 1992 on a platform that included tax increases on the affluent, and he delivered on that promise starting in tax year 1993, when the top federal tax rate increased from 31 percent to 39.6 percent. Proponents of this policy argued that it was appropriate that high-income taxpayers pay their "fair share" of the necessary increase in tax burden. Opponents cautioned that the revenue projections were overstated because they ignored the inevitable behavioral response of high-income taxpayers.

Once the initial evidence on tax year 1993 was compiled, Daniel Feenberg and Martin Feldstein of Harvard University examined tabulations of tax return data for 1992 and 1993. They concluded that compared to previous trend growth and the income growth of other taxpayers, the reported taxable incomes of very high-income families *fell* by 7.8 percent in 1993, the year of the tax increase. If correct, then the Treasury collected only half of the revenue that it had claimed it would collect from the rate increase.[126] Feenberg and Feldstein argued that this large behavioral response indicated that the ratio of the efficiency cost due to distorted behavior to the revenue raised was high—much higher than for alternative ways to raise revenue. The policy implication: high taxes on the rich are a bad idea.[127]

There's more to this story, though. Bill Clinton was elected in early November 1992, leaving plenty of time for many high-income taxpayers to shift taxable income that would otherwise have been received in 1993 and afterward into 1992, when it would be taxed at a rate no higher than 31 percent. In December, the financial press was full of stories advising readers to do just that and full of stories about prominent citizens who already had. Walt Disney executives Michael Eisner and Frank Wells cashed in stock options worth $257 million. The New York State Bureau of the Budget's annual survey of the year-end bonuses paid to Wall Street high flyers revealed that about two-thirds were paid in December of 1992 and one-third in January of 1993, compared to the usual breakdown of one-third in December and two-thirds in January.[128]

For all these reasons, the fact that the 1993 incomes of the highest-income group were lower than their 1992 incomes could reflect nothing more than the fact that taxable income was shifted backward from 1993 to 1992 to escape the expected higher taxes. In fact, compared to data from 1991, which would not be contaminated by the shifting, the 1993 incomes of affluent taxpayers do not look particularly low.[129] The evidence from years surrounding announced or anticipated tax changes clearly reveals a mixture of timing responses and the more permanent responses to tax changes, and it is difficult to sort out one from the other. All in all, although affluent taxpayers surely take note of and respond to the tax system, no clear evidence shows that they altered their behavior enough to undermine the tax increases of 1990 and 1993.

Figure 4.8 puts this debate into a longer-term historical perspective, based on a study of tax-return data by Thomas Piketty and Emmanuel Saez.[130] It shows, for the years 1913 through 2015, before-tax income (excluding capital gains) reported by people in the top 1 percent of the income distribution as a share of the total of such income in the United States and the marginal tax rate in the top bracket of the personal income tax.

The short-run relationship between marginal rates and the share of income earned by the top 1 percent of earners suggests that a number of features are not particularly consistent with the notion that a behavioral response to tax rates is the main factor driving the recent surge of incomes at the top of the distribution. While the very large surge in income following the Tax Reform Act of 1986 is readily apparent, the incomes of the top 1 percent increased nearly as fast during the 1990s as during the 1980s. Between 1990 and 2000, the share of income (excluding capital gains) reported by the top 1 percent surged from 13.0 percent to 16.5 percent. Capital gains also increased dramatically for this group during the 1990s, but because these gains mainly reflect the stock market boom, we exclude them from the analysis. The sharp rise in incomes at the top of the distribution occurred despite increases in the top marginal tax rate in 1990 and 1993. Thus, the soaring reported incomes of the affluent continued until 2000, nearly a decade and a half after the last tax cut and a few years after two tax increases, which casts some doubt on the hypothesis that movements in the top tax rate were the principal cause of the striking changes in the reported income of high-income households since 1980. Top marginal tax rates were cut in 2001 and 2003, and then increased again in 2013. Since 2000, the share of income going to the top 1 percent has bounced around a bit, but overall seemed to continue its upward trajectory, reaching 18.4 percent by 2015.

Other instances of patterns that do not suggest a strong response to incentives include the Kennedy-Johnson tax cut, which cut the top rate from 91 percent to 70 percent between 1963 and 1965 and was not accompanied by a surge in top reported incomes anything like what happened in the 1980s. Nor is there any discernible sign of a response in figure 4.8 of the 1971 cut in the maximum tax rate on labor income from 70 percent to just over 50 percent.[131]

Over the longer run, however, a clear negative relationship does appear between the top marginal income tax rate and the reported incomes of the top 1 percent. At the beginning and end of the time

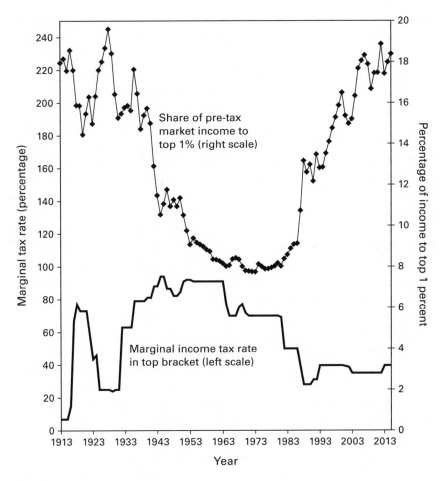

Figure 4.8
Share of total U.S. pre-tax market income, excluding capital gains, going to top 1 percent of income distribution, versus marginal personal income tax rate in top bracket, 1913–2015.
Sources: Piketty and Saez (2003, updated 2016), and Internal Revenue Service (2016a).

period shown in figure 4.8, marginal tax rates were relatively low, and incomes of the rich were very high. In the middle of the twentieth century, by contrast, marginal tax rates were high and incomes were low. Thus, there is some broad support for responsiveness to incentives here. One reasonable interpretation of the data would be that very high marginal rates like those imposed in the middle of the century have a negative impact on reported income of the rich but that modest changes around the levels of the marginal rates we have today do not necessarily have a significant effect (as evidenced by the experience of the 1990s). Some of the response to changes in incentives might also take time to materialize.

International evidence also lends some support to the notion that the surge in incomes among the rich in the United States over the past few decades had something to do with taxes. For instance, research by Saez, Piketty, and others has found that while the share of income going to the top 1 percent has risen dramatically since 1970 in English-speaking countries such as the United States, Canada, and the United Kingdom, it has remained fairly flat in continental European countries such as France, the Netherlands, and Switzerland. If rising incomes for highly skilled individuals had been driven primarily by globalization or technical change, we might have expected the patterns to look more similar across these countries. There is some correlation between which countries had the largest tax cuts on high-income people and which ones had the largest surges in shares of before-tax income reported by the top 1 percent, although this correlation is far from perfect. On the one hand, France and the Netherlands had no significant cuts in top tax rates and no increases in top income shares, while the United States and United Kingdom both had large cuts in marginal tax rates and large income surges at the top. On the other hand, the rising share of income going to the top 1 percent in Canada has been only slightly less pronounced than that in the United States, despite much smaller tax cuts there. The rise in incomes in Canada—which has been concentrated in English-speaking regions—may reflect either the influence of some non-tax factor unique to English-speaking cultures or perhaps competitive pressures on the wages of highly skilled (and potentially internationally mobile) English-speaking Canadians arising from the rapidly increasing after-tax wages for highly skilled U.S. workers across the border.[132]

Finally, the data in figure 4.8 and in the international comparisons noted above are based on income reported to the tax authorities. Thus, to the extent that the share of income reported by the top 1 percent responded to tax rates, the data reflect a combination of "real" behavioral responses (like altered labor supply) and other responses (such as avoidance and evasion). Figure 4.8 and the international evidence strongly suggest that in times when statutory tax rates are as high as 70 to 90 percent, affluent taxpayers report, and perhaps also earn, relatively less income. That evidence does not tell us, however, to what extent the reduced reported earnings are due to less real productive economic activity, more avoidance and evasion, or something else (e.g., corporate executives bargaining harder with the board of directors for higher pay). Research by Piketty, Saez, and Stantcheva (2014) finds that there was no correlation between which countries had the largest cuts in top marginal income tax rates between the 1960s and the early 2000s, and which countries had the fastest growth in real GDP per person over that same time period. That raises doubts about the extent to which the faster rise in top incomes in the countries that had the big tax cuts on top earners actually reflected increases in real productive economic activity.

How Do Tax Cuts Affect Revenues?
The proposition that across-the-board tax cuts would cost the government no tax revenue is associated with the economist Arthur Laffer, who claimed in the 1970s that high tax rates might be harming the economy so much that tax cuts would provide more, rather than less, revenue. The free lunch promised by Laffer proved irresistible to politicians and was one of the ideological underpinnings of the tax cuts pushed by President Reagan in 1981. The massive increase in the budget deficit following that tax cut weakened support for such views, but some such support still persists today. For example, on the presidential campaign trail in 1996 and 2000, one of Steve Forbes's mantras was that tax cuts in the United States have always increased revenues. The 2008 Republican presidential candidate John McCain apparently agreed, saying in early 2007 that "Tax cuts, starting with Kennedy, as we all know, increase revenues. So what's the argument for increasing taxes? If you get the opposite effect out of tax cuts?"[133] The 2015 presidential candidate Ted Cruz said his tax plan was conceived with help from Dr. Laffer.[134]

With three decades of hindsight, most economists now believe that Laffer's claim was not proven correct by the response to tax rate cuts of 1981. It did not accurately characterize the effects of the Bush-era tax cuts of the first decade of the twenty-first century either. This should not be surprising given all of the evidence we discussed above, such as the apparently small responsiveness of labor supply to taxes. A reduction in tax rates does not cause the economy to expand enough to recoup the revenues, at least at the levels of tax rates applying in recent U.S. history. Revenues in the 1980s and in the 2000s turned out to be significantly lower than what they would have been had there been no tax cut. All but the most ardent "supply-siders" now concede this point.

Certainly, individual income tax revenues fell relative to GDP after 1981. From 1981 to 1984, they dropped from 9.1 percent of GDP down to 7.5 percent, despite continued inflation-induced "bracket creep" that pushed taxpayers into higher tax rates. President George H. W. Bush's Treasury Department estimated that by 1990 the rate reductions of the 1981 act alone were costing the federal government $164 billion per year, assuming no departure from the normal trend of economic growth.[135] The only way such facts could be reconciled with claims that the 1981 cut caused revenues to *increase* would be if it caused the economy to grow significantly faster than it otherwise would have. As table 4.1 shows, however, the productivity growth rate of the 1980s was about the same as in the 1970s, as well as below that of the 1990s. Some point to the growth rate experienced in the years immediately after 1982, but this confuses the recovery from a deep recession with sustainable long-run growth.

The Bush tax cuts enacted in 2001 definitely reduced government revenue. When measured in constant (inflation-adjusted) 2009 dollars, federal personal income tax revenue declined from $1,221 billion in 2000 to $1,109 billion in 2012, and the decline relative to what revenues would have been without the tax cut was undoubtedly much larger.[136] Overall federal revenues dropped from 20.0 percent of GDP in 2000 to 15.3 percent of GDP in 2012.[137] And, once again, there is no clear evidence that the tax cuts improved economic growth. Productivity growth was strong from 2001 to 2006 but was only slightly stronger than it had been from 1995 to 2000, and average annual real per capita GDP growth was much slower from 2001 to 2006 (1.6 percent per year) than it had been from 1995 to 2000 (2.8 percent).[138] There is room for argument about whether *some* of the revenue loss from the Bush tax cuts was recouped through economic growth that was higher than it would have been otherwise, but not about whether the tax cuts actually increased revenue.

Dynamic Scoring

Even if we dismiss the claim that tax cuts "pay for themselves," a legitimate and important question remains: exactly how do revenues respond to changes in tax rates? As we've already discussed, the more that behavior responds to tax rates, the more costly high tax rates are likely to be. Moreover, advocates of tax cuts often complain that official analyses of their proposals fail to take into account *any* possibility of induced economic growth and that they therefore make tax cut proposals appear to cost more revenue than they really would. They argue that the revenue-estimating process of the government should be made *dynamic* (assuming that economic growth will be affected) rather than *static* (assuming that growth is unaffected).[139]

Some background is necessary to understand this issue. The budget act of 1974 assigned to the Congressional Budget Office (CBO) the tasks of making baseline projections of revenues and outlays and of estimating the budget effects of the spending proposals reported by committees. It assigned to the Joint Committee on Taxation (JCT) of Congress the task of preparing estimates for most revenue legislation. The two groups coordinate their efforts on estimates of complex pieces of legislation that affect both revenues and outlays. This process is designed to provide Congress with the information it needs to evaluate budgetary proposals independently. *Scoring* refers to the official estimates of the revenue and spending effects of each proposal, which are used to determine whether the proposal is consistent with whatever congressional budget rules are in effect at that time. In practice, these tend to become the numbers most often cited in the media in connection with any big tax or spending proposals.

Under current practice, both CBO and JCT already incorporate into their revenue estimates a wide variety of behavioral changes in response to economic incentives. In his May 2002 testimony to the House Budget Committee about dynamic scoring, outgoing CBO director Dan Crippen cited two examples of the CBO methodology.[140] First, he noted that when CBO does a revenue estimate of an increase in the capital gains tax, it accounts for the fact that this tax will accelerate the realization of gains to avoid the higher tax rate. (Note that this is a timing response, at the top of the hierarchy of behavioral responses.) He then said that when CBO does cost estimates of a change in marginal income tax rates, it includes the effect on the tax base that comes from re-characterizing compensation from taxable wages and salaries to nontaxable fringe benefits. (This is a *renaming effect*.)

Until very recently, though, the macroeconomic effect of proposed legislation and the budgetary implications of those effects were not included. In other words, gross domestic product was not allowed to be affected by tax policy in calculating a revenue estimate. In 2015, a congressional resolution mandated that henceforth the official revenue estimates for major legislation considered by Congress must incorporate the budgetary effects of induced macroeconomic changes. One argument for dynamic scoring is that an imprecisely right answer that recognizes behavioral responses is better than a precisely wrong answer—the precisely wrong answer being that tax cuts or changes have absolutely *no* effect on the macro economy. Argument number two is that non-dynamic, or *static*, scoring biases decision making toward bigger government because it overestimates both the revenue cost of tax cuts and the revenue gain from tax increases. It is by no means obvious that this latter point is true, however. For instance, if a tax cut is not accompanied by a cut in government spending and the economy is operating at capacity, then the negative economic effects of the resulting budget deficit are likely to outweigh the positive economic effects of improved incentives. In that case, the tax cut will reduce economic growth and cut revenues even further, so that the static estimate would *understate* the revenue cost of the tax cut.

The principal arguments against dynamic scoring are that (1) the uncertainty about its true impact would politicize the revenue scoring process and threaten its integrity, (2) it would bias the process toward fiscally irresponsible outcomes, and (3) because it is infeasible to do for all proposals, it would favor *big* proposals if only big proposals are dynamically scored and favor tax expenditure proposals rather than regular expenditure programs if only tax proposals are dynamically scored.[141]

In evaluating these claims, it is important to keep in mind that cutting taxes without cutting expenditures is not a free ride. A plan to cut taxes is not a plan to spend less of the taxpayers' money; it is instead a plan to put off assigning to our citizens the burden of that spending. One dynamic effect that is indisputable is that large, persistent budget deficits are unsustainable. Thus, a proper dynamic scoring of a tax cut that is not offset elsewhere in the budget should show it eventually having a negative effect on the economy. As we noted above, if taxes are cut and government spending is not cut, the resulting deficit is bad for the long-run economy. Moreover, taxes will eventually have to go up in the future, which harms incentives then. If it does not recognize this, dynamic scoring can obfuscate the nature of the choices we face rather than improve the accuracy of the trade-offs we face.

But now dynamic scoring of official revenue estimates is the law of the land. In its first use by the Joint Committee on Taxation, the revenue cost of the two-year tax extension of dozens of tax breaks was $86.6 billion, compared to $96.9 billion under a "static" revenue scoring, cutting the cost by 11 percent. Unsurprisingly, instituting dynamic scoring does not eliminate controversy over *how* the scoring is done. For example, the conservative Heritage Foundation criticized how the revenue impact of extending bonus depreciation was calculated.[142]

Government agencies do not have a monopoly on revenue estimates. In the run-up to the 2016 presidential election, the Washington-based Tax Foundation, a nonpartisan tax policy research organization, achieved much prominence by scoring all of the candidates' tax proposals, using both a static and dynamic analysis. The dynamic analysis is based on an economic model consisting of a small number of simultaneous equations that determine output, capital stock, and labor usage in four sectors (private corporate, private noncorporate, government enterprises, and households), and a few summary measures of effective marginal and average tax rates on labor and capital.[143] Although anyone without an economics PhD viewing these equations on the Tax Foundation website will undoubtedly be put off, and possibly impressed, by the equations sprinkled with Greek letters and logarithmic notation, the model is actually very simple as macroeconomic models go. It also builds in some fairly extreme assumptions, such as that the after-tax world interest rate is unaffected by U.S. tax policy or U.S. aggregate investment. Given our large role in the world economy, this is unlikely to be true, and exacerbates the effect of tax changes that reduce the tax on business investment and capital income. In a world in which the world interest rate does depend on what happens in the United States, an investment-increasing tax change would drive up interest rates, choking off some (but not all) of the increase.

Conclusion

Our tax system unquestionably imposes costs on the economy, but exactly how large those costs are no one knows for sure. Although no tax system can eliminate these costs entirely, tax reform could succeed in reducing them. Some tax changes that are "good for the economy" eliminate unnecessary and misguided features that are violations of neutral tax treatment of economic activities. In other cases, the economic gains are achieved by reducing tax progressivity and thus loosening the link between tax liability and economic success. Depending on one's views about equity, it may be reasonable to reject any economic gains that come only at the cost of penalizing the poor and middle class. For this reason, these cases must be carefully distinguished. This is a major theme of chapters 6 through 8, where we discuss options for tax reform. Before moving on, however, two other aspects of a good tax system need to be considered—simplicity and enforceability.

5   Simplicity and Enforceability

To this point, we have explored the two fundamental criteria for judging a tax system—how it assigns tax burden to people, and how it affects people's well-being through its effect on the level and growth of prosperity. Both of these desirable features of a tax system are affected by how simple and easy to enforce it is. This chapter begins by examining just how complex our income tax is, what makes it complex, and how one might simplify it. Then we look in more depth at one cause of complexity—tax evasion—and discuss the features of a tax system that make it easy or difficult to enforce.

How Complicated Is Our Tax System?

For several years, *Money* magazine invented a tax situation of moderate but not exceptional complexity and asked a few dozen tax professionals to calculate tax liability. The last time it did this was in 1997, but tax matters haven't gotten easier since then. It got back forty-six different answers from the forty-six professionals who submitted returns, with tax liability ranging from $34,420 to $68,192. The actual tax liability was $35,643, although some legitimate differences in interpreting the law could have changed that total a bit. Not a single preparer turned in an error-free return.[1]

Another springtime ritual of *Money* was to call the Internal Revenue Service (henceforth the IRS) helpline and ask a set of common questions that people face when filling out their tax returns. In 2002, the IRS workers answered only 75 percent of the questions accurately, far short of a perfect score but a large improvement over the 55 percent correct figure reported in 1988.[2] The accuracy percentage jumped even higher to 95 percent in 2014, but the average wait time was nearly twenty minutes and only 64 percent of callers seeking live help received it that same year.[3] In 2014, the Government Accountability Office sent under-cover employees out to have nineteen tax returns prepared at several different outlets of major retail tax preparation chains. Seventeen of the nineteen returns were prepared with errors that led to incorrect refund amounts, with many involving substantial consequences for tax liability. Six returns had errors leading to underpayment of tax by above $3,000 each, and the only return that had errors leading to overpayment of tax led to an overpayment of about $50.[4]

The fact that, in some situations, neither tax professionals nor the IRS itself can be sure of a taxpayer's tax liability is just one indicator of the tax system's complexity. Another is the sheer length of the tax code. Commerce Clearing House's 2015 edition of the unabridged *Internal Revenue Code* sections on income, estate, gift, employment, and excise taxes is 5,296 pages long, while the accompanying *Income Tax Regulations* spans 14,260 pages.[5] As of 2012, the Internal Revenue Code contained nearly four million words.[6] Between 1991 and 2012, the number of sections, subsections, and cross references in the Internal Revenue Code increased from less than 50,000 to nearly 70,000.[7] The number of pages in the instruction book for Form 1040 and associated schedules increased from 60 in 1988 to 214 by 2012.[8]

Although these figures are eye-catching, they are not of direct concern to most taxpayers. Does it matter whether the tax code has 4, 40, or 400 million words, as long as your own tax affairs are straight-forward? In some situations, having a detailed set of rules could even make things simpler if it clears up gray areas in the tax law. Many of these rules have been adopted to stop the increasingly complicated tax-avoidance strategies that some taxpayers and their advisers are continually inventing. Clearly, one needs to dig more deeply than anec-dotes and word or page counts to get a good picture of how complex our tax system is and whether it needs to be simplified.

The Costs of Compliance

One of the most informative measures of tax complexity is the total cost incurred in the process of collecting taxes. This cost includes the budget of the IRS, which in fiscal year 2014 spent $11.6 billion enforcing all varieties of federal taxation, or about 0.4 percent of the gross revenue it collected.[9] The IRS budget—the *administrative cost* of raising taxes—is, however, only the tip of the iceberg of the total cost of collection. It is dwarfed by the cost borne directly by taxpayers, which comprises much of what is known as *compliance cost*. Part of this cost is the money spent on accountants and other tax preparers, software, and tax guidebooks. Compliance cost also includes the expense incurred by third parties to the tax-collection process, such as employers who withhold and remit tax on behalf of their employees and provide information reports to the IRS about these payments. But the largest resource cost of compliance consists of the time that taxpayers devote to doing their taxes and keeping track of the information needed to document their tax liability. Both the monetary outlay and the time spent are resource costs because they could be used for some valuable purpose if it weren't for the tax system.

In order to estimate the compliance cost of taxation, researchers have conducted surveys that ask people, and in some cases businesses, detailed questions about how much time and money they devote to various aspects of the taxpaying process. Analysis of such a survey for tax year 2010, conducted by researchers at the IRS and the Treasury Department's Office of Tax Analysis, suggests that, on average, each taxpayer spent 12.5 hours of his or her own time complying with the federal individual income tax.[10] That amounts to 1.8 billion total hours in aggregate for the United States.[11] In addition, on average, individual taxpayers paid $198 in out-of-pocket tax preparation expenses such as the cost of tax software or help from an accountant.[12] The methodology values each hour taxpayers spend on their taxes at their estimated after-tax wage rates, and adds out-of-pocket expenses for tax preparation, to come up with an overall average compliance cost of $373 per individual income tax return, which amounts to an aggregate cost of $53 billion for the United States as a whole in 2010.[13]

Comparison with similar surveys from previous years suggests that despite the apparent increase in tax complexity, the average amount of time that individual taxpayers spend on their own taxes has been declining over time, and this has only been partly offset by increased out-of-pocket expenditures on tax preparation. An IRS survey for tax year 2007 indicated that the average time spent complying with the individual income tax was nineteen hours per return.[14] A similar study for tax year 2000 implied that individual taxpayers spent an average of 25.5 hours each complying with individual income taxation (about twice as much as in 2010), and spent $182 (in constant year 2010 dollars) out-of-pocket on tax preparation costs on average.[15] That 2000 estimate implied that 3.2 billion hours were spent in aggregate complying with individual income taxation in that year.[16] A survey of Minnesota tax-payers for tax year 1989 suggested each taxpayer devoted 27.4 hours, on average, complying with individual income taxation, and spent an average of $104 (in constant year 2010 dollars) out-of-pocket on tax preparation costs.[17] Increasing use of tax preparation software might explain some of the apparent decline in the amount of taxpayers' own time spent on tax compliance, but varying methodologies across the studies could explain some of the differences as well, creating some uncertainty about the true costs and especially the trends in these costs.[18]

Analysis of the 2010 IRS survey suggests that a bit more than half of the federal individual income tax compliance burden involves "reporting and substantiating income," with deductions, credits, the alternative minimum tax, and other taxes reported on the individual income tax form accounting for the rest.[19] Higher-income people tend to have higher compliance costs in absolute terms, but lower-income people have higher compliance costs relative to their incomes. Taxpayers with AGI of $200,000 or above spent an average of 29.8 hours a year on taxes and had an average compliance cost of $2,331, or 0.5 percent of AGI. Taxpayers with AGI between $50,000 and $75,000 spent an average of 13.4 hours per year on taxes and had an average compliance cost of $380, or 0.6 percent of AGI. Those with AGI between $10,000 and $15,000 spent an average of 10.3 hours per year on taxes and had an average compliance cost of $192, or 1.5 percent of AGI.[20] The IRS data for 2010 also suggests that income tax compliance costs are particularly burdensome for the self-employed, who accounted for 62 percent of the total individual income tax compliance cost in the survey.[21]

While the estimate of $53 billion of compliance costs for individual taxpayers does include costs imposed on sole-proprietorship businesses, it does not count compliance costs imposed on other businesses, such as corporations and partnerships. To be sure, there are many fewer corporate and partnership tax returns than there are personal returns—10.7 million corporate and partnership returns, versus 147.4 million individual returns, were filed in fiscal year 2014.[22] But the amount of time and money spent per corporate and partnership return is much greater. The most up-to-date evidence on this comes from an analysis of a survey of corporations and partnerships of all sizes for the tax year 2009 by IRS and Treasury Department researchers. They estimate that the total cost to corporations and partnerships of complying with federal income taxation in 2009, including direct monetary outlays and the value of the time of personnel devoted to tax compliance, was $104 billion, including $25 billion for C corporations, $36 billion for S corporations, and $43 billion for partnerships.[23] Their data suggest that, similar to individuals, smaller firms face larger tax compliance costs per dollar of sales, which is consistent with the findings of several prior studies.[24] In 2009, the 97.5 percent of corporations and partnerships that had assets below $10 million accounted for just 23 percent of sales receipts but 81 percent of tax compliance costs, which averaged $9,600 per firm, or 1.3 percent of sales receipts. The 2.5 percent of corporations and partnerships that had assets of $10 million or above accounted for 77 percent of sales receipts but only 19 percent of tax compliance costs, which averaged $89,000 per firm, or 0.09 percent of sales receipts.[25]

Surveys of large corporations conducted during the 1990s shed further light on tax compliance costs of big business, and the factors contributing most to those costs. In 1996 the average Fortune 500 company spent about $5.5 million per year on tax matters (in 2014 dollars).[26] That same 1996 survey and another from 1992 suggested that some of the biggest sources of complexity for large corporations were depreciation rules, the alternative minimum tax, lack of uniformity among states and between the federal income tax rules and those used by the states, and the set of rules governing income earned abroad.[27] The last of these was a particularly important source of complexity, accounting for 40 percent of the total cost of compliance for these companies, although foreign operations accounted for less than a quarter of assets, sales, or employment for these large corporations.[28]

The IRS/Treasury studies of 2010 individual income tax compliance costs and 2009 corporate and partnership compliance costs, together with data on the IRS budget, suggest a total annual cost of enforcing and complying with the federal individual and corporate income taxes of about $170 billion.[29] This amounts to 15.6 percent of individual and corporate income tax receipts in fiscal year 2010.[30] That percentage is probably atypically high because tax collections, the denominator of the ratio, were unusually low in 2010, due to a combination of the lasting impact of the 2001 and 2003 tax cuts, a severe recession, and further large temporary tax cuts enacted in an attempt to fight it. Congressional Budget Office projections suggest that nominal personal and corporate income tax receipts will be 79 percent higher in fiscal year 2016 than they were in fiscal year 2010, and it is highly unlikely that

income tax compliance and administrative costs will increase by anywhere near 79 percent over that time span. If compliance and administrative costs were to grow at the same rate as GDP over those years,
for example, then they would amount to 11 percent of personal and
corporate income tax revenue in 2016.[31]

After adjusting for inflation and growth in the number of returns,
the $170 billion estimate for 2010 would be in the same ballpark as our
previous best estimate of the total compliance and enforcement costs
of the income tax: $135 billion (in nominal dollars) for 2004, which
amounted to 13.5 percent of income tax receipts in that fiscal year.[32]
Earlier editions of our book suggested compliance costs in the vicinity
of 10 percent of income tax revenue. The rising percentage over time
reflects a shrinking denominator more than anything—nominal personal and corporate income tax receipts were smaller in 2010 than they
were in 2000.[33] It also reflects significantly higher estimated business
compliance costs in the 2009 tax year study, compared to previous
estimates, which seem to be driven mainly by a combination of better
survey coverage of small businesses and revised methodologies for
estimating costs.

Caution is warranted because any survey-based estimate of tax compliance costs faces the difficulty of separating out the incremental costs
imposed by the tax system from the recordkeeping and accounting
activities that would have been done anyway for personal or business
purposes. Survey designers do the best they can to elicit from respondents just the incremental costs imposed by the tax system, but it is
unclear how accurately survey respondents can separate those out.
Moreover, survey respondents may have a tendency to exaggerate the
costs they incur, for example due to frustration with the tax system and
hope that their answers might help spur reform. On the other hand,
the estimates above do leave out certain compliance costs related to the
tax system, such as costs to nonprofit organizations of maintaining
tax-exempt status, and they make no effort to quantify the "psychic"
costs the tax imposes in the form of anxiety suffered by taxpayers concerned about getting their taxes done on time, having them done right,
and the possibility of an audit.

Others have argued that compliance costs are even higher. For
example, in the 2010 version of "A Roadmap for America's Future,"
Congressman Paul Ryan claimed "The total cost of complying with
the individual and corporate income tax ... amounts to roughly $200
billion per year."[34] Writing for the Tax Foundation, Arthur P. Hall

estimated income tax compliance costs for 1995 that would have amounted to about 19 percent of federal income tax receipts in that year.[35] We think these are overestimates, but agree that the costs are still substantial.

A cost of $170 billion per year is worth taking seriously. This is the dollar value of the time, goods, and services that would be freed up if it were not for the complexity of the tax system. For both cost and fairness reasons, we should take seriously proposals to simplify the tax system. To properly evaluate these proposals, however, it's important to put this cost into its proper perspective.

It's Not Complicated for Everyone

How complex the tax system is depends on who you are. For millions of people without complicated financial affairs, filing a tax return requires writing down, or entering online, wage and interest income, subtracting the personal exemption and standard deduction, and then looking up the tax owed (and in some cases the Earned Income Tax Credit) in the tax tables. If you prefer, the IRS will even do the tax liability calculation for you.

In the 1989 survey of Minnesota taxpayers, unfortunately the most recent such study that sheds light on the heterogeneity of compliance costs, 30 percent of taxpayers spent fewer than five hours on all tax matters over an entire year; 45 percent spent fewer than ten hours, and 66 percent spent fewer than twenty.[36] And as noted above, the average number of hours spent by individuals on tax preparation seems to have declined substantially since then. In any attempt to reform the tax system, we must be careful not to throw the baby out with the bath water and destroy the relative simplicity that already exists for many millions of taxpayers. The tax system is highly complex only for a minority of taxpayers with relatively complicated financial affairs.

However, tax complexity affects even the millions of taxpayers with fairly simple tax returns. For one thing, many of these people believe that others are taking advantage of the complexity to find loopholes that lower their tax liability, leaving them holding the revenue bag. To these people, one attraction of a simple tax system such as a flat tax is its promise of ensuring that high-income people have no way to avoid paying their share. Second, the cost directly borne by businesses due to tax complexity is undoubtedly passed on to individuals in the form of higher prices, lower wages, or lower business or capital income, in just the same way as an explicit tax liability on businesses would be passed through. Although businesses directly incur these costs, the ultimate burden is borne by individuals.

Computers and the Internet are rapidly changing how taxpayers file their tax returns. Increasing numbers of taxpayers are using computers to help prepare and file their tax returns. The IRS estimates that in fiscal year 2014, a total of 125 million individual returns, or 84 percent of the total, were filed electronically, while only 23 million were filed on paper. Of the electronically filed returns, 77 million were submitted by paid preparers and 47 million were submitted by the taxpayers themselves.[37] Since 2012, all professional preparers who file 11 or more tax returns in a year are required to file the returns electronically.[38] In 2014, over 3 million returns were filed using the Free File program, under which the IRS provides free tax preparation software and filing services to people with low and moderate incomes (those with AGI below $60,000 for 2015 returns) and non-software assistance to people with incomes above the cut-off.[39]

There's no question that tax preparation software reduces the burden of filling out tax forms and calculating tax liability; taxpayers need not muck through special worksheets with a calculator at their side to figure out such things as the phase-ins and phaseouts of exemptions, deductions, and credits. However, filling out the form is only one component of the overall compliance burden of the tax system. Tax preparation software does little to reduce the burden of recordkeeping or of transactions undertaken to avoid taxes, although other technologies may be helping to reduce those costs as well.

Is Our Tax System Too Complex?

Is a cost of collecting income taxes somewhere in the range of 10 to 16 cents on the dollar outrageously high, remarkably low, or about right? It is somewhat higher than estimates for European countries, but because the methodologies used are not comparable, it is impossible to know for sure whether our cost per dollar is higher. We suspect it is, though. Even if the U.S. cost of collection is higher, however, a simple comparison of cost per dollar raised could be misleading. A lower cost could mean that the tax is being raised in a sloppy, inequitable way. As an extreme example, we could easily reduce the cost of the taxpaying process if we stopped enforcing it, making it effectively voluntary. But this would place the tax burden entirely on those who view taxpaying as a duty, allowing everyone else to escape with no obligations. Most everyone would agree this is patently unfair and not worth the cost saving of a voluntary tax system. This example illustrates the point that before we dismiss the U.S. system as unnecessarily complex and therefore too costly, we must consider what, if anything, this complexity is buying us. If it is buying us nothing—or something that is not worth the cost—the tax system certainly ought to be simplified.

What Makes a Tax System Complicated?

Tax complexity arises for many reasons. The desire to achieve equity and fairness in the assignment of tax burdens is one. The attempt to encourage certain activities deemed socially or economically beneficial is another. Sometimes, complexity arises as an unfortunate and probably unintended by-product of political compromises and maneuvering. Below, we discuss these and other causes of tax complexity.[40]

Measuring Ability to Pay

One reason that paying for government via the tax system is complicated, costly, and time-consuming is that we are not willing to have one price for all. The line for tickets at a movie theater moves fairly quickly when there is one basic admission price; it moves a bit less quickly when there is a separate charge for seniors, children, and those with discount coupons. It would move more slowly still if each senior citizen and child had to produce identification to prove his or her age; to speed things along, most theaters are willing to take people's word for it. Paying for a meal at a restaurant is usually a simple process, but imagine what it would be like if the bill depended not only on what was ordered but also on the income, number of children, charitable contributions, and annual medical expenditures of each person at the table.

In part, our system is complex because we think that simpler methods of assigning tax burdens are inequitable. Achieving vertical and horizontal equity puts demands on the tax system. First, consider *vertical equity*—the appropriate sharing of tax burdens across families of different levels of well-being. A lump-sum tax, under which each year every adult pays the same amount of tax, period, is the essence of simplicity but is unacceptable to most everyone on equity grounds.[41] Instead, we require that tax liability be tied to how well-off a family is. But as soon as tax liability is tied to some indicator of well-being such as income or consumption, things can start to get complicated fast.

In the income tax system, the basic indicator of well-being is constructed from adding up various sources of income, some more difficult to measure than others. Measuring labor compensation is often straightforward, although it runs into difficulties when fringe benefits are involved or when the compensation can be relabeled as capital income to receive more generous tax treatment. For example, employers can substitute untaxed benefits such as free parking in lieu of wages. Fringe benefits can be a valuable source of labor compensation, but assessing their precise value is difficult. Similarly, the income from working can be repackaged as a capital gain—for instance, by spending time fixing up a home and then selling it. Much executive compensation comes in the form of stock options, the value of which is notoriously difficult to measure accurately when they are granted.

Income earned from owning a business or from financial investments is especially difficult to measure precisely. For example, measuring business income requires assessing how much the business's capital assets have depreciated in value, which is impossible to do precisely. Even the standardized but approximate depreciation deductions used by our tax code require considerable recordkeeping and calculation. When a car is used for business and personal use, how much of the cost of operating the car should be deductible as a business expense? At the personal level, including capital gains in the tax base as they accrue would be prohibitively complex for assets where market values are not readily obtained, and even including capital gains in taxable income only when the asset is sold raises nettlesome problems. Anyone who has sold shares of a mutual fund acquired over many years knows this problem all too well. Other requirements of a completely accurate measure of capital income, such as including the rental value of services from a home and adjusting capital income for inflation, are so complicated that we—and nearly every other country[42]—don't even attempt them. Despite all the compromises we make in our tax code, measuring and reporting capital income are still burdensome tasks for many taxpayers.

The difficulty of administering and complying with taxes based on consumption rather than income depends on how it is done. Imagine the incredible hassle if each household had to keep track of all of its expenditures over the course of the year and report the total to the tax authorities. Alternatively, we could measure each household's consumption as income minus saving, which, if done appropriately, could avoid most of the complexities of measuring income but would require keeping track of all deposits and withdrawals from savings. For the consumption taxes in wide use, such as retail sales taxes or value-added tax (VAT), all tax liabilities are remitted by businesses rather than individuals, which in principle greatly simplifies the taxpaying process relative to a U.S.-style income tax. But removing individuals from the taxpaying process would limit the degree to which tax burdens would vary according to ability to pay or other household characteristics, highlighting the policy trade-off between simplicity and other desirable criteria of a tax system.

Achieving *horizontal equity*—the equal treatment of people with equal ability to pay—also exacts a cost of complexity. If we accept some measure of income or consumption as the basic measure of well-being, how much fine-tuning needs to be done? If two families with the same income are not equally well-off because one has high unavoidable medical expenses and the other doesn't, should that be reflected in tax liabilities? Probably so, but accomplishing this and other adjustments to accurately measure ability to pay inevitably complicates the tax system—in this case, by allowing some medical expenses to be subtracted in calculating taxable income. Again there is a tax policy choice that must be made—how to trade off fine-tuning tax liability for family circumstances against the complexity required to implement that fine-tuning. Substantial simplification will require that we give up on the notion that tax burden must be finely personalized and settle instead on rough justice only.

Taxing Individuals Instead of Taxing at the Business Level
How simple a tax is to administer depends crucially on the mechanics of how the revenue is collected. For example, a consumption tax that (only) requires retail businesses to remit to the government a fixed percentage tax on every sale (a retail sales tax) is much simpler to operate than one that would require each individual consumer to keep records of each purchase and then remit (to the government) some percentage of total purchases. Similarly, in an income tax it is simpler to have employers, financial institutions, and corporations remit tax on various items of income paid to individuals than to have each individual keep track of the income he or she receives and remit tax based on those receipts.

Our income tax system is relatively simple in the areas where it follows this principle and is more complex where it does not. Taxation of wage and salary income is facilitated because employers are required to withhold and remit tax to the IRS based on the wages and salaries of each employee. The information reports they send to the IRS—which detail the payments and provide the Social Security number of the recipient—make it easier to monitor that tax liabilities are collected in a timely manner. Both withholding and information reporting add some compliance burden for the employer but save even more for the employee and, in addition, reduce enforcement costs for the IRS. The more income we treat in this fashion, the simpler the taxpaying process can become. As we discuss in greater detail below, in Japan, the United Kingdom, and indeed about half of all industrialized countries, most employees don't even have to file tax returns in most years.[43] This can work in part because their systems for withholding on wages are more precise than ours and because taxes are withheld not only for wages and salaries but also on other types of income such as interest.

Graduated Tax Rates

The graduation of the income tax rate schedule, with increasing rates applying to swaths of income known as brackets, does not by itself directly contribute any significant complexity to the taxpaying process. Once taxable income is computed, looking up tax liability in the tax tables is a trivial operation that is not perceptibly simplified by having fewer brackets. For those using tax preparation software, it is completely inconsequential for compliance costs because the tax liability calculation is done automatically and instantaneously.

But a graduated rate structure does indirectly add to the complexity of the tax system because it implies that, due to the need to measure income (as an approximation of ability to pay) family by family, the tax system cannot rely solely on tax collection at the business level, but rather must involve individuals in the collection process. For this reason, in conjunction with other changes, having only one tax rate could facilitate a major simplification. If most everyone were subject to the same tax rate, then taxes on some types of income could be remitted at the source of the income payment rather than by the recipient, with little or no reconciliation required of the individual.

The implementation advantage of a single rate is also central to the simplicity of the value-added or retail sales tax. With a single rate with no exemptions, a tax base of aggregate consumption can be achieved with tax remitted entirely by businesses with no involvement of individuals.

A Messy Tax Base

Although society's insistence that the distribution of the tax burden meets some fundamental standards of fairness is responsible for some of the complexity of our current tax system, much additional complexity arises from reasons that may be neither fundamental nor justifiable. Consider the deductions and other tax preferences that complicate and narrow the tax base. The personal code has numerous adjustments, credits, and itemized deductions for things such as home mortgage interest, state and local tax payments, child-care payments, tuition expenses, and the like. At the business level, there are various tax credits, special depreciation rules, and other provisions that apply to certain industries only. Each of these features requires recordkeeping and calculation. Moreover, each deduction or credit involves ambiguities about exactly what kinds of activities qualify. As but one example, the Lifetime Learning Credit is available for "qualified tuition and related expenses." In 2014, the credit could be taken for fees required for enrollment and attendance but not for fees associated with meals, lodging, transportation, or insurance.[44] Further complexity ensues as regulations are written to clarify the ambiguities and as taxpayers come up with new ways to circumvent them.

Just about any time someone comes up with a bright idea about how the government should encourage one activity or discourage another, the tax system gets the call. This is especially true because the current political environment favors tax credits rather than outright expenditures, even if they add up to essentially the same thing. A tax credit for child care expenses is more politically palatable than a direct payment from the government to qualifying families or to child care providers. As a result, our tax system is now an awkward mixture of a revenue-raising system plus scores of incentive and reward programs, and it is much more complicated than it would be if its only function was raising revenue in the most equitable and cost-efficient way possible. Most leading income tax reform plans, including the one proposed in 2010 by President Obama's deficit commission, call for eliminating many of these programs, called *tax expenditures*. (We discuss some of these plans in detail in chapter 8.)

The notion of a "tax expenditure" admittedly seems oxymoronic on the surface. *The Daily Show*'s Jon Stewart mocked President Obama's allusions to cutting tax expenditures, saying, "You managed to talk about a tax hike as a spending reduction. Can we afford that and the royalty checks you'll have to send to George Orwell?"[45] But as we emphasized in the previous chapter, the distinction between government spending and tax cuts can be pretty arbitrary. The late Princeton University economist David Bradford memorably pointed out that we could greatly shrink "the size of government," without changing anything real, by eliminating all government spending on military weapons procurement, and enacting a refundable "weapons supply tax credit" of an equal dollar amount.[46] While this example seems ridiculous, a close examination of the tax code reveals examples only slightly less ridiculous, including, for example, a federal tax credit for chicken manure.[47] The important point for our purposes here is that the practical and political advantages of running what are essentially expenditure programs through the tax code explain a lot of the complexity of our tax system.

As for the practical advantages, although it is generally more efficient to leave economic decisions to the free market, in some situations subsidizing certain activities is entirely appropriate—for example, when an activity generates positive externalities. In these cases, it may be cheaper and simpler to deliver the subsidy through the tax code rather than through a separate program.[48] After all, the administrative machinery already exists for the government to collect money from and, in some cases, remit money to, over 147 million households in their roles as tax filers, and more than 10 million corporations and partnerships.[49] If we as a society decide to subsidize, say, child care expenditures, from a purely administrative point of view it doesn't make sense to set up a separate system for processing child care credit applications and remitting checks to eligible people. Because the IRS is already set up to process tax forms and either subtract the credit from tax liability or send out checks, piggybacking a child care credit onto the taxpaying process is surely cost-effective.[50] Why not keep just one set of accounts—one-stop shopping—between the government and its citizens?

One problem with piggybacking policies onto the revenue-raising system is that some important economic policies that would never be enacted as stand-alone policies are "hidden" in the tax system and therefore remain in place year after year. As an example, consider the political prospects of the following proposal. Suppose that the federal government has decided to subsidize the activities of state and local governments. It has decided not to limit the kinds of activities it will subsidize: municipal swimming pools and golf courses will be treated the same as primary education and fire departments. The subsidy payments will not be made to the state and local governments but instead will be given directly to the resident taxpayers based on their share of state and local tax liabilities. The rate of subsidy, though, will not be the same for all citizens. In fact, only about one-third of households, mostly high-income ones, will receive any subsidy at all; no one else is eligible. Those who do receive subsidies will do so according to several rates of subsidy: 10, 15, 25, 28, 33, 35, and 39.6 percent. Moreover, the higher is a household's income, the higher the rate of subsidy!

This is certainly a very peculiar kind of subsidy program and one that, presumably, would never be passed by Congress. Strange as it sounds, this hypothetical subsidy program is essentially the same as the current federal income tax deduction for state and local taxes. This deduction can be claimed only by the 30 percent of taxpayers who itemize their deductions, who are typically the most affluent of families.[51] The value of the deduction, in terms of tax saved, depends on the household's marginal tax rate, which ranges between 10 and 39.6 percent, and is larger for higher-income households.[52]

Similar parables could be told about the deduction for home mortgage interest, the exclusion of employer-provided health insurance, and a host of other features of the tax code. The point is that these features are enormously popular because they have been enshrined as "tax reductions," but exactly the same features probably wouldn't be as popular, and we surmise would not even survive, as stand-alone spending policies.

Eliminating all of the "bells and whistles" and starting over with a clean tax base would go a long way toward simplifying the taxpaying process. Chapter 6 examines the merits of major preferences in our tax code, considering the equity, economic efficiency, and simplicity aspects of each one. Even when all these factors are considered, many of the exceptions to a clean base are difficult to justify. Whether the political system is ready to undertake such a hard-headed analysis remains an open question.

Institutional Pressures Favoring Complexity

One reason that our tax base is a mess has nothing to do with principles: strong political and institutional factors bias the U.S. tax system toward greater complexity. Under the current system, being a member of one of the tax-writing congressional committees— either the House Ways and Means Committee or the Senate Finance

Committee—is a plum assignment. For example, the average political action committee (PAC) contribution given to a member of the House Ways and Means Committee was 55 percent larger than the average PAC contribution given to other members of the House of Representatives during the 2012 election cycle.[53] Clearly, representatives' potential influence over tax policy leads lobbyists to curry their favor.[54] If Congress were to bind itself to make no major changes in tax law during the next congressional session—or ever again—the contributions would start to dry up, these members' lunch and dinner invitations would taper off, and so on.[55]

Once adopted, tax preferences develop strong lobbies that fight to retain them by financing media campaigns and making campaign contributions to like-minded politicians. For example, the oil industry's leading trade association mounted a newspaper and radio ad campaign in 2012 to defend its tax breaks, such as unusually generous depreciation deductions, against a proposal to limit them that was being considered in the Senate (and that ultimately failed to pass).[56] In contrast, no well-organized constituency opposes the complexity (and inefficiency!) that these tax breaks generate. Yes, business groups bemoan complexity and support tax simplification. But when push comes to shove, they are quite willing to accept a new provision that saves their member corporations $100 million per year in tax liability, even if it means adding a few more staffers and buying some expensive software to do tax and project planning. Yes, individual taxpayers complain about having to keep records of their deductible charitable contributions, but they'd complain even more if this deduction were eliminated—and so would the charities themselves.

To counterbalance these institutional pressures toward greater complexity, several countries have instigated a formal mechanism for making compliance costs more visible during the policy process. For over two decades, the United Kingdom has required its officials to produce compliance cost assessments (CCAs) for all regulations affecting business, including tax regulations. The Netherlands has required qualitative CCAs for changes in tax legislation since 1985, and both New Zealand and Australia have similar requirements. The Internal Revenue Service Restructuring and Reform Act of 1998 contains a provision requiring the Joint Committee on Taxation to provide a "tax complexity analysis" for any change in tax law being considered by Congress that has widespread applicability to individuals or small businesses.[57] This analysis includes an estimate of the cost to taxpayers of complying with the provision and a statement about whether tax-payers would be required to keep additional records. As in the other countries with CCAs, this provision is designed to focus attention on complexity and offset the built-in institutional biases that perpetuate it. These reports attract virtually no media attention and seem to have little or no impact on policy, however.

Phaseouts, Phase-Ins, and Floors

In some cases, complexity creeps into the tax system because legislators desire to obfuscate their true intent. This was certainly the case in 1990, when Republicans averse to further increases in the top income tax rate settled instead for a variety of difficult-to-administer luxury taxes. Another example is the proliferation of "phase-ins" and "phaseouts" of various exemptions, deductions, and credits that now litter the tax code. In almost all cases, these features are exactly equivalent to raising the marginal tax rate a few percentage points in certain income ranges, and so they are just a way of raising tax rates without making it obvious to the public.[58] In other cases, the goal is to limit the benefits of certain credits such as the Earned Income Tax Credit (EITC) and the child and dependent care credits to families below a certain income range. Again, one effect of these phaseouts is to increase the effective marginal tax rate on income: losing a credit as your income rises has the same effect as paying more tax. In the 2015 version of the personal income tax, there are 18 separate provisions that are gradually phased out as income increases.[59]

Attempts to Limit Tax Avoidance and Evasion

Taxpayers can reduce their tax liabilities in a wide variety of ways. The legal ways, such as using legitimate itemized deductions or taking advantage of tax code provisions in ways unintended by Congress, are called by economists *tax avoidance*. The illegal ways, such as failing to report income or overstating deductions, are called *tax evasion*. Because of the amount of money at stake, people and companies are continuously developing new and ingenious ways of achieving both. Government attempts to curb these activities often make the tax code even more complicated and burdensome, even to those who never contemplate pursuing evasion or even avoidance. Countless intricate regulations—such as the alternative minimum tax and passive-loss restrictions—are geared toward minimizing or preventing tax-reduction strategies.

It follows that one way of achieving simplification would be to scale back government efforts to curb avoidance and evasion. But in some other cases, halting these efforts could have a major cost in terms of additional avoidance and evasion, making the tax system considerably less fair and less efficient.

Minimum Taxes

Eliminating the alternative minimum taxes (AMTs) in the personal and corporate codes must come high on the list of options for simplifying the tax system. The personal AMT, discussed in chapter 2, is a complicated tax that has little justification on policy grounds. It was originally enacted in an effort to ensure that high-income people could not lower their tax liability below some minimum level through aggressive use of questionable deductions and loopholes. But by 2012, 89 percent of the value of "tax preference" items that make people subject to the AMT came from the itemized deduction for state and local taxes, personal exemptions, and the standard deduction, which are not the sort of "loopholes" that motivated the adoption of the tax.[60] Moreover, if the concern is that some of the deductions taken by high-income taxpayers are unjustified, a simpler and more logical approach would be to limit those deductions directly. Now that the American Taxpayer Relief Act of 2013 (ATRA) has made a higher AMT exemption "permanent" and indexed it for inflation, the threat that the AMT would grow to affect a huge portion of taxpayers is gone, and the share of individual taxpayers affected by the AMT is projected to fluctuate between 4.3 and 4.6 percent over the next ten years.[61]

At the corporate level, the AMT requires many businesses to do a tremendous amount of extra accounting, often without even knowing whether they will be subject to it. The corporate AMT raised only $3.5 billion of revenue in 2012, yet many corporations cite this as one of the most complicated and burdensome aspects of the taxpaying process.[62] The AMT is also in many cases inefficient because it mismeasures income and sometimes can force companies with real economic losses to owe tax.

Eliminating both the corporate and personal AMTs would substantially simplify the taxpaying process and reduce compliance burdens. The stumbling block in practice is that eliminating the personal AMT, in particular, would cost a large amount of revenue—an estimated $372 billion from 2016 through 2025.[63] Of course, the revenue losses from eliminating the AMT could be offset by an upward adjustment in the ordinary tax rates that apply over income ranges where many people would otherwise face the AMT. In the long run, this would give us a simpler tax system, and it could on average have little net impact on the tax liabilities faced by people in each income class.

The AMTs are symptomatic of a tendency in U.S. politics to offer ever more tax preferences throughout the code, and then to enact additional complex provisions to limit the resulting damage in terms of revenue and distributional effects. They are akin to the extensive use of "phaseouts" in this regard. We see a similar tendency potentially playing out in the debate over the "Buffett Rule." As we discussed in chapter 3, while the income tax is indeed quite progressive *on average*, there is considerable diversity in effective tax rates across high-income people, with some of the very rich paying individual income taxes that are a smaller percentage of their incomes than typical people in the middle class. The Obama administration and billionaire Warren Buffett have advocated for tax reform that would rectify this situation, producing a tax system that is more uniformly progressive and horizontally equitable. While this is a principled position about which reasonable people can differ, some incremental proposals to address this issue, such as the "Fair Share Tax" proposed in the Obama administration's fiscal year 2014 budget (roughly similar to the Buffett tax proposals discussed in chapter 3), take the unattractive approach of adding yet another complicated minimum tax with many of the same drawbacks as the AMT. If one thinks that the provisions that cause variation in effective income tax rates among high-income people—such as excessive deductions and preferential tax rates on dividends and capital gains—are objectionable on equity grounds, it would certainly be better from the perspective of reining in the growth of tax code complexity to modify those provisions directly, as opposed to maintaining them in their current forms while adopting another complicated minimum tax to reduce their effects.[64]

Duplicative Provisions

Another aspect of the income tax code that causes largely needless complication is the duplication of features that serve the same purpose. For example, numerous different tax credits, deductions, and special accounts are designed to subsidize higher-education expenditures, and a multitude of others to promote retirement saving. The same goals can be achieved while consolidating the programs. Similarly, the EITC, Child Tax Credit, and personal exemption all serve similar purposes

but have different rules (for instance, each imposes a different definition of an "eligible dependent child") and require different calculations.
These could be consolidated into a single feature that accomplishes
essentially the same objectives and does so much more simply. Many
of the current tax reform proposals, some of which we will consider
later in this book, aim to consolidate and simplify these provisions.[65]

Reason for Hope: Technological Improvements and the Promise of a Return-Free System

Modernization of IRS operations and advances in tax preparation technology promise continual, although gradual, improvement in the tax-
filing process. The most notable recent innovations are electronic filing
and, especially, the use of software to prepare tax returns. As noted
above, a lot of progress has already been made in shifting toward electronic filing, and the rapid growth in the use of tax preparation software may have contributed to an apparently substantial decline over
time in the number of hours that taxpayers report devoting to the
tax-filing process. By fiscal year 2014, 84 percent of individual income
tax returns were filed electronically.[66] Technological advance promises
continued gradual improvements of this nature in the future.

Before we get too self-congratulatory, we should point out that in
many other countries, such as the United Kingdom and Japan, most
taxpayers need not file a return at all! These countries manage this by
having a very simple tax base for most taxpayers and a sophisticated
system of employer withholding (called PAYE, or Pay As You Earn, in
the United Kingdom) that ensures that at year-end exactly the appropriate amount of tax has been withheld and remitted to the tax authority by employers: no refund is received, and no tax is due. This system
is facilitated by the fact that interest and dividend income are taxed at
the source of payment at a fixed rate applying to the vast majority of
taxpayers; in addition, because the system is individual-based rather
than family-based, it is easier to get withholding of tax liabilities right
for two-earner couples. Withholding can accurately reflect itemized
deductions if they are implemented in certain ways. For instance, in
the United Kingdom, when there was still a income tax subsidy for
mortgage interest, the tax saving from deductibility of mortgage interest at a flat 15 percent rate was applied directly at the bank level.[67]
Similarly, the United Kingdom's government directly provides
approved charitable organizations with a matching contribution equal
to 25 percent of individual donations to those organizations, and many

taxpayers take advantage of this through payroll deductions administered by the employer. For most taxpayers this is the only tax benefit available for donations, so there is no need to file a tax return to report donations and claim tax benefits. Only the small minority of taxpayers with marginal income tax rates above 25 percent need file "self-assessment" returns to claim additional tax benefits for their charitable donations.[68] The United Kingdom's experience clearly demonstrates the potential for operating an income tax system where most people don't have to file a return.[69]

In fact, at least thirty-four countries use some version of a no-return system for some of their taxpayers.[70] Almost all of these countries use some form of exact withholding as in the United Kingdom, but some countries such as Denmark and Sweden achieve it with a system called *tax agency reconciliation* (TAR).[71] Under a TAR system, the tax authority calculates tax liability based on information provided by the taxpayer, employers, and other institutions, and then provides taxpayers with a prefilled, or pre-populated return. Taxpayers have a chance to review (and contest) these calculations, after which refunds or additional tax payments may be needed. The OECD reports that in 2013, eight countries (Chile, Denmark, Finland, Lithuania, Malta, Norway, Spain, and Sweden) provided prefilled income tax returns to the majority of their taxpayers, and in six other countries some, but less than half, of all taxpayers used prefilled returns.[72]

In 2004, the state of California instituted a pilot TAR system with prefilled returns called ReadyReturn for the 11,620 taxpayers who volunteered to use it.[73] Joseph Bankman, a Stanford law professor who helped design and promote the ReadyReturn program, emphasizes that tax authorities already have the information needed to fill out much of the tax return for most people, just as credit card companies have the information necessary to deliver an itemized bill to their customers, and notes that unlike the U.S. tax authorities, VISA does not send its customers "a blank sheet and ask [them] to write down all their transactions."[74] In 2013, 77,611 California taxpayers took advantage of the ReadyReturn program, while 2 million were eligible to do so.[75] The program has reportedly worked smoothly for those who participated (97 percent of participants who responded to a survey about it reported they would use it again), but growth was hampered by lack of a marketing budget, low public awareness, and a lobbying campaign against it funded by the makers of TurboTax. In 2015, the state of California replaced the ReadyReturn program with a new electronic tax filing service called CalFile, which incorporated many of ReadyReturn's best features, including the ability to import information already in government records while filing a return.[76] Lobbying campaigns financed by tax preparation software companies, together with opposition by conservative anti-tax activist Grover Norquist, have also hindered nascent efforts to promote a return-free system at the federal level.[77]

Note that establishing either a return-free or tax agency reconciliation system for many taxpayers accomplishes what might be called "populist simplification," because while it completely eliminates the hassle of tax filing for a large number of people it does not address the difficult issues of complexity that would continue to affect businesses and many high-income households. For example, neither system could handle business income, nor could they handle some of the credits and itemized deductions in our current system. Thus, unless there is substantial simplification of the tax base, a significant fraction of taxpayers would still have to compile and file a return.

Some experts advocate that the United States institute a data retrieval system, under which taxpayers and paid preparers could view, access, and download tax information from a secure database maintained by the federal government, thus relieving them of having to obtain this information form employers, financial institutions, and other third parties as they have to now. Supporters argue that having such a platform would facilitate communication between the IRS on the one hand, and between taxpayers and preparers on the other.[78]

Tax Evasion, Avoidance, and Enforcement

Tax evasion, tax avoidance, and IRS enforcement of the tax law have drawn a lot of attention lately. For example, in 2010 news broke of a whistle-blowing former Swiss banker named Rudolf Elmer, who gave documents to the IRS that allegedly detailed offshore tax evasion by "more than 100 trusts, dozens of companies and hedge funds and more than 1,300 individuals," achieved in part by routing money through subsidiaries in the Cayman Islands.[79] Apparent aggressive use of international tax shelters by some of America's largest corporations, including General Electric, Starbucks, and Apple, has made headlines repeatedly in recent years in the United States, and even more so in the United Kingdom.[80] And in mid-2013, the news featured two IRS scandals: one involving IRS employees who allegedly used political criteria to help determine which applications for tax-exempt status should get extra scrutiny, and another involving excessive spending on conferences and training videos.[81] The Republican-controlled House Appropriations Committee voted to slash the IRS budget by 24 percent as punishment.[82] Meanwhile, Nina Olson, the National Taxpayer Advocate, who heads the Taxpayer Advocate Service (mission statement: "As an independent organization within the IRS, we help taxpayers resolve problems with the IRS and recommend changes that will prevent the problems"), issued reports arguing that an already shrinking IRS budget was hindering the agency's ability to effectively and fairly administer the tax code in the face of an increasingly complex mission.[83]

Why Enforcement Is Necessary

Human nature being what it is, announcing a tax-base definition, setting tax rates, and then relying on taxpayers' sense of duty to collect over a trillion dollars of taxes every year just won't work. If the IRS did not exist, undoubtedly some dutiful people would pay what they owe, but many others would not. Over time, the ranks of the dutiful would shrink as they see how they are being taken advantage of by others.

We cannot rely on voluntary contributions because the benefits of citizenry that are funded by taxation do not depend on one's payment of income taxes.[84] The auto mechanic who on the weekends also paints houses for cash without reporting his painting income to the IRS still has access to the national parks. The trucker who overstates his expenses on gas will still be protected by our system of national defense. The same goes for the investment banker who sets up a credit card account in the Cayman Islands to evade taxes. Even if everyone agrees that the government should collect taxes to provide highways, defense, and everything else the government does, with no enforcement system many would still not find it in their individual economic interest to contribute voluntarily to the government's coffers. Each citizen has a strong incentive to "free ride" on the tax "contributions" of others because one individual's contribution is just a drop in the bucket and doesn't materially affect what that person gets back from the government.

For this reason, paying taxes must be made a legal responsibility of citizens. In the United States, failure to pay taxes in a timely manner is a civil offense that subjects taxpayers to a variety of penalties. Fraud can lead to criminal charges and jail sentences, although this is a rare occurrence. Even in the face of those penalties, substantial tax evasion persists—how much we discuss below.

Tax Evasion and the Case of the 7 Million Vanishing Exemptions
Stories of tax evasion by the wealthy and famous tend to make the headlines. For example, in 2008, movie actor Wesley Snipes was sentenced to three years in federal prison for failing to file federal income tax returns from 1999 through 2001 despite earning millions of dollars during those years.[85] In 2012, Grammy winning musical artist Lauryn Hill pled guilty to failing to pay income taxes on over $1.8 million of income.[86] More recently the news has been full of stories of tax avoidance and evasion by wealthy individuals and corporations through offshore tax havens, an issue we'll consider in more depth a bit later. But evasion on a smaller scale is also a pervasive phenomenon.

One fascinating example from the 1980s involved exemption allowances for dependents. For a long time, the IRS had suspected that many taxpayers were claiming exemptions for dependents that either did not exist or did not qualify as dependents under the tax law. An IRS employee by the name of John Szilagyi thought that this was costing the Treasury—and ultimately all other taxpayers—hundreds of millions of dollars each year, and he suggested the following change in the tax return: to claim an exemption allowance for a dependent over the age of five, you must report the dependent's Social Security number.

When implemented in tax year 1987, the effect of this change was astonishing to everyone, with the possible exception of Szilagyi himself. Between tax years 1986 and 1987, the number of dependent exemption allowances claimed fell by 7 million. This simple change increased tax revenues by about $3 billion per year, or approximately $28 per taxpayer.[87] Undoubtedly, a few of the 7 million cases represented legitimate dependents whose parents or guardians just hadn't gotten around to obtaining Social Security numbers for them, and a few others were children who had been improperly claimed by both parents after a divorce. But certainly the great majority represented people who were simply inventing dependents.[88]

Fraudulent tax refund claims provide another salient example of a small-time tax evasion scheme that is starting to add up to some real money. In 2014, the IRS identified 2.2 million tax returns claiming $15.7

billion in fraudulent refunds.[89] Prisoners, in growing numbers, have been filing fraudulent returns claiming refundable credits. The number of fraudulent prisoner tax returns identified by the IRS more than quintupled from 18,103 tax returns in 2004 to 137,883 tax returns in 2012, while the value of refunds claimed by prisoners that were ruled fraudulent and blocked by the IRS rose from $54.6 million to $936 million during the same period.[90]

How Much Tax Evasion Is There?

Most people don't have to read about such episodes of tax evasion to be convinced that it exists. Moreover, reciting anecdotes does not convey any sense about whether tax evasion is a big problem or a little problem, or what kinds of evasion are important. For obvious reasons— would you answer honestly survey questions about tax evasion?—it is difficult to determine the magnitude of tax evasion. Although measuring how much tax is collected is easy enough, measuring what *should* be paid is not at all easy.

The IRS has, though, periodically estimated what it calls the *tax gap*, meaning the amount of tax that should have been paid but wasn't. The IRS calculates the tax gap by combining information obtained from a special program of intensive random audits with information from special studies about sources of income, such as tips, that are difficult to uncover even in an intensive audit.[91] The procedure for estimating the tax gap is an imperfect one, and even the IRS would admit that its measures are only approximations. In addition, some types of evasion that are especially difficult to uncover, such as unreported income from illegal activities, are not included in the estimate.

The most recent tax gap study was completed in 2016, based on data from the tax years 2008 through 2010.[92] Considering all federal taxes, the overall gross tax gap estimate came to an average of $458 billion per year, which amounted to 18.3 percent of actual (paid plus unpaid) tax liability. Of the $458 billion, the IRS expected to recover $52 billion in enforced tax payments, fines, and late fees, resulting in a "net tax gap"—that is, the tax that should have been paid but that is never collected—of $406 billion on average for the tax years 2008 through 2010, which was 16.3 percent of the tax that should have been reported.

The gross individual income tax gap was estimated to average $319 billion annually during 2008 through 2010. The corporate income tax gap was estimated at $44 billion per year. About 7.0 percent of the gross tax gap was due to non-filing, another 8.5 percent due to tax underpayments, and the remaining 84.5 percent was due to underreporting.

Why Is Tax Evasion a Problem?

For the sake of argument, let's take the IRS tax gap study's conclusion at face value and assume that between 2008 and 2010 there was about $406 billion of tax evasion per year for all federal taxes taken together. Why is that a problem? One straightforward answer is that if evasion vanished, then the deficit could be $406 billion lower than otherwise. Alternatively, we could spend $406 billion more per year to finance health research, job training, transportation infrastructure, a stronger military, and a host of other potentially worthy projects. Or the revenues raised from eliminating evasion could be used to finance a cut in tax rates for everyone, thus benefiting compliant taxpayers.

But these are not very satisfactory answers to the question. Deficit reduction or expanding government programs could be achieved in a number of other ways, such as raising tax rates or broadening the income tax base. A tax rate reduction could be financed by cuts in overall spending. The real question is whether policies that curb evasion would improve the equity and efficiency of how we tax ourselves.

Consider the following hypothetical example. Imagine that all Americans automatically "discounted" their legal tax liability by 20 percent, sort of the way that most car buyers presume that the actual price of a car is considerably below the sticker price. Thus, all families whose true tax liability was $15,000 remitted (or had their employers remit for them) $12,000; families that legally owed $50,000 forked over $40,000, and so on. Imagine further that the IRS looked the other way.

In this imaginary world, tax evasion wouldn't matter much at all. Government would simply readjust everyone's "sticker-price" tax liability upward so that the desired amount of tax would be collected, even after the 20 percent "discount" was taken. Each taxpayer might think that he or she is beating the system, but in fact no one gains compared to a world with no evasion. In this example, evasion is just a shell game that no one wins or loses, and spending money on enforcing the tax laws would be a waste.

But a lot of things are wrong with this picture as a description of real-life tax evasion, things that turn tax evasion from the benign phenomenon of this imaginary world to one that has important negative implications for equity and efficiency. First and foremost, not everyone evades tax by the same proportionate amount. Some people evade a great deal, while others engage in little or no evasion at all. Not surprisingly, in surveys that ask outright about past tax evasion, the vast majority deny cheating. But some do admit it, and a small minority express no moral compunction about it. In a 1991 Gallup poll, 95 percent of respondents answered "no" to the question "have you ever cheated on your federal income taxes, or not?"[93] In a 2005 Blum & Weprin / NBC poll, 85 percent of respondents said they had never even been "tempted" to cheat on their taxes.[94] A survey conducted by the IRS Oversight Board in 2014 asked an anonymous random sample of Americans "how much, if any, do you think is an acceptable amount to cheat on your income taxes?" In the survey, 86 percent chose "not at all," 6 percent chose "a little here and there," 5 percent chose "as much as possible," and 2 percent chose not to answer.[95]

By contrast, analysis of the data from the IRS randomized audits used to estimate the 2001 tax gap suggested that 32 percent of individual income tax payers in that year had misreported items on their tax return that led to an understatement of tax liability of at least $100.[96] Another analysis of the same data suggested that about 13 percent of all individual income tax returns had "errors" in the reporting of itemized deductions for cash charitable contributions, which amounted to 45 percent of returns claiming such deductions. On average, returns with such errors overstated the contributions by $811.[97] Overall, audit data suggest that cheating on taxes in the United States is significantly more common than self-reported survey data would indicate, but that the majority of people are reporting tax liabilities that are accurate or quite close to true liabilities, with tax evasion involving large dollar amounts confined to a small minority.

The propensity of individuals to evade varies because of differences in personal characteristics, such as intrinsic honesty and willingness to gamble, and also because of varying opportunities and potential rewards for evasion. As long as people differ in these characteristics or opportunities, evasion can cause substantial inequities and inefficiencies. Evasion creates horizontal inequity because otherwise equally well-off people end up with different burdens. Unlike the imaginary 20 percent "discount" example presented above, tax rates cannot be adjusted to offset the advantage gained by the free-riding evaders. To the extent that opportunities or predilections for evasion are related to level of well-being (for instance, if the rich could evade more easily than the poor), the tax rate schedule can, in principle, be adjusted to offset on average the systematic income-related evasion; but, even in that case, evasion makes it difficult to achieve whatever degree of progressivity we deem to be consistent with vertical equity.

In a sense, tax evasion is a gamble like any other, with a chance of coming out ahead and a chance of coming out behind. Indeed, the standard economic model of evasion is essentially the same as the model used to explain other choices people make under uncertainty, such as how risky a portfolio to have or how much insurance to purchase.[98] As you would expect, the evidence clearly shows that the lower the chance of getting caught, the more likely people are to try to get away with tax evasion. This is borne out by the data in table 5.1, which presents information from IRS tax gap studies about the compliance rates (the percentages of true income that is reported) for different types of income in tax years 2001 and 2008–2010. In 2001, the compliance rate ranges from 99 percent for wages and salaries (taxes on which are difficult to evade successfully because of employer reports to the IRS) down to 28 percent for farm net income. Strikingly, the reporting percentage for nonfarm sole proprietors is estimated to be only 43 percent, so in other words 57 percent of true income of this group is *not* reported, according to the IRS. Moreover, noncompliance of sole proprietors by itself accounted for 35 percent of the overall individual tax gap. The 2008–2010 data groups types of income into broader categories, but basically corroborates the findings from 2001. In 2008–2010, for "amounts of income subject to little or no information reporting," including self-employment and farm income, rents and royalties, etc., about 37 percent of income was reported to the IRS, and this accounted for 72 percent of all income underreporting. The estimated compliance rates in 2008–2010 were again much higher for the types of income that involve more and better information reporting and especially withholding. These facts suggest that significant horizontal inequities persist because of evasion, with caveats noted below in some cases where market adjustments mitigate these inequities.

On average, higher-income people underreport a larger share of their true incomes. Analysis of data from the intensive random audits conducted by the IRS for the 2001 tax gap study suggests that those with true AGI above $100,000 on average failed to report 15.2 percent of their true AGI to the IRS, compared to 7.0 percent for those with true AGI below $100,000. Once again, there was a large amount of heterogeneity in underreporting across people within the same

Table 5.1
Compliance estimates for selected types of personal income, 2001 and 2008–2010

Type of personal income	Examples	Reported net income as a percentage of true net income from this source	Percentage of individual income tax underreporting of income contributed by this item
In **2001**:			
Wages and salaries		99	5
Pensions and annuities		96	2
Interest and dividends		96	2
Capital gains		88	6
Partnerships, S corporations, estates, and trusts		82	11
Nonfarm proprietor income		43	35
Farm net income		28	3
In **2008–2010**:			
Amounts subject to substantial information reporting and withholding	Wages and salaries	99	3
Amounts subject to substantial information reporting	Pensions and annuities, unemployment compensation, dividend income, interest income, Social Security benefits	93	8
Amounts subject to some information reporting	Partnership and S corporation income, capital gains, alimony income	81	17
Amounts subject to little or no information reporting	Nonfarm proprietor income, other income, rents and royalties, farm income, Form 4797 income	37	72

Source: Internal Revenue Service (2007, 2016b).

income groups, with most of the underreporting coming from people with substantial self-employment, pass-through-entity, or capital gains income.[99]

Tax evasion not only compromises the equitable sharing of tax burdens; it also imposes economic costs. Other things being equal, income tax evasion requires higher tax rates, which makes extra work and saving less attractive to honest taxpayers. This is partially offset by lower effective tax rates on the evaders but not enough to make up fully for the distortion to income-earning activities.

More important, because it is easier to get away with tax evasion in certain circumstances, there is an incentive—which is inefficient from a social point of view—to pursue these circumstances. As an example, consider the market for house painting, where payment is often made in cash, to facilitate tax evasion. Because the cash income from house painting is hard for the IRS to detect, this occupation is more attractive than otherwise. The supply of eager housepainters bids down the market price of a house-painting job, so that the amount of taxes evaded overstates the benefit of being a tax-evading housepainter, and comparing taxes actually remitted may overstate the extent of horizontal inequity. The biggest loser in this game is the honest housepainter, who sees his or her wages bid down by the competition but who dutifully pays taxes.

Although a supply of eager and cheap housepainters undoubtedly is greeted warmly by most prospective buyers of that service, it is also a symptom of an economic cost of tax evasion. The work of the extra people drawn to house painting, or to any activity that facilitates tax evasion, would have higher value in some alternative occupation. This is just an example of the principle, discussed in chapter 4, that deviations from a uniform tax system, uniformly enforced, have economic costs.

Corporate Tax Shelters and Profit Shifting by Multinational Firms
In 2013, a congressional panel concluded that Apple Inc., which had recently become the world's most valuable company, had avoided billions of dollars in corporate income taxes through the use of international tax shelters, shifting "at least $74 billion [of income] from the reach of the Internal Revenue Service between 2009 and 2012."[100] In 2010, General Electric reported $14.2 billion in worldwide profits, and claimed to owe no U.S. corporate income tax.[101] Also in 2010, it was reported that Google had reduced its effective corporate tax rate to 2.4

percent through the use of complex tax planning strategies with names such as "Double Irish" and "Dutch Sandwich," saving the company $3.1 billion in taxes from 2007 through 2009.[102] Earlier in the 2000s, newspapers were filled with headlines about corporations such as Enron that were dodging their U.S. corporate income tax obligations at the same time they were deceiving their shareholders about their financial health and prospects.

Something is going on for sure, but the headlines don't capture the subtleties of this topic. First of all, there is no consensus even on how to define a *tax shelter*. Some would apply the term to a broad range of activities that help taxpayers to either (legally) avoid taxes or (illegally) evade taxes, while others would limit the term to transactions that have no purpose but to reduce taxes and that technically violate the law. Avoidance opportunities often arise from the difficulty of measuring true economic income and the resulting compromises that the tax code makes in defining income. Tax avoidance often involves principles such as tax arbitrage (taking advantage of differences in tax rates applied to technically different, but essentially similar, entities or different types of income or deductions) and deferral of taxes (made possible, for example, by taxation of capital gains on realization or reinvestment of profits earned by an offshore subsidiary in a low-tax country). These activities may be combined with efforts to improperly re-characterize income or payments into forms that receive favorable tax treatment (for example, converting ordinary income into capital gains or labeling nondeductible repayments of debt principal as deductible interest payments) or to create fictional losses, many of which cross over the line into tax evasion. Efforts of this sort can be embedded in a series of complicated transactions that are extraordinarily difficult to track. Some of these activities are perfectly legal and some are not, and in many cases it is unclear whether they are legal or not. Tax shelters often capitalize on ambiguities in the law or on complicated situations that were not foreseen by drafters of the law. These ambiguities are sometimes resolved eventually by the IRS, the courts, or Congress, but can produce significant tax savings in the meantime.

The most obvious, and probably most consequential, form of corporate tax shelter involves multinational corporations artificially shifting profits from countries with high corporate tax rates (such as the United States) to foreign subsidiaries in low-tax countries. As explained in chapter 2, foreign subsidiaries of U.S. corporations do not owe U.S.

corporate income tax on their profits until those profits are repatriated to the United States (usually in the form of dividends). When the profits are eventually repatriated to the United States, the U.S. parent corporation must remit to the United States the amount by which the U.S. corporate income tax on those profits exceeds the corporate tax already remitted on those profits to the government of the country where the foreign subsidiary is located. So for example, if the Irish foreign subsidiary of a large U.S. corporation earns $100 million in taxable profits, it will owe $12.5 million in corporate tax in that year to the Irish government (because Ireland has a 12.5 percent corporate tax rate), and will owe $22.5 million to the United States (the difference between U.S. tax liability at the 35 percent U.S. corporate tax rate and Irish tax liability) only when the profits are sent back to the United States. The liability to the United States may be deferred indefinitely by reinvesting the profits in the foreign country. U.S. owners of the company can still benefit from the foreign profits right away, because they increase the value of the firm and produce capital gains on shares of ownership. As explained in more detail in chapter 2, deferring the U.S. portion of the tax can greatly reduce the present value of the tax burden, because the U.S. tax that otherwise would have been due when the profits are made can instead be reinvested and earn returns for the duration of time that the tax is deferred.[103]

One way that multinational corporations shift U.S. profits to foreign subsidiaries in low-tax countries is by manipulating "transfer pricing." Transfer prices are the prices that different parts of the same company pay to each other for things such as business inputs or the right to use intellectual property. Profits can be shifted from the United States to low-tax countries if the U.S. parent firm charges artificially low prices for what it sells to its foreign subsidiaries, and pays artificially high prices for what it purchases from its foreign subsidiaries. So, for example, a U.S. auto manufacturer with an Irish subsidiary might sell auto parts that are worth $100 to the subsidiary for only $40. Or a U.S. pharmaceutical firm might have its Irish subsidiary manufacture and sell its drugs, and charge artificially low royalty rates for the intellectual property embodied in those drugs, when the research and development for the drug was done in the United States. Alternatively, the parent firm could try to claim that the (deductible) research and development leading to the drug was mostly done by the U.S. parent company, and then sell the patent for the drug to its Irish subsidiary for an artificially low price.

U.S. tax law requires that firms use an "arm's length" standard to determine transfer prices—that is, goods and services should be bought and sold between different parts of the firm at the same price as they would sell for on the competitive open market between unrelated parties. But this represents an intractable monitoring problem for the IRS, and it is often difficult or impossible for the IRS to prove what the arm's length price would be. This is especially difficult in the case of intellectual property, such as drug patents, computer software, or the customer goodwill that goes with a heavily marketed and trademarked brand such as Coca Cola. Such intellectual property is almost by definition unique to the particular firm that owns it. It is virtually impossible for the IRS to prove what the intellectual property would have sold for in a transaction between unrelated parties, and sometimes it is difficult to determine in which country the development of the intellectual property really occurred.

Is transfer-pricing manipulation an example of legal tax avoidance or illegal tax evasion? Corporations are generally very careful to do only what they can legally get away with. On the other hand, the IRS has successfully prosecuted scores of cases that require companies to remit more tax plus penalties. For example, in 2006 the IRS reached a settlement with pharmaceutical company GlaxoSmithKline that required the company to pay the IRS $3.4 billion for violations of the arm's length transfer-pricing standard from 1989 through 2005.[104] Arguably, abusive transfer-pricing practices that violate the arm's length standard *should* qualify as tax evasion, but in many cases the IRS has neither the resources nor the information necessary to prove it and enforce the law.

It is also worth noting that this problem is by no means unique to the United States. Multinational corporations based in countries other than the United States potentially stand to gain even more by shifting profits to low-tax countries, because almost all other countries now operate a "territorial" corporate tax system that only attempts to tax profits arising from economic activity occurring within their borders. As a result, for multinationals based in countries other than the United States, profits reported as being earned by foreign subsidiaries are usually not ever subject to the corporate income tax of the parent company's home country, even when the profits are repatriated to that country.

Manipulation of transfer pricing is just one particularly important example of a number of different strategies for shifting profits to low-tax countries. For example, multinational corporations also have an incentive to shift their debts to high-tax countries, so that they can deduct the interest on those debts at higher tax rates. One example of a debt-shifting strategy is "earnings-stripping," a classic tax arbitrage maneuver where, for example, a U.S. subsidiary of a foreign parent company located in a low-tax country borrows from the parent firm, producing deductions against the high U.S. tax rate, and interest income that is taxed at the low-tax country's rate.[105] There is also the phenomenon of "stateless income," where some of a multinational firm's profits are not taxed by *any* country. For example, a U.S. multinational corporation might, through a complicated series of transactions, arrange for royalty payments on intellectual property to be paid to a firm that the U.S. tax law treats as a company based in Luxembourg, but that the Luxembourg tax law treats as a company based in the United States, so that neither country ends up taxing the income.[106]

For the same reason that the enforcement arm of the IRS has difficulty proving that tax-motivated international profit shifting is happening and violates the law, it is also difficult for researchers to determine how much U.S. corporate income tax is avoided or evaded in this manner. The IRS estimate of a corporate "tax gap" of $44 billion annually in 2008–2010, that we mentioned earlier, includes at best a tiny portion of the kind of international tax sheltering activity that we are talking about here.[107] There is, however, plenty of compelling circumstantial evidence suggesting that the amount of U.S. corporate tax avoided by shifting profits to low-tax countries is quite large. For example, in 2012, U.S. corporations reported that half of their foreign profits were earned in just seven foreign locations—Bermuda, Ireland, Luxembourg, the Netherlands, Switzerland, Singapore, and the U.K. Caribbean Islands (including, for example, the Cayman Islands and British Virgin Islands)—that had *effective* corporate tax rates (defined here as corporate tax paid to the governments of those countries as a percent of profits reported in those countries) of less than 5 percent. But these locations accounted for only about 5 percent of U.S. multinational corporations' foreign workforce.[108] In 2008, the average profit per worker in foreign subsidiaries of U.S. multinationals was $520,640 in Ireland and $2.6 million in Bermuda, compared to a $40,372 average profit per worker in foreign subsidiaries of U.S. companies worldwide.[109] There is no evidence that employees of multinational corporations' subsidiaries in Ireland and Bermuda are truly endowed with the nearly superhuman productivity these numbers seem to imply, so this surely reflects tax-motivated profit shifting to a large extent.

Economist Kimberly Clausing of Reed College has attempted to systematically estimate how much corporate tax revenue the United States loses through profit shifting based on a statistical analysis of data on the aggregate amount of U.S. multinational corporation profits that were reported as being earned in each foreign country between 1983 and 2012.[110] She estimates how differences in corporate tax rates across countries affect the value of U.S. multinational profits reported in each country, controlling for factors that ought to influence real economic activity such as the level of GDP per capita. She finds that a 1 percentage point increase in the foreign corporate tax rate is associated with between a 1.9 percent to 4.6 percent decline in profits reported in that country, and that shifting of profits to low-tax countries reduced U.S. corporate tax revenues by between $77 billion and $111 billion, or between 24 and 31 percent of corporate tax revenues that would have been collected in the absence of profit shifting. Her estimates also suggest that the fraction of U.S. corporate tax revenue lost to profit shifting has been growing rapidly over time. Interestingly, Clausing does not find evidence that the foreign locations of U.S. multinational corporations' employment or physical capital (plant, property, and equipment) are significantly responsive to corporate tax rates.

A number of other researchers have attempted to estimate the magnitude of corporate profit shifting and its responsiveness to tax rates. Our interpretation is that the best available evidence corroborates the general notion that profit shifting is significant and is responsive to corporate tax rates, although there's significant uncertainty, for example, because all such studies must infer the quantity of profit shifting indirectly from data that are imperfect for this purpose. Gabriel Zucman, an economist at the University of California, Berkeley, infers that the United States loses about 20 percent of its corporate tax revenue to profit shifting by multinationals, based on national accounts data on the share of U.S. corporate profits held in tax haven countries, and evidence on the low rate of repatriation of those profits.[111] Tim Dowd, Paul Landefeld, and Anne Moore of the Joint Committee on Taxation estimate the influence of corporate tax rates on the location of reported profits of U.S. multinational firms using data on those firms' U.S. tax returns from 2002 to 2012. They find that the location of reported corporate profits is more sensitive to changes in corporate tax rates when the tax rate is low than when it is high—at a tax rate of 5 percent, a 1 percent reduction in the tax rate is associated with a 4.7 percent increase in reported corporate profits, whereas at a tax rate of 30 percent, a 1 percent reduction in the tax rate is associated with a 0.7 percent increase in reported corporate profits.[112] Compared to Clausing's study, Dowd, Landefeld, and Moore's evidence implies that relatively more U.S. multinational profits are shifted to countries with very low tax rates, and relatively less are shifted to countries with tax rates that are closer to the U.S. rate (but still below it). Clausing reports in her 2016 study that if she were to adjust her calculations to take this into account, the implied overall amount of tax-motivated profit shifting by U.S. multinationals would be even larger than her main estimates that we reported above.

In a recent review of the broader literature on this topic, Dhammika Dharmapala of the University of Chicago Law School discusses a number of recent studies using firm-level data that seem to suggest a smaller degree of profit shifting than the evidence cited above.[113] These studies estimate the extent to which reported profits of foreign subsidiaries change when the corporate tax rate differential between a subsidiary's host country and its parent company's home country changes. Dharmapala notes, however, that the smaller degree of profit shifting suggested by these studies seems inconsistent with the very large share of profits of multinational corporations that are located in tax havens, leading to something of a "puzzle." It could be, for example, that tax-motivated profit shifting is indeed as large as Clausing suggests, but that the firm-level studies that Dharmapala cites—which focus on the effects of incremental changes in corporate tax rates over time—are finding small effects because both before and after incremental changes in the corporate tax rates of high-tax countries, differentials in tax rates between those countries and tax havens were already so large as to induce companies to shift as much profit to the tax havens as possible. In addition, Clausing and others have emphasized that the firm-level data used in the studies discussed by Dharmapala are actually missing many affiliated firms located in tax havens, so that these studies fail to capture much of the kind of profit shifting activity that the evidence of Dowd, Landefeld, and Moore suggests is most responsive to changes in host-country tax rates.[114] While there is still some uncertainty, we think Clausing's estimates are nonetheless reasonably suggestive of the magnitude of the problem.

There are other kinds of corporate tax shelters, but less evidence is available on how much corporate income escapes taxation through them. Much evidence on tax shelters is anecdotal, but some of these anecdotes are striking, indeed. For example, in 2003 the Joint Tax Committee issued a 2,700-page report largely devoted to explaining the tax shelters used by the Enron Corporation. The eleven specific shelters that could be identified were estimated to have reduced Enron's U.S. tax liability by a total of $257 million, while at the same time increasing the profits Enron reported to its shareholders between 1995 and 2001 by $651 million![115] Following the Enron episode, new regulations and laws were adopted in an effort to combat this kind of tax sheltering activity and to improve the accuracy of reported corporate financial information. For example, the Sarbanes-Oxley Act of 2002 required certification of financial reports by chief executive officers and chief financial officers, among other things. Such regulations and laws have apparently had some impact, but there is little systematic evidence about their effect on the magnitude and nature of corporate tax shelter use.

Regardless of its legality, corporate tax sheltering activity is economically wasteful. While it often makes sense from the individual corporation's perspective, it is inefficient from a societal perspective. It uses up real resources (including the time and effort of the lawyers, accountants, and investment bankers who devise and implement the shelters) that could have otherwise been devoted to some socially productive purpose. It also diverts resources toward particular types of investments or other activities that help facilitate such avoidance behavior. For example, as noted above, the more important intellectual property is to one's business, the easier it is to avoid U.S. corporate taxes by shifting profits to subsidiaries in low-tax countries. This greatly reduces effective corporate tax rates on investments in industries such as pharmaceuticals, computer software, and electronics, favoring them over investments in industries where intellectual property is a smaller part of the business or industries that operate mostly domestically. This helps explain the apparent success of Apple, General Electric, and Google at avoiding U.S. corporate income tax.[116]

In 2011, economist Martin Sullivan estimated effective corporate tax rates of numerous companies based on their most recent company annual reports. General Electric, Merck, and Cisco Systems faced effective tax rates of 3.6 percent, 12.5 percent, and 19.8 percent, respectively, while Aetna, United Health Group, and Walmart were estimated to face effective tax rates of 34.6 percent, 35.4 percent, and 33.6 percent, respectively.[117] Keep in mind that not all multinational corporations are using tax havens to reduce their taxes—the best available estimate suggests that about 41 percent of U.S. corporations with significant foreign operations did not have subsidiaries in tax haven countries.[118] Differences in effective tax rates across firms with different opportunities and willingness to exploit tax shelters can have an economic cost, as they may divert investment away from where it is most productive, and toward marginal investments that are less productive but more tax advantaged.

Policy Responses to Corporate Tax Shelters and Profit Shifting by Multinational Firms

What can be done about corporate tax shelters? Addressing tax shelters is to some extent an issue of enforcement. Expanding efforts by the IRS to uncover tax shelter activities, clarify their legality, and impose penalties for abusive behavior could all reduce sheltering activity. The IRS is faced with a particularly difficult job here, though, as the people who devise tax shelters are highly compensated and highly skilled and seem able to come up with ever more ingenious—indeed, almost diabolical— methods of sheltering corporate income from tax. In 2003, the IRS implemented a regulation creating a list of specific tax-shelter-related transactions that corporations must now disclose to the IRS if the transactions exceed a certain value. This is intended to make it easier for the IRS to monitor such transactions.

Another set of suggestions would exploit the fact that managers of corporations have an incentive to maximize *book income*, the measure of corporate profits reported in financial statements to shareholders, in order to boost share prices. Therefore, many tax shelters attempt to reduce taxable income while leaving unchanged or even increasing reported book income. Some have argued that requiring corporations to report to the public more detailed and informative numbers regarding their taxable income and tax remittances might reduce the incentive to engage in tax shelters and to artificially inflate reported book income. This could have benefits not only for the tax system but also for the efficiency of financial markets. A large gap between profits reported to shareholders and profits reported to the IRS might be taken as a signal that the company has been misleading investors about its true profits. This signal would certainly have been informative in the case of Enron, for example. On the other hand, shareholders' desire for accurate information may be swamped by their desire for low taxes, so it is unclear whether requiring firms to publicly disclose more informative accounting would actually reduce managers' incentives to shrink taxable income and inflate book income. Better information disclosure could make tax shelters more transparent to the public, which might lead to greater pressure to address them. One positive step in this direction was taken starting in 2004, when the IRS added a new schedule in the corporate income tax, the M-3, which requires a more informative accounting of the reasons for differences between book income and taxable income.[119] This allows the IRS to more easily identify and investigate potential tax shelters and to target its resources more effectively. Public disclosure of the M-3, or part of it, could be used to strengthen the effectiveness of the other measures mentioned above.

The measures mentioned above are at best partial solutions, and in particular are unlikely to have a huge effect on international corporate tax avoidance and evasion. In the case of international transfer-pricing manipulation, many tax experts have concluded that better disclosure and administratively feasible efforts at tougher enforcement of the arm's length standard for transfer pricing could help, but would at best make a small dent in the problem.[120] For this reason, making serious progress in cleaning up the mess described above may require major reforms of our tax laws.

One approach would be to try to subject the worldwide profits of U.S.-based multinational firms to U.S. corporate tax (less the credit for foreign taxes paid) immediately, instead of allowing the difference between U.S. tax and foreign tax to be deferred until profits are repatriated to the United States. This would eliminate the gains from transfer-pricing manipulation, and would also increase revenues substantially in present value, which in turn could be used to reduce the corporate tax rate so as to avoid outflow of capital from the United States (a potential response to the fact that now more corporations would actually have to remit U.S. corporate tax on the full value of their U.S. and foreign profits, instead of on just the smaller portion of their U.S. profits that they could not shift offshore). A more targeted approach would be to eliminate deferral just in cases where objective and easily observable indicators suggest abusive transfer-pricing manipulation is likely (e.g., cases of investment in subsidiaries located in countries on a designated list of "tax havens").[121]

A potential problem with ending deferral is that this would also increase the incentive for a U.S. parent company to change its country of incorporation, enabling it to avoid U.S. tax on its non-U.S. profits altogether. Indeed, this has already been happening in the form of corporate "inversions," where U.S. multinational companies merge with companies in low-tax countries that do not tax foreign income, changing their legal domicile. Between 1982 and early 2016, more than fifty U.S. corporations moved their tax residences to low-tax countries through inversions, with twenty of those occurring since 2012. Prominent recent examples of inversions have included Eaton Corporation and Medtronic (both to Ireland) and Burger King (to Canada).[122] One potential response to this is to change the tax laws and regulations governing inversions so as to make "inverting" more difficult. The Obama administration's Treasury Department took this approach in early April 2016, releasing over 300 pages of administrative regulations addressing various aspects of international corporate tax avoidance, including inversions. For example, existing U.S. law already specified that if a U.S. corporation merges with a foreign firm, the foreign acquirer must own more than 20 percent of the combined new company in order for the IRS to accept that the tax residence of the combined company has moved to the foreign nation for tax purposes, and it must own more than 40 percent to avoid certain onerous regulations. Foreign firms planning to merge with U.S. firms, with the goal of inverting the U.S. firm's tax residence out of the United States, would routinely "fatten themselves up" by acquiring other U.S. firms in the years leading up to the inversion, so as to meet those thresholds. The new 2016 Treasury regulation disregards the value of any firms acquired in the three years prior to a new merger for purposes of meeting the 20 percent and 40 percent thresholds. This regulation in particular seems to have caused the almost immediate collapse of a planned $160 billion merger between U.S. pharmaceutical giant Pfizer and the Irish pharmaceutical firm Allergan, which was intended to establish the tax residence of the combined firm in Ireland.[123]

Many other countries around the world have responded to the problems of international corporate tax avoidance by reducing their corporate tax rates, and relying more heavily on taxes that are less prone to these sorts of problems, such as the value-added tax or taxes on labor income. Few countries now have statutory corporate tax rates higher than the U.S. rate. KPMG reports that in 2015 the average statutory corporate tax rate in OECD countries was 25 percent, and the average around the globe was 24 percent.[124] A lower corporate tax rate reduces the incentive to shift profits to low-tax countries, by reducing the gain from doing so. But even if a reduction in corporate rates were to reduce international tax avoidance significantly, it would still be likely to reduce tax revenue collections overall, as many firms are not currently engaging in international tax avoidance so aggressively or at all, and because lowering the corporate tax rate increases the attractiveness of sheltering personal income in corporations to avoid taxes. Moreover, as Eric Toder of the Urban-Brookings Tax Policy Center puts it, "If a company is trying to reduce its income tax rate from 35 percent to zero, I don't know why it wouldn't do the same at a 28 or 25 percent rate."[125] Evidence from Dowd, Landefeld, and Moore cited above suggests that's a good question.

Another potential reform, advocated by both Clausing and Zucman, is "formulary apportionment." The idea here is that each country would tax a portion of the current worldwide income of each corporation operating in that country; the portion of that income allocated to any particular country would depend on factors that are more difficult to fake than the location of profits, such as the share of the firm's worldwide employment, sales, and/or physical property that are located in the country. This is already how state corporate income taxes divide up the corporate tax base in the United States. While this would ameliorate problems of transfer-pricing manipulation and other forms of cross-border profit shifting, it could also pose new problems if implemented by any one country unilaterally, as it would lead to situations where some corporate income is taxed more than once while other income is not taxed by any jurisdiction. Thus, making this work well could require international cooperation and coordination, which have so far been in short supply on this issue. Formulary apportionment would also introduce new distortions to the incentives of multinational corporations, while removing some old ones, and it is not obvious in advance whether the new distortions or the old ones are worse. With that said, the problems with the current system are widely agreed to be quite bad.[126]

Our discussion here only scratches the surface of possible reforms for addressing international corporate tax problems. For example, most other countries have moved away from the attempt to tax worldwide income and have switched to territorial systems, which to a rough approximation only levy corporate income tax on profits from capital located within the borders of the country. Compared to a system like that in the United States, this has the advantage of ending the incentive to defer repatriation of profits. The hope is that this might encourage more investment in the United States, or at least reduce the inefficient game-playing that firms engage in to effectively repatriate profits without incurring tax. But it would only exacerbate incentives to engage in profit shifting to low-tax countries. Other proposed reforms offer various combinations of approaches discussed above, such as lowering the corporate tax rate, limiting or eliminating deferral, broadening the corporate tax base, and imposing rules and regulations that put more frictions in the way of inversions and profit shifting. Other ideas involve defining the business tax base according to the locations where the goods and services produced by businesses are consumed, instead of the locations where the businesses claim to earn their profits. Still others involve shifting taxation of more capital income to the personal level, for example by treating more business income as pass-through entity income, and by taxing capital gains on corporate equities at the personal level as they accrue.[127]

Recently, the combination of growing evidence about the magnitude of the problem, concerns about increasing inequality of income and wealth, and government budget problems in the wake of the financial crisis, have contributed to political pressure for action on multinational corporation tax avoidance. The problem has even acquired its own snappy acronym, "BEPS," which stands for "base erosion and profit shifting."

In lieu of fundamental reforms, countries have been adopting a variety of ad hoc fixes, and international organizations have been engaging in efforts to make the existing corporate tax system work better in the face of profit shifting challenges. The United Kingdom and Australia acted first, enacting measures such as what is known in the United Kingdom as the "Google tax," a new 25 percent tax on so-called taxable diverted profits, meaning any profits that the tax authority deems to have been improperly shifted out of the country.[128] In 2015, the OECD "BEPS Project" culminated in a set of guidelines intended to limit such tax-saving strategies. Although countries aren't required to follow the OECD's recommendations, in the past many countries have adopted the group's guidelines as their own international tax rules. The wide array of recommendations includes, for example, calls for increased information sharing among governments and encouragement for coordination of tax laws across countries (e.g., harmonizing countries' rules for determining residence of companies to prevent problems of "stateless income"). There is much unhappiness about the OECD's guidelines, and not only among the multinational companies themselves.[129] Some are cautiously optimistic that the BEPS initiative may lead to incremental improvements, but much depends on the willingness of those who are benefitting from the existing system to cooperate and share information. Critics call these measures band-aids that don't go far enough and will be ultimately ineffective, and argue that the international corporate tax system needs a fundamental reworking, perhaps along the lines of some of the reforms discussed earlier.[130]

Offshore Tax Evasion by Individuals
Multinational corporations are not the only ones that can reduce their tax liabilities through offshore shenanigans. There is a long history of wealthy individuals from around the world evading taxes on capital income through secret foreign accounts, such as the infamous Swiss bank account. Here, there's no question about the legality. The basic idea is to engage in outright evasion of one's own country's tax laws, by hiding one's wealth in a jurisdiction that supports financial secrecy and is uncooperative with international efforts to promote information sharing with tax authorities, so that interest, dividends, and capital gains can accumulate tax-free. In recent years, much of the policy and media attention surrounding evasion has focused on the role of off-shore accounts.

Gabriel Zucman of the University of California, Berkeley has recently shed new light on this topic by digging into the data.[131] His main strategy for inferring how much wealth is hidden in offshore accounts exploits the fact that in international financial statistics, there is a large excess of reported financial liabilities (e.g., stocks and bonds issued by corporations) over reported financial assets (e.g., stocks and bonds owned by individuals), when in principle the two should be equal. The gap presumably represents wealth that is kept secret by its owners. Based on this, Zucman estimates that about 8 percent of global wealth is hidden in tax havens. His estimates further suggest that U.S. residents stash about $1.2 trillion, or 4 percent of their wealth, in tax-haven accounts, resulting in a tax revenue loss of $36 billion annually. To put that in perspective, he notes: "Assuming that all unrecorded offshore wealth belongs to the top 0.1%, eradicating offshore evasion would thus raise as much revenue as increasing the top 0.1%'s federal income tax bill by close to 18%."[132] He corroborates the kind of evidence described above with evidence from newly released records of financial institutions, such as those demonstrating that Swiss banks hold $2.3 trillion in foreign-owned wealth.[133]

While getting precise numbers on such secretive behavior is difficult and fraught with potential for error, most observers agree with Zucman that a lot of this is going on. Certainly the U.S. government thinks so. In the past decade, the United States has tried a series of enforcement measures, including offers of amnesty from the harshest penalties for such evasion. The first U.S. amnesty in 2009 drew around 15,000 disclosures of offshore accounts and resulted in the collection of $3.4 billion in back taxes and penalties, nothing to sneeze at but small potatoes compared to Zucman's estimates of the size of the problem.[134] Also in 2009, the United States struck a deal with the Swiss financial services company UBS to get access to the names of Americans who had accounts there, resulting in a $780 million fine for UBS; since then hundreds of other Swiss banks have come to similar arrangements with the United States, including a guilty plea from Credit Suisse in 2014 resulting in a $2.6 billion fine.[135]

The latest, and most ambitious, U.S. enforcement effort is the Foreign Account Tax Compliance Act, known by its acronym FATCA, enacted in 2010 by Congress to target noncompliance by U.S. taxpayers using foreign accounts. FATCA requires foreign financial institutions to report to the IRS information about financial accounts held by U.S. taxpayers. In case you're wondering how the U.S. government can compel foreign financial institutions to comply with its wishes, the answer is that U.S. financial institutions and other U.S withholding agents must both withhold 30 percent on certain payments to foreign entities that do not document their FATCA status and report information about certain nonfinancial foreign entities. Wealth held in Swiss bank accounts and other offshore accounts is generally invested in corporate equities and bonds, often from U.S. corporations, so the threat of withholding a 30 percent tax on the dividend and interest payments on those stocks and bonds has real bite. With this stick, as of 2014, more than 80 countries, including China and Russia, and more than 77,000 financial institutions had agreed to comply.[136] The idea behind FATCA has spread to the rest of the world: by early 2016, 97 countries (but not the United States yet!) had agreed to automatically exchange information on residents' assets and incomes beginning in 2017 or 2018, with the FATCA rules as a template for what some refer to informally as GATCA or the "Common Reporting Standard" (but which is formally called the OECD Standard for Automatic Exchange of Financial Account Information).[137]

While FATCA certainly represents real progress in the fight against offshore tax evasion, Zucman argues that it has a number of important holes.[138] First, even with information sharing, it is not always possible to identify the individual owners of offshore accounts, especially because accounts are often registered in the names of "shell corporations," the ownership of which can be difficult to trace. Second, it can be quite difficult to monitor whether foreign financial institutions are complying in a complete and honest fashion. Without looking at the bank's internal records, how is one to know whether the bank is really sharing *all* of the relevant information? The holes in the Common Reporting Standard are even more significant, given that it does not yet involve any sanctions against financial institutions or countries that do not cooperate.[139]

For these reasons, Gabriel Zucman argues that the ultimate solution to these issues will have to involve the creation of a unified and transparent worldwide register that records the owners of financial wealth, accessible to tax authorities around the world and managed by an international agency such as the International Monetary Fund. Many private registries, such as the Depository Trust Company in the United States and Clearstream in Europe, already exist to record who really owns various assets such as corporate stocks and bonds, as that information needs to be recorded *somewhere* in order for ownership of the assets to be secure. But these private institutions do not share information with tax authorities. Zucman argues that governments should cooperate to take over and merge these registries so that tax authorities can trace ownership of assets to individuals in a reliable fashion.[140] It is hard to envision achieving the extent of international consensus needed to make this happen, nor have the practical problems of implementation yet been seriously addressed.

These issues all became front page headlines in April 2016, when it was revealed that 2.6 terabytes of data from Mossack Fonseca, a Panamanian law firm that specializes in setting up shell companies, had been leaked to a German newspaper that then turned them over to the International Consortium of Investigative Journalists. These data, known as the "Panama Papers," shed unprecedented light on the shadowy worlds of shell corporations, offshore tax evasion, criminal money laundering, and networks of political corruption. Shell corporations can be used for legitimate purposes, but they are often used to make ownership of offshore accounts less transparent. This helps some wealthy individuals evade taxes, and helps corrupt politicians and their associates keep the proceeds of their unscrupulous activities out of sight, so as to avoid the scrutiny of their citizens. For example, the papers revealed that associates of Russian president Vladimir Putin had about $2 billion hidden in offshore shell companies. Offshore wealth of important political figures and their relatives and associates in many other parts of the world, including China and the Middle East, along with 29 billionaires included in the Forbes list of the 500 wealthiest people in the world, was also exposed.[141] This evidence was a reminder that wealth hidden in offshore accounts is a particularly important problem in the parts of the world where corruption is most endemic. Zucman estimates that the share of financial wealth held in offshore accounts is as high as 30 percent for Africa, 52 percent for Russia, and 57 percent for the Gulf countries.[142]

Interestingly, at least initially, a disproportionately small share of people revealed to be using Panamanian shell corporations to hide wealth were Americans. This might reflect the fact that Americans have numerous other places where they can set up shell companies, together with the fact that the United States signed a trade agreement with Panama in 2010 that obliged Panama to share information on ownership of companies with the United States, making Panama a relatively unattractive place for Americans to set up shell companies.[143]

Ironically, in light of aggressive efforts by the United States to stamp out bank secrecy in other countries, in recent years U.S. states such as Delaware, Nevada, Wyoming, and South Dakota have become leading destinations for the wealth of foreigners who wish to evade their own countries' taxes. These states have laws that facilitate the establishment of anonymous shell companies, accounts that are kept secret from foreign authorities, or both. The refusal of the United States to comply with foreign efforts such as the Common Reporting Standard or to compel U.S. financial institutions to automatically share information with foreign tax authorities makes this possible. This led one U.S. lawyer involved in setting up such accounts to say that "the U.S. is effectively the biggest tax haven in the world." The U.S. Department of the Treasury is working on regulations that would comply with the OECD Common Reporting Standard, but opposition from congressional Republicans and the banking industry has derailed such efforts in the past.[144]

How the IRS Operates

Widespread evasion endangers the fairness of how we tax ourselves and may have a substantial economic cost. Thus, an enforcement agency like the IRS is a necessity for any tax system. But how should it operate, and how intensively should we track down and penalize tax evasion?

Mention the IRS, and most people think of the dreaded tax audit. But you may be surprised to learn that the IRS now examines slightly less than 1 percent of all individual tax returns and only slightly more than 1 percent of corporation income tax returns.[145] This fraction has declined dramatically over the last three decades; it was typically about 4 percent during the 1960s.[146]

Does this mean that if you file your tax return and happen to omit reporting your salary, there is only about a 1 in 100 chance of being caught in the act? Absolutely not, for several reasons.

First of all, the IRS does not just pick out of a hat which returns to audit, which would mean that everyone has the same chance of being audited. Instead, the probability that a return will be examined is influenced by a carefully developed secret formula, called the *discriminant index formula* (DIF). This formula assigns a score to each return that reflects the estimated likelihood of significant noncompliance for that taxpayer, based on the amounts stated on the return for each type of income and deduction. Returns that fit the profile of those that have a significant dollar amount of evasion are the most likely to be examined. For example, in fiscal year 2014, the fraction of returns audited was 1.0 percent for people with some business income and income under $25,000, but was 2.7 percent for those with some business income and income above $200,000.[147] Among very large corporations, most are audited every year by a team of IRS examiners. In 2014, 84.2 percent of the 494 corporations with assets exceeding $20 billion were audited, compared to only about 1.0 percent of corporations with assets below $5 million.[148]

Audits are by no means the only way the IRS checks on the accuracy of tax returns. Another important tool for the IRS is *information reporting*. For example, employers are required to send information reports on wages and salaries for all their employees to the IRS. The IRS computers then match up most of these information reports against tax returns. About 76.5 percent of the audits that go into the 1.0 percent audit rate for all individual returns mentioned above refer to correspondence by tax examiners generated by computer matching of returns to information reports.[149] If the computer detects a discrepancy, a computer-generated notice is automatically sent out to the taxpayer asking him or her to pay up or provide an explanation. Most interest and dividend payments and pension disbursements are also subject to information reporting. It is therefore no accident that these types of income, together with wages and salaries, have near 100 percent compliance rates, as reported in table 5.1. In fiscal year 2014, the IRS received 2.3 billion information reports, 86 percent of which were transmitted in electronic form.[150] The increased use and efficiency of computer checks based on information reporting has clearly substituted, to some extent, for the decline in face-to-face audits.

Another major enforcement tool of the IRS is withholding of taxes on wage and salary income, a practice it has followed since 1943. All firms above a certain size are required to remit payments directly to the IRS based on an estimate of the personal income taxes owed by their employees on their labor income. In 2013, 86 percent of personal income tax liability was withheld in this manner.[151] The amount withheld for an employee is usually greater than actual tax liability over the course of the year, so the vast majority of individual taxpayers (78 percent of all returns in 2012) receive a refund.[152] This creates an added incentive for taxpayers to file their returns in a timely manner. Withholding and remittance by employers is an effective enforcement tool because it allows the IRS to concentrate its resources on collecting taxes from a relatively small number of firms that have sophisticated accounting capabilities rather than from a much larger number of individuals.

Together, information reporting and withholding are powerful enforcement tools. A stark illustration of that is provided by the IRS study of the tax gap during the years 2008–2010. As shown in table 5.1, it separates taxable income into four types depending on the extent to which the income is covered by information reporting and withholding and calculates a misreporting rate for each. For income (such as wages and salaries) subject to both withholding and substantial information reporting, the misreporting rate is just 1 percent. For income not subject to withholding, the misreporting rate is 7 percent and 19 percent, respectively, for income subject to substantial and "some" information reporting. Strikingly, the misreporting rate is 63 percent for income (such as self-employment income) not subject to withholding and subject to "little or no" information reporting.[153]

The Housing and Economic Recovery Tax Act of 2008 expanded the scope of information reporting to credit card receipts of most small- and medium-sized businesses. As a result, since 2012, financial firms that process credit or debit card payments have been required to send to their clients and, more importantly, to the IRS, an annual form documenting the previous year's transactions. This documentation requirement is designed to improve compliance for the category of income that had a 63 percent misreporting rate in 2008–2010 in table 5.1, by enabling the IRS to compare information on payments to a firm through credit and debit cards with the income that the firm reports to the IRS, and to investigate cases involving large discrepancies.[154]

Of course, not all misstatement of tax liability is intentional; taxpayers make mistakes in both directions. One additional way the IRS makes sure the proper tax liability gets paid is by helping taxpayers understand and comply with the tax law. For this reason, the IRS makes help available over the phone and on the Internet and operates education and outreach programs.

Why More Enforcement May Not Be the Answer

With a net tax gap of at least $406 billion, why don't we devote more resources to enforcement? Wouldn't this make the tax system fairer and more efficient and generate money that could be used to reduce the national debt, cut tax rates, or advance some other worthwhile purpose? The answer is that, although extra enforcement may indeed bring many benefits, we must also consider the costs. Just as stationing a police officer at every corner would certainly reduce street crime, more audits and higher penalties could almost certainly make a dent in the extent of tax evasion. But as a society, we choose not to have police everywhere and not to impose the death penalty for minor infractions. We accept some level of crime because we judge that the benefits of eliminating crime would not outweigh the costs of achieving zero crime. The same is true of the crime of tax evasion.

Would the benefits of extra enforcement by the IRS outweigh the costs? One analysis has suggested that for every extra $1 the IRS spends on auditing returns, it could gain between $4 and $7 of additional revenue directly from the audited returns.[155] Such a yield could not be achieved immediately because time would be needed to train new agents, but it is plausible that eventually the gain could be realized. Indeed, this amount probably underestimates the potential revenue yield because it doesn't take into account the deterrent effect of extra enforcement. For instance, if the audit rate were increased, the greater likelihood that evasion would be detected probably would persuade some people who were not audited to become more compliant.

Although a 4-to-1 or a 7-to-1 ratio of extra revenues collected to spending is certainly impressive, this comparison does not correctly compare the true costs and benefits of engaging in extra enforcement and, for that reason, we should not jump to the conclusion that tax enforcement ought to be vastly expanded. An apples-and-oranges fallacy is lurking here. The expenditure on expanded IRS enforcement activities certainly represents a real resource cost to the country: the people and computers doing the auditing could be employed elsewhere in the economy to produce valuable goods and services. But the increased revenue from greater enforcement does not by itself represent a gain to the economy: $7 handed from a taxpayer to the IRS does not create $7 worth of new goods and services, but rather transfers control of the resources from taxpayers to the government.

To the extent it reduces evasion, increased tax enforcement does produce important social benefits by establishing a more efficient and equitable tax system. The benefits of reduced evasion, however, are not at all well measured by the extra revenue that more enforcement will produce and are less concrete than dollar revenue. Although the size of the tax gap and the revenue yield from extra expenditures on the IRS are informative, by themselves they do not resolve the question of whether the level of enforcement is about right or whether it should be increased or decreased.

Bruno Frey of Zeppelin University in Germany has argued that heavy-handed enforcement can even backfire to reduce tax compliance based on a distinction between what he calls intrinsic and extrinsic motivation. With *intrinsic* motivation, taxpayers remit their tax liability because they admire "civic virtue"—they are dutiful. With *extrinsic* motivation, they do so because they fear punishment. Frey argues that increasing extrinsic motivation—say, with more punitive enforcement policies—can in some situations "crowd out" intrinsic motivation by making people feel that they pay taxes because they have to rather than because they want to. He suggests that where the relationship between the individual and the tax authority is seen as involving an implicit contract sustained by trust, individuals will comply due to high "tax morale." To sustain citizens' commitment to the contract and therefore their morale, the tax authority must act respectfully toward citizens and protect the honest from the free rider. It does this, he argues, by giving taxpayers the benefit of the doubt when it finds a mistake, by sanctioning small violations more mildly, and by sanctioning large and basic violations more heavily.[156]

Problems at the IRS

The IRS has periodically been embroiled in controversies over excessive intrusiveness and unfair treatment of taxpayers, with the 2013 accusations of politically biased scrutiny of applications for a certain kind of tax-exempt status being just the most recent case. These episodes have led to some constructive reforms, but in conjunction with an increasingly polarized political atmosphere, they have also contributed to a political environment where the IRS has not been allocated the budgetary resources to keep up with an increasingly difficult job, with negative consequences for enforcement of the tax code and service to taxpayers.

For every anecdote about flagrant tax evasion, there is another about heavy-handed IRS handling of a taxpayer. Some taxpayers are concerned about the intrusiveness of the IRS into their lives. Balancing the rights of taxpayers against the desire for an equitably enforced tax system raises critical issues of, among other things, privacy. Many Americans do not want the IRS to get "too good" at its job and legitimately object to procedures that would facilitate enforcement of the tax law.

In 1997 and 1998, Congress held highly publicized hearings that highlighted supposedly inappropriate practices by the IRS. Spurred on by the hearings, Congress enacted and the president signed the Internal Revenue Service Restructuring and Reform Act of 1998. This act set up an oversight board for the IRS that includes six private sector members, ordered the IRS to undertake major organizational restructuring and management changes, and included several provisions designed to improve service provided to taxpayers by the IRS and to protect taxpayers' rights. Most controversially, the new law shifted the burden of proof in civil court cases from the taxpayer to the IRS.

While we can't expect an agency tasked with making people pay their taxes to be particularly *popular*, public opinion polls do suggest that, at least until recently, Americans' satisfaction with the IRS had been improving a bit since 1998. The share of Americans who said in public opinion polls that they had a "favorable" opinion of the IRS had dropped from 51 percent in 1983 to a nadir of 32 percent in 1999, shortly after the congressional hearings on IRS abuses, but gradually recovered to 47 percent by 2010, perhaps reflecting some combination of the IRS's "kinder and gentler" approach and some improvements in IRS "customer service."[157] A 2012 poll by the IRS Oversight Board asked people about their own interactions with the IRS. Forty-one percent of respondents said they were "very satisfied" with these interactions, 35 percent said they were "somewhat satisfied," and only 15 percent said they were "not very satisfied" or "not at all satisfied."[158] Whatever progress the IRS was making in public perception was dealt a blow in May 2013, when IRS officials acknowledged that low-level IRS employees reviewing applications for a particular kind of tax-exempt status had targeted certain applications for extra scrutiny in a way that suggested bias against conservative organizations. This led to high-profile congressional hearings, the resignation of the acting Commissioner of the IRS along with some other senior IRS officials, and harm to the reputation of the IRS and the Obama administration.

To understand what this rather complex scandal was about, one needs to know something about the tax laws governing tax-exempt organizations, and also about campaign finance law. In general, only donations to charitable organizations that do *not* participate in political campaigns for public office are eligible to be itemized deductions on individual income tax returns. Donations to other organizations, such as political parties and political action committees, are not tax deductible. Campaign finance laws distinguish between those organizations that must disclose the names of their donors, and those that need not, and this distinction was the crux of the 2013 kerfuffle. The Supreme Court's 2010 decision in the "Citizens United" case invalidated portions of campaign finance reform laws that had imposed limits on political contributions by corporations and unions. Ever since then, the IRS has been flooded by applications for 501(c)(4) status (which does not require organizations to disclose donors' names) from organizations that were arguably ineligible for this status because they were "primarily" involved in attempting to influence election outcomes. A prominent example of such a 501(c)(4) organization is Crossroads GPS, for which Karl Rove (formerly George W. Bush's chief political adviser) plays a large role; Crossroads spends millions of dollars on political ads during election seasons. In an effort to comply with the letter of the law, they are careful to only produce ads that attack candidates' positions on policies, rather than directly calling for the defeat of particular candidates. But there is considerable controversy over whether organizations such as Crossroads are primarily engaged in influencing elections, in which case they should instead be classified as "527" organizations, which do have to disclose their donors. This sort of thing led to calls for greater IRS scrutiny of applications of 501(c)(4) status.[159]

The 2013 scandal arose because low-level IRS employees tasked with reviewing a huge backlog of 501(c)(4) applications searched for certain "key words" to help them identify which applications deserved closer scrutiny, so as to determine whether they were violating the stipulation against too much political activity. Such targeted applications tended to be subject to long delays and many intrusive requests for further information. Initial reports suggested that targeted applications were disproportionately those involving terms, like "tea party," that would tend to single out conservative organizations. It was later revealed that the IRS employees were also using terms associated with liberal organizations, such as "progressive," to help flag applications for closer scrutiny. Critics still maintained that the probability of scrutiny and delay was greater for applications by conservative organizations. Everyone seemed to agree that it was wrong for the IRS to treat applications by political groups in a way that was not even-handed, and the scandal resonated with the public partly because it recalled dark episodes in the past, such as when President Nixon apparently ordered the IRS to conduct audits of political opponents. There was never any credible evidence to suggest that the Obama administration had been involved in any way in the decisions about which applications for 501(c)(4) status to review; most evidence suggested that this was an issue of overwhelmed low-level employees exhibiting poor judgment, rather than an effort to promote a particular political agenda.[160]

To address these and other problems at the IRS, the National Taxpayer Advocate issued reports proposing a long list of specific reforms at the IRS, while also calling for an increase in the IRS budget to give it sufficient resources to operate in a way that would better protect taxpayers' rights (e.g., by substantially reducing long delays when reviewing applications). It is unclear whether any of these reforms will be implemented, and if anything it appears that the IRS budget will continue to shrink. In late 2013, the Treasury and IRS proposed revised regulations in an effort to establish clearer and more objective criteria for defining unacceptable types of political activity for 501(c)(4) organizations. These proposals were immediately criticized by Republicans as a threat to free speech. At the time we wrote this in August 2016, the

Treasury and IRS were still reviewing over 150,000 public comments on the proposed regulations, and were planning revisions before putting the new regulations into effect.[161]

The scandal did serious damage to the reputation of the IRS. In May 2013, 43 percent of respondents to a Gallup poll said the IRS was doing a "poor" job, up from 20 percent in July 2009. The same month, a Fox News poll found 57 percent of respondents said the amount of confidence they had in the IRS was "not much" or "none at all," which was up dramatically from 32 percent in May 2003.[162] On October 27, 2015, a group of Republicans in the House of Representatives sponsored a resolution to impeach IRS Commissioner John Koskinen, citing his failure to follow up on this episode; it was denounced by Democrats as "political grandstanding."

While most headlines about the IRS in 2013 related to this scandal, reports by the National Taxpayer Advocate and the Treasury's Inspector General for Tax Administration also called attention to worrisome declines in the quality of IRS service and its ability to fairly enforce the tax code, which they attributed to sharp reductions in budget and staff, despite increasing demands on the agency.[163]

Resources devoted to the IRS have been growing more slowly than the economy, and considerably more slowly than its responsibilities, for a long time. Between the 1992 and 2014 fiscal years, the share of GDP spent on the IRS shrank by 34 percent, from 0.102 percent to 0.067 percent, and the number of IRS employees declined by 29 percent, despite a 28 percent increase in the number of individual income tax returns processed by the IRS.[164] In the meantime, the complexity of the tax law and the sophistication of abusive tax shelters and other means of evading taxes has certainly not decreased at all. Moreover, the IRS recently has been tasked with implementing an increasing number of social policies incorporated into the tax code—including refundable tax credits for low-income people and portions of the Affordable Care Act (because approximately 50 of its 500 total provisions are in the Internal Revenue Code).[165] IRS resources have declined particularly sharply in recent years. Between fiscal years 2010 and 2015, the IRS budget was cut by 17 percent in real terms and the IRS training budget was cut by 83 percent.[166] Between fiscal years 2010 and 2014, the number of IRS employees decreased 11 percent.[167]

One consequence of reduced IRS resources has been an apparent decline in enforcement activity. The percentage of corporate returns audited fell from 2.7 percent in 1997 to 1.3 percent in 2014. Audits of individual returns went from 1.3 percent of returns in 1997 to 0.9 percent in 2014.[168] The Treasury Inspector General for Tax Administration reports that between fiscal years 2010 and 2013, IRS enforcement revenue fell by 7 percent, from $57.6 billion to $53.3 billion.[169] The apparent decline in resources devoted to enforcement, relative to the difficulty of the task, poses the danger that tax evasion will increase as people respond to the incentives created by a reduced probability of being caught or punished, and as public confidence that other people are paying their legally required taxes declines.

There is also evidence that the quality of service provided by the IRS has eroded over time as its budget has not kept up with increasing demands on the agency. Between 2004 and 2014, the percentage of taxpayers seeking to speak on the phone to an IRS "customer service representative" who actually succeeded in getting through to such a representative declined from 87 percent to 64 percent, and the average waiting time to speak to such a representative increased from 3 minutes to 20 minutes. The IRS has also eliminated the opportunity for low-income and elderly people to get help completing their tax returns at IRS walk-in centers, has stopped answering tax law questions over the phone in a tax year after April 15, and has sharply reduced the set of tax topics it is willing to discuss over the phone before then. Increasingly, taxpayers must turn to expensive private tax preparers for help. While most private tax preparers behave in a professional manner, there are growing concerns about unqualified, unscrupulous, and fraudulent private tax preparers. About half of all private tax preparers are not enrolled with the IRS, and IRS efforts to regulate these preparers have been stymied by a federal court ruling in 2013 declaring that the IRS does not have the authority to regulate them.[170]

What Facilitates Enforcement?

Congress has handed the IRS a difficult if not impossible task—to fairly and efficiently administer a tax code that is plagued with inequities and complexities. Just as bill collectors are never popular, the IRS will never be, but the tax enforcement process could be less painful and costly if the tax system were different. What features of a tax system facilitate enforcement?

As we discussed earlier in this chapter, some of the aspects that make a tax system simpler also facilitate enforcement. Information reporting and also tax withholding and remittance at the source of payment are the best examples. The effectiveness of these measures is amply demonstrated by compliance rates that are vastly higher for income that is subject to them (such as employee wages and salaries) than for income that is not (such as income of informal suppliers), shown in table 5.1. Another feature that facilitates enforcement is limiting the number of credits, deductions, and other non-revenue-raising aspects of the tax system that stretch IRS resources. But a number of other factors also strongly influence the effectiveness of tax enforcement.

At first blush, the most direct cause of tax evasion might seem to be high tax rates. To lower evasion, therefore, why not simply lower tax rates? This is too simplistic an answer when a fixed amount of revenue must be raised. A more appropriate question is whether evasion would be curtailed if marginal tax rates were reduced, holding revenues constant, either by making the system less progressive or broadening the base. In either case, the quantitative evidence is not decisive. Even on theoretical grounds, the argument that lower tax rates reduce evasion is not certain. This is a case where economists hesitate to accept something that is a no-brainer for most everyone else. But bear with us for a second, and consider the following argument. If penalties for detected evasion are proportional to the understated tax, then lowering the tax rate automatically proportionally lowers the penalty for a dollar of evasion; thus the terms of the tax-evasion gamble—the gain if undetected relative to the cost if caught—remains unchanged, making the effect on evasion indeterminate.[171] Furthermore, for some kinds of evasion, such as non-filing, the marginal tax rate is immaterial because the entire tax liability is at stake; what matters is the average tax rate that would apply to the reported income.

Much of the tax evasion in our country occurs on types of income that are difficult for the IRS to monitor. Self-employment and small business income are the most important examples. Some types of capital income are also relatively easy to conceal, at least when compared to wages and salaries. Thus, in some sense the tax system could become considerably easier to enforce if we simply give up on trying to tax some of these types of income. For example, a retail sales tax, VAT, or Hall-Rabushka flat tax (discussed in chapter 7) would not attempt to tax capital income; furthermore, most VAT systems exempt from tax all businesses below a certain size.

This observation is reminiscent of the assertion that drug crimes could be eliminated by legalizing drugs. In this analogy, the crime is evading taxes on capital income, which could be eliminated by making this type of income exempt from taxation. Whether this is vertically equitable is questionable—capital income is disproportionately received by affluent families—but it would at least improve horizontal equity between honest and dishonest people who earn capital income. Keep in mind, though, that even "legalization" solutions like this have enforcement problems of their own, particularly when they are introduced in a piecemeal fashion. For example, eliminating all tax on difficult-to-enforce capital gains would greatly increase the incentive to convert ordinary income into capital gains and would thus put more, rather than less, pressure on enforcement.

A complex tax system makes complying with the rules more difficult for conscientious taxpayers. It is also frustrating and puts people in less of a mood to comply. Moreover, if people feel that other taxpayers are taking advantage of complexity to avoid paying their "fair share," they may feel less morally obligated to pay their own taxes honestly. Evidence from surveys and laboratory experiments provides some support for this notion, although the evidence does not speak with one voice.[172]

These arguments are often cited by advocates of simpler alternatives to the income tax, such as the flat tax, and they undoubtedly have some merit. Simplifying the tax code could well improve people's attitudes toward compliance. But we can't rely entirely on public goodwill. It's unclear whether moving to a streamlined tax system that is perceived to be fairer would by itself have a dramatic impact on compliance, and it certainly wouldn't eliminate the need for an enforcement authority, as some have implied.

The more that taxpayers are required to document their incomes and deductions, the easier it is for the IRS to ensure that people's tax liability is accurate. The current requirement that a Social Security number be provided for each dependent exemption is one particularly effective example. But for most types of deductions, such as those for charity or for employee business expenses, the IRS only requires a taxpayer to supply documentation in the event that the taxpayer is audited. Requiring documentation for more items would curtail evasion and improve the accuracy of tax liabilities. For example, analysis of 2001 randomized IRS audit data from the United States suggests that about 16 percent of cash charitable donation deductions claimed in that year represented misreporting, and there is solid evidence that when France started requiring more documentation to claim tax benefits for charitable donations, it dramatically reduced overreporting of such donations.[173] A potentially even more effective approach would be to have the IRS check most or all returns, requiring taxpayers to provide some justification for each item. This may seem far-fetched, but in the Netherlands, the tax authority has in the past audited every single personal income tax return, at least briefly.[174]

Of course, requiring more documentation from taxpayers and expanding auditing could make the taxpaying process considerably more complicated for both the taxpayer and the IRS, even as it cuts down on evasion. In this case, there is a clear trade-off among the multiple objectives of tax policy. In other situations, costs of enforcement can be transferred from the government budget to the private sector with substantial flexibility. For example, requiring more documentation of taxpayers who make some personal use of a business car may facilitate monitoring this behavior, but it certainly increases the taxpayers' cost of compliance. For a given degree of enforcement effectiveness, whether this is a good idea depends on whether the sum of these costs declines. Shifting the costs off the budget onto the taxpayers does not necessarily constitute an improved process.

Conclusion

Other things equal, a tax system should be simple and enforceable. In some cases, such as requiring more taxpayer documentation, efforts to achieve one of these goals are costly in terms of the other. But many policies can foster both goals. For example, settling for rough justice and getting rid of all of the bells and whistles in the tax code would clean up the tax base, making the system simpler and easier to enforce. So would more dramatic changes, such as moving to a single rate or changing to a business-remitted consumption tax, especially to the extent that they would allow wider use of withholding and less involvement of individuals in the taxpaying process. The simplicity and enforcement benefits of these approaches are a major reason that they are often at the heart of radical tax reform proposals. But what else is sacrificed by moving to these simpler ways to tax ourselves?

One important lesson of the past three chapters is that policy debates often involve conflicts and trade-offs among the criteria by which we evaluate the tax system. More progressivity generally is accompanied by greater disincentives to work and to otherwise seek economic advancement. More fine-tuning of the tax system to achieve equitable sharing of the tax burden has a cost of complexity. Many of the most radical and most simplifying tax reform options abandon or sharply reduce progressivity, and they eliminate all or nearly all personalization of the tax burden. Others would maintain or increase the existing degree of progressivity while still arguably reducing complexity and increasing enforceability and efficiency substantially. In the next chapter, we turn to the elements that many tax reform plans have in common, and in subsequent chapters we consider particular approaches to tax reform and how they balance the competing objectives of the tax system.

6 Elements of Fundamental Reform

In this chapter, we examine the common elements of many proposals for fundamental tax reform. We frame this exercise by analyzing the components of so-called *flat* taxes, a moniker proudly adopted by many reform proposals that may differ tremendously from each other.

There are three possible distinct dimensions of flatness in a tax—a single tax rate, a consumption tax base, and a clean tax base. The single rate is what most people pick up on, but the other two dimensions would represent even more fundamental changes in the way we tax ourselves. The essential distinguishing feature of a consumption tax base is that it eliminates distortions to incentives for saving and investment—in effect, making the rate of taxation on consumption at different points in the life cycle flat. Cleaning the tax base often means flattening tax rates across different choices, for example by removing various exemptions, deductions, and credits that arguably create economically inefficient or inequitable variation in tax rates across choices, and contribute to complexity. It can also mean cleaning up messy aspects of the tax system that lead to arbitrary differences in effective tax rates across different methods of saving and investing, so that tax rates are once again flatter and more uniform across choices. Examples of such messiness include the double taxation of corporate income, the uneven treatment of debt versus equity, depreciation deductions that differ from economic depreciation, the realization-based taxation of capital gains, and estate taxation. Some proposals seek reform in all three dimensions; other plans focus on only one or two of these aspects. In what follows, we consider each of these elements of fundamental tax reform in detail.

A Single Rate

The most eye-catching feature of flat taxes is the flat *rate*. In place of our current income tax system of graduated tax rates that increase with higher incomes, all or most taxpayers under a flat tax system would be subject to a single rate of tax. Other reform proposals would flatten the rate structure, without moving to just one rate, by cutting the top rate of tax and thus reducing the range of tax rates. Because in most flat tax proposals the single rate applies only to the base in excess of some exemption level, even these are really a form of graduated tax, with an initial bracket to which a zero tax rate applies, plus an open-ended bracket subject to a single tax rate. Under such a system, the ratio of tax liability to the tax base (i.e., the average tax rate) is zero until the exemption level is reached and then increases gradually with the tax base until, for very high incomes, the average rate is nearly the single rate. Moreover, the degree of progressivity can be varied by adjusting the level of tax-exempt income and the tax rate. A flat-rate tax that exempts all income below $100,000 and levies a 50 percent tax on income above $100,000 is considerably more progressive than a flat tax rate that exempts only $10,000 of income and levies a 20 percent tax above that.

To distinguish this aspect of flatness from the others, we refer to a tax system with one tax rate as a *single-rate tax*. Replacing the graduated tax rates with a single rate can be accomplished independently of any and all of the changes in the tax base we discuss below that are often associated with flat tax proposals. A single rate, or flattened rates, can be applied to a narrow, preference-ridden base or to a broad, clean base, and it can be applied to all of income or just to the portion that is consumed. Similarly, we can certainly clean up the tax base while maintaining graduated rates and implement a consumption tax in a way that allows us to preserve graduated rates.

If nothing else changed, replacing the graduated income tax rate structure with a single tax rate would make the distribution of tax liabilities dramatically less progressive. Figure 6.1 illustrates this point. The thick black line depicts how average income tax rates varied with adjusted gross income in 2013 for typical married couples with two children who have average deductions, capital gains, and dividends for their income levels, and earn the rest of their income from wages and salaries.[1] One thing to note about current law is that tax liability is *negative* for low-income families, due mainly to the refundable portions

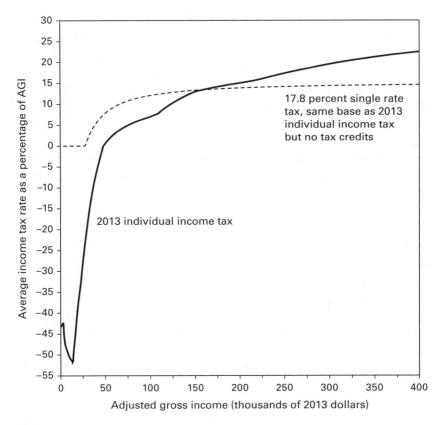

Figure 6.1
Effect of a revenue-neutral elimination of graduated tax rates, tax credits, the AMT, and reduced tax rates on capital gains and dividends on average personal income tax rates for typical married couples with two children in 2013.
Source: Authors' calculations based on data from Internal Revenue Service *Statistics of Income—2013 Individual Income Tax Returns*, Publication 1304 and Bakija (2016).

of the Earned Income Tax Credit and the Child Tax Credit. A second is that the tax-exempt threshold is already quite large: in 2013, a couple with two children did not face any positive income tax liability until its income reached just above $48,300. Third, above that tax-exempt threshold, income tax burdens were still distributed very progressively, as *marginal* rates in 2013 gradually rose from 10 percent at the lowest levels of taxable income up to 39.6 percent above $450,000. As a result, *average* tax rates continue to rise well into the upper end of the income distribution.

The dashed line in figure 6.1 illustrates the effects of switching to a single-rate tax with a large tax-exempt threshold, in the spirit of some flat tax proposals floated in recent years. To isolate the effects of switching to a single rate from the effects of other components of tax reform, we eliminate the main features that contribute to the current system's progressivity or that create multiple marginal tax rates—the graduated rate structure, tax credits, reduced marginal tax rates on capital gains and qualified dividends, and the alternative minimum tax—but keep all the existing deductions, personal exemptions, and exclusions. We calculate that to raise the same revenue as the income tax did in 2013, such a tax would require a tax rate of approximately 17.8 percent.[2] The standard deduction and personal exemption would continue to provide a large tax-exempt threshold ($27,800) for these families. The exemption of the first $27,800 of income from tax makes the distribution of tax burdens somewhat progressive (i.e., average tax rates do rise with income), but it is significantly less progressive than the current system. The reform makes a family with $20,000 of AGI worse off by about $7,400, or 37 percent of AGI, by eliminating refundable credits. For a family with $75,000 of AGI, tax liability goes up by about $4,400, or 6 percent of AGI, mainly due to replacing the 10 percent and 15 percent tax brackets with a flat 17.8 percent tax rate and eliminating the Child Tax Credit. A family with $1 million in AGI, by contrast, gets a tax cut of about $111,000, or 11 percent of AGI.

This exercise points out starkly how much the impact of a single-rate tax depends on exactly what rate is enacted, to what extent the rate change is accompanied by measures that broaden the tax base, and whether tax credits are preserved. In practice, most advocates of a flat tax are also advocates of a flat, *low* tax rate, usually in the high teens or low twenties. As shown above, switching to such a rate by itself, while still raising the same tax revenue overall, would radically shift tax burdens away from upper-income families and toward low- and middle-income families. The same conclusion applies to flattened, but not literally flat, rate schedules. In either case one must cut back on exclusions and itemized deductions that disproportionately benefit upper-income families if one wishes to mitigate the negative impact on low- and moderate-income families through tax credits and larger exemptions, while raising the same revenue as the existing system. Even with substantial base broadening, however, it would be practically impossible to design a tax system with a single rate that is significantly below the current top rate of 39.6 percent that replicates the current tax liabilities on people with extremely high incomes. As a result, somebody else will have to owe more in taxes.

Why flatten the rate structure, or go whole hog to a single rate? Perhaps the most commonly cited reason is to improve economic incentives. Raising the same amount of revenue with a more graduated rate structure requires that, on average, people face higher *marginal* tax rates, which, as discussed in chapter 4, can discourage work and saving and cause a whole host of other economic distortions and inefficiencies. Thus, tax policy design must confront a trade-off between progressivity and economic prosperity. In principle, improved economic growth could eventually compensate some of the people who initially face higher tax burdens as a result of switching to a less graduated rate structure. As shown in chapter 4, however, the economic costs of progressivity are uncertain and are almost certainly not as high as they are often made out to be by many political advocates of a flat rate. Other things being equal, lower marginal rates are better for the economy, but economics reveals nothing magical about a single rate. For example, the economic cost of having two low marginal rates—say, 15 percent and 25 percent—is not likely to be significantly higher than the cost of a single 20 percent rate.

Some argue that a single-rate tax structure is "neutral" toward distributional issues and thereby avoids "class warfare." By advocating a single rate, they suggest they are transcending the controversy over fairness and are promoting the system that maximizes economic performance. Neither of these arguments is correct. A flat-rate tax with a low rate generates a distribution of tax burdens that is less progressive than the current graduated tax rate structure, but it certainly affects the distribution of income and is not *neutral* in any meaningful sense. The only tax system that would truly eliminate all the economic costs of taxation is a lump-sum tax under which tax *liability*, not the tax *rate*, is the same for everyone, rich or poor. In place of all federal taxes, we could have a fixed annual charge of $12,795 per adult, whether that adult is Mark Zuckerberg, a homeless person, or you.[3] This eliminates any tax penalty tied to work, saving, or investing. Presumably, the reason that the proponents of a single-rate tax prefer it to a lump-sum tax is that they find the latter abjectly unfair (or else they are too timid to admit the opposite). Thus, the single-rate tax structure already reflects a balancing between equity and efficiency. A two-rate or multiple-rate structure reflects another balancing, as does a lump-sum tax. We can argue about how best to make this balancing, but no tax system avoids this trade-off, and any tax system takes a stand on distribution.

When it comes to simplicity and enforceability, however, there is indeed something special about a single rate, although it's not what most people think. As discussed in chapter 5, a single rate doesn't really simplify your tax return; in fact, applying the tax rate schedule to your taxable income to calculate how much you owe is the least complicated part of the whole taxpaying process and is automatic for the majority of returns filed using software. The real advantage of a single-rate tax structure is that it facilitates much simpler, business-based, systems of collecting taxes under which no individuals need file tax returns or remit taxes to the tax authority. Even under an income tax that nominally features an individual tax component, a single rate makes it easier to rely on employers withholding and remitting taxes on behalf of employees, banks withholding and remitting on behalf of those who receive interest, and so on, a major simplification and enforcement advantage.

Reducing the disparity of tax rates also reduces the incentives for individuals to shift taxable income from high-rate to low-rate taxable entities and from high-tax to low-tax periods. Moreover, it minimizes the horizontally inequitable treatment accorded to those with fluctuating incomes. Under a graduated income tax, comparing two families with the same lifetime income, the one with fluctuating income will pay more total tax than a family with a more stable income flow; a flatter-rate system reduces this disparity.

Although these are important advantages, it's debatable whether they offset the distributional consequences of a low flat rate, and economic reasoning alone cannot resolve the question. Moreover, adding another rate on top of the main flat rate doesn't entirely destroy the simplicity advantages. The United Kingdom greatly simplified its income tax system by moving to a single rate for most people and improving its withholding system but still retained a higher marginal rate for a small percentage of high-income individuals.[4] And having the same *top* rate across individuals, businesses, and different types of income eliminates many of the opportunities for complex income-shifting and tax-avoidance schemes, even if there are graduated rates below that top rate.

A Consumption Base

The second element of many fundamental tax reform plans is to change the system so that tax liability is triggered by consumption rather than by income. Admittedly, non-economists do not associate this aspect of a tax system with flatness. But to economists, a consumption tax imposes a uniform (call it flat, if you like) tax on current consumption and future consumption, in the sense that it does not alter the reward for postponing consumption (that is, saving). In contrast, an income tax, because it taxes the return to saving, makes consumption in the future more expensive than consumption now. We explain further below.

What Is a Consumption Tax?

For some readers, the word *consumption* may conjure up memories of their introductory college economics class, where they may have first encountered consumption as being something other than an old-fashioned word for tuberculosis. Consumption is just economists' language for what people do when they use up (i.e., consume) goods and services. A consumption tax simply means that the tax base is consumption, as opposed to income, wealth, or some other concept.

There are many ways to measure consumption, and many varieties of consumption tax. Because annual income—for a family or for the country as a whole—is equal to annual consumption plus saving, consumption can be measured directly or, alternatively, by subtracting saving from income. It is also true by definition that the total income of a country equals the value of output of factors of production (labor and capital) owned by its residents, and the amount of saving done by a country equals the amount of investment on which its residents have a claim to the returns, and so another way of measuring consumption is output minus investment. Note that, following the convention in economics, the term *investment* here refers to a business purchase of a capital good such as a plant or equipment, and not a portfolio choice such as an individual purchasing some General Electric stock.

Varieties of Consumption Tax

To make our discussion more concrete, let's consider some examples of consumption taxes. The *retail sales tax* is the type most familiar to Americans, as almost all states already levy one. Under this approach, tax liability is triggered by the final sales of goods and services at the retail level, and the tax is collected entirely from retailers (that is, businesses that sell directly to individual consumers).

The world's most common consumption tax, the *value-added tax* (VAT), is not levied in the United States. Instead of collecting tax only from retailers, under a VAT businesses at each stage of the production and distribution process must remit tax. Each firm pays tax on its "value added," which is simply its total sales minus the cost of the inputs it purchases from other businesses. Because downstream businesses deduct from their tax base all of their purchases from upstream businesses, all business-to-business sales and purchases exactly cancel each other out, so that the aggregate tax base is just final sales to consumers—the same as it is with a retail sales tax.

A close relative to the value-added tax is what economists refer to as "the" flat tax, or more specifically, the "Hall-Rabushka" flat tax, named after its inventors. Businesses owe tax on sales minus inputs purchased, just like under a VAT, but—unlike with a VAT—they can also deduct payments to workers. The critical difference from a VAT is that workers owe tax on their labor income at the same rate of tax as do businesses. Thus, the flat-tax approach to taxing consumption is essentially equivalent to a VAT—the only difference being that labor compensation is taken out of the business tax base and then taxed separately, and at the same rate, at the personal level. Under this tax system it is easier to introduce some progressivity by incorporating a large exemption and perhaps graduated tax rates in the personal tax on labor compensation. Further progressivity could be introduced into this tax by imposing graduated tax rates on labor income, in which case the tax is known as an "X-tax."

Finally, under a *personal consumption tax,* each year individual taxpayers would calculate and report both income and net saving, and the tax base would be the difference between the two—that is, income minus saving, which equals consumption. This kind of tax could easily accommodate tax progressivity by applying a graduated rate schedule to the individual consumption base. To get from the current system to a personal consumption tax would require allowing the equivalent of unlimited (traditional) Individual Retirement Accounts, so that all contributions to the account (net saving) would be subtracted from the tax base, and all withdrawals (dissaving) would be added to the tax base.

The various methods of taxing consumption differ in how they *appear* to assign the tax burden among consumers, workers, and businesses, both because the location of the official tax liability varies and because different parties remit the tax (i.e., write checks to the IRS). As explained in chapter 3, however, except for implementation issues, these differences are irrelevant to which people ultimately bear the burden of the tax and to its economic effects. Thus, the different approaches have more in common than it might appear on the surface. In chapter 7, we examine in more detail how each of these approaches would work, explore the differences among them, and evaluate them. Next, though, we focus on the many elements that are common to all consumption taxes.

Consumption Taxes, Income Taxes, and Incentives to Save and Invest

The key distinction between an income tax and a consumption tax is that income taxes reduce the incentive to save and invest, whereas consumption taxes do not. The easiest way to see this is to work through an example. Suppose you get a $100 bonus at work and are trying to decide whether to spend it today or to put it in the bank and save it for next year at a 10 percent interest rate. If there were no taxes, you'd have a choice between consuming the $100 today or saving it so you have $110 next year, a 10 percent reward for saving.

Now let's see how things change when there's a single-rate 20 percent income tax. If you choose to spend your raise immediately, you'll get to consume $80—your take-home pay after the income tax. If you decide instead to save it, your $80 will earn an extra $8 in interest. An income tax, however, subjects that interest to taxation as well. After taxes, you only get $6.40 in interest—so your choice is between consuming $80 today and $86.40 next year. Thus, the income tax not only reduces your take-home pay but also reduces the reward to saving from 10 percent to 8 percent.

Now consider what happens when, instead of an income tax, there is a retail sales tax levied at a rate of 20 percent of the value of purchases (inclusive of the tax).[5] If you spend your $100 bonus today, you are subject to a 20 percent tax, so you get to consume $80 after taxes, just like you would under the income tax. But what if you prefer to save the bonus so you can buy goods and services next year? Then you put the $100 bonus in the bank, and because it earns 10 percent interest, you'll have $110 in your account next year; note that, unlike under an income tax, no tax is triggered by the interest earned. When you withdraw your money and spend it, you owe the 20 percent sales tax, leaving you with 80 percent of $110, or $88, of after-tax consumption. Thus, under the consumption tax, your choice is to consume $80 today or consume $88 in a year. The reward for saving is still 10 percent, exactly what it would be in the absence of any tax at all. The 20 percent income tax leads to the same result as the 20 percent consumption tax if you consume today—the difference is that the income tax reduces next year's consumption from $110 to $86.40, which is equivalent to what would happen under a consumption tax with a 21.45 percent rate. So the income tax is like a consumption tax with a tax rate that rises when you defer consumption.

This is what economists mean when they say that a consumption tax is "neutral" between current and future consumption: the terms of the choice between consumption today and consumption in the future are the same as they would be in the absence of taxes. In our example, you get the 10 percent reward under the consumption tax, just as you would if there were no taxes, while the income tax leaves you with only an 8 percent reward for saving. To put it another way, the consumption tax imposes the same tax rate on your consumption regardless of when you decide to consume, whereas the income tax effectively imposes a higher tax rate on your consumption the longer you choose to defer that consumption. Our example is admittedly simplified, but complicating it in any number of ways, such as considering multiple time periods or allowing inflation, would not change the basic result.[6] Moreover, the argument applies to *any* form of consumption tax, including not only retail sales taxes but also value-added taxes, the flat tax, and a personal consumption tax.

Some of these tax systems require businesses to remit taxes, so to show that under a consumption tax there is no reduction in the return to saving *or investing*, we need to investigate further. It turns out that there is a key difference between how business investment is treated under a consumption tax versus an income tax system. An income tax allows deductions for the cost of capital goods as they *depreciate* (i.e., lose their value due to wearing out or technological obsolescence), while a consumption tax allows the cost of capital goods to be deducted from the tax base in full immediately, which is known as *expensing*. Modifying our example a bit can show why expensing removes the tax system's impact on the incentive of business to invest in the same way that a consumption tax has no impact on the return to saving.

Suppose you're the owner of a small business that has just earned a $100 profit. You could take the portion that is left over after taxes out of the business today and use it to buy a new (cheap) smart phone. Alternatively, you could invest the profits in the business by purchasing a new piece of equipment that will enable the business next year to produce goods that are worth 10 percent over and above the cost of the investment. You know that immediately after producing the goods, the equipment will break down and produce nothing more.

Under either an income or a consumption type of business tax, if you pay the profit to yourself today and consume it, it will be subject to tax. If the tax rate is 20 percent, you have the option of consuming $80 worth of stuff today. The difference is in what happens if you invest in the business by buying some new equipment. Under the income tax, you would still pay a 20 percent tax on your $100 profit today, even if you were to invest in the equipment; there is no deduction for the cost of the equipment because it hasn't worn out yet. So you have $80 left over to invest, which will produce $88 in goods for you next year. Next year, you will have $8 in taxable income—$88 in sales, minus an $80 deduction for depreciation. You would pay 20 percent of taxable income, or $1.60, in tax next year, leaving you with $86.40 to consume. So the business income tax leaves you with a choice of consuming $80 today or, if you invest your profits, $86.40 next year—reducing the reward to investing from 10 percent to 8 percent, just as in the personal saving example.

In contrast, under expensing the tax on business income has no effect on the return to investing. If you decide to spend all of your profit on the equipment, you face no tax liability today because you get to deduct the full purchase price of the equipment immediately, which makes your tax base today $0. This leaves you with $100 to invest in the equipment. Next year, you'll have $110 of output to sell but no depreciation deductions. After paying a 20 percent tax on that $110, you will have $88 dollars left. Thus, you have a choice between consuming $80 today or $88 next year. This is, of course, a 10 percent return, the same as what you would get in the absence of taxes. Although our example could be made more complicated—for instance, by allowing the equipment to depreciate over several years—this would not change the basic conclusion that with expensing the rate of return to investment is the same as it would be in the absence of taxes.

Similarities and Differences between a Consumption Tax and a Wage Tax, and the Fairness of a Transition to a Consumption Tax

Another way to eliminate the effect of taxes on the incentive to save and invest is to base tax liability on labor compensation, while exempting from tax all interest income and other returns from saving and investment. This approach is generally called a *wage tax*, although tax scholars sometimes refer to it as a *yield-exempt tax*, because the yield (i.e., return) from saving and investment does not trigger tax liability. Extending our example to this case is straightforward. Under a 20 percent wage tax, when you earn $100, you receive $80 after tax. Saving it at a 10 percent interest rate would give you $88 next year, and there's no tax on the interest. So just like a consumption tax, the wage tax gives you a choice of consuming $80 today or $88 in a year. Not only is there no impact on the reward to saving—the rate of return remains at 10 percent—but the amount you get to consume after tax is exactly the same in both periods under either the wage tax or the retail sales tax.

These two alternative methods for exempting the return to saving— a consumption tax and a wage tax—are reflected in the two different kinds of IRAs in the current system. A traditional IRA allows a deduction for contributions to the account, exempts capital income on the account from taxation while it accrues, and then taxes withdrawals (which are presumably made to finance consumption). A Roth IRA, on the other hand, does not allow an initial deduction, does exempt capital income on the assets in the account from tax, but does not impose tax on withdrawals. Thus, the traditional IRA works like a consumption tax does to eliminate the tax penalty on the return to saving, while the Roth IRA works like a wage tax. Except for some technicalities (for example, marginal tax rates may differ at the time of contribution and the time of withdrawal), the two approaches are similar in the same way that consumption and wage taxes are similar.

Despite their similarity, the consequences of switching cold turkey from an income tax to a wage tax versus a consumption tax would be different in one important way. If we switch to a consumption tax, any preexisting wealth that gets spent on consumption after the transition will be taxed as it is spent. However, if we eliminate the income tax and replace it with a wage tax, all preexisting wealth can be spent on consumption tax-free forever. This is indeed an enormous difference, as accumulated wealth in the United States was approximately $83.3 trillion by the end of 2014.[7] To see the difference, imagine how a just-retired professor would feel if, the day after his retirement party, the United States replaced its income tax with a consumption tax: he would not be happy. He would not be happy because he had expected to be pretty much done with tax burden, but now as he spends down his retirement savings he triggers the consumption tax, so his savings will not provide him the standard of living he had expected. If, instead, the United States had switched to a wage tax on his first day of retirement, he would not be unhappy; indeed he would be pleased because not only would he escape any wage tax, but also the income tax liability on his capital income would be eliminated. The potential windfall tax on existing wealth can be relieved to some extent by building transitional provisions into the reform. However, the more transition relief that is provided to existing assets in the switch to any consumption tax, the more it becomes like a wage tax.

What characterizes the owners of wealth who will be affected most by these transitional gains or losses? They are, on average, very wealthy; for example, the richest 1 percent of the population owns approximately one-third of the nation's private wealth.[8] They are also disproportionately older people. In 2013, 42 percent of families were headed by someone aged 55 or older, but these families owned 66 percent of the nation's wealth.[9]

Whether it is "fair" to hit wealth holders, elderly or not, with such an unexpected burden is an equity issue about which economic analysis cannot be decisive. The fact that moving to a consumption tax with no transition relief places a burden on the wealthy is probably appealing to many people. But experience suggests that wealth owners and their representatives would have their interests defended by strong lobbying, a powerful voting bloc, and some public support from people who view the unexpected transitional burden as unfair, so some kind of transitional relief would probably happen.

Because many important prices are inflexible in the short run, the transition to a consumption tax can also lead to a variety of other, often capricious redistributions. Depending on whether the Federal Reserve allows the price level to change, all sorts of redistributions can occur surrounding contracts written in fixed nominal terms, such as bonds, mortgages, and long-term wage contracts. For example, if a switch to a consumption tax is accompanied by an increase in consumer prices, bondholders suffer the same one-time loss as stockholders because the real value of their bonds declines. On the other hand, if prices do not rise, the switch to a consumption tax will not hurt bondholders because firms are legally obligated to pay them the full nominal value of their bonds. In this case, the owners of businesses who borrowed from those bondholders are hit hard because they cannot pass through the cost of lost depreciation deductions to the bondholders. Some of these firms might be forced into bankruptcy or layoffs, hurting the employees as well.

One other notable issue of transitional fairness concerns government transfer payments that are not automatically indexed for price changes, such as food stamps and welfare. If a consumption tax is accompanied by a price increase, and transfer payments are not increased in value to keep real benefits constant, the tax change levies an extra burden on the poor.

Not All "Capital Income" Represents the Return to Saving

So far, we've seen that a hallmark of both consumption taxes and wage taxes is that they exempt from taxation the return to saving. The return to saving can be thought of as the reward to deferring consumption. Certainly some of what we loosely call "capital income" (interest, dividends, capital gains, small-business income, and so on) represents returns to deferring consumption. But some of it represents something else entirely. In what follows, we consider what the other components of capital income represent and how they are treated under different tax systems.[10]

Consumption Taxes, Income Taxes, and Inflation

As we have noted before, some portion of capital income represents compensation for the fact that inflation erodes the real purchasing power of the underlying wealth. Consumption and wage taxes automatically exempt this compensation for inflation from tax. For instance, if half of the 10 percent interest in our examples above reflected inflation, the consumption and wage taxes wouldn't tax it because they exempt the full 10 percent from tax. In contrast, under our current income tax, to the extent that capital income is taxed, the inflationary component is taxed too. As we discuss in chapter 4, when inflation is more than a few percentage points per year, this can greatly increase the effective tax rate on the return to saving.

Compensation for inflation does not have to be taxed by an income tax. But designing an income tax that has this feature is difficult, while it is automatic under a consumption or wage tax. The key difference is that an income tax must distinguish what portion of capital income was compensation for inflation and what portion was not, instead of just exempting the whole thing. Accurately distinguishing the two would require not only a measure of the dollar amount of capital income, which is what we currently report on the tax form, but also a measure of the value of the underlying wealth that generated the return, which can be administratively difficult to obtain, as well as the rate of inflation over the period the capital asset was held. For example, suppose that someone receives $10 of interest income and the rate of inflation has been 5 percent. If that interest was earned on $100 of wealth, we should be exempting 5 percent of $100, or $5. But if it were earned on $125 of wealth, we should be exempting 5 percent of $125, or $6.25. If we don't know whether the underlying wealth was $100 or $125, we don't know exactly how much of the $10 to exempt to offset the fact that, in addition to generating the $10 of interest income, the real value of the investment has been eroded by the inflation. It would be possible to come up with rough approximations—for example, based on average interest rates in the economy in a particular year— but these would be just that, rough approximations. Obtaining a correct measure of real, inflation-adjusted, personal capital income would also require adjusting dividends and capital gains (i.e., the increase in value of assets held in one's portfolio) for inflation. At the business level, the value of depreciation deductions, interest deductions, and inventory allowances would also need to be adjusted for inflation. For similar reasons as above, this is difficult in an income tax and unnecessary under a consumption or wage tax. This is not a big concern when inflation is as low as it has been recently, but of course, inflation may rise again.

Consumption Taxes, Income Taxes, and Risk

An important component of capital income is the compensation—or *premium*—for bearing risk. On average, riskier opportunities for saving and investment yield higher returns because people prefer to avoid risk and need to be compensated to be willing to accept it. For example, corporate stocks have historically earned a higher return, on average, than government bonds, partly because the return on stocks is much more variable. Therefore, there is a trade-off between risk and expected average return, and in choosing their portfolio savers need to choose some optimal balance between them.

Compensation for bearing risk is also exempt under both consumption taxes and wage taxes. To illustrate, consider a risky asset that offers a 1-in-2 chance of earning a 40 percent return and a 1-in-2 chance of losing 10 percent of its value, so the return is expected to be 15 percent on average. Suppose once again that you've got $100 before taxes available to save and there's a 20 percent consumption tax rate, so you have the option of consuming $80 after taxes today. Under a consumption tax, if the money is saved, no tax is paid today, $100 gets saved, and it yields either $140 or $90 next year. After paying the 20 percent consumption tax, you get to consume either $112 or $72 next year. Relative to the $80 you can consume today, that still translates to a 40 percent return if you have good luck, a 10 percent loss if you have bad luck, and a 15 percent return on average. Under a wage tax, you pay tax immediately today even if you save, leaving $80 to be saved. Next year you get to consume $112 (= 1.4 × $80) if you have good luck or $72 (= 0.9 × $80) if you have bad luck, exactly the same outcomes as under the consumption tax. So under either a consumption tax or a wage tax, your average return from investing in the risky asset is 15 percent, the same as it would be without any taxes, and there is no distortion to your decisions regarding how much risk to take. Comparing a consumption tax to a wage tax, the people who are lucky after the fact remit more tax, and the unlucky people remit less tax. But this distinction is in fact meaningless. What people actually get to consume either today or tomorrow, whether they have good luck or bad, is exactly the same under both taxes.

A more surprising fact is that under a proportional *income* tax that allows full deductions for losses, the compensation for risk is also effectively exempt from tax. The argument for why, which dates back to an article written by economists Evsey Domar and Richard Musgrave in the early 1940s, is based on the key insight that an income tax absorbs some of the risk from your portfolio. If an investment turns out well, the income tax takes away some of the resulting capital income, but if it turns out badly, the tax system partly compensates you by allowing you to deduct the loss, reducing tax liability. Thus, the income tax reduces both the expected after-tax return *and* the variance in the after-tax return. Over seventy years ago these two economists showed that the reduction in the expected after-tax return is exactly equal to the fair market price for the reduction in risk, so that even though on average the government collects revenue from imposing income tax on the portion of the return that represents compensation for bearing risk, that part of the tax does not place a burden on the taxpayer. In fact, by increasing the share of one's portfolio invested in risky assets, an investor can exactly replicate the risk-return possibilities that would have been available if only the risk-free portion of returns were taxed. Because the income tax on the risky portion of the return leaves the investor with exactly the same opportunities he or she would have had with no tax at all on that portion of the return, it is in a sense equivalent to not taxing that portion of the return at all.[11]

This example relies on a presumption that the income tax treats gains and losses symmetrically, which in reality it does not. Progressive tax rates and limitations on deductibility of losses both mean that the government takes a larger share of capital income if you have good luck with your portfolio than if you have bad luck. However, this is not an inherent or unique feature of income taxes. Indeed, the reasons for the asymmetric treatment of gains and losses (the desire for *ex post* vertical equity and the need to limit tax-avoidance schemes) can apply to consumption tax plans as well.[12] A consumption tax with these features would also tax some of the compensation for bearing risk.

"Supernormal" Returns and Mislabeled Labor Compensation

Aside from compensation for postponement of consumption, inflation, and risk, some of what we loosely call "capital income" may reflect a variety of factors such as returns to innovation, returns to entrepreneurial skill and effort, returns to establishing a monopoly in some market, returns to early units of investment that may be more productive than the last "marginal" units of investment, or simply mislabeled returns to labor effort. What all of these have in common from an economic point of view is that they are *supernormal returns*—meaning they produce income that is larger than the "normal" return that would be earned on a marginal investment in capital, which is competed down to a fairly low level. It turns out that these supernormal returns are effectively taxed by both income taxes and consumption taxes. A wage tax, on the other hand, would not tax them.

A highly visible example of a supernormal return would be Bill Gates's income, which comes mainly from his share of the profits of Microsoft. Only a tiny portion of that income represents a reward for postponing consumption or taking on risk. Mostly, it represents some combination of a return to his labor (including effort put into innovation and entrepreneurship) and the return to being in the right place at the right time and gaining an early lead in what turned out to be a fantastically lucrative market that naturally tends toward monopoly (because computer software tends to be more valuable to a user when most other people are using the same software). Under the current income tax, these returns are indeed taxed, mainly by the corporate income tax and also by the personal income tax to the extent that Gates realizes any of his capital gains by selling shares or receives dividends from Microsoft.

A wage tax, on the other hand, would never tax these returns as long as Microsoft pays Gates only a nominal salary. Under a wage tax, relabeling your labor compensation as capital income would be a potentially attractive way to escape taxation altogether. The difficulty of distinguishing what is labor income and what is capital income is an important reason that a pure wage tax would almost certainly end up being highly inequitable and costly to enforce.[13]

In contrast, a consumption tax does indeed tax supernormal returns and mislabeled returns to labor (like those received by Bill Gates) in the same way as an income tax does. No matter what these returns are labeled, they will eventually trigger tax liability when the recipient, or his or her heirs, spend the supernormal returns. For consumption taxes that have a business tax component, like a flat tax, the normal return to saving and investment is exempt from tax because investments in physical capital (such as productive machinery and factories) are expensed (deducted immediately). The factors that produce supernormal returns for someone like Bill Gates lead to big increases in the taxable revenues of his company but do nothing to increase the size of the expensing deduction that the company gets to take early on: the supernormal returns did not result from larger than usual investments in physical capital. Similarly, under the Hall-Rabushka flat tax, if a firm mislabels the labor compensation of its proprietor as "dividends" or "capital gains," no tax will be due on that income at the personal level, but tax is due at the business level, and the mislabeling produces no expensing deduction for capital investment to offset it. Thus, as long as the tax rates on the personal and business bases in the flat tax are the same, mislabeling labor income as returns to capital and vice versa makes no difference to the total tax liability.

How Different Is the Current Income Tax from a Consumption Tax?

The bottom line of the above discussion is that an income tax taxes the return to saving while a consumption tax does not. Compensation for the loss in real value of assets caused by inflation need not be taxed under either type of tax, but it is administratively easier to exempt it from a consumption tax. Compensation for bearing risk need not be taxed under either approach: the features that make it partly taxable (including progressive rates and limitations on loss deductibility) might apply under either type of tax. Finally, supernormal returns and labor compensation mislabeled as capital income are generally taxable under either approach. Thus, much of what is generally thought of as capital income can be treated similarly by income taxes and consumption taxes. In sharp contrast, a wage tax would completely exempt *all* of these forms of capital income.

The difference between a consumption tax and the system that we have now is mitigated further by the fact that, as we detail in chapter 2, our current tax system is in many ways a hybrid between an income tax and a consumption tax. For example, although revenue is collected from taxing nominal (not real, inflation-adjusted) interest income, even more revenue may be lost due to the *deduction* of nominal interest payments, both because those deducting interest payments tend to be in higher tax brackets than those receiving interest and because so much interest income is sheltered from tax (largely because it is earned in tax-exempt pension accounts or IRAs). Large portions of dividend and capital gains income are excluded from personal tax, and generous depreciation allowances further reduce the effective tax on capital income.

One rough metric of how different the current income tax is from a consumption tax is the amount of revenue that would be lost if the tax base was switched from income to consumption, while leaving the other features of the current system intact. To see this, consider that the existing income tax could be almost entirely converted to a type of consumption tax in just three steps: (1) exempt all interest, dividends, and capital gains from tax; (2) replace depreciation deductions with expensing of all new investment, while eliminating depreciation deductions for past investment; and (3) eliminate all interest deductions. One study calculated that taking these steps in 2004, while leaving the rest of the tax code (including the rate structure) the way it is, would have reduced revenues from personal and corporate income taxes by a total of $64 billion that year, or only approximately 6 percent of income tax revenues.[14] Thus, in 2004, taken altogether, our tax system raised only a modest amount of net revenue more than an otherwise-similar consumption tax would raise. In that sense, we are not that far from a consumption tax, although our system is still rife with many distortions to incentives that would be avoided under a clean consumption tax. This should not be taken to mean that transforming our income tax into a consumption tax would be easy, though. The calculation above relies heavily on the politically challenging steps of eliminating depreciation deductions on past investments and/or interest deductions. Skipping either or both of those steps would make the switch to consumption taxation very costly indeed in terms of revenue.

Now that we've examined how income taxes and consumption taxes differ in their treatment of capital income, let's consider how they treat the other major source of income, labor.

Consumption Taxes, Income Taxes, and the Incentive to Work

Popular discussion of tax alternatives often misses the fact that both consumption taxes and income taxes reduce the reward for working (the quantity of goods and services that can be purchased per hour of work). The reward for working can be reduced in either of two ways— by lowering take-home pay and holding fixed the prices of the things you buy, or by increasing the prices of everything you buy while keeping take-home pay the same: "pay me now or pay me later." A comprehensive 20 percent tax on wages and salaries has about the same effect on reducing the reward for working as a comprehensive 20 percent sales tax.[15]

It is sometimes argued that a consumption tax reduces the incentive to work *more* than an income tax does. The argument goes like this. Total consumption is smaller than the total amount of income. There-fore, the tax rates required to raise a given amount of revenue must be higher under a consumption tax than under an income tax with an equally broad base, and a higher tax rate means a greater disincentive to work. The problem with this argument is that it ignores the fact that, because a consumption tax allows you to earn higher after-tax returns on the portion of your labor income that you save, working becomes more financially attractive. This helps offset the effect of the higher tax rates (on an apparently smaller base) that would be required under a consumption tax.

Is a Consumption Tax More or Less Fair Than an Income Tax?

On a year-by-year basis, a consumption-based tax can appear to be much more regressive than an income tax with the same rate structure. This is because people who have low incomes in any given year on average spend a very high fraction of their incomes—often more than their income—while people with high incomes in a given year save a relatively larger portion of theirs.[16] One might conclude from this observation that shifting from an income tax to a consumption tax with the same rate structure would greatly increase the tax burden on low-income people relative to high-income people.

This argument is somewhat misleading, though, because a snapshot of income-saving patterns for a single year of data significantly over-states the regressivity of the consumption tax compared to an income tax. First of all, in any given year some people with temporarily low income continue spending at a rate corresponding to their usual income. Conversely, some people who had an exceptionally good income-earning year might not expect their good fortune to continue and therefore keep their spending well below their income, saving up for the years of relatively bad fortune. In both cases, one year's income is not a good measure of how well off those people are, and the fact that the consumption-income ratio varies widely across persons, being high for the temporarily low-income people and low for the temporarily high-income people, overstates how much more regressive a consump-tion tax is relative to an income tax.

Second, most people have a natural life-cycle pattern of earning and saving. In the early years of working life, family expenses are pressing and income relatively low, so savings are minimal or even negative, as families borrow to finance consumption, including housing. In the later working years, incomes have grown to the point where many families begin to save for their retirement and higher education for their children. In retirement, the pattern reverses again, as people live off their accumulated savings, spending more than they earn. Looking across people of different ages, low-income people (on average the young and old) would appear to do little (or even negative) saving, and high-income people would seem to be relatively big savers. That picture would be misleading because—leaving aside for a moment bequests, inheritances, other gifts, and government transfers—over a lifetime people cannot spend more than they earn, and over a lifetime people end up spending all of what they earn.[17] Thus, from a lifetime perspective it doesn't make a huge difference whether the tax base is income or consumption: it all adds up the same. Big savers age 45 to 65, who might appear to be getting off easy under a consumption tax because they consume a relatively small fraction of their annual income, will eventually pay more tax when they take their trip around the world and otherwise live the high life when they retire. A single-rate tax on consumption and a single-rate tax on labor income both end up being single-rate levies on lifetime resources. Similarly, over a lifetime, a consumption tax with graduated rates could in principle achieve about the same degree of progressivity as a graduated income tax: *one is not inherently more progressive than the other*. Rather, the degree of progressivity depends largely on the kind of tax rates that we impose, which is in principle a separate issue than the tax base the rates apply to.

Many economists would also argue that a consumption tax is more horizontally equitable than a comprehensive income tax. This is because when comparing families with equal lifetime labor incomes, a consumption tax collects the same present value of taxation regardless of a family's saving propensity. In contrast, under an income tax savers have a higher lifetime tax burden than non-savers because the return to their saving triggers an additional tax liability that does not arise under a consumption tax. If two people earn the same labor incomes, but one prefers to save more of that labor income early in life so as to defer more consumption until later in life, under an income tax that person will effectively face higher tax rates on more of his or her consumption, compared to another person who had the same opportunities (because of equal labor earnings) but had a stronger preference for present consumption over future consumption. Thus, a consumption tax arguably penalizes people whose tastes are more future-oriented, and rewards those who are inclined toward present consumption.

A caveat to these arguments arises because across people there are apparently positive empirical correlations among natural ability, lifetime labor earnings, and propensity to save and defer consumption. In other words, better-off people tend to save larger fractions of their incomes.[18] One reason that a tendency to defer consumption is positively correlated with lifetime labor income may be that patience and willingness to defer gratification are traits that also promote success in the labor market, and tend to go along with other traits that also make one more productive. Another is that better-off people are more likely to be willing and able to save for the purpose of passing on wealth to their heirs. All of this means that to achieve the same level of progressivity overall as an income tax, a consumption tax would tend to need a more progressive pattern of tax rates. Some economists who favor a consumption tax would go further than this, and tax a bequest as if it were an act of consumption by the bequeathor.[19] A tax on bequests, however, might be viewed as a double tax on deferring consumption, as a tax is levied both when the bequest is made and then again when the heirs consume it. If people leave bequests because they value the consumption of their heirs, then this would reduce the incentive to save for bequests in much the same way as an income tax does. We consider these issues in more detail when we discuss the estate tax later in this chapter.

Economic Reasons for Switching to a Consumption Tax

What would be the long-term economic impact of switching to a consumption tax? The most talked-about potential benefits arise from increasing the incentive to save and invest. A less publicized but perhaps more important benefit is that a consumption tax could make it easier to "level the playing field" among different types of investment. Finally, the windfall tax burdens that arise in the transition to a new system could have important economic effects, apart from whether they are fair or not.

Switching to a consumption tax would remove any negative impact of the tax system on the incentive to save and invest. Thus, a consumption tax distorts one less decision—and a critical one, to boot—compared to an income tax. By itself, this is a step toward a more efficient tax system because individuals' choices between current and future consumption will more closely reflect the social return to saving rather than the influence of the tax system. However, it is not necessarily true that this makes a consumption tax more economically efficient overall than an income tax; the tax that distorts the smallest *number* of choices is not necessarily the most efficient.[20]

In theory, a reform that removes the tax distortion to saving decisions while raising the same revenue should increase saving and capital accumulation, which many economists argue would be beneficial. By providing workers better machines and tools to work with, increased capital accumulation could improve productivity and long-run living standards. As shown in chapter 4, however, the magnitude of any increase in saving that would arise from improved incentives is highly uncertain. This is a crucially important question on which the available evidence is simply not very good. In recent history, the periods with the highest incentives to save coincided paradoxically with the *lowest* rates of saving. This might have occurred for many different reasons, each with different policy implications, and it is difficult to distinguish empirically among these reasons. Nonetheless, the best guess of most economists is that private saving is probably not very responsive to the after-tax rate of return, so that switching to a consumption tax would be unlikely to increase the quantity of saving much. Because we can find more direct ways to increase national saving (for example, by reducing the budget deficit), the likely but not guaranteed prospect of a somewhat higher saving rate does not appear to be, by itself, a reason to undertake a wholesale transformation of the tax system.

A second possible benefit of a consumption tax is that achieving "neutrality" or "uniformity" in the tax treatment of various types of investment would be made easier. Under the current income tax, different types of investment are effectively taxed at varying rates. For example, corporate business investments are taxed more heavily than noncorporate business investments, which are in turn taxed more heavily than investments in owner-occupied housing. Investments in certain types of capital equipment or in certain lines of business are capriciously favored relative to others by depreciation schedules that are more front-loaded, or accelerated, relative to true economic depreciation. Business endeavors that can be packaged into assets that appreciate in value are more attractive than those that pay their returns in the form of dividends or interest because of the preferential treatment of capital gains. Inflation can introduce arbitrary variation in tax rates. All of these deviations from "neutrality" are economically harmful because they attract investment into the tax-favored investments even though their social return is not higher than the social return to the investments that are not tax-favored.

A consumption tax would eliminate all of these distortions to the choice among different types of investment because it would equalize the effective marginal tax rate on the returns to all investment to a single uniform rate—zero. In principle, an income tax could also be made more neutral, taxing the returns to investment at a uniform but positive rate. Thus, to some extent, this is a separate issue from the choice between an income tax and a consumption tax: it's a matter of having a "clean," or uniform, base. But this particular aspect of uniformity is much easier to achieve in a consumption tax than in an income tax. Some of the existing distortions are hard to avoid in an income tax because capital income is difficult to measure accurately. For example, measuring economic depreciation exactly right is impossible, so some distortions will inevitably be caused by implicitly favoring investments in assets whose depreciation for tax purposes is especially generous relative to true depreciation. Similarly, including all capital gains in taxable income as they accrue is probably infeasible, so appreciating assets will be favored. It is theoretically possible to adjust the measurement of capital income for inflation, but in practice doing so would be complicated and inevitably imperfect. Because a consumption tax eliminates the need to address any of these issues, it can achieve this aspect of uniformity in a simple way.

The transition to a consumption tax can also have significant efficiency consequences. For example, from an efficiency point of view, placing a surprise, one-time tax on holders of existing wealth, as moving to a consumption tax could, is not unattractive. Raising revenue from the returns to *past* investments has no effect on the incentive to invest, to work, or to do anything else. Shifting tax burdens onto the elderly—whose work and saving decisions are nearly finished—also avoids costly disincentives. Moreover, because the elderly have a relatively low propensity to save, transferring some of the tax burden onto them and away from others could give a boost to national saving. This last effect is likely to be offset, however, by the fact that the wealthy as a whole have a much higher propensity to save than everyone else, and placing an extra burden on them through a consumption tax might reduce their contribution to national saving. As we see in the next chapter, models that attempt to work out the economic impact of switching to a consumption tax suggest that, all things considered, a very large portion of any economic gain from the switch comes from replacing other, distorting, taxes with this one-time tax on already accumulated wealth.

As we have emphasized, we now have a messy hybrid between an income tax and a consumption tax. This is a mixed blessing for the case for switching entirely to a consumption tax. To the extent that saving already receives consumption tax treatment due to tax-preferred pensions, IRAs, and the like, the potential increase in saving and corresponding economic benefits that could arise from going all the way to a consumption tax are apparently reduced. This should not be overstated, however. Although a large share of capital income is already sheltered from taxation, a large share of the capital income that would arise from *additional* saving, which matters for decisions about how much to save, is still taxed. This is largely because pensions, IRAs, and similar plans shelter saving only up to some limit. For anyone whose saving is at or above those limits, the marginal incentive to save is still distorted by tax. On the positive side, this means that switching entirely to a consumption tax would still improve incentives substantially for the people who do most of the saving—and at a lower cost in terms of lost revenue (which must be recouped somehow) than if we were starting from a pure income tax. But it also means that the capital income that remains unsheltered from the current tax disproportionately goes to high-income people, which heavily influences the distributional impact of such a reform.

Simplification and Enforcement Aspects of a Consumption Tax
Even with all the compromises that we make in our current system, calculating and reporting capital income can be a complex and burdensome process. These compromises, in turn, create opportunities to achieve tax savings in complicated and socially unproductive ways, such as devising schemes to rearrange financial and business transactions. In principle, measuring consumption accurately is simpler than measuring income, even a version of income that makes concessions to measurability, mainly because the need for measuring capital income can be completely avoided. But, in practice, a consumption tax could end up being just as, or even more, difficult to administer and comply with than the current income tax. The simplicity and enforceability of moving to a consumption tax depend crucially on which approach is chosen and how it is operated. These issues are addressed in chapter 7.

Here, too, transitional issues are critically important. Moving cold turkey to a consumption tax like a VAT or flat tax could immediately make the taxpaying process simpler. But the pleadings of those likely to suffer windfall losses will be difficult to resist, so a switch to a consumption tax is likely to offer various forms of transition relief. Special transitional provisions can be exceedingly complex because they require the simultaneous operation of parallel tax systems, at least for a while. For example, interest on mortgages taken out before the switch might remain tax-preferred in some way, while interest on new mortgages is not. The real choice is not between the current system and a clean consumption tax but between the current system and a new tax encumbered by as yet unspecified rules for how to get from here to there, which can be unaesthetic at best, and complicated and loophole-ridden at worst.

One other transitional issue has important implications for evaluating a new system. Depending on how it is implemented, the switch to a consumption tax can lead to enormous incentives to postpone or speed up transactions around the date of switchover. Firms will post-pone investment until the expensing rules are in place, and under some plans, individuals will rush to consume as much as possible before the implementation date. This could cost a great deal of revenue and raises a very delicate problem of minimizing the short-run economic disruption at the time of transition. Evidence from past VAT rate increases in other countries suggests that acceleration of purchases, especially of durable goods, can be substantial.[21]

A Clean Tax Base

A third element of proposals for fundamental tax reform is to eliminate many or all of the features that provide special treatment of particular types of consumption or investment. The aim is variously described as "broadening" the tax base, "leveling the playing field," or making the tax system more "neutral." We refer to this aspect of tax reform proposals as a *clean* tax base.

Preferences for particular types of expenditures or activities are major contributors to the messiness in the tax base. Important examples are housing, health care, charity, funds raised by state and local governments, and education. Although we concentrate here on a few important examples, the current personal and corporate income taxes feature scores of other deviations from a clean-base system, from incentives to invest in low-income housing to tax breaks for the production of ethanol.[22] Each needs to be evaluated on its own merits.

Some ambitious proposals for overhauling the tax system, such as the one in President Obama's deficit commission report or the Hall-Rabushka flat tax, would eliminate many preferences of this sort. Other proposals tackle some of these preferences but do not eliminate the most prominent, and popular, of them. Beginning in the 1980s, the U.S. income tax system has moved closer to a consumption base and toward flatter rates. But at the same time it has rapidly *increased* the extent and generosity of deductions, exclusions, and credits. Any attempt to remove the most cherished and politically entrenched of these tax goodies would undoubtedly engender a fierce political fight, as the negative reaction to the report of the 2005 President's Advisory Panel on Federal Tax Reform showed.

Throughout this book, we have discussed a host of reasons why special incentives and rewards in the tax base can be a problem. Every reward is a penalty for someone else and every incentive is a disincentive for un-preferred activities, because the rewards and incentives require tax rates to be higher than otherwise. Moreover, tax deductions are a regressive way to subsidize activities: people with larger incomes receive bigger subsidies from deductions because on average they engage more in the deductible activities and have higher marginal tax rates. Those who don't itemize receive no subsidy, or benefit, from the deductions. Except in special cases, tax preferences are inefficient because they create an incentive to engage "too much" in the lightly taxed activity and too little in other activities, relative to what the free market would generate. And, finally, they are a big reason that our tax code is so complicated.

For all of these reasons, the burden of proof should rest on those who defend deviations from a clean tax base. There are three main acceptable lines of defense. First, allowing certain deductions can make the tax system fairer if, by so doing, the tax base provides a more accurate measurement of well-being. Second, a tax preference can improve economic efficiency if it corrects a significant market failure—that is, a situation where the incentives in the market do not lead to an economically efficient outcome by themselves. An example would be an externality, which occurs when an activity generates important benefits or costs for others that are not reflected in the incentives faced by the individual undertaking the action. Third, as we discussed in chapter 4, if we take as given the fact that any tax that is related to ability-to-pay will discourage work and encourage leisure, then it can be economically efficient to offset this distortion by subsidizing complements to work, such as child care, or by taxing complements to leisure. These are necessary, but not sufficient, conditions for a tax preference to be justified. For example, even if a significant market failure is identified, the tax preference must be the best alternative for dealing with it. As specific exceptions to a clean base are examined below, each of them is evaluated in light of these criteria.

Consider one more compelling argument for maintaining a clean base: the political system is incapable of distinguishing legitimate arguments from illegitimate ones and often succumbs to the political clout of powerful pleaders. Once any preference is allowed, we may begin to slide down the slippery slope to more preferences.

Aside from the sorts of preferences mentioned above, another important source of messiness in the tax base has to do with compromises or peculiarities involved in the taxation of capital income, such as the failure to index capital income for inflation and the double taxation of corporate income. These can also cause inefficiency, inequity, and complexity. As discussed above, a consumption tax could do away with many of these problems. In the latter part of this section we will consider in greater detail how the current design of the income tax and estate tax contribute to this sort of messiness, and what might be done about it.

Housing and the Mortgage Interest Deduction

Owner-occupied housing is favored by our tax system in a number of ways. By far, the deduction for home mortgage interest payments is the most visible and traditionally the most politically sacred aspect of these. Notably, its "sacredness" is now being challenged, as some recent prominent tax reform plans, such as those offered in 2015 by presidential candidates Jeb Bush and Marco Rubio, have proposed limiting it.[23]

The home mortgage interest deduction is an expensive one, costing $67 billion in revenues in fiscal year 2014. It requires personal tax rates to be about 4.8 percent (not 4.8 percentage *points*) higher than they otherwise could be.[24] About 82 percent of the revenue loss from the deduction goes to benefit households with incomes above $100,000.[25] So a lot is at stake in this debate. What are the issues?

First of all, let's consider whether there is any good economic reason to favor housing over other types of consumption or investment. To answer yes to this question requires demonstrating that an owner-occupied house provides important benefits to people other than the residents themselves; that the residents themselves take pleasure in ownership is an inadequate argument. Although undoubtedly neighbors prefer to gaze out their window at a well-kept rather than ramshackle house and owner-occupiers arguably maintain their houses better than the combination of renters and landlords, these benefits are certainly quite localized and probably fairly small. Sometimes vague appeals are made to the role of homeownership in maintaining a strong democracy, but these arguments are not convincing. Remember that to the extent that the tax system attracts investment into housing, it diverts funds from other business investments made by, for example, corporations outside the housing sector. Why isn't broad stock ownership a healthy aspect of democracy? All in all, preferential treatment of housing, in general, is difficult to justify on economic grounds.[26]

Some evidence shows that homeowners are more likely to engage in home maintenance, especially gardening. Homeowners are also more apt to join organizations and socialize with their neighbors compared to renters. In addition, homeowners are more likely to be politically informed and active than renters. All of these activities may create positive externalities. However, the correlation between homeownership and these behaviors may not be indicative of a causal relationship, and could instead arise from personal characteristics that make certain people more likely to be homeowners and also make them join more clubs, be more conscientious gardeners, and so on.[27] And, let's be honest, inadequate resources devoted to *gardening* should not justify $67 billion worth of annual tax subsidies for owner-occupied housing.

One might be tempted to defend the home mortgage interest deduction as necessary to correctly measure the tax base in a comprehensive income tax. After all, to achieve a comprehensive measure of income, interest payments ought to be deductible, just as interest receipts are taxable. The catch to this argument is that, if the goal is to measure income comprehensively, the rental value of owner-occupied housing, net of depreciation and maintenance expenses, should also be subject to tax. To be sure, most homeowners don't think of the rental value of their home as income in the same way that they think about, say, their salary. But the failure to include the services provided by housing in the tax base, in conjunction with the deductibility of mortgage interest, adds up to a big preference for residential housing.

To see this, consider a family that is trying to decide whether to buy a $300,000 house or instead to buy a more modest $200,000 house and invest the extra $100,000 in the stock market. Suppose further that the annual rent for such houses would be 10 percent of their value and that stocks provide an annual pre-tax return of 10 percent, so that each would be an equally attractive investment in the absence of taxes. Living in the more expensive house will certainly make the family better off; they'll have nicer living quarters, more rooms, a better view, a safer neighborhood, and so on. How much better off they are per year is approximated by the rental value of the extra housing, or $10,000 per year. Investing the $100,000 in stocks, on the other hand, will yield considerably less than $10,000 per year because of the taxes that would be due on the investment return.

The preferential tax treatment could tip the scales in favor of investing in the more expensive house. As a result, in some cases nonhousing investments are passed up in favor of more expensive homes even though, taxes aside, the return to these investments equals or exceeds the value of the housing services; from a social point of view, this is wasteful. Allowing the deductibility of mortgage interest exacerbates this problem because it enables homeowners to use borrowing with tax-deductible interest to finance an investment for which the return, the rental value of the housing, is untaxed. In addition, families and individuals who, for one reason or another, prefer to rent housing, end up being penalized. Because the net rental income of landlords is taxed, rental housing does not get the same preferential tax treatment afforded to owner-occupied housing. This generates an additional source of inefficiency. Not only is there an excessive amount of housing and an insufficient amount of other types of investment, but also some households are induced to own housing when, taxes aside, they would find it more attractive to rent housing.

Even if we wanted to, however, there is no clean and easy way to put owner-occupied housing on a level playing field with other investments because taxing the net rental value of owner-occupied housing would be complicated and imprecise, as it probably would have to rely on homeowners' annually self-assessing the value of their house or condo. Moreover, it would undoubtedly be resisted strenuously by the public, so it is probably not a practical option. It is not inconceivable, however, as several European countries have attempted to do this, albeit in a very rough fashion.

A simpler approach to reducing the tax preference for owner-occupied housing (that is, the penalty for everything else) would be to eliminate the deduction for home mortgage interest; Canada, Germany, and the United Kingdom are three countries that take this approach. This would certainly make mortgage-financed housing less attractive, reducing the inefficient bias toward housing investment. But this is not a flawless option because it would eliminate the bias only for taxpayers who must borrow to finance their houses. For those who are wealthy enough (or who have wealthy-enough relatives) to pay cash or later pay off their loans, part of the opportunity cost of housing is the (generally taxed) return on what asset would otherwise be held. The taxation of the alternative investment still makes buying one's own house look more attractive than otherwise. Thus, without a mortgage deduction, it would cost mortgage holders the pre-tax rate of interest to own housing (because interest is not deductible), but for wealthy individuals who need not borrow, the cost would be the lower after-tax interest rate.

No such dilemma arises under a consumption tax. Although under some variants of the Hall-Rabushka flat tax proposed in Congress the deduction for mortgage interest is retained, it is completely incongruous in such a consumption tax because other interest payments are not deductible and all forms of capital income are untaxed. A consumption tax that treats purchasing housing just like other purchases and does not allow mortgage interest deductions would be a clean and simple way of eliminating the existing bias toward housing. Tax preferences for owner-occupied housing are often defended on the grounds that their elimination would lead to unfair transitional effects. In particular, homeowners are understandably concerned about what eliminating the mortgage interest deduction would do to house prices. By itself, eliminating the home mortgage deduction makes it more expensive to buy a house for anyone who relies on mortgage financing and could expect to itemize deductions. This would tend to reduce the demand for housing, which in turn would cause housing prices to drop. The greatest decline in demand would be for the high-priced homes that itemizers in high tax brackets favor, so that eliminating the tax preference for housing should shift demand from more to less expensive homes.[28]

The historical experience in the United States and other countries casts doubt on predictions of large impacts on either housing prices or the extent of homeownership. After all, dire predictions for the housing market were made about the Tax Reform Act of 1986, which made the deductibility of mortgage interest less valuable by lowering marginal tax rates, but it has been difficult to discern any negative effects on housing prices from that reform.[29] Canada has no deduction for mortgage interest at all but has a slightly higher homeownership rate than we do in the United States.[30] Indeed, many countries without deductibility have higher homeownership rates than we do, and some with deductibility have lower rates.[31] William Gale of the Brookings Institution points out that mortgage interest subsidies have been reduced dramatically in the United Kingdom since the mid-1970s, yet homeownership rates, mortgage debt, and housing as a share of the capital stock actually grew faster than in the United States.[32] Gale argues that a fundamental reform that eliminates all tax preferences for housing and moves to a consumption tax could, though, have a fairly large impact, with real house prices falling by about 7 to 10 percent in the short run and from 2 to 6 percent in the long run.

In search of an explanation of the housing market crash that began in 2007, some have pointed to the mortgage interest deduction. Surely it provides an incentive for more people to own houses, for homeowners to own bigger houses than otherwise, and for people to finance their houses with bigger mortgages than otherwise. A problem with the argument that the mortgage interest deduction was a major cause of the bubble or crash is timing. The mortgage interest deduction had been around for decades, and nothing about it changed during the years when the bubble inflated and then popped. In fact, by historical standards, the value of tax savings from the deduction was unusually low throughout the whole episode because of very low nominal interest rates (due to low inflation). With that said, the home mortgage interest deduction does encourage ordinary people to make highly leveraged bets on owner-occupied housing, which the recent crash reminds us is a rather risky asset. In that sense, it is at least possible that the deduction could make it more likely that bubbles in housing prices will arise from time to time, and exacerbate the fallout when they pop.[33]

Health Care and Health Insurance

Tax policy has played a big role in the markets for health care and health insurance in the United States for a long time. The Affordable Care Act (ACA), also known as "Obamacare," enacted in 2010, greatly expanded that role in some important ways, but also involved provisions that may eventually curtail the role in some respects. In what follows, we'll first summarize how the markets for health care and health insurance worked and how tax policy influenced them before the ACA, and then discuss the reforms enacted in the ACA.

The most important tax preference for health care has long been the exclusion from tax of employer contributions to employee medical insurance plans. Since World War II, these contributions have been deductible from the employing businesses' taxable income just the way wage and salary payments are, but the value of the health insurance—unlike wages and salary receipts—has not been part of employees' taxable income. In fiscal year 2014, this treatment cost an estimated $195 billion in revenues, requiring personal tax rates to be 14 percent (not percentage points) higher than otherwise.[34]

Does health care merit preferential tax treatment? This argument cannot be dismissed out of hand, because health insurance is plagued by serious market failures arising from imperfect information.[35] First, a problem of *adverse selection* arises because individuals know more about their health risks and status than insurers do. Insurance companies charge premiums based on the average level of risk for a particular population and in some cases a perfunctory medical examination. Some healthier, lower-risk people will find this price unattractive and leave the market, which increases the average risk level of people left in the insurance pool. This, in turn, pushes up premiums, driving out even more low-risk people, and a vicious cycle ensues. As a result, many people end up without insurance, even though the insurance could be both valuable to the buyer and profitable for the insurance company in the absence of the adverse selection problem.

The system of employer-provided insurance helps mitigate the adverse selection problem; because employees work for firms for reasons generally unrelated to health risks, an insurance provider has reason to expect that any firm's employees are a mix of high-risk and low-risk people. Employer-based insurance thus automatically pools risks. By encouraging employer-provided insurance, the tax preference for it has helped to offset the adverse selection problem that would otherwise plague this market. Nevertheless, before provisions in the ACA meant to address adverse selection in the individual health insurance market were implemented starting in 2014, adverse selection remained a serious problem for people who were not covered by employer-provided insurance and who were faced with high premium rates. It was also arguably partly responsible for the almost complete absence of a market for long-term contracts for health insurance that would be fully portable across jobs and would not skyrocket in price if you developed a chronic illness *after* purchasing it.

A second market failure associated with health insurance is known as *moral hazard*. This means that because health insurance changes the incentives faced by insured people, they may change their behavior in a way that drives up expenditures on health care. For instance, because most people with insurance face a low or zero out-of-pocket charge for additional medical services, they may consume extra medical services for which the true social costs (which are higher than their out-of-pocket costs) exceed the benefits. However, for reasons we explain below, the tax preference for employer-provided health insurance tends to exacerbate the moral hazard problem rather than reducing it.

Special treatment of health care might also be justified by equity objectives. The itemized deduction for medical expenditures is consistent with horizontal equity concerns; families that experience large, unavoidable, out-of-pocket medical costs arguably have a lower ability to pay taxes than other families with the same income. Furthermore, vertical equity concerns might motivate a desire to redistribute resources to the poor, or to those burdened by extraordinary medical expenses, in the form of health care. In some cases, voters may prefer redistribution for a specific meritorious (in their eyes) purpose such as health care over redistribution of resources that can be used for any purpose, meritorious or not. Moreover, "luck egalitarian" arguments of the sort discussed in chapter 3 imply that there is an especially strong moral rationale for redistribution to protect people from poor health status to the extent that it is due to bad luck, as it usually is. Finally, low-income uninsured people often end up getting care anyway—for example, through uncompensated care from a public or charitable hospital. This creates a kind of moral hazard problem by reducing the incentive to buy insurance. While such care does help the poor who receive it, both the benefits and the costs are distributed in a capricious fashion. For instance, whether a particular uninsured individual has access to uncompensated care is largely a matter of luck, and the costs may be borne through higher insurance premiums for certain people or perhaps lower compensation for health-care providers who happen to be willing to work in certain areas. Arguably, a more systematic government policy could provide a fairer and more efficient way of helping the poor than uncompensated care.

Although solid rationales can be found for some form of government intervention in the market for health care, the tax preference for employer-provided health insurance is poorly designed for addressing these problems and may even make some of them worse. It provides no help at all to people whose incomes are too low to be subject to income tax, and it provides very large amounts of help to those high-income people who have high marginal tax rates.

In 2010, prior to implementation of the ACA, about 50 million Americans per year went the entire year with no health insurance coverage, and nearly 50 million more went without health insurance for some part of the year.[36] In 2012, which was still before the most important provisions of the ACA had been implemented, 75 percent of the uninsured had incomes below 250 percent of the federal poverty line ($57,625 for a family of four in 2012). Moreover, 63 percent of the uninsured in 2012 lived in a household with at least one full-time worker, and another 16 percent lived in a household with at least one part-time worker, so this was mostly an issue for the self-employed and people who work for employers that do not offer health insurance.[37] Proposals for health care reform have long featured measures to redirect more of our health care subsidies toward the low- and moderate-income people who are disproportionately likely to be uninsured.

The tax exclusion of employer-provided insurance is also inefficient because it provides an incentive not only to buy health insurance in the first place (which may be desirable for the reasons discussed earlier) but also to buy expensive health insurance (which is not desirable). Consider an employee who faces a 20 percent marginal tax rate. If an employer wants to give that worker $80 more in net-of-tax compensation, the firm would pay only $80 to grant that compensation in the form of a better health insurance policy but $100 to provide compensation in the form of a higher cash salary. This creates a strong incentive for employers to offer, and employees to prefer, much more generous health benefits than otherwise, which exacerbates the moral hazard problem considerably, leading to some wasteful expenditure on medical care.

The ACA included many provisions designed to address the problems discussed above, most of which were implemented starting in 2014.[38] To address concerns about equity between the sick and healthy, as well as concerns about the absence of long-term health insurance contracts that would protect people against changes in health status that lead to increased premiums, the act imposed a number of regulations on insurance companies. Health insurance premiums can no longer vary based on health status or factors that predict it, except for age, tobacco use, and geographic region. Moreover, health insurers can no longer deny coverage to anyone, regardless of health status, and cannot drop customers when they become sick.

If that were all the ACA had done, it would have greatly exacerbated the adverse selection problem, as people could simply wait until they get sick to buy health insurance, and it would have done little to help low- and moderate-income people purchase insurance. This is where some of the most important tax provisions of the ACA come in. First, the ACA introduced an income tax penalty for individuals who are not covered by health insurance. Second, it instituted a substantial refundable income tax credit to help subsidize the cost of purchasing health insurance. This credit is available to people with incomes below 400 percent of the federal poverty line ($97,200 for a family of four in 2016) who do not receive insurance from their employers and who are not covered by Medicare or Medicaid.[39] The credit is sufficient to cover the amount by which the cost of a standardized health insurance package exceeds a percentage of household income; this percentage gradually rises from 3 percent for families with incomes at 133 percent of the federal poverty line up to 9.5 percent for families with incomes at 400 percent of the federal poverty line. It must be used to purchase insurance from an "exchange," which is a marketplace for insurance organized by the federal or a state government. The value of the credit is significantly larger than the value of the tax exclusion for employer-provided insurance for most low- and middle-income workers. In order to reduce the incentive for employers to drop their health insurance plans, the ACA requires all employers with 50 or more full-time workers to either provide health insurance or pay a fee. Eligibility for Medicaid was also expanded to cover a larger fraction of the population.

To mitigate moral hazard problems and help pay for the cost of coverage-expanding provisions, the ACA included a provision that has come to be known as the "Cadillac tax." This provision was originally scheduled to take effect starting in 2018, and would impose an "excise tax" remitted by plan administrators (insurers) equal to 40 percent of the cost of health coverage that exceeds threshold amounts, tentatively set at $10,200 per year for individual coverage and $27,500 for family coverage in 2018, and then adjusted for inflation thereafter. This was meant to roughly approximate the effects of removing the tax exclusion for employer-provided health insurance, offsetting the inefficient incentive that exclusion creates to choose more expensive insurance plans. The hope was that labeling this a tax on insurers would make it more politically palatable. In December 2015, the Protecting Taxpayers from Tax Hikes Act of 2015 delayed the implementation of the Cadillac tax until 2020, and also made the tax itself tax-deductible for the plan administrator. Peter Orszag, former director of the Office of Management and Budget, expressed a worry shared by many economists who understand the efficiency and cost-control advantages of this provision: "the big concern with delay is, it's not a delay, it becomes a rolling permanent deferral."[40]

Because most provisions of the ACA were only implemented starting in 2014, it's still too early to know much about its effects. Early evidence suggests that it is succeeding in extending health insurance coverage to more people. Between the last quarter of 2013 and the first quarter of 2015, the percentage of Americans that are uninsured dropped from 16.2 percent to 10.7 percent. By June 2015, about 10 million people were enrolled in private insurance through ACA exchanges, and enrollment in Medicaid had increased by about 14 million people relative to October 2013.[41] The ACA also included many provisions intended to reduce the growth of health care costs and improve the quality and efficiency of health care, but as of late 2015 it was too early to know much about whether these would succeed, and the most important such provision, the Cadillac tax, has just been delayed.[42]

The ACA will undoubtedly continue to be a source of controversy going forward. One concern regards the budgetary impact. Over the near term, the various new taxes and fees introduced by the ACA bring in more than enough revenue to cover its costs. But this is unlikely to be true over the long term, as ACA tax revenues would tend to grow at a rate similar to economic growth while health care costs tend to grow faster than economic growth.[43] It is even less likely to be true over the long run if the Cadillac tax gets deferred indefinitely. A second concern regards how the ACA will affect labor supply. For example, the gradual phaseout of premium tax credits as income rises causes an increase in effective marginal tax rates on labor income, which might lead some people to work less. A third concern is that various features of the ACA distort incentives in ways that might lead to outcomes such as employers dropping insurance coverage (which would raise government budgetary costs), or a reduction in the share of employment that is in large firms (which could have costs in terms of productivity).[44] The size of such costs is an empirical question for which the evidence is not yet in, and in any event, the costs must be weighed against the benefits of the ACA.

Charitable Contributions

Under current law, contributions to qualifying charitable organizations are deductible from taxable income for those who itemize deductions. Let's subject this provision—which is in effect a penalty on those who are not charitably inclined—to our two-tiered test. First, are charitable contributions an indication that the contributing family is less well-off than their income would suggest? Some would argue yes—that people who make charitable contributions are sacrificing some of their own well-being for an altruistic or moral purpose. However, these are *voluntary* contributions. The contributors must be getting some satisfaction from the act of giving. Otherwise they would not have done so. Perhaps they are motivated by the "warm glow" they feel when they help others. So their level of well-being is really no different than that of people with equal incomes who don't give to charity. If that is the case, we cannot invoke an ability-to-pay justification for providing a tax preference for charitable donations.

Test number two is whether there is something inherent about charity that justifies subsidies to encourage charitable giving. In this case, the answer is arguably yes, as charitable contributions involve positive externalities. For one thing, the beneficiary of the contribution is better off. Second, charitable contributions may provide benefits to people who do not make contributions themselves. For example, many noncontributors might feel better knowing that homeless people are provided with food and shelter by charities. But in these cases, people have an incentive to free ride on the contributions of others; economists call such a situation a *public goods problem*. Charitable giving still occurs because some people are motivated by the satisfaction they receive from giving, but because of free riding, an inefficiently low amount of giving is done. To the extent this occurs, an extra incentive from the tax code may lead to a higher level of charitable activity that makes everyone better off. Of course, another approach would be for the government to provide the public goods directly, instead of relying on private contributions. However, some things that are arguably public goods would tend to be under-provided by the combination of government and unsubsidized charity. For example, the U.S. government could not contribute directly to religious institutions because of the constitutionally mandated separation of church and state, and some public goods that are valued only by a minority of the population might not be provided by a majority-rule government. Some argue, in addition, that private charitable contributions are a more efficient and less intrusive way of financing public goods such as aid to the poor than is government intervention.

The charitable contribution deduction is not without its costs, however. In fiscal year 2014, it reduced income tax revenues by about $51 billion. It adds to complexity and recordkeeping requirements.[45] A broad array of activities qualifies as "charity," so there's no guarantee that the gifts will go to activities that really deserve to be subsidized by the tax system.[46] For example, only a small portion of subsidized giving goes to help the poor; much of it goes to higher education and cultural institutions, which may or may not deserve subsidy.[47] Contributions can also be difficult to monitor, so unfortunately some inequity arises from abusing the system.[48]

There is empirical evidence that high-income people, in particular, do respond to tax incentives for charitable donations by donating more. The tax saving from donating an additional dollar to charity is larger when marginal income tax rates are higher—for instance, someone in the 35 percent tax bracket who itemizes deductions saves at least 35 cents in taxes for every additional dollar that is donated.[49] At the top of the income distribution, incentives to donate to charity were much stronger during the 1970s than they have been since 1988, because marginal income tax rates were much higher at the top of the distribution during the 1970s. Households with incomes above $500,000 (in constant year 2007 dollars) reported charitable donations that were 8.2 percent of their after-tax incomes, on average, during the 1970s. This figure dropped to 5.1 percent, on average, during 1988 through 2007, which is consistent with a behavioral response to reduced incentives to donate. In other income groups that experienced much smaller changes in the incentive to donate over this period, donations as a share of after-tax income did not change much at all.[50] There is also evidence that, after controlling for other factors that influence donation behavior such as income and religion, high-income taxpayers donate more to charity in states where the tax system creates a stronger incentive to donate, and that charitable donations went down relatively more over time for high-income people living in states where tax incentives for donations declined relatively more over time during 1979 through 2006. This evidence suggests that charitable tax subsidies cause high-income people to increase their donations by a bit more than the value of the tax subsidy. Evidence on the responsiveness of donations to tax incentives is more uncertain for low- and middle-income people.[51]

On balance, some form of incentive for charity may be justified. With that said, it is by no means clear that the current approach is appropriate in terms of either efficiency or equity. Currently, the rate of subsidy is tied to the donor's tax rate, and is zero for taxpayers who do not itemize or who have incomes below the filing threshold. In 2014, about 68 percent of the revenue loss from the federal income tax deduction for charity went to subsidize the donations of people with incomes above $200,000.[52] Replacing the itemized deduction for charitable donations with a fixed credit per dollar donated that is available to all taxpayers would subsidize all charitable contributions at the same rate, instead of subsidizing more heavily the contributions of affluent taxpayers. That is arguably fairer, and is perhaps more efficient, as there's no obvious reason to think that the positive externalities produced by donations are larger if they come from higher-income people. It could also facilitate adoption of a system of direct government matching grants to qualifying charitable organizations, as is used in the United Kingdom, which would have advantages in terms of reducing administrative and compliance costs (see chapter 5). Moreover, some empirical evidence suggests that a match would have a greater "bang for the buck" in terms of increased resources received by charities per dollar of forgone tax revenue, compared to a deduction that offers the same economic incentives to the same people.[53] On the other hand, if donation behavior is less responsive to incentives among low- and middle-income people compared to high-income people, then replacing a deduction that targets most of the incentives to high-income people with a flat-rate credit would mean *less* "bang for the buck," because relatively more of the tax subsidy for donations would be spent on windfalls for donations that would have happened anyway, and relatively less would be spent on people who actually respond by donating more.

State and Local Government Taxes and Borrowing

Two important preferences in our tax code have to do with state and local governments. The itemized deduction for tax payments to state and local governments cost the federal government about $77 billion in revenues in fiscal year 2014. Households with incomes above $200,000 accounted for about 58 percent of the revenue loss from this provision in that year.[54] The exclusion from federal income tax of interest on state and local government bonds cost an estimated $39 billion in fiscal year 2014.[55] Are these features justifiable?

One potential rationale for the deductibility of state and local taxes is that families that have the same income but live in high-tax states and municipalities have less "ability to pay" and therefore should owe less federal taxes than families who live in low-tax places. The flaw in this argument is that many of the people who live in high-tax states presumably benefit from a higher level of public expenditures. Why should someone who chooses to live in a low-tax state and make do with fewer government services be penalized for that choice? Of course, the relationship between state and local taxes and the benefits from public services is certainly not one-to-one, and those who bear the tax burden and those who benefit from government programs need not be the same people. So the ability-to-pay argument against deductibility has some merit, although it is limited.

Another problem with the deduction is that it provides an inefficient subsidy to state and local spending. The cost to (itemizing) taxpayers of a dollar of such spending is less than a dollar because of the deduction; in effect, part of the cost is shifted to taxpayers in other states. On the margin, this may encourage state and local governments to undertake projects that would not meet taxpayer approval in the absence of the tax incentive and that therefore use up resources that would be more efficiently used for other purposes. Moreover, because it is linked to itemized deductions, this subsidy is larger for governments that have relatively more high-income (and therefore high-tax-rate, itemizing) residents.

Such a subsidy for state and local expenditures might be desirable if those expenditures provide benefits that have spillover effects that spread beyond the state's or municipality's borders. In this case, some programs that are worthwhile from the country's perspective might not be undertaken by a state or local government. This argument certainly does not apply for many types of programs, such as garbage collection or municipal swimming pools. It makes more sense for primary education, on the grounds that it builds an "educated citizenry," which benefits all Americans. Although this argument has some intuitive appeal, it is hard to prove or quantify and, in any event, it applies only to a subset of what state and local governments do and therefore does not justify the general deductibility of state and local taxes. Nor does it justify effectively giving a larger subsidy to more affluent communities where the residents are more likely to itemize and tend to be subject to higher tax rates.

On balance, although the deduction for state and local taxes has some merit as an adjustment for ability to pay and perhaps as an encouragement of certain worthy public expenditures, it also involves significant inefficiency, unfairness, and complexity. Some of these same arguments apply to the other major income tax provision related to state and local government—the exclusion of interest on state and local bonds from taxable income. In this case, there is no ability-to-pay rationale because the decision to buy bonds issued by municipal governments is entirely voluntary, and thus holders of such bonds are certainly not worse off for doing so. The main effect of the interest exclusion is to subsidize debt-financed expenditures in the states and municipalities because it enables these governments to borrow money at a lower interest rate than otherwise. High-tax-rate investors are willing to accept the lower interest rates because they owe no tax on the interest. The increased demand by investors drives up the prices of these bonds—or, in other words, pushes the yields on these bonds down toward the after-tax rate of interest offered on similar, but taxable, bonds.

Not all of the benefits of the interest exclusion go to state and local governments, however. If all potential buyers of these bonds had the same tax rate—say, 20 percent—the interest rates on the bonds would end up being about 20 percent lower than on other bonds, so the purchasers would gain little or no benefit. Their *implicit* tax (because they have a lower interest rate) would equal the *explicit* tax on other investments. But in a system of graduated rates and both taxable and nontaxable potential purchasers, to sell all the bonds that state and local governments want to issue, the rate of interest must be high enough to attract not only those taxpayers with the highest tax rate but also many investors with lower tax rates. This means that taxpayers in the top tax brackets benefit because they can invest at a higher after-tax rate of return than otherwise.

Given that the case for subsidizing state and local expenditures is shaky, the interest exclusion seems hard to justify. Because a substantial portion of the subsidy represents a windfall to very high-income people, it is even harder to justify. An alternative to both the exclusion of bond interest and the deductibility of state and local tax payments that would avoid these problems would be for the federal government to provide direct subsidies to these governments for the intended class of expenditures. This idea has always been resisted by state and local governments, largely due to their fear that once the tax preference becomes a straightforward appropriation it could more easily go onto the budget chopping block. This is another good example of how the tax system can sustain implicit subsidies that would probably not survive as equivalent stand-alone programs.

The Standard Deduction and Rough Justice

To this point, we have addressed the most important itemized deductions. Only about 30 percent of taxpayers—those who itemize—deduct these expenses, and these are predominantly affluent families.[56] This is because all taxpayers are offered the option of bypassing the itemizing process and instead claiming a *standard deduction*, which varies only by marital status. In 2015, the standard deduction amounted to $12,600 for a married couple filing jointly, $6,300 for a single taxpayer, and $9,250 for a head of household.[57]

Offering the option of a standard deduction makes sense because it would not be cost-efficient for the IRS to have to monitor and occasionally audit the deductions claimed by the 70 percent of people who file tax returns but do not now itemize, not to mention the cost in time and monetary expense of these taxpayers having to keep track of their expenses.[58] By having a standard deduction, however, the tax system loses its ability to finely differentiate among taxpayers with differing abilities to pay. As it stands now, two otherwise identical families, both with $30,000 of income and both taking the standard deduction, owe the same tax even though one family has incurred $5,000 in medical expenses and the other hasn't. Although in principle the tax system allows extraordinary medical expenses to reduce income subject to tax, in practice we settle for "rough justice" by differentiating tax liability only when relatively large sums of money are involved.

If some or all itemized deductions end up being retained, a larger standard deduction could still simplify taxpaying for many people by cutting down on the number of itemizers. This could save substantial administrative and compliance costs. It would mean settling for even more rough justice, but the trade-off might be worth it. One simplifying change that would cost no revenue would be to couple a reduction or elimination of personal exemption allowances for the adults in a family with a corresponding increase in the standard deduction. Similarly, if some itemized deductions are retained in a flat tax, the family allowance could be treated as a large standard deduction.

Savings Incentives in the Income Tax

A variety of income tax provisions—including IRAs, Keogh plans, 401(k) and 403(b) pension plans, and numerous other tax-preferred pension plans and saving accounts—reduce the tax on the return to savings. In recent years, these kinds of plans have been expanded considerably. Their popularity partly reflects a growing enthusiasm for consumption taxation, perhaps combined with a skeptical appraisal of the likelihood of fundamental tax reform, so that tax-preferred savings accounts are seen as a feasible way to move toward consumption taxation.

These plans have three essential features. First, the ordinary return on contributions to such plans is exempt from tax. In most cases, this is accomplished by excluding employer and employee contributions from tax; allowing interest, dividends, and other returns on the assets in the account to accumulate tax-free; and then taxing withdrawals from the accounts. In some cases, such as Roth IRAs, contributions cannot be deducted from taxable income, but no tax is charged on either the assets' returns or on withdrawals, which also effectively exempts the return to saving from tax. Second, maximum limits are imposed in various ways on the amount of contributions that can receive favorable tax treatment. For example, in 2015, annual individual contributions to IRAs were limited to $5,500 for those under age 50 and $6,500 for those aged 50 and over.[59] Third, in some cases, eligibility is limited to people with incomes below a certain level. For example, in 2015, eligibility for conventional IRAs was phased out for married couples with AGI between $98,000 and $118,000 (unless neither spouse has access to an employer-provided pension plan) and eligibility for Roth IRAs was phased out for married couples with AGI between $183,000 and $193,000.[60]

Advocates of tax-preferred saving plans argue that they provide many people with the opportunity to accumulate wealth tax-free but that they do so in a "limited" way that, compared to abandoning completely all taxation of returns to saving, costs less government revenue and restricts the size of the tax advantage obtained by very high-income people with large amounts of capital income. However, in some cases this compromise essentially provides the worst of both worlds— losing revenue without actually affecting the incentive to save or increasing saving.

To see the problem, consider the implications of contribution limits— for example, the current $5,500 limit on contributions to IRAs for those under age 50. This limit makes no difference to taxpayers who would not in any event want or be able to contribute as much as $5,500 in a year, so for them an IRA could provide an incentive to save more than they otherwise would. However, for those taxpayers who would otherwise save more than that and don't mind subjecting their funds to a penalty for early withdrawal, the IRA deduction is a nice gift, but *at the margin* it will have absolutely no influence on how much they save. If you're trying to decide whether to save $6,000 or $7,000, the IRA program is immaterial because you've already maxed out on your contribution. Thus, the IRA provides a reward for saving you would have done anyway rather than an inducement to do more saving. In fact, because the tax reduction you obtain from it adds to your disposable income, having an IRA should therefore increase your consumption, which *reduces* rather than increases national saving. Moreover, reducing taxes without improving incentives is inefficient because it means we have to forgo some other equal tax reduction that would have improved incentives. This is a major reason why, in the Tax Reform Act of 1986, eligibility for deductible IRAs was restricted mainly to people with incomes low enough that they would have been unlikely to save more than the contribution limits anyway.

The other key problem is that, while IRAs and other tax-favored saving plans are intended to encourage saving, they actually subsidize deposits into an account, and making a deposit is not at all the same as saving. As a result, people who have assets outside of these accounts or an ability to borrow can use IRAs and pensions to reduce their taxes without doing any new saving at all. To see how this works, consider an individual who over the years has saved up $16,500, which is now invested in stocks and bonds. If she takes $5,500 of this and deposits it into a traditional IRA account, she gets the tax benefits even though her saving has not increased or decreased; it's just been moved from one account to another. Of course, if she deposits $5,500 every year into an IRA account and does no more new saving, after three years she will have transferred all of her wealth into the IRA account. At that time, she may face the decision that the IRA is designed to alter: to get any further tax benefit, she might have to do some new saving. But even then, she could avoid actually doing any net saving by increasing her borrowing by the same amount that she contributes to her account (or equivalently, reducing the rate at which she pays back an outstanding loan). The taxpayer makes money on this strategy as long as the interest on the loan is deductible from tax, as it would be on a home mortgage, for example.

One reason that current savings incentives subsidize deposits rather than saving itself is that deposits are a lot easier to measure. Accurately measuring saving would probably require every taxpayer to keep track of all additions to assets, subtract out all withdrawals, and record and report to the IRS all borrowing. As discussed earlier, this procedure would substantially complicate the tax system.

Some basic facts about IRAs and pensions can help illustrate the nature and extent of the problem. In 2010, when the IRA contribution limit was $5,000 for those under 50 and $6,000 for those 50 and over, 40 percent of people who contributed to either a traditional or Roth IRA contributed exactly the maximum amount for their age group.[61] For many IRA participants, therefore, the IRA probably provided a windfall rather than an incentive to save.[62] Moreover, the vast majority of people *eligible* to contribute to a deductible IRA simply didn't contribute anything. In 2010, only 7.9 percent of taxpayers eligible to contribute to tax-deductible IRAs actually did so.[63]

The story for pensions is a bit more complicated. In 2013, 36.2 percent of families had at least one member participating in an employer-provided pension plan, 30.1 percent had a defined-contribution plan such as a 401(k), and 12.1 percent had a defined-benefit plan, with some overlap between the two groups.[64] Defined-benefit plans have essentially no impact on individuals' incentive to save at the margin because individual workers have no control over how much is saved in these plans on their behalf. Most participants in defined-contribution plans do have the opportunity to increase their tax-deductible contributions, so that these plans do increase the incentive to save (or at least to contribute to the account). For example, a study by the Congressional Research Service found that in 2006, only 8 percent of defined-contribution pension-plan participants were making employee contributions of $1,000 per month, which corresponded to the annual employee tax-deductible contribution limit of $12,000 that was then applicable. Thus, the vast majority could have contributed more but did not.[65]

The bottom line is that, between IRAs and defined-contribution pension plans, most people probably have the opportunity to do additional retirement saving that receives consumption tax treatment, although apparently many do not take advantage of this opportunity. On the other hand, a substantial fraction of the people who actually participate in IRAs are making the maximum allowable contribution. For these people, the special tax treatment applied to such plans generally provides a windfall rather than an incentive to save.

Some economists maintain that retirement saving accounts provide an important institutional commitment device that helps people overcome their natural tendency not to do the retirement saving that they ultimately know is good for them. Traditional economic models assume that people are forward-looking, well-informed, and fully rational with regard to their saving (and all other) behavior. But much recent evidence shows that many people suffer from problems like temptation to spend cash in hand today, have a poor understanding of basic principles of financial planning, and put little thought into saving decisions. For example, recent research suggests that employee decisions regarding pension saving often follow the "path of least resistance," accepting whatever default plan the employer provides. By contrast, a model of fully rational saving behavior would tend to predict that employees would take advantage of options provided by these plans to finely tailor the amount and kind of saving they do to match their tastes, circumstances, and incentives. This research suggests that institutions like employer-provided pensions may have important impacts on saving independent of their effects on incentives.[66] Thus, tax preferences that create an incentive for employers to operate such plans might increase saving. But switching all the way to a consumption tax could conceivably weaken the employer-provided pension system, as the tax advantage to setting up such plans with an employer would disappear. As a result, this theory suggests that such a reform might actually reduce saving.

Many economists now take seriously the idea that certain people are unable to commit to save as much as they "should" and that the problem is particularly severe for low- and moderate-income people, as both the pressures to spend today and the consequences of under-saving are the worst for this group.[67] Moreover, low- and moderate-income workers are also much less likely to be enrolled in a pension plan and thus do not benefit from private pensions' role as a commitment device. This could support a case for going beyond removing distortions and perhaps subsidizing saving among low-income people, as well as creating institutions that do a better job of getting low- and moderate-income people in the habit of saving. The 2001 tax act took a step in this direction by creating a tax credit, known as the Savers Credit, of up to 50 percent for contributions to retirement savings accounts such as IRAs by low-income people, with a maximum annual credit of $1,000 for an individual or $2,000 for a couple.[68]

Increasing contribution limits reduces the number of people who are constrained by contribution limits, and for those people the plans might now provide an incentive to do additional saving rather than serving solely as a windfall.[69] On the other hand, it would increase the size of the windfall going to those who remain above the limits. Extending eligibility for contribution-limited saving accounts like IRAs to higher-income people might improve incentives to save for some of them, but for many it would just provide an opportunity to shift assets from taxable to tax-free accounts. The vast majority of people, who are already contributing less than the limits, would be unaffected, and most of the benefits of the changes would go to upper-income people.

All in all, the array of tax-preferred saving plans is an inefficient way to reduce the disincentives to save under an income tax. If people are presumed to systematically under-save—and this is by no means obvious—then other policies, such as providing refundable credits for low-income savers and expanding their participation in pension plans, are worth considering. Finally, if private pensions are the key to more saving, the tax incentive for employers may be the most important incentive of all. The fact that, under a consumption tax system, employer-provided pensions might be cut back, because they would no longer be tax-advantaged relative to any other form of saving, suggests that private saving might actually decline.

Integration: Addressing the Double Taxation of Corporate Income
Economists have long considered the tax treatment of corporate income to be an important problem with the U.S. income tax system. The current system, under which corporation income can be taxed twice—first by the corporation tax and then again when the income is received by shareholders—can put an inefficient penalty on business activity carried out in corporate form, and it distorts corporate financial structure toward debt finance. It also may make investment in corporate stock particularly unattractive relative to nonbusiness investments such as owner-occupied housing, causing too much high-priced housing to be built at the expense of more socially productive corporate investments.

The argument for eliminating the double taxation of corporate income is largely one of economic efficiency and not fairness, although it is often sold politically as an issue of fairness. The sound economic argument is that uneven taxation of different forms of investment causes investment to be allocated in a less productive manner than it could be. But uneven treatment is not necessarily unfair because putting savings into corporate stock is a voluntary choice. To the extent that the return to corporate stocks is taxed more heavily than other assets, demand for corporate stocks declines, and their prices go down until they offer a similar expected rate of return (after adjusting for risk) as other assets. The double taxation arguably caused horizontal inequity for people who owned stocks at the time it was originally instituted because they suffered a capital loss. But most people who own stocks today have not been penalized relative to other asset owners because they were largely compensated for the higher tax burden by paying a lower price for the stocks. As we noted above, a horizontal equity argument can be made for removing taxes on the return to saving in general, but there's nothing special about the double taxation of corporate income in this regard.

For similar reasons, if double taxation of corporate income is removed, some of the benefits will be dissipated into a windfall gain for current shareholders, as demand for stocks should rise in anticipation of their more favorable tax treatment, pushing up their prices and generating an immediate capital gain. There is no good reason to think that such a windfall is in any way "deserved." The immediate rise in share prices also mitigates the degree to which the after-tax incentive to save rises, thus limiting any long-term economic gains. Taxpayers will still have improved incentives to channel saving toward more productive uses, though (reflected in increased demand for corporate stocks relative to other assets), and that's the best argument for addressing the problem.

At first blush, the obvious solution to the problem of double taxation is simply to eliminate the corporate income tax altogether. The obvious solution is not the right one. Just eliminating the corporation income tax would create formidable new problems, mainly because a large fraction of corporate income goes untaxed at the individual level. Recall that accrued capital gains are not taxed until they are realized and are not taxed at all if held until death and passed on to heirs. Even when realized, capital gains are taxed at preferential rates. With no corporate income tax at all, taxpayers would have a strong (and inefficient) incentive to keep as much income in corporations as possible, deferring or perhaps eliminating taxation on that income altogether. Individuals would have a great incentive to incorporate themselves and devise schemes to "pay" themselves in ways that escape personal taxation, such as providing company cars, apartments, and so on. As a practical matter, an income tax system such as ours requires some form of corporate tax as a backstop to the personal taxation of capital, and possibly labor, income.

For these reasons, most proposals for mitigating the double taxation of corporate income involve some form of tax relief at the personal level for dividends and sometimes capital gains, on which corporate income tax has already been paid. This is known as *integration* of the corporate and personal tax systems. Indeed, many countries have in the past adopted such an approach. Traditionally, a common policy has been to grant taxable individual shareholders a credit against personal tax liability for a portion of the corporate tax attributable to the dividends they receive. Recently, though, some of the European countries who had this type of system have abandoned it for a preferential tax on dividends.

The 2003 tax act was a step toward one type of integration because it reduced the top tax rate on capital gains (not just those on corporate stock), as well as all dividends, to 15 percent. The 15 percent rate was increased to 20 percent as of 2013. This preferential rate does indeed reduce the extent of double taxation of corporate income. However, because the capital gains tax cut applied to past as well as future accumulations of gains, a substantial portion of its revenue cost represented windfall gains related to past decisions and so had no incentive effects. Furthermore, there was no provision to limit tax relief at the personal level to cases where tax was actually paid at the corporate level, so there was no reduction in incentives for corporate tax sheltering.

It is instructive to compare the 2003 tax change to a more fundamental approach to removing the inefficient tax treatment of corporate investment that was set out in a 1992 U.S. Treasury report called the *comprehensive business income tax*, or CBIT.[70] The CBIT plan would go further than the 2003 changes by excluding from AGI any dividends that come from profits on which corporate income tax had been paid, as well as any capital gains that arise from new retained earnings on which corporate tax had been paid. The CBIT also would make radical changes in the tax treatment of interest, eliminating interest deductions from the corporate tax and excluding corporate bond interest from taxation at the personal level. Moreover, it would apply to almost all businesses, not just corporations. The change in the treatment of corporate interest, in particular, would raise revenue because some interest income that currently escapes taxation at any level would now be taxed at the corporate level. As a result, the Treasury estimated that the plan as a whole (including the provision for capital gains) could reduce the corporate tax rate by 3 percentage points and still be roughly revenue-neutral. The CBIT would eliminate any tax preference for debt finance relative to equity finance of corporations because the returns to both would be taxed once at the same corporate rate under the CBIT.

In its treatment of dividends, interest, and capital gains, the CBIT proposal resembles a consumption tax along the lines of a Hall-Rabushka flat tax or the X-tax, discussed in chapter 7. It would still be a type of income tax, however, because business investment would continue to be depreciated rather than expensed. In this way, the normal return to corporate investment would be taxed at the firm level.

Corporate Welfare

The 2003 tax changes regarding dividends and capital gains focused attention on the *double* taxation of corporate income that can occur under the U.S. income tax structure. Ironically, at the same time the public spotlight was directed toward cases of egregious corporate tax avoidance, tax evasion, and preferential tax treatment, all of which suggest that some corporate income is not double taxed, single taxed, or even taxed at all. We addressed issues of corporate tax avoidance and evasion in chapter 5, and turn to preferential tax treatment next.

One frequent rhetorical target of politicians is *corporate welfare*. Although everyone claims to be against corporate welfare, not everyone defines it the same way. Defining it as "programs and subsidies that primarily benefit profitable corporations," a Stop Corporate Welfare Coalition of organizations drawn from all across the political spectrum could come up with only twelve programs that cost slightly more than $11 billion over five years. A *Time* magazine exposé put the bill for federal corporate welfare at $125 billion per year, a small part of which represented tax breaks.[71]

Some provisions in the tax code provide preferences for investments done by certain types of corporations or businesses. The most obvious example is the generous depreciation deductions granted to oil, gas, and mining operations. Other industries that tend to be favored include rental housing, real estate, insurance, and financial services.[72] The libertarian Cato Institute argues that targeted tax breaks are not corporate welfare because allowing corporations to keep more of their own earnings is not a form of welfare. Even the Cato Institute admits, though, "While targeted tax breaks are not welfare, they are bad policy and should be eliminated."[73]

As with double taxation of corporate income, the main problem with these types of preferences once they are in place is inefficiency, not unfairness. For example, the preference for oil drilling has caused investment funds to flow into that line of business at the expense of other, more productive investments. The uneven playing field that results prevents the country's resources from going toward their most efficient use.

Capital Gains

The treatment of capital gains is one of the most controversial and publicly debated issues about the income tax, with Republicans generally wanting to reduce rates on capital gains as much as possible and Democrats wanting to keep them near rates on other income. It is a particularly divisive issue because realized capital gains are highly concentrated among high-income individuals. In 2011, for example, 78 percent of gains were received by households whose AGI exceeded $200,000, and capital gains constituted 12 percent of the AGI of these taxpayers.[74] Because of this concentration, preferential tax treatment of capital gains is the archetypical example of "trickle-down economics," where the immediate benefits go to a small group of highly affluent people and the extent of longer-term, more widely distributed, benefits is hotly disputed.

According to the economist's definition of income (consumption plus the change in wealth), increases in the real value of capital assets are certainly income. When a stock you own increases in value from $1,000 to $1,100, you are $100 wealthier, just as you would be if you won $100 in the lottery or got paid $100 for overtime work.[75] The $100 gain is income you have "accrued" at the time the increase in value occurs, regardless of whether you convert it into cash by selling the asset. By this logic, all of capital gains should be included in taxable income as they accrue with no preferences.

Implementing this logic in a comprehensive way is not simple, however. For many capital assets, obtaining a market value that can be verified by the IRS or even be known to the owner is extremely difficult. It's no problem for highly liquid securities such as shares of companies traded on the NASDAQ or the New York Stock Exchange. But it is a real problem for closely held businesses, real estate, and other assets such as paintings. From an administrative standpoint, requiring taxpayers to value all their capital assets each year (so that they could report as income the increase in value) and having the IRS monitor these reports would be very cumbersome.

Rather than requiring taxpayers to annually value all their capital assets and include the change in value as income, capital gains are taxed only on *realization*, which usually means when the asset is sold.[76] One implication of postponing the taxation of the gain until the time of sale, rather than when the asset appreciated, is that it confers on the taxpayer the time value of money: remitting the tax liability later rather than sooner is almost always better. In one sense, the IRS offers the asset holder an interest-free loan that is equal to the tax due at the time the asset appreciates and that begins when the gain is made and is repaid at the time the asset is sold. This interest-free loan is more valuable the higher nominal interest rates are and the longer an asset is held.

Because of the advantage of deferring the tax liability, taxing capital gains at the time of sale rather than at the time of accrual provides an incentive to hold appreciated assets longer than otherwise. This "lock-in effect" is greatly exacerbated because of another feature of current law that is discussed further below: there is no tax at all on capital gains if the asset is not sold during the holder's lifetime. Empirical evidence suggests that capital gains realizations are indeed sensitive to income tax rates on capital gains, which supports the existence of a lock-in effect. For example, in the United States, capital gains realizations grew relatively more slowly between the 1950s and the 2000s in states where tax rates on capital gains went up by more, compared to states where those tax rates did not change as much.[77]

This combination—the deferral of tax until sale and the eventuality that all the gain will be forgiven from tax—makes potentially appreciating assets much more attractive than assets (like taxable bonds) that pay out their return in a taxable form. This provides a purely tax-related advantage to investments (such as real estate) that more easily can provide returns to their investors in the form of appreciation.

Tax preferences accorded to capital gains also create a tremendous incentive to repackage ordinary income into capital gains. People who buy fixer-upper houses take advantage of this feature because their time and effort is not taxed as labor income. Instead, they are reflected in a higher sale price for the house and hardly taxed at all due to generous rules about capital gains on owner-occupied housing. Other sophisticated taxpayers make use of stock options or "collapsible" corporations to convert labor compensation into capital gains. Some lawyers speculate that before the Tax Reform Act of 1986 (when the capital gains tax rate preference was especially large—a 30 percentage-point difference for top-bracket taxpayers), about half of all the transactional complexity of the tax law was due to this feature of the law.[78]

The 1986 tax reform virtually eliminated the rate differential on capital gains, although the advantages of deferral and tax exemption at death remained. The rate differential has since crept back up, as taxpayers in the 39.6 percent tax bracket for ordinary income now pay no more than 20 percent on their realized capital gains.

For all the problems caused by preferential taxation, taxing capital gains realizations like other income poses its own problems, particularly given other features of the current tax code. For one thing, in inflationary periods much capital appreciation represents not a real increase in income but only a catching up to higher prices. Second, the income that generates capital gains on corporate shares is already taxed to some extent by the corporate income tax. Third, given the realization-based tax system, imposing higher rates of tax will inevitably provide some deterrent to efficient sales of capital assets—the lock-in effect already discussed. Fourth, allowing full deductibility of realized capital *losses* is not feasible because investors with diversified portfolios could "cherry-pick" their assets, selling only those with losses and holding those with gains and thereby consistently generating losses for tax purposes.[79] But the current asymmetrical treatment of losses and gains makes the private investor's prospects look less attractive: she owes a share to the government if the investment turns out well but gets little help if it turns out badly. Such treatment can inefficiently deter risky investments.

Lock-in effects and tax avoidance could be further reduced by addressing the exclusion from tax of capital gains that are held until death. For income tax purposes, the taxable capital gain is calculated as the difference between the proceeds from selling an asset and the basis of that asset, where the basis is generally the amount the individual originally paid to buy the asset. Under current law, heirs are able to *step up* the basis of inherited assets to the value at the date of the donor's death so that any unrealized capital gains accumulated to that point escape income taxation forever. This provides an effective avenue for avoiding income taxes. In fact, the income arising from unrealized capital gains can effectively be consumed during the lifetime of the asset's owner without the owner ever paying tax on it, and the owner can even reduce other taxes in the process. For example, someone could hold an appreciated asset until his or her death and thus never pay tax on the gains, borrow through a home equity loan and use the proceeds to consume, and deduct the interest payments on the loan from the income tax. When the heir sells the asset (with no tax) after the asset owner's death, he or she can use the appreciated asset to pay off the debt.

One reform option would tax unrealized capital gains at death as if they were sold, which would greatly reduce the lock-in effect and avoidance opportunities. Another option would require heirs to carry over the donor's basis on inherited assets, so capital gains that had accumulated prior to the donor's death would eventually be taxed whenever the heirs sell the assets, an approach that was actually implemented for a small number of wealthy decedents in 2010 during the temporary repeal of the estate tax, as discussed in chapter 2.

Estate Taxes

Elimination of the estate tax is a frequent target of proposals for fundamental tax reform, especially those emanating from the right side of the political spectrum. This is partly because the estate tax is relevant to all three of the elements of fundamental tax reform considered in this chapter. Its highly progressive nature goes against the spirit of single-rate taxes. The fact that it reduces incentives to save and invest goes against the motivation for switching taxation to a consumption base. And schemes to avoid and evade the estate tax, together with preferential treatment in the estate tax for certain types of property such as farms, small businesses, and closely held businesses that can benefit from valuation discounts, contribute to uneven taxation of capital income and thus "messiness."

The estate tax directly affects only the richest of Americans. Indeed, the main argument made by proponents of the estate tax is that it is an important component of a progressive tax system. In 2013, there were only 4,687 taxable estate tax returns filed, which represented approximately the richest 0.2 percent of adult deaths in the United States.[80] The exemption in 2013 was $5.25 million, and it is now automatically indexed for inflation, so that it had risen to $5.43 million by 2015. The substantial exemption amount means that it applies to a thin slice of the very wealthiest segment of society. In 2013, the 698 taxable estate tax returns filed which had gross estates over $20 million accounted for 63 percent of the $12.7 billion in federal estate tax revenues.[81] Above the exempt level, a tax rate of 40 percent applies, although unlimited deductions are allowed for bequests to a spouse or to charity. These features make the estate tax by far the most progressive component of the tax system.

Although the $20.9 billion of estate and gift tax revenues collected in 2013 represent only about 1 percent of federal tax revenues, they represent a nontrivial portion of the tax burden placed on the very rich.[82] For instance, in 2013, taxpayers with adjusted gross income above $1 million represented the top 0.2 percent of income tax returns filed ranked by income, and the personal income tax raised $306 billion in revenue from that group. Estate and gift tax liability was equal to 6.8 percent of that.[83]

The cases for and against a progressive tax system are addressed in chapter 3. But if the goal of the estate tax is to achieve progressivity, this raises the question of why an estate tax is preferable to levying somewhat higher *income* tax rates on upper-income people. One argument for using an estate tax as a supplement to income taxation is that our income tax fails to tax a considerable portion of income, which may make it difficult to achieve the degree of vertical and horizontal equity that society might desire. For instance, estimates by economists James Poterba of MIT and Scott Weisbenner of the Federal Reserve Board of Governors suggest that 42 percent of the value of estates over $5 million represents unrealized capital gains, income that would never be taxed by the personal income tax.[84] Taxing estates is also an administratively convenient way of raising tax revenue from the very wealthy. Even in the absence of taxes, estates are required to go through a detailed legal process that reveals much information about the decedent's economic resources that would be difficult to obtain in any other way.

Horizontal equity arguments are invoked by both supporters and opponents of the estate tax. Supporters of the estate tax contend that people who receive very large inheritances start off unfairly with a big unearned advantage in life. Opponents of the tax focus on the donor rather than the donee, questioning whether people who prefer to "spend" their money on their children via bequests should be penalized relative to people who prefer to spend their money while they are alive. Between two people who earn the same incomes over their lives, the one who saves more of it will face a higher estate tax burden (if they are sufficiently wealthy to face the tax, that is).

The estate tax is also defended on the grounds that it creates a strong incentive for the wealthy to give to charity, both during life and at death. Because charitable bequests are fully deductible from the estate tax, someone who faces a 40 percent marginal estate tax rate can leave $1 to charity while sacrificing only 60 cents of bequests to heirs. Thus, the estate tax effectively cuts the relative price of a charitable bequest in half for the wealthiest members of society. The estate tax also increases the incentive to give to charity during life, since anything given to charity while alive is not available at death to be included in the taxable estate. In 2013, $13.6 billion of charitable bequests were reported on estate tax returns (taxable and nontaxable), and $75 billion of charitable donations were reported on income tax returns with AGI above $200,000.[85] Most empirical research done on this topic suggests that charitable giving can be expected to decline if the estate tax is repealed. For example, over the twentieth century, as the marginal tax rate on the typical estate tax return increased, the share of the value of estates that was left to charity also increased significantly.[86] Although this correlation could conceivably have been caused by other influences on charitable behavior that changed over time, research that controls for these influences and takes advantage of the fact that estate tax and inheritance tax rates changed in different ways over time across different real wealth levels and different states also finds that charitable bequests respond strongly to incentives and that repeal of the estate tax is likely to reduce charitable giving.[87]

The estate tax reduces the incentive to save for those wealthy families whose saving is at least partly motivated by the desire to leave a large bequest. After all, one way to avoid estate tax liability is to consume all of one's wealth while alive and leave nothing for the kids. Wojciech Kopczuk of Columbia University and Joel Slemrod found evidence that aggregate reported estates in the United States were somewhat smaller than would be predicted based on other variables during periods when federal marginal estate tax rates were relatively high. However, this result could reflect increased tax avoidance as well as reduced wealth accumulation in high-tax periods.[88]

The estate tax's disincentive effect on saving may be fairly small for several reasons. While some bequests undoubtedly occur because people desire to provide a gift to their heirs, bequests also occur because people accumulate enough wealth to ensure that they do not outlive their resources, and some of these people die holding substantial precautionary wealth. In those cases, people may put relatively little value on what happens to the wealth after their death. If so, taxing that wealth after death would be economically efficient, as it would have little effect on peoples' behavior. And to the extent that the estate tax reduces inheritances received by heirs, it *increases* their need to do saving on their own.[89]

The other main economic argument against the estate tax is the same argument that can be made against any progressive tax—that it reduces the incentive to do any of the things that make people better off, including working hard, taking risks, or starting a business. The estate tax could plausibly have an important impact on these kinds of decisions among the very wealthy (or those who think they have a realistic prospect of becoming very wealthy), given the high marginal tax rates it imposes. For example, a person of advanced age who has already achieved a comfortable level of wealth may be motivated to continue working by the prospect of leaving a bequest, and a high tax rate on such bequests could affect that decision. With the estate tax, in particular, there is little evidence one way or the other on this question. There is evidence that large inheritances *reduce* the labor supply of the heirs who receive them, however.[90]

Public discussion of the estate tax has focused heavily on the extent to which it forces sales of farms and other small businesses to pay the tax. This concern, however, has been greatly exaggerated. In 2013, only 14.1 percent of taxable estates reported having farm assets, and the value of these assets represented 2.4 percent of the aggregate value of taxable estates. Business assets aside from publicly traded stock accounted for about 16.4 percent of the value of the net worth of taxable estates, but much of this represented businesses that were not in any way "small."[91] The value of small businesses and farms included in a taxable estate is eligible to receive discounts that can reduce the value of the taxable estate by up to $1,090,000 for decedents in 2014.[92] In addition, the tax need not be paid in one lump sum at death. Taxes on businesses and farms can be paid in installments over a fourteen-year period after death, and a standard element of estate planning is to purchase a life insurance policy sufficient to pay the estate tax liability so that the payments are spread out over many years before death as well. Given this, the impact of the tax need not be much different from that of any other progressive tax for which payment would be spread in smaller installments over many years, such as the income tax. Nor is there any compelling ethical or economic reason to provide preferential treatment to someone who has a farm or small business relative to someone with equal wealth who just happened to accumulate it in some other form. Nevertheless, the image of someone having to sell the family farm or business because of taxes serves as a particularly vivid symbol of how a highly progressive estate tax could impact the well-being and incentives to create wealth of the people affected.

The estate tax is not a popular tax. This goes especially for conservatives, as evidenced by the fact that it would be eliminated in *all* of the tax plans proposed by those seeking to be the Republican presidential candidate in 2016. Two-thirds of respondents in a 2009 Harris Interactive / Tax Foundation online survey favored its elimination.[93] Part of this opposition undoubtedly reflects a visceral dislike of associating the unhappy event of death with the unhappy event of paying taxes. But there is another reason for its unpopularity. A large number of people who support abolition of the estate tax are apparently under the erroneous impression that it applies to people who are not particularly wealthy. In a 2003 NPR poll, 57 percent of respondents favored eliminating the estate tax, 39 percent of respondents said that they opposed the estate tax because "it might affect YOU someday," and 49 percent of those who favored elimination of the tax said they thought "most families have to pay the federal estate tax when someone dies." Thus, some combination of wild optimism and misunderstanding of how the tax works appears to play a role in opposition to the estate tax.[94] As we noted in chapter 3, more recent research by Ilyana Kuziemko and co-authors suggests that survey respondents increase their support for the estate tax dramatically when they learn that it only applies to the very rich.[95]

Conclusion

This chapter has addressed the policy issues that arise in contemplating any major tax reform. As with most contentious policy choices, evaluating these proposals often requires a balancing among the desirable characteristics of a tax system. Having now addressed these issues in the abstract, in the next two chapters we turn to examining specific proposals for overhauling the tax system. All of these proposals involve some combination of the three elements discussed in this chapter—a single rate (or at least low marginal rates), a consumption base, and a clean base. Each of these three elements of tax reform is conceptually and practically distinct from the others so that a reform could achieve any or all to varying degrees.

7 Consumption Tax Alternatives

This chapter and the next examine specific proposals for improving the tax system. Options for replacing or pairing the current system with a tax based on consumption—including the retail sales tax, the value-added tax (VAT), the "flat tax," and the mysteriously named X-tax—are addressed in this chapter, and reform plans based on the current income tax are addressed in chapter 8.

First, we explain how each of these four varieties of consumption taxation works and why, despite cosmetic differences, they are all close relatives. Second, to make the discussion more concrete, the chapter examines the tax rates that would have to be levied to make up for the revenue lost from the income tax. With this as background, we can then move on to how to evaluate the consumption tax approaches and how they stack up to the current system. Because each of the four approaches to consumption taxation can achieve the same basic economic goal—eliminating the negative impact of the tax system on the reward for saving—a choice among them must depend on other factors. As is so often the case with issues as complex as this one, the devil is in the details. Deciding which approach is best depends crucially on administrative factors—simplicity and enforceability—and the ease with which the tax base can be adjusted for ability to pay so as to deliver the degree of progressivity desired. This chapter shows that the VAT and flat tax emerge as superior to the other choices for simplification and enforcement reasons. If you are especially concerned about the progressivity of the tax burden, the X-tax, which allows for a graduated tax rate structure, is the best choice among consumption taxes. Finally, we consider estimates of the distributional and economic effects of some specific proposals to start the tax system over from scratch.

How the Consumption Tax Plans Work

How a Retail Sales Tax Works

To Americans (but not to residents of other countries), the most familiar type of consumption tax is the retail sales tax (RST). As of July 2015, forty-six states and the District of Columbia had either a state or a local retail sales tax or both, with state rates ranging from 2.9 percent in Colorado to 7.5 percent in California, and local rates typically being no more than 1 or 2 percent but reaching as high as 7 or 8 percent in parts of some states.[1] It has attracted some attention—including from a few of the candidates in the 1996, 2000, 2008, 2012, and 2016 Republican presidential primaries—as a replacement for the federal personal and corporate income taxes.[2] Starting a few years ago, a well-financed lobbying campaign has been trying to drum up support for a particular plan for a national retail sales tax dubbed the FairTax.

The retail sales tax is a tax remitted by businesses triggered by all sales to consumers. In principle, it excludes from tax all goods and services sold from one business to another for use as an input to what they produce, but as discussed later, existing state retail sales tax regimes often violate this principle.[3]

A pure, clean-base, single-rate retail sales tax would tax *all* sales to consumers of both goods and services. It would be a completely "impersonal" tax in the sense that the rate of tax would not be adjusted to account for any characteristic of the consumer, such as income, marital status, number of dependents, or personal tastes—all of which a personal income tax can in principle account for. In practice, most states exempt certain items, such as food and medicine, in an attempt to exempt "necessities" and ease the burden on the poor. Many consumption items, particularly certain services, are also frequently exempt. Under a pure retail sales tax the aggregate tax base is the total value of final sales to consumers. Recall from chapter 3 that, administrative and compliance issues aside, who writes the checks and which side of a transaction bears legal liability for a tax on a given base do not ultimately matter for either the economic ramifications or for which people bear the burden of the tax. This point is critical to keep in mind when investigating some other tax systems that, judging from their mechanics, look to be very different from a retail sales tax but in fact are close relatives.

How a Value-Added Tax Works

One close relative to the sales tax is the value-added tax, widely known by its acronym, VAT (usually pronounced to rhyme with *flat*), which we mentioned briefly in chapter 6. The VAT has been a staple of European tax systems since the late 1960s and is now levied in almost every country in the world—more than 160 countries worldwide.[4] As Sijbren Cnossen of the University of Maastricht has remarked, "The nearly universal introduction of the value added tax should be considered the most important event in the evolution of tax structure in the last half of the twentieth century."[5] The United States stands out starkly among the countries of the world by *not* levying a value-added tax.[6] Not yet, at least.

In the aggregate, the VAT base is exactly the same as the retail sales tax—total final sales from businesses to consumers. The difference is entirely in the mechanics of how the tax liability is remitted from the private sector to the government. Although under the retail sales tax only retail businesses remit, under the VAT *all* businesses remit. The tax base for a firm under a VAT is simple—total sales revenue minus the cost of inputs purchased from other businesses. Note that the definition of purchased inputs does *not* include payments to a firm's workforce but does include purchases from other businesses of material inputs and capital goods. Unlike with an income tax, under a VAT business purchases of machinery, factories, and other capital goods can be deducted immediately instead of being deducted over several years according to a schedule of depreciation allowances. If investment goods were depreciated rather than being immediately deductible by the firms that purchase them, the aggregate tax base would be consumption plus net investment: in other words, it would be a form of income tax instead of a consumption tax.

A simple example can help show why the tax base for a VAT is equal to final sales of goods and services to consumers, just as it is for a retail sales tax. Say you go to a bakery and buy a loaf of bread for $2. Under a retail sales tax, the tax base is simply $2 (assuming that food isn't tax-exempt). To illustrate the VAT, let's greatly simplify the process of making bread into just two steps. First, suppose there is a farmer who grows wheat, grinds it into flour, and sells it to the baker for $1. Then the baker turns the flour into dough, bakes it into bread, and sells it to you for $2. The value added by the baker is $1—the sale price of the bread minus the cost of the flour. Under the VAT, the tax base is $1 for the farmer and $1 for the baker, adding up to a total of $2, the same tax base as under the retail sales tax. The example could be complicated by adding the cost of other ingredients, an oven, a tractor and seeds for the farmer, a separate flour company, and so on, but the net result would turn out to be identical: the tax base would still be $2.

At first blush it might appear that the retail sales tax is a tax "on" consumers while the VAT is a tax "on" businesses. But because the key difference between the two taxes concerns which parties remit (i.e., write the check to cover) the same total tax triggered by the same actions, there is no difference between these two taxes in who bears the burden of the tax or its economic effects (aside from administrative and enforcement issues, discussed below). And don't forget that business entities cannot bear the burden of taxation: only people can. What's more, if you've ever been to Europe or Canada, you know that a VAT need not even *look* different from a retail sales tax to the consumers. For instance, in a country with a 10 percent VAT, your cash register receipt may show the before-tax sales price and then tack on the 10 percent VAT, just like it does with a retail sales tax in the United States.[7] Some advocates of a national retail sales tax have argued that a retail sales tax would somehow be more inherently "visible" to the consumer than a VAT and thereby more accurately reflect the cost of taxation, but this need not be true.

There are a couple of different ways that a VAT can be implemented. Under the rarely used *subtraction method*, each tax period (which may be a year or a quarter) a firm reports to the government the total amount of sales minus the total cost of purchased inputs and multiplies that amount by the tax rate to find the tax it must remit to the government.[8] However, virtually every country that has a VAT uses a second approach, known as the *credit-invoice* method. Under this approach, the VAT is administered more like a sales tax; tax is triggered by each individual transaction. With a 10 percent VAT, every sale a firm makes incurs a 10 percent tax liability, and every purchase it makes from other firms[9] entitles it to a "credit" for the amount of tax that was remitted by the businesses it buys from—10 percent of the purchase price. Under this approach, the net amount of tax remitted by each firm to the government is identical to the tax that would be remitted under the subtraction method, but there's more of a paper trail. If a business is audited, it must have invoices to back up the credits it claims: it needs to demonstrate that the VAT has been remitted on its purchases by the businesses it purchased from. Thus, firms have an incentive to purchase goods and services from tax-law-abiding suppliers; otherwise, they may get no tax credit for their purchased inputs.

"Zero-rating" a consumption good means that at the final stage of the production and distribution chain within the country (for example, at the point of sale to the consumer, or at the point of export), no tax is due, but credit is received for taxes at earlier stages. This is equivalent to levying no tax at all on the zero-rated good, because all tax remitted by firms at earlier stages is credited back to firms at the final stage, with no tax due at that stage.

When applied to a firm, "exemption" means that the firm is completely outside of the tax net, with no filing requirement. This, of course, implies that no tax is owed on sales, but also that no credit is received for any tax that had been remitted at earlier stages. In addition, firms that purchase inputs from the exempt firm cannot claim any credits on those purchases. When applied to a good, exemption means that no VAT is due upon the sale of the good, no credit can be taken for inputs used to make that good, and no credit can be taken by other firms that purchase the good.

One crucial and often misunderstood aspect of how VATs operate involves the treatment of imports and exports. Most countries zero-rate exported goods; in other words, no VAT is due on the goods and services sold to people or businesses located in other countries. At the same time, a domestic firm owes VAT on any goods imported into the country. If the imported good is used as an input to production rather than sold to a consumer, then credit can be taken by the purchasing firm for the VAT remitted at the border on the imported input. Some observers in the United States have envied this aspect of the VAT, viewing it as an ingenious export promotion scheme that puts competing American producers at a disadvantage. They are, though, simply confused. As explained in detail in chapter 4, no VAT or any other tax system can so simply give us any kind of edge in international competition.[10] A VAT with this treatment of exports and imports essentially levies tax on goods and services consumed within the country, regardless of where they are produced. This is exactly what a retail sales tax does, and the VAT offers no more competitive advantage than does a retail sales tax—that is, none at all.[11]

Like the retail sales tax, the VAT is often much messier in practice than it is in theory. For example, many countries levy preferential or zero rates on certain "necessary" or hard-to-tax goods and services, exempt some kinds of businesses from tax remittance responsibility altogether, and levy special high rates on luxury goods.

If a VAT has the same consequences as a retail sales tax but involves more (non-retail) businesses in the collection process, why go through all the extra trouble? Why is it the tax success story of the last half century, almost totally replacing retail sales taxes everywhere but the United States? In a nutshell, the answer is that the retail sales tax suffers from important administrative and enforcement problems that are greatly magnified as the rate gets higher, while the VAT moderates these problems in clever ways. Most tax experts believe that a retail sales tax large enough to replace our personal and corporate income taxes would be unadministrable, but that a VAT of that size could be run (and *has* been run) fairly smoothly. Later in this chapter, when we discuss the simplicity and enforceability aspects of consumption taxes, we explain why.

After many years out of the U.S. policy debate, the value-added tax has recently been advocated by many who believe the long-term fiscal imbalance must be addressed.[12] Usually these people argue for a VAT as an addition to, rather than a replacement for, the income tax. For example, the Domenici-Rivlin tax reform plan proposed in November 2010 featured a 6.5 percent "Debt Reduction Sales Tax" that is a value-added tax under a different name.[13] The *Roadmap for America's Future* plan proposed by Paul Ryan (R-WI) in 2008 featured an 8.5 percent value-added tax, once again called something else (a "business con-sumption tax"),[14] although the VAT was notably dropped from the revised versions of the plan proposed in 2010, 2012, and 2016.[15] In the 2016 Republican presidential nomination campaign, two candidates' tax proposals prominently featured a VAT, called something else. Rand Paul's tax plan contained a 14.5 percent VAT, called a business-activity tax, and Ted Cruz's plan featured a 16 percent VAT, called a business flat tax. In Cruz's plan, 71 percent of total federal taxes would eventually be collected by the VAT, according to the Tax Foundation.[16]

How the Hall-Rabushka Flat Tax and X-Tax Work

The original flat tax was developed in 1981 by economist Robert E. Hall and political scientist Alvin Rabushka, both of Stanford University, and was first laid out in detail in their 1983 book *Low Tax, Simple Tax, Flat Tax* (titled *The Flat Tax* in its 1995 edition). Hall and Rabushka first attracted attention by claiming that flat tax returns could fit on a postcard. Ever since, the flat tax has had a devoted but small band of supporters. It formed the basis of a few proposals introduced in Congress during the years leading up to the Tax Reform Act of 1986, but the proposals did not receive much serious consideration then. The idea attracted more attention after the Republicans took control of Congress in the 1994 elections. The House majority leader at the time, Richard Armey (R-TX), and Senator Richard Shelby (R-AL) introduced legislation based on the Hall-Rabushka plan in Congress in 1995, and Steve Forbes then made it the centerpiece of his bids for the Republican presidential nomination in 1996 and 2000. He and the flat tax made the covers of *Newsweek* and *Time* magazines in the same week in January of 1996. Since then many politicians have argued for tax reforms that have at least one element of flatness discussed in chapter 6—a single rate, a consumption base, or a clean base. But the innovative design of the Hall-Rabushka plan, which involves all three elements of "flatness," has earned it the right to be called *the* flat tax.

Readers vaguely familiar with the flat tax may be surprised that we lump it together with the retail sales tax and the VAT. The flat tax looks a lot more like the current income tax system than either of the other two, mostly because along with a tax remitted by businesses it imposes a separate tax on individuals, who must annually file returns, albeit simple ones. Recall that under either a sales tax or a VAT, individuals are completely outside the tax system and need never fill out and send in personal tax returns.

Although the flat tax looks superficially like our existing income tax, it is fundamentally different. It is a reconfigured VAT or, in other words, a reconfigured sales tax. Under the flat tax, businesses pay tax on their total sales, minus purchases of goods and services from other businesses (the cost of which is deducted immediately), just like a VAT— with only one main difference. Unlike a VAT, the flat tax also allows firms to subtract from their tax base payments of wages and salaries (but not fringe benefits) to their workers.

Now comes the key innovation of the flat tax. Although, unlike a VAT, wages and salaries are deductible by employers, these same wages and salaries are then taxed separately, at the same rate as the business tax, at the personal level. Thus compared to a VAT the flat tax takes payments to employees out of the business tax base and makes them part of the employees' tax base. This is where the discussion of "tax incidence" in chapter 3 leads to a truly surprising insight. Apart from administrative and compliance issues, which side of a transaction is technically subject to the tax—in this case, the employer or the employee—ultimately makes no difference, so a Hall-Rabushka flat tax with a single rate and no exemptions is no different than a VAT or a comprehensive sales tax.

That the flat tax is a consumption tax (in sheep's or wolves' clothing, depending on your point of view) is not widely understood. For example, a former chair of the House Ways and Means Committee, Bill Archer, who favored a consumption tax, rejected the flat tax by saying, "In my common sense, if your wages are going to be taxed before you get them, that's an income tax."[17] Widely accepted economic theory makes clear that whether a tax on the flow of labor is remitted by the employer or the employee makes no fundamental difference to the impact of the tax, regardless of what one calls it.

If a flat tax is just a VAT in disguise, why go through the extra trouble of having employees fill out returns and perhaps remit tax on their wages and salaries? The main reason is that this scheme facilitates the adjustment of individual tax liabilities, and tax burdens, according to ability to pay. The individual wage portion of most flat tax proposals features a large family allowance (i.e., tax-exempt amount), similar to but larger than the standard deduction under the current income tax, as well as personal exemptions. Thus, people with low wage and salary income have no personal tax liability. As illustrated in the last chapter, the ratio of personal tax to labor income gradually increases from zero for families with labor income at or below the exemption, up to close to the uniform flat rate for high-income families. This means that the flat tax is more progressive than a value-added tax. Having a standard deduction and personal exemptions is a much simpler and more efficient method of introducing progressivity than would be possible under either a retail sales tax or a VAT.

Although the Hall-Rabushka flat tax is quite similar to a VAT, it differs critically from the existing personal income tax. Just two kinds of payments would be reported on the personal tax return: (1) wages and salaries and (2) pension receipts.[18] That's it. All of the other capital income components of what we are used to being part of taxable income—interest, dividends, capital gains, rents, royalties, and so on—would be completely exempt from tax at the personal level. All of the familiar deductions and credits would also be eliminated, including the deduction for mortgage interest payments, charitable contributions, state and local taxes, and medical expenses. This is what gives the Hall-Rabushka flat tax a clean base as well as a consumption base.

The business portion of the flat tax is also fundamentally different from the current corporation income tax. For one thing, all businesses, not just corporations, would remit this tax. So instead of sole proprietorships and partnerships reporting their income on their personal tax return as they do now, this income would be subject to a separate business tax. One implication of this is that noncorporate business losses could not offset wage and salary income, as they do—with some limits—now.

The business tax base would differ from the current one in three principal ways. First, in keeping with the consumption-tax concept, capital expenditures would be deducted immediately when made instead of generating deductions as they depreciate. (On enactment of a flat tax, all remaining depreciation deductions for past investments would be disallowed unless special transition rules were introduced.) Second, interest payments (and other financial outflows) would no longer be deductible, nor would interest receipts (and financial inflows) be subject to tax.[19] (In the absence of transition rules, deductions for interest payments due on past borrowing would also be disallowed.) Third, employer contributions to Social Security, health insurance, and other non-pension benefits would no longer be deductible by businesses, nor would tax payments to state and local governments. All would therefore be effectively subject to the flat rate of tax.

The essence of the Hall-Rabushka flat tax is the way that it defines the tax base, dividing a VAT into a business component and a wage component. Many of its details could be changed, while retaining its essential character. For example, certain itemized deductions could be allowed under the personal tax.

What if you like the flat tax but don't think that a single low rate with an exempt level of labor income provides enough progressivity, and are willing to sacrifice the extra efficiency cost of higher marginal tax rates to achieve that progressivity? Then you should consider a "graduated flat tax," which may sound as self-contradictory as jumbo shrimp. Such a tax, known as the X-tax, was developed and championed by the late and widely respected economist David Bradford of Princeton University.[20] The X-tax business and personal tax bases are the same as the flat tax, but the X-tax sets the business tax rate and the top personal rate on labor income at a higher level (say, 35 percent) and imposes lower, graduated rates on lower levels of labor income in addition to a tax-exempt level. The point of introducing graduated tax rates on labor income is to roughly replicate the overall degree of progressivity of the current system.

We emphasize that many tax systems labeled "flat" do not adopt the Hall-Rabushka VAT-like base, often being income taxes with a single tax rate and a more or less clean base. For example, in the last decade or two, over forty mostly low- and middle-income countries around the world have adopted single-rate taxes, but none has adopted the Hall-Rabushka tax base, so they are not consumption taxes. Rather, in all cases they are some form of income tax.[21] To keep things straight, whenever we refer to *the flat tax* in this chapter, we are talking about taxes with a consumption tax base, as in the original Hall-Rabushka proposal.

Other Approaches to Consumption Taxation
In this chapter, we focus on the varieties of consumption tax that have played or may play a major role in the U.S. tax reform debate. It is worthwhile to mention one other variety that is unlikely to get much of a public airing. This kind of consumption tax goes by a variety of names, including "personal consumption tax," "savings-exempt tax," and "consumed income tax." The basic idea of this tax is that each household would calculate its own consumption for the year by first computing income and then subtracting a measure of net saving. Either a flat-rate or a progressive tax-rate structure can then be applied to that base. In 1995, former Georgia senator Sam Nunn and Senator Pete Domenici of New Mexico introduced a version of this tax and called it the "USA tax," where USA stands for "unlimited savings allowance." The Achilles heel of this approach is that it is considerably more complicated than the other consumption tax options, mostly because it requires the tracking of transactions that now need not be tracked for tax purposes. The Hall-Rabushka flat tax (or its X-tax variant) can be designed in such a way that it achieves essentially the same economic and distributional goals as the personal consumption tax but in a simpler fashion.[22]

At What Rate?

Advocates of replacing the current income tax (and sometimes other taxes, as well) with a consumption tax often advertise rates that look low compared to the current income tax. Of course, this can make any tax system look attractive indeed. Unfortunately, in some cases the government would collect less revenue at the advertised rates than under the current system—sometimes a lot less. This section focuses on the rates that would be required for the consumption tax alternatives to raise the same amount of revenue as the current corporate and personal income tax systems—so-called *revenue-neutral* rates.

Any discussion of tax rates needs to be clear about the tax base to which the tax rate is applied because equivalent taxes can appear quite different if the tax base—and therefore the effective tax rate—is defined differently. Rates of sales tax or value-added tax are often quoted as a percentage of the price of a good excluding the tax—that is, on a *tax-exclusive* basis. In contrast, income tax rates and flat tax rates are generally quoted as a percentage of the tax base including the tax—that is, on a *tax-inclusive* basis. So, for example, if $20 of retail sales tax is charged on a good that costs $100 exclusive of the tax (so that you pay a total of $120, including tax, at the cash register), we usually say the tax rate is 20 percent—that is, (20/100)*100%. But an equivalent flat tax rate would be reported as 16.67 percent—that is, (20/120)*100%.

If any one of the consumption tax proposals discussed so far was somehow able to tax *all* personal consumption expenditures in the United States with a single rate and no exemptions whatsoever, the revenue-neutral rate needed to replace personal and corporate income taxation in 2014 would have to have been about 15.3 percent (tax-exclusive) or 13.3 percent (tax-inclusive).[23] In practice, however, a higher—and perhaps much higher—rate would be needed to make it be revenue-neutral. First of all, many types of consumption are difficult to tax and almost certainly would not be included in the tax base. Moreover, there will always be some evasion. As already discussed, several hundred billion dollars of taxable income now goes unreported. Although reducing evasion somewhat might be possible under an alternative system, undoubtedly a significant amount will persist. Finally, most consumption tax proposals purposely exclude some categories of spending from the base in an effort to ease the tax burden on those with low incomes; these exemptions must lead to higher rates of tax on what is not exempt to hit any revenue target.

How high would the rate have to go in practice? First, consider the retail sales tax. Among the states, it is common to exempt medical expenditures (including insurance), food for home consumption, clothing, the imputed rental value of housing, religious and charitable activities, and most services. If the federal sales tax base were to look like that of the average state, replacing the personal and corporate income taxes in 2012 would require a tax-exclusive rate of about 28.3 percent.[24] Emulating the states with the very broadest sales tax bases could lower the rate to perhaps 17.1 percent.[25] At that level of coverage, the sales tax might fully tax food, which is the most expensive exemption, comprising nearly a quarter of potential sales tax revenue.[26]

Both of these figures are gross underestimates for a *clean* national sales tax rate, however, because a great deal of state sales tax revenue comes from taxing purchases of business inputs, which are supposed to be exempt from a retail sales tax. One recent study estimated that on average only 56 percent of state sales tax revenues in 2011 came from final purchases by resident consumers; the rest represented taxation of business inputs.[27] Taxing business inputs with a retail sales tax is economically harmful and becomes much more so as the tax rate gets higher. If business inputs were to be completely eliminated from the base and the base was otherwise that of an average state, the national tax-exclusive rate would have to be 50.6 percent.[28]

A few years ago a proposal for replacing income and other taxes with a national retail sales tax garnered some attention—the so-called FairTax advocated by the organization Americans for Fair Taxation, and popularized by radio talk show host Neal Boortz. The FairTax is a national retail sales tax that includes a cash rebate intended to introduce some progressivity. Advocates of the FairTax tend to advertise a tax-inclusive rate of 23 percent, which corresponds to a rate of approximately 30 percent using the tax-exclusive definition we are accustomed to, from our experience with state retail sales taxes; thus an item that is priced at $100 would cost $130, where the $30 tax is 30 percent of $100 but only 23 percent of $130.[29] Proponents claimed that this would produce enough revenue to replace personal and corporate income taxes, payroll taxes, and estate and gift taxes and also to pay for the rebate. The rebate would be paid in cash to each and every household in the United States and would equal the tax-inclusive rate times the federal poverty line for that size household. So, for example, in 2014 the annual rebate would be a cash payment of $2,684 for a single person or $5,368 for a couple, plus $934 per dependent.[30] If the full burden of the sales tax is passed on to consumer prices, then for a household with consumption right at the poverty line, the rebate exactly offsets the sales tax burden, but for households with consumption below the poverty line, the rebate refunds more than the sales tax burden.[31]

Even the 30 percent tax-exclusive rate for the FairTax is misleadingly low. First, the proposal would impose sales tax not only on personal consumption expenditures but also on government purchases (which effectively implies a very large reduction in real government spending).

Second, the national sales tax base is assumed to include essentially all consumption with no avoidance, evasion, or special exemptions, except for education. The Treasury Department has estimated that if the FairTax were adjusted to maintain the real purchasing power of government spending and if a moderate amount of tax evasion (15 percent of the tax base) is assumed, the tax-exclusive rate necessary to replace just personal and corporate income taxes and to pay for the rebate would have been 34 percent in 2006. Going further to also replace payroll taxes and estate taxes as the FairTaxers intend would naturally require a considerably higher rate than that. If, instead of assuming a virtually comprehensive consumption base, one assumes a base similar to that of the median state's retail sales tax, the tax-exclusive rate necessary to replace income taxation in 2006 rises from 34 percent to 64 percent![32]

In principle, because the VAT base is the same as the retail sales tax base, the same calculations for estimating the revenue-neutral rate should apply. In practice, the VAT does a much better job of avoiding the taxation of business inputs and probably generates considerably less evasion. Still, many types of consumption would be difficult, if not impossible, to tax under either a sales tax or a VAT. Just two among many examples are the imputed rental value of the existing housing stock and the value of financial services, such as check-writing privileges, that are paid for implicitly through lower interest rates rather than fees.

A 2012 study by Eric Toder, Jim Nunns, and Joseph Rosenberg of the Tax Policy Center sheds light on the rates that would be needed if a VAT were to replace income taxation in the United States.[33] They considered three VAT options that differ by the breadth of the tax base and whether there is a rebate. Option 1 features a relatively broad base, amounting to 57 percent of all consumption, which excludes (zero-rates) government health expenditures, other general government spending, education, religious and nonprofit expenditures, along with a few other small items (mostly things that are administratively difficult to tax, such as the kind of financial services income discussed above). Option 2 involves a narrower base, amounting to 36 percent of consumption, which in addition to the exclusions in option 1 also zero-rates food consumed at home, health care, and housing expenditures. Option 3 uses the broad base but also provides a refundable rebate to households equal to the VAT rate times "employment income" (including current wage and salary and self-employment income, together with deferred employment income such as payouts from pension plans and withdrawals from retirement accounts), up to a maximum of $12,000 of such income for single adults and $24,000 of such income for married adults.[34] This rebate is roughly similar to the FairTax rebate for childless adults with employment income above the poverty line. But it is significantly less generous than the FairTax rebate for larger families, because there is no adjustment to the rebate for children. It is also less generous to families with employment income below the poverty line, because unlike the FairTax, the rebate is zero for people with no employment income and then gradually rises with employment income up to a maximum amount. Our extrapolations from their estimates suggest that a revenue-neutral replacement of individual and corporate income tax revenues in fiscal year 2016 would require a tax-exclusive VAT rate of 20.5 percent for option 1, 32.4 percent for option 2, and 28.8 percent for option 3.[35]

When measured in comparable (tax-inclusive or tax-exclusive) terms, a flat tax requires a higher rate than a VAT without a rebate, because the family allowances in the flat tax reduce the tax base significantly. The version of the Hall-Rabushka flat tax that was introduced in Congress in 1995 had a $31,400 exemption for a family of four in 1996 and a tax rate of 17 percent (tax-inclusive) when fully phased in, but it was designed explicitly to be a tax cut.[36] Subsequently, the U.S. Department of the Treasury has estimated that a similar plan with a perfectly clean base and an exemption level of $38,600 ($44,458 in 2014 dollars) for a family of four in 2006 would require a 21 percent tax-inclusive rate to replace personal and corporate income tax revenues.[37] Adding back in some itemized deductions or changing the tax base in other ways could raise the revenue-neutral rate for a flat tax significantly.[38]

In assessing these revenue estimates, it should be kept in mind that, to the extent that tax reform induces greater economic growth, a given amount of revenue could be raised with a somewhat lower rate. However, if rates are set too low at the outset and thus increase budget deficits, long-run economic growth is less likely to increase, and might decline.

The estimates above all refer to the level of tax rates that would be necessary to replace revenues from the personal and corporate income taxes in recent years, when the revenue raised by these taxes, taken together, was in the vicinity of 10 to 11 percent of GDP.[39] But as we have discussed, the projected path of spending and taxes generates large deficits with potentially severe negative consequences. This is why some have looked to the VAT as part of a package of reforms that will raise more tax revenue and curtail government spending, especially on the entitlement programs whose projected future cost soars.

In this context our discussion about the revenue potential of the VAT must be revisited—how much revenue could a VAT raise for each percentage point of the levy? Estimates from the 2012 Toder, Nunns, and Rosenberg VAT study discussed above suggest that, when implemented as an add-on to the existing tax system, each percentage point of the VAT rate would reduce the federal budget deficit in 2015 by $75 billion (0.40 percent of GDP) under option 1 (the broad-based VAT), $48 billion (0.25 percent of GDP) under option 2 (the narrow-based VAT), and $49 billion (0.26 percent of GDP) under option 3 (the broad-based VAT with a rebate).[40]

Simplicity and Enforceability of the Consumption Tax Plans

We now begin an evaluation of these consumption tax plans. Some important practical questions must be addressed first: how simple or complicated is each approach, and how easy is it to enforce? The answers to these questions turn out to be crucial for determining which approach to consumption taxation is the best. These issues are also important in deciding whether any of the approaches would be better than the existing system or a reformed income tax, or attractive as an additional tax to raise more revenue.

Administrative Problems of a Retail Sales Tax Compared to a VAT

On the surface, the retail sales tax seems like a fairly simple and straightforward way to raise money, and to the average citizen, it probably appears to work reasonably well. But as mentioned before, the VAT has become the world standard, and virtually every developed country that ever had a national retail sales tax has by now replaced it with a VAT. One important reason is that serious administrative problems arise with the retail sales tax that most average Americans never hear about, even though they ultimately bear the burden of the costs these problems generate. These problems are not too glaring when rates are low, as they are in most states. But at the 30 percent (or higher) rate that would be required to replace U.S. personal and corporate income taxation, these problems would be serious, indeed.

Our current state retail sales taxes appear to be simpler and relatively less costly to administer than our income tax system. Some reputable studies suggest that the total cost of enforcing and complying with current state retail sales taxes is about 4 percent of revenues raised.[41] This is lower than the 11 to 16 percent that we estimated in chapter 5 for the income tax system, but it is not necessarily a reliable indicator of what the costs would be like for a national retail sales tax because current administrative costs do not give a flavor of the kinds of problems that could be created at high rates.

The first problem with the retail sales tax (henceforth RST) is the taxation of business inputs. An RST is supposed to tax only the final purchases of consumers and not the purchases of businesses. If tax is triggered both when businesses purchase their inputs and then again when they sell their outputs, a problem of *cascading* develops. Consumer goods and services that involve relatively more businesses in their production and distribution end up being taxed more heavily. This inefficiently distorts incentives in two ways—inducing vertical integration of businesses that would not otherwise occur to minimize the cascading tax, and discouraging production and consumption of goods that cannot easily be vertically integrated. States try to avoid this problem by giving businesses a registration number to present when purchasing goods from other firms, exempting them from sales tax liability. But this procedure often works poorly, as evidenced by the high percentage of RST revenues that apparently come from business purchases. Another problem with the retail sales tax is that, at high tax rates, it becomes difficult to enforce because it collects all the money from what is, for compliance purposes, the weakest link in the production and distribution chain—retail. Consumers have no incentive to make sure retailers are paying their sales tax, and retailers have no incentive to pay aside from the threat of audit.[42] Moreover, consumers have the incentive to inappropriately acquire business registration numbers to avoid the sales tax. A study by the Florida Department of Revenue estimated that 5 percent of tax-free business purchases involved abuse or misuse of business exemption certificates, and it recounts how "paper" businesses are created solely as a means of obtaining business exemption certificates and avoiding taxes on purchases intended for personal use.[43] Florida has a sales tax rate of 6 percent, and the magnitude of this problem for a rate five times higher is likely to be much larger.

In contrast, under a standard credit-invoice-style VAT, firms have an incentive to make sure that any other firm they are buying from has paid its VAT because otherwise they cannot claim credit for the tax remitted by their suppliers. A retailer that evades a 10 percent RST costs the government tax revenue equal to the full 10 percent of the retail price. In contrast, under a VAT, evasion by a retailer puts at risk, at most, only the tax due on the value added by the retailer, which is generally a fairly small percentage of the retail price. For a firm at an intermediate point in the production and distribution chain, failure to file a return or collect VAT on sales may actually *increase* total VAT revenue because the tax credit to businesses that are downstream in the production and distribution chain, for taxes paid at earlier stages, is lost. Although evasion of current state RSTs may not appear that serious, the problem would be much worse at higher rates. As Alan Tait, a leading expert on consumption taxation around the world has stated, "At 5 percent, the incentive to evade tax is probably not worth the penalties of prosecution; at 10 percent, evasion is more attractive, and at 15–20 percent, it becomes extremely tempting."[44]

Just as with an income tax, all sorts of difficult issues of interpretation arise under the sales tax. The difference is that unless you run a retail sales business, most people never hear about these issues. Whenever some commodities are exempt from tax, where the line is drawn is important. Consider the problem if expenditures on food but not on restaurant meals are exempt. What is the appropriate tax treatment of salad bars in grocery stores or fast-food restaurants, where the customer may eat in or take out? These sorts of problems become much more troublesome as the rate rises because the payoff to taxpayers of misclassifying goods into the low-taxed category increases.

Worst of all, no historical precedent is available to reassure us that these problems are manageable in a retail sales tax. Undoubtedly for the reasons discussed above, only six countries have operated retail sales taxes at rates over 10 percent, and all of them have since switched to a VAT.[45] Based on a review of worldwide practice, Vito Tanzi, the former director of the Fiscal Analysis Division of the International Monetary Fund, concludes that 10 percent is probably the maximum rate feasible for a retail sales tax.[46] We believe that because of compliance and enforcement problems, replacing the income tax with a retail sales tax would be unwise, especially given that a VAT can achieve the same goals while avoiding most of these problems.

Just How Simple and Easy to Enforce Is a VAT?

The VAT clearly has many administrative advantages over a retail sales tax, but how does it compare to the current system? Replacing the income tax with a comprehensive, single-rate VAT *could* provide an enormous amount of simplification. Individual income tax returns could be completely eliminated, and business tax returns could be significantly simplified, requiring little more information than is now collected in the normal course of business. No longer would tax-payers have to deal with complex depreciation allowances or the laby-rinthine rules concerning financial instruments. It would also be easier to enforce than the combined personal and corporate income tax codes.

A few studies have estimated the enforcement and compliance costs of adopting a VAT in the United States. Several of them suggest that a broad-based, single-rate VAT could involve considerably lower enforce-ment and compliance costs than the current income tax in the United States.[47] For instance, a 1992 Congressional Budget Office study con-cluded that the combined administrative and compliance costs of raising $150 billion in 1988 from a relatively clean European-style VAT would be between $4 and $7 billion, or between 2.7 and 4.7 percent of revenues collected. That would be the equivalent of between $7 and $12 billion in administrative and compliance costs to raise $263 billion in 2014.[48] They note that these costs would be "largely independent" of the amount of revenue raised. This suggests that the cost-revenue ratio for a trillion-dollar VAT could be substantially lower than the 15.6 percent of revenue we estimate for the 2010 U.S. income tax system, but to an unknown degree. Before jumping to this conclusion, however, several caveats should be noted.

First, a portion of the apparent compliance cost saving of replacing the income tax with a VAT stems from the elimination of individual tax returns. Much of this saving would disappear if the states did not abolish their own personal income tax systems. Because most of the information required to calculate income is currently used for both federal and state income tax purposes, eliminating only the federal return requirement would not spare most individuals of the need to file returns and keep track of the requisite information. And, of course, these calculations do not apply at all to any proposal that introduces a VAT *in addition* to the income tax, unless the plan featured substantial income tax simplification.

Second, the cost estimates done by the CBO and others presume that firms with total sales less than a certain amount would be exempt from VAT liability. In a VAT, an exempt firm is completely outside the tax system and therefore does not remit tax to the government on its sales, cannot take credit for VAT remitted on its purchases from suppliers, and cannot issue invoices that would enable firms that purchase inputs from it to claim credits. Exemptions for retailers cost the government revenue on the final slice of a product's value. But exempting a firm in the middle of the production and distribution chain can *increase* revenues because neither the exempt firm nor the next firm in the chain can take a credit for taxes paid at earlier stages in the chain, similar to what happens when a firm in the middle of the chain evades the tax. So overall, exempting small firms may not cost the government much revenue.[49] It does involve some economic costs, however. It can distort firms' decisions about size and organizational form, and it can tax different types of goods more heavily or lightly depending on how many firms in the production and distribution chain are exempt and where in the chain these firms are located. The conventional wisdom among VAT experts is that the administrative and compliance cost savings from exempting firms with revenues below some moderate threshold outweighs the efficiency cost of this approach.[50] For this reason, most countries that operate a VAT do exempt firms with sales below a certain threshold—for example, below about $125,669 or 81,000 pounds for 2014 in the United Kingdom.[51] In any event, the hidden efficiency cost arising from exemption of small firms offsets some of the administrative and compliance cost saving from switching to a VAT.

Finally, the VAT poses some tricky implementation issues of its own, such as how to tax financial transactions. Recall that the VAT base is equal to the cash flow from the firm's real operations (sales revenue minus the cost of inputs) and thus is not affected by the financial operations of a firm (its borrowing, lending, issuance of new shares, and so on). For example, in a VAT interest receipts are not part of taxable income, and interest payments are not deductible. But for a financial institution, the financial operations *are* the real purpose of the business, and the pricing of the services offered is often implicit in the interest charges and payments. Thus, by placing interest receipts and payments outside of the tax base, we may be seriously mismeasuring the true value added of a financial firm or of a nonfinancial firm with financial operations. To be sure, taxing financial services can be problematic in an income tax or a retail sales tax, so it is not obvious that things would be significantly worse under a VAT. But some unique problems do arise under a consumption tax like the VAT. For example, procedures would have to be developed to deal with installment sales of automobiles because a car dealer would have the incentive to characterize payments as (untaxed) interest, while a consumer would be indifferent as to how the payment is labeled.[52]

Although these implementation problems are undeniable, we also have more than four decades of experience in other countries, particularly in Europe, on which to draw. In contrast to the retail sales tax, VAT systems at the rate necessary to replace the U.S. income tax are not out of the range of historical experience. In several European countries, the standard rate that is applied to most goods and services is 20 percent or more. Although the ratio of federal personal and corporate income tax receipts to gross domestic product in the United States—10.5 percent in 2014—is higher than what is collected by most other countries' VATs, it is not higher by much.[53] As of 2013, the OECD countries with the largest VAT revenues as a percentage of GDP were Denmark (9.6 percent), New Zealand (9.4 percent), and Finland (9.3 percent). Of the big European countries, France raised 6.9 percent of GDP with its VAT, Germany raised 7.0 percent, and the United Kingdom raised 6.9 percent.[54]

The fact that VATs have been around a while, at levels comparable to what the United States would need to replace the income tax, is both the good news and the bad news for advocates. It is good news because we would not be stepping into unknown territory, as would be the case with a retail sales tax. It is bad news because the experience from other countries is not encouraging about the possibility of realizing the simplification potential of a VAT. For the most part, the European countries do not levy the kind of broad-base, uniform-rate VAT we have been discussing or perhaps fantasizing about. Instead, the European VATs have multiple rates and numerous exemptions, features that require difficult-to-make distinctions, invite abuse, and require close and costly monitoring.

The evidence suggests that, warts and all, the European countries' VATs are no less costly to collect than their income taxes. A careful although now somewhat outdated study of the British VAT concluded that the ratio of collection cost to revenue raised was only slightly lower for the VAT compared to the personal income tax—4.7 percent for the VAT (1.0 percent for administration, 3.7 percent for taxpayer costs) and 4.9 percent for the personal income tax (1.5 percent for administration,

3.4 percent for taxpayer costs).[55] A study of the Swedish tax system suggests that its VAT is *more* expensive to operate than its income tax, costing 3.1 percent of revenue to collect compared to 2.7 percent for the income tax, prompting the author of the study to remark that "the VAT is evidently not the simple tax it has been marketed as."[56] Undoubtedly, in both these cases the failure of the VAT to display a collection-cost advantage reflects both that actual VATs are more complex than ideal VATs and also that European income taxes are less costly to collect than the U.S. income tax.

Nor do enforcement problems disappear under a VAT, in spite of the advantages of the invoice-credit method of administration. The 2012 "VAT gap" (the difference between actual VAT revenues, and what those revenues would be in the absence of evasion and fraud) has been estimated at 16 percent of potential revenues for the European Union as a whole, in the same ballpark as our best guess for the U.S. income tax.[57] A VAT requires a strong enforcement system to monitor such things as unregistered businesses, exaggerated refund claims, unrecorded cash purchases, underreported sales, and false export claims. In one growing type of VAT noncompliance, known as "carousel fraud," goods are sold through multiple business-to-business transaction chains across the borders of European countries. Exporters claim credit for VAT remitted at earlier stages on their exports, and importers of those goods "disappear" before remitting VAT to the importing country's government. Then, on the next turn of the "carousel," firms later in the distribution chain may reexport those same goods and claim credit again for VAT that was never actually remitted by firms earlier in the chain.[58]

All in all, a VAT *potentially* represents a major simplification compared to our current income tax. But the failure of European VATs to be as simple as the drawing-board version of a VAT suggests caution when comparing the messy real world to an ideal. More practically, this lack of simplicity is a warning that if the United States were to adopt a VAT, either as a replacement for the income tax or as an additional tax, it would be well advised to keep it simple and, in particular, to levy a uniform rate on all goods and services.

Simplicity and Enforceability of a Flat Tax or X-Tax

As stressed earlier, the Hall-Rabushka flat tax adds an extra step to the VAT by taking wages and salaries out of the business tax base and requiring individuals to fill out their own returns on which they report that income. Although this extra step greatly facilitates adjusting households' tax burdens according to ability to pay, it also adds extra compliance costs. Nevertheless, advocates argue that if the personal tax base is kept relatively clean and simple, the flat tax would not be much more difficult to administer or comply with than a VAT. In that case, like a VAT, the flat tax would have the *potential* to greatly reduce the costs of compliance and enforcement relative to the current income tax, but it could also end up quite messy, as with many real-world VATs.

Unlike the VAT, however, the flat tax is a relatively new concept. No country has ever actually adopted it, and in fact, no flat tax proposal has ever been written out in enough legal detail that it could actually be implemented.[59] For that reason, there is greater uncertainty surrounding it. Since the flat tax first garnered significant attention in the mid-1990s, academic tax experts have begun to put some serious thought into the administrative and enforcement problems that it might introduce.[60] They point out that some of the problems that arise under the existing income tax would remain, some would be eliminated, and some new problems would be introduced. The consensus of this literature is that, on balance, the flat tax would very likely be simpler and easier to enforce and administer than the current income tax but that the advantage is a lot smaller than initially indicated by Hall and Rabushka.

The flat tax would suffer from some of the same problems as a VAT, such as the incentive for businesses to redefine taxable sales to consumers as nontaxable interest received from consumers. Many of the potential problems with the flat tax, however, arise from differences in the way the flat tax and VATs are implemented. First of all, taxing labor compensation separately at the individual level (with an exemption level and possibly at different rates) necessitates using a deduction-based, or subtraction, method of implementation rather than a credit-invoice-based tax system. The Hall-Rabushka flat tax proposal thus features what is essentially a subtraction-method VAT (with labor costs deductible) at the business level. A subtraction-method VAT lacks some of the enforcement advantages of a credit-invoice VAT, which is why almost all countries use the latter method. Because a fixed tax rate can no longer be charged on each transaction, it becomes harder to monitor whether all transactions are reported for tax purposes. The leading flat tax blueprints do not feature a small-business exemption, and in its absence, they do not take advantage of the potentially large cost savings of being able to ignore the hardest-to-tax sector. In principle, it would be possible to exempt small-business income from the Hall-Rabushka flat tax, although this does invite some problems. For example, it would create an incentive to start a small business and then pay oneself an artificially low salary to shelter labor income from taxation.[61]

What about the trademark postcard-size tax form? Contrary to what the flat tax inventors Hall and Rabushka claim, flat tax business returns would not be able to fit on postcards without combining many different items into single entries, making it difficult for the IRS to verify the results. In any event, the postcard would merely summarize what could be millions of transactions, and thus the metaphor of the post-card tax return misleadingly understates the difficulty of monitoring the tax system. Still, some aspects of the flat business tax make it simpler and easier to enforce than a corporate income tax, in part because of the replacement of depreciation deductions with expensing and the fact that financial transactions generally have no tax conse-quences. The flat business tax would also have the advantage of elimi-nating many of the complicated special provisions in the current corporate code, although some of this could be accomplished within the context of the income tax as well.

At the personal level, the flat tax is obviously more complicated than a VAT because a VAT eliminates personal returns altogether. But the flat tax is vastly simpler and easier to enforce than the current income tax system. Since only wages and salaries plus pension income need be reported, all of the complications associated with measuring and reporting capital income are eliminated. Personal returns could cer-tainly fit on postcards. To be sure, the self-employed would continue to pose an administrative and compliance problem. For example, the knotty issue of whether a car is for personal purposes or business pur-poses (and therefore deductible as a business expense) remains and might even be worse because the designation of personal or business, or something in between, must be made at the time of purchase. It is difficult to come up with a precise estimate of the compliance and enforcement costs associated with a flat tax, especially because no other country has ever operated such a system. If it were kept clean and care were taken to address some of the implementation issues identified above, the total cost could surely be much lower than our estimate of $170 billion per year for the current system.

The simplification promise of the flat tax depends on a lot of big "ifs." What starts as a very simple plan could end up becoming a mess as it winds its way through the political process. For instance, allowing lots of itemized deductions would make the personal system more complicated. Transition rules could make things even more complicated than the current system in the short run. Some flat tax advocates have also proposed eliminating withholding of taxes on wages, which would undoubtedly cause major enforcement problems.[62] And simplifying the federal code would only help taxpayers to the extent that the states followed suit. It's also worth noting that some of the simplification, such as eliminating itemized deductions, could be achieved while retaining the existing income tax structure. Nonetheless, the potential simplicity of the flat tax approach to progressive consumption taxation cannot be denied.

Distributional Effects of the Consumption Tax Alternatives

Of course, simplicity and enforceability are not the only issues that arise in choosing a tax system, nor are they necessarily the most important. Most everyone also has a strong and abiding interest in the distributional consequences of tax reform: which plans will make *your* tax burden larger or smaller, and more generally, how will the total tax burden be shared among us? Next we examine the progressivity of the leading consumption taxes, with emphasis on a value-added tax. This is relevant both to the question of replacing our current system with a consumption tax and to the question of enacting a VAT to supplement the existing income tax.

Tax Burden Progressivity of a Retail Sales Tax or VAT

In chapter 6, we argued that over a lifetime a single-rate VAT or sales tax would exact from most individuals a burden that is approximately proportional to their lifetime incomes and would be regressive to the extent that inheritances and bequests escape tax. Given this presumption, a complex analysis is not needed to reach the conclusion that—compared to an income tax with a generous level of tax-free income, graduated rates, and an earned income credit for the working poor—a VAT or sales tax without a rebate would substantially increase the tax burden on low-income households. For example, someone who spends an entire lifetime at the poverty level would be liable for no income tax under the current system because tax-exempt levels are currently set above the poverty line. In fact, if such a person were poor in spite of working, he or she would currently receive a potentially substantial refund because of the Earned Income Tax Credit. In stark contrast, a 20 percent VAT would impose a tax burden equal to approximately 20 percent of that person's lifetime income.

Table 7.1 presents estimates of the distributional impacts of three different options for adding a VAT to the existing tax system. Each option involves a VAT that raises enough revenue to reduce the federal budget deficit by 2 percent of GDP in 2015, based on the 2012 analysis by Toder, Nunns, and Rosenberg discussed earlier.[63] The table depicts the combined transitional and long-run burden of each tax, expressed as a percentage of after-tax income. The analysis underlying the results shown assumes that in the long run, the burden of the VAT is borne in proportion to labor income, "super-normal" returns to capital, and cash transfers received, with adjustments for the distributional effects of changes in relative prices of different types of consumption (e.g., due to excluding some items from the tax base). It also assumes that the transitional burden of adopting a new consumption tax is borne in proportion to wealth. These assumptions make sense for reasons we discussed in chapter 6. Option 1 is a broad-based 5.0 percent VAT. Option 2 is a narrow-based 7.9 percent VAT, which relative to option 1 removes all expenditures on housing, health care, and food consumed at home from the base. Option 3 is a broad-based 7.7 percent VAT, with a rebate equal to the VAT rate multiplied by employment income, up to a maximum employment income of $12,000 for single people and $24,000 for married couples (see our earlier section on VAT rates for further details).

As table 7.1 shows, for VAT options 1 and 2, burdens are borne roughly proportionately to after-tax income, except that in both cases the burden is a somewhat lower percentage of after-tax income for households in the top 5 percent of the income distribution. The fact that the distribution of burdens across income classes for option 2 is very similar to that for option 1 suggests that in this analysis, removing housing, health care, and food consumed at home from the VAT base is *not* an effective way to make a VAT more progressive. By contrast, the burden of option 3, the broad-based VAT with a rebate, is distributed progressively. The net-of-rebate VAT burden is 0.6 percent of after-tax income in the lowest quintile, 2.9 percent of after-tax income in the middle quintile, and 3.7 percent of after-tax income for people in the top 1 percent of the income distribution. The rebate causes the burden as a share of after-tax income to rise steadily from the bottom through the middle of the income distribution, but it does not produce

Table 7.1
Distributional effect of adding a VAT to the existing tax system that is large enough to reduce the federal budget deficit by 2 percent of GDP in 2015, expressed as a percentage change in after-tax income

Rank in distribution of cash income	Percentage change in after-tax income		
	Broad-based VAT	Narrow-based VAT	Broad-based VAT with rebate
	(1)	(2)	(3)
Overall	−3.3	−3.3	−3.2
Top 1 percent	−2.5	−2.6	−3.7
Rest of top 5 percent	−2.8	−2.8	−3.6
Bottom half of top decile	−3.2	−3.2	−3.8
Bottom half of top quintile	−3.4	−3.4	−3.8
Second highest quintile	−3.6	−3.6	−3.5
Middle quintile	−3.6	−3.6	−2.9
Second lowest quintile	−3.6	−3.5	−1.8
Lowest quintile	−3.9	−3.8	−0.6

Source: Toder, Nunns, and Rosenberg (2012, table 7).
Note: The tax-exclusive VAT rates are 5.0 percent in column (1), 7.9 percent in column (2), and 7.7 percent in column (3).

much progressivity at income levels above that—the VAT burden as a share of after-tax income is fairly equal across different slices of the top half of the income distribution.

An important lesson from table 7.1 is that abandoning tax rate uniformity to impose a zero tax rate on goods and services such as food, shelter, and health care may not actually succeed at making the distribution of VAT burdens more progressive. If the authors had made different, but still reasonable, assumptions about how VAT burdens are shifted across consumers, labor, and capital, it might have suggested that option 2 was a bit more progressive. But even then, in aggregate most purchases of the preferentially taxed commodities are made by middle- and high-income families (e.g., not only low-income households buy food), so this is a very poorly targeted way to increase the progressivity of a VAT or sales tax. Moreover, European experience with the VAT shows that multiple-rate VAT systems are significantly more complex and therefore more expensive to run. Preferential taxation of necessities also sharply reduces revenues, requiring an even higher tax rate on other goods to raise any given dollar amount. Finally, it causes significant economic distortions, creating an inefficient incentive to consume more of the goods and services that are untaxed and less of the ones that are taxed. The analysis by Toder, Nunns, and Rosenberg suggests that replacing income taxation with a narrow-base VAT that zero-rates health care, housing, and food consumed at home would require a 32 percent tax rate. At a rate that high, the distortion to incentives would be nontrivial. Compared to the zero-rated goods and services, the taxed ones become 32 percent more expensive, causing people to switch away from them even though they would otherwise prefer not to. The attempt to achieve progressivity causes an unintended distortion in what people consume.

As table 7.1 demonstrates, cash rebates are a much more effective means of introducing progressivity into a VAT (or sales tax). This approach is also more economically efficient, because it generates less distortion to decisions about what to consume.

Table 7.2 presents one attempt to quantify the distributional consequences of replacing federal income taxes with a very broad-based national retail sales tax, performed by the Treasury Department in 2005 for the President's Advisory Panel on Federal Tax Reform.[64] Column (1) shows an estimate of the percentage of total federal personal and corporate income taxes that were borne by each income class in 2006. Column (2) shows the percentage of the sales tax that would be borne by each income class if income taxation were replaced by a retail sales tax with no rebate (which the Treasury estimates would require a tax-exclusive rate of 22 percent). The distribution of tax burdens shifts sharply. Under 2006 law, households with incomes above $230,000 (in 2014 dollars) owed 53.5 percent of income taxes. Under the sales tax with no rebate, those same households would have owed just 33.0 percent of sales taxes. Thus, under this plan 20.5 percent of the 2006 income tax burden gets shifted to people lower in the income distribution. The bottom 80 percent of taxpayers ranked by income experience a tax increase totaling $288 billion per year (in 2014 dollars), and the average annual tax hike per taxpayer in the bottom 80 percent is over $2,419 (in 2014 dollars).[65]

Column (3) of table 7.2 depicts the distributional consequences of a FairTax-style approach. The plan examined here has a 34 percent tax-exclusive rate, which is what the Treasury estimated would be necessary to replace income taxation and fund a rebate of an amount that would offset the tax burden on a family at the poverty level, while maintaining real government spending and allowing for modest

Table 7.2
Estimated effect on the distribution of tax burdens if 2006 federal income taxes were replaced with a national retail sales tax

Cash income range (thousands of 2014 dollars)	Percentage of federal income taxes or sales taxes borne		
	(1)	(2)	(3)
	2006 income taxes	22% sales tax, no rebate	34% sales tax with rebate
Below 17	-0.7	1.4	-6.3
17–35	-0.5	5.1	-0.3
35–46	1.5	4.8	2.8
46–58	2.6	5.5	4.2
58–86	9.5	14.0	12.9
86–115	9.2	12.0	12.4
115–230	24.8	24.7	29.1
230 and over	53.5	33.0	45.9

Source: President's Advisory Panel on Federal Tax Reform (2005).

evasion. The rebate envisioned in the FairTax plan does mitigate the regressive redistribution of tax burdens caused by a national sales tax, but is not large enough to undo it. Households with incomes above about $230,000 (in 2014 dollars) paid 53.5 percent of income taxes in 2006 but would have paid 45.9 percent of sales taxes, with the difference shifted to lower-income classes. Households with incomes between about $17,000 and $230,000 are estimated to bear an increased tax burden under this plan. Those with incomes below about $17,000 do end up better off, though, as the rebate more than offsets the sales tax and lost refundable income credits for this group.

The distributional effects of the plan could be moved closer to the current income tax with a larger rebate and a higher tax rate. But the single rate and uniform rebate provide only limited flexibility to match the existing distribution, so there would inevitably be big winners and losers. More complicated, income-related rebate schemes could more finely tailor the distributional impact but would require household-level information on the amount of annual income or consumption, defeating one of the main advantages of impersonal tax systems like the sales tax or VAT. Moreover, the rebate in the FairTax-style plan analyzed in table 7.2 would already cost about $600 billion in 2006, or 23 percent of federal spending.[66] The government would be writing a check for several thousand dollars every year to each household in the United States, and it is not clear how voters would feel about such a large new transfer program or whether this would have an important impact on political support for efforts to ease tax burdens on low- and moderate-income people. A rebate or credit would require that a whole new administrative apparatus be set up in addition to the one needed to run the sales tax or VAT. Tracking low-income people to ensure that they received rebates could prove difficult, as the IRS has difficulty dealing with this population, as evidenced by pervasive fraudulent claims for the Earned Income Tax Credit.[67]

Tables 7.1 and 7.2 illustrate the key policy questions. With respect to replacing the income tax with a VAT or RST, do the potential gains from simplification and stimulation of economic growth (assessed later in this chapter) justify a tax burden redistribution of this magnitude? With respect to enacting a VAT in addition to the income tax, do the benefits of addressing the long-term fiscal imbalance in part by increasing tax revenues justify imposing a tax that is either slightly regressive or slightly progressive, but inevitably raises burdens significantly across most of the distribution? Economic analysis by itself cannot provide decisive answers to these questions because they involve evaluating policies that make some people better off and others worse off. Even with the possibility that overall economic growth could increase and thereby eventually offset to some extent the real income decline of some people who initially suffer increased tax burdens, such an evaluation inescapably involves value judgments that must ultimately be resolved by our political system. We suspect, though, that most Americans would not support a retail sales tax or VAT as a replacement for the income tax because they do not favor such a dramatic shift in the tax burden, except perhaps if some simple and appealing method could be found to undo much of the distributional impact.

We are less sure about whether there could be political support for an *add-on* value-added tax in the United States at some point in the near future. Of course, its attractiveness depends on the politically viable alternatives. But the fact that most of the expected future increase in government spending comes from politically popular and thus difficult-to-cut programs, especially Medicare, together with the fact that essentially every other rich country has adopted an add-on VAT to pay for their larger governments, suggests that this is a path the United States should consider. This approach need not necessarily be regressive once the government spending financed by the VAT is taken into account. Indeed, many rich countries, especially the Nordic ones, do more through public policy than the United States does to mitigate economic inequality and inequality of opportunity, despite levying high-rate value-added taxes, because of the way they spend their VAT revenues.[68]

Distributional Consequences of a Flat Tax

A flat tax more naturally addresses the vertical equity issue, which is not surprising considering its genesis as a scheme to administer a VAT while achieving some progressivity. The tax-exempt level of labor income in the flat tax makes it equivalent to a VAT plus a (nonrefundable) credit set at the flat tax rate times the portion of labor income that is below the exemption. So the flat tax is economically equivalent to a VAT paired with a rebate scheme like the one considered by Toder, Nunns, and Rosenberg that we discussed earlier. But unlike that kind of scheme, the flat tax does not require an additional administrative mechanism to distribute rebates. As labor income rises above the flat tax exemption, the tax saving from the exemption effectively shrinks as a percentage of labor income, which is what makes the exemption useful as a device for enhancing progressivity.[69]

How would a flat tax distribute the burden of taxes relative to the current system? First, as illustrated in chapter 6, replacing the current graduated rate structure with a single rate unambiguously shifts the tax burden dramatically away from those with the highest incomes and toward everyone else. If the Earned Income Tax Credit and Child Tax Credits are eliminated, the negative impact on the poor would be particularly large. Second, the flat tax would exempt from tax the returns to postponing consumption (i.e., to saving) that are not already exempt under the current system. This also mainly benefits upper-income people, and thus necessarily comes at the expense of everyone else in a revenue-neutral reform. These two effects are offset to some extent by the transitional tax on preexisting wealth (unless this is removed by transitional relief) and by eliminating various deductions and exclusions, both of which can be expected to be somewhat progressive.

To illustrate the distributional consequences of a flat tax, table 7.3 presents an analysis of the 1995 Armey-Shelby flat tax proposal (with the tax rate adjusted to a then revenue-neutral 20.8 percent), conducted by the U.S. Department of the Treasury's Office of Tax Analysis in 1996. Their calculations were done on an annual basis rather than on the

Table 7.3
Treasury estimates of the distributional impact of replacing the 1996 income tax with a revenue-neutral flat tax: percentage change in after-tax incomes

Percentile rank	Economic income range (thousands of 2014 dollars)	Percentage change in after-tax income caused by flat tax
Lowest quintile	0–24	–6.8
Second quintile	24–44	–5.4
Middle quintile	44–71	–2.9
Fourth quintile	71–117	–2.4
Next 10 percent	117–161	–2.7
Next 5 percent	161–214	–1.8
Next 4 percent	214–516	1.2
Top 1 percent	over 516	11.7

Source: U.S. Department of the Treasury, Office of Tax Analysis (1996).
Notes: Depicts the effects of replacing 1996 personal and corporate income taxes and estate tax with a 20.8% Hall-Rabushka flat tax, with an exemption of $46,439 (in year 2014 dollars) for a couple with two dependents, and no deductions or credits.

theoretically preferable, but difficult-to-implement, lifetime basis. The estimates depend on a number of assumptions about tax incidence. In particular, the Treasury's analysis assumes that both the existing corporate income tax and the new business tax are borne by individuals in proportion to their capital income, that the existing individual income tax is borne by those households that remit the tax, and that all taxes on labor compensation are borne by workers.

These assumptions are by no means uncontroversial, but they provide a reasonable starting point for assessing the distributional impact of a change to a flat tax.[70] Certainly the analysis is better than one that considers only the individual wage portion of the flat tax. Ignoring the business tax and (implicit, because of the loss of deductibility at the business level) new taxes on employer contributions for Social Security and fringe benefits can give a misleading impression of the true impact on tax burdens.

Table 7.3 illustrates the Treasury's estimates of the initial percentage change in after-tax income that would be caused at different points in the income distribution if the 1996 personal and corporate income taxes, as well as the estate tax, were replaced by a revenue-neutral version of the Armey-Shelby plan, a 20.8 percent Hall-Rabushka flat tax with an exemption of $46,439 (in year 2014 dollars) and no other deductions or credits for a couple with two dependents. Income is here defined broadly to approximate as closely as possible economic income. The exemptions are lower for single individuals and smaller families, as in the current system.

The Treasury analysis suggests that the plan causes a stark shifting of the tax burden away from those with very high incomes and onto everyone else. Tax burdens drop sharply for those in the top 1 percent of the income distribution, drop moderately for those in the next highest 4 percent, and go up for all other income groups. Thus, all groups outside of the top 5 percent would see their after-tax incomes decline. The largest percentage declines occur among the poorest families. For example, people in the bottom fifth of the income distribution, with incomes below $24,000, would see their after-tax incomes decline by 6.8 percent. Much of this is due to the elimination of the refundable Earned Income Tax Credit.

A more recent but less detailed analysis of the distributional effects of a Hall-Rabushka flat tax was included in the 2005 report of the President's Advisory Panel on Federal Tax Reform, and it came to broadly similar conclusions. The plan analyzed there had an exemption of $38,600 for a couple with two children ($44,458 in 2014 dollars), and the rate required to replace 2006 income taxes was estimated to be 21 percent. The share of total federal taxes paid by the highest-income quintile was estimated to decline from 70.2 percent to 64.0 percent, and the share paid by every other income group was estimated to increase.[71] Given that taxes on upper-income people were increased significantly starting in 2013, if a similar analysis were conducted today, it would suggest an even larger shift of tax burdens off of high-income people and onto everyone else.

Some aspects of these distributional estimates are debatable. For example, some economists argue that assuming that the burden of the business portion of the flat tax is proportional to capital income, as table 7.3 does, may understate burdens imposed on upper-income households and overstate them for everyone else.[72] As noted in chapter 6, relative to the current income tax, the flat tax would exempt the return to saving but the two systems would treat similarly other components of capital income, such as rewards to entrepreneurship, innovation, and risk taking; some experts argue that the kinds of capital income that are treated similarly constitute a disproportionately large share of capital income at the upper end of the income distribution. A number of economists have attempted to infer the likely impact of this consideration using information on the types of assets owned by people at different points in the income distribution. Some find this makes only a small difference to the estimated distributional effects.[73] These distributional estimates also ignore any improvements to the economy that might arise from tax reform. Some economists' estimates of the likely size of the boost are discussed below. In anticipation of that discussion, note that table 7.3 illustrates, to a rough approximation, how much economic growth would have to increase someone's income to make up for any change in their tax burden.

In weighing the impact of a flat tax on different peoples' levels of well-being, we shouldn't forget the benefits of having a much simpler tax. As discussed above, these benefits could be substantial for a flat tax, which has the *potential* to save a significant fraction of the estimated $170 billion in annual compliance costs of the current system. For most of the people who would owe higher taxes under a revenue-neutral flat tax, however, the income tax is already fairly simple, so the simpler flat tax will deliver little or no direct offset. Most of the gains from simplification would go directly to people with higher incomes because they're typically the ones with the complicated tax affairs. This doesn't diminish the fact that increased simplicity is valuable; other things being equal, all that time and effort devoted to tax affairs is a waste that doesn't do anybody any good. But it also means that the gains from simplicity don't significantly change the overall distributional impact of a switch to a flat tax.

It is also worth remembering that special transition rules, which would be likely to accompany any reform that is enacted, could have a major influence on the distributional effects of a flat tax. In particular, transitional relief for depreciation deductions on existing capital would greatly reduce the revenues available from the business tax, forcing tax-rate increases and therefore tax burdens to rise on wage earners, which would make the flat tax considerably less progressive. Table 7.3 assumes no transition relief at all.

Distributional Consequences of an X-Tax

The X-tax retains many of the efficiency and simplification advantages of a flat-rate consumption tax but, because of its graduated personal tax rate structure, assigns the tax burden in a more progressive way. Because it is more progressive, it does not achieve the incentive advantages of a lower marginal rate of tax. But the X-tax has not as yet garnered as much attention as the flat tax or VAT, undoubtedly because it does not have the easy-to-understand attraction of a single low rate.

To convey a sense of what a consumption tax that is approximately as progressive as the current income tax would entail, consider the X-tax plan that was described (without endorsement) in the 2005 report of the President's Advisory Panel on Federal Tax Reform. At the personal level, it would impose three tax rates of 15 percent, 25 percent, and 35 percent, with a business tax rate of 35 percent. The plan included a credit scheme that closely replicates the effects of personal exemptions, the standard deduction, the Earned Income Tax Credit, and the Child Tax Credit of the current income tax but in a simpler fashion; this was critical to replacing the progressivity of the income tax at the low end of the income distribution. All other deductions and exclusions are eliminated, except for a capped credit for home mortgage interest, a deduction for charitable giving above 1 percent of income, and a capped deduction for health insurance premium payments. Some limited transition relief is granted for depreciation on old capital and for interest above the deductible cap on preexisting mortgages.

A U.S. Department of the Treasury analysis suggested that this package would come very close to replicating the 2006 distribution of federal income tax burdens across income percentiles. It was not quite as progressive but could easily get there with small tweaks. It is also worth noting that although the distribution of burdens across income percentiles is indeed fairly close to that of the current system on average, there would still be substantial winners and losers within given income classes, which is not surprising given the substantial nature of the tax base reforms involved.[74]

The *perceived* fairness of a proposed tax reform might end up being even more decisive in its political fate than its effect on the actual distribution of tax burden. Americans are accustomed to an individual tax base that includes not only wages and salaries but also interest, dividends, and capital gains. With this frame of reference, we suspect that many people will think the personal tax base of the flat tax just doesn't smell right and it will therefore fail the "sniff test" they apply to determine what's fair and what isn't. That one family with $50,000 in dividends and interest remits no personal tax while another family with $50,000 in wages does will just not fly for many Americans. This is true in spite of the economic arguments that, because of the changes in the business tax, the flat tax is no better or worse on this criterion than a VAT or retail sales tax. This state of affairs is a bit ironic because the flat tax and X-tax are supposed to be more progressive alternatives to the RST or VAT. Nevertheless, their political prospects may founder because, although in some ways they look like our current system, in other possibly critical dimensions they do not at all look like what people are accustomed to—people don't expect that a sales tax will apply to, say, dividends, and so may not find this feature to be salient. Indeed, this aspect of the flat tax and X-tax, together with concerns about potentially disruptive transitional effects and the untested nature of the new system, likely contributed to the failure of the bipartisan 2005 Advisory Panel to reach consensus in favor of recommending the X-tax plan.

Economic Effects of Consumption Tax Plans

Chapter 4 considers all of the major channels through which the tax system affects how well the economy performs. The consumption tax proposals discussed in this chapter affect many of these channels. Replacing income taxation with consumption taxation would remove taxation's negative impact on the incentive to save and invest. To the extent that households and firms respond to these improved incentives, the resulting increase in saving and investment would lead to a larger capital stock, which in turn would make U.S. workers more productive and improve our long-run standard of living. The consumption tax reforms would eliminate capricious variation in tax rates on different types of investment, leading to a more efficient allocation of our capital stock and risk-bearing. All of the consumption tax plans also promise to clean up the tax base to some degree, removing distortions among different types of consumption. To the extent that the consumption taxes shift tax burdens onto existing wealth and the elderly, they also provide an economic boost. The retail sales tax, VAT, and flat tax lower marginal tax rates by scaling back progressivity, which would reduce the tax system's drag on incentives to achieve success through hard work, initiative, innovation, and risk-taking.

At the outset, the economic effects of tax *reform* (such as switching to a consumption base, cleaning the tax base, and changing the rate structure) must be distinguished from the economic effects of tax cuts or increases. Tax cuts or increases raise issues regarding the economic effects of budget deficits and the appropriate level of government spending that have nothing inherently to do with tax reform. We addressed the economics of deficits in detail in chapter 4, and in the rest of the discussion here we focus on the economics of tax reforms that are designed to raise the same revenue as the taxes they replace.

The potential economic benefits of switching to, or toward, a consumption tax are real, but how large would these benefits be? Ideally, we would want to quantify the impacts of each of the elements of the proposals and then see how the economic impacts add up in various packages. But as shown in chapter 4, the evidence on each of these effects is uncertain. In many cases, the best evidence suggests only a moderate effect.

Despite the uncertainty, bounds can be put on the kind of economic benefit that can be reasonably expected. Clearly, promises of miraculously higher growth rates forever are unjustified by the existing evidence. For instance, while some have claimed that switching to a flat-rate consumption tax could double our long-term rate of economic growth indefinitely,[75] this result is unsupported by the evidence, and no serious economist has made such claims. In fact, switching to a consumption tax is unlikely to permanently increase our rate of growth at all. Rather, even if the tax change were successful at raising saving, growth would increase only for a while as we added to the economy's level of capital intensity, moving us to a level of income permanently higher than we would otherwise achieve. The effect on growth rates reaches a limit because eventually a higher level of saving will be needed just to maintain that greater degree of capital intensity. The incentives to undertake the kind of activities that, if stimulated, could arguably induce a persistent increase in growth rates, such as investment in R&D or human capital, are either left untouched or dampened by a consumption tax and so are unlikely to noticeably increase.

Putting aside such overly optimistic estimates, how can we get a sense of the size of economic benefits we can expect from reform proposals? One approach is to make an educated guess, considering all the types of evidence we discussed in chapter 4. Robert Hall and Alvin Rabushka, the inventors of the flat tax and therefore hardly disinterested observers, take this approach and claim that their plan would increase real incomes by a total of 6 percent after seven years.[76]

A careful reading of the evidence presented in chapter 4, however, could easily suggest an even more modest economic impact. Based on historical experience, many important areas of economic behavior, especially hours worked, do not appear to be very responsive to moderate changes in incentives. A stronger economic response cannot be ruled out, though, because some areas of economic behavior that might be responsive to incentives, such as entrepreneurial effort, are hard to measure. But there's no compelling evidence either way on these latter issues.

Some economists have taken a more ambitious approach to gauging the potential economic benefits of reform. They have put together stylized quantitative models of the U.S. economy that can be used to simulate the effects of adopting a new tax system. Although these models produce precise answers, these should not be taken to be anything more than what they are, which is just a more sophisticated kind of educated guess that is nevertheless subject to a wide margin for error. The results of any such modeling exercise depend heavily on the assumptions that are made about the responsiveness of economic behaviors, such as saving and labor supply, to incentives. And these assumptions can be derived only from a review of the same uncertain historical evidence that we've discussed in this book. Moreover, both the tax system and economic behavior are incredibly complicated, so any feasible model must leave out potentially important aspects of the problem and must rely on potentially restrictive simplifying assumptions. Nonetheless, the models are still useful because they help us work out in a systematic way the implications of reasonable assumptions regarding the evidence and how the economy works. It is difficult to see how everything fits together in any other way.

One such modeling exercise, done by economists David Altig, Alan Auerbach, Laurence Kotlikoff, Kent Smetters, and Jan Walliser,[77] simulated the long-run economic and distributional impacts from each of several tax reforms. The results are intriguing. For example, their model simulations suggest that switching to a single-rate income tax that eliminates all deductions and exemptions would increase per capita income by 4.4 percent. Replacing the current system with a single-rate consumption tax, such as a retail sales tax or VAT, would increase long-run per capita income by more than twice as much—9.4 percent. A flat tax is estimated to increase long-run per capita income by 4.5 percent.

Perhaps the most valuable insight of this modeling exercise is *why* the economic impact varies so much across reform plans. The smaller estimated economic impact of a flat tax relative to a VAT arises from two factors. First, the flat tax is more progressive than a VAT, and thus features higher distorting marginal tax rates; this is just a quantification of the trade-off between progressivity and efficiency. Second, the model assumes that, unlike a VAT, the flat tax exempts housing (which accounts for about half of the capital stock) from the efficient transitional tax on preexisting wealth, thus requiring higher tax rates on the remaining tax base. The importance of the transitional tax to any potential economic gains is further illustrated by their estimate that a flat tax with transition relief, allowing continued deductions for depreciation on old capital, would increase per capita income by only 1.9 percent in the long run.

To this point, we've been focusing on projected increases in per capita income or output, but neither is necessarily a good measure of how much better off people might be as a result of a tax change. For example, the higher output is achieved in part through a higher saving rate, which means that some consumption today must be sacrificed. Similarly, some of the increased output occurs because people are induced to work longer hours. But, of course, working longer hours has a cost in terms of lost leisure, so the increased output is an overestimate of the net benefit. *Welfare* is the economists' term for a dollar measure of well-being that takes these factors into account. Table 7.4 shows that simulated increases in welfare from tax reform are considerably smaller than the simulated increases in income or output.

Also of interest is that the impact on welfare depends both on one's income level and on one's age at the time of the tax reform. As shown in table 7.4, among those aged 55 when the reform is enacted, the poor lose under the proportional income and consumption tax plans, but middle- and upper-income people at this age are predicted to experience at least modest gains. Similarly for those aged 21 at the time of enactment, the proportional income and consumption taxes tend to significantly hurt low- and moderate-income people and benefit upper-income people, which is not surprising given the elimination of progressive rates and exemptions. Among people who are young at the date of enactment, the flat tax improves the welfare of the highest- and lowest-income people by a small amount and reduces the welfare of those in the middle class by a similar proportion. An important qualification is that whether the poor would gain or lose from any of the reform plans depends critically on what happens to the Earned Income Tax Credit, which is not considered in the analysis by Altig, Auerbach, Kotlikoff, Smetters, and Walliser.

Members of future generations at all income levels are predicted to roughly break even or gain slightly under the flat tax. Adding transition relief to the flat tax, though, causes most young and future middle-income people to be worse off than under current law: only the highest-income people are better off in the long run. Finally, under the

Table 7.4
Estimated percentage change in remaining lifetime welfare under various tax reform proposals

Age and percentile of lifetime labor income distribution	Proportional income tax	Proportional consumption tax	Flat tax	Flat tax with transition relief	X-tax
Future generations					
Top 2 percent	3.0	4.5	1.5	1.0	1.0
70th–80th percentile	0.5	2.0	0.0	–1.5	1.0
40th–50th percentile	–0.5	1.0	0.0	–1.5	1.0
10th–20th percentile	–1.5	–1.0	0.5	–1.0	1.5
Bottom 2 percent	–6.0	–4.5	1.5	0.0	2.0
Aged 21 at date of enactment					
Top 2 percent	3.0	3.0	1.0	1.0	0.0
70th–80th percentile	0.0	1.0	–1.0	–2.0	0.0
40th–50th percentile	–1.0	–0.5	–1.0	–2.0	0.0
10th–20th percentile	–3.0	–2.0	–0.5	–1.0	0.5
Bottom 2 percent	–6.5	–6.0	1.0	–0.5	1.0
Aged 55 at date of enactment					
Top 2 percent	3.0	2.0	0.5	3.5	1.0
70th–80th percentile	2.0	1.0	1.0	2.0	0.5
40th–50th percentile	1.0	0.5	1.0	2.0	0.5
10th–20th percentile	0.5	–0.5	1.0	2.0	0.5
Bottom 2 percent	–1.5	–2.0	2.5	1.0	0.5

Source: Altig, Auerbach, Kotlikoff, Smetters, and Walliser (2001).
Notes: Depicts percentage change in remaining potential lifetime earnings that would leave someone as well off as they would be under the tax reform. "Future generations" are represented by those born 25 years after enactment of the reform. Percentage changes are rounded to the nearest 0.5 percent.

X-tax, almost all income groups and generations gain on average, with the largest gains going to low-income people. Even here, however, there are some losers. Middle- and upper-income people who are elderly at the time the X-tax is adopted (who are not shown in table 7.4) face welfare reductions due to the large transitional tax on preexisting wealth.

The bottom line of this analysis is that, even after taking into account the positive effects of tax reform on the economy, there will be both winners and losers. Although these results are not far from what most reputable analyses suggest, a number of modeling choices can produce different results. For example, Eric Engen of the Board of Governors of the Federal Reserve System and William Gale of the Brookings Institution have shown that a large portion of saving in the United States is done for precautionary reasons, and that precautionary saving is relatively insensitive to incentives. This implies that the impact of tax reform on saving and capital accumulation would be small.[78] On the other hand, a number of changes could be made to the modeling that could increase the positive economic impact relative to what the Altig, Auerbach, Kotlikoff, Smetters, and Walliser study found. For instance, their model does not address the positive effects of making the tax treatment of different types of investment more neutral. Nor does it address the potential effects of tax reform on innovation and technological development, an important issue about which unfortunately there is little or no good evidence. In addition, incorporating international considerations could strengthen the positive economic impact of tax reform somewhat—for example, because increases in domestic saving are more valuable if they can take advantage of good investment opportunities overseas.[79] No one will be surprised to learn that a lot of disagreement still exists among economists about the potential economic benefits of tax reform. In our judgment, the kinds of tax reforms discussed here would likely yield important economic improvements—but these would not be nearly large enough to provide a free lunch. For instance, dramatically cutting tax rates on high-income people will still impose significant costs on other people. Economists pride themselves on emphasizing the ubiquity of trade-offs, and we believe that tax reform is no exception to this rule. As we have stressed, economic reasoning is an essential input to an informed opinion of the likely effects, but the evidence is highly imperfect, so there's still plenty of uncertainty. In such an environment, *someone* can always provide an economic argument, often with a supporting model, that the economic benefits will be tremendous and maybe there's a free lunch after all. For reasons detailed throughout this book, a skeptical attitude toward such claims is appropriate.

Conclusion

Where does our discussion of alternatives to the income tax leave us? A national retail sales tax is an unproven alternative, which is likely to be administratively infeasible at the rates necessary to replace the federal income tax. The VAT is a proven alternative that accomplishes the same economic goals. But either tax entails a radical shift in tax burden from affluent to poor and middle-class families, and for this reason each is likely to be unacceptable to most Americans as a replacement for the income tax, although this is a value judgment rather than a matter of economics. The personal consumption tax complicates rather than simplifies the personal tax system and is unacceptable on these grounds. So the flat tax (or its more progressive version, the X-tax) is the most attractive of the consumption tax alternatives to the income tax.

We are not faced, however, with an either-or choice between the flat tax and the tax system we have now, warts and all. On the contrary, many tax experts favor substantial reform that stays within the basic framework of the current system. Indeed, in the history of U.S. taxation, abolishing the whole tax system and starting over from scratch is unprecedented, but incremental changes happen all the time and are the stuff of political battles every day. Moreover, the growing imperative to raise more revenue as part of a comprehensive plan to address the long-term fiscal imbalance has drawn attention to enacting a value-added tax *in addition to* the (hopefully reformed) income tax. The next chapter discusses the prospects and problems of changes to the way we tax ourselves that build on the system we have now.

8 Starting from Here

In his book *Untangling the Income Tax*, David Bradford relates the old story of a tourist who asks a native of Ireland for the best route to Dublin. The Irishman responds: "If I was you, I wouldn't start from here."[1] The analogy to tax reform is apt in more ways than one. Bradford means to illustrate his point that, having himself gained the familiarity of a native in the strange territory of comprehensive income measurement, his advice to a visitor thinking about tax reform would be to start somewhere else. He argues that because economic income is so difficult to measure, any tax system based on income will inevitably be something of a mess. In his view, completely untangling the tax system would require switching to a consumption tax.

Ironically, Bradford's story also illustrates that we have no choice but to start from where we are. Any reform effort will have to begin from the tax system we've got now. Our income tax evolved into its present state over the course of a century, forged by political compromise in a democratic system, the inevitable influence of special interests, and the government's responses to efforts by taxpayers to devise ever more sophisticated ways of avoiding and evading taxes. The structure that has already been built up over time has important implications for who would win and who would lose from any reform, for how well any reform would work, and for the likelihood that any particular reform will actually happen. Historically, policy changes that are as ambitious as eliminating the income tax and starting over from scratch have been extremely rare.[2]

Whether completely replacing the income tax would be a good idea is a fascinating and important question. But significant, if not radical, changes to the tax system are being debated and enacted all the time. The purpose of this chapter is to discuss and evaluate some possible changes in the way we tax ourselves that start from the system we have now. Constructing a tax system that is simpler, fairer, and better for the economy than what we have now is certainly possible to do without throwing out the whole current system. Changes that more or less stay within the general framework of the current system are the subject of this chapter.

Many recent proposals for tax reform take this general approach, but they differ widely in their priorities and details. Some would move in the direction of flatter tax rates, while others would increase progressivity by adding more tax brackets applying to upper-income taxpayers, expanding credits for low-income taxpayers, or increasing the estate tax. Some would move us more in the direction of a consumption tax, for example by exempting dividends and capital gains from personal taxation, allowing the expensing of business investment, eliminating the estate tax, or replacing part of the income tax with a VAT. Others move in the opposite direction, for example by proposing to tax dividends and capital gains at the same rates as ordinary income. Many proposals broaden and clean the tax base by removing various deductions and exclusions or by making taxation of capital income more uniform, while others add complicated new wrinkles to the tax code to promote equity goals or to raise revenue. As we demonstrate below, elements of tax reform we've considered in earlier chapters can be added, subtracted, and combined in a variety of ways, leading to disparate consequences for tax revenue, for the degree of economic inequality in society, and for incentives to work, save, and invest.

Talk of tax reform is in the air again. But whether that talk will lead to action is not at all clear. It's been thirty years since the last comprehensive income tax reform in the United States—the Tax Reform Act of 1986, or TRA86—and there are good reasons for that. Fundamental tax reform is politically divisive, especially when it is designed to be revenue-neutral or to raise revenue, because there are clear winners and losers. To provide some context for our look at the major income tax reform proposals, we begin by going back to take a closer look at the 1986 income tax reform. Considering its origin and nature provides valuable context for assessing the plans now being discussed.[3]

The Tax Reform Act of 1986

The origin of TRA86 can be traced back to the local tax revolts of the 1970s, highlighted by Proposition 13 and the Jarvis-Gann Amendment in California that severely limited property taxes. Much of the tax revolt was directed at property taxes, but discontent with the income tax was also simmering. The brackets of the individual income tax were then fixed in nominal terms, so the high inflation of the 1970s and early 1980s, exceeding 10 percent in 1979 and 1980, pushed families into higher tax brackets even if their real income did not increase. While this provided Congress with the opportunity to occasionally cut tax rates without continually losing revenue, in the five years before 1981, federal individual income tax receipts as a share of GDP rose by nearly a quarter, from 7.4 percent in fiscal year 1976 to 9.1 percent in 1981.[4] Once elected, Ronald Reagan delivered on his campaign promise to cut income tax rates across the board, which was enacted in the Economic Recovery Tax Act (ERTA) of 1981. ERTA also substantially accelerated depreciation allowances for capital goods purchased by businesses. These tax cuts were partially reversed when Congress passed significant tax increases in 1982 and 1984, in reaction to the revenue losses from ERTA and the large deficits that appeared in the early 1980s.

Also brewing in the early 1980s was a sense that tax loopholes had rendered the income tax system highly dysfunctional. The ability to deduct interest payments, with nominal long-term interest rates exceeding 10 percent from 1980 to 1985, combined with the generous post-1981 tax depreciation write-offs, contributed to the proliferation of tax shelters. By borrowing to finance lightly taxed investments, individuals could generate negative taxable income even though their investments were not necessarily unprofitable, after taxes. "See-through" buildings—which could be profitable for tax reasons even at low occupancy rates—grabbed headlines and were symptomatic of an inefficient misallocation of the economy's resources. Even more important, the spectacle of some people reducing, or eliminating, their tax liability through such tax schemes led to a perceived lack of fairness in the tax system.

These concerns prompted a series of proposals over several years, beginning with the "Fair Tax Act," a bill introduced in 1983 by Senator Bill Bradley (D-NJ) and Representative Richard Gephardt (D-MO). The Bradley-Gephardt proposal contained the most central elements of what was to become TRA86 and of most of today's income tax reform plans: lower top individual and corporate tax rates, few (in this case three) tax brackets, a broadening of the tax base at both corporate and individual levels aimed at taxing income more accurately and uniformly. Unlike some current proposals, though, it was designed to preserve the existing tax burden distribution and revenue level.

During the 1984 presidential campaign President Reagan promised to study tax reform, and after the election the U.S. Department of the Treasury released a proposal and then, after much public debate, released a revised plan that itself underwent substantial modification as the bill moved through the House of Representatives, the Senate, and the House-Senate conference committee and was eventually signed by President Reagan on October 22, 1986.[5] TRA86's most distinctive feature was its reduction in individual marginal tax rates. The Act reduced the number of marginal rate brackets and compressed the marginal rate structure so that the sharpest decline applied to the highest-income individuals, whose rate fell from 50 percent to just 28 percent. In addition to this compression of marginal income tax rates, the reform raised the levels of the standard deduction and the personal exemption, which together substantially reduced the number of tax-payers at or below the poverty level that incurred a positive individual income tax liability. Also affecting low-income individuals and representing an effective reduction in their marginal tax rates on labor income was an expansion of the Earned Income Tax Credit. To make up some of the large loss in revenue from the lower rates and more generous exemption, standard deduction, and credits, the Act repealed income averaging and the "second-earner" deduction, limited tax incentives for retirement savings, eliminated the itemized deductions for state and local sales taxes and interest on consumer debts, and removed preferential treatment for capital gains and dividend income. TRA86 also included limitations on the deductibility of passive losses, which had been an important part of tax shelter strategies, and strengthened the individual AMT.

At the corporate level the reform followed the same approach of reducing marginal tax rates and broadening the tax base. The headline corporate rate that affected most income was cut from 46 percent to 34 percent. At the same time, though, it repealed the 10 percent investment tax credit for machinery and equipment and scaled back the accelerated depreciation schedules introduced in 1981, primarily by extending the lifetimes over which residential and nonresidential structures could be written off. In many cases the rate reduction was more than offset by the base broadening, so that the net disincentive effect on the incentive to invest increased. In addition, in part to reduce the attractiveness of tax shelters and other avoidance schemes, TRA86 introduced a corporate alternative minimum tax.

All in all, the Tax Reform Act of 1986 lowered marginal tax rates and broadened the tax bases at both the individual and corporate levels. It made the tax treatment of different types of income and different industries more uniform, and introduced several other provisions to restrict the ability of high-income individual and corporate taxpayers to pay little or no tax. Taken together, these changes were designed to be roughly revenue-neutral, but with a shift in tax collections from the individual income tax to the corporate income tax.

Polls taken a few years after TRA86 suggested that most of the public did not think that it had significantly improved economic performance, or the fairness or simplicity of the tax system.[6] On all three issues the modal response was that TRA86 had little effect; of those that detected an effect, more found it to be negative rather than positive. This is especially true of fairness, where the fraction that judged the new distribution of tax burden to be less fair outnumbered those that concluded the opposite by 37 percent to 9 percent. This does not bode well for the public reception and political attractiveness of a future base-broadening, rate-lowering tax reform initiative.

Bush, Clinton, and Bush

Many supporters of TRA86 hoped that its low-rate, broad-base spirit would hold up against the continual pressure to provide special tax breaks to particular sectors or activities. But that hope proved to be Pollyannaish. Tax bills after 1986 added preferential provisions, increased the number and level of marginal tax rates, and added back a lot of the complexity that the 1986 reform sought to remove.

The 1990 tax act increased the top statutory rate from 28 percent to 31 percent (but kept the top rate on capital gains at 28 percent), thus breaking George H. W. Bush's promise at the 1988 Republican convention: "read my lips—no new taxes." The broken promise helped contribute to his electoral defeat in 1992 to Bill Clinton. Clinton campaigned explicitly on raising income tax rates for high-income people and after his election Congress imposed in 1993 two additional top rates of 36 percent and 39.6 percent, increased the individual income AMT tax rates, and raised the top corporate income tax rate by 1 percentage point to 35 percent. The 1997 tax act further increased the disparity between the top rate on capital gains and on other income, by reducing the top rate on capital gains from 28 percent to 20 percent.

Like Ronald Reagan, George W. Bush pledged if elected to slash income tax rates, and beginning in 2001 a series of tax bills did just that. The 2001 legislation set the stage, featuring a sharp reduction in income tax rates and a reduction and eventual repeal (for 2010 only) of the estate tax. The top rate fell from 39.6 percent to 35 percent, the other tax rates fell by about a tenth, and a new 10 percent tax bracket was created from the 15 percent bracket. It also introduced or expanded a wide range of tax breaks for education, families with children, married couples, and contributions to certain kinds of savings accounts. Legislation in 2003 introduced a preferential lower tax rate on dividend income and further reduced the tax rates that applied to capital gains, so that for both the rate became 0 percent (in brackets where the ordinary income tax rate was 15 percent or below) or 15 percent (in brackets where the ordinary income tax was higher than 15 percent). The cut in the personal tax on dividends was applauded by many economists who had been concerned about the deleterious effects of the system of "double taxing" corporate income, but also raised concerns about widening the budget deficit and reducing the progressivity of the tax system.

The President's Advisory Panel on Federal Tax Reform

In an effort to focus attention on reforming the tax system, in January 2005 President Bush appointed a Presidential Advisory Panel to outline alternatives and modifications to the current system.[7] The panel was co-chaired by two savvy former Senators—Connie Mack (R-FL) and John Breaux (D-LA)—and included prominent academics, a former congressman, a top investment strategist at Charles Schwab, a former chair of the Federal Trade Commission, and the previous IRS commissioner.

The charge to the panel mandated that any proposal it came up with had to be revenue-neutral. At least one policy option had to be based on the current income tax system. Any proposal had to simplify compliance, distribute the tax burden in "an appropriately progressive" manner, and promote growth and job creation while "recognizing the importance of homeownership and charity in American society." This latter phrase was widely interpreted as code for preserving some tax preferences for mortgage interest and charitable contributions, thus limiting two potentially important ways to broaden the tax base. Early in its deliberations, the panel decided to interpret delivering "appropriate" progressivity as not substantively tampering with the current distribution of the tax burden.

The report was released on November 1, 2005.[8] It is still well worth reading, as it nicely lays out the trade-offs that tax system design must confront. Besides discussing the issues, it outlined two alternative reform proposals without tipping its hat toward one or the other—the Simplified Income Tax (SIT) plan and the Growth and Investment Tax (GIT) plan. Although the plans differed in important ways, it was the aspects they shared—namely, the restructuring of deductions much loved by the middle class—that captured headlines.

Both would replace the existing mortgage interest deduction for those who itemize with a 15 percent credit available to all taxpayers, and would reduce significantly the cap on mortgage debt eligible for a tax deduction. Both would extend the charitable deduction to all taxpayers—not just itemizers—but only to the extent that the contributions exceed 1 percent of a taxpayer's income. Under both plans employer-paid health insurance premiums costing over $11,500 for a family policy would be taxed as income to the employees. Both proposals would also eliminate deductions for state and local taxes for both individuals and businesses and repeal the individual and corporate alternative minimum tax (AMT).

Both plans would replace the current hodgepodge of personal exemptions, standard deductions, and child credits with a simpler system of credits and replace the Earned Income Tax Credit and low-income Child Tax Credit with a simplified work credit. The myriad tax-advantaged savings plans available—most notably, individual retirement accounts and 401(k) plans—would be replaced by three streamlined savings plans and a savings credit for low-income workers. The infamous 1040 tax form would shrink from seventy-five lines to thirty-two lines, and the assorted worksheets, schedules, and other attachments would be trimmed from fifty-two to ten.

The tax panel wrestled with whether to propose that a tax on consumption replace the current system. The panel rejected a retail sales tax as a replacement for the income tax on the grounds that it would generate a more regressive distribution of the tax burden and would cause insuperable administrative difficulties if levied at the historically unprecedented rates (probably over 30 percent) needed to replace all income tax revenues. The panel also ended up rejecting the VAT on the grounds that it would operate as a "hidden" tax, encouraging policymakers to raise rates because taxpayers would not notice the burden. The panel also flirted with—but did not propose—the X-tax, the variant of the Hall-Rabushka flat tax that features the flat-tax base but levies a set of graduated rates rather than a single, flat rate on wages and salaries. That the panel did not present a pure consumption tax was unfortunate in that it did not thus starkly pose this fundamental choice about tax structure—income tax versus consumption tax. Indeed, both of the panel's proposals were hybrids—an income tax framework with generous tax-preferred savings accounts that would eliminate taxes on the savings of most Americans, and a consumption tax framework with tax on capital income flows at the personal level (the GIT).

The proposed changes in tax rates in both plans were rather modest. The SIT featured rates of 15 percent, 25 percent, 30 percent, and 33 percent at the personal level and a corporate rate of 33 percent, while the GIT had rates of 15 percent, 25 percent, and 30 percent on labor income, 15 percent on personal capital income, and 30 percent on corporations. Despite getting rid of many popular deductions, the panel found it impossible to lower rates considerably and still meet the revenue and distributional constraints, mainly because of the need to replace the revenues of the eliminated AMT and because both plans reduced taxation of capital income.

The panel's report made hardly a ripple in Washington's political waters. "Tax Overhaul Proposal Gets Lukewarm Welcome," trumpeted *The Wall Street Journal* the next day.[9] Indeed, Senator Charles Schumer of high-tax New York (with a disproportionate number of residents who would suffer from the elimination of the state tax deduction) called it—before the report was officially released—a "pernicious proposal…that would slap a $12 billion tax on New Yorkers."[10] Associations of realtors and home builders were upset, too, warning that the mortgage interest proposals could mean "the value of the nation's residential property could decline 15 percent or more" and labeling them as "the biggest tax hike for homeowners ever considered."[11] This response illustrates the political difficulty of a comprehensive overhaul—those who perceive their interest to be endangered cry loudly, while those who perceive they would benefit keep relatively quiet. TRA86 managed to overcome this political dynamic, but had the clear support of a popular president and widespread popular and congressional concern about tax shelters and horizontal inequities. No bill based on the panel's recommendations made any progress through

Congress, although some of its suggestions—such as consolidating the personal exemption, Child Tax Credit, and Earned Income Tax Credit into a simplified credit system and converting itemized deductions into a flat, above-the-line credit—attracted considerable interest and have resurfaced as parts of more recent reform packages we discuss below.

Wyden-Gregg

A good example of tax reform proposals that do not start very far from the current system is the Bipartisan Tax Fairness and Simplification Act of 2010, introduced in February 2010 by Senators Ron Wyden (D-OR) and Judd Gregg (R-NH) and later, after the retirement of Gregg, sponsored by Wyden, Senator Dan Coats (R-IN), and Senator Mark Begich (D-AK)[12]. It reduces the number of individual income tax rates from six to three (15, 25, and 35 percent), and increases the basic standard deduction amounts to $30,000 for joint filers, $22,500 for heads of households, and $15,000 for singles, nearly tripling the 2010 amounts. The special tax rates that apply to long-term capital gains and qualified dividends would be replaced by a 35 percent exclusion of such income, thus increasing the maximum rates on long-term gains and qualified dividends to 22.75 percent; in addition, the holding period for the capital gains exclusion would be reduced to six months for the first $500,000 of gains.

Several individual income tax base changes are worthy of note. The current law exclusion for interest on state and local bonds would be eliminated and replaced with a nonrefundable 25 percent credit. The individual AMT would be repealed. The proposal also consolidates the current tax system's incentives for higher education. It would replace the current graduated corporate rate structure and top rate of 35 percent with a flat rate of 24 percent, while reducing a slew of business tax preferences—such as accelerated depreciation, the tax preference for income from domestic production activities, and tax credits for enhanced oil recovery costs—and would simplify tax accounting for small businesses.

Obama Deficit Commission

In February 2010, President Obama created the National Commission on Fiscal Responsibility and Reform, known informally as the "deficit commission." Comprised of eighteen lawmakers, it was charged with issuing a set of recommendations to address the growing gap between revenues and expenditures. They issued a report in December of 2010, but a subsequent commission vote failed to achieve the fourteen votes required to send the recommendations on to be debated in Congress. Nevertheless, these recommendations were widely seen as influencing whatever fiscal plan might eventually be adopted, so the report's contents are worth a look.[13]

The tax side of the deficit commission report outlines a rate-lowering, base-broadening plan in the tradition of the Tax Reform Act of 1986. It lowers the top personal income tax rate to 28 percent (exactly where it was under TRA86 until 1990). Moreover, it repeals the AMT and the preferential rates for capital gains and dividends. Thus, it moves away from integration of the corporate and individual taxes as a way to address the double taxation of corporate income. Itemized deductions are eliminated, replaced by a 12 percent nonrefundable credit for mortgage interest and charitable giving. Almost all income tax expenditures are eliminated, with the prominent exception of the Earned Income Tax Credit and Child Tax Credit. A distributional analysis by the Urban-Brookings Tax Policy Center found that the plan as a whole would make the tax system slightly more progressive.[14]

On the corporate side, the proposal features one tax rate of 28 percent and removal of all business credits and corporate tax expenditures. It also recommends abandoning the worldwide basis for the taxation of multinational corporations, and adopting instead a territorial system.

The Domenici-Rivlin plan

Approximately in parallel with the Obama deficit commission, in February 2010 the Bipartisan Policy Center's Debt Reduction Task Force began meeting to develop a budget plan that addresses the nation's future fiscal problems. The group was chaired by former Senator Pete Domenici (R-NM) and former Congressional Budget Office Director and Vice Chair of the Federal Reserve Board of Governors Alice Rivlin. They released their own plan, called Restoring America's Future, in November 2010.[15]

The tax part of the Task Force plan has several features in common with the Obama deficit commission proposal. First of all, it would dramatically reduce both individual and corporate income tax rates. In place of the current six-bracket system for the individual income tax, with rates ranging from 10 percent to 39.6 percent, the plan would substitute a two-bracket system with rates of 15 and 27 percent. The top corporate rate would drop from 35 percent to 27 percent. That's the rate-lowering part. Deductions for mortgage interest and charity would be replaced with flat-rate credits. Because the credits are flat-rate, universal (i.e., not just for itemizers as currently), and refundable, households will not have to file a tax return to claim them; rather than be reimbursed directly to taxpayers, the credits will go to the institutions. Qualifying charities and mortgage lenders would apply for the tax credits, as has been done in the United Kingdom; presumably much of the mortgage interest credit would be shifted to benefit borrowers in the form of lower interest rates. The Task Force proposal would eliminate itemized deductions for state and local taxes. It would combine the Earned Income Tax Credit, Child Tax Credit, exemptions for children, and the child and dependent care tax credit with two new provisions: a universal child credit of $1,600 per child and an earnings credit of 21.3 percent of the first $20,300 of earnings for each worker, both indexed for inflation. Like the Obama deficit commission, the Task Force plan would eliminate the preferential rates on capital gains and dividends. Notably, it proposes a new broad-based value-added tax on goods and services at a rate of 6.5 percent with, of course, a new name.

The Lee-Rubio Plan

Slightly more radical is the plan proposed in 2015 by Republican Senators Mike Lee of Utah and Marco Rubio[16] of Florida, who was at the time running for the Republican presidential nomination.[17] On the individual side, the plan would consolidate the code into two brackets: 15 percent and 35 percent, a drop of 4.6 percentage points in the top rate. It would eliminate all itemized deductions except the two most popular—the mortgage interest and charitable donation deductions—and retain the exclusion of employer-provided health care benefits, but would abolish the deduction for state and local taxes. It would abolish the alternative minimum tax. Its most controversial aspect, at least among Republicans, is its child tax credit of $2,500, which would be refundable against income tax and against payroll taxes as well, so that it would benefit working families whose income is too low to incur income tax liability. As with just about every Republican-sponsored tax reform plan, it would end the estate and gift tax.

The Lee-Rubio plan features a thoroughgoing reform of the taxation of business income. Capital expenditures would be fully expensed, rather than depreciated. It would integrate the individual and corporate tax code by eliminating individual taxes on capital gains, dividends, and corporate interest payments, and, at the same time, abolish interest deductions in the calculation of business income; a separate tax regime would apply to financial institutions. It would cut the federal corporate tax rate to 25 percent and cap the tax rate that applies to the income from sole proprietorships, partnerships, and other pass-through entities at 25 percent. Finally, it would move to a territorial tax system, thus exempting business income earned outside the United States. According to the Tax Foundation, the plan would be short $414 billion per year on revenue compared to current law not counting any impact it might have on GDP or GDP growth.[18]

The People's Budget and Bernie Sanders' Tax Plan

Most of the plans we've discussed feature cuts in tax rates and many would reduce revenues and thereby raise deficits. Not every plan, though. In 2011, the Congressional Progressive Caucus, comprised of one senator and 75 members of the House who pledged to, among other things, "[fight] for economic justice and security for all," released their own plan called "The People's Budget."[19]

Rather than cutting income tax rates, The People's Budget would rescind the Bush-era tax cuts so that income tax rates revert to their Clinton-era levels, but would extend marriage penalty relief (increased standard deduction, Earned Income Tax Credit phaseout, and the 15 percent bracket for married couples), the expanded child tax credit, education incentives, and other incentives for children and families enacted in the Bush years. On top of that, it would create five additional income tax brackets, starting at 45 percent for married couples making over $1 million dollars a year and increasing to 49 percent for people making $1 billion and over. It would end preferential rates for capital gains and dividends, and would not only return the estate tax to its 2009 rates, brackets, and exemption, but would add new higher rates as follows: a 45 percent rate on the taxable portion of estates up to $50 million, a 55 percent rate on the taxable portion of estates up to $500 million, and a 65 percent rate on the taxable portion of estates worth over $500 million. Like the Gregg-Wyden plan, it would replace the tax exclusion for interest on state and local bonds with a subsidy (in this case 15 percent) for the issuer.

Unlike most of the other plans, The People's Budget corporate tax reform includes no rate cuts. Quite the contrary, as its major thrust is to change the tax treatment of U.S. multinational corporations by taxing their foreign income as it is earned rather than when earnings are repatriated to the United States, with the objective of increasing domestic investment and making it less attractive for corporations to move jobs offshore. Foreign tax credits would still be allowed, although treated differently. Note that this is 180 degrees opposite from the deficit commission proposal to move to a territorial system that would effectively exempt foreign-source income from U.S. tax. In addition, as in many of the other tax reform plans we've discussed, the proposal would also eliminate tax preferences for oil, gas, and coal companies, and the domestic manufacturing deduction. Finally, it would enact a "financial crisis responsibility fee" as proposed—but not passed—in President Obama's 2011 budget request at a rate of 0.15 percent on a base of covered liabilities on banks with more than $50 billion in assets.[20]

Obviously, this plan embraces a view that the progressivity of our tax system ought to be expanded, not cut back, in light of the rapid growth of income and wealth inequality. Democratic presidential candidate Bernie Sanders has not embraced this plan, but he has definitely embraced tax progressivity as a weapon against inequality, saying that the tax rate the wealthiest Americans pay should be "a damned lot higher than it is now."[21]

In the Sanders tax plan, the top tax rate on taxable income is capped at 30.2 percent, but on top of that there would be a new graduated tax on adjusted gross income that would reach as high as 24 percent, so that the maximum total marginal tax rate would be 54.2 percent on adjusted gross income over $10 million. Moreover, the top tax rate on dividends and capital gains would rise from the current 23.8 percent (20 percent from the income tax plus 3.8 percent from the net investment income surtax) to as high as 64.2 percent (54.2 percent from the income tax plus a proposed 10 percent net investment surtax), in part because the preferential rates on dividends and capital gains would be eliminated for high-income taxpayers. Unrealized capital gains in gifts and bequests would be taxed at death. The Social Security payroll tax, which currently applies only to the first $118,500 of an individual's earned income in 2016, would be extended to also apply to the portion of an individual's earnings above $250,000. Carried interest (discussed in chapter 2) would be taxed as ordinary income. Sanders would also replace the current estate tax rate of 40 percent with a graduated rate structure that tops out at 55 percent on the value of an estate in excess of $50 million. A 6.2 percent payroll tax would be imposed on employers to help pay for a universal single-payer health insurance plan, and a carbon tax with a rebate for low-income households would be adopted to both raise revenue and fight climate change. Sanders would also eliminate the deferral of U.S. corporate tax on foreign profits of U.S. multinationals that are reinvested overseas, a change which would greatly reduce corporations' ability to shift profits into tax havens through manipulation of transfer prices, but which would also make taxation of multinational corporations headquartered in the United States much heavier than that which applies to multinational corporations based in almost all other countries. To counter the threat that more corporations would move their headquarters overseas in response, he would also introduce various impediments to qualifying for a corporate inversion (an issue we discussed in chapter 5).[22]

Hillary Clinton's 2016 Campaign Tax Proposals

Democratic presidential candidate Hillary Clinton's 2016 tax proposals featured much more modest increases in progressivity and revenues than either of the two plans noted immediately above, and a much less thoroughgoing restructuring of the tax code than many of the tax reform packages discussed earlier in the chapter. Her plan included a number of proposals that had been in President Obama's proposed budgets, but to no avail in the face of opposition from a Republican-controlled Congress, along with a few new proposals. Clinton proposed the imposition of a 4 percent income tax surcharge on adjusted gross income above $5 million, and a limitation of the tax savings from itemized deductions (other than charity) and certain exclusions (such as for employer-provided health insurance) to no more than 28 percent of the value of the deductions and exclusions, which would only directly affect upper-income taxpayers. She would also seek to increase the tax rate on capital gains held for less than six years. In addition, she supported taxing carried interest as ordinary income, and advocated a version of the Buffett Rule that would ensure that everyone faced a minimum average rate, which we discussed in chapters 3 and

5. Clinton also proposed to adopt various rules to limit tax avoidance by multinational corporations. For example, the plan would only allow a corporate merger to qualify as an inversion if the foreign acquiring company is at least as valuable as the U.S. firm being acquired. Clinton also promised further measures that would reduce taxes on low- and middle-income working families, but had not yet laid out the details of those measures at the time we wrote this.[23]

Other Alternatives

We close our discussion of tax reform options with two plans that have not been embraced by any American politicians, but are worth mentioning. The first recognizes that the either-or policy choice between income and consumption taxation is false and embraces a "third way" that features a drastically scaled-back income tax and a VAT. The other responds to the global mobility of capital by enacting a separate flat low-rate tax on capital income while retaining a graduated tax on labor income.

The Graetz Plan

In chapter 7 we addressed the value-added tax, how it works, and its strengths and weaknesses. Two of the deficit plans we have looked at include a VAT. In recent years, Michael Graetz of Columbia University Law School has forcefully advocated introducing a value-added tax, using some of the revenue it would raise to reduce personal tax rates substantially and—here's the interesting part—to exempt most people from personal income taxation altogether.[24] He proposes adopting a broad-based VAT with a single rate of approximately 15 percent—about double the rate of the proposals discussed heretofore in this chapter—and replacing the standard deduction, personal exemption, and various credits of the current personal income tax with a standard deduction of $100,000 ($50,000 for singles). The income tax rate on personal income above the standard deduction would be 25 percent. This large of a standard deduction would exempt over 80 percent of current filers from the personal income tax altogether, and would cause most remaining taxpayers to eschew itemized deductions.

The shift would offer many of the economic advantages of the VAT we've discussed, although the simplification gains would be mitigated by the need to maintain the administrative infrastructure of the federal income tax system for high-income taxpayers and for many others still subject to state income taxation. This is an excellent example of "populist simplification" because by raising the income threshold for filing, it relieves millions of taxpayers of any obligation to file a (federal) tax return, and at the same time it induces many others who still file to pass up itemizing their deductions. On the other hand, this plan retains the income tax infrastructure for just those people (and corporations) for whom the tax is most complicated. Although it would greatly reduce the number of individual income tax returns, it would not reduce by much the number of complex returns. The reduction in the aggregate cost of compliance would be proportionately much smaller than the reduction in the number of filers.

While using a VAT to finance a large increase in the standard deduction could be done in a way that has little net impact on tax burdens faced by most of the middle class, it would dramatically increase tax burdens on low-income people who already pay no income tax and in fact often receive large refundable credit payments. So this approach at first glance seems like a particularly bad compromise, combining the most unsatisfactory elements of each kind of tax—the regressive shift in the distribution of taxes caused by a VAT for low-income people as well as the complications and inefficiencies of the income tax for high-income people.

Graetz argues that these defects can be fixed by offering a rebate or credit tied to the level of reported labor earnings for the Social Security payroll tax. Given the way the payroll tax is currently administered, such a provision would have to be based on individual rather than family labor income, but this could conceivably be changed. Even if it could, the payroll tax would not be helpful for administering tax relief to nonworking low-income people. To replicate the current system's degree of progressivity, the refundable tax relief paid out in this manner would have to be very large, as it would need to replace features like the Earned Income Tax Credit and Child Tax Credit and also offset the new burden imposed by the VAT. Graetz estimates that a 15 percent VAT rate and a 25 percent income tax rate would be sufficient to finance enough of this sort of relief to, on average, render low-income people no worse off and raise the same revenue as under the current system.

Professor Graetz emphasizes one other potential advantage of the VAT-income tax hybrid—that it would greatly reduce political pressures to adopt deductions, exclusions, and credits that clutter up the tax base because the tax would contain no "personal" element for most taxpayers. Given the proliferation of various forms of preferential treatment such as exemptions in real-world VATs, we probably should not be overly optimistic about this claim. It is at least plausible, however, that convincing the middle class to give up itemized deductions, a major obstacle to many fundamental reform plans, might be easier if at the same time they were offered freedom from filing income tax returns altogether.

As we've mentioned, one very recent development is the embrace of the (renamed) VAT by some American politicians. Plans proposed by Republicans Paul Ryan, Rand Paul, and Ted Cruz featured it prominently. At the time we were writing this, none of these politicians had yet been nominated for president by the Republicans, and if they were they'd have to defend against the inevitable negative ads howling about a "new tax," even if the proposal sharply reduces the bite of an "old tax," the income tax, by sharply reducing its tax rates or, in the Graetz version, sharply increasing the exemption level.

Some conservatives believe that VATs are somehow responsible for the higher levels of government spending in Europe relative to the United States: in other words, the VAT is *too* efficient for those who believe that big government is a more important problem than an inefficient tax system. This argument carried the day in the Bush tax panel of 2005, but it is not clear that there is any truth to it: certainly other influences, such as culture, must dominate in determining the size of countries' governments. All in all, though, we may finally be seeing the future as once envisioned by former Secretary of the Treasury Larry Summers, who said "The United States will get a VAT when conservatives realize it is regressive and when liberals realize it is a money machine."[25]

Dual Income Tax

If the VAT is the world's tax success story of the past half century, then a contender for the success story of the next fifty years is a Scandinavian innovation known as the dual income tax (DIT). Denmark introduced it in 1987, Sweden in 1991, Norway in 1992, and Finland in 1993, with all of these countries making modifications since their initial enactment. The basic structure of the DIT is straightforward: combine a graduated tax rate schedule on labor income with a low flat tax on all capital income.[26] In a pure version of the system the flat tax rate on capital income is equal to the corporate income tax rate and the marginal tax rate on labor income in the first bracket; with this set-up, the

DIT can be thought of as levying a flat tax on all income plus a progressive surtax on labor income. Alternatively, the DIT may be seen as a compromise between the comprehensive income tax and the expenditure tax: while an expenditure tax completely exempts the normal return to capital from tax, the DIT imposes a positive tax on income from capital, but at a low flat rate below the top marginal tax rate on labor income.

The argument for the DIT, which is especially relevant for small open economies like the Scandinavian countries, is that a low capital income tax rate would lessen the incentive both for domestic wealth owners to invest capital outside the country and to invest in hard-to-measure types of capital that aren't included in the tax base. A flat rate also simplifies the administration of the tax because it can be easily withheld and remitted since the tax rate is the same for all individuals regardless of other income. It may come as a shock that the Nordic countries, with a reputation for highly progressive tax and other policies, would abandon a graduated tax schedule for capital income. Apparently they believe that a highly progressive tax on at least some forms of capital income is an inefficient means of redistributing income compared to a progressive labor income tax, and that inequalities stemming from large inherited stocks of wealth may be better addressed through instruments such as an inheritance tax. One major drawback of the dual income tax is the incentive to reclassify labor income as generally lower-taxed capital income. This arises especially for self-employed people or owners of small closely held businesses, where business income has to be divided up between labor and capital income and the tax rate is generally lower on the latter. To address this issue, the dual income tax system assigns a rate of return to the assets in the business to calculate capital income and treats any additional income as labor income.

Tax at the Crossroads of Economic Policy

As we write this chapter, the course of near-term U.S. fiscal policy is unclear. What is perfectly clear, however, is that tax policy will be central to what unfolds. Looking down the road, a massive fiscal imbalance looms, which most experts agree must be addressed soon to avoid potentially large negative consequences. But experts, politicians, and the public do not agree on how to address this issue, especially on the right mix of tax increases (if any), and cuts in spending that, to make a dent in projected deficits, must include popular entitlement programs such as Social Security and Medicare. And there is continuing disagreement about whether the lingering short-term economic danger from the recent financial crisis has receded enough that we can safely turn our focus to addressing the long-term fiscal imbalance.

Into this mix we add tax reform. Rationalizing the tax system to improve the economy's efficiency is good policy at any time, but comprehensive reform is highly divisive and succeeds rarely, as evidenced by the thirty-year gap since the Tax Reform Act of 1986. The major deficit reduction plans include major tax reform, for both economic and political reasons. A rationalizing tax reform might cushion the negative economic impact of tax increases, to be sure. But note that while some of the tax changes proposed are indeed what most experts would think of as tax reform, others—such as abandoning preferential rates for dividends and capital gains on corporate stock—are now less widely regarded as reform. While most base broadeners raise revenue, not all constitute good tax policy. In the discussion of deficit-reducing tax changes, this distinction should not be lost.

But the visible feature of reduced tax *rates* might also distract the public's attention from the reality of an increased tax burden that would likely be part of a compromise long-term fiscal agreement. Whether or not that is a good idea depends in part on one's views about whether the end of addressing our dire long-term fiscal imbalance justifies the means of obfuscating tax policy.

Conclusion

The reform options discussed so far represent only a subset of the possible alternatives, and the political process may eventually focus on other possibilities. Any alternative, though, can be classified according to what it does to the rate structure, how clean the tax base is, and how much it relies on an income or consumption base.

Where does this leave the intelligent citizen who is convinced that the income tax system needs fixing but is unsure about what should be done? One option is to pull the tax system out "by its roots" and replace it with a clean-base, single-rate system based on consumption rather than income. We have argued that a national retail sales tax is not administrable at the usual standards of equity and intrusiveness we should expect of a tax system. Its close cousin, the value-added tax, is administrable, but because without other policy changes it would starkly shift the burden of tax from affluent families to everyone else, we suspect that it will be rejected by a majority of Americans as a stand-alone option. It might be more acceptable if used in parallel with a more progressive income tax. That leaves the flat tax and X-tax (or "gradu-ated flat tax") as the best consumption tax options. But these plans are untested, often still entail a regressive change in the distribution of tax burdens, and could produce large windfall gains and losses. Moreover, the critical but potentially complex details about how to get from here to there are still to be fleshed out. Aside from the substantive issues of equity, efficiency, and simplicity, we sense that they will fail a simple "sniff test" administered by Americans accustomed to a personal tax on all income, who will find that a tax that appears to be only on labor income just doesn't smell right. Indeed, surveys suggest that most Americans think it's fair that families with higher charity, medical expenses, or mortgage interest pay less tax than otherwise similar families, but a majority of Americans think it is not fair for families with the same income to be liable for different taxes depending on what share of that income comes from labor or from capital.[27]

Contemplating this sort of change is not for the meek. We are reminded of a sketch from the old British television series *Monty Python's Flying Circus*. In the sketch, an accountant comes to a job-change counselor, complaining of his boring job and inquiring about the career possibilities of being a lion tamer. Once the counselor makes abundantly clear how ferocious a lion is (the accountant had thought it to be a more domesticated sort of animal), the accountant decides to settle for pursuing opportunities in banking.

Can the income tax be fixed enough to be worthy of saving? The base can certainly be thoroughly cleaned, eliminating substantial com-plexity and inefficiency. By so doing, the tax rates can be lowered, which reduces the cost of those bugs that remain. And remain they will, because any system based on income contains inherent difficulties that have no simple solution. But the way toward income tax reform has been illuminated by a number of serious studies of the trade-offs that must be faced.

9 A Voter's Guide to the Tax Policy Debate

Many people's views about tax policy can be boiled down to one question: which system is best for me? If you've read this far, however, the odds are that your interest in tax policy goes beyond which plan offers you and your family the best deal and extends to which tax policy is best for the country.

Coming to a reasoned judgment about tax policy requires clarifying your own values about fairness, sifting through some subtle conceptual issues, and, perhaps hardest of all, evaluating conflicting claims about the economic impact of tax alternatives. This is particularly difficult because the public debate about tax reform is dominated by advocates whose purpose is not to educate but rather to persuade. In this book, we have attempted to explain clearly the conceptual issues and have presented what is known and what is not known about economic impacts. You must supply your own value judgments.

In this environment, a citizen must learn how to ask the right questions. To help you do that, in this last chapter we offer a voter's guide to tax policy choices to keep by your television as the issue is debated, in the same way that newspapers offer viewers' guides to the Super Bowl or the Academy Awards. But unlike either of those, in this election you have a say in the outcome.

Tax Cuts versus Tax Reform

Tax cuts are politically popular in part because advocates can plausibly claim that most, or even all, taxpayers come out ahead. But that claim is highly misleading because the revenue shortfall they cause will certainly have further repercussions. Either some kinds of expenditures will be cut, or the deficit will grow, requiring higher tax or fewer government services or both at some point in the future. This caveat applies both to making tax cuts in the context of the current tax system and to evaluating a radically different kind of tax system that will raise much less revenue. Before you buy into a tax proposal, kick the tires to learn how big a hole in the deficit it would create.

Tax Cuts as a Trojan Horse

For many advocates of tax cuts, the real objective is not the tax system but rather the size of government, and tax cuts are really a tactical weapon in the battle to downsize government ("starve the beast"). The idea is to lower taxes and hope that politicians' (and voters') fear of deficits and dislike of tax increases will force expenditures below what they would otherwise be. Because the ultimate objective is to limit spending initiatives, this is a good idea only if the benefits of the spending that is cut or forestalled fall short of their cost. So the real issue is not the tax system but the proper size and scope of government.

One response to a tax cut as Trojan horse policy proposal is to inquire about the rest of the plan. Exactly what spending programs do tax cut advocates want cut back or eliminated? Is it farm subsidies, the Head Start program, or Medicare benefits? What proposed programs do they wish would never see the light of day? Is it prescription drug subsidies or homeland security enhancements? Only when the whole strategy is known can an informed judgment be made. The other appropriate response is to ask whether a starve-the-beast strategy will work. The experience since 2000 suggests that it may not, so that tax cuts lead to deficits.

The Devil Is in the Details

More than one hundred years since its inception, the U.S. income tax system has grown encrusted and Byzantine. In comparison, a two-page sketch of a replacement is bound to look breathtakingly simple. But be warned that, in taxation, the devil is in the details.

Any tax system has gray areas that require rules and regulations if it is to be administered in a transparent way. All tax systems require an enforcement agency to see that the tax burden is shared equitably and not unfairly shouldered by those who feel morally obligated to pay taxes or have no opportunity to avoid them. All tax systems will be subject to the same political pressures from special interests that have contributed to the current system's problems. Finally, a tax reform plan that includes transition rules or other aspects "to be fleshed out later" will almost always turn out to be a lot more complicated than it appears.

The Tax System Can't Encourage Everything

In defending a tax break, politicians always point out how it will encourage or reward some laudable activity, such as housing, charity, or investment in the United States. Every time you hear the word *encourage*, though, remember that the break, by virtue of the higher tax rates it requires, discourages all other endeavors. Every time you hear the word *reward*, remember that it penalizes other activities.

It might make sense to implement social or economic policy through the tax code in some cases, but these must clear a high hurdle. Tax preferences in the tax code are too easily hidden from plain view, leading to what is in effect a hidden industrial or distributional policy.

Fairness Is a Slippery Concept, But an Important One

No politician and certainly no economist has the one true answer to what is fair. This is an ethical judgment that each person must make. It is also an issue that cannot be avoided in tax policy. A century ago, the leading American scholar of taxation, Edwin R. A. Seligman of Columbia University, remarked that "the history of modern taxation is the history of ... class antagonisms."[1] These days, *class* has become a four-letter word used derisively to attack another political party's concern about the distributional implications of tax policy, as in "That's class warfare!" But this issue cannot be dismissed with a slogan. Using less inflammatory language, the *distribution* of incomes—and not just total income—matters. We may disagree about how to trade off total income against the distribution of total income—and in the end this involves values as well as economics—but because policy implicitly makes this trade-off, we must face up to it and not only by name calling.

Be Skeptical of Claims of Economic Nirvana

High tax rates can certainly stifle initiative, and wrong-headed taxes can cause us to waste resources as we rearrange our affairs in an attempt to reduce tax liability. To some degree, these problems can be reduced by tax reform. But another part is an unavoidable consequence of the desire for an equitable distribution of tax burden, which requires that tax liability be linked with indicators of well-being such as income, consumption, or wealth. The terms of this trade-off between justice and prosperity are uncertain.

The unresolvable differences about what is fair could be put aside if we could adapt to a tax system that is so good for the economy that *everyone* ends up better off. But don't hold your breath. Tax plans proposed by politicians almost always come with claims about the stupendous growth in GDP, jobs, and wages that would ensue. But vague promises of an economic nirvana caused by a new tax system are just that. Neither tax reform nor tax cuts will double the growth rate forever. The fact that advocates overpromise is not a reason to dismiss the issue: tax reform can deliver long-term economic gains that are well worth pursuing.

Tax policy can help the economy in the short term if it can increase demand and thereby reduce excess capacity. But so can spending increases. It is not a coincidence that liberal economists tend to think that the best countercyclical policy is either tax cuts for low-income households or social spending directed to the same folks and that conservative economists generally think that the best stimulus is a tax cut designed to stimulate saving and investment and maybe just investment in the stock market. The underlying and generally unspoken concern is that these alternative stimulus plans benefit different people and have different implications for the long-term level of government spending. These things matter, to be sure, but they have nothing to do with which is the best short-term economic stimulus.

The Tax System Can Be Improved

Recall the plight of Hercules, who, as penance for having killed his wife and children in a fit of madness, was given twelve tasks of immense difficulty. The fifth of these tasks was one of the most daunting of all—to clean, in one day, thirty years of accumulated manure left by thousands of cattle in the stables of Augeas. (The analogy to the tax system is, we fear, obvious.) Hercules did not attempt to clean out the stables one shovelful at a time. Instead, Hercules diverted the rivers Alpheus and Peneus through the stables, ridding them of their filth at once.

There is much to clean in the tax system, and contemplating a Herculean approach is an appropriate part of a serious debate about tax reform. But the best should not become the enemy of the good. If fundamental reform is not to be, then the debate ought to continue because the tax system is too important for us to neglect.

The U.S. tax system can be made simpler. It can be made fairer. It can be made more conducive to economic growth. Some changes can accomplish all three, but in most cases difficult choices among these objectives must be made. We hope this book will help to clarify those choices and guide us toward the best way to tax ourselves.

Notes

Preface

1. According to a post on Garson O'Toole's "Quote Investigator" website, available at <http://quoteinvestigator.com/2011/03/07/einstein-income-taxes> (accessed October 11, 2016), this quote was attributed to Einstein by his friend and tax preparer Leo Mattersdorf in a letter to the editor of *Time* magazine in 1963.

Chapter 1

1. Further details and documentation for the history detailed in the first eight paragraphs of this chapter can be found in chapters 2 and 8 of this book.

2. Ryan (2008, 2011).

3. Descriptions of Republican candidate tax plans and revenue loss estimates are based on Nunns, Burman, Rohaly, and Rosenberg (2015), Rosenberg, Burman, Nunns, and Berger (2016), and Maag, Williams, Rohaly, and Nunns (2016). John Kasich did not release enough details about his tax plan to estimate the potential revenue consequences.

4. Congressional Budget Office (2016a).

5. Authors' calculations based on Gale and Potter (2002) and Congressional Budget Office (2001).

6. The House Republican tax plan released in June 2016 is described in Ryan (2016). The revenue cost and distributional projections for the House GOP tax plan are based on estimates reported in Nunns, Burman, Rohaly, Rosenberg, and Page (2016). Estimates from the Tax Foundation imply that the ten-year revenue cost of the June 2016 House Republican tax plan would be 1.1 percent of GDP (authors' calculations based on Pomerleau 2016 and Congressional Budget Office 2016a). August 2016 revisions to the Trump tax plan are described in Gleckman (2016) and Greenberg (2016). Our description of the September 2016 revisions to the Trump tax plan is based on Cole (2016) and Appelbaum (2016). Revenue cost projections for the September revision of the Trump plan are authors' calculations based on Tax Foundation estimates reported in Cole (2016) and baseline revenue projections from Congressional Budget Office (2016a). The difference between the 2.0 percent of GDP and 2.6 percent of GDP estimates reflects uncertainty about whether pass-through entity income would be taxed at ordinary personal income tax rates or a reduced tax rate of at most 15 percent.

7. The description of Hillary Clinton's tax plan and estimates of its revenue impact is based on Auxier, Burman, Nunns, and Rohaly (2016).

8. Discussions of the Sanders tax plan and revenue estimates (which are net of the carbon tax rebate) are based on Sammartino, Nunns, Burman, Rohaly, and Rosenberg (2016).

9. Compañía General de Tabacos de Filipinas v. Collector of Internal Revenue (1927).

10. We address survey evidence regarding public opinion on the size of government in chapter 4.

11. Marcuss et al. (2013, table 3).

12. The 900,000 employee figure comes from dividing the 1.8 billion annual hours spent complying with taxes by a 2,000 hour work year.

13. In tax year 2012, 56 percent of all individual tax returns bore the signature of a paid preparer (authors' calculation based on data in Internal Revenue Service 2015i and 2015m). Presumably, many of these taxpayers use a preparer not because their returns are complex but because they hope to maximize and speed up their tax refund.

14. See chapter 5, section on "The Costs of Compliance" for the basis of the estimates in the final two sentences in this paragraph.

15. Parisi (2015).

16. Internal Revenue Service (2015g, tables 2 and 4).

17. See chapter 5, section on "The Costs of Compliance," for the basis of these numbers and citations.

18. Internal Revenue Service (2015g, table 29). This figure is the actual fiscal year 2014 operating cost for the IRS.

19. Figures on the number of returns filed and examined are for fiscal year 2014 and are from Internal Revenue Service (2015g, tables 2 and 9a). Figures on computer-generated notices and information reporting are for fiscal year 2014 and are from Internal Revenue Service (2015g, table 14).

20. Internal Revenue Service (2016b). All statistics reported in this paragraph and the next one are authors' calculations based on data from this source. See chapter 5 for further details.

21. See chapter 5 for further details and documentation of these facts.

22. U.S. Bureau of Economic Analysis (2015, tables 1.1.5, 3.2, 3.3, and 5.11). The figures include current tax receipts, contributions for government social insurance, and estate and gift tax receipts.

23. Gallup (2015).

24. Gray (1995, p. 18), quoting Bill Archer (R-TX).

25. Rieschick (1997, p. 1661).

26. Lim, Slemrod, and Wilking (2013, table 1).

27. McIntyre (1995, p. 1).

Chapter 2

1. Authors' calculations based on U.S. Bureau of Economic Analysis (2015, table 3.6, lines 3, 4, 21, and 22).

2. The OECD figure for tax revenue as a percentage of GDP in the United States in 2014 is 26 percent (Organisation for Economic Co-operation and Development 2015c, table A). We report figures for 2013 in table 2.2 because data was not yet available for all OECD countries for 2014.

3. Organisation for Economic Co-operation and Development (2014b, p. 18).

4. Authors' calculations based on U.S. Bureau of Economic Analysis (2015, table 3.2).

5. These estimates are based on authors' calculations, which start with federal budget deficits projected by the Congressional Budget Office (2015c, summary table 1) in August 2015, and then adjust them by the CBO's December 2015 estimates of the impact of H.R. 2029, enacted in December 2015, on future budget deficits (Congressional Budget Office 2015d).

6. Total federal, state, and local tax revenues in 2014 and 1969 are calculated based on data from U.S. Bureau of Economic Analysis (2015), using the same procedure as in table 2.1 of this chapter, and adjusting for inflation using the GDP deflator, from U.S. Bureau of Economic Analysis (2015, table 1.1.4, line 1).

7. Milazzo and Thorndike (2012).

8. The Supreme Court decision barring income taxation was in *Pollock v. Farmers Loan and Trust Company*, 158 U.S. 601 (1895). The eminent economist Edwin Seligman called this the "Dred Scott decision of government revenue" (Seligman 1914).

9. Histories of the U.S. personal income tax are provided in Brownlee (1989), Goode (1976), Pechman (1987), and Witte (1985).

10. *Congressional Record* 63d Cong., 1st sess., vol. 50 (1913): 3840 (Statement of Senator Lodge, August 28).

11. Goode (1976) discusses the history of deductions and exclusions in the personal income tax base. Later additions include the standard deduction (1941), the deduction for medical expenses (1942), and the deduction for child and dependent care expenses (1954), which was later turned into a tax credit.

12. Data on the percentage of households filing tax returns presented throughout this section are from Piketty and Saez (2003, updated 2016, table A0). The number of households in the United States is defined for these purposes as the sum of married men, divorced and widowed men and women, and single men and women aged 20 and over.

13. Data up to 2009 was computed by Baneman and Nunns (2012). Data for 2010–2012 are authors' calculations based on data from the 2010 through 2012 editions of Internal Revenue Service, *Statistics of Income—Individual Income Tax Returns, Complete Report, Publication 1304*, table 3.4, following Baneman and Nunns' methodology. As we discuss below, some forms of income, such as capital gains, are often subjected to special reduced marginal tax rates. Figure 2.2 depicts marginal tax rates on "ordinary" income that does not receive such special treatment. The figure shows the "statutory" marginal tax rate, which is the marginal tax rate that is written into the tax law and the tax tables in the Form 1040 instructions. It does not take into account certain features of the income tax

that sometimes change the true effective marginal tax rate, such as some phaseouts of credits and deductions, or the alternative minimum tax.

14. Romer and Romer (2014).

15. Witte (1985) discusses the story of the introduction of income tax withholding. The United States already had experience with the withholding of Social Security payroll taxes prior to 1942, and numerous other countries had previously implemented withholding systems (Lent 1942). Economist Milton Friedman helped design the U.S. income tax withholding system while working at the Treasury department, and later came to regret it because he thought that it made the cost of government less salient to voters (Thorndike 2005).

16. Baneman and Nunns (2012).

17. See Reynolds (2011) for a recent example.

18. Brownlee (1989, p. 1615) addresses the special Civil War tax on corporations. Thorndike (2002) and Kornhauser (2002) discuss problems with corporate financial reporting at the time the corporate income tax was adopted. Pechman (1987, p. 135) discusses the constitutional questions surrounding the 1909 corporate income tax.

19. von Schanz (1896); Haig (1921); Simons (1938).

20. Nohlgren (2013) describes the options offered to Powerball winner Gloria MacKenzie.

21. Numbers cited in this paragraph are based on data from U.S. Bureau of Economic Analysis (2015, tables 1.12 and 6.11d) and Parisi (2015, table 1). "National income" is a broad measure of income that is similar to Haig–Simons income, but with some important differences, such as excluding capital gains that do not arise directly from retained earnings of firms in that year. In chapter 5, we demonstrate that only a small portion of wage and salary income evades taxation in the United States. Moylan (2008) discusses the treatment of executive stock options in the national accounts. Under the income tax, the gains on most executive stock options are treated as wage and salary income when they are exercised. Those designated as "incentive" stock options are treated as capital gains income on the personal income tax returns, but unlike other executive stock options, are not deductible from the taxable income of the employer.

22. Joint Committee on Taxation (1999). In 1943 the IRS ruled that employer contributions to group health insurance were excludable, but in 1953 the IRS ruled that employer contributions to individual health insurance plans were not excludable. The 1954 law reversed the latter ruling and codified the exclusion for employer contributions to both group and individual health insurance plans for their employees.

23. Numbers cited in this paragraph are based on U.S. Bureau of Economic Analysis (2015, tables 1.12 and 6.11d).

24. U.S. Bureau of Economic Analysis (2015, tables 1.12 and 6.11d).

25. For more detailed coverage of these issues, see for example Graetz and Schenk (2013).

26. According to the Office of Management and Budget (2015, Historical Table 2.1 and *Analytical Perspectives* table 14.1), in Fiscal Year 2014, individual income tax receipts totaled $1.395 trillion, the exclusion of employee meals and lodging (other than military) reduced individual income tax revenues by $2.59 billion (or 0.19 percent) relative to what they would have otherwise been, the exclusion for employer-provided child care benefits

cost $890 million (0.06 percent) of individual income tax revenue, and the exclusion of employer-provided educational assistance cost $750 million (or 0.05 percent) of individual income tax revenue.

27. The estimate for capital and business income is from table 2.4 in this chapter. Employee compensation is calculated based on U.S. Bureau of Economic Analysis (2015, table 1.12, row 2, and table 1.1.4, row 2).

28. The inflation rate is measured here using the consumer price index for urban consumers. The inflation rate for the twelve months leading up to August 1, 2016 is calculated by the authors based on data from the FRED database at the Federal Reserve Bank of St. Louis, <https://fred.stlouisfed.org/series/CPIAUCSL> (accessed September 17, 2016), and is seasonally adjusted. The forecast for the next ten years is from Federal Reserve Bank of Cleveland (2016).

29. If $100 is saved at a 3 percent interest rate, then after twenty years there will be $100 × 1.03^{20} = $181, the original $100 plus $81 of accumulated interest.

30. As we discuss later in the chapter, there was a temporary exception to this rule in the case of very wealthy people who died in 2010.

31. McCaffery (2002, p. 32).

32. This is derived from authors' calculations based on Board of Governors of the Federal Reserve System (2015). Pension and individual retirement account (IRA) assets are the sum of pension fund reserves owned by households (table B.101, line 28), which include both defined-contribution and defined-benefit plans, and total amount held in IRAs (table L.226, line 7), less IRAs held at life insurance companies (table L.226, line 7), which are already included in the pension totals.

33. Authors' calculations based on Board of Governors of the Federal Reserve System (2013). The estimate for nonprofit institution assets as a percentage of total assets is for 2000 because that is the last year for which all the necessary data is available, and is based on table L.100.a, line 1, and table B.100, lines 1, 5, and 6.

34. Board of Governors of the Federal Reserve System (2015, table B.101, lines 1 and 4).

35. See table 2.3.

36. Note that there are variations across organizational forms in how the business income must be divided up among owners for tax purposes. For example, S corporation income must be allocated to owners strictly in proportion to their shares of ownership, whereas partnerships specify the allocations in a partnership agreement, which allows much greater flexibility, subject to some constraints imposed by the tax law. See Joint Committee on Taxation (2012a) for further information.

37. When both spouses in a married couple are "material participants" in and owners of a business, they can choose to have the business treated as a "qualified joint venture," which is treated as a sole proprietorship instead of as a partnership. In the IRS data used to construct table 2.3, the number of sole proprietorships is actually the number of personal income tax returns that include at least one Schedule C (nonfarm sole proprietorship), plus the number of personal income tax returns that have at least one Schedule F (farm sole proprietorships). It does not correspond exactly to the number of separate businesses, because a given personal income tax return can have multiple Schedule C or Schedule F businesses.

38. Authors' calculations based on data from Internal Revenue Service (2015a).

39. For purposes of the rule limiting the number of owners of an S corporation to 100, a married couple and certain family members may be treated as a single owner.

40. Nonetheless, *some* large and relatively well-known firms are not C corporations. Companies such as Cargill, Koch Industries, Dell, Bechtel Group, PricewaterhouseCoopers, Mars, Publix Supermarkets, and Enterprise Holdings (parent company of Enterprise Rent-A-Car) are privately owned, and thus likely organized as pass-through entities. Some large publicly traded firms, such as StoneMor Partners LP (one of the nation's leading cemetery companies), are organized as publicly traded partnerships, thus qualifying for pass-through status. See Murphy (2014) and McKinnon (2012).

41. Table 2.3 excludes two special classes of C corporations: regulated investment companies (RICs); and real estate investment trusts (REITs). RICs are mutual funds, investing for example in diversified portfolios of corporate stocks, while REITs invest in bundles of commercial real estate or mortgages. Unlike other C corporations, RICs and REITs are allowed to deduct income distributed to shareholders (usually as dividends) when computing corporate income tax. They distribute almost all of their income, so that less than 0.15 percent of their income ends up subject to corporate income taxation (more specifically, "taxable income" was 0.13 percent of "net income less deficit" in 2011). RICs and REITs account for less than 1 percent of C corporation returns. We exclude them from table 2.3 to reduce double-counting of income (for example, much RIC income is derived from other C corporations already counted in table 2.3). Sources: authors' calculations based on data from Internal Revenue Service (2014b; *Statistics of Income—2011 Corporation Income Tax Returns Complete Report*; and *Statistics of Income—2011 Corporation Source Book, Publication 1053*).

42. Partnerships that are publicly traded are treated as C corporations for tax purposes, and are counted as such in table 2.3, with one exception. If at least 90 percent of the gross income received by a partnership is "qualifying income," which includes for example interest, dividends, capital gains, and rents, then the partnership can be publicly traded, yet still be treated as partnership rather than as a C corporation for tax purposes. See our earlier discussion of "publicly traded partnerships" in Joint Committee on Taxation (2015b) for further details.

43. According to Strumpf (2014), there were 4,916 publicly traded U.S. firms at the end of 2012. There were 1,635,369 C corporations in 2012, according to tables 1.1 and 4.1 of the Internal Revenue Service's *Statistics of Income—2012 Corporation Source Book, Publication 1053*.

44. Roberts (2008).

45. Authors' calculations based on Internal Revenue Service (2015a) and *Statistics of Income—1980 Individual Income Tax Returns, Complete Report, Publication 1304*.

46. Figures in this paragraph are based on Wilson and Liddell (2010, table 1a).

47. See Internal Revenue Service (2015b) and Ramirez (2012).

48. See Instructions for Schedule C, line 26 in Internal Revenue Service (2014c).

49. Orszag (2007, p. 3).

50. The same bottom-line result would apply if the carried interest were treated as ordinary partnership income. Changing the character of the carried interest income from capital gain to ordinary partnership income raises the tax liability of the fund managers, but if limited partners face the same tax rates as general partners, it reduces the tax

liability of the limited partners by the same amount by replacing ordinary partnership income (which becomes reallocated to the fund managers) with more lightly taxed capital gains on the limited partners' returns.

51. For further discussion (and disagreement) on the carried interest controversy, see Fleischer (2008, 2015), Judge (2013), Viard (2008), Sanchirico (2008), and Orszag (2007). Schler (2008) discusses issues with legislative proposals to tax carried interest as ordinary income. Table 1 of Orszag suggests that the vast majority of capital invested in private equity funds in 2006 came from tax-exempt entities.

52. Marr and Huang (2016) discuss the taxation of pass-through entities in the December 2015 Trump tax proposal. Applebaum (2016) reports that during the roll-out of the September 2016 revisions to the Trump tax plan, members of the Trump campaign apparently told the Tax Foundation that pass-through entity income would be taxed at ordinary personal income tax rates, but also assured the National Federation of Independent Businesses that pass-through entities would be taxed at a rate no higher than 15 percent. The $1.5 trillion revenue cost of the provision is based on estimates from the Tax Foundation reported in Cole (2016) and refers to whether or not it is included in the September 2016 version of Trump's plan. The House Republican tax plan of June 2016 is discussed in Ryan (2016), Pomerleau (2016), and Nunns, Burman, Rohaly, Rosenberg, and Page (2016).

53. In table 2.4, total capital gains in the U.S. economy are estimated based on Board of Governors of the Federal Reserve System (2015, table R.101, line 9), "holding gains on assets stated at market value" for households and nonprofit institutions. Total interest, dividend, S corporation, partnership, sole proprietorship, rental, royalty, estate, and trust income in the U.S. economy is from U.S. Bureau of Economic Analysis (2015), table 2.1, row 15 plus table 1.12, row 9 plus table 2.1, row 14 plus table 1.12, row 12 minus table 7.12, row 164. Imputed rental value of owner-occupied housing, less expenses other than taxes and interest is from U.S. Bureau of Economic Analysis (2015), table 7.12, row 158 plus row 160 plus row 164. Total property tax on nonbusiness real estate in the economy is from U.S. Bureau of Economic Analysis (2015, table 7.12, row 158). Total interest payments by persons are from U.S. Bureau of Economic Analysis (2015), table 2.1, row 30 plus table 7.12, row 160. Data on amounts of each type of income included on personal income tax returns are from IRS *Individual Income Tax Returns, Complete Report,* Publication 1304, various years, and Parisi (2015). All numbers are converted to constant year 2013 dollars using the price index for personal consumption expenditures, U.S. Bureau of Economic Analysis (2015, table 1.1.4, row 2). Adjustment for the erosion of real value of net worth by inflation takes total net worth of households and nonprofits at the end of the previous year from Board of Governors of the Federal Reserve System (2015, table R.101, line 9), converts it to constant year 2013 dollars using the price index for personal consumption expenditures, and then multiplies it by the inflation rate for the year as measured by the price index for personal consumption expenditures. One form of capital income that we do not attempt to estimate in column (a) of table 2.4 is the value of the net service flow from consumer durables.

54. Our estimates of the economic income of businesses in table 2.4 are based on U.S. Bureau of Economic Analysis (2015), which offers only a rough approximation of the true economic value of depreciation. Nonetheless, these estimates are undoubtedly much closer to economic income than what is included in taxable income.

55. Authors' calculations based on IRS *Individual Income Tax Returns Complete Report,* Publication 1304, 2004 (table 1.4), Ledbetter (2006), and unpublished data provided by Mark Ledbetter of the U.S. Bureau of Economic Analysis. Further details behind these

calculations are available in the 4th edition of *Taxing Ourselves*, and from the authors upon request.

56. The average annual inflation rate was 2.3 percent during 1987–2013, as measured by the price index for personal consumption expenditures (authors' calculations based on U.S. Bureau of Economic Analysis 2015, table 1.1.4). As noted earlier in the chapter, inflation has recently been lower than this, which would reduce the size of this adjustment if we were to focus just on very recent years.

57. For years through 2007, C corporation income subject to tax is from Internal Revenue Service (2013c). For later years, it is from the 2008 through 2012 editions of Internal Revenue Service, *Statistics of Income—Corporation Source Book,* Publication 1053 and Internal Revenue Service, *Statistics of Income—Corporation Income Tax Returns, Complete Report.*

58. The 54 percent is the sum of the 27 percent real economic capital income that was included in gross income on personal income tax returns 1987 through 2012, plus 27 percent of real economic capital income that was included in the corporate tax base during that period.

59. Pension contribution and benefit limits are from Internal Revenue Service (2014d).

60. IRA contribution limits are from Internal Revenue Service (2015c).

61. The deduction for tuition expenses is described in Joint Committee on Taxation (2015d, pp. 72–73). It cannot be used for the tuition expenses of an individual who benefits from one of the federal higher education expense credits described below.

62. Authors' calculations based on data from Parisi (2015).

63. Joint Committee on Taxation (2015d, pp. 11–12).

64. Rules for deductibility of home mortgage interest can be found in Internal Revenue Service (2015d).

65. U.S. Department of the Treasury, Internal Revenue Service, Internal Revenue Code (2015, Section 213(f)).

66. We discuss why this is so and whether it is a good idea in chapter 3. There is also a "married filing separately" filing status, but this is rarely used because it usually results in higher total tax liability for a married couple compared to "married filing jointly" status.

67. The graduated tax system ensures that, ignoring phaseouts as in the Earned Income Tax Credit, a taxpayer's marginal tax rate is always larger than his or her average tax rate.

68. Above an AGI threshold ($309,900 for a joint return in 2015), 2 percent of the value of exemptions is phased out for every additional $2,500 of AGI. Similarly, most types of itemized deductions are reduced in value by 3 percent of the amount by which AGI exceeds a threshold ($309,900 for joint returns in 2015), but no more than 80 percent of these itemized deductions can be lost. For example, consider a family of four in the 33 percent tax bracket with $380,000 in AGI. Earning 1 more dollar of income causes them to lose 3 cents of itemized deductions and $(1/2500) \times 2\% \times \$4,000 \times 4 = 12.8$ cents worth of personal exemptions. At a 33 percent tax rate, this increases their tax bill by 5.21 cents, in effect increasing the family's marginal rate by 5.21 percentage points to 38.21 percent.

69. Williams and Austin (2015) describe all of the phaseouts that applied in the federal income tax as of 2015.

70. Values of AMT exemption, AMT tax bracket thresholds, and threshold for phaseout of AMT exemption are from Internal Revenue Service (2014a).

71. The AMT exemption phaseout causes taxpayers to lose 25 cents of AMT exemption for every dollar by which AMT taxable income exceeds the threshold. For a taxpayer in the 26 percent AMT tax bracket, each additional dollar of income causes $0.25 of AMT exemption to be lost, which in turn increases AMT liability by $0.25 \times 26\% = \$0.065$, raising the marginal tax rate to $26\% + 6.5\% = 32.5\%$. For someone in the 28 percent AMT tax bracket who has not already lost the whole exemption, the phaseout raises the marginal tax rate to $28\% + 0.25 \times 28\% = 35$ percent.

72. The percentage of returns subject to AMT in 2013 is calculated from data in Parisi (2015).

73. Authors' calculations based on Parisi (2015). Explanations of the meanings of Earned Income Tax Credit "used to offset income tax before credits," "used to offset all other taxes," and "refundable portion" can be found in Internal Revenue Service, *Statistics of Income—2010 Individual Income Tax Returns, Complete Report*, Publication 1304, pp. 161 and 186–187.

74. Statements in the previous two sentences, except for the comparison to Medicaid, are based on Bitler and Hoynes (2010, table 3). In 2009, total federal and state spending on Medicaid was $374.9 billion (Centers for Medicare and Medicaid Services 2014b, table 3).

75. For a full description of EITC "qualifying child" requirements, see Internal Revenue Service (2014e, chapter 2).

76. All EITC parameters are from Internal Revenue Service (2014a). The income threshold at which the phaseout begins is $18,111 for an unmarried parent with three qualifying children.

77. Even this procedure is imperfect because it makes no allowance for whether the firm's combine was in better or worse condition than the ones for sale on the market.

78. The recent history of bonus depreciation provisions is described in Joint Committee on Taxation (2015c, pp. 160–164, and 2015d, pp. 60–67).

79. For further information on the depreciation rules, see Joint Committee on Taxation (2012b, 2013a, 2015c, and 2015d).

80. In 2012, 74 percent of firms with income tax after credits of less than $15,000 had *zero* income tax *before* credits, and thus definitely faced a statutory marginal tax rate of either 0 percent or 15 percent. Income tax *before* credits was $13,750 at the top of the 25 percent bracket. So among the 26 percent of firms with income tax after credits below $15,000 that had positive income tax after credits, many probably faced statutory marginal tax rates of 15 or 25 percent. Nonetheless, some portion of that 25 percent of C corporations had taxable incomes that put them in the lower part of the 34 percent tax bracket, or had even higher taxable incomes but large credits.

81. Numbers cited in this paragraph are authors' calculations based on data from Internal Revenue Service, *Statistics of Income—2012 Corporation Income Tax Returns, Complete Report*, tables 5 and 22, and Internal Revenue Service (2015e). "Business

receipts" are proceeds from sales of goods and services, and exclude income from financial investments. Statistics on C corporations classified by size of income tax after credits exclude REITs and RICs, while statistics classified by size business receipts include REITs and RICs. But the latter classify REITs and RICs as having no business receipts, and REITs and RICs account for a trivial portion of income subject to corporate tax and corporate income tax liability.

82. U.S. Department of the Treasury (2011, p. 2) notes that the research and experimentation credit had been extended fourteen times and was scheduled to expire December 31, 2011. Joint Committee on Taxation (2013a, p. 141) notes that the American Taxpayer Relief Act of 2012 extended the expiration date from December 31, 2011 to the end of 2013. The Tax Increase Prevention Act of 2014 extended the credit to the end of 2014 (Joint Committee on Taxation 2015c, p. 134–137).

83. Joint Committee on Taxation (2015d).

84. Internal Revenue Service (2015f, pp. 18–19) lists twenty-six different "general business credits" available to small businesses, including among other things the research and experimentation credit.

85. Authors' calculations based on data from Internal Revenue Service (2014b, pp. 16, 20, 46, 52, 68, 78, 90, 112, 116, 120, and 122) and Internal Revenue Service *Statistics of Income—2011 Corporation Income Tax Returns, Complete Report* (table 4).

86. U.S. Bureau of Economic Analysis (2015, tables 1.1.5, 3.4, and 3.6).

87. For purposes of the payroll tax, taxable "self-employment income" includes income from sole proprietorships and income from a partnership if the taxpayer actively works for the partnership. The cap on earnings subject to OASDI tax is reported in U.S. Social Security Administration (2015).

88. Employers are only required to remit the 0.9 percent HI tax on the portion of each individual's wage and salary income that exceeds $200,000, regardless of what the combined wage and salary and self-employment income of that individual and his or her spouse are. Therefore, two-earner married couples with high incomes will often need to ask employers to adjust withholding rates in order to avoid penalties for underpayment.

89. The tax provisions of the ACA are described in Joint Committee on Taxation (2011).

90. Urban-Brookings Tax Policy Center (2013).

91. Joint Committee on Taxation (2015a, p. 13), and Internal Revenue Service (2014a).

92. Urban-Brookings Tax Policy Center (2012a).

93. Internal Revenue Service (2014a).

94. Stevenson (2001) and Kestenbaum (2011).

95. Brief summaries of the major components of the tax plans proposed by Bush and Gore during the 2000 Presidential election campaign, along with some analysis, can be found in Citizens for Tax Justice (2000a, 2000b). During the first debate of the 2000 Presidential election campaign, Gore referred to a "lockbox" for Social Security and/or Medicare seven times, and George W. Bush referred to the budget surplus as "your money" four times (Commission on Presidential Debates, 2012). Dizikes (2001) describes Bush's shifting rationales for the tax cut.

96. See Kiefer et al. (2002) and Joint Committee on Taxation (2003a) for detailed descriptions of EGTRRA 2001. Greenhouse (2000) discusses the *Bush v. Gore* decision.

97. Joint Committee on Taxation (2003a).

98. In many of those years, the top effective marginal tax rate on long-term capital gains was somewhat higher than the rates listed in the text due to phaseouts of various deductions, exemptions, and credits. Urban-Brookings Tax Policy Center (2012d) provides historical data on top effective marginal tax rates on long-term capital gains.

99. See Joint Committee on Taxation (2005, 2007) for further description of the changes in tax law discussed in this paragraph.

100. Joint Committee on Taxation (2009) provides further details on the tax cuts described in this paragraph.

101. See Burman, Khitatrakun, Rohaly, Toder, and Williams (2008) for description and analysis of the tax proposals made by Obama and McCain in the 2008 presidential campaign.

102. Estimates of the expenditure and revenue costs of ARRA reported in the text are slightly larger than those made at the time of enactment, reflecting new information available through June 2012, and are from Recovery.gov (2012).

103. Tax legislation enacted in 2009 is described in Joint Committee on Taxation (2011).

104. Liptak (2012) summarizes the 2012 Supreme Court decision on President Obama's health care law.

105. Tax changes in this paragraph are described in more detail in Joint Committee on Taxation (2011) and U.S. Senate Committee on Finance (2012).

106. The number of AMT taxpayers between 1970 and 1998 comes from Leiserson and Rohaly (2006b, table 2), and the total number of tax returns comes from Internal Revenue Service (2015m, 2015o).

107. Authors' calculations based on data from Internal Revenue Service (2015i).

108. Slemrod and Kopczuk (2003) analyze historical federal estate tax return data and find evidence that when federal estate tax rates declined from one year to the next, there were an unusually low number of deaths in the high-tax year and an unusually high number of deaths in the low-tax year, suggesting that people may actually have delayed their dates of death to leave larger after-tax bequests to their heirs. On the basis of this research, they were awarded the 2001 Ig Nobel Prize in the field of economics.

109. Mayoras and Mayoras (2010) report estimates of the value of Steinbrenner's net worth at death, estate tax liability avoided, the purchase price for his share of the Yankees, and that he owned 55 percent of the Yankees. Ozanian (2012) reports that the estimated value of the Yankees in March 2012 was $1.85 billion, so a 55 percent stake would have been worth $1.0175 billion. If that was sold, then after subtracting the $10 million basis and the $4.5 million of applicable exemptions, there would be $1.003 billion of taxable capital gains, which at a 15 percent tax rate yields $150 million of tax liability.

110. Gale and Potter (2002).

111. Gale and Potter (2002, table 2), and Joint Committee on Taxation (2003d).

112. See, for example, Rosenbaum and Stevenson (2001) and Stevenson (2003).

113. See, for example, Auerbach and Gale (2001).

114. Authors' calculations based on Ruffing and Horney (2011, table 1) and Office of Management and Budget (2012); see also *Economic Report of the President* (2012, p. 83).

115. Kogan (2013) explains the spending caps and sequesters required by the Budget Control Act of 2011.

116. The $1.9 trillion figure is from Auerbach and Gale (2012, p. 2), based on Congressional Budget Office projections. Projected GDP for fiscal years 2013–2022 is from Congressional Budget Office (2012b).

117. Congressional Budget Office (2012a).

118. Most of the Obama administration's 2012 tax proposals are laid out in Office of Management and Budget (2012); proposals for business tax reform can be found in U.S. Department of the Treasury (2012). President's Economic Recovery Advisory Board (2010) provides more details on options for making up revenue loss from lowering corporate tax rates, including options for changing the tax treatment of certain businesses currently treated as pass-through entities. See Toder et al. (2012) for a description and analysis of the tax plans outlined in the Obama administration's budget proposal for fiscal year 2013.

119. Romney (2012) lays out the basic outline of Romney's tax proposal, and further possible details were floated during the presidential debates (ABC News 2012a, 2012b, 2012c). Urban-Brookings Tax Policy Center (2012b) offers description and analysis of the Romney campaign's tax proposals.

120. ABC News (2012a).

121. Romney (2012).

122. ABC News (2012b).

123. ABC News (2012b).

124. ABC News (2012a, 2012b, 2012c).

125. Marron (2012) explains the basis of the $5 trillion estimate.

126. This is derived by dividing the $5 trillion revenue loss estimate by the estimated $202 trillion of nominal GDP projected for fiscal years 2013 through 2022, reported in Auerbach and Gale (2012, appendix table 1).

127. The Urban-Brookings Tax Policy Center analysis referred to here is in Brown, Gale, and Looney (2012a). They estimate that making Romney's income tax plan revenue-neutral would require $86 billion of tax increases on those with incomes below $200,000 in 2015. That represents 0.5 percent of the Congressional Budget Office (2012c) projection of calendar-year 2015 GDP.

128. Urban-Brookings Tax Policy Center (2012c).

129. Hubbard (2012) contends that Brown, Gale, and Looney (2012a) underestimated the economic growth effects of the Romney plan. Brown, Gale, and Looney (2012b, 2012c) offer a rebuttal.

130. ABC News (2012a).

131. Weisman (2013a), Steinhauer (2013), and Joint Committee on Taxation (2013a, p. 86).

132. Kogan (2013).

133. Plumer (2013a) and Weisman (2013b) describe some of the effects of the sequester.

134. Harwood (2013) discusses the state of budget politics as of mid-2013.

135. Weisman and Parker (2013) summarize the story of the 2013 government shutdown and its resolution.

136. Plumer (2013b) describes the December 2013 budget deal.

137. Weisman (2014) describes the January 2014 budget agreement.

138. Weisman and Parker (2014).

139. Steinhauer (2015).

140. Herszenhorn (2015a).

141. Herszenhorn (2015b).

142. Joint Committee on Taxation (2015d).

Chapter 3

1. Whitney (1990) describes the protesting and rioting over the U.K. poll tax. Smith (1991) offers an analysis of its failure.

2. British Broadcasting Corporation (2011).

3. McHardy (1992, p. xxiv). Accounts of the peasant revolt of 1381 are also given in McKissack (1959) and Powell (1894).

4. Fisher (1996, p. 37).

5. *New York Times* (2012a).

6. *New York Times* (2012b).

7. Boxer (2011).

8. Knowlton and Calmes (2011).

9. Stein (2006).

10. As we discuss below, if age is the issue, any apparent disparity is less important because most people pass through most ages during their lifetime, while most people do not live in all regions of the country over their lifetime, or smoke for the same number of years.

11. Although in this illustration we use income as the tax base and measure of well-being, the definitions would apply to any alternative measure of well-being.

12. A tax system can be progressive over some income ranges and not others. Similarly, when comparing two tax systems, one might be more progressive over some income ranges and not over others.

13. Clinton (1992, pp. 644–645).

14. Safire (1995, p. A19).

15. Hall and Rabushka (1995, p. 26). Political supporters of the flat tax advocate a large exempt level of income, which would add some progressivity. But they tend to oppose having multiple tax rates, which almost certainly means that their systems would impose less of a tax burden on high-income families than the current income tax. Professor Hall later changed his mind about the appropriate degree of progressivity, and came out for applying a graduated rate structure to the individual Hall-Rabushka flat tax base (see Hall 2005).

16. Higgins (1995, p. A11).

17. vos Savant (1994, p. 12), quoted in Miller (2000, p. 529).

18. Davies (1995, p. A11).

19. In the *Wealth of Nations*, Adam Smith (1937 / 1776) stated his first principle of taxation: "The subjects of every state ought to contribute towards the support of the government, as nearly as possible, in proportion to their respective abilities; that is, in proportion to the revenue they enjoy under the protection of the state. The expense of government to the individuals of a great nation is like the expense of management to the joint tenants of a great estate, who are all obliged to contribute in proportion to their respective interests in the estate." *Wealth of Nations* was originally published in 1776; the quote is from pp. 777–778 of the 1937 edition.

20. Gates and Collins (2003).

21. Mankiw (2010). More specifically, he says that the distribution of tax burdens should be guided by the principle that "people should get what they deserve," but makes many benefit-principle-style arguments, similar to those mentioned in connection with Adam Smith above, in discussing how the tax burden should be distributed, and why progressive taxation and transfers to the poor might be justified.

22. Friedman (1962), Hayek (2007, ch. 3, and 2011, ch. 20), and Mankiw all favor government involvement in the economy to address a broader array of "market failures," such as public goods or externalities, which we discuss in chapter 4. Nozick (1989, ch. 25) allows for a considerably larger role for government than Nozick (1974).

23. A similar argument is an important element of Rawls's (1971) theory of justice. Varian (1980) provides a formal economic argument along these lines.

24. Jeremy Bentham's *An Introduction to the Principles of Morals and Legislation* (1789) and John Stuart Mill's *Utilitarianism* (1871) are the classic works on utilitarian philosophy, although note that in *Principles of Political Economy* (1877, vol. II, pp. 394–402), Mill advocates the equal sacrifice principle for taxation that we described above. Economist and Nobel Prize winner James A. Mirrlees (1971) is a major contributor to working out the theory of what a tax-and-transfer system that maximizes the sum of human happiness would entail when redistribution involves costs in terms of economic efficiency. Kaplow and Shavell (2006) offer a detailed argument in favor of exclusive reliance on welfarist ethics (of which utilitarianism is a leading example) as a guide for policy.

25. Note that the Rawlsian approach would still generally stop short of complete equality of income, because responses to the incentive effects of such extreme redistribution could reduce total income so much that it makes everyone worse off. More concretely, if taxes on the rich reduce their tax base so much that tax revenue declines, there is *less* revenue to fund programs that benefit low-income households.

26. Dworkin (2000) and Roemer (1998).

27. Varian (2001).

28. Krugman (2001, p. 36).

29. Simons (1938, p. 24).

30. Piketty and Saez (2003, updated 2016, table A6).

31. There is also a difference between the Piketty-Saez and CBO studies in how they rank households to determine their position in the income distribution. Piketty and Saez rank households (or more precisely, "tax units," which are approximately the same thing) by their total pre-tax market incomes, with no adjustments for household size, and assign an equal number of households to each percentile of the distribution. In contrast, when CBO ranks households to assign them to segments of the income distribution, the ranking is based on income divided by the square root of the number of people in the household, to reflect the notion that each person in a large household is less well-off than each person in a smaller household with the same income. CBO assigns equal numbers of people, rather than equal numbers of households, to each percentile of the distribution. The average household incomes from the CBO data reported here are the simple averages of *unadjusted* household incomes (i.e., *not* divided by the square root of household size) for people in each segment of the income distribution ranked by the method described above.

32. Armour, Burkhauser, and Larrimore (2013) argue that replacing realized capital gains with imputed values for accrued capital gains weakens the conclusion that income inequality has been increasing over time. However, they rely on Census Current Population Survey data that is not very informative about what is happening at the top of the income distribution (due to small sample size and top-coding of incomes), and their conclusions are largely driven by comparing two individual years: 2007 (a year with relatively low accrued capital gains) and 1989 (a year with relatively high accrued capital gains). Making the comparison over a longer time span that averaged accrued capital gains and income over multiple years would likely strengthen the conclusion that inequality has been increasing dramatically over time. Bernstein (2013) offers a more detailed critique.

33. The CBO data used here adjusts for inflation using the Bureau of Economic Analysis chained personal consumption expenditure (PCE) price index. Compared to the more commonly used consumer price index (CPI), the PCE index does a better job of dealing with factors that would otherwise bias measured inflation upward, such as introduction of new goods, changing quality of goods, and substitution toward cheaper goods when relative prices change. Boskin, Dulberger, Gordon, Griliches, and Jorgenson (1998) discuss biases in the measure of inflation, and McCully, Moyer, and Stewart (2007) explain differences between the PCE price index and the CPI. Between 1979 and 2013, cumulative inflation is 29 percentage points lower when calculated by the PCE price index compared to the CPI-U-RS, and 50 percentage points lower compared to the CPI-U (authors' calculations based on data from U.S. Bureau of Economic Analysis 2015 and U.S. Bureau of Labor Statistics 2015, series CUUR0000SA0 and CPI-U_RS, all items, https://www.bls.gov/cpi/cpiursai1977-2015.xlsx). CBO switched from using CPI-U-RS to using the PCE price index after the previous edition of our book, which helps explain why reported real income growth across the distribution is higher in this edition of our book compared to earlier editions.

34. Government policy could also have indirect effects on income inequality because it changes incentives, which might affect how much pre-tax market income people choose to earn and report. We address this later in this chapter and in chapter 4.

35. The CBO data are reported on an annual basis and re-rank households each year. Thus, in our table 3.1, the set of people used to compute the three-year averages of income in each segment of the income distribution varies from year to year, as people move up and down the income distribution across years. The data that would be needed to compute three-year averages of income for a fixed set of households are not publicly available. We address this issue and its potential consequences in the text below.

36. Authors' calculations based on data in Congressional Budget Office (2016b, Supplemental Data tables 3 and 13).

37. Cilke, Cronin, McCubbin, Nunns, and Smith (2001). Note that these estimates are not directly comparable to those from the CBO analysis cited earlier, because Cilke and co-authors use a different, less comprehensive measure of income than CBO, because their unit of analysis is the individual rather than the household, and because their analysis includes only people who filed federal income tax returns, as opposed to the whole population in the CBO analysis. Congressional Budget Office (2005) performs a similar analysis and finds that the highest quintile's share of all income going to the top four quintiles from 1991 to 1997 is 71 percent when they use single-year measures of income and re-rank each year (similar to what we do in table 3.1), and 69.5 percent when they compute a seven-year average annual income for the whole 1991 to 1997 period for particular households followed over time, and then rank based on that.

38. This claim is based on tabulations of 1994 and 1995 individual tax returns provided to us by the Office of Tax Analysis, United States Treasury. For 1995, the top 1 percent of earners received 14.8 percent of expanded adjusted gross income. For taxpayers in the age class 45 to 54, the top 1 percent received 15.3 percent of income, and for those in the age class 55 to 64, the fraction was 18.2 percent. Income was less concentrated for those age classes below age 45.

39. Kopczuk, Saez, and Song (2010). Similarly, Gerald Auten and Geoffrey Gee (2009) of the U.S. Department of the Treasury analyzed tax-return data following the same individuals over time from 1987 through 1996 and 1996 through 2005, and found that, although there was indeed significant economic mobility throughout this period, there is no evidence that mobility was any higher in 1996 through 2005 compared to 1987 through 1996.

40. The Consumer Expenditure Survey is a random sample of about 7,500 households each year. Thus, even if high-income people responded to these surveys as often as lower-income people, the sample would only include about 75 households in the top 1 percent, which is not nearly enough to say anything reliable about the entire high-income population given the huge variability of incomes and income sources among households within the top 1 percent. For this reason statistics on the top 1 percent and even the top 5 percent are generally not reported in studies on consumption inequality. The CBO income inequality data relies on samples of tax returns including well over 100,000 households per year, with a higher sampling probability for higher-income households, together with census surveys containing information on around 60,000 households per year.

41. Meyer and Sullivan (2011). Articles by Furchtgott-Roth (2012) and Hassett and Mathur (2012) make similar points, but then go further to argue that the consumption data suggests that inequality has not increased over time. That conclusion is unwarranted given the lack of reliable data on consumption in the upper part of the distribution discussed above. Meyer and Sullivan also argue that adequately correcting for upward bias in measured inflation would require reducing the inflation rate as measured by the

CPI-U-RS by 0.8 percentage points per year. That approach would reduce cumulative inflation between 1979 and 2009 by 41 percentage points relative to the PCE price index used by CBO, and that in turn would raise real income growth rates similarly throughout the income distribution. Broda and Romalis (2008) estimate that cumulative inflation between 1994 and 2005 was about 6 percentage points less for people in the bottom decile of the income distribution than for people in the top decile. But a difference of this order of magnitude is not nearly large enough to substantially undermine the conclusion that real income grew much faster over time at the top of the income distribution than elsewhere.

42. Authors' calculations based on data in Kennickell (2009, tables 2 and A1 and figure A3a) and Bricker et al. (2014, table 4).

43. Saez and Zucman (2016, Online Appendix table B1).

44. Bricker, Henriques, Krimmel, and Sabelhaus (2016, figure 5). Kopczuk (2015) provides further information on estimates of wealth inequality from a variety of sources including estate tax return data, and discussion of reasons for differences in estimates across data sources.

45. Gallup (2015).

46. Bowman, Sims, and O'Neil (2015, pp. 32–33) report these polling results, along with results of a large number of other polls conducted between 2011 and 2014, which mostly find roughly similar levels of support for propositions like these.

47. National Public Radio, Kaiser Family Foundation, and Kennedy School of Government (2003). A January 2015 *Huffington Post* / YouGov poll (reported in Edwards-Levy 2015) seems to corroborate this. When asked "do you think America's tax system favors the wealthy over the middle class and poor, favors the middle class and poor over the wealthy, or treats everyone equally," 62 percent said it "favors the wealthy." The interpretation of this result is less clear, though; for instance, some may reasonably interpret "treats everyone equally" to mean it demands equal sacrifice, as opposed to equal average tax rates.

48. McKee and Gerbing (1989), cited in Roberts, Hite, and Bradley (1994).

49. Hite and Roberts (1991) conducted a survey of a random, nationally representative sample of adults, and found fairly close correspondence between average tax rates volunteered as "fair" at each income level, and actual average tax rates at those income levels. An October 1995 Roper Center / *Reader's Digest* poll (reported in Bowman, Sims, and O'Neil, 2015, pp. 39–40) found a broadly similar result, although the correspondence with actual average tax rates was less close. Hite, Hasseldine, and Fatemi (2007) conducted a survey of undergraduate accounting majors who had not yet taken a tax course, and their findings roughly corroborate those of the earlier Hite and Roberts survey. The 2007 study finds evidence that students' assessment of the "fair" level of taxes at each income level was closer to the actual levels of taxes when students were first given information on the actual levels of taxes, supporting the notion that views about what is fair in taxation are influenced by the status quo. However, students' "fair" levels of taxation were still reasonably close to actual levels of taxation at each income level even when they were not first given information about status quo tax levels. A February 2012 survey by the Capitol Hill newspaper *The Hill* asked what the "most appropriate top tax rate for families earning $250,000 or more" was, and 75 percent of respondents chose a tax rate of 30 percent or below. This, in conjunction with the fact that the top marginal tax rate in the federal income tax in 2012 was 35 percent, might seem to contradict the

notion that people would prefer to make the tax system more progressive than it is now (Schroeder 2012). But the ambiguous wording of the question leaves open to interpretation whether it is meant to refer to an average tax rate or a marginal tax rate, and what kinds of taxes should be included.

50. Poll results in the previous two sentences are reported in Bowman, Sims, and O'Neil (2015, pp. 42 and 45).

51. In a survey sponsored by National Public Radio, the Kaiser Family Foundation, and the Kennedy School of Government (2003), 41 percent of people answered that under a flat-rate system high-income people would pay more income tax than now, 35 percent said they'd pay less, 18 percent said they'd pay about the same amount, and 6 percent said they didn't know. A 2011 McClatchy / Marist poll found that 36 percent thought the wealthy would pay higher taxes than now under a flat tax, 38 percent thought they would pay lower taxes than now under a flat tax, and 21 percent thought they would pay about the same amount as now under a flat tax (Bowman, Sims, and O'Neil 2015, p. 47). A January 2005 CBS / *New York Times* poll found 53 percent of respondents thought rich people would "benefit most from a flat tax system," while 25 percent thought middle income people would benefit the most (Bowman, Sims, and O'Neil, 2015, p. 47).

52. Slemrod (2006) performs a statistical analysis of data from a survey sponsored by National Public Radio, the Kaiser Family Foundation, and the Kennedy School of Government (2003). Even after holding constant other factors such as family income, political party affiliation, age, gender, and stated beliefs about the fairness and complexity of the current income tax, the probability that someone supported replacing the income tax with a flat tax was 24 percentage points higher if that person believed that high-income people would pay *more* under a flat tax than they do now.

53. Kuziemko, Norton, Saez, and Stantcheva (2015, table 2).

54. The estimate is based on IRS data and is reported in the Kuziemko, Norton, Saez, and Stantcheva online survey available at <https://hbs.qualtrics.com/SE/?SID=SV _77fSvTy12ZSBihn>, accessed July 8, 2013.

55. Numbers cited in this paragraph are from Kuziemko, Norton, Saez, and Stantcheva (2015, tables 4 and 5).

56. To be precise, individual taxpayers pay the difference between tax liability and withheld taxes *plus* estimated tax payments.

57. The importance of mobility in escaping the burden of taxes was recognized by the group of tax scholars popularly known as the Who, who wrote in their song "Going Mobile": "Watch the police and tax man miss me, I'm mobile."

58. With heavily advertised goods like Coke and Pepsi, even if all consumers could not distinguish them in a blind taste test, many still might strongly prefer to buy one or the other. This example presumes that consumers think the two products are identical and choose solely on the basis of price.

59. Christensen, Cline, and Neubig (2001, p. 498).

60. Gallup (2015).

61. Parker (2011).

62. Indeed, the corporation tax could even be somewhat shifted to workers, if the corporate sector is more labor-intensive than the noncorporate sector, because the

tax-induced shift of activity from the corporate sector to the noncorporate sector will thus reduce the overall demand for labor.

63. As Martin Feldstein (1994) of Harvard University has argued, although there is certainly foreign investment over short periods, over the long term a country's investment is limited by its own citizens' saving. If this is true, the link between domestic savings and domestic investment is restored.

64. See, for example, Feldstein and Horioka (1980). Coakley, Kulasi, and Smith (1998) provide a review of the subsequent literature on the topic.

65. Gravelle and Smetters (2006) and Baldwin and Krugman (2004) provide compelling theoretical and empirical support for the notion that much of the burden of corporate income taxes falls on domestic owners of capital. Clausing (2013) presents evidence from cross-country panel data suggesting that workers bear at most a small portion of the burden of corporate income taxation, and Suárez Serrato and Zidar (2016) come to a similar conclusion based on analysis of cross-state panel data from the United States, exploiting variation in state corporate tax rates across states and time.

66. Bastiat ([1850] 1964, p. 1).

67. See Urban-Brookings Tax Policy Center (2015d) for further information on the incidence assumptions and methodology behind the estimates in table 3.2. Note that percentiles of the income distribution are defined here such that each percentile contains an equal number of people, not an equal number of households.

68. The Urban-Brookings Tax Policy Center (2015d) defines "expanded cash income" as "adjusted gross income (AGI) plus: above-the-line adjustments (e.g., IRA deductions, student loan interest, self-employed health insurance deduction, etc.), employer-paid health insurance and other nontaxable fringe benefits, employee and employer contributions to tax-deferred retirement savings plans, tax-exempt interest, nontaxable Social Security benefits, nontaxable pension and retirement income, accruals within defined benefit pension plans, inside buildup within defined contribution retirement accounts, cash and cash-like (e.g., Supplemental Nutrition Assistance Program) transfer income, employer's share of payroll taxes, and imputed corporate income tax liability."

69. Urban-Brookings Tax Policy Center (2006a, 2006b). Note that this analysis assumed that the burden of corporate taxation was borne in proportion to receipt of capital income. Our discussion below suggests that this is unlikely to make a major difference to the overall conclusion emphasized in the text.

70. Buffett (2011).

71. Confessore and Kocieniewski (2012).

72. *Economic Report of the President* (2012, pp. 86–88). The Treasury definition of "cash income" is broadly similar to that used by the Urban-Brookings Tax Policy Center.

73. A "Buffett Rule" bill was introduced in the Senate on February 1, 2012 under the name "Paying a Fair Share Act of 2012," and can be found at <http://www.gpo.gov/fdsys/pkg/BILLS-112s2059is/pdf/BILLS-112s2059is.pdf> (accessed August 18, 2012). The similar "Paying a Fair Share Act of 2013" died in Congress and the "Paying a Fair Share Act of 2015" was introduced to Congress in January 2015 but not seriously considered. These bills can be found at <http://www.gpo.gov/fdsys/pkg/BILLS-113s321is/pdf/BILLS-113s321is.pdf> and <http://www.gpo.gov/fdsys/pkg/BILLS-114hr362ih/pdf/BILLS-114hr362ih.pdf> (accessed June 29, 2015).

74. Congressional Budget Office (2016b, Supplemental Data table 2).

75. Piketty and Saez (2007). The average tax rate estimates cited in the text and below are from their online appendix, <http://elsa.berkeley.edu/~saez/jep-results-standalone. xls>, table A3 (accessed August 21, 2012). Their analysis includes personal income taxes, corporate income taxes, payroll taxes, and estate taxes. They assume that the burden of the corporate income tax is borne in proportion to capital income received, and that each percentile (or fraction of a percentile) of the income distribution bears the burden of the estate tax paid by the same percentile (or fraction of a percentile) of the wealth distribution among decedents in that year. According to Piketty and Saez, the average federal tax rate for the top 0.1 percent of the income distribution declined from 60.6 percent in 1976 to 33.6 percent in 2004. This included the combined effects of a decline in the average personal income tax rate from 31.8 percent to 24.8 percent, an increase in the average payroll tax rate from 0.6 percent to 2.1 percent, a decline in the average corporate tax rate from 14.4 percent to 4.4 percent, and a decline in the average estate tax rate from 13.7 percent to 2.2 percent. The minimum income to qualify for the top 0.1 percent reported in the text is from Piketty and Saez (2003, updated 2016), and refers to income including capital gains.

76. An Urban-Brookings Tax Policy Center analysis by Leiserson and Rohaly (2006a) confirms the 2001 and 2003 federal tax cuts produced larger reductions in average federal tax rates and tax liability per household for upper-income people, but reduced federal tax liability by a larger percentage for moderate-income people.

77. Authors' calculations based on data in Congressional Budget Office (2016b, Supplemental Data table 6).

78. Kaiser Commission on Medicaid and the Uninsured (2013a, figure 21). All references to years in this paragraph are to fiscal years.

79. Kaiser Commission on Medicaid and the Uninsured (2010, p. 1) and Paradise (2015). Maximum household income levels to qualify for Medicaid are higher for children than for adults in most states.

80. Although Medicaid is targeted to low-income people, table 3.3 shows that some Medicaid benefits go to people in households in the upper parts of the income distribution. One reason this occurs is that an adult may qualify for Medicaid benefits based on his or her own income and assets, but be counted as part of a higher-income household for purposes of the CBO analysis. For example, an elderly parent with high long-term care expenses covered by Medicaid can sometimes count as part of the household belonging to his or her adult son or daughter in the CBO data. In addition, Medicaid receipt is inferred based on responses to the U.S. Census Bureau's Current Population Survey, which involves some misreporting. For further information on how CBO calculates the value of Medicaid and Medicare benefits and allocates it to households, see Congressional Budget Office (2016b) and U.S. Census Bureau (1992).

81. Elmendorf, Furman, Gale, and Harris (2008).

82. All estimates except for those in the final two sentences are from the Urban-Brookings Tax Policy Center, and are reported in studies by Nunns, Burman, Rohaly, and Rosenberg (2015), Rosenberg, Burman, Nunns, and Berger (2016), Maag, Williams, Rohaly, and Nunns (2016), Auxier, Burman, Nunns, and Rohaly (2016), and Sammartino, Nunns, Burman, Rohaly, and Rosenberg (2016). Revenue cost estimates for the September revision of the Trump plan in the final two sentences are authors' calculations based on Tax Foundation estimates reported in Cole (2016) and baseline revenue projections from

Congressional Budget Office (2016a). Other estimates for the presidential primary tax plans include those from the Tax Foundation, including Pomerleau and Schuyler (2015, 2016), Schuyler and McBride (2015), Cole (2015), and Cole and Greenberg (2016), and those from Citizens for Tax Justice (2015a, 2015b) and McIntyre (2015). Static revenue estimates for given plans differ across these studies mainly because of different assumptions about how unspecified details would later be filled in by the candidates. So for example, the Tax Foundation estimates suggest static revenue loss amounting to about 5.5 percent of GDP during 2015–2024 for the original Trump plan, and 1.6 percent for the Cruz plan. The Tax Foundation also reports dynamic estimates which incorporate feedback effects from the changes in economic growth that their model suggests will happen as a result of each tax plan, and these estimates do differ substantially from the static Urban-Brookings Tax Policy Center estimates reported in the text. We'll consider economic effects of tax changes in chapter 4.

83. Kogan and Friedman (2014). The 2.2 percent of GDP figure is authors' calculation, which divides the $4.8 trillion nominal value of the proposed spending cuts for fiscal years 2015 through 2024 by the $218.3 trillion projected value of nominal GDP for fiscal years 2015 through 2024 from Congressional Budget Office (2015c).

84. Shapiro (2016) offers some analysis of the magnitude of spending cuts implied by the Cruz and Trump tax plans.

85. Donmoyer (1997, p. 1305).

86. At present, the federal government doesn't levy a special tax on movies. But in 1990 it did impose a "luxury" tax of 10 percent of the purchase price over $10,000 for furs and jewelry, over $30,000 for autos, over $100,000 for boats, and over $250,000 for airplanes. The luxury taxes have since been repealed.

87. For this reason, the deduction for medical expenses is limited to "involuntary" expenses and specifically excludes such things as elective cosmetic surgery. Some readers may be interested to know that in 2012 Brazil made cosmetic surgery—including breast implants, liposuction, and tummy tucks—deductible from income taxes, and allowed the deductions to be retroactive to procedures performed as far back as 2004. See <http://www.allure.com/beauty-trends/blogs/daily-beauty-reporter/2012/04/brazil-makes-plastic-surgery-tax-deductible.html>.

88. The interest rate spread between tax-exempt and taxable bonds is, however, significantly less than the top individual marginal tax rate, so that top-bracket investors can indeed receive a strictly higher after-tax rate of return by investing in those securities.

89. As the late eminent Irish economist, W.M. (Terence) Gorman (1976, p. 215) put it so eloquently, "When you have a wife and a baby, a penny bun costs threepence."

90. Note that an application of the benefit principle might suggest that larger families should have *higher* tax liabilities, reflecting the fact that many tax-funded benefits, like public education, increase with family size. This argument is made by Kaplow (1999).

91. Carasso and Steuerle (2005, figure 3).

92. Another way to reduce these horizontal inequities is to make the rate structure less progressive, but this comes at the expense of what many people view as a desirable degree of vertical equity.

93. One reason for abandoning the earlier system of taxing each spouse separately was that spouses in community property states could claim to earn half of family income,

thus lowering the couple's total taxes. Many states adopted community property laws, apparently so their residents could receive this benefit.

Chapter 4

1. Bush (2003).

2. The candidates' tax plans are summarized by Urban-Brookings Tax Policy Center (2015e).

3. Cruz (2015). Cruz's claim is based on a Tax Foundation "dynamic scoring" analysis reported in Pomerleau and Schuyler (2015). We discuss dynamic scoring and its uncertainties later in this chapter.

4. Haddon (2015).

5. The 2.7 percent growth rate is for the years 1974 through 2014, and its source is authors' calculation based on data from U.S. Bureau of Economic Analysis (2015, table 1.1.6).

6. Tankersley and Guo (2016) and Nunns, Burman, Rohaly, and Rosenberg (2015). Costa and O'Keefe (2015) and *The Economist* (2016) discuss Trump's statements on Social Security and Medicare.

7. Friedman (2016) and Drum (2016).

8. Krueger, Goolsbee, Romer, and Tyson (2016), and Romer and Romer (2016).

9. Clinton (2015a).

10. Keynes (1936, 1937) and Friedman (1962). Compared to Keynes, Friedman was considerably more optimistic that stable, rules-based monetary policy would smooth economic fluctuations sufficiently on its own, and was much less sanguine about the use of discretionary fiscal policy as a counter-cyclical measure. Friedman (1962, chapter 5) did admit that when the economy was constrained by the zero lower bound on interest rates, the argument for expansionary fiscal policy makes sense, although he thought that even in that case monetary policy might be able to solve the problem (Wessel 2010).

11. The data on interest rates on Baa corporate bonds is from the FRED database at the Federal Reserve Bank of St. Louis, <https://research.stlouisfed.org/fred2/series/BAA> (accessed August 28, 2015).

12. *MarketWatch* (2015).

13. Short- and long-term interest rate data is from the FRED database at the Federal Reserve Bank of St. Louis, <https://research.stlouisfed.org/fred2> (accessed August 28, 2015).

14. Sablik (2013b).

15. In fact, interest rates on some bonds have actually declined into slightly negative territory in recent years. For instance, in April 2015 the interest rate on 10-year Swiss government bonds fell to -0.055 percent (Moore and Giugliano 2015). Although at first blush this may seem impossible because one can always hold cash that earns a zero interest rate, a negative return can arise because holding wealth in cash or checking accounts is not costless and involves some risk (e.g., of a mattress fire), whereas some assets such as Swiss government bonds are considered to be extremely safe. Anderson

and Liu (2013) provide further discussion of these issues. Nonetheless, even in these cases, the negative nominal interest rates are close enough to zero that it is still appropriate to talk about an approximate zero lower bound on nominal interest rates.

16. Federal Reserve Bank of Cleveland (2016).

17. Krugman (2009 and 2012), Summers (2014), and Romer (1993) provide accessible arguments and evidence to support each of these assertions.

18. Krugman (2001, pp. 27–28).

19. An alternative solution would be for the central bank to somehow get people to expect a higher rate of inflation in the future, which would reduce *real* interest rates and stimulate the economy. This is difficult to achieve in an environment where short-term nominal interest rates have already been pushed to zero. Perhaps the central bank could somehow persuade people that in the future, it will let inflation rise higher than it normally would once the economy recovers. But that is difficult given how much effort rich-country central banks have exerted since the early 1980s to establish credible reputations for never letting inflation rise much above a target of around 2 percent per year.

20. Office of Management and Budget (2015, historical table 8.1). Note that "debt held by the public" includes debt held by the Federal Reserve System. Excluding debt held by the Fed would bring the debt number down to 30 percent of GDP in 2007 and 60 percent of GDP in 2014.

21. Federal Reserve Bank of St. Louis FRED data base, <https://research.stlouisfed.org/fred2/series/IRLTLT01USM156N#> (accessed September 24, 2015).

22. See Shapiro and Slemrod (2003a, 2003b) and Johnson, Parker, and Souleles (2006) for details of how taxpayers behaved on receiving the 2001 tax rebates, and Parker, Souleles, Johnson, and McClelland (2013) for evidence on the consumption response to the 2008 tax cut.

23. Sahm, Shapiro, and Slemrod (2012).

24. See, for example, Chodorow-Reich, Feiveson, Liscow, and Woolston (2012), Feyrer and Sacerdote (2011), and Wilson (2012). Nakamura and Steinsson (2014) provide corroborating evidence for a longer time period, based on the response of U.S. state economies to changes in federal military spending in the state. Romer (2011) and Auerbach (2012) offer accessible overviews of this and other evidence on the effectiveness of expansionary fiscal policy as a recession-fighting measure.

25. Ramey (2015) provides a review of this literature, and DeLong and Summers (2012) discuss why estimates from such studies may underestimate the impact of fiscal policy on the economy when we are at the zero lower bound. Examples of such studies include Romer and Romer (2010), Auerbach and Gorodnichenko (2012), Favero and Giavazzi (2012), Owyang, Ramey, and Zubairy (2013), Perotti (2012), and Riera-Chrichton, Vegh, and Vuletin (2016).

26. U.S. Bureau of Labor Statistics (2016, Series LNS14000000).

27. Yellen (2015) provides insight into the nature of the debate at the Fed over whether to raise interest rates in 2015.

28. U.S. Bureau of Labor Statistics (2016, Series LNS12300060). The unemployment rate is calculated as the number of people who do not have jobs but who are actively looking for work, divided by the number of people who have jobs plus the number of people

who do not have jobs but are actively looking for work. People who lack jobs and who have abandoned the search for a job are removed from both the numerator and the denominator.

29. Summers (2014, 2015, and 2016). Bernanke (2015a, 2015b, and 2015c) offers an interesting rejoinder to Summers.

30. Office of Management and Budget (2015, historical table 3.1). For projections of future interest spending, see figure 4.1.

31. Andrews (2003).

32. Speech at the Dallas Regional Chamber, Dallas, Texas, April 7, 2010. "Economic Challenges: Past, Present, and Future."

33. This judgment applies to deficits created (or surpluses reduced) by reducing taxes collected, holding constant government expenditure on consumption. It may not apply to increasing government-funded investment in infrastructure or education, which provide current and future benefits.

34. U.S. House of Representatives, Committee on the Budget (2015).

35. Okun (1975) and Saez and Stantcheva (2016).

36. Congressional Budget Office (2015b). The federal poverty line is from Office of the Assistant Secretary for Planning and Evaluation, U.S. Department of Health and Human Services (2016).

37. Finkelstein (2009).

38. Dusek (2006).

39. See Becker and Mulligan (1998) for an expression of this point of view.

40. Friedman (2003, p. A10).

41. For opposing views on the evidence about whether tax cuts automatically lead to lower government spending, see Calomiris and Hassett (2002) and Gale and Potter (2002).

42. Niskanen (2004).

43. Authors' calculations based on data in Office of Management and Budget (2015, historical tables 3.1 and 8.5).

44. According to authors' calculations based on data from Centers for Medicare and Medicaid Services (2014a, table 13.10), in fiscal year 2011, 18 percent of Medicaid expenditures were made on the behalf of people age 65 and over, and 43 percent of expenditures were made on behalf of disabled beneficiaries.

45. Authors' calculations based on Office of Management and Budget (2015, historical tables 3.1 and 8.5). Note that Affordable Care Act tax credits that offset liability from taxes are counted as tax reductions in figure 4.1.

46. Congressional Budget Office (2015a, table 2–1).

47. The health care cost growth projections in the Government Accountability Office study are from Centers for Medicare and Medicaid Services Office of the Actuary (2014), and assume that some planned cost-control measures in Medicare, such as a reduction in physician payments, will not be implemented, which would be consistent with recent

congressional behavior. See also Auerbach and Gale (2014) for further discussion of the cost growth assumptions in that report. Holahan and McMorrow (2015) discuss the recent slowdown in health care costs, possible explanations, and implications for the future.

48. Auerbach and Gale (2014, table 1).

49. Stein (1998, p. 32).

50. Pew Research Center (2013).

51. Authors' calculations based on data from Office of Management and Budget (2015, tables 3.1 and 8.5).

52. See Bakija, Kenworthy, Lindert, and Madrick (2016, chapter 3) for evidence on other rich countries. Jones (1995) pointed out the remarkable stability of long-run growth rates in real GDP per person in rich countries since the late 1800s, and performs formal statistical tests which generally reject the hypothesis that there have been any *permanent* changes in those growth rates in almost any of these countries. He argues that this poses a challenge for any theories that purport to show that a factor that exhibits permanent changes (such as taxes as a percentage of GDP) could be causing permanent changes in the growth rate of real GDP per person.

53. Bergeaud, Cette, and Lecat (2014) provide evidence on productivity growth rates in the United States and other countries since 1890.

54. See figure 4.2.

55. See figure 4.2.

56. Although, see Gordon (1998) for an argument that high personal tax rates, by providing an incentive to reclassify earnings as corporate rather than personal income for tax purposes, encourage corporate entrepreneurial activity because entrepreneurs can easily reclassify income for tax purposes. This could in theory cause a boost to economic growth to the extent that corporate entrepreneurial activity is an important driver of innovation and technological progress.

57. Bakija, Kenworthy, Lindert, and Madrick (2016, figure 3.1).

58. Ten of the current OECD countries—Chile, the Czech Republic, Estonia, Hungary, Iceland, Israel, Mexico, Poland, the Slovak Republic, and Slovenia—are missing data for substantial portions of the 1970 to 2012 period and so are not included in figure 4.4.

59. See Bakija, Kenworthy, Lindert, and Madrick (2016, chapter 3) for documentation of this fact for the 23 industrialized nations for which data on taxes as a percentage of GDP are available on a continuous basis going back to the early 1960s.

60. Slemrod (1995), Myles (2000), Huang and Frentz (2014), and Gale and Samwick (2014) review the literature and express skepticism that the cross-country or historical evidence establishes that higher taxes harm long-run economic growth. Bergh and Henrekson (2011), McBride (2012), and Gemmell and Au (2013) review the literature and argue that more recent cross-country evidence does show negative effects of taxes on economic growth. Even the authors arguing that taxes have negative effects on economic growth tend to qualify it in important ways. For example, Gemmell and Au suggest that the negative effects of taxes on long-run economic growth are largely offset by the positive effects on economic growth of the government spending that they finance. A big question about recent studies that claim to find a negative effect of taxes on growth is whether they distinguish the short-run correlation between changes in taxes and

movements of real GDP around its long-run trend, which are largely about the business cycle, from effects of taxes on the long-run trend. See Bakija, Kenworthy, Lindert, and Madrick (2016) and Bakija and Narasimhan (2016) for further discussion and evidence on this point, suggesting that better methods of isolating the long-run effects yield no evidence of negative effects of a permanent change in the level of taxes as a percentage of GDP on the long-run growth rates or levels of real GDP per person.

61. For the rest of this chapter, we refer to taxes other than lump-sum taxes.

62. U.S. Bureau of Economic Analysis (2015, table 1.12).

63. This argument applies even more directly when the base broadening refers to eliminating the deductibility of state and local income taxes. This may allow a lowering of the federal tax rate, but it does not permit an overall reduction in the combined rate of tax from local, state, and federal levels.

64. In fact, $50 is a lower bound on how much everyone is better off because we know that Roger's customers value his carpentry work at no less than $200 but possibly more. The numerical example assumes that this value is just exactly $200.

65. As discussed earlier, this is but one example where our country's (and every other country's) national income statistics will incorrectly measure the economic cost of tax disincentives. The statistics will record the $200 decrease due to lost labor income, but since the value of leisure is not included in national income, they ignore the $150 worth of extra leisure that Roger enjoys when taxed.

66. McClelland and Mok (2012).

67. Heim (2007, 2009) and Blau and Kahn (2007).

68. Imbens, Rubin, and Sacerdote (2001), Cesarini, Lindqvist, Notowidigdo, and Östling (2015), and Jacob and Ludwig (2012).

69. See Eissa and Liebman (1996), Meyer and Rosenbaum (2001), and Eissa and Hoynes (2004). Hoynes (2014) provides an accessible overview of this evidence.

70. Blundell, Duncan, and Meghir (1998).

71. Chetty, Guren, Manoli, and Weber (2013, table 1) review 9 studies on labor force participation, and find that on average a 10 percent increase in after-tax wage is associated with a 2.5 percent increase in the probability of working. Chetty (2012, table 1) reviews seven studies on hours worked, and finds that on average a 10 percent increase in after-tax wage is associated with a 1.5 percent increase in hours worked among those who are working. Summing the two effects yields the 4 percent figure cited in the text.

72. Meghir and Phillips (2010).

73. Meghir and Phillips (2010, p. 204).

74. Meghir and Phillips (2010, p. 252).

75. See Moffitt and Wilhelm (2000).

76. Eissa (1995) and Liebman and Saez (2006).

77. Keane (2011).

78. An example of an empirical study that attempts to take this into account is Imai and Keane (2004). See Keane (2011) for further discussion of the possible implications of that

study for the efficiency costs of taxation. Meghir and Phillips (2010, pp. 237–238) explain why Imai and Keane's findings are subject to multiple plausible interpretations, some of which imply large efficiency costs of taxation and some of which do not.

79. Chetty (2012).

80. Chetty, Guren, Manoli, and Weber (2013, figure 2) show a scatter plot of the logarithm of hours worked per adult versus the logarithm of one minus the tax rate on labor, using data from a small number of rich countries in the 1970s and the 1990s. The scatter plot implies a 10 percent increase in the after-tax wage is associated with about a 7 percent reduction in hours worked.

81. Kleven (2014).

82. Bakija, Kenworthy, Lindert and Madrick (2016, figure 3.6 and associated discussion).

83. Prescott (2004).

84. Alesina, Glaeser, and Sacerdote (2005). Jäntti, Pirttilä, and Selin (2015) perform an econometric analysis of micro data from numerous OECD countries between the 1970s and 2004 to estimate the effects of cross-country and cross-educational-group variation in wages on hours worked and labor force participation, while controlling for nonlabor income, time-invariant aspects of countries, education groups, and global annual average changes. Their conclusions about responsiveness are roughly similar to that of the literature reviews of Chetty and co-authors noted above. See Bakija, Kenworthy, Lindert, and Madrick (2016, chapter 3) for an accessible explanation of their strategy and findings.

85. For a few countries shown in figure 4.6, data on tax as a percentage of GDP is available for 1960 and from 1965 on, but missing for 1961 through 1964. In those cases, we compute the 1960–1969 average of tax as a percentage of GDP by replacing the 1961 through 1964 values with linear interpolations.

86. The line drawn through the scatter plot is the regression line estimated by an ordinary-least-squares regression. It implies that a 10 percent of GDP tax increase is associated with an increase of sixteen hours worked per year per working-age adult, although the relationship is not statistically significant.

87. Kleven (2014) corroborates the latter point. It is also worth noting that Davis and Henrekson (2005, table 2.4) fail to find evidence of a statistically significant negative effect of taxes on hours worked per adult when controlling for country fixed effects and year fixed effects in a panel of rich countries covering the years 1977, 1983, 1990, and 1995.

88. Kleven (2014).

89. Technically, these taxes eliminate the tax on the "normal" return to saving and investment and do exact a burden on above-normal returns. We discuss this issue in more detail in chapter 6.

90. Data for the saving rate are from the U.S. Bureau of Economic Analysis (2015). Net private saving is from table 5.1, line 3. Disposable personal income is gross national product (table 1.7.5, line 4) minus private consumption of fixed capital (table 1.7.5, line 6) minus total government receipts (table 3.1, line 1). We follow Gravelle (1994) in defining the after-tax rate of return but use somewhat different sources of data to construct a consistent series for 1960 to 2012. The marginal income tax rate on interest income is

from National Bureau of Economic Research (2015), the interest rate on Baa corporate bonds is from *Economic Report of the President 2015* (2015), and expected inflation data are from Federal Reserve Bank of Philadelphia (2015).

91. See Gale and Sabelhaus (1999) for a discussion of this issue.

92. Chetty, Friedman, Leth-Petersen, Nielsen, and Olsen (2014).

93. Gelber (2011).

94. Chirinko, Fazzari, and Meyer (1999) estimate that the effect is at the lower end of the range cited in the text, using panel data on U.S. firms from 1981 through 1991. Hassett and Hubbard (2002) review the broader literature and conclude that it suggests a 10 percent increase in the user cost of capital would be associated with a 5 to 10 percent decline in investment. Some recent studies have investigated this question by applying econometric techniques to panel data that follow firms over very long spans of time. Relative to the previous literature, this approach is better at identifying the long-run effect of persistent changes in the user cost of capital on investment, and purging the estimates of contamination from re-timing of investment in response to temporary changes in the user cost of capital. Smith (2008) applies this approach to panel data on firms from the United Kingdom and estimates that a 10 percent increase in the user cost of capital is associated with a 4 percent decline in investment, whereas Dwenger (2014) applies it to a panel of firms from Germany and estimates that a 10 percent increase in the user cost of capital is associated with a 10 percent decline in investment.

95. Chirinko, Fazzari, and Meyer (1999, pp. 73–75) and Auerbach (1996, table 2.3, column 2).

96. See House and Shapiro (2008) and Zwick and Mahon (2017).

97. It is difficult to determine the degree to which this is true in their studies, because data from the period after the temporary accelerated depreciation provisions expired were not yet available.

98. Yagan (2015).

99. Djankov, Ganser, McLiesh, Ramalho, and Shleifer (2010, tables 5B, 5C, and 5D, column 3). See Gravelle (2014) for a critique of this study, including discussion of problems with their measure of marginal effective tax rates, and evidence that correcting some of these problems reduces the magnitude of the estimated effect.

100. Zodrow (2010) reviews the empirical literature on the sensitivity of the location of overall investment and foreign direct investment to differences in corporate tax rates across countries, and concludes that corporate tax rate differentials do have an effect. In chapter 5 we discuss a study by Clausing (2016) which presents evidence that decisions of U.S. multinational companies about where to report that their profits are earned are very responsive to corporate tax rates, but that the location of their employment and physical capital is not.

101. Kawano and Slemrod (2016).

102. Lee and Gordon (2005) find that countries have higher economic growth rates during five-year periods when their statutory corporate tax rates are lower, based on an analysis of cross-country panel data that includes seventy countries from 1980 through the mid-1990s. Gemmell, Kneller, and Sanz (2015) find a much smaller negative effect of corporate tax rates on growth in a panel of OECD countries. In both cases, there are

questions about whether the studies are really picking up long-run effects. Bakija and Narasimhan (2016) use panel cointegration techniques, which are better for identifying long-run equilibrium relationships purged of short-run correlations that might be driven by the business cycle, and find no evidence that cuts in corporate tax rates are associated with real GDP per person rising above its long-run historical trend.

103. See Kleven (2014).

104. Technically the tax credit is for research and *experimentation* activities, not research and development.

105. Office of Management and Budget (2015, "Analytical Perspectives," table 14.1).

106. Congressional Budget Office (2014, p. 10).

107. Compared to taxation of commodities, deviating from uniform taxation of investment on efficiency grounds—say, by favoring machinery over structures or manufacturing over agriculture—is much harder to justify. See Slemrod (1990) for a nontechnical review of optimal tax theory.

108. Congressional Budget Office (2014) provides evidence of wide variation in effective income tax rates on the returns to different industries and different types of productive capital assets.

109. Already in the tax code is a 50 percent exclusion for capital gains for an original investor in a "qualified small business stock" who held the stock for at least five years; the gross assets of the business cannot exceed $50 million.

110. Hall and Rabushka (1995, p. 87) make this case. Hubbard (1998) and Gentry and Hubbard (2004) review the implications of capital market imperfections that prevent entrepreneurs from obtaining external financing.

111. For an expansion of this view, see Krugman (1994) or Slemrod (1992).

112. Hines (1999) and Wilson (1999) offer good summaries of the issues relating to taxation of multinational companies and tax competition. Rodrik (1997) and Baldwin and Krugman (2004) also offer interesting perspectives and evidence.

113. Rodrik (1997, p. 64).

114. By saying this, we are by no means endorsing export subsidies, which would cause an inefficient allocation of resources just as import tariffs would. See Slemrod (2011a, 2011b) for more discussion.

115. Kornblut and Blanton (2003).

116. Pomerleau (2015).

117. Some policies, such as the minimum wage, can in principle lead to involuntary unemployment even when the economy is operating normally. We leave these aside here to focus on tax policy issues. Because taxes reduce after-tax wages, they also can cause people who would be willing to work at the pre-tax wage to voluntarily decline employment at the after-tax wage.

118. See Davies and Whalley (1991) for a review of this issue.

119. Chapman (2006).

120. We focus on the subject of tax evasion in chapter 5.

121. Authors' calculations based on Internal Revenue Service, Statistics of Income Division, *Corporation Income Tax Returns, Complete Report* (various years).

122. See Feenberg and Poterba (1993). The figures they reported were slightly misleading because they failed to account for changes in the definition of adjusted gross income over the time period of the study. The text cites the corrected numbers presented in Slemrod (1996a).

123. See Saez, Slemrod, and Giertz (2012) for a critical survey of recent analyses of the high-income response to changes in marginal tax rates since the 1980s.

124. Sherwin Rosen of the University of Chicago discussed this "superstar" phenomenon in a 1981 article. A 1995 book written by Robert H. Frank of Cornell University and Philip J. Cook of Duke University, *The Winner-Take-All Society* (1995), documents many examples of it in the U.S. economy.

125. See Moffitt and Wilhelm (2000).

126. Feldstein and Feenberg (1996).

127. Whether tax increases on the rich are a bad idea depends on a person's views about the benefit of a more equal distribution of well-being. But regardless of how much one values equality, progressivity is less desirable the higher is the economic cost of higher marginal tax rates, which depends on the magnitude of the behavioral response they cause. In the extreme, consider the case of a "high-income Laffer curve," in which a higher top-bracket rate causes enough response as to *lower* the amount of tax collected on those affluent families. In this case, no one is better off, certainly not the high-income families that face the higher tax rate, and not anyone else because there is no extra revenue collected that could be used to lower others' tax burden or to increase social expenditures.

128. Fastis (1992) and Peers and Tannenbaum (1992).

129. See Parcell (1996).

130. Piketty and Saez (2003, updated 2016). We focus on income excluding capital gains both because capital gains tax rates changed in different ways than tax rates on ordinary income over time and because capital gains realizations fluctuate a great deal, mainly for reasons (such as stock-market valuations) that are unrelated to taxpayers' responses to incentives created by the tax code. In any event, using a measure that includes capital gains yields the same general patterns and in particular yields an even larger increase in incomes of the top 1 percent between 1980 and 2015. See Piketty and Saez (2003) for more details.

131. Goolsbee (1999) provides a formal analysis of how incomes at the top of the distribution responded to five major tax reforms between 1924 and 1966, finding mixed results.

132. Saez (2006). See also Piketty, Saez, and Stantcheva (2014).

133. Ponnuru (2007).

134. Cruz (2015).

135. Revenue as a percentage of GDP is from figure 2.2. The $164 billion estimate is reported in Steuerle (1992, p. 186).

136. Authors' calculations based on U.S. Bureau of Economic Analysis (2015, table 3.2), adjusted for inflation using the GDP deflator from line 1 of table 1.1.4.

137. Office of Management and Budget (2015, table 1.2).

138. This is calculated from the fourth quarter of 1994 to the fourth quarter of 2000 and from the fourth quarter of 2000 to the fourth quarter of 2006, based on data from U.S. Bureau of Economic Analysis (2015, table 7.1, row 19).

139. Each year for many years, former Senator Bob Packwood (R-OR) asked the Joint Committee on Taxation (JCT) to prepare an analysis of a 100 percent marginal tax rate applied to income over $100,000 or $200,000. Senator Packwood was not really considering supporting such a proposal but wanted to illustrate that the official government procedures would overestimate the amount of revenue a confiscating tax rate would generate. JCT responded reasonably to this request, calculating the revenue that would be raised if there were no behavioral responses but adding that "if the 100 percent tax rate were to be in effect for a substantial period of time ... then in our judgment there would be a substantial reduction in income-producing activity in the economy and, thus, a significant reduction in tax receipts to the federal government." This episode is discussed in written testimony of the staff of the Joint Committee on Taxation (1995).

140. Crippen (2002).

141. See Auerbach (2005) for a discussion of the pros and cons of dynamic revenue estimation.

142. Dubay (2015).

143. A description of the Tax Foundation's dynamic scoring model can be found at <http://taxfoundation.org/overview-tax-foundation-s-taxes-and-growth-model> (accessed August 26, 2016).

Chapter 5

1. Tritch (1998, p. 104).

2. Garcia (2002).

3. Government Accountability Office (2014a).

4. Government Accountability Office (2014b).

5. Commerce Clearing House (2015a, 2015b).

6. National Taxpayer Advocate (2012, p. 6).

7. Marcuss et al. (2013, figure 1).

8. Internal Revenue Service (1989, 2013a).

9. Internal Revenue Service (2015g, table 29).

10. Marcuss et al. (2013, table 3).

11. Marcuss et al. (2013, table 3) report that the average time spent per return was 12.54 hours, and the number of returns was approximately 142,985,000. Multiplying one by the other yields 1.8 billion hours.

12. Marcuss et al. (2013, table 3).

13. Marcuss et al. (2013, table 3) report that the average compliance cost per return was $373, and the number of income tax returns was approximately 142,985,000; multiplying the two yields $53 billion. The authors of that study compute the opportunity cost of time spent complying with individual income taxation by multiplying estimated hours spent on each return by an individual-specific estimated after-tax wage rate, with hourly wages and tax rates inferred from information reported on the income tax return. The average estimated opportunity cost of an hour is $14 (which we infer by subtracting the out-of-pocket cost of $198 per return from the total compliance cost of $373 per return, and then dividing the result by the 12.54 average of hours spent per return).

14. Contos, Guyton, Langetieg, and Vigil (2010, table 6).

15. Guyton, O'Hare, Starrianos, and Toder (2003, table 4). They report an average out-of-pocket cost of $149 per return for 2000, which we adjust to 2010 using the PCE price deflator from U.S. Bureau of Economic Analysis (2015, table 1.1.4, last updated July 30, 2015).

16. Guyton, O'Hare, Starrianos, and Toder (2003, table 5).

17. Blumenthal and Slemrod (1992, table 1). They report an average out-of-pocket cost of $66 per return for 1989, which we adjust to 2010 using the PCE price deflator from U.S. Bureau of Economic Analysis (2015, table 1.1.4, last updated July 30, 2015).

18. Another difference is that the estimates for 1989 include time and money spent to comply with both federal and state of Minnesota income taxes (Blumenthal and Slemrod 1992), whereas in the later IRS surveys incremental compliance costs from state and local income taxes are excluded (Contos, Guyton, Langetieg, Lerman, and Nelson 2012, p. 4).

19. Marcuss et al. (2013, table 5).

20. Figures in the previous three sentences are from Marcuss et al. (2013, table 3).

21. Authors' calculations based on data in Marcuss et al. (2013, table 5).

22. Internal Revenue Service (2015g, table 2).

23. Contos, Guyton, Langetieg, Lerman, and Nelson (2012, table 9).

24. Slemrod and Blumenthal (1996), Hall (1995, table 2), and Sandford (1995) show that compliance costs as a percentage of many different measures of firm size, such as sales, assets, and tax liability, are larger for smaller firms.

25. Estimates in the previous four sentences are for tax year 2009, and are authors' calculations based on data from Contos, Guyton, Langetieg, Lerman, and Nelson (2012, table 8), Internal Revenue Service, *Statistics of Income–2009 Corporation Source Book* (table 1), and Internal Revenue Service (2013d).

26. According to Slemrod (1997, p. 7), in 1996 the average Fortune 500 company spent $3.93 million to comply with corporate income tax laws at the federal, state, and local levels of government, which translates to $5.50 million in 2014 dollars, when adjusted by the PCE price deflator (U.S. Bureau of Economic Analysis 2015, table 1.1.4, updated July 30, 2015). About 75 percent of this amount was spent on complying with federal tax laws.

27. Slemrod (1997) and Slemrod and Blumenthal (1996).

28. Slemrod and Blumenthal (1996).

29. This is the rounded sum of the $53.3 billion of individual income tax compliance costs for 2010 from Marcuss et al. (2013, table 5), the $104.1 billion of corporate and partnership income tax compliance costs for 2009 reported in both Contos, Guyton, Langetieg, Lerman, and Nelson (2012, table 8) and Marcuss et al. (2013, table 6), and the $12.4 billion IRS budget for fiscal year 2010 reported in Internal Revenue Service (2015g, table 29).

30. According to Office of Management and Budget (2015, historical tables, table 2.1), individual and corporate income tax receipts were $1.090 trillion in fiscal year 2010, and are projected to be $1.820 trillion in fiscal year 2015.

31. Author's calculations based on Congressional Budget Office (2015c, 2015d) and Office of Management and Budget (2015, historical tables, tables 1.2 and 2.1).

32. The $135 billion compliance cost estimate for 2004 was based on extrapolations from some of the earlier surveys discussed above, and is explained in Slemrod (2004). Relative to the 2010 estimate, the 2004 estimate suggested higher individual income tax compliance costs ($85 billion), and lower business tax compliance costs ($40 billion). The 13.5 percent figure is calculated relative to individual and corporate income tax receipts of $998 billion in fiscal year 2004 (Office of Management and Budget, 2015, historical tables, table 2.1).

33. Office of Management and Budget (2015, historical tables, table 2.1).

34. Ryan (2010, p. 36).

35. Hall (1995) estimated individual and corporate income tax compliance costs were $140 billion. According to Office of Management and Budget (2015 historical tables, table 2.1), individual and corporate income tax receipts were $747 billion in fiscal year 1995, so Hall's estimate would be about 19 percent of that. Hall's study relies on a flawed Arthur D. Little (1988) estimate of the total hours spent by business for tax compliance and uses very high estimates of the cost per hour for both individuals and businesses, arbitrarily based on an average of the IRS budget per employee hour and the total revenues of a large accounting firm per employee hour. See Slemrod (1996b).

36. Blumenthal and Slemrod (1992, table 1).

37. Internal Revenue Service (2015g, tables 3 and 4).

38. Internal Revenue Service (2013b).

39. The 3.3 million returns filed through the Free File program are during fiscal year 2014 (Internal Revenue Service 2015g, table 4). A description of the Free File program, including eligibility rules, is available at Internal Revenue Service (2015h).

40. We consider here what makes any given tax structure complex, but continuous change in the tax system is itself complex, as time and effort are needed for taxpayers to learn and adjust to the new environment. This raises a classic problem of policy reform: should adopting a better policy be put off because of the costs of getting there?

41. As the British experience discussed in chapter 3 suggests, a lump-sum tax like a poll tax would likely also be difficult to enforce if it is widely perceived to be unfair and for this reason resisted.

42. In Europe, Iceland, Luxembourg, the Netherlands, Slovenia, and Switzerland do it (Andrews, Caldera Sánchez, and Johansson 2011).

43. Organisation for Economic Co-operation and Development (2015d, table 9.5), indicates that 19 of the 34 OECD countries operate "cumulative withholding" systems, under

which for the majority of employees the total amount of taxes withheld over the course of a fiscal year exactly matches their full-year tax liability.

44. Internal Revenue Service (2015k).

45. Burman (2011) includes the quote from Stewart, and offers a spirited (and funny) defense of the tax expenditure concept.

46. Bradford (2003, p. 98).

47. Section 45 of the Internal Revenue Code, discussed in Burman (2011).

48. This argument applies to negative externalities, as well. To reduce pollution-generating activities, it might be appropriate to levy a tax on them.

49. These represent the number of returns filed in fiscal year 2014, from Internal Revenue Service (2015g, table 2).

50. On the other hand, delivering subsidies to low-income families through the tax code means that they can no longer be exempted from filing returns. It also postpones the receipt of the tax credit to when the return is filed, unless the subsidy can be integrated into the employer withholding system. Currently, employers are allowed to make a limited portion of refundable EITC payments available to eligible workers throughout the year through their withholding systems, but this option is rarely used.

51. The 30 percent figure represents the percentage of all 2013 individual income tax returns that itemized deductions, and is the authors' calculation based on data from table 1.4 of Internal Revenue Service *Statistics of Income—2013 Individual Income Tax Returns*, Publication 1304.

52. There is no reason that the tax system could not provide a subsidy that is a constant rate for all taxpayers. If this is desired, it should be a refundable credit rather than an itemized deduction.

53. Authors' calculations based on data from the Center for Responsive Politics (2013a, 2013b) and U.S. House of Representatives, Committee on Ways and Means (2013).

54. The fact that Ways and Means Committee members receive greater-than-average contributions is undoubtedly partly due to the fact that those selected may be more prominent, or promising, politicians.

55. Strict limitations constrain what members of Congress can accept from lobbyists. For example, members of Congress can accept a dinner invitation but cannot accept payment for meals or gifts totaling more than $100 from any one source per year. The House gift rule can be found at U.S. House of Representatives, Committee on Ethics (2013).

56. Dlouhy (2012).

57. The analysis of tax complexity for the Jobs and Growth Tax Relief Reconciliation Act of 2003 can be found in Joint Committee on Taxation (2003c).

58. To see this, note that disallowing $1 of tax credit for every additional $10 of income imposes a 10 percent marginal tax rate on earning additional income.

59. Williams and Austin (2015).

60. Authors' calculations based on data from Urban-Brookings Tax Policy Center (2015f).

61. Urban-Brookings Tax Policy Center (2015g).

62. Corporate AMT tax revenue data is from Internal Revenue Service (2015j). In a survey of large businesses, 35.9 percent of respondents cited the AMT as the tax feature "contributing most to compliance costs" (Slemrod and Blumenthal 1996).

63. Authors' calculations based on Urban-Brookings Tax Policy Center (2015g).

64. Williams (2013) offers further explanation of the Fair Share Tax proposal.

65. For an example of a proposal to consolidate and simplify such provisions, see President's Advisory Panel on Federal Tax Reform (2005).

66. Internal Revenue Service (2015g, tables 3 and 4).

67. Gale and Holtzblatt (1997). Income tax subsidies for home mortgage interest no longer apply in the United Kingdom (Figari et al. 2012, table 3).

68. Almunia, Lockwood, and Scharf (2015, section 2.1) describe the tax treatment of charitable contributions in the United Kingdom.

69. Gale and Holtzblatt (1997) survey how no-return systems have worked around the world, and Organisation for Economic Co-operation and Development (2015d) offers an update on what many countries have been doing in this regard recently.

70. Organisation for Economic Co-operation and Development (2015d, table 9.5 and pp. 297–298) surveys fifty-five countries (including all thirty-four OECD countries plus a selection of twenty-one "emerging market" countries such as Russia, India, China, and South Africa), and reports that thirty-three of them use a "cumulative withholding" system which is intended to "ensure that for the majority of employees the total amount of taxes withheld over the course of a fiscal year matches their full-year tax liability," adding "… [t]o the extent this is achieved, employees are freed of the obligation to prepare and file an annual tax return …" (p. 297). In addition, as discussed in the text, Sweden, which does not operate a cumulative withholding system, achieves something similar with a TAR system.

71. Cordes and Holen (2010) discuss Tax Agency Reconciliation systems, including those in Sweden and Denmark.

72. Organisation for Economic Co-operation and Development (2015d, table 7.3).

73. State of California Franchise Tax Board (2006).

74. Bankman (2005).

75. State of California Franchise Tax Board (2014a).

76. State of California Franchise Tax Board (2014b) describes the replacement of ReadyReturn with CalFile. The new version of CalFile can be found at State of California Franchise Tax Board (2015).

77. The discussion of lobbying activity in this paragraph reflects the findings of a ProPublica investigation reported in Day (2013).

78. See, for example, National Taxpayer Advocate (2013b, section 5), Bankman (2008), and Ventry (2011).

79. Browning (2010).

80. See, for example, Kocieniewski (2011), Schwartz and Duhigg (2013), and Sullivan (2013).

81. The various parts of the evolving 2013 IRS scandals are detailed in Confessore, Kocieniewski, and Luo (2013), Norris (2013), Weisman (2013c, 2013d), Shesgreen (2013), and Nyhan (2013).

82. Hicks (2013).

83. The description of the Taxpayer Advocate Service is from their mission statement, available at <http://www.irs.gov/Advocate/The-Taxpayer-Advocate-Service-Is-Your -Voice-at-the-IRS> (accessed July 1, 2015). National Taxpayer Advocate (2012, 2013a, 2014) details problems caused by insufficient resources at the IRS.

84. A notable exception is the Social Security payroll tax, where benefits do depend on the amount of tax "contributions" made, although the relationship between contributions and benefits is far from one-for-one.

85. Lukacs (2008).

86. Hoffman (2012).

87. For his idea, Mr. Szilagyi received a check for $25,000 (Dubner and Levitt 2006).

88. The dependent exemption episode is chronicled in Lewin (1991) and Szilagyi (1990). A change in the information requirements for claiming the child care credit produced similar results. Beginning in tax year 1989, taxpayers who wanted to claim a child care credit had to report the name of the care provider plus the provider's Social Security number or employer identification number. As in the dependent exemption case, the results were immediate and striking. The number of taxpayers claiming child care credits dropped from 8.7 million in 1988 to 6 million in 1989, and the dollar amount claimed fell from $3.7 billion to $2.4 billion. Even more incredible, the number of taxpayers reporting self-employment income from child care services rose from 261,000 in 1988 to 431,000 in 1989, a 65 percent increase. The combination of the decrease in child care credits taken and increase in income reported by self-employed child care providers resulted in a $1.5 billion increase in tax revenues. See O'Neil and Lanese (1993).

89. Treasury Inspector General for Tax Administration (2015, figure 5).

90. Treasury Inspector General for Tax Administration (2012, figure 1; 2014a, figure 1).

91. The principal purpose of these studies is not to measure the tax gap but rather to help the IRS to devise a formula, based on the information provided on tax returns, for determining which returns are cost-effective to audit.

92. Internal Revenue Service (2016b). All statistics reported in this paragraph and the next one are authors' calculations based on data from this source.

93. Survey of the Gallup Organization, March 28–30, 1991, reported in Roper Center on Public Opinion Research (1993).

94. April 2005 Blum & Weprin / NBC poll reported in Bowman, Rugg, and Marsico (2013a, p. 129).

95. Internal Revenue Service Oversight Board (2014).

96. Bennett (2005, p. 8).

97. Turk, Muzikir, Blumenthal, and Kalambokidis (2007, p. 53) report the $811 figure and that 45 percent of returns claiming deductions for cash contributions had errors. We calculate that 29 percent of all returns in 2001 claimed itemized deductions for cash

contributions in 2001, based on Internal Revenue Service *Statistics of Income—2001 Individual Income Tax Returns, Complete Report,* Publication 1304, tables 1.1 and 2.1. The 13 percent figure comes from multiplying 45 percent by 29 percent.

98. The seminal article is Allingham and Sandmo (1972), who adapted to tax evasion the classic 1968 article of Nobel Laureate Gary Becker of the University of Chicago laying out a rational model of the decision to commit crime.

99. Johns and Slemrod (2010, pp. 404–405).

100. Schwartz and Duhigg (2013). Sullivan (2011b) provides further evidence of Apple's tax avoidance. Browning, Russolillo, and Vascellaro (2012) document Apple's becoming the most valuable company in the world by market capitalization.

101. Kocieniewski (2011).

102. Drucker (2010).

103. KPMG <http://www.kpmg.com/global/en/services/tax/tax-tools-and-resources/pages/corporate-tax-rates-table.aspx> (accessed July 3, 2015) reports an Irish statutory corporate tax rate of 12.5 percent for 2015. Hines (1999) offers an accessible explanation of tax rules applying to U.S. multinational corporations and how various avoidance strategies work.

104. Internal Revenue Service (2006).

105. Gravelle (2015a) provides a concise summary of tax avoidance strategies involving allocation of debt and earnings stripping, and existing and proposed policy responses to these strategies.

106. See, for example, Kleinbard (2016).

107. The tax gap estimate is from Internal Revenue Service (2016b). Gravelle (2015a, p. 19) reports: "There are no official estimates of the cost of international corporate tax avoidance … In general, the estimates are not reflected in the overall tax gap estimate."

108. In the previous two sentences, the data on profits, effective tax rates, and workforce are from Clausing (2016, figure 1) and Keightley and Stupak (2015, figure 2).

109. Sullivan (2011a).

110. Clausing (2016).

111. Zucman (2014; 2015, chapter 5). Gravelle (2015a) surveys other estimates of the magnitude of profit shifting and some of the challenges involved in measuring it.

112. Dowd, Landefeld, and Moore (2014).

113. Dharmapala (2014).

114. Clausing (2016).

115. Joint Committee on Taxation (2003b).

116. Kocieniewski (2011) notes that General Electric's tax avoidance strategies rely not just on ambiguity over appropriate transfer prices for intellectual property, but also on extensive foreign lending and leasing operations that help facilitate effective tax shelters.

117. Sullivan (2011a).

118. Desai, Foley, and Hines (2006) cited in Dharmapala (2014, p. 444).

119. The new M-3 filing requirement was effective for any taxable year ending on or after December 31, 2004. A proposal like the new M-3 is discussed in Mills and Plesko (2003). Lenter, Shackelford, and Slemrod (2003) discuss the pros and cons of greater public disclosure of corporate tax return information.

120. See, for example, Sullivan (2011a) and testimony before Congress by former Joint Committee on Taxation chief of staff Edward Kleinbard discussed in Sheppard (2008).

121. Sullivan (2011a) discusses and advocates the targeted approach. Government Accountability Office (2013) offers an accessible discussion of the pros and cons of ending deferral.

122. Mider and Drucker (2016).

123. Fleischer (2016) and Humer and Pierson (2016).

124. KPMG <http://www.kpmg.com/global/en/services/tax/tax-tools-and-resources/pages/corporate-tax-rates-table.aspx> (accessed July 1, 2015).

125. Quoted in Sablik (2013a, p. 30).

126. Clausing and Avi-Yonah (2008) and Zucman (2014, 2015) make the case for formulary apportionment, while Altshuler and Grubert (2010) provide a critique.

127. For insightful discussion of these and other creative approaches for reforming taxation of multinational corporations, see Gravelle (2015a, 2015b), Grubert and Altshuler (2013), Toder and Viard (2014), Auerbach (2010), Kleinbard (2015), and Shaviro (2014).

128. Khadem (2015) and Kahn and Penny (2016).

129. Organisation for Economic Co-operation and Development (2015e) offers a concise summary of the final recommendations.

130. Further discussion of, and reactions to, the OECD BEPS recommendations can be found in Keightley and Stupak (2015), Clausing (2016), and Avi-Yonah and Xu (2016).

131. Zucman (2014, 2015).

132. Zucman (2015, p. 53).

133. Zucman (2015, p. 3).

134. Internal Revenue Service (2014h).

135. Browning (2009), Protess and Silver-Greenberg (2014), and Zucman (2015).

136. Wood (2014).

137. Drucker (2016), *South China Morning Post* (2014), Tax-News.com (2015), and Tax Justice Network (2014).

138. Zucman (2015).

139. Tax Justice Network (2014).

140. Zucman (2015).

141. Information so far in this paragraph is based on Hall and Taylor (2016).

142. Zucman (2015, table 1).

143. Cassidy (2016).

144. Information in this paragraph is from Drucker (2016). The quotation is from Andrew Penney of Rothschild & Co., quoted in Drucker.

145. Internal Revenue Service (2015g, table 9a).

146. Internal Revenue Service, *Internal Revenue Service Data Book*, Publication 55B (various years).

147. Internal Revenue Service (2015g, table 9a).

148. Internal Revenue Service (2015g, table 9a).

149. Internal Revenue Service (2015g, table 9a).

150. Internal Revenue Service (2015g, table 14).

151. The 86 percent figure is the amount of individual income tax payments withheld, divided by total income tax, both based on final data for tax year 2013, from Internal Revenue Service (2015i).

152. This represents the number of returns with overpayment refunds divided by the total number of individual income tax returns, based on preliminary data for 2012, from Internal Revenue Service (2015i).

153. Internal Revenue Service (2012a).

154. The new information reporting requirements enacted in the Housing and Economic Recovery Tax Act of 2008 are described in Joint Committee on Taxation (2009, pp. 249–252). Subsequent developments in the implementation of the law are described in Elliott (2009) and Coder (2012).

155. Steuerle (1986, p. 27). Former IRS Commissioner Douglas Shulman (2011) refers to a 6-to-1 return on requested additional enforcement personnel.

156. For a detailed account of this argument, see Frey and Jegen (2001). Luttmer and Singhal (2014) review the theory and evidence on this and other related forms of "tax morale." Gneezy and Rustichini (2000) find evidence broadly consistent with Frey's hypothesis, but in the context of Israeli day care centers. They randomly assigned some day care centers to implement a policy of fining parents who show up more than ten minutes late to pick up their children. No fine was imposed in the control group. They find that lateness *increased* in the treatment group compared to the control group, and interpret this as evidence that a fine can cause deterioration in pro-social behavior. Perhaps having to pay a monetary fine reduced the guilty conscience associated with lateness, having the perverse effect of reducing the deterrent to lateness.

157. Public opinion data is from Bowman, Rugg, and Marsico (2013a, p. 128; 2013b, p. 1). The Government Accountability Office (2005) found evidence of reduced waiting times and improved accuracy of answers on the IRS toll-free telephone helpline and noted substantial improvements in the services provided through the IRS website.

158. Internal Revenue Service Oversight Board (2014, p. 8).

159. See, for example, Luo and Strom (2010).

160. Confessore, Kocieniewski, and Luo (2013) discuss the early stages of the 2013 scandal. Cohen (2013), Weisman (2013d), Nyhan (2013), and Shesgreen (2013) discuss later revelations that IRS reviews also targeted liberal groups, continuing disputes over the degree to which treatment was or was not evenhanded, and the absence of evidence that the Obama administration was involved. Nagourney and Shane (2011) report that tape recordings capture Nixon "ordering the use of tax audits against opponents."

161. Confessore (2013) discusses the proposal for revised regulations. National Taxpayer Advocate (2013c) presents an extensive set of proposals for reforms. The IRS statement regarding public comments on the proposed 501(c)(4) regulations and planned revisions is available at <https://www.irs.gov/uac/newsroom/irs-update-on-the-proposed-new-regulation-on-501-c-4-organizations> (accessed August 28, 2016).

162. Clement (2013).

163. The reports mentioned in the text are National Taxpayer Advocate (2013a) and Treasury Inspector General for Tax Administration (2013).

164. The source of the figures on the IRS budget as a percentage of GDP is authors' calculations based on Internal Revenue Service (2015g, table 29) and Office of Management and Budget (2015, historical tables, table 1.2). Sources for IRS employment and returns filed are authors' calculations based on data from Internal Revenue Service (2015g, tables 2 and 30; 1992, tables 2 and 30). Figures for numbers of employees are based on "average positions realized."

165. Treasury Inspector General for Tax Administration (2013, "Highlights" section).

166. National Taxpayer Advocate (2014, p. 2).

167. Internal Revenue Service (2015g, table 30; 2012b, table 30).

168. Statistics in the previous two sentences are from Internal Revenue Service (2015g, table 9a; 1998, table 11).

169. Treasury Inspector General for Tax Administration (2014b, "Highlights" section; 2013, "Highlights" section).

170. National Taxpayer Advocate (2013a, p. 28 and p. xiv) and Government Accountability Office (2014a).

171. This argument is presented in Yitzhaki (1974).

172. Luttmer and Singhal (2014), Torgler (2007), Alm and Jacobson (2007), and Alm (2012) review various aspects of the relevant empirical literature.

173. Turk, Muzikir, Blumenthal, and Kalambokidis (2007) present the evidence from the United States, and Fack and Landais (2016) present the evidence from France.

174. Hessing, Elffers, Robben, and Webley (1992, p. 298).

Chapter 6

1. We computed the average tax rates in figure 6.1 with the tax calculator program described in Bakija (2016) applied to data on hypothetical married couples with two dependent children at AGI levels that are multiples of 100. To impute typical values of line items on Form 1040 at each AGI level we first compute the average amount of

statutory adjustments, each type of itemized deduction (conditional on itemizing), qualified dividends, capital gains, and credits (other than the EITC and Child Tax Credit,
which are computed by the tax calculator) all as shares of gross income, in each of many
ranges of AGI from data in tables 1.4, 2.1, and 3.3 of Internal Revenue Service, *Statistics
of Income—2013 Individual Income Tax Returns,* Publication 1304. We assign the shares for
each AGI range to families with AGI at the midpoint of that range, linearly interpolate
the shares for AGI values between the midpoints, and then multiply the shares by gross
income to impute the values of each line item on the tax form (setting itemized deductions to zero for non-itemizers). At each income level, we compute tax once for an item-
izer and once for a non-itemizer. The average tax rate at each income level shown in
figure 6.1 is a weighted average of the two, where the weights represent the share of
returns at that income level that do and do not itemize deductions.

2. We compute the revenue-neutral single tax rate to be 17.77 percent, based on data
from Internal Revenue Service *Statistics of Income—2013 Individual Income Tax Returns,*
Publication 1304 in the following way. The numerator is "total income tax, all returns,
total" (table 3.3, column 51, first row), minus the sum of "refundable credits used to offset
all other taxes" (table 3.3, column 67, first row) and "refundable credits refundable
portion, all returns, total" (table 3.3, column 93, first row). Note that "total income tax"
already subtracts out the nonrefundable portion of all credits, and includes the effects of
the alternative minimum tax and reduced rates on capital gains and qualified dividends.
The denominator is "taxable income, all returns, total" (table 1.4, column 132, first row).

3. The $12,795 is approximately $3,138 billion in federal tax revenue raised in 2014 (from
table 2.1), divided by a population of 245 million people age 18 or over in 2014 (from
U.S. Census Bureau, 2015b).

4. It also introduced a rate below the basic rate in 1992, which applied only to savings
income after 2008, and was completely dropped in 2015. Starting in 2010, an even higher
rate was added, leaving the United Kingdom with three rates at present. See <https://
www.gov.uk/government/uploads/system/uploads/attachment_data/file/418669/
Table-a2.pdf>.

5. The tax described here would be a 25 percent tax on the value of purchases *excluding*
tax, which is the more common practice for retail sales taxes. We use the equivalent tax-
inclusive tax rate to simplify the exposition. The alternative ways of describing the rate
of tax under alternative consumption taxes are discussed in more detail in chapter 7.

6. The assertion does, though, depend on other aspects of the example, especially that
the rate of consumption tax does not change from year to year.

7. This is net worth of households and nonprofit organizations. Board of Governors of
the Federal Reserve System (2015, table B.101.e).

8. Estimate is for 2013, and is from Bricker, Henriques, Krimmel, and Sabelhaus (2016,
figure 5).

9. Authors' calculations based on data in Bricker et al. (2014, table 2) and U.S. Census
Bureau (2014, table H-10).

10. Warren (1996) offers a more detailed treatment of the following discussion.

11. Domar and Musgrave (1944).

12. For instance, the Hall-Rabushka flat tax proposal places limitations on the deductibility of business losses.

13. The difficulties associated with distinguishing labor income from capital income become particularly acute in the context of the *dual income tax* system adopted in some Scandinavian countries, an approach that we discuss in chapter 8.

14. Gordon, Kalambokidis, Rohaly, and Slemrod (2004).

15. Recall that if the consumption tax were levied on the price exclusive of tax, it would have to be set at a 25 percent rate to be equivalent to a 20 percent tax on wage and salary income.

16. See Sabelhaus (1993) for an examination of consumption and saving rates by income level.

17. The precise statement is that the present discounted value of consumption must equal the present discounted value of labor earnings and inherited wealth.

18. See Dynan, Skinner, and Zeldes (2004) for evidence that high-income people save a larger share of their lifetime incomes.

19. Aaron and Galper (1985) present an argument for accompanying a consumption tax with a tax on bequests.

20. Discussion of various reasons why a consumption tax is not *necessarily* more economically efficient than an income tax can be found in Slemrod (1990, pp. 160–161), Saez (2002), Shaviro (2007), Bankman and Weisbach (2010), and Diamond and Saez (2011).

21. Cashin (2013) finds evidence that household expenditures on durable goods increased in response to preannounced future increases in VAT rates in Japan and New Zealand.

22. We mention ethanol here because, for a few months in most every presidential election cycle, the tax preference for ethanol attracts a lot of attention. Ethanol is an alternative fuel made from corn, and the caucuses in the corn state of Iowa are the first major event of the U.S. presidential election process. Under current law, the federal excise tax on gasoline is reduced for ethanol-blended fuel or, alternatively, refiners can claim an income tax credit per gallon of ethanol used to produce ethanol-blended gasoline. In 2011, the issue caused a public dispute between conservative former Senator Tom Coburn (R-OK) and conservative Grover Norquist of Americans for Tax Reform (ATR). Coburn favored eliminating the subsidy and Norquist said this would break ATR's Taxpayer Protection Pledge, in which lawmakers promise not to raise taxes, unless it includes an offsetting tax cut. See Bolton (2011).

23. Bush's plan would eliminate deductions for state and local taxes, and would limit all other itemized deductions other than charitable contributions to no more than 2 percent of AGI (Burman et al. 2015). Rubio's plan would allow interest on only the first $300,000 of mortgage debt to be deducted (Schuyler and McBride 2015).

24. Office of Management and Budget (2015, "Analytical Perspectives," table 14.1). Personal income tax revenues were $1,395 billion in fiscal year 2014 (Office of Management and Budget, 2015, "Analytical Perspectives," table 12.1). This latter figure is used to calculate the increase in personal income tax rates necessary to finance deductions and exclusions throughout the rest of this chapter.

25. Authors' calculation based on data from Joint Committee on Taxation (2015e, table 3).

26. The best argument may be that a federal tax preference offsets a bias against housing due to the heavy reliance of local governments on property taxes. Many economists argue, however, that property taxes on housing act not as a disincentive to purchase housing but rather as the price for obtaining local public services, predominantly elementary and secondary education; houses cost more in places where the government provides better services, and that is taken into account when people choose where to live. To the extent that local property taxes are a user charge for public services, they do not act as a disincentive to purchase housing, and the argument for offsetting preferences in the federal income tax does not apply.

27. This evidence is discussed in Glaeser and Shapiro (2003). Note, though, that Glaeser and Shapiro conclude that, whatever the spillover benefits of homeownership, the effect of the home mortgage interest deduction on the homeownership rate is minimal.

28. If, however, tax reform leads to lower interest rates, the hit to housing prices could be eased. Lower interest rates would make house buying less expensive, which would help support demand and prices. Moving to a consumption tax should put downward pressure on interest rates because it eliminates the tax on lenders' interest income and eliminates the deductibility of borrowers' interest payments; as a result, lenders should be willing to accept a lower pre-tax interest rate, and borrowers will be less willing to tolerate a high pre-tax interest rate. On the other hand, because a consumption tax removes tax on the normal return to investment, firms would probably increase their demand for loanable funds, which would push up interest rates. In an analysis that takes many of the relevant factors into account, Martin Feldstein of Harvard University concluded that interest rates are more likely to go up than down if the current income tax were replaced with a consumption tax. See Feldstein (1995) and Hall and Rabushka (1995, pp. 94–95).

29. Poterba (1990) finds that single-family housing starts showed similar patterns in the United States and Canada after 1986, despite the fact that Canada did not have a tax reform that made owner-occupied housing less attractive. Moreover, in the 1970s and 1980s, movements in the real price of single-family homes in the United States were only partially consistent with tax-induced changes in the cost of housing.

30. In 2013, the homeownership rate was 67.6 percent in Canada; it was 64.5 percent in the United States in 2014. The Canadian rate is from Statistics Canada (2015). The U.S. rate is from the U.S. Census Bureau (2015a).

31. See Bourassa, Haurin, Hendershott, and Hoesli (2013). Of course, this does not rule out the possibility that the deduction leads to a higher homeownership rate, other things equal.

32. See Gale (2001) and Bruce and Holtz-Eakin (2001) for more details.

33. See Glaeser (2010) and Shiller (2014) for further discussion of these issues.

34. Office of Management and Budget (2015, "Analytical Perspectives," tables 12.1 and 14.1).

35. See Glied and Remler (2002) for a more detailed discussion of the economic issues involved in health insurance.

36. Cutler (2014, p. 3).

37. The facts noted in the previous two sentences are taken from Kaiser Commission on Medicaid and the Uninsured (2013b, figure 3).

38. The description of the provisions of the Affordable Care Act below draws on Cutler (2010, 2014) and the Henry J. Kaiser Family Foundation (2013).

39. The federal poverty line is from Office of the Assistant Secretary for Planning and Evaluation, U.S. Department of Health and Human Services (2016).

40. The quote from Orszag is from Goldstein (2015). The original provisions of the Cadillac tax are described in Joint Committee on Taxation (2011, pp. 303–304), and the 2015 changes are described in Goldstein (2015) and Blase (2015).

41. Facts in the previous two sentences are from Kaiser Commission on Medicaid and the Uninsured (2015, p. 3).

42. Kliff (2015) describes the many different provisions of the ACA that are intended to improve the efficiency of providing health care and slow the growth of costs, and summarizes some early evidence.

43. Cutler (2014, pp. 6–9).

44. See Mulligan (2015) and Cutler (2013) for further discussion of these concerns.

45. The revenue cost of the charitable contribution deduction in the personal income tax is from Office of Management and Budget (2015, "Analytical Perspectives," table 14.1).

46. Stern (2013) offers an accessible account of problems of this nature.

47. According to the Center on Philanthropy at Indiana University (2007, p. 28), about 31 percent of the dollar value of charitable donations were "focused on the needs of the poor," which includes giving to help the poor meet basic needs, and giving that supports college financial aid for low-income students. Our calculations based on data from table 9 of the same report suggest that among households with incomes of $200,000 or above, who as noted above receive 68 percent of the value for income tax subsidies for charity, 30 percent of the aggregate value of their donations went to education, 21 percent went to religion, 15 percent went to the arts, and 13 percent to went to health. Indiana University Lilly Family School of Philanthropy (2015) indicates that for all donors, in 2014, the three largest categories of charitable donations were religion (32 percent), education (15 percent), and human services (12 percent).

48. Internal Revenue Service audit data suggests that, in 2001, misreporting accounted for 15 percent of the value of cash contributions deductions and 16 percent of the value of noncash contributions deductions (Turk, Muzikir, Blumenthal, and Kalambokidis 2007). Donations of cars offer a fascinating example of potential abuse of the deduction system. Donors used to be allowed to deduct the "fair market value" of the donated car, but the IRS suspected that many were claiming significantly more than that, so that the deduction sometimes saved more in taxes than the car was actually worth. Comparing eBay prices to taxpayer valuations, Ackerman and Auten (2006) concluded that average taxpayer valuations in 2003 and 2004 were implausibly high. The regulations were changed so that, as of 2005, if the claimed value exceeds $500, the deduction is limited to the gross proceeds from the sale of the donated item by the charitable organization.

49. The tax savings could be higher than 35 cents due to state taxes and various other considerations, such as the fact that donating appreciated assets enables one to avoid tax on capital gains.

50. This evidence is discussed in Bakija (2013).

51. See Bakija (2013) and Bakija and Heim (2011) for the evidence discussed in the previous two sentences.

52. Authors' calculations based on data from Joint Committee on Taxation (2015e, table 3).

53. A number of laboratory and field experiments find that a given incentive for donations has a larger impact on resources received by a charity when it is framed as a match compared to when it is framed as a deduction. See Andreoni and Payne (2013) and Blackman (2015) for overviews of this evidence.

54. Authors' calculations based on Joint Committee on Taxation (2015e, table 3).

55. Office of Management and Budget (2015, "Analytical Perspectives," table 14.1).

56. Authors' calculation based on data in table 1.4 of Internal Revenue Service *Statistics of Income—2013 Individual Income Tax Returns*, Publication 1304.

57. Internal Revenue Service (2014a).

58. Authors' calculation based on data in table 1.4 of Internal Revenue Service *Statistics of Income—2013 Individual Income Tax Returns*, Publication 1304.

59. Internal Revenue Service (2015c).

60. Internal Revenue Service (2015l).

61. Authors' calculations based on data in Bryant and Gober (2013, tables 5 and 6). There were 3.5 million contributors to traditional IRAs and 5.8 million contributors to Roth IRAs in 2010.

62. Some of those IRA contributors might have been members of a family where at least one spouse was not contributing at the limit, and a few might have been people who otherwise would have saved less than the limit but were induced by the IRA to save enough extra to get exactly to the limit.

63. Bryant and Gober (2013).

64. Copeland (2014, figure 2), based on data from the 2013 Survey of Consumer Finances. 6.5 percent of families participated in both a defined-benefit and a defined-contribution plan.

65. This comes from Purcell (2009, table 3), based on an analysis of the Survey of Income and Program Participation. It is possible that some of the 92 percent of participants who were contributing less than $1,000 per month were constrained by a lower limit imposed by their employers, but this situation is rare. For instance, a Government Accountability Office (2001) study of data on 1,831 defined-contribution pension participants provided by a New York law firm that administers pension plans found that only 4 percent of participants were constrained by a contribution limit imposed by employers.

66. Choi, Laibson, Madrian, and Metrick (2002) and Thaler and Benartzi (2004) discuss evidence on the effects of default options in employer-provided pensions. Bernheim (2002) discusses theory and evidence for behavioral models of saving more generally.

67. In one plan, called "Save More Tomorrow™" and outlined in Thaler and Benartzi (2004), employees agree in advance to save a portion of future salary raises for retirement.

68. However, the plan is not effectively designed for achieving its intended purpose, as the credit is nonrefundable and therefore few people can benefit. In addition, the program suffers from the problem, discussed above, that it subsidizes deposits into an account rather than saving.

69. Such a proposal was floated in 2003 by the Bush administration. U.S. Department of the Treasury (2003) describes the administration's proposal, and Burman, Gale, and Orszag (2003) provide a critique.

70. See U.S. Department of the Treasury (1992).

71. Barlett and Steele (1998).

72. Congressional Budget Office (2014) presents estimates of how marginal effective tax rates on investment differ across industries, which corroborates the claims made in the text.

73. Cato Institute (2003).

74. Authors' calculations based on data in Parisi (2015, table 1).

75. For this example, we ignore inflation and therefore the issue just discussed—that some of the increase in the stock price (the part that just keeps up with price level increases) does not represent income at all.

76. For example, if you bought a share of Pfizer stock at $100, you would owe no tax until you sold it. If you sold it five years later at $300, $200 of capital gains would be taxable in the year of sale, even if the $200 increase all occurred in the first year that you held the stock.

77. Bakija and Gentry (2016).

78. This problem was eloquently stated by the economics Nobel Laureate William Vickrey (1977): "It cannot be too strongly emphasized that there is no way in which capital gains can be distinguished from other forms of income without creating a host of arbitrary and capricious distortions, which on the one hand will place a heavy burden on the administration of the tax, and on the other will lead to a whole complex of unnatural practices designed to convert what might ordinarily appear as ordinary income fully taxable into the capital gains eligible for various kinds of special favor. ... There is no reason to suppose that the types of capital formation that might be promoted through special favors to capital gains will have any special advantage over others, and every reason to suppose that the distortions introduced by this form of investment promotion will materially detract from the advantages that might be secured."

79. Indeed, allowing capital losses to be fully deductible against other income would provide an incentive to purposely hold portfolios with negatively correlated (when one goes up in price, the other goes down) assets, so that there are always assets to be sold with losses that can be offset against other income.

80. The number of estate tax returns filed in 2013 is from <http://www.irs.gov/file _source/pub/irs-soi/13es01fy.xls> (accessed July 20, 2015). We divide this by the number of deaths of people aged 25 or above in 2012, which is when most 2013 estate tax return filers died. The number of 2012 deaths is from Centers for Disease Control and Prevention (2014) <http://www.cdc.gov/nchs/data/nvsr/nvsr63/nvsr63_09.pdf> (accessed July 20, 2015).

81. Authors' calculations based on Internal Revenue Service *Statistics of Income* data found at <http://www.irs.gov/file_source/pub/irs-soi/13es01fy.xls> (accessed July 20, 2015).

82. Federal tax revenues is defined here as the sum of current tax receipts, contributions for government social insurance, and estate and gift tax receipts (U.S. Bureau of Economic Analysis, 2015, tables 3.2 and 5.11).

83. Data on estate tax revenue is from U.S. Bureau of Economic Analysis (2015, table 5.11). Data on individual income tax returns is from Internal Revenue Service *Statistics of Income –2013 Individual Income Tax Returns*, Publication 1304. Figure for income tax revenue is "total income tax" from table 3.3.

84. Poterba and Weisbenner (2001, p. 440) estimate, based on the 1998 Survey of Consumer Finances, that expected decedents in 1998 with estates above $5 million would have $21.3 billion of net worth and that $8.9 billion of that net worth would represent unrealized capital gains. Some portion of these unrealized gains would represent compensation for inflation, and some would be generated by corporate earnings already taxed by the corporation income tax.

85. Estate tax return data is from <http://www.irs.gov/file_source/pub/irs-soi/13es01fy.xls> (accessed July 21 2015), and income tax return data is from Parisi (2015, table 1).

86. Kopczuk and Slemrod (2003, figure 7.2), based on data from IRS, Statistics of Income Division (various years).

87. See Bakija, Gale, and Slemrod (2003) for evidence on the impact of estate and inheritance taxes on charitable bequests. Joulfaian (2001) and Auten and Joulfaian (1996) find evidence that giving during life is sensitive to estate tax rates.

88. See Kopczuk and Slemrod (2001). Holtz-Eakin and Marples (2001) find evidence that people who are born in states with larger inheritance and estate taxes tend to accumulate somewhat less wealth by the time they are old. However, their data (from the Health and Retirement Survey, a random sample of about 8,000 elderly households) contain hardly any very rich people, so it is not clear whether this result extends to the people who would be affected by repeal of the estate tax.

89. Gale and Perozek (2001) discuss the theory of how estate tax repeal might affect saving.

90. Holtz-Eakin, Joulfaian, and Rosen (1993).

91. Estate tax return data is from <http://www.irs.gov/file_source/pub/irs-soi/13es01fy.xls> (accessed July 21, 2015). Business assets aside from publicly traded stock is defined here as the sum of closely held stock, private equity and hedge funds, other limited partnerships, and other noncorporate business assets for all taxable returns. Net worth of taxable estates is the value of gross estate for tax purposes for all taxable returns minus the value of debts and mortgages for all taxable returns.

92. Internal Revenue Service (2014f).

93. Harris Interactive and Tax Foundation (2009, question 645, p. 5).

94. The poll results are from National Public Radio, Kaiser Family Foundation, and Kennedy School of Government (2003). From the NPR poll, the 39 percent figure is the

product of the 57 percent who say they favor eliminating the estate tax, and the 69 percent of those people who agree that "it might affect YOU someday" is one of the reasons they favor eliminating it. Overall, 52 percent of respondents supported keeping the estate tax if the exemption were raised to $5 million.

95. Kuziemko, Norton, Saez, and Stantcheva (2015).

Chapter 7

1. Sales Tax Institute (2015).

2. Senator Richard Lugar (1995) advocated a national retail sales tax in the 1996 Republican presidential primaries. Alan Keyes (2000) advocated a similar plan in the 2000 Republican presidential primaries. Mike Huckabee supported the "FairTax" national retail sales tax plan in 2008 (Redburn 2008) and again in 2016, and Ron Paul supported a similar plan in 2012 (*New York Times* 2012c), but his son, Rand Paul, supported a different kind of consumption tax (a VAT) in his 2016 campaign for the Republican nomination.

3. Some states, such as Michigan, Ohio, and Texas, have enacted modified versions of a *gross receipts tax*, which has a tax base that is all sales of businesses regardless of whether the purchaser is another business or a final consumer. This type of tax is subject to *cascading*, where the total tax penalty on a product is higher, the more businesses are involved in the production and distribution chain. The gross receipts tax has (thankfully) not yet been prominent in discussions of federal tax reform. See Pogue (2007) for more information on gross receipts taxes.

4. Organisation for Economic Co-operation and Development (2014b, p. 18).

5. Cnossen (1998, p. 399).

6. From 1976 until 2007, Michigan levied a form of a value-added tax known as the *single business tax*.

7. A VAT may be levied either on the price inclusive of the tax or the price before tax, as with a retail sales tax. Almost all countries report the VAT rate on a tax-exclusive basis.

8. As of 2014, the only national VAT implemented using the subtraction method is that of Japan.

9. As noted above, a credit-invoice method VAT need not necessarily visibly charge the tax as a percentage of the before-tax price, but nearly every country that has one does.

10. Indeed, Desai and Hines (2002) find evidence that, other things equal, the more countries make use of the VAT, the *less* foreign trade they have.

11. See Slemrod (2011a) for further details on why the VAT does not promote exports.

12. The lack of political support—and the tendency of supporters to find a different name for it—is often attributed to the 1980 stunning electoral defeat of Al Ullman (D-OR), the powerful twelve-term chair of the House Ways and Means Committee, blamed at the time in part on his advocacy of a national value-added tax. The fact that several Republican politicians now support a VAT, albeit with a different name, may signal that the "Ullman curse" is fading.

13. Domenici and Rivlin (2010, pp. 38–41).

14. Ryan (2008, Title VI). The name "business consumption tax" grates on an economist's ear, as businesses do not consume, people do.

15. Ryan (2010, 2012, 2016).

16. Tax Foundation descriptions and analyses of the Rand Paul and Ted Cruz tax plans are in Lundeen and Schuyler (2015) and Pomerleau and Schuyler (2015).

17. Rieschick (1997, p. 1661).

18. As in the current system, pension contributions would be deductible by businesses, and benefits paid would be included in the recipients' taxable income.

19. Financial institutions may be subject to special tax rules.

20. See, for example, Bradford (1986).

21. Rabushka (2015) reports forty-four countries with flat-rate income taxes as of March 2015. See Keen, Kim, and Varsano (2006), Gorodnichenko, Martinez-Vasquez, and Peter (2009), Ji and Ligthart (2012), and Adhikari and Alm (2016) for further information on how these taxes are designed and what effects they've had.

22. See Ginsburg (1995) for a discussion of the USA Tax and its administrative problems.

23. In 2014, federal corporate and personal income taxes raised $1,815 billion. Personal consumption expenditures in 2014 were $11,866 billion (U.S. Bureau of Economic Analysis, 2015, tables 3.2 and 1.1.5).

24. We calculate the 28.3 percent figure as follows. According to Mikesell (2013), the average state's retail sales tax base was equal to 38.8 percent of personal income in 2012. Personal income for 2012 was $13,915 billion (U.S. Bureau of Economic Analysis, 2015, table 1.7.5), and we would need to raise $1,528 billion in revenue (federal corporate and personal income taxes from U.S. Bureau of Economic Analysis, 2015, table 3.2). The necessary tax-exclusive rate is then [1528 / (13915 × 0.388)] × 100 = 28.3 percent.

25. According to Mikesell (2013), leaving aside Hawaii, the five states with the broadest sales tax coverage in 2012 were Wyoming, North Dakota, South Dakota, New Mexico, and Nevada. These five have a sales tax base equal to 64 percent of personal income, on average. The tax-exclusive rate is [1528/ (13915 × 0.640)] × 100 = 17.1 percent. Hawaii is an outlier, with a retail sales tax base equal to 105.1 percent of personal income. Mikesell indicates that Hawaii's unusually large base arises partly from high tourist spending relative to personal income of residents and partly from heavy taxation of business inputs (Hawaii explicitly imposes a "multistage" sales tax that taxes business inputs).

26. The seven states that included groceries in their sales tax base in 2012 were all in the top half of states with the broadest sales tax coverage. Breadth of sales tax coverage is from Cline, Phillips, and Neubig (2013). State tax treatment of groceries is from Tax Foundation (2012). Due and Mikesell (1994, p. 75) estimate that a food exemption costs a state between 20 and 25 percent of sales tax revenue.

27. Cline, Phillips, and Neubig (2013).

28. We calculate the 50.6 percent rate as follows. According to Mikesell (2013), the average state retail sales tax base was equal to 38.8 percent of personal income in 2012. As personal income in 2012 was $13,915 billion (U.S. Bureau of Economic Analysis, 2015, table 1.7.5), this gives us a retail sales tax base of $13,915*0.388=$5,399. We then multiply

this by the percent of retail sales not from business inputs to get \$5,399*0.56= \$3,023. Since we need to raise \$1,528 billion in revenue (U.S. Bureau of Economic Analysis, 2015, table 3.2), the tax exclusive rate would have to be \$1,528/\$3,023=0.506.

29. See, for example, Americans for Fair Taxation (2016).

30. Americans for Fair Taxation (2014).

31. Alternatively, if some of the burden of the VAT is shifted onto workers in the form of lower wages, the offset will be less exact, but there will still be a tendency for the rebate to exceed the VAT burden by a wider margin the further below the poverty line one is.

32. President's Advisory Panel on Federal Tax Reform (2005, chapter 9). Gale (2005) also calculates the rates that would be required for a retail sales tax to replace current major federal taxes and draws broadly similar conclusions.

33. Toder, Nunns, and Rosenberg (2012).

34. The rebate considered in the Toder, Nunns, and Rosenberg (2012) analysis also includes an adjustment to help offset the eventual reduction in Social Security benefits that occurs because the VAT reduces the measure of wage income that goes into the Social Security benefit calculation formula.

35. Taking into account the effects of the Protecting Americans from Tax Hikes Act of 2015, our calculations based on data from the Congressional Budget Office (2015c, 2015d) suggest that individual and corporate income tax revenue in fiscal year 2016 will be 10.5 percent of GDP. To estimate the VAT rate that would be required to raise 10.5 percent of GDP under each of the three options described in the text, we use data from Toder, Nunns, and Rosenberg (2012, tables 4, 5, and 6). They report that the tax-exclusive VAT rate needed to raise \$377 billion in calendar year 2015 would be 5.0 percent under option 1, 7.9 percent under option 2, and 7.7 percent under option 3. To the \$377 billion, we add their reported "individual income tax offset" and "corporate income tax offset" for each option, as these would not be applicable if the VAT were used to completely replace individual and corporate income taxes; this implies that at the VAT rates specified above, options 1 and 2 would each raise 2.56 percent of GDP in revenue and option 3 would raise 2.81 percent of GDP in revenue. We then compute the percentage VAT rates needed for a revenue-neutral replacement of individual and corporate income taxes reported in the text as $5.0 \times (10.5/2.56) = 20.5$ for option 1, $7.9 \times (10.5/2.56) = 32.4$ for option 2, and $7.7 \times (10.5/2.81) = 28.8$ for option 3.

36. The 1995 Armey-Shelby flat tax proposal can be found in U.S. Congress (1995).

37. President's Advisory Panel on Federal Tax Reform (2005, chapter 4).

38. For instance, Sullivan (1996, p. 490) calculated that allowing deductibility of home mortgage interest and charitable deductions would push the revenue-neutral rate on the July 1995 Armey-Shelby flat tax plan from 20.8 percent to about 22.7 percent. Gale (1996, p. 721) comes up with a similar estimate.

39. Individual and corporate income tax revenue was 9.8 percent of GDP in calendar year 2005 and 10.5 percent of GDP in calendar year 2006 (U.S. Bureau of Economic Analysis 2015, tables 1.1.5, 3.2, and 3.4). Taking into account the effects of the Protecting Americans from Tax Hikes Act of 2015, our calculations based on data from the Congressional Budget Office (2015c, 2015d) suggest that individual and corporate income tax revenue in fiscal year 2016 will be 10.5 percent of GDP.

40. Authors' calculations based on Toder, Nunns, and Rosenberg (2012, tables 4, 5, and 6). Note that in this paragraph, we are considering the VAT as an add-on to the existing system, so unlike our earlier calculations meant to illustrate the VAT rates necessary to replace income taxation, the estimates in this paragraph include the adjustments Toder, Nunns, and Rosenberg made for the revenue loss caused by how the VAT interacts with the individual and corporate income tax bases. The TPC estimates are not far from those in Congressional Budget Office (2011), which suggest that 5 percent VAT implemented as an add-on to the existing tax system would yield $260 billion in revenues in 2015, or $52 billion per percentage point.

41. Due and Mikesell (1994) report that, for a sample of eight states from 1991 to 1993, the administrative cost as a percentage of revenue ranged from 0.41 to 1. A survey in Federation of Tax Administrators (1993) reported an overall average compliance cost of 3.18 percent. Adding the two together gives a range of 3.59 to 4.18 percent.

42. The difficulty of enforcing tax due from retailers is also true of a VAT. Some jurisdictions that impose a VAT, most notably Sao Paolo in Brazil, have induced consumers to check on the tax compliance of retailers by turning receipts into lottery tickets and providing rewards to consumers whose receipts do not match to retailers' tax filings listed on the online database. Naritomi (2015) describes this system.

43. Florida Department of Revenue (1994).

44. Tait (1988, p. 18).

45. Tait (1988, p. 18) notes that Iceland, Norway, South Africa, Sweden, and Zimbabwe all at one time had retail sales taxes with rates over 10 percent. Sweden and Norway switched to VATs many years ago, Iceland switched to a VAT in 1990, and South Africa switched in 1991. In 1996, Slovenia's new tax administration levied a national retail sales tax of 20 percent, but it was replaced with a VAT in 1999. Zimbabwe switched to a VAT in 2004—see International Bureau for Fiscal Documentation (2007). Information was obtained from "Country Surveys, Zimbabwe, Section B.7.1," which is a subscription-only authoritative database. A number of countries have had other types of sales taxes, such as wholesale sales taxes or turnover taxes on the gross sales revenues of manufacturing firms, with rates higher than 10 percent, but most of these have switched to VATs as well. For example, Australia replaced its wholesale sales tax with a VAT in 2000.

46. Tanzi (1995, pp. 50–51).

47. See the U.S. Department of the Treasury (1984), Congressional Budget Office (1992), and the Government Accountability Office (1993), all of which are discussed in Cnossen (1994).

48. Values were adjusted for inflation using the Personal Consumption Expenditure Indices (U.S. Bureau of Economic Analysis, 2015, table 1.1.4).

49. Note, however, that if all firms in the production and distribution chain are exempt, then the tax revenue on the full value of the final consumption good is lost. Research by de Paula and Scheinkman (2010) in Brazil finds that exempt firms tend to do business with each other, to avoid the cascading of tax burdens that occurs when exempt firms deal with nonexempt firms. To the extent that exempt firms deal only with each other, this increases the revenue cost of exempting small firms.

50. See, for example, International Monetary Fund (2015, pp. 56–58).

51. Issues surrounding the tax-exempt threshold for the VAT and the levels for various countries are discussed in Ebrill, Keen, Bodin, and Summers (2001, pp. 113–124). The

current threshold for the United Kingdom is from Her Majesty's Revenue and Customs (2016).

52. Bradford (1996) discusses how income and consumption taxes treat financial services, argues that important problems arise under either type of tax, and discusses some options for addressing the problems.

53. See tables 2.1 and 2.2 in this book.

54. Figures in the previous two sentences are authors' calculations based on data from Organisation for Economic Co-operation and Development (2015c).

55. The corporation income tax was the lowest of the three at 2.7 percent of revenue, comprised of 0.5 percent administration and 2.2 percent compliance costs. See Godwin (1995, p. 75).

56. Malmer (1995, p. 258). The income tax cost consisted of 1 percent for administrative cost and 1.7 percent for taxpayer cost. For VAT, it was 0.6 percent for administrative cost and 2.5 percent for taxpayer cost.

57. Center for Social and Economic Research (2014, p. 15).

58. Keen and Smith (2006) provide an overview of how VAT fraud schemes work and what is known about them.

59. As noted above, many countries and jurisdictions have adopted flat income taxes.

60. See Feld (1995), Weisbach (2000), Calegari (1998), and Pearlman (1998).

61. See Weisbach (2000) for a discussion of the pros and cons of a small business exemption in the context of the Hall-Rabushka flat tax.

62. Representative Armey's original flat tax proposal, introduced in 1994 as H.R. 4585, proposed to eliminate withholding and replace it with monthly payments. This provision was eliminated from Armey's later flat tax proposal, H.R. 1040.

63. Toder, Nunns, and Rosenberg (2012).

64. The sales tax base in the Treasury analysis is modeled after the FairTax proposal, which promised it "would exempt only educational services, expenditures abroad by U.S. residents, food produced and consumed on farms, and existing housing" (President's Advisory Panel on Federal Tax Reform 2005, p. 209).

65. President's Advisory Panel on Federal Tax Reform (2005, chapter 9). We calculate the $2,411 figure by converting the $250 billion figure cited in the Advisory Panel report to 2014 dollars and then dividing it by the number of tax units in the bottom 80 percent of the income distribution in 2006, which we derive from estimates in Urban-Brookings Tax Policy Center (2007).

66. President's Advisory Panel on Federal Tax Reform (2005, p. 212).

67. See Gillis, Mieszkowski, and Zodrow (1996) for a discussion of these issues.

68. Kenworthy (2014) demonstrates this and argues that, in the long run, the United States is likely to follow suit. See also Burman (2014), who makes the case for using a VAT to fund increased federal health care spending.

69. To see this equivalence, assume that a (tax-inclusive) 20 percent VAT imposes a burden that is proportional to labor income. Granting a nonrefundable $5,000 per family

credit with the VAT is equivalent to imposing a 20 percent tax on labor income in excess of $25,000.

70. Assuming the burden falls on individuals or families according to their consumption would make the change in tax burdens caused by adopting the flat tax look more regressive. See Mieszkowski and Palumbo (2002), who provide evidence on this, as well as a review of the literature on distributional effects of fundamental tax reform.

71. President's Advisory Panel on Federal Tax Reform (2005, figure 4.6).

72. See, in particular, Bradford (1998) and Gentry and Hubbard (1997).

73. See Cronin, Nunns, and Toder (1996) and Dunbar and Pogue (1998).

74. President's Advisory Panel on Federal Tax Reform (2005, chapter 7).

75. This is the claim made in the Kemp Commission report on tax reform. See National Commission on Economic Growth and Tax Reform (1996).

76. Hall and Rabushka (1995).

77. See Altig, Auerbach, Kotlikoff, Smettters, and Walliser (2001).

78. See Engen and Gale (1996).

79. Ballard (2002) addresses the various ways in which international considerations could affect the economic case for fundamental tax reform. He concludes that international considerations likely increase the potential economic benefits of reform, but not by very much.

Chapter 8

1. Bradford (1986, p. 312).

2. One might argue that the 1996 elimination of the welfare system and its replacement by Temporary Assistance for Needy Families was one example of a wholesale policy change.

3. See Auerbach and Slemrod (1997) for a detailed discussion of the origin and economic impact of TRA86.

4. Office of Management and Budget (2015, historical tables, table 2.3).

5. The Tax Reform Act of 1986 is Public Law 99–514 — Oct. 22, 1986–100 Stat. 2085.

6. The poll data is analyzed in Auerbach and Slemrod (1997, pp. 618–619).

7. This account is based on Slemrod and Blauvelt (2006).

8. President's Advisory Panel on Federal Tax Reform (2005).

9. Matthews (2005).

10. Schumer (2005).

11. The first quotation is taken from Evans (2005) and the second quotation is taken from Brand (2005).

12. Nunns and Rohaly (2010).

13. See National Commission on Fiscal Responsibility and Reform (2010).

14. The analysis can be found in Urban-Brookings Tax Policy Center (2010).

15. Domenici and Rivlin (2010).

16. Disclosure: Slemrod's son, Jonathan, was policy director for Rubio's presidential campaign.

17. Rubio (2015).

18. Schuyler and McBride (2015).

19. Miller (2011).

20. See White House, Office of the Press Secretary (2010) for a definition of covered liabilities and a justification of the tax.

21. ABC News (2015).

22. See Sammartino, Nunns, Burman, Rohaly, and Rosenberg (2016) for a description and analysis of Sanders' tax plan.

23. Details of the Clinton plan are in Clinton (2015b) and Auxier, Burman, Nunns, and Rohaly (2016).

24. This discussion is based on the proposal in Graetz (2002). See also Graetz (1999) for arguments in favor of this general approach.

25. Summers' statement is mentioned in Bartlett (2009).

26. The dual income tax model is outlined in Sørensen (2005).

27. National Public Radio, Kaiser Family Foundation, and Harvard Kennedy School of Government (2003). For each of several items, the poll asked, "When two families have the same income, do you think it is fair that one family pays less tax because they …?" When the sentence was completed with "give more to charity than the other family," 62 percent said it was fair. When it was completed with "have more medical expenses than the other family," 71 percent said it was fair. When completed with "have a home mortgage while the other family does not," 55 percent said it was fair. And when completed with "receive more of their income from investments than the other family," 42 percent said it was fair and 52 percent said it was unfair.

Chapter 9

1. Seligman (1915, p. 14).

References

Aaron, Henry J., and Harvey Galper. 1985. *Assessing Tax Reform*. Washington, DC: Brookings Institution.

ABC News. 2012a. *Presidential Debate Transcript. President Barack Obama and Former Gov. Mitt Romney, R-Mass., Presidential Candidate, Participate in a Candidates Debate, University of Denver, Colorado, October 3, 2012*. <http://abcnews.go.com/Politics/OTUS/presidential-debate-transcript-denver-colo-oct/story?id=17390260> (accessed September 7, 2016).

ABC News. 2012b. *Second Presidential Debate Transcript: President Barack Obama and Former Gov. Mitt Romney Participate in a Candidates Debate, Hofstra University, Hempstead, New York, October 16, 2012*. <http://abcnews.go.com/Politics/OTUS/2012-presidential-debate-full-transcript-oct-16/story?id=17493848> (accessed September 7, 2016).

ABC News. 2012c. *Third Presidential Debate Full Transcript: President Barack Obama and Former Gov. Mitt Romney, R-Mass., Participate in a Candidates Debate, Lynn University, Boca Raton, Florida, October 22, 2012* . <http://abcnews.go.com/Politics/OTUS/presidential-debate-full-transcript/story?id=17538888> (accessed September 7, 2016).

ABC News. 2015. *This Week with George Stephanopoulos*, October 18. <http://abc.go.com/shows/this-week-with-george-stephanopoulos/episode-guide/2015-10/18-this-week-101815-aftermath-from-the-1st-democratic-debate-of-the-2016-presidential-campaign> (accessed January 9, 2017).

Ackerman, Deena, and Gerald Auten. 2006. "Floors, Ceilings, and Opening the Door for a Non-Itemizer Deduction." *National Tax Journal* 59 (3): 509–530.

Adhikari, Bibek, and James Alm. 2016. "Evaluating the Economic Effects of Flat Tax Reforms Using Synthetic Control Methods." *Southern Economic Journal*. doi:10.1002/soej.12152.

Alesina, Alberto, Edward L. Glaeser, and Bruce Sacerdote. 2005. "Work and Leisure in the U.S. and Europe: Why So Different?" In *NBER Macroeconomics Annual 2005*, eds. Mark Gertler and Kenneth Rogoff, 1–64. Cambridge, MA: MIT Press.

Allingham, Michael, and Agnar Sandmo. 1972. "Income Tax Evasion: A Theoretical Analysis." *Journal of Public Economics* 1 (3–4): 323–338.

Alm, James. 2012. "Measuring, Explaining, and Controlling Tax Evasion: Lessons from Theory, Experiments, and Field Studies." *International Tax and Public Finance* 19 (1): 54–77.

Alm, James, and Sarah Jacobson. 2007. "Using Laboratory Experiments in Public Economics." *National Tax Journal* 60 (1): 129–152.

Almunia, Miguel, Benjamin Lockwood, and Kimberley Scharf. 2015. "The Price Elasticity of Charitable Donations: Evidence from UK Tax Records." Working paper, University of Warwick, May 5. <https://editorialexpress.com/cgi-bin/conference/download.cgi?db_name=NTA2015&paper_id=356> (accessed September 7, 2016).

Altig, David, Alan J. Auerbach, Laurence J. Kotlikoff, Kent A. Smetters, and Jan Walliser. 2001. "Simulating Fundamental Tax Reform in the United States." *American Economic Review* 91 (3): 574–595.

Altshuler, Rosanne, and Harry Grubert. 2010. "Formula Apportionment: Is It Better than the Current System and Are There Better Alternatives?" *National Tax Journal* 63 (4), part 2: 1145–1184.

Americans for Fair Taxation. 2014. *The FairTax Prebate Explained.* Houston, TX. <https://www.flfairtax.org/Documents/Whitepapers/PrebateExplaination-revised-May-2014.pdf> (accessed September 7, 2016).

Americans for Fair Taxation. 2016. *FAQs.* <http://fairtax.org/faq> (accessed September 18, 2016).

Anderson, Richard, and Yang Liu. 2013. "How Low Can You Go? Negative Interest Rates and Investors' Flight to Safety." *The Regional Economist,* Federal Reserve Bank of St. Louis, January. <https://www.stlouisfed.org/~/media/Files/PDFs/publications/pub_assets/pdf/re/2013/a/investments.pdf> (accessed September 7, 2016).

Andreoni, James, and A. Abigail Payne. 2013. "Charitable Giving." In *Handbook of Public Economics,* eds. Alan J. Auerbach, Raj Chetty, Martin Feldstein, and Emmanuel Saez, vol. 5, 1–50. Amsterdam: North-Holland.

Andrews, Dan, Aida Caldera Sánchez, and Asa Johansson. 2011. "Housing Markets and Structural Policies in OECD Countries." OECD Economics Department Working Papers No. 836, January. <http://dx.doi.org/10.1787/5kgk8t2k9vf3-en> (accessed September 7, 2016).

Andrews, Edmund L. 2003. "Greenspan Throws Cold Water on Bush Arguments for Tax Cut." *New York Times,* February 12, A1.

Appelbaum, Binyamin. 2016. "Conflicting Policy from Trump: To Keep, and Remove, Tax Cut." *New York Times,* September 16.

Armour, Philip, Richard V. Burkhauser, and Jeff Larrimore. 2013. "Levels and Trends in United States Income and It's Distribution: A Crosswalk from Market Income Towards a Comprehensive Haig-Simons Income Approach." NBER Working Paper No. 19110, June. <http://www.nber.org/papers/w19110> (accessed September 7, 2016).

Arthur D. Little, Inc. 1988. *Development of Methodology for Estimating the Taxpayer Paperwork Burden.* Final Report to the U.S. Department of the Treasury, Internal Revenue Service, Washington, DC, June.

Auerbach, Alan J. 1996. "Tax Reform, Capital Allocation, Efficiency, and Growth." In *Economic Effects of Fundamental Tax Reform,* eds. Henry J. Aaron and William G. Gale, 29–73. Washington, DC: Brookings Institution Press.

Auerbach, Alan J. 2005. "Dynamic Scoring: An Introduction to the Issues." *American Economic Review* 95 (2): 421–425.

Auerbach, Alan J. 2010. "A Modern Corporate Tax." The Hamilton Project, December. <http://www.hamiltonproject.org/assets/legacy/files/downloads_and_links/FINAL _AuerbachPaper.pdf> (accessed September 7, 2016).

Auerbach, Alan J. 2012. "The Fall and Rise of Keynesian Fiscal Policy." *Asian Economic Policy Review* 7 (2): 157–175.

Auerbach, Alan J., and William G. Gale. 2001. "Tax Cuts and the Budget." *Tax Notes* 90 (March 26): 1869–1879.

Auerbach, Alan J., and William G. Gale. 2012. "The Federal Budget Outlook: No News Is Bad News." Working paper, University of California, Berkeley, June 14. <http:// elsa.berkeley.edu/~auerbach/Auerbach-Gale%202012-06-14.pdf> (accessed September 7, 2016).

Auerbach, Alan J., and William G. Gale. 2014. "Forgotten but Not Gone: The Long-Term Fiscal Imbalance." Working paper, University of California, Berkeley, September. <http:// eml.berkeley.edu/~auerbach/AG%202014-09-04.pdf> (accessed September 7, 2016).

Auerbach, Alan J., and Yuriy Gorodnichenko. 2012. "Measuring the Output Responses to Fiscal Policy." *American Economic Journal: Economic Policy* 4 (2): 1–27.

Auerbach, Alan J., and Joel Slemrod. 1997. "The Economic Effects of the Tax Reform Act of 1986." *Journal of Economic Literature* 35 (2): 589–632.

Auten, Gerald, and Geoffrey Gee. 2009. "Income Mobility in the United States: New Evidence from Income Tax Data." *National Tax Journal* 62 (2): 301–328.

Auten, Gerald, and David Joulfaian. 1996. "Charitable Contributions and Intergenerational Transfers." *Journal of Public Economics* 59 (1): 55–68.

Auxier, Richard C., Leonard E. Burman, James R. Nunns, and Jeffrey Rohaly. 2016. "An Analysis of Hillary Clinton's Tax Proposals." Urban-Brookings Tax Policy Center, March 3. <http://www.taxpolicycenter.org/publications/analysis-hillary-clintons-tax -proposals/full> (accessed September 7, 2016).

Avi-Yonah, Reuven S., and Haiyan Xu. 2016. "Evaluating BEPS." University of Michigan Public Law Research Paper #493, January 15. <http://papers.ssrn.com/sol3/papers .cfm?abstract_id=2716125> (accessed September 7, 2016).

Bakija, Jon. 2013. "Tax Policy and Philanthropy: A Primer on the Empirical Evidence for the U.S. and Its Implications." *Social Research* 80 (2): 557–584.

Bakija, Jon. 2016. "Documentation for a Comprehensive Historical U.S. Federal and State Income Tax Calculator Program." Working paper, Williams College, September 13. <http://web.williams.edu/Economics/wp/Bakija_Documentation_IncTaxCalc _2016.pdf> (accessed September 13, 2016).

Bakija, Jon, William G. Gale, and Joel Slemrod. 2003. "Charitable Bequests and Taxes on Inheritances and Estates: Aggregate Evidence from across States and Time." *American Economic Review* 93 (2): 366–370.

Bakija, Jon, and William Gentry. 2016. "Capital Gains Taxes and Realizations: Evidence from a Long Panel of State-Level Data." Working paper, Williams College. <http:// web.williams.edu/Economics/wp/BakijaGentryCapitalGainsStatePanel.pdf> (accessed September 7, 2016).

Bakija, Jon, and Bradley T. Heim. 2011. "How Does Charitable Giving Respond to Incentives and Income? New Estimates from Panel Data." *National Tax Journal* 64 (2): 615–650.

Bakija, Jon, Lane Kenworthy, Peter Lindert, and Jeff Madrick. 2016. *How Big Should Our Government Be?* Berkeley: University of California Press.

Bakija, Jon, and Tarun Narasimhan. 2016. "Effects of the Level and Structure of Taxes on Long-Run Economic Growth: What Can We Learn from Panel Time-Series Techniques?" Working paper, Williams College. <http://web.williams.edu/Economics/wp/BakijaNarasimhanTaxEconomicGrowthPanelTimeSeries.pdf> (accessed September 7, 2016).

Baldwin, Richard E., and Paul Krugman. 2004. "Agglomeration, Integration and Tax Harmonisation." *European Economic Review* 48 (1): 1–23.

Ballard, Charles. 2002. "International Aspects of Fundamental Tax Reform." In *United States Tax Reform in the Twenty-first Century*, eds. George R. Zodrow and Peter Mieszkowski, 109–139. Cambridge: Cambridge University Press.

Baneman, Dan, and Jim Nunns. 2012. "Changes in the Distribution of Top Marginal Tax Rates, 1958–2009." *Tax Notes* 134 (March 5): 1321.

Bankman, Joseph. 2005. "Simplifying Tax for the Average Citizen." Presentation before the President's Advisory Panel on Federal Tax Reform, Washington, DC, May 17. <http://govinfo.library.unt.edu/taxreformpanel/meetings/docs/bankman_05172005.ppt> (accessed September 7, 2016).

Bankman, Joseph. 2008. "Using Technology to Simplify Individual Tax Filing." *National Tax Journal* 61 (4), part 2: 773–789.

Bankman, Joseph, and David Weisbach. 2010. "Consumption Taxation Is Still Superior to Income Taxation." *Stanford Law Review* 60 (3): 789–802.

Barlett, Donald L., and James B. Steele. 1998. "Corporate Welfare." *Time* 152, November 9, 36–39.

Bartlett, Bruce. 2009. "VAT Time?" *Forbes*, June 5. <http://www.forbes.com/2009/06/04/value-added-tax-opinions-columnists-bartlett.html> (accessed September 7, 2016).

Bastiat, Frédéric. [1850] 1964. *Selected Essays on Political Economy. Reprint.* Irvington-on-Hudson, NY: Foundation for Economic Education.

Becker, Gary S. 1968. "Crime and Punishment: An Economic Approach." *Journal of Political Economy* 76 (2): 169–217.

Becker, Gary, and Casey Mulligan. 1998. "Deadweight Costs and the Size of Government." *Journal of Law & Economics* 46 (2): 293–340.

Bennett, Charles. 2005. "Preliminary Results of the National Research Program's Reporting Compliance Study of Tax Year 2001 Individual Returns." In *Proceedings of the 2005 IRS Research Conference*, eds. James Dalton and Beth Kilss, 3–14. Washington, DC: Internal Revenue Service, Statistics of Income Division. <http://www.irs.gov/file_source/pub/irs-soi/05bennett.pdf> (accessed January 8, 2014).

Bentham, Jeremy. 1789. *An Introduction to the Principles of Morals and Legislation.* Oxford: Clarendon Press.

Bergeaud, Antonin, Gilbert Cette, and Rémy Lecat. 2014. "Productivity Trends from 1890 to 2012 in Advanced Countries." Working paper, Banque de France, February.

<https://www.banque-france.fr/uploads/tx_bdfdocumentstravail/DT_475.pdf>
(accessed September 7, 2016).

Bergh, Andreas, and Magnus Henrekson. 2011. "Government Size and Growth: A Survey and Interpretation of the Evidence." *Journal of Economic Surveys* 25 (5): 872–897.

Bernanke, Ben S. 2015a. "Why Are Interest Rates So Low?" *Ben Bernanke's Blog*, March 30. <http://www.brookings.edu/blogs/ben-bernanke/posts/2015/03/30-why-interest -rates-so-low> (accessed September 7, 2016).

Bernanke, Ben S. 2015b. "Why Are Interest Rates So Low, Part 2: Secular Stagnation" *Ben Bernanke's Blog*, March 31. <http://www.brookings.edu/blogs/ben-bernanke/ posts/2015/03/31-why-interest-rates-low-secular-stagnation> (accessed September 7, 2016).

Bernanke, Ben S. 2015c. "Why Are Interest Rates So Low, Part 3: The Global Savings Glut." *Ben Bernanke's Blog*, April 1. <http://www.brookings.edu/blogs/ben-bernanke/ posts/2015/04/01-why-interest-rates-low-global-savings-glut> (accessed September 7, 2016).

Bernheim, B. Douglas. 2002. "Taxation and Saving." In *Handbook of Public Economics*, vol. 3, eds. Alan J. Auerbach and Martin Feldstein, 1173–1249. Amsterdam: Elsevier Science.

Bernstein, Jared. 2013. "When the Results Look Weird, Check the Methods … Carefully!" *On the Economy*, June 29. <http://jaredbernsteinblog.com/when-the-results-look-weird -check-the-methods-carefully> (accessed September 7, 2016).

Bitler, Marianne P., and Hilary W. Hoynes. 2010. "The State of the Social Safety Net in the Post-Welfare Reform Era." *Brookings Papers on Economic Activity* (Fall): 71–127.

Blackman, Andrew. 2015. "The Surprising Relationship between Charitable Giving and Taxes: Researchers Have Learned a Lot by Putting Donors Under the Microscope; Policy Makers Might Want to Pay Attention." *The Wall Street Journal*, December 14.

Blase, Brian. 2015. "Delaying and Weakening Obamacare's Cadillac Tax Is a Move in Wrong Direction." *Forbes*, December 16. <http://www.forbes.com/sites/ theapothecary/2015/12/16/delaying-and-weakening-obamacares-cadillac-tax-a-bad -outcome> (accessed September 7, 2016).

Blau, Francine D., and Lawrence M. Kahn. 2007. "Changes in the Labor Supply Behavior of Married Women: 1980–2000." *Journal of Labor Economics* 25 (3): 393–438.

Blomquist, Sören, and Laurent Simula. 2012. "Marginal Deadweight Loss When the Income Tax Is Nonlinear." Working paper, Uppsala University. <http://www.vanderbilt .edu/econ/conference/taxation-theory/documents/Blomquist-Simula.pdf> (accessed September 7, 2016).

Blumenthal, Marsha, and Joel Slemrod. 1992. "The Compliance Cost of the U.S. Individual Income Tax System: A Second Look after Tax Reform." *National Tax Journal* 45 (2): 185–202.

Blundell, Richard, Alan Duncan, and Costas Meghir. 1998. "Estimating Labor Supply Responses Using Tax Reforms." *Econometrica* 66 (4): 827–861.

Board of Governors of the Federal Reserve System. 2013. *Flow of Funds Accounts of the United States*. <http://www.federalreserve.gov/releases/z1/Current/data.htm> (accessed September 7, 2016).

Board of Governors of the Federal Reserve System. 2015. *Flow of Funds Accounts of the United States.* <http://www.federalreserve.gov/releases/z1/Current/data.htm> (accessed September 7, 2016).

Bolt, Jutta, and Jan Luiten van Zanden. 2014. "The Maddison Project: Collaborative Research on Historical National Accounts." *Economic History Review* 67 (3): 627–651.

Bolton, Alexander. 2011. "Coburn Spars with Norquist over Tax Breaks for Ethanol." *The Hill*, March 29. <http://thehill.com/homenews/senate/152609-coburn-spars-with -norquist-over-tax-breaks-for-ethanol> (accessed September 7, 2016).

Boskin, Michael J., Ellen R. Dulberger, Robert J. Gordon, Zvi Griliches, and Dale W. Jorgenson. 1998. "Consumer Prices, the Consumer Price Index, and the Cost of Living." *Journal of Economic Perspectives* 12 (1): 3–26.

Bourassa, Steven, Donald Haurin, Patric Hendershott, and Martin Hoesli. 2013. "Mortgage Interest Deductions and Homeownership: An International Survey." *Journal of Real Estate Literature* 21 (2): 181–203.

Bowman, Karlyn, Andrew Rugg, and Jennifer Marsico. 2013a. "Public Opinion on Taxes: 1937 to Today." American Enterprise Institute for Public Policy Research, April. <https:// www.scribd.com/document/134669474/Polls-on-Attitudes-on-Taxes-2013> (accessed September 7, 2016).

Bowman, Karlyn, Andrew Rugg, and Jennifer Marsico. 2013b. "The IRS: Opinions over Time." *AEI Political Report* 9 (6): 1–2. <https://www.aei.org/wp-content/uploads/ 2013/06/-political-report-june-2013_143029439789.pdf> (accessed September 7, 2016).

Bowman, Karlyn, Heather Sims, and Eleanor O'Neil. 2015. *Public Opinion on Taxes: 1937 to Today.* Washington, DC: American Enterprise Institute for Public Policy Research. <https://www.aei.org/wp-content/uploads/2015/04/Bowman_Taxes_March-2015.pdf> (accessed September 7, 2016).

Boxer, Sarah B. 2011. "Romney: Wall Street Protests 'Class Warfare.'" *National Journal*, October 4. <http://www.nationaljournal.com/2012-presidential-campaign/romney -wall-street-protests-class-warfare--20111004> (accessed August 3, 2012 – only available with subscription).

Bradford, David F. 1986. *Untangling the Income Tax.* Cambridge, MA: Harvard University Press.

Bradford, David F. 1996. "Treatment of Financial Services under Income and Consumption Taxes." In *Economic Effects of Fundamental Tax Reform*, eds. Henry J. Aaron and William G. Gale, 437–464. Washington, DC: Brookings Institution Press.

Bradford, David F. 1998. "Review of *Taxing Ourselves* (1st ed.)." *Regulation* 21 (1): 70–72.

Bradford, David F. 2003. "Reforming Budgetary Language." In *Public Finance and Public Policy in the New Century*, eds. Sijbren Cnossen and Hans-Werner Sinn, 93–116. Cambridge, MA: MIT Press.

Brand, Madeleine. 2005. "The Marketplace Report: Bush Tax Reform Proposals." *National Public Radio*, November 2. <http://www.npr.org/templates/story/story.php?storyId =4986412> (accessed September 7, 2016).

Bricker, Jesse, Lisa J. Dettling, Alice Henriques, Joanne W. Hsu, Kevin B. Moore, John Sabelhaus, Jeffrey Thompson, and Richard A. Windle. 2014. "Changes in U.S. Family

Finances from 2010 to 2013: Evidence from the Survey of Consumer Finances." *Federal Reserve Bulletin* 100 (4). <http://www.federalreserve.gov/pubs/bulletin/2014/pdf/scf14.pdf> (accessed September 7, 2016).

Bricker, Jesse, Alice Henriques, Jacob Krimmel, and John Sabelhaus. 2016. "Measuring Income and Wealth at the Top Using Administrative and Survey Data." *Brookings Papers on Economic Activity*, Spring.

British Broadcasting Corporation. 2011. "Vodafone Shops Blockaded in Tax Protest." <http://www.bbc.co.uk/news/business-11658950> (accessed September 7, 2016).

Broda, Christian, and John Romalis. 2008. "Inequality and Prices: Does China Benefit the Poor in America?" Working paper, University of Chicago.

Brown, Samuel, William G. Gale, and Adam Looney. 2012a. "On the Distributional Effects of Base-Broadening Income Tax Reform." Urban-Brookings Tax Policy Center, August 1. <http://www.taxpolicycenter.org/UploadedPDF/1001628-Base-Broadening-Tax-Reform.pdf> (accessed September 7, 2016).

Brown, Samuel, William G. Gale, and Adam Looney. 2012b. "Implications of Governor Romney's Tax Proposals: FAQs and Responses." Urban-Brookings Tax Policy Center, August 16. <http://www.taxpolicycenter.org/UploadedPDF/1001631-FAQ-Romney-plan.pdf> (accessed September 7, 2016).

Brown, Samuel, William G. Gale, and Adam Looney. 2012c. "The Tax Policy Center's Analysis of Governor Romney's Tax Proposals: A Follow-up Discussion." Urban-Brookings Tax Policy Center, November 7. <http://www.brookings.edu/~/media/research/files/papers/2012/11/07-romney-tax-followup-brown-gale-looney/07-romney-tax-followup-brown-gale-looney.pdf> (accessed September 7, 2016).

Browning, Lynnley. 2009. "UBS to Pay $780 Million Fine over Offshore Services." *New York Times*, February 18.

Browning, Lynnley. 2010. "Swiss Banker Blows Whistle on Tax Evasion." *New York Times*, New York Edition, January 19, B1.

Browning, E. S., Steven Russolillo, and Jessica E. Vascellaro. 2012. "Apple Now Biggest-Ever U.S. Company." *The Wall Street Journal*, August 20.

Brownlee, W. Elliot. 1989. "Taxation for a Strong and Virtuous Republic: A Bicentennial Retrospective." *Tax Notes* 45 (December 25): 1613–1621.

Bruce, Donald, and Douglas Holtz-Eakin. 2001. "Will a Consumption Tax Kill the Housing Market?" In *Transition Costs of Fundamental Tax Reform*, eds. Kevin A. Hassett and R. Glenn Hubbard, 96–114. Washington, DC: American Enterprise Institute Press.

Bryant, Victoria L., and Jon Gober. 2013. "Accumulation and Distribution of Individual Retirement Arrangements, 2010." *IRS Statistics of Income Bulletin* 33 (2): 193–210.

Buffett, Warren. 2011. "Stop Coddling the Super-Rich." *New York Times*, August 14.

Burman, Leonard E. 2011. "Jon Stewart's Fake News on Tax Expenditures." *Forbes* 10, May 10. <http://www.forbes.com/sites/leonardburman/2011/05/10/jon-stewarts-fake-news-on-tax-expenditures> (accessed September 7, 2016).

Burman, Leonard E. 2014. "The Tax Reform that Just Won't Die. And Shouldn't." *Milken Institute Quarterly* (Second Quarter): 17–23.

Burman, Leonard E., William G. Gale, John Iselin, James R. Nunns, Jeffrey Rohaly, Joseph Rosenberg, and Roberton Williams. 2015. "An Analysis of Governor Bush's Tax Plan." Urban-Brookings Tax Policy Center, December 8. <http://www.taxpolicycenter.org/UploadedPDF/2000547-analysis-of-bush-tax-plan.pdf> (accessed September 7, 2016).

Burman, Leonard E., William G. Gale, and Peter R. Orszag. 2003. "The Administration's New Tax-Free Saving Proposals: A Preliminary Analysis." *Tax Notes* 98 (March 3): 1423–1446.

Burman, Leonard E., Surachai Khitatrakun, Jeffrey Rohaly, Eric Toder, and Roberton Williams. 2008. "An Updated Analysis of the 2008 Presidential Candidates' Tax Plans: Revised August 15, 2008." Urban-Brookings Tax Policy Center. <http://www.taxpolicycenter.org/sites/default/files/alfresco/publication-pdfs/411749-An-Updated-Analysis-of-the-Presidential-Candidates-Tax-Plans-Updated-September--.PDF> (accessed September 7, 2016).

Bush, George W. 2003. *The President's Agenda for Tax Relief.* Washington, DC, April 25. <https://georgewbush-whitehouse.archives.gov/news/reports/taxplan.html> (accessed September 7, 2016).

Calegari, Michael. 1998. "Flat Taxes and Effective Tax Planning." *National Tax Journal* 51 (4): 689–713.

Calomiris, Charles W., and Kevin A. Hassett. 2002. "Marginal Tax Rate Cuts and the Public Tax Debate." *National Tax Journal* 55 (1): 119–131.

Carasso, Adam, and C. Eugene Steuerle. 2005. "The Hefty Penalty on Marriage Facing Many Households with Children." *Marriage and Child Well-Being* 15 (2): 157–175.

Carter, Susan B., Scott Sigmund Gartner, Michael R. Haines, Alan L. Olmstead, Richard Sutch, and Gavin Wright, eds. 2006. *Historical Statistics of the United States, Millennial Edition.* Cambridge: Cambridge University Press. <https://hsus.cambridge.org/HSUSWeb/HSUSEntryServlet> (accessed October 18, 2016).

Cassidy, John. 2016. "Panama Papers: Why Aren't There More American Names." *The New Yorker*, April 5. <http://www.newyorker.com/news/john-cassidy/panama-papers-why-arent-there-more-american-names> (accessed September 7, 2016).

Cashin, David. 2013. "The Household Expenditure Response to Pre-announced Tax Changes." PhD diss., University of Michigan.

Cato Institute. 2003. *Cato Handbook for Congress: Policy Recommendations for the 107th Congress.* Washington, DC. <http://www.cato.org/cato-handbook-policymakers/cato-handbook-congress-policy-recommendations-107th-congress-2001> (accessed September 7, 2016).

Center on Philanthropy at Indiana University. 2007. "Patterns of Household Charitable Giving by Income Group, 2005." Indianapolis, IN. <http://www.philanthropy.iupui.edu/files/research/giving_focused_on_meeting_needs_of_the_poor_july_2007.pdf> (accessed September 7, 2016).

Center for Responsive Politics. 2013a. "2012 Election Overview: Members of Congress Only." <http://www.opensecrets.org/overview/index.php?cycle=2012&display=T&type=M> (accessed January 8, 2017).

Center for Responsive Politics. 2013b. "Overview: House Ways and Means Committee." <http://www.opensecrets.org/cmteprofiles/overview.php?cycle=2012&cmteid=H22&cmte=HWAY&congno=113&chamber=H> (accessed September 7, 2016).

Center for Social and Economic Research. 2014. "2012 Update Report to the Study to Quantify and Analyse the VAT Gap in the EU-27 Member States." Report No. TAXUD/2013DE321, Warsaw, September. <https://ec.europa.eu/taxation_customs/sites/taxation/files/resources/documents/common/publications/studies/vat_gap2012.pdf> (accessed September 7, 2016).

Centers for Disease Control and Prevention. 2014. *Deaths: Final Data for 2012. National Vital Statistics Reports* 63 (9). <http://www.cdc.gov/nchs/data/nvsr/nvsr63/nvsr63_09.pdf> (accessed September 7, 2016).

Centers for Medicare and Medicaid Services. 2014a. *Medicare and Medicaid Statistical Supplement, 2013 Edition.* <http://www.cms.gov/Research-Statistics-Data-and-Systems/Statistics-Trends-and-Reports/MedicareMedicaidStatSupp/2013.html> (accessed September 7, 2016).

Centers for Medicare and Medicaid Services. 2014b. *National Health Expenditure Data.* <https://www.cms.gov/Research-Statistics-Data-and-Systems/Statistics-Trends-and-Reports/NationalHealthExpendData/NationalHealthAccountsHistorical.html> (accessed September 7, 2016).

Centers for Medicare and Medicaid Services Office of the Actuary. 2014. *Projected Medicare Expenditures under Current Law, the Projected Baseline, and an Illustrative Alternative Scenario.* <https://www.cms.gov/Research-Statistics-Data-and-Systems/Statistics-Trends-and-Reports/ReportsTrustFunds/Downloads/2014TRAlternativeScenario.pdf> (accessed September 7, 2016).

Cesarini, David, Erik Lindqvist, Matthew J. Notowidigdo, and Robert Östling. 2015. "The Effect of Wealth on Individual and Household Labor Supply: Evidence from Swedish Lotteries." NBER Working Paper No. 21762, December. <http://www.nber.org/papers/w21762> (accessed September 7, 2016).

Chapman, Bruce. 2006. "Income Contingent Loans for Higher Education: International Reforms." In *Handbook of the Economics of Education,* vol. 2, eds. Eric Hanushek and Finis Welch, 1437–1503. Amsterdam: Elsevier.

Chetty, Raj. 2012. "Bounds on Elasticities with Optimization Frictions: A Synthesis of Micro and Macro Evidence on Labor Supply." *Econometrica* 80 (3): 968–1018.

Chetty, Raj, John N. Friedman, Soren Leth-Petersen, Torben Helen Nielsen, and Tore Olsen. 2014. "Active vs. Passive Decisions and Crowd-Out in Retirement Savings Accounts: Evidence from Denmark." *Quarterly Journal of Economics* 129 (3): 1141–1219.

Chetty, Raj, Adam Guren, Day Manoli, and Andrea Weber. 2013. *"Does Indivisible Labor Explain the Difference between Micro and Macro Elasticities? A Meta-Analysis of Extensive Margin Elasticities." NBER Macroeconomics Annual 2012* 27 (1): 1–56. <http://www.journals.uchicago.edu/doi/10.1086/669170> (accessed October 19, 2016).

Chirinko, Robert S., Steven M. Fazzari, and Andrew P. Meyer. 1999. "How Responsive Is Business Capital Formation to Its User Cost? An Exploration with Micro Data." *Journal of Public Economics* 74 (1): 53–80.

Chodorow-Reich, Gabriel, Laura Feiveson, Zachary Liscow, and William Gui Woolston. 2012. "Does State Fiscal Relief during Recessions Increase Employment? Evidence from the American Recovery and Reinvestment Act." *American Economic Journal: Economic Policy* 4 (3): 118–145.

Choi, James J., David Laibson, Brigitte Madrian, and Andrew Metrick. 2002. "Defined Contribution Pensions: Plan Rules, Participant Decisions, and the Path of Least Resistance." In *Tax Policy and the Economy*, vol. 16, ed. James M. Poterba, 67–114. Cambridge, MA: MIT Press.

Christensen, Kevin, Robert Cline, and Tom Neubig. 2001. "Total Corporate Taxation: 'Hidden,' Above-the-Line, Non-Income Taxes." *National Tax Journal* 54 (3): 495–506.

Cilke, James, Julie-Anne M. Cronin, Janet McCubbin, James R. Nunns, and Paul Smith. 2001. "Distributional Analysis: A Longer-Term Perspective." In *Proceedings of the Ninety-Third Annual Conference on Taxation*, 248–258. Washington DC: National Tax Association.

Citizens for Tax Justice. 2000a. "Overview of the George W. Bush Tax Plan." <http://www.ctj.org/html/bushpage.htm> (accessed September 7, 2016).

Citizens for Tax Justice. 2000b. "Preliminary Summary of the Gore Tax Plan." August 30. <http://www.ctj.org/pdf/gore0800.pdf> (accessed September 7, 2016).

Citizens for Tax Justice. 2015a. "Marco Rubio's Tax Plan Gives Top 1% An Average Tax Cut of More than $220,000 a Year," November 3. <http://ctj.org/pdf/rubio11315.pdf> (accessed September 7, 2016).

Citizens for Tax Justice. 2015b. "Donald Trump's $12 Trillion Tax Cut." November 4. <http://ctj.org/pdf/trump1142015.pdf> (accessed September 7, 2016).

Clausing, Kimberly A. 2013. "Who Pays the Corporate Tax in a Global Economy?" *National Tax Journal* 66 (1): 151–184.

Clausing, Kimberly A. 2016. "The Effect of Profit Shifting on the Corporate Tax Base in the United States and Beyond." *National Tax Journal* 69 (4): 905–934.

Clausing, Kimberly A., and Reuven Avi-Yonah. 2008. "Reforming Corporate Taxation in a Global Economy: A Proposal to Adopt Formulary Apportionment." In *Path to Prosperity: Hamilton Project Ideas on Income Security, Education, and Taxes*, eds. Jason Furman and Jason E. Bordoff, 319–344. Washington, DC: Brookings Institution Press.

Clement, Scott. 2013. "The IRS' Approval Ratings are Free Fallin'." Washington Post *The Fix Blog*, May 28. <http://www.washingtonpost.com/blogs/the-fix/wp/2013/05/28/the-irs-approval-ratings-are-free-fallin> (accessed September 7, 2016).

Cline, Robert, Andrew Phillips, and Thomas Neubig. 2013. "What's Wrong with Taxing Business Services." *State Tax Notes* 68 (April 22): 311.

Clinton, Hillary. 2015a. "Building the 'Growth and Fairness Economy.'" Speech given July 13 at the New School for Social Research, New York. Transcript available at *Wall Street Journal Washington Wire*. <http://blogs.wsj.com/washwire/2015/07/13/hillary-clinton-transcript-building-the-growth-and-fairness-economy/> (accessed September 7, 2016).

Clinton, Hillary. 2015b. "A Plan to Raise American Incomes." Hillary Clinton website. <https://www.hillaryclinton.com/issues/plan-raise-american-incomes/> (accessed January 10, 2016).

Clinton, William. 1992. "Acceptance Address: Democratic Nominee for President." Delivered at the Democratic National Convention, New York, July 16. *Vital Speeches of the Day* 58 (21), August 15: 642–645.

Cnossen, Sijbren. 1994. "Administrative and Compliance Costs of the VAT: A Review of the Evidence." *Tax Notes International* 8 (June 20): 1649-1668.

Cnossen, Sijbren. 1998. "Global Trends and Issues in Value Added Taxation." *International Tax and Public Finance* 5 (3): 399–428.

Coakley, Jerry, Farida Kulasi, and Ron Smith. 1998. "The Feldstein-Horioka Puzzle and Capital Mobility: A Review." *International Journal of Finance & Economics* 3 (2): 169–188.

Coder, Jeremiah. 2012. "IRS Initiating Form 1099-K Compliance Program." *Tax Notes* 137 (December 3): 1049.

Cohen, Tom. 2013. "IRS Inspector General: Liberals Also on Target List." CNN.com. <http://www.cnn.com/2013/07/18/politics/irs-scandal/> (accessed September 7, 2016).

Cole, Alan. 2015. "Details and Analysis of Donald Trump's Tax Plan." Tax Foundation Fiscal Fact No. 482, September 29. <http://taxfoundation.org/article/details-and -analysis-donald-trump-s-tax-plan> (accessed September 7, 2016).

Cole, Alan. 2016. "Details of the Donald Trump Tax Reform Plan, September 2016." Tax Foundation Fiscal Fact No. 528, September 19. <http://taxfoundation.org/sites/ taxfoundation.org/files/docs/TaxFoundation_FF528_FINAL3.pdf> (accessed September 20, 2016).

Cole, Alan, and Scott Greenberg. 2016. "Details and Analysis of Bernie Sanders' Tax Plan." Tax Foundation Fiscal Fact No. 498, January 28. <http://taxfoundation.org/ sites/taxfoundation.org/files/docs/TaxFoundation-FF498.pdf> (accessed September 7, 2016).

Commerce Clearing House. 2015a. "Internal Revenue Code: Income, Estate, Gift, Employment and Excise Taxes." <https://www.cchgroup.com/store/products/internal -revenue-code-income-estate-gift-employment-excise-taxes-summer-2015-prod -10037776-0001/book-softcover-item-1-10037776-0001> (accessed September 7, 2016).

Commerce Clearing House. 2015b. "Income Tax Regulations." <https://www.cchgroup .com/store/products/income-tax-regulations-summer-2015-prod-10037777-0001/book -softcover-item-1-10037777-0001> (accessed September 7, 2016).

Commission on Presidential Debates. 2012. *October 3, 2000 Transcript: The First Gore-Bush Presidential Debate.* <http://www.debates.org/index.php?page=october-3-2000 -transcript> (accessed September 7, 2016).

Compañía General de Tabacos de Filipinas v. Collector of Internal Revenue. 1927. 275 U.S. 87.

The Conference Board. 2015. *The Conference Board Total Economy Database™ May 2015.* <http://www.conference-board.org/data/economydatabase/> (accessed September 7, 2016).

Confessore, Nicholas. 2013. "New Rules Would Rein In Nonprofits' Political Role." *New York Times*, November 26.

Confessore, Nicholas, and David Kocieniewski. 2012. "For Romneys, Friendly Code Reduces Taxes." *New York Times*, January 24.

Confessore, Nicholas, David Kocieniewski, and Michael Luo. 2013. "Confusion and Staff Troubles Rife at I.R.S. Office in Ohio." *New York Times*, May 18.

Congressional Budget Office (CBO). 1992. *Effects of Adopting a Value-Added Tax*. February. <https://www.cbo.gov/sites/default/files/102nd-congress-1991-1992/reports/1992_02_effectsofadloptingavat.pdf> (accessed September 7, 2016).

Congressional Budget Office (CBO). 2001. *The Budget and Economic Outlook: An Update*, August. https://www.cbo.gov/sites/default/files/107th-congress-2001-2002/reports/entirereport_2.pdf (accessed September 7, 2016).

Congressional Budget Office (CBO). 2005. *Effective Tax Rates: Comparing Annual and Multiyear Measures*, January. <http://www.cbo.gov/sites/default/files/cbofiles/ftpdocs/60xx/doc6051/01-06-longitudinaltaxrates.pdf> (accessed September 7, 2016).

Congressional Budget Office (CBO). 2011. *Reducing the Deficit: Spending and Revenue Options*, March. <http://www.cbo.gov/sites/default/files/03-10-reducingthedeficit.pdf> (accessed September 7, 2016).

Congressional Budget Office (CBO). 2012a. *Economic Effects of Reducing the Fiscal Restraint That Is Scheduled to Occur in 2013*, May 22. <http://www.cbo.gov/publication/43262> (accessed September 7, 2016).

Congressional Budget Office (CBO). 2012b. *Updated Budget Projections: Fiscal Years 2012 to 2022*, March. <http://www.cbo.gov/sites/default/files/cbofiles/attachments/March2012Baseline.pdf> (accessed September 7, 2016).

Congressional Budget Office (CBO). 2012c. *Additional Data: Economic Baseline Projections*, January. <http://www.cbo.gov/sites/default/files/cbofiles/attachments/Jan2012_EconomicBaseline_Release.xls> (accessed September 7, 2016).

Congressional Budget Office (CBO). 2014. *Taxing Capital Income: Effective Marginal Tax Rates under 2014 Law and Selected Policy Options*, December. <https://www.cbo.gov/sites/default/files/113th-congress-2013-2014/reports/49817-Taxing_Capital_Income_0.pdf> (accessed September 7, 2016).

Congressional Budget Office (CBO). 2015a. *The 2015 Long-Term Budget Outlook*, June. <https://www.cbo.gov/sites/default/files/114th-congress-2015-2016/reports/50250-LongTermBudgetOutlook-3.pdf> (accessed September 7, 2016).

Congressional Budget Office (CBO). 2015b. *Effective Marginal Tax Rates for Low- and Moderate-Income Workers in 2016*, November. <https://www.cbo.gov/publication/43709> (accessed September 7, 2016).

Congressional Budget Office (CBO). 2015c. *An Update to the Budget and Economic Outlook: 2015 to 2025*, August 25. <https://www.cbo.gov/publication/50724> (accessed September 7, 2016).

Congressional Budget Office (CBO). 2015d. *Cost Estimate for H.R. 2029, as Cleared for the President's Signature on December 18, 2015*, December 18. <https://www.cbo.gov/sites/default/files/114th-congress-2015-2016/costestimate/cboestimateofhr2029asclearedforthepresidentssignatureondecember182015.pdf> (accessed September 7, 2016).

Congressional Budget Office (CBO). 2016a. *Updated Budget Projections: 2016 to 2026*, March. <http://www.cbo.gov/publication/51384> (accessed September 7, 2016).

Congressional Budget Office. 2016b. *The Distribution of Household Income and Federal Taxes, 2013,* June 8. <https://www.cbo.gov/publication/51361> (accessed September 7, 2016).

Contos, George, John Guyton, Patrick Langetieg, Allen H. Lerman, and Susan Nelson. 2012. "Taxpayer Compliance Costs for Corporations and Partnerships: A New Look." In *IRS Research Bulletin: Proceedings of the 2012 IRS Research Conference,* ed. Alan Plumley, 3–16. Washington, DC: U.S. Department of the Treasury. <https://www.irs.gov/pub/irs-soi/12rescon.pdf> (accessed September 7, 2016).

Contos, George, John Guyton, Patrick Langetieg, and Melissa Vigil. 2010. "Individual Taxpayer Compliance Burden: The Role of Assisted Methods in Taxpayer Response to Increasing Complexity." In *IRS Research Bulletin: Proceedings of the 2010 IRS Research Conference,* eds. Martha Eller Gangi and Alan Plumley, 191–220. Washington, DC: U.S. Department of the Treasury. <http://www.irs.gov/pub/irs-soi/10rescon.pdf> (accessed September 7, 2016).

Copeland, Craig. 2014. "Individual Account Retirement Plans: An Analysis of the 2013 Survey of Consumer Finances." EBRI Issue Brief No. 406, November. <http://www.ebri.org/pdf/briefspdf/EBRI_IB_406_Nov14.IAs1.pdf> (accessed July 20, 2015).

Cordes, Joseph, and Arlene Holen. 2010. "Should the Government Prepare Individual Income Tax Returns?" Working paper, Technology Policy Institute, September. <https://techpolicyinstitute.org/wp-content/uploads/2010/09/should-the-government-prepare-2007495.pdf> (accessed December 23, 2015).

Costa, Robert, and Ed O'Keefe. 2015. "Debate over Medicare, Social Security, Other Federal Benefits Divides GOP." *Washington Post,* November 4.

Crippen, Daniel. 2002. *Testimony before the House Budget Committee on Federal Budget Estimating,* Washington, DC, May 2.

Cronin, Julie-Anne, James Nunns, and Eric J. Toder. 1996. "Distributional Effects of Recent Tax Reform Proposals." Paper presented at the James A. Baker III Institute for Public Policy, Rice University, Second Annual Conference, Houston, TX, November 12–13.

Cruz, Ted. 2015. "A Simple Flat Tax for Economic Growth." *The Wall Street Journal* op-ed, October 28.

Cutler, David. 2010. "The Simple Economics of Health Reform." *The Economists' Voice,* December.

Cutler, David. 2013. "The Economics of the Affordable Care Act." *New York Times Economix Blog,* August 7. <http://economix.blogs.nytimes.com/2013/08/07/the-economics-of-the-affordable-care-act/> (accessed December 28, 2015).

Cutler, David. 2014. *The Quality Cure.* Berkeley: University of California Press.

Davies, A. J. 1995. "Only One Name for It: Bureaucratic Theft." *The Wall Street Journal,* April 5, A11.

Davies, James, and John Whalley. 1991. "Taxes and Capital Formation: How Important Is Human Capital?" In *National Saving and Economic Performance,* eds. Douglas Bernheim and John Shoven, 163–197. Chicago: University of Chicago Press.

Davis, Steven J., and Magnus Henrekson. 2005. "Tax Effects on Work Activity, Industry Mix and Shadow Economy Size: Evidence from Rich Country Comparisons." In *Labour*

Supply and Incentives to Work in Europe, eds. Ramon Gomez-Salvador, Ana Lamo, Barbara Petrongolo, Melanie Ward, and Etienne Wasmer, 44–104. Cheltenham, UK: Elgar.

Day, Liz. 2013. "How the Maker of TurboTax Fought Free, Simple Filing." *ProPublica*, March 26. <http://www.propublica.org/article/how-the-maker-of-turbotax-fought-free -simple-tax-filing> (accessed September 7, 2016).

DeLong, J. Bradford, and Lawrence H. Summers. 2012. "Fiscal Policy in a Depressed Economy." *Brookings Papers on Economic Activity* (Spring): 233–274.

de Paula, Aureo, and Jose A. Scheinkman. 2010. "Value-Added Taxes, Chain Effects, and Informality." *American Economic Journal: Macroeconomics* 2 (4): 195–221.

Desai, Mihir A., C. Fritz Foley, and James R. Hines Jr. 2006. "The Demand for Tax Haven Operations." *Journal of Public Economics* 90 (3): 513–531.

Desai, Mihir, and James R. Hines Jr. 2002. "Value-Added Taxes and International Trade: The Evidence." Working paper, University of Michigan, Ann Arbor, December.

Dharmapala, Dhammika. 2014. "What Do We Know About Base Erosion and Profit Shifting? A Review of the Empirical Literature." *Fiscal Studies* 35 (1): 421–448.

Diamond, Peter, and Emmanuel Saez. 2011. "The Case for a Progressive Tax: From Basic Research to Policy Recommendations." *Journal of Economic Perspectives* 25 (4): 165–190.

Dizikes, Peter. 2001. "Bush Presses for Tax Cut." *ABC News*, January 4. <http://abcnews .go.com/Politics/story?id=121888&page=1&singlePage=true> (accessed September 7, 2016).

Djankov, Simeon, Tim Ganser, Caralee McLiesh, Rita Ramalho, and Andrei Shleifer. 2010. "The Effect of Corporate Taxes on Investment and Entrepreneurship." *American Economic Journal: Macroeconomics* 2 (3): 31–64.

Dlouhy, Jennifer A. 2012. "Oil Industry Campaigns to Keep Its Tax Breaks." *Houston Chronicle*, March 23. <http://www.chron.com/business/article/Oil-industry-campaigns -to-keep-its-tax-breaks-3431361.php> (accessed September 7, 2016).

Domar, Evsey, and Richard Musgrave. 1944. "Proportional Income Taxation and Risk-Taking." *Quarterly Journal of Economics* 58 (2): 388–422.

Domenici, Pete, and Alice Rivlin. 2010. *Restoring America's Future: Reviving the Economy, Cutting Spending and Debt, and Creating a Simple Pro-Growth Tax System*. Bipartisan Policy Center, Washington, DC, November. <http://bipartisanpolicy.org/sites/default/files/ files/BPC%20FINAL%20REPORT%20FOR%20PRINTER%2002%2028%2011.pdf> (accessed September 7, 2016).

Donmoyer, Ryan J. 1997. "Flat Tax Strategy: The IRS as Poster Boy for Tax Reform." *Tax Notes* 77 (December 22): 1305.

Dowd, Tim, Paul Landefeld, and Anne Moore. 2014. "Profit Shifting of U.S. Multinationals." Joint Committee on Taxation Working Paper, January 8. <http://papers.ssrn.com/ sol3/papers.cfm?abstract_id=2711968> (accessed September 7, 2016).

Drucker, Jesse. 2010. "Google 2.4% Rate Shows How $60 Billion Lost to Tax Loopholes." *Bloomberg*, October 21. <http://www.bloomberg.com/news/print/2010-10-21/google -2-4-rate-shows-how-60-billion-u-s-revenue-lost-to-tax-loopholes.html> (accessed September 7, 2016).

Drucker, Jesse. 2016. "The World's Favorite New Tax Haven Is the United States." *Bloomberg Businessweek*, January 27. <http://www.bloomberg.com/news/articles/2016-01-27/the-world-s-favorite-new-tax-haven-is-the-united-states> (accessed September 7, 2016).

Drum, Kevin. 2016. "Is Bernie Sanders Responsible for Gerald Friedman's Economic Analysis?" *Mother Jones*, February 18. <http://www.motherjones.com/kevin-drum/2016/02/bernie-sanders-responsible-gerald-friedman> (accessed September 7, 2016).

Dubay, Curtis S. 2015. "JCT Dynamic Score of Bonus Depreciation: Highly Flawed." Heritage Foundation Issue Brief No. 4478, November 3. http://thf-reports.s3 .amazonaws.com/2015/IB4478.pdft (accessed September 7, 2016).

Dubner, Stephen J., and Steven D. Levitt. 2006. "Filling in the Tax Gap." *New York Times*, April 2.

Due, John F., and John L. Mikesell. 1994. *Sales Taxation: State and Local Structure and Administration*. Washington, DC: Urban Institute Press.

Dunbar, Amy, and Thomas Pogue. 1998. "Estimating Flat Tax Incidence and Yield: A Sensitivity Analysis." *National Tax Journal* 51 (2): 303–324.

Dusek, Libor. 2006. "Do Governments Grow When They Become More Efficient? Evidence from Tax Withholding." Working paper, CERGE-EI, Prague, Czech Republic, January 4. <http://congress.utu.fi/epcs2006/docs/E2_dusek.pdf> (accessed September 7, 2016).

Dwenger, Nadja. 2014. "User Cost Elasticity of Capital Revisited." *Economica* 81 (321): 161–186.

Dworkin, Ronald. 2000. *Sovereign Virtue: The Theory and Practice of Equality*. Cambridge, MA: Harvard University Press.

Dynan, Karen E., Jonathan Skinner, and Stephen P. Zeldes. 2004. "Do the Rich Save More?" *Journal of Political Economy* 112 (2): 397–444.

Ebrill, Liam, Michael Keen, Jean-Paul Bodin, and Victoria Summers. 2001. *The Modern VAT*. Washington, DC: International Monetary Fund.

Economic Report of the President 2012. 2012. Transmitted to the Congress, February. Washington, DC: Government Printing Office. <http://www.whitehouse.gov/administration/eop/cea/economic-report-of-the-President/2012> (accessed September 7, 2016).

Economic Report of the President 2015. 2015. Transmitted to the Congress, February. Washington, DC: Government Printing Office. <https://www.whitehouse.gov/administration/eop/cea/economic-report-of-the-President/2015> (accessed September 7, 2016).

The Economist. 2016. "Buttonwood: Donald Ducks the Big Questions," February 27. <http://www.economist.com/node/21693538/> (accessed September 7, 2016).

Edwards-Levy, Ariel. 2015. "America's Tax System Is Widely Seen as Favoring the Rich, Poll Shows." *Huffington Post*, January 28. <http://www.huffingtonpost.com/2015/01/28/tax-system-poll_n_6566388.html> (accessed September 7, 2016).

Eissa, Nada. 1995. "Taxation and Labor Supply of Married Women: The Tax Reform Act of 1986 as a Natural Experiment." NBER Working Paper No. 5023, February.

Eissa, Nada, and Hilary W. Hoynes. 2004. "Taxes and the Labor Market Participation of Married Couples: The Earned Income Tax Credit." *Journal of Public Economics* 88 (9–10): 1931–1958.

Eissa, Nada, and Jeffrey B. Liebman. 1996. "Labor Supply Response to the Earned Income Tax Credit." *Quarterly Journal of Economics* 111 (2): 605–637.

Elliott, Amy S. 2009. "Long-Awaited Proposed Credit Card Reporting Regs Released." *Tax Notes* 125 (November 30): 961.

Elmendorf, Douglas W., Jason Furman, William G. Gale, and Benjamin Harris. 2008. "Distributional Effects of the 2001 and 2003 Tax Cuts: How Do Financing and Behavioral Responses Matter?" *National Tax Journal* 61 (3): 365–380.

Engen, Eric, and William G. Gale. 1996. "The Effects of Fundamental Tax Reform on Saving." In *The Economic Effects of Fundamental Tax Reform*, eds. Henry Aaron and William G. Gale, 83–121. Washington, DC: Brookings Institution Press.

Evans, Blanche. 2005. "Why Loss of Homeowner Tax Benefits Will Cause Real Estate Bust." *RealtyTimes*, November 8. <http://realtytimes.com/todaysheadlines1/item/9369-20051109_taxbenefits> (accessed January 10, 2016).

Fack, Gabrielle, and Camille Landais. 2016. "The Effect of Tax Enforcement on Tax Elasticities: Evidence from Charitable Contributions in France." *Journal of Public Economics* 133 (January): 23–40.

Favero, Carlo, and Francesco Giavazzi. 2012. "Measuring Tax Multipliers: The Narrative Method in Fiscal VARs." *American Economic Journal: Economic Policy* 4 (2): 69–94.

Fastis, Stefan. 1992. "Big Earners Cash in Early to Beat Tax Bite." *San Francisco Chronicle*, December 29, C1.

Federal Reserve Bank of Cleveland. 2016. "Inflation Expectations." News Release, August 16. <https://www.clevelandfed.org/our-research/indicators-and-data/inflation-expectations/inflation-expectations-archives/ie-20160816.aspx> (accessed August 24, 2016).

Federal Reserve Bank of Philadelphia. 2015. "Historical Data: Livingston Survey." <http://www.phil.frb.org/research-and-data/real-time-center/livingston-survey/historical-data/> (accessed September 7, 2016).

Federation of Tax Administrators. 1993. "Vendor Collection of State Sales and Use Tax." *Tax Administrator News* 57: 88.

Feenberg, Daniel R., and James M. Poterba. 1993. "Income Inequality and the Incomes of Very High-Income Taxpayers: Evidence from Tax Returns." In *Tax Policy and the Economy*, vol. 7, ed. James M. Poterba, 145–177. Cambridge, MA: MIT Press.

Feld, Alan. 1995. "Living with the Flat Tax." *National Tax Journal* 48 (4): 603–618.

Feldstein, Martin. 1994. "Tax Policy and International Capital Flows." *Weltwirtschaftliches Archiv* 130 (4): 675–697.

Feldstein, Martin. 1995. "The Effect of a Consumption Tax on the Rate of Interest." NBER Working Paper No. 5397, December. <http://www.nber.org/papers/w5397.pdf> (accessed January 10, 2017).

Feldstein, Martin, and Daniel Feenberg. 1996. "The Effect of Increased Tax Rates on Taxable Income and Economic Efficiency: A Preliminary Analysis of the 1993 Tax Rate Increases." In *Tax Policy and the Economy*, vol. 10, ed. James M. Poterba, 89–118. Cambridge, MA: MIT Press.

Feldstein, Martin, and Charles Horioka. 1980. "Domestic Savings and International Capital Flows." *Economic Journal* 90 (358): 314–429.

Feyrer, James, and Bruce Sacerdote. 2011. "Did the Stimulus Stimulate? Real Time Estimates of the Effects of the American Recovery and Reinvestment Act." NBER Working Paper No. 16759, February. <http://www.nber.org/papers/w16759.pdf>(accessed September 22, 2016).

Figari, Francesco, Alari Paulos, Holly Sutherland, Panos Tsaklogu, Gerlinde Verbist, and Francesca Zantomio. 2012. "Taxing Home Ownership: Distributional Effects of Including Net Imputed Rent in Taxable Income." IZA Discussion Paper No. 6493, April. <http://ftp.iza.org/dp6493.pdf> (accessed December 22, 2015).

Fisher, Glenn W. 1996. *The Worst Tax? A History of the Property Tax in America*. Lawrence: University Press of Kansas.

Florida Department of Revenue. 1994. *Examination of Resale Abuse/Misuse: Summary of Findings*, Tallahassee, FL, June.

Fleischer, Victor. 2008. "Two and Twenty: Taxing Partnership Profits in Private Equity Funds." *New York University Law Review* 83 (1): 1–59.

Fleischer, Victor. 2015. "How a Carried Interest Tax Could Raise $180 Billion." *New York Times*, June 5.

Fleischer, Victor. 2016. "On Inversions, the Treasury Department Drops the Gloves." *New York Times DealBook*, April 5. <http://nyti.ms/1q3wwlY> (accessed September 7, 2016).

Finkelstein, Amy. 2009. "E-ZTax: Tax Salience and Tax Rates." *Quarterly Journal of Economics* 124 (3): 969–1010.

Fox, Cynthia G. 1986. "Income Tax Records of the Civil War Years." *Prologue Magazine* 18 (4): 250–259. <http://www.archives.gov/publications/prologue/1986/winter/civil-war-tax-records.html> (accessed September 7, 2016).

Frank, Robert H., and Philip J. Cook. 1995. *The Winner-Take-All Society*. New York: Free Press.

Frey, Bruno, and Reto Jegen. 2001. "Motivation Crowding Theory." *Journal of Economic Surveys* 15 (5): 589–611.

Friedman, Gerald. 2016. "What Would Sanders Do? Estimating the Economic Impact of Sanders Programs." Working paper, University of Massachusetts at Amherst, January 28. <http://www.dollarsandsense.org/What-would-Sanders-do-013016.pdf> (accessed September 7, 2016).

Friedman, Milton. 1962. *Capitalism and Freedom*. Chicago: University of Chicago Press.

Friedman, Milton. 2003. "What Every American Wants." *The Wall Street Journal*, January 15, A10.

Furchtgott-Roth, Diana. 2012. "The Myth of Increasing Income Inequality." Manhattan Institute for Policy Research, March. <http://www.manhattan-institute.org/pdf/ir_2.pdf> (accessed September 7, 2016).

Gale, William G. 1996. "The Kemp Commission and the Future of Tax Reform." *Tax Notes* 70 (February 5): 717–729.

Gale, William G. 2001. "Commentary on 'Will a Consumption Tax Kill the Housing Market?'" In *Transition Costs of Fundamental Tax Reform*, eds. Kevin A. Hassett and R. Glenn Hubbard, 115–122. Washington, DC: American Enterprise Institute Press.

Gale, William G. 2005. "The National Retail Sales Tax: What Would the Rate Have to Be?" *Tax Notes* 107 (May 16): 889–911.

Gale, William G., and Janet Holtzblatt. 1997. "On the Possibility of a No-Return System." *National Tax Journal* 50 (3): 475–485.

Gale, William G., and Maria Perozek. 2001. "Do Estate Taxes Reduce Saving?" In *Rethinking Estate and Gift Taxation*, eds. William G. Gale, James R. Hines Jr., and Joel Slemrod, 216–247. Washington, DC: Brookings Institution Press.

Gale, William G., and Samara R. Potter. 2002. "An Economic Evaluation of the Economic Growth and Tax Relief Reconciliation Act of 2001." *National Tax Journal* 55 (1): 133–186.

Gale, William G., and John Sabelhaus. 1999. "Perspectives on the Household Saving Rate." *Brookings Papers on Economic Activity* 1: 181–214.

Gale, William G., and Andrew A. Samwick. 2014. "Effects of Income Tax Changes on Economic Growth." Working paper, Economic Studies at Brookings Institution, September. <http://www.brookings.edu/~/media/research/files/papers/2014/09/09-effects-income-tax-changes-economic-growth-gale-samwick/09_effects_income_tax_changes_economic_growth_gale_samwick.pdf>. (accessed September 7, 2016).

Gallup. 2015. *Taxes.* <http://www.gallup.com/poll/1714/taxes.aspx> (acccessed September 7, 2016).

Garcia, Erica. 2002. "Checking Up on the IRS: MONEY Tested the IRS Agents Who Help You File Your Taxes. They Did Well—Sometimes." *Money* 31 (May): 125.

Gates, William H., Sr., and Chuck Collins. 2003. *Wealth and Our Commonwealth: Why America Should Tax Accumulated Fortunes.* Boston: Beacon Press.

Gelber, Alexander M. 2011. "How Do 401(k)s Affect Saving? Evidence from Changes in 401(k) Eligibility." *American Economic Journal: Economic Policy* 3 (4): 103–122.

Gemmell, Norman, and Joey Au. 2013. "Do Smaller Governments Raise the Level or Growth of Output? A Review of Recent Evidence." *Review of Economics* 64 (2): 85–116. http://www.review-of-economics.com/download/Gemmell_Au_2013.pdf (accessed September 7, 2016).

Gemmell, Norman, Richard Kneller, and Ismael Sanz. 2015. "The Growth Effects of Tax Rates in the OECD." *Canadian Journal of Economics. Revue Canadienne d'Economique* 47 (4): 1217–1255.

Gentry, William M., and R. Glenn Hubbard. 1997. "Distributional Implications of Introducing a Broad-Based Consumption Tax." In *Tax Policy and the Economy*, vol. 11, ed. James M. Poterba, 1–47. Cambridge, MA: MIT Press.

Gentry, William M., and R. Glenn Hubbard. 2004. "Entrepreneurship and Household Saving." *Advances in Economic Analysis & Policy* 4 (1): 1-55.

Gillis, Malcolm, Peter Mieszkowski, and George R. Zodrow. 1996. "Indirect Consumption Taxes: Common Issues and Differences among the Alternative Approaches." *Tax Law Review* 51 (Summer): 725–774.

Ginsburg, Martin. 1995. "Life under a Personal Consumption Tax: Some Thoughts on Working, Saving, and Consuming in Nunn-Domenici's Tax World." *National Tax Journal* 48 (4): 585–602.

Glaeser, Edward L. 2010. "A Tax Break That Is Breaking Us." *Boston Globe*, May 7.

Glaeser, Edward L., and Jesse M. Shapiro. 2003. "The Benefits of the Home Mortgage Interest Deduction." In *Tax Policy and the Economy*, vol. 17, ed. James M. Poterba, 37–82. Cambridge, MA: MIT Press.

Gleckman, Howard. 2016. "We Are Learning Less About Trump's Tax Plan, Not More." Urban-Brookings Tax Policy Center *TaxVox Blog*, August 18. <http://www.taxpolicycenter.org/taxvox/we-are-learning-less-about-trumps-tax-plan-not-more> (accessed September 7, 2016).

Glied, Sherry A., and Dahlia K. Remler. 2002. "What Every Public Finance Economist Needs to Know about Health Economics: Recent Advances and Unresolved Questions." *National Tax Journal* 55 (4): 771–788.

Gneezy, Uri, and Aldo Rustichini. 2000. "A Fine Is a Price." *Journal of Legal Studies* 29 (1): 1–17.

Godwin, Michael. 1995. "The Compliance Costs of the United Kingdom Tax System." In *Tax Compliance Costs: Measurement and Policy*, ed. Cedric Sandford, 73–100. Bath, UK: Fiscal Publications.

Goldstein, Amy. 2015. "Congress to Delay ACA's 'Cadillac' Tax on Pricey Health Plans Until 2020." *Washington Post*, December 16.

Goode, Richard. 1976. *The Individual Income Tax*. Washington, DC: Brookings Institution Press.

Goolsbee, Austan. 1999. "Evidence on the High-Income Laffer Curve from Six Decades of Tax Reform." *Brookings Papers on Economic Activity* 2: 1–64.

Gordon, Roger H. 1998. "Can High Personal Tax Rates Encourage Entrepreneurial Activity?" *IMF Staff Papers* 45 (1): 49–80.

Gordon, Roger H., Laura Kalambokidis, Jeffrey Rohaly, and Joel Slemrod. 2004. "Toward a Consumption Tax, and Beyond." *American Economic Review* 94 (2): 161–165.

Gorman, William M. 1976. "Tricks with Utility Functions." In *Essays in Economic Analysis: Proceedings of the 1975 AUTE Conference*, eds. M. J. Artis and A. R. Nobay, 211–244. Cambridge: Cambridge University Press.

Gorodnichenko, Yuriy, Jorge Martinez-Vazquez, and Klara Sabirianova Peter. 2009. "Myth and Reality of Flat Tax Reform: Micro Estimates of Tax Evasion Response and Welfare Effects in Russia." *Journal of Political Economy* 117 (3): 504–554.

Government Accountability Office. 1993. *Value-Added Tax: Administrative Costs Vary with Complexity and Number of Businesses*. Study No. GAO/GGD-93–78, Washington, DC, May. <http://www.gao.gov/products/GGD-93-78> (accessed November 3, 2016).

Government Accountability Office. 2001. *Private Pensions: Issues of Coverage and Increasing Contribution Limits for Defined Contribution Plans.* Publication No. GAO-01–846, Washington, DC, September. <http://www.gao.gov/products/GAO-01-846> (accessed November 3, 2016).

Government Accountability Office. 2005. *IRS Modernization: Continued Progress Requires Addressing Resource Management Challenges.* Publication No. GAO-05–707T, Washington, DC, May. <http://www.gao.gov/new.items/d05707t.pdf> (accessed September 7, 2016).

Government Accountability Office. 2013. *Corporate Tax Expenditures: Evaluations of Tax Deferrals and Graduated Tax Rates.* Publication No. GAO-13–789, Washington, DC, September. <http://www.gao.gov/assets/660/657896.pdf> (accessed September 7, 2016).

Government Accountability Office. 2014a. *2014 Performance Highlights the Need to Better Manage Taxpayer Service and Future Risks.* Publication No. GAO-15–163, Washington, DC, December. <http://www.gao.gov/assets/670/667563.pdf> (accessed September 7, 2016).

Government Accountability Office. 2014b. *Paid Tax Return Preparers: In a Limited Study, Preparers Made Significant Errors.* Testimony before the Committee on Finance, U.S. Senate. Publication No. GAO-14-467T, Washington, DC, April 8. <http://www.gao.gov/assets/670/662356.pdf> (accessed September 7, 2016).

Government Accountability Office. 2015a. *ALTERNATIVE SIMULATION: Trustees' Assumptions for Social Security and Medicare.* <http://www.gao.gov/assets/670/669525.pdf> (accessed September 7, 2016).

Government Accountability Office. 2015b. *The Federal Government's Long-Term Fiscal Outlook, Spring 2015 Update.* <http://www.gao.gov/assets/670/669538.pdf> (accessed September 7, 2016).

Graetz, Michael J. 1999. *The U.S. Income Tax: What It Is, How It Got That Way, and Where We Go from Here.* New York: Norton.

Graetz, Michael J. 2002. "One Hundred Million Unnecessary Returns: A Fresh Start for the U.S. Tax System." *Yale Law Journal* 112 (2): 261–310.

Graetz, Michael J., and Deborah H. Schenk. 2013. *Federal Income Taxation: Principles and Policies.* 7th ed. New York: Foundation Press.

Gravelle, Jane. 1994. *The Economic Effects of Taxing Capital Income.* Cambridge, MA: MIT Press.

Gravelle, Jane. 2014. "Corporate Tax Reform: Issues for Congress." Congressional Research Service Report No. RL34229, January 6. <http://www.ctj.org/pdf/crscorporatetaxreformissuesforcongress.pdf> (accessed September 7, 2016).

Gravelle, Jane. 2015a. "Tax Havens: International Tax Avoidance and Evasion." Congressional Research Service Report No. R40623, January 15. <https://www.fas.org/sgp/crs/misc/R40623.pdf> (accessed September 7, 2016).

Gravelle, Jane. 2015b. "Reform of U.S. International Taxation: Alternatives." Congressional Research Service Report No. RL34115, June 3. <https://www.fas.org/sgp/crs/misc/RL34115.pdf> (accessed September 7, 2016).

Gravelle, Jane G., and Kent A. Smetters. 2006. "Does the Open Economy Assumption Really Mean That Labor Bears the Burden of a Capital Income Tax?" *B.E. Journal of Economic Analysis and Policy: Advances in Economic Analysis and Policy* 6 (1): 1–42.

Gray, Robert T. 1995. "Blockbuster Tax Reform." *Nation's Business* 83 (April): 18–24.

Greenberg, Scott. 2016. "Donald Trump Revises His Tax Plan." Tax Foundation, August 8. <http://taxfoundation.org/blog/donald-trump-revises-his-tax-plan> (accessed September 7, 2016).

Greenhouse, Linda. 2000. "Bush Prevails; By Single Vote, Justices End Recount, Blocking Gore After 5-Week Struggle." *New York Times*, December 13.

Grubert, Harry, and Rosanne Altshuler. 2013. "Fixing the System: An Analysis of Alternative Proposals for the Reform of International Tax." *National Tax Journal* 66 (3): 671–712.

Guyton, John, John F. O'Hare, Michael P. Starrianos, and Eric Toder. 2003. "Estimating the Compliance Cost of the U.S. Individual Income Tax." *National Tax Journal* 56 (3): 673–688.

Haddon, Heather. 2015. "Donald Trump Says Tax Plan Could Lift GDP Growth to 6%." *The Wall Street Journal*, September 28.

Haig, Robert M. 1921. "The Concept of Income—Economic and Legal Aspects." In *The Federal Income Tax*, ed. Robert M. Haig, 1–28. New York: Columbia University Press.

Hall, Arthur P. 1995. "Compliance Costs of Alternative Tax Systems." Testimony before the House Ways and Means Committee. Tax Foundation Special Brief, Washington, DC, June. <http://taxfoundation.org/article/compliance-costs-alternative-tax-systems> (accessed September 7, 2016).

Hall, Kevin G., and Maris Taylor. 2016. "Massive Leak Exposes How the Wealthy and Powerful Hide Their Money." *McClatchy DC*, April 3. <http://www.mcclatchydc.com/news/nation-world/national/article69994502.html> (accessed September 7, 2016).

Hall, Robert E. 2005. "Guidelines for Tax Reform: The Simple, Progressive Value-Added Consumption Tax." In *Toward Fundamental Tax Reform*, eds. Alan Auerbach and Kevin A. Hassett, 70-80. Washington, DC: AEI Press.

Hall, Robert E., and Alvin Rabushka. 1995. *The Flat Tax*. 2nd ed. Stanford, CA: Hoover Institution Press.

Harris Interactive and Tax Foundation. 2009. "2009 Tax Attitudes Study: Tax Foundation: Datasheeted Questionnaire," April 8. <http://taxfoundation.org/article/topline-results-tax-foundations-2009-survey-us-attitudes-taxes-government-spending-and-wealth> (accessed September 7, 2016).

Harwood, John. 2013. "Puzzle Awaits the Capital: How to Solve 3 Fiscal Rifts." *New York Times*, August 15.

Hassett, Kevin A., and R. Glenn Hubbard. 2002. "Tax Policy and Business Investment." In *Handbook of Public Economics*, vol. 4, eds. Alan J. Auerbach and Martin Feldstein, 1293–1343. Amsterdam: Elsevier Science, North-Holland.

Hassett, Kevin A., and Apaarna Mathur. 2012. "A New Measure of Consumption Inequality." Working paper, American Enterprise Institute, June. <http://www.aei.org/files/2012/06/25/-a-new-measure-of-consumption-inequality_142931647663.pdf> (accessed September 7, 2016).

Hayek, Friedrich A. 2007. *The Road to Serfdom: Text and Documents*. Chicago: University of Chicago Press.

Hayek, Friedrich A. 2011. *The Constitution of Liberty*. Chicago: University of Chicago Press.

Heim, Bradley T. 2007. "The Incredible Shrinking Elasticities: Married Female Labor Supply, 1978–2002." *Journal of Human Resources* 42 (4): 881–918.

Heim, Bradley T. 2009. "Structural Estimation of Family Labor Supply with Taxes: Estimating a Continuous Hours Model Using a Direct Utility Specification." *Journal of Human Resources* 44 (2): 350–385.

Henry J. Kaiser Family Foundation. 2013. "Summary of the Affordable Care Act," updated April 2013. <http://files.kff.org/attachment/fact-sheet-summary-of-the-affordable-care-act> (accessed September 7, 2016).

Her Majesty's Revenue and Customs. 2016. "VAT Notice 700/1: Supplement," February 24. <https://www.gov.uk/government/publications/vat-notice-7001-should-i-be-registered-for-vat/vat-notice-7001-supplement--2#registration-limits-taxable-supplies> (accessed September 7, 2016).

Herszenhorn, David M. 2015a. "A Budget Deal Promising Peace Is Rooted in Modest Goals." *New York Times*, October 27.

Herszenhorn, David M. 2015b. "Congress Passes $1 Trillion Spending Measure." *New York Times*, December 18.

Hessing, Dick J., Hank Elffers, Henry S. J. Robben, and Paul Webley. 1992. "Does Deterrence Deter? Measuring the Effect of Deterrence on Tax Compliance in Field Studies and Experimental Studies." In *Why People Pay Taxes: Tax Compliance and Enforcement*, ed. Joel Slemrod, 291–305. Ann Arbor: University of Michigan Press.

Hicks, Josh. 2013. "House Subcommittee Approves GOP Plan to Slash IRS Budget by 24 Percent." *Washington Post*, July 10.

Higgins, Heather Richardson. 1995. "Tax Fairness: Treat All Dollars Equally." *The Wall Street Journal*, April 5, A11.

Hines, James R., Jr. 1999. "Lessons from Behavioral Responses to International Taxation." *National Tax Journal* 52 (2): 305–322.

Hite, Peggy A., John Hasseldine, and Darius Fatemi. 2007. "Tax Rate Preferences: Understanding the Effects of Perceived and Actual Current Tax Assessments." In *IRS Research Bulletin: Proceedings of the 2007 IRS Research Conference*, eds. James Dalton and Martha Gangi, 23-50. Washington, DC: U.S. Department of the Treasury. <http://www.irs.gov/pub/irs-soi/07resconfhite.pdf> (accessed September 7, 2016).

Hite, Peggy A., and Michael L. Roberts. 1991. "An Experimental Investigation of Taxpayer Judgments on Rate Structure in the Individual Income Tax System." *Journal of the American Taxation Association* 13 (2): 47–63.

Hoffman, William. 2012. "Tax Controversies of the Suddenly Wealthy and Famous." *Tax Notes* 136 (August 27): 981.

Holahan, John, and Stacey McMorrow. 2015. "The Widespread Slowdown in Health Spending Growth: Implications for Future Spending Projections and the Cost of the Affordable Care Act." Robert Wood Johnson Foundation and Urban Institute report, Washington, DC, April. <http://www.rwjf.org/content/dam/farm/reports/reports/2015/rwjf419172> (accessed September 7, 2016).

Holtz-Eakin, Douglas, David Joulfaian, and Harvey S. Rosen. 1993. "The Carnegie Conjecture: Some Empirical Evidence." *Quarterly Journal of Economics* 108 (2): 413–435.

Holtz-Eakin, Douglas, and Donald Marples. 2001. "Distortion Costs of Taxing Wealth Accumulation: Income Versus Estate Taxes." NBER Working Paper No. w8261, April. <http://papers.nber.org/papers/w8261> (accessed September 7, 2016).

House, Christopher L., and Matthew D. Shapiro. 2008. "Temporary Investment Tax Incentives: Theory with Evidence from Bonus Depreciation." *American Economic Review* 98 (3): 737–768.

Hoynes, Hillary 2014. "A Revolution in Poverty Policy: The Earned Income Tax Credit and the Well-Being of American Families." *Pathways: A Magazine on Poverty, Inequality, and Social Policy*, Stanford, Summer. https://web.stanford.edu/group/scspi/_media/pdf/pathways/summer_2014/Pathways_Summer_2014_Hoynes.pdf (accessed September 7, 2016).

Huang, Chye-Ching, and Nathaniel Frentz. 2014. "What Really Is the Evidence on Taxes and Growth?" Center on Budget and Policy Priorities, February 18. <http://www.cbpp.org/sites/default/files/atoms/files/2-18-14tax.pdf> (accessed September 7, 2016).

Hubbard, R. Glenn. 1998. "Capital-Market Imperfections and Investment." *Journal of Economic Literature* 36 (1): 193–225.

Hubbard, R. Glenn. 2012. "Flawed Criticism of Mitt Romney's Tax Plan." *Washington Post*, August 21.

Humer, Caroline, and Ransdell Pierson. 2016. "Obama's Inversion Curbs Kill Pfizer's $160 Billion Allergan Deal." *Reuters*, April 6. <http://www.reuters.com/article/us-allergan-m-a-pfizer-idUSKCN0X21NV> (accessed September 7, 2016).

Imai, Susumu, and Michael P. Keane. 2004. "Intertemporal Labor Supply and Human Capital Accumulation." *International Economic Review* 45 (2): 601–641.

Imbens, Guido W., Donald B. Rubin, and Bruce Sacerdote. 2001. "Estimating the Effect of Unearned Income on Labor Earnings, Savings, and Consumption: Evidence from a Survey of Lottery Players." *American Economic Review* 91 (4): 778–794.

Indiana University Lilly Family School of Philanthropy. 2015. *Giving USA 2015: The Annual Report on Philanthropy for the Year 2014*. Giving USA Foundation, Chicago. <https://givingusa.org/product-category/2015-products/> (accessed November 3, 2016).

Internal Revenue Service (IRS). Various Years. *Internal Revenue Service Data Book*. Publication 55B, Washington, DC. <https://www.irs.gov/pub/irs-pdf/p55b.pdf?_ga=1.234236439.86000257.1473445197> (accessed November 3, 2016).

Internal Revenue Service (IRS). Various Years. *Statistics of Income—Corporation Income Tax Returns, Complete Report*. <http://www.irs.gov/uac/SOI-Tax-Stats-Corporation-Complete-Report> (accessed September 7, 2016).

Internal Revenue Service (IRS). Various Years. *Statistics of Income—Corporation Source Book*. Publication 1053, Washington, DC. <http://www.irs.gov/uac/SOI-Tax-Stats-Corporation-Source-Book:-U.S.-Total-and-Sectors-Listing> (accessed September 7, 2016).

Internal Revenue Service (IRS). Various Years. *Statistics of Income—Individual Income Tax Returns, Complete Report*. Publication 1304, Washington, DC. <https://www.irs.gov/

uac/soi-tax-stats-individual-income-tax-returns-publication-1304-complete-report (accessed September 7, 2016).

Internal Revenue Service (IRS). 1989. *Instructions for Form 1040, U.S. Individual Income Tax Return, and Schedules A, B, C, D, E, F, J, L, M, and SE, 1988.* <http://www.irs.gov/pub/irs-prior/i1040--1988.pdf> (accessed September 7, 2016).

Internal Revenue Service (IRS). 1992. *1992 Annual Report.* <http://www.irs.gov/file_source/pub/irs-soi/92dbfullar.pdf> (accessed September 7, 2016).

Internal Revenue Service (IRS). 1998. *1997 Data Book.* <http://www.irs.gov/file_source/pub/irs-soi/97dbfullar.pdf> (accessed September 7, 2016).

Internal Revenue Service (IRS). 2006. *IRS Accepts Settlement Offer in Largest Transfer Pricing Dispute,* September 11. <https://www.irs.gov/uac/IRS-Accepts-Settlement-Offer-in-Largest-Transfer-Pricing-Dispute> (accessed September 7, 2016).

Internal Revenue Service (IRS). 2007. *Reducing the Federal Tax Gap: A Report on Improving Voluntary Compliance,* August 2. <http://www.irs.gov/file_source/pub/irs-news/tax_gap_report_final_080207_linked.pdf> (accessed September 7, 2016).

Internal Revenue Service (IRS). 2012a. *Tax Gap for Tax Year 2006: Overview,* January 6. <http://www.irs.gov/file_source/pub/newsroom/overview_tax_gap_2006.pdf> (accessed September 7, 2016).

Internal Revenue Service (IRS). 2012b. *Data Book 2011.* Publication 55B, Washington, DC. <http://www.irs.gov/pub/irs-soi/11databk.pdf> (accessed September 7, 2016).

Internal Revenue Service (IRS). 2012c. *2011 Instructions to Form 1120,* January 23. <http://www.irs.gov/pub/irs-prior/i1120--2011.pdf> (September 7, 2016).

Internal Revenue Service (IRS). 2013a. *Instructions for Form 1040, U.S. Individual Income Tax Return, and Schedules A, C, D, E, F, J, R, and SE, 2012.* <http://www.irs.gov/pub/irs-prior/i1040--2012.pdf> (accessed September 7, 2016).

Internal Revenue Service (IRS). 2013b. *Most Tax Return Preparers Must Use IRS e-file.* <http://www.irs.gov/Tax-Professionals/e-File-Providers-&-Partners/Most-Tax-Return-Preparers-Must-Use-IRS-e-file> (accessed September 7, 2016).

Internal Revenue Service (IRS). 2013c. *SOI Tax Stats—Historical Table 15.* <http://www.irs.gov/uac/SOI-Tax-Stats---Historical-Table-15> (accessed July 31, 2013).

Internal Revenue Service (IRS). 2013d. *SOI Tax Stats—Table 15. All Partnerships: Total Assets, Trade or Business Income and Deductions, Portfolio Income, Rental Income, and Total Net Income, by Size of Total Assets, 2009.* <http://www.irs.gov/file_source/pub/irs-soi/09pa15.xls> (accessed September 7, 2016).

Internal Revenue Service (IRS). 2013e. *2012 Instructions to Form 1120,* January 25. <https://www.irs.gov/pub/irs-prior/i1120--2012.pdf> (accessed September 7, 2016).

Internal Revenue Service (IRS). 2014a. "Revenue Procedure 2014-61." *Internal Revenue Bulletin 2014–47,* November 17. <http://www.irs.gov/irb/2014-47_IRB/ar14.html> (accessed September 7, 2016).

Internal Revenue Service (IRS). 2014b. *2011 Corporation Income Tax Returns Line Item Estimates.* <http://www.irs.gov/pub/irs-soi/11colineitemestimates.pdf> (accessed September 7, 2016).

Internal Revenue Service (IRS). 2014c. *2014 Instructions for Schedule C*, December 22. <http://www.irs.gov/pub/irs-pdf/i1040sc.pdf> (accessed September 7, 2016).

Internal Revenue Service (IRS). 2014d. *IRS Announces 2015 Pension Plan Limitations.* IR-2014–99, Washington, DC, October 23. <http://www.irs.gov/uac/Newsroom/IRS -Announces-2015-Pension-Plan-Limitations-1> (accessed September 7, 2016).

Internal Revenue Service (IRS). 2014e. *Earned Income Credit.* Publication 596, Washington, DC, December 18. <http://www.irs.gov/pub/irs-pdf/p596.pdf> (accessed September 7, 2016).

Internal Revenue Service (IRS). 2014f. "Estate and Gift Tax Returns." *Internal Revenue Manual 21.7.5.* <http://www.irs.gov/irm/part21/irm_21-007-005r.html> (accessed July 21, 2015).

Internal Revenue Service (IRS). 2014g. *SOI Tax Stats—Historical Table 24.* Page last reviewed or updated May 9, 2014. <https://www.irs.gov/uac/SOI-Tax-Stats-Historical -Table-24> (accessed January 10, 2016).

Internal Revenue Service (IRS). 2014h. *IRS Offshore Voluntary Disclosure Efforts Produce $6.5 Billion; 45,000 Taxpayers Participate,* June. <https://www.irs.gov/uac/Newsroom/ IRS-Offshore-Voluntary-Disclosure-Efforts-Produce-$6.5-Billion%3B-45,000-Taxpayers -Participate> (accessed September 7, 2016).

Internal Revenue Service (IRS). 2015a. *SOI Tax Stats—Integrated Business Data.* <http:// www.irs.gov/uac/SOI-Tax-Stats-Integrated-Business-Data> (accessed September 7, 2016).

Internal Revenue Service (IRS). 2015b. *S Corporation Compensation and Medical Insurance Issues.* Last updated April 27. <http://www.irs.gov/Businesses/Small-Businesses-& -Self-Employed/S-Corporation-Compensation-and-Medical-Insurance-Issues> (accessed June 23, 2015).

Internal Revenue Service (IRS). 2015c. *Retirement Topics-IRA Contribution Limits.* Updated January 22. <http://www.irs.gov/Retirement-Plans/Plan-Participant,-Employee/ Retirement-Topics-IRA-Contribution-Limits> (accessed June 23, 2015).

Internal Revenue Service (IRS). 2015d. *Home Mortgage Interest Deduction: For Use in Preparing 2014 Returns,* January 8. <http://www.irs.gov/pub/irs-pdf/p936.pdf> (accessed September 7, 2016).

Internal Revenue Service (IRS). 2015e. *SOI Tax Stats–Table 4–Returns of Active Corporations, Form 1120S,* January 8. Page last reviewed or updated April 30, 2015. <http:// www.irs.gov/uac/SOI-Tax-Stats-Table-4-Returns-of-Active-Corporations,-Form-1120S> (accessed June 24, 2015).

Internal Revenue Service (IRS). 2015f. *Tax Guide for Small Business, for Use in Preparing 2014 Returns.* Publication 334, Washington, DC. <http://www.irs.gov/pub/irs-pdf/ p334.pdf> (accessed September 7, 2016).

Internal Revenue Service (IRS). 2015g. *Internal Revenue Service Data Book 2014,* Publication 55B, Washington, DC. <http://www.irs.gov/pub/irs-soi/14databk.pdf> (accessed September 7, 2016).

Internal Revenue Service (IRS). 2015h. *Free File: Do Your Federal Taxes for Free.* <http:// www.irs.gov/uac/Free-File:-Do-Your-Federal-Taxes-for-Free> (accessed June 29, 2015).

Internal Revenue Service (IRS). 2015i. *SOI Tax Stats—Historical Table 1.* Page last reviewed or updated October 6, 2015. <http://www.irs.gov/uac/SOI-Tax-Stats-Historical-Table-1> (accessed January 10, 2016).

Internal Revenue Service (IRS). 2015j. *SOI Tax Stats—Historical Table 13.* <http://www.irs.gov/uac/SOI-Tax-Stats-Historical-Table-13> (accessed June 30, 2015).

Internal Revenue Service (IRS). 2015k. *Lifetime Learning Credit.* Publication 970, February 25. <http://www.irs.gov/publications/p970/ch03.html#en_US_2014_publink1000178191> (accessed July 6, 2015).

Internal Revenue Service (IRS). 2015l. *Contributions to Individual Retirement Accounts (IRAs).* Publication 590A, Washington, DC, January 13. <http://www.irs.gov/pub/irs-pdf/p590a.pdf> (accessed July 20, 2015).

Internal Revenue Service (IRS). 2015m. *SOI Tax Stats—Historical Table 22.* <http://www.irs.gov/uac/SOI-Tax-Stats-Historical-Table-22> (accessed June 30, 2015).

Internal Revenue Service (IRS). 2015n. *2014 Instructions to Form 1120.* <https://www.irs.gov/pub/irs-pdf/i1120.pdf> (accessed September 7, 2016).

Internal Revenue Service (IRS). 2015o. *SOI Tax Stats—Historical Table 9.* Last reviewed or updated October 6, 2015. https://www.irs.gov/uac/SOI-Tax-Stats-Historical-Table-9> (accessed January 10, 2016).

Internal Revenue Service (IRS). 2016a. *SOI Tax Stats—Historical Table 23.* Page last reviewed or updated May 17, 2016. <https://www.irs.gov/uac/SOI-Tax-Stats-Historical-Table-23> (accessed August 20, 2016).

Internal Revenue Service (IRS). 2016b. *Tax Gap Estimates for Tax Years 2008–2010,* April 28. <https://www.irs.gov/PUP/newsroom/tax%20gap%20estimates%20for%202008%20through%202010.pdf> (accessed September 7, 2016).

Internal Revenue Service Oversight Board. 2014. *2014 Taxpayer Attitude Survey,* December. <http://www.treasury.gov/IRSOB/reports/Documents/IRSOB%20Taxpayer%20Attitude%20Survey%202014.pdf> (accessed September 7, 2016).

International Bureau for Fiscal Documentation. 2007. *Africa: Taxation & Investment* (online subscription database) (accessed August 29, 2007).

International Monetary Fund. 2015. *Current Challenges in Revenue Mobilization: Improving Tax Compliance,* April. <http://www.imf.org/external/np/pp/eng/2015/020215a.pdf> (accessed September 7, 2016).

Jacob, Brian A., and Jens Ludwig. 2012. "The Effects of Housing Assistance on Labor Supply: Evidence from a Voucher Lottery." *American Economic Review* 102 (1): 272–304.

Jäntti, Markus, Jukka Pirttilä, and Håkan Selin. 2015. "Estimating Labour Supply Elasticities Based on Cross-Country Micro Data: A Bridge between Micro and Macro Estimates?" *Journal of Public Economics* 127 (July): 87–99.

Ji, Kan, and Jenny E. Ligthart. 2012. "The Causes and Consequences of the Flat Income Tax." Tilburg University, August. <https://editorialexpress.com/cgi-bin/conference/download.cgi?db_name=res_phd_2013&paper_id=116> (accessed September 7, 2016).

Johns, Andrew, and Joel Slemrod. 2010. "The Distribution of Income Tax Noncompliance." *National Tax Journal* 63 (3): 397–418.

Johnson, David A., Jonathan A. Parker, and Nicholas S. Souleles. 2006. "Household Expenditure and the Income Tax Rebates of 2001." *American Economic Review* 96 (5): 1589–1610.

Joint Committee on Taxation. 1995. *Written Testimony of the Staff of the Joint Committee on Taxation Regarding the Revenue Estimating Process.* Report No. JCX-1–95, Washington, DC, January 10. <https://www.jct.gov/publications.html?func=startdown&id=1183> (accessed September 7, 2016).

Joint Committee on Taxation. 1999. *Present Law and Background on Federal Tax Provisions Relating to Retirement Savings Incentives, Health and Long-Term Care, and Estate and Gift Taxes.* Report No. JCX-29–99, Washington, DC, June 15. <http://www.jct.gov/jct _html/x-29-99.htm> (accessed September 7, 2016).

Joint Committee on Taxation. 2003a. *General Explanation of Tax Legislation Enacted in the 107th Congress.* Report No. JCS-1-03. Washington, DC: Government Printing Office. <https://www.gpo.gov/fdsys/pkg/CPRT-108JPRT83912/pdf/CPRT-108JPRT83912 .pdf> (accessed September 7, 2016).

Joint Committee on Taxation. 2003b. *Report of Investigation of Enron Corporation and Related Entities Regarding Federal Tax and Compensation Issues, and Policy Recommendations.* Report No. JCS-3–03, Washington, DC, February. <https://www.jct.gov/s-3-03-vol1.pdf> (accessed September 7, 2016).

Joint Committee on Taxation. 2003c. "Tax Complexity Analysis." *Congressional Record.* H4699–H4703, May 22.

Joint Committee on Taxation. 2003d. *Estimated Budget Effects of the Conference Agreement for H.R. 2, the "Jobs and Growth Tax Relief Reconciliation Act of 2003."* Report No. JCX-55–03, Washington, DC, May 22. <https://www.jct.gov/publications.html?func =startdown&id=1746> (accessed September 7, 2016).

Joint Committee on Taxation. 2005. *General Explanation of Tax Legislation Enacted in the 108th Congress.* Report No. JCS-5–05. Washington, DC: Government Printing Office. <https://www.jct.gov/publications.html?func=download&id=2314&chk=2314&no _html=1> (accessed September 7, 2016).

Joint Committee on Taxation. 2007. *General Explanation of Tax Legislation Enacted in the 109th Congress.* Report No. JCS-1–00. Washington, DC: Government Printing Office. <https://www.jct.gov/publications.html?func=download&id=2023&chk=2023&no _html=1> (accessed September 7, 2016).

Joint Committee on Taxation. 2009. *General Explanation of Tax Legislation Enacted in the 110th Congress.* Report No. JCS-1–09. Washington, DC: Government Printing Office. <https://www.jct.gov/publications.html?func=download&id=1990&chk=1990&no _html=1> (accessed September 7, 2016).

Joint Committee on Taxation. 2011. *General Explanation of Tax Legislation Enacted in the 111th Congress.* Report No. JCS-2–11, Washington, DC, March. <https://www.jct.gov/ publications.html?func=download&id=3775&chk=3775&no_html=1> (accessed September 7, 2016).

Joint Committee on Taxation. 2012a. *Selected Issues Relating to Choice of Business Entity.* Report No. JCX-20–12, Washington, DC, March 7. <https://www.jct.gov/publications.htm l?func=download&id=4402&chk=4402&no_html=1> (accessed September 7, 2016).

Joint Committee on Taxation. 2012b. *Background and Present Law Relating to Cost Recovery and Domestic Production Activities.* Report No. JCX-19–12, Washington, DC, February 27. <https://www.jct.gov/publications.html?func=download&id=4401&chk=4401&no_html=1> (accessed September 7, 2016).

Joint Committee on Taxation. 2013a. *General Explanation of Tax Legislation Enacted in the 112th Congress.* Report No. JCS-2-13. Washington, DC: Government Printing Office.<https://www.jct.gov/publications.html?func=download&id=4509&chk=4509&no_html=1> (accessed September 7, 2016).

Joint Committee on Taxation. 2013b. *Overview of the Federal Tax System as in Effect for 2013.* Report No. JCX-2–13R, Washington, DC, January 8. <https://www.jct.gov/publications.html?func=download&id=4498&chk=4498&no_html=1> (accessed September 7, 2016).

Joint Committee on Taxation. 2014. *Overview of the Federal Tax System as in Effect for 2014.* Report No. JCX-25–14, Washington, DC, March 28. <https://www.jct.gov/publications.html?func=startdown&id=4568> (accessed September 7, 2016).

Joint Committee on Taxation. 2015a. *Overview of the Federal Tax System as in Effect for 2015.* Report No. JCX-70–15, Washington, DC, March 30. <https://www.jct.gov/publications.html?func=startdown&id=4763> (accessed September 7, 2016).

Joint Committee on Taxation. 2015b. *Choice of Business Entity.* Report No. JCX-71–15, Washington, DC, April 10. <https://www.jct.gov/publications.html?func=startdown&id=4765> (accessed September 7, 2016).

Joint Committee on Taxation. 2015c. *General Explanation of Tax Legislation Enacted in the 113th Congress.* Report No. JCS-1–15, April 1. Washington, DC: Government Printing Office. <https://www.jct.gov/publications.html?func=startdown&id=4741> (accessed September 7, 2016).

Joint Committee on Taxation. 2015d. *Technical Explanation of the Revenue Provisions of the Protecting Americans from Tax Hikes Act of 2015, House Amendment #2 to the Senate Amendment to H.R. 2029 (Rules Committee Print 114–40).* Report No. JCX-144–15, Washington, DC, December 17. <https://www.jct.gov/publications.html?func=download&id=4861&chk=4861&no_html=1> (accessed September 7, 2016).

Joint Committee on Taxation. 2015e. *Estimates of Federal Tax Expenditures for Fiscal Years 2015–2019.* Report No. JCX-141R–15, Washington, DC, December 7. <https://www.jct.gov/publications.html?func=download&id=4857&chk=4857&no_html=1> (accessed September 7, 2016).

Jones, Charles I. 1995. "Time Series Tests of Endogenous Growth Models." *Quarterly Journal of Economics* 110 (2): 495–525.

Joulfaian, David. 2001. "Charitable Giving in Life and at Death." In *Rethinking Estate and Gift Taxation,* eds. William G. Gale, James R. Hines Jr., and Joel Slemrod, 350–374. Washington, DC: Brookings Institution Press.

Judge, Steve. 2013. "Why Carried Interest Is a Capital Gain." *New York Times*, March 4.

Kahn, Jeremy, and Thomas Penny. 2016. "Google Tells Parliament It Won't Pay 'Google Tax' in U.K." *Bloomberg Technology*, February 11. <http://www.bloomberg.com/news/articles/2016-02-11/google-tells-parliament-it-won-t-pay-google-tax-in-u-k> (accessed September 7, 2016).

Kaiser Commission on Medicaid and the Uninsured. 2010. *The Medicaid Program at a Glance*, June. <http://www.kff.org/medicaid/upload/7235-04.pdf> (accessed August 20, 2012).

Kaiser Commission on Medicaid and the Uninsured. 2013a. *Medicaid and Its Role in State/Federal Budgets and Health Care Reform*, April. <https://kaiserfamilyfoundation.files .wordpress.com/2013/04/8162-03.pdf> (accessed September 7, 2016).

Kaiser Commission on Medicaid and the Uninsured. 2013b. "Key Facts about the Uninsured Population," September. <https://kaiserfamilyfoundation.files.wordpress .com/2013/09/8488-key-facts-about-the-uninsured-population.pdf> (accessed September 7, 2016).

Kaiser Commission on Medicaid and the Uninsured. 2015. "Key Facts about the Uninsured Population," October. <http://files.kff.org/attachment/fact-sheet-key-facts -about-the-uninsured-population> (accessed September 7, 2016).

Kaplow, Louis. 1999. "Tax Treatment of Families." In *Encyclopedia of Taxation and Tax Policy*, 120–122. Washington, DC: Urban Institute Press.

Kaplow, Louis, and Steven Shavell. 2006. *Fairness versus Welfare*. Cambridge, MA: Harvard University Press.

Kawano, Laura, and Joel Slemrod. 2016. "How Do Corporate Tax Bases Change When Corporate Tax Rates Change? With Implications for the Tax Rate Elasticity of Corporate Tax Revenues." *International Tax and Public Finance* 23 (3): 401–433.

Keane, Michael P. 2011. "Labor Supply and Taxes: A Survey." *Journal of Economic Literature* 49 (4): 961–1075.

Keen, Michael, Yi Tae Kim, and Recard Varsano. 2006. "The 'Flat Tax(es)': Principles and Evidence." IMF Working Paper No. 06/218, September..

Keen, Michael, and Stephen Smith. 2006. "VAT Fraud and Evasion: What Do We Know and What Can Be Done?" *National Tax Journal* 59 (4): 861–887.

Keightley, Mark P., and Jeffrey M. Stupak. 2015. "Corporate Tax Base Erosion and Profit Shifting (BEPS): An Examination of the Data." Congressional Research Service Report No. R44013, April. <https://www.fas.org/sgp/crs/misc/R44013.pdf> (accessed September 7, 2016).

Kennickell, Arthur. 2009. "Ponds and Streams: Wealth and Income in the U.S., 1989 to 2007." Finance and Economics Discussion Series Working Paper No. 2009–13. Board of Governors of the Federal Reserve System, Washington, DC, January 7. <http:// www.federalreserve.gov/pubs/feds/2009/200913/200913pap.pdf> (accessed September 7, 2016).

Kenworthy, Lane. 2014. *Social Democratic America*. New York: Oxford University Press.

Kestenbaum, David. 2011. "What If We Paid Off the Debt? The Secret Government Report." *NPR Planet Money*, October 20. <http://www.npr.org/blogs/money/2011/10/ 21/141510617/what-if-we-paid-off-the-debt-the-secret-government-report> (accessed September 7, 2016).

Keyes, Alan. 2000. "Alan Keyes on Tax Reform." *On the Issues*. <http://www.issues2000 .org/Celeb/Alan_Keyes_Tax_Reform.htm> (accessed June 17, 2003).

Keynes, John Maynard. 1936. *The General Theory of Employment, Interest, and Money*. New York: Harcourt Brace.

Keynes, John Maynard. 1937. "The General Theory of Employment." *Quarterly Journal of Economics* 51 (2): 209–223.

Khadem, Nassim. 2015. "Why the United States Hate Britain and Australia's 'Google Tax.'" *Sydney Morning Herald*, June 25. <http://www.smh.com.au/business/comment -and-analysis/why-the-united-states-hates-britain-and-australias-google-tax -20150625-ghxj0n.html> (accessed September 7, 2016).

Kiefer, Donald, Robert Carroll, Janet Holtzblatt, Allen Lerman, Janet McCubbin, David Richardson, and Jerry Tempalski. 2002. "The Economic Growth and Tax Relief Reconcili- ation Act of 2001: Overview and Assessment of Effects on Taxpayers." *National Tax Journal* 55 (1): 89–117.

Kleinbard, Edward D. 2015. "Reimagining Capital Income Taxation." Working paper, University of Southern California Gould School of Law, June 5. <http://www.sbs.ox. ac.uk/sites/default/files/Business_Taxation/Events/conferences/symposia/2015/ kleinbard-paper.pdf> (accessed September 7, 2016).

Kleinbard, Edward D. 2016. "Stateless Income and Its Remedies." In *Global Tax Fairness*, eds. Thomas Pogge and Krishen Mehta, 129-152. Oxford: Oxford University Press.

Kleven, Henrik Jacobsen. 2014. "How Can Scandinavians Tax So Much?" *Journal of Economic Perspectives* 28 (4): 77–98.

Kliff, Sarah. 2015. "Obamacare's Changes to Doctor Payments, Explained." *Vox*. <http:// www.vox.com/cards/how-doctors-are-paid> (accessed September 7, 2016).

Knowlton, Brian, and Jackie Calmes. 2011. "Republicans Call Obama's Tax Plan 'Class Warfare.'" *New York Times*, September 18.

Kocieniewski, David. 2011. "G.E.'s Strategies Let It Avoid Taxes Altogether." *New York Times*, March 24.

Kogan, Richard. 2013. "The Pending Automatic Budget Cuts: How the Two 'Sequestra- tions' Would Work." Center on Budget and Policy Priorities, February 26. <http:// www.cbpp.org/files/2-26-13bud.pdf> (accessed August 16, 2013).

Kogan, Richard, and Joel Friedman. 2014. "Ryan Plan Gets 69 Percent of Its Budget Cuts from Programs for People with Low or Moderate Incomes." Center for Budget and Policy Priorities, April 8. <http://www.cbpp.org/research/ryan-plan-gets-69 -percent-of-its-budget-cuts-from-programs-for-people-with-low-or-moderate> (accessed September 7, 2016).

Kopczuk, Wojciech. 2015. "What Do We Know about the Evolution of Top Wealth Shares in the United States." *Journal of Economic Perspectives* 29 (1): 47–66.

Kopczuk, Wojciech, Emmanuel Saez, and Jae Song. 2010. "Earnings Inequality and Mobility in the United States: Evidence from Social Security Data since 1937." *Quarterly Journal of Economics* 125 (1): 91–128.

Kopczuk, Wojciech, and Joel Slemrod. 2001. "The Impact of the Estate Tax on the Wealth Accumulation and Avoidance Behavior of Donors." In *Rethinking Estate and Gift Taxation*, eds. William Gale, James R. Hines Jr., and Joel Slemrod, 299–349. Washington, DC: Brook- ings Institution Press.

Kopczuk, Wojciech, and Joel Slemrod. 2003. "Tax Impacts on Wealth Accumulation and Transfers of the Rich." In *Death and Dollars: The Role of Gifts and Bequests in America*, eds. Alicia Munnell and Annika Sunden, 213–257. Washington, DC: Brookings Institution Press.

Kornblut, Anne E., and Kimberly Blanton. 2003. "Bush Wants \$670B Cut in Taxes over Ten Years: Would Abolish Dividend Levies." *Boston Globe*, January 8, A1.

Kornhauser, Marjorie E. 2002. "More Historical Perspective on Publication of Corporate Returns." *Tax Notes* 96 (July 29): 745.

Krueger, Alan, Austan Goolsbee, Christina Romer, and Laura D'Andrea Tyson. 2016. "An Open Letter from Past CEA Chairs to Senator Sanders and Professor Gerald Friedman," February 17. <https://lettertosanders.wordpress.com/2016/02/17/open-letter -to-senator-sanders-and-professor-gerald-friedman-from-past-cea-chairs/> (accessed September 7, 2016).

Krugman, Paul. 1994. *Peddling Prosperity*. New York: W. W. Norton & Co.

Krugman, Paul. 2001. *Fuzzy Math: The Essential Guide to the Bush Tax Plan*. New York: W. W. Norton & Co .

Krugman, Paul. 2009. *The Return of Depression Economics and the Crisis of 2008*. New York: W.W. Norton & Co.

Krugman, Paul. 2012. *End This Depression Now!* New York: W.W. Norton & Co.

Kuziemko, Ilyana, Michael I. Norton, Emmanuel Saez, and Stefanie Stantcheva. 2015. "How Elastic Are Preferences for Redistribution? Evidence from Randomized Survey Experiments." *American Economic Review* 105 (4): 1478–1508.

Ledbetter, Mark A. 2006. "Comparison of BEA Estimates of Personal Income and IRS Estimates of Adjusted Gross Income." *Survey of Current Business* (November): 29–36.

Lee, Young, and Roger H. Gordon. 2005. "Tax Structure and Economic Growth." *Journal of Public Economics* 89 (5–6): 1027–1043.

Leiserson, Greg, and Jeffrey Rohaly. 2006a. "The Distribution of the 2001–2006 Tax Cuts: Updated Projections, November 2006." Urban-Brookings Tax Policy Center.

Leiserson, Greg, and Jeffrey Rohaly. 2006b. "The Individual Alternative Minimum Tax: Historical Data and Projections, Updated November 2006." Urban-Brookings Tax Policy Center. <http://www.urban.org/sites/default/files/alfresco/publication-pdfs/901012 -The-Individual-Alternative-Minimum-Tax.PDF> (accessed September 7, 2016).

Lent, G. E. 1942. "Collection of the Personal Income Tax at the Source." *Journal of Political Economy* 50 (5): 719–737.

Lenter, David, Douglas Shackelford, and Joel Slemrod. 2003. "Public Disclosure of Corporate Tax Return Information: Accounting, Economics, and Legal Perspectives." *National Tax Journal* 56 (4): 803–830.

Lewin, Tamar. 1991. "I.R.S. Sees Evidence of Wide Tax Cheating on Child Care." *New York Times*, January 6.

Liebman, Jeffrey, and Emmanuel Saez. 2006. "Earnings Responses to Increases in Payroll Taxes." Working paper, University of California, Berkeley, September. <http:// eml.berkeley.edu//~saez/liebman-saezSSA06.pdf> (accessed September 7, 2016).

Lim, Diane, Joel Slemrod, and Eleanor Wilking. 2013. "Expert and Public Attitudes towards Tax Policy: 2013, 1994, and 1934." *National Tax Journal* 66 (4): 775–805.

Liptak, Adam. 2012. "Supreme Court Upholds Health Care Law 5-4, in Victory for Obama." *New York Times*, June 28.

Lugar, Richard. 1995. "My Plan to End the Income Tax." Cato Policy Report, Washington, DC, April 5. <https://www.cato.org/policy-report/julyaugust-1995/plan-end-income-tax> (accessed September 7, 2016).

Lukacs, Oliver. 2008. "Snipes Sentenced to Three Years in Prison." *Tax Notes* 119 (April 28): 352.

Lundeen, Andrew, and Michael Schuyler. 2015. "The Economic Effects of Rand Paul's Tax Reform Plan." The Tax Foundation, June 18, updated October. <http://taxfoundation.org/blog/economic-effects-rand-paul-s-tax-reform-plan> (accessed November 9, 2015).

Luo, Michael, and Stephanie Strom. 2010. "Donor Names Remain Secret as Rules Shift." *New York Times*, September 20.

Luttmer, Erzo F. P., and Monica Singhal. 2014. "Tax Morale." *Journal of Economic Perspectives* 28 (4): 149–168.

Maag, Elaine, Roberton Williams, Jeffrey Rohaly, and James R. Nunns. 2016. "An Analysis of Marco Rubio's Tax Plan." Urban-Brookings Tax Policy Center, February 11. <http://www.taxpolicycenter.org/publications/analysis-marco-rubios-tax-plan/full> (accessed September 7, 2016).

The Maddison Project. 2013. *The Maddison Project, 2013 Version.* <http://www.ggdc.net/maddison/maddison-project/home.htm> (accessed September 7, 2016).

Malmer, Håkan. 1995. "The Swedish Tax Reform in 1990–1991 and Tax Compliance Costs in Sweden." In *Tax Compliance Costs: Measurement and Policy*, ed. Cedric Sandford, 226–262. Bath, UK: Fiscal Publications.

Mankiw, N. Gregory. 2010. "Spreading the Wealth Around: Reflections Inspired by Joe the Plumber: Presidential Address." *Eastern Economic Journal* 36 (3): 285–298.

Marcuss, Rosemary, George Contos, John Guyton, Patrick Langetieg, Allen Lerman, Susan Nelson, Brenda Schafer, and Melissa Vigil. 2013. "Income Taxes and Compliance Costs: How Are They Related?" *National Tax Journal* 66 (4): 833–854.

MarketWatch. 2015. "Timeline: A Short History of QE and the Market." <http://projects.marketwatch.com/short-history-of-qe-and-the-market-timeline/> (accessed August 28, 2015).

Marr, Chuck, and Cye-Ching Huang. 2016. "Trump Tax Plan Includes Major Tax Break for Wealthiest Taxpayers." Center on Budget and Policy Priorities, August 8. <http://www.cbpp.org/sites/default/files/atoms/files/8-8-16tax2.pdf> (accessed September 7, 2016).

Marron, Donald. 2012. "Five Things You Should Know about Mitt Romney's $5 Trillion Tax Cut." Urban-Brookings Tax Policy Center *TaxVox Blog*, October 12. <http://taxvox.taxpolicycenter.org/2012/10/12/five-things-you-should-know-about-mitt-romneys-5-trillion-tax-cut/> (accessed September 7, 2016).

Matthews, Robert Guy. 2005. "Tax Overhaul Proposal Gets Lukewarm Welcome." *The Wall Street Journal*, November 2, D3.

Mayoras, Danielle, and Andrew Mayoras. 2010. "Steinbrenner Goes Out a Real Winner." *Forbes.com*, July 20. <http://www.forbes.com/2010/07/20/yankees-estate-tax-intelligent -investing-steinbrenner.html> (accessed September 7, 2016).

McBride, William. 2012. "What Is the Evidence on Taxes and Growth?" Special Report No. 207, The Tax Foundation, December 18. <http://taxfoundation.org/article/what -evidence-taxes-and-growth> (accessed September 7, 2016).

McCaffery, Edward J. 2002. *Fair Not Flat: How to Make the Tax System Better and Simpler.* Chicago: University of Chicago Press.

McClelland, Robert, and Shannon Mok. 2012. "A Review of Recent Research on Labor Supply Elasticities." Congressional Budget Office Working Paper 2012–12, October. <https://www.cbo.gov/sites/default/files/112th-congress-2011-2012/workingpaper/ 10-25-2012-Recent_Research_on_Labor_Supply_Elasticities_0.pdf> (accessed September 7, 2016).

McCully, Clinton P., Brian C. Moyer, and Kenneth J. Stewart. 2007. "Comparing the Consumer Price Index and the Personal Consumption Expenditures Price Index." *Survey of Current Business* (November): 26–33. <http://www.bea.gov/scb/pdf/2007/11%20 november/1107_cpipce.pdf> (accessed August 4, 2012).

McHardy, A. K. 1992. *Clerical Poll-Taxes of the Diocese of Lincoln, 1377–1381.* Woodbridge, Suffolk, UK: Boydell Press.

McIntyre, Robert S. 1995. *Statement Concerning Proposals for a Flat-Rate Consumption Tax before the Joint Economic Committee.* Washington, DC, May 17. <http://www.ctj.org/html/ tjmjec.htm> (accessed September 30, 2003).

McIntyre, Robert S. 2015. "Ted Cruz's Tax Plan Would Cost $16.2 Trillion over 10 Years —Or Maybe Altogether Eliminate Tax Collection." *Tax Justice Blog*, November 12. <http://www.taxjusticeblog.org/archive/2015/11/ted_cruzs_tax_plan_would _cost.php> (accessed September 7, 2016).

McKee, T. C., and M. D. Gerbing. 1989. "Taxpayer Perceptions of Fairness: The TRA of 1986." Paper presented at the Internal Revenue Service Research Conference, 1989, Washington, DC.

McKinnon, John D. 2012. "More Firms Enjoy Tax-Free Status." *The Wall Street Journal*, January 10.

McKisack, May. 1959. *The Oxford History of England: The Fourteenth Century, 1307–1399.* Oxford: Clarendon Press.

Meghir, Costas, and David Phillips. 2010. "Labour Supply and Taxes." In *Dimensions of Tax Design: The Mirrlees Review*, eds. James Mirrlees, Stuart Adam, Timothy Besley, Richard Blundell, Stephen Bond, Robert Chote, Malcom Gammie, Paul Johnson, Gareth Myles and James Poterba, 203–274. Oxford: Oxford University Press.

Mermin, Gordon, Leonard E. Burman, and Frank Sammartino. 2016. "An Analysis of Senator Bernie Sanders's Tax and Transfer Proposals." Urban-Brookings Tax Policy Center, May 9. <http://www.taxpolicycenter.org/sites/default/files/alfresco/ publication-pdfs/2000786-an-analysis-of-senator-bernie-sanderss-tax-and-transfer -proposals.pdf> (accessed September 7, 2016).

Meyer, Bruce D., and Dan T. Rosenbaum. 2001. "Welfare, the Earned Income Tax Credit, and the Labor Supply of Single Mothers." *Quarterly Journal of Economics* 116 (3): 1063–1114.

Meyer, Bruce D., and James X. Sullivan. 2011. "The Material Well-Being of the Poor and the Middle Class Since 1980." American Enterprise Institute Working Paper No. 2011–04, October 25. <http://www.aei.org/files/2011/10/25/Material-Well-Being-Poor-Middle -Class.pdf> (accessed September 7, 2016).

Mider, Zachary R., and Jesse Drucker. 2016. "Tax Inversion: How U.S. Companies Buy Tax Breaks." *Bloomberg QuickTake*, April 6. <http://www.bloombergview.com/quicktake/ tax-inversion> (accessed September 7, 2016).

Mieszkowski, Peter, and Michael Palumbo. 2002. "Distributive Analysis of Fundamental Tax Reform." In *United States Tax Reform in the Twenty-First Century*, eds. George R. Zodrow and Peter Mieszkowski, 140–178. Cambridge: Cambridge University Press.

Mikesell, John L. 2013. "State Retail Taxes in 2012: The Recovery Continues." *State Tax Notes* 68 (June 24): 1001.

Milazzo, Paul, and Joseph J. Thorndike. 2012. *Tax History Project: Tax History Museum.* Tax Analysts. <http://www.taxhistory.org/www/website.nsf/Web/TaxHistoryMuseum ?OpenDocument> (accessed September 7, 2016).

Mill, John Stuart. 1871. *Utilitarianism.* 4th ed. London: Longmans, Green, Reader, and Dyer.

Mill, John Stuart. 1877. *Principles of Political Economy.* 5th ed. New York: D. Appleton and Company.

Miller, John A. 2000. "Equal Taxation: A Commentary." *Hofstra Law Review* 29 (Winter): 529-545.

Miller, John. 2011. "The People's Budget: A Plan to Get Deficit-Reduction Off Our Backs." *Dollars & Sense: Real World Economics.* <http://www.dollarsandsense.org/archives/ 2011/0911ein.html> (accessed September 7, 2016).

Mills, Lillian F., and George A. Plesko. 2003. "Bridging the Reporting Gap: A Proposal for More Informative Reconciling of Book and Tax Income." *National Tax Journal* 56 (4): 865–893.

Mirrlees, James A. 1971. "An Exploration in the Theory of Optimum Income Taxation." *Review of Economic Studies* 38 (2): 175-208.

Moffitt, Robert, and Mark Wilhelm. 2000. "Taxation and the Labor Supply Decisions of the Affluent." In *Does Atlas Shrug? Economic Consequences of Taxing the Rich*, ed. Joel Slemrod, 193–234. Cambridge, MA and New York: Harvard University Press and the Russell Sage Foundation.

Moore, Elaine, and Ferdinando Giugliano. 2015. "Switzerland Becomes First to Sell 10-Year Debt at Negative Yield." *Financial Times*, April 8.

Moylan, Carol E. 2008. "Employee Stock Options and the National Economic Accounts." *Survey of Current Business* 88 (2): 7–13.

Mulligan, Casey. 2015. *Side Effects and Complications: The Economic Consequences of Health Reform.* Chicago: University of Chicago Press.

Murphy, Andrea. 2014. "America's Largest Private Companies." *Forbes*, November 5. <http://www.forbes.com/sites/andreamurphy/2014/11/05/americas-largest-private -companies-2014/> (accessed September 7, 2016).

Murphy, Liam B., and Thomas Nagel. 2002. *The Myth of Ownership: Taxes and Justice*. Oxford: Oxford University Press.

Myles, Gareth. 2000. "Taxation and Economic Growth." *Fiscal Studies* 21 (1): 141–168.

Nagourney, Adam, and Scott Shane. 2011. "Newly Released Transcripts Show a Bitter and Cynical Nixon in '75.'" *New York Times*, November 10.

Nakamura, Emi, and Jon Steinsson. 2014. "Fiscal Stimulus in a Monetary Union: Evidence from US Regions." *American Economic Review* 104 (3): 753–792.

Naritomi, Joana. 2015. "Consumers as Tax Auditors." Working paper, London School of Economics, July. <https://www.dropbox.com/s/vppbq1wwlp9deim/naritomi _enforcement.pdf?dl=0> (accessed September 7, 2016).

National Bureau of Economic Research. 2015. "Marginal Tax Rates by Income Type." <http://users.nber.org/~taxsim/marginal-tax-rates/> (accessed June 21, 2015).

National Commission on Economic Growth and Tax Reform. 1996. *Unleashing America's Potential: A Pro-Growth, Pro-Family Tax System for the Twenty-first Century*. Galen Institute, Alexandria, VA, January 1.

National Commission on Fiscal Responsibility and Reform. 2010. *The Moment of Truth*. Washington, DC, December. <https://www.fiscalcommission.gov/sites/ fiscalcommission.gov/files/documents/TheMomentofTruth12_1_2010.pdf> (accessed September 7, 2016).

National Public Radio, Kaiser Family Foundation, and Kennedy School of Government. 2003. "National Survey of Americans' Views on Taxes," April. <http://www.npr.org/ news/specials/polls/taxes2003/index.html> (accessed September 7, 2016).

National Taxpayer Advocate. 2012. *2012 Annual Report to Congress, Volume 1*. <http:// www.taxpayeradvocate.irs.gov/2012-Annual-Report/downloads/Volume-1.pdf> (accessed September 7, 2016).

National Taxpayer Advocate. 2013a. *2013 Annual Report to Congress, Volume 1*. <http:// www.taxpayeradvocate.irs.gov/userfiles/file/2013FullReport/Volume-1.pdf> (accessed September 7, 2016).

National Taxpayer Advocate. 2013b. *2013 Annual Report to Congress, Volume 2*. <http:// www.taxpayeradvocate.irs.gov/userfiles/file/2013FullReport/Volume-2-TAS-Research -And-Related-Studies.pdf> (accessed September 7, 2016).

National Taxpayer Advocate. 2013c. *Special Report to Congress: Political Activity and the Rights of Applicants for Tax-Exempt Status*. <http://www.taxpayeradvocate.irs.gov/ userfiles/file/FullReport/Special-Report.pdf> (accessed September 7, 2016).

National Taxpayer Advocate. 2014. *2014 Annual Report to Congress*. <http:// www.taxpayeradvocate.irs.gov/userfiles/file/2014-Annual-Report-to-Congress -Executive-Summary.pdf> (accessed September 7, 2016).

New York Times. 2012a. "Times Topics: Tea Party Movement," updated May 11. <http:// topics.nytimes.com/top/reference/timestopics/subjects/t/tea_party_movement/> (accessed August 3, 2012).

New York Times. 2012b. "Times Topics: Occupy Movement (Occupy Wall Street)," updated May 2. <http://topics.nytimes.com/top/reference/timestopics/organizations/o/occupy_wall_street/> (accessed August 3, 2012).

New York Times. 2012c. "Republican Presidential Candidates on the Issues: Taxes and Spending." <http://elections.nytimes.com/2012/primaries/issues#issue/taxes-spending> (accessed February 11, 2014).

Niskanen, William. 2004. "'Starve the Beast' Does Not Work." *Cato Policy Report* 26 (2): 2.

Nohlgren, Stephen. 2013. "What to Do if You Win the Lottery." *Tampa Bay Times*, South Pinellas Edition, June 7, 1B.

Norris, Floyd. 2013. "A Fine Line Between Social and Political." *New York Times*, May 16.

Nozick, Robert. 1974. *Anarchy, State, and Utopia*. New York: Basic Books.

Nozick, Robert. 1989. *The Examined Life: Philosophical Meditations*. New York: Simon & Schuster.

Nunns, James R., Leonard E. Burman, Jeffrey Rohaly, and Joseph Rosenberg. 2015. "An Analysis of Donald Trump's Tax Plan." Urban-Brookings Tax Policy Center, December. <http://www.taxpolicycenter.org/UploadedPDF/2000560-an-analysis-of-donald-trumps-tax-plan.pdf> (accessed September 7, 2016).

Nunns, James R., Leonard E. Burman, Jeffrey Rohaly, Joseph Rosenberg, and Benjamin R. Page. 2016. "An Analysis of the House GOP Tax Plan." Urban-Brookings Tax Policy Center, September 16. <http://www.taxpolicycenter.org/publications/analysis-house-gop-tax-plan> (accessed September 18, 2016).

Nunns, James R., and Jeffrey Rohaly. 2010. "Preliminary Revenue Estimates and Distributional Analysis of the Tax Provisions in the Bipartisan Tax Fairness and Simplification Act of 2010." Urban-Brookings Tax Policy Center, May 24. <http://www.taxpolicycenter.org/UploadedPDF/412098_wyden_gregg.pdf> (accessed September 7, 2016).

Nyhan, Brendan. 2013. "Shifting the Goalposts on the IRS Scandal." *Columbia Journalism Review*, August 5.

Office of Management and Budget (OMB). 2012. *Budget of the United States Government, Fiscal Year 2013*. Washington, DC: Government Printing Office. <http://www.gpo.gov/fdsys/browse/collectionGPO.action?collectionCode=BUDGET> (accessed September 7, 2016).

Office of Management and Budget (OMB). 2015. *Budget of the United States Government, Fiscal Year 2016*. Washington, DC: Government Printing Office. <http://www.gpo.gov/fdsys/browse/collectionGPO.action?collectionCode=BUDGET> (accessed September 7, 2016).

Office of the Assistant Secretary for Planning and Evaluation, U.S. Department of Health and Human Services. 2016. *Poverty Guidelines*. <https://aspe.hhs.gov/poverty-guidelines> (accessed August 24, 2016).

Okun, Arthur. 1975. *Equality and Efficiency: The Big Tradeoff*. Washington, DC: Brookings Institution Press.

O'Neil, Cherie J., and Karen B. Lanese. 1993. "T.I.N. Requirements and the Child Care Credit: Impact on Taxpayer Behavior." Working paper, University of South Florida, Tampa.

Organisation for Economic Co-operation and Development. 2014a. *Revenue Statistics 2014*. Paris: OECD Publishing. <http://www.oecd-ilibrary.org/taxation/revenue-statistics-2014_rev_stats-2014-en-fr;jsessionid=6ffb85me9bejh.x-oecd-live-02> (accessed September 7, 2016).

Organisation for Economic Co-operation and Development. 2014b. *Consumption Tax Trends 2014: VAT/GST and Excise Rates, Trends and Policy Issues*. Paris: OECD Publishing. <http://dx.doi.org/10.1787/ctt-2014-en> (accessed September 7, 2016).

Organisation for Economic Co-operation and Development. 2015a. *National Accounts of OECD Countries, Volume 2015 Issue 1: Main Aggregates*. <http://www.oecd-ilibrary.org/economics/national-accounts-of-oecd-countries-volume-2015-issue-1_na_ma_dt-v2015-1-en> (accessed September 7, 2016).

Organisation for Economic Co-operation and Development. 2015b. *OECD Economic Outlook, Statistics and Projections*, No. 97, Edition 2015/1 (database). <http://dx.doi.org/10.1787/data-00759-en> (accessed September 7, 2).

Organisation for Economic Co-operation and Development. 2015c. *Revenue Statistics 2015*. Paris: OECD Publishing. <http://www.oecd-ilibrary.org/taxation/revenue-statistics-2015_rev_stats-2015-en-fr> (accessed September 7, 2016).

Organisation for Economic Co-operation and Development. 2015d. *Tax Administration 2015: Comparative Information on OECD and Other Advanced and Emerging Economies*. Paris: OECD Publishing. <http://dx.doi.org/10.1787/23077727> (accessed September 7, 2016).

Organisation for Economic Co-operation and Development. 2015e. *OECD/G20 Base Erosion and Profit Shifting Project, 2015 Final Reports: Explanatory Statement*. Paris: OECD Publishing. <http://www.oecd.org/ctp/beps-explanatory-statement-2015.pdf> (accessed September 7, 2016).

Orszag, Peter R. 2007. "The Taxation of Carried Interest." *Statement before the Committee on Ways and Means, U.S. House of Representatives*, Washington, DC, September 6. <http://www.cbo.gov/sites/default/files/cbofiles/ftpdocs/85xx/doc8599/09-06-carriedinterest_testimony.pdf> (accessed September 7, 2016).

Owyang, Michael T., Valerie A. Ramey, and Sarah Zubairy. 2013. "Are Government Spending Multipliers Greater during Periods of Slack? Evidence from Twentieth-Century Historical Data." *American Economic Review* 103 (3): 129–134.

Ozanian, Mike. 2012. "The Business of Baseball." *Forbes.com*, March 21. <http://www.forbes.com/sites/mikeozanian/2012/03/21/the-business-of-baseball-2012/> (accessed September 7, 2016).

Paradise, Julia. 2015. "Medicaid Moving Forward." The Henry J. Kaiser Family Foundation Issue Brief, March 9. <http://kff.org/health-reform/issue-brief/medicaid-moving-forward/> (accessed September 7, 2016).

Parcell, Ann D. 1996. "Income Shifting in Response to Higher Tax Rates: The Effects of OBRA 93." Paper presented at the Allied Social Science Associations Meetings, San Francisco, January.

Parisi, Michael. 2015. "Individual Income Tax Returns, Preliminary Data, 2013." *IRS Statistics of Income Bulletin* 34 (4): 1–13. <http://www.irs.gov/pub/irs-soi/soi-a-inpd-id1505.pdf> (accessed June 19, 2015).

Parker, Ashley. 2011. "'Corporations Are People,' Romney Tells Iowa Hecklers Angry Over His Tax Policy." *New York Times*, New York Edition, August 12, A16.

Parker, Jonathan A., Nicholas S. Souleles, David S. Johnson, and Robert McClelland. 2013. "Consumer Spending and the Economic Stimulus Payments of 2008." *American Economic Review* 103 (6): 2530–2553.

Pearlman, Ronald A. 1998. "Fresh from the River Styx: The Achilles Heels of Tax Reform Proposals." *National Tax Journal* 51 (3): 569–578.

Pechman, Joseph A. 1987. *Federal Tax Policy.* 5th ed. Washington, DC: Brookings Institution Press.

Peers, Alexandra, and Jeffrey A. Tannenbaum. 1992. "Insiders Race to Exercise Stock Options." *The Wall Street Journal*, December 16, C1.

Perotti, Roberto. 2012. "The Effects of Tax Shocks on Output: Not So Large, but Not Small Either." *American Economic Journal: Economic Policy* 4 (2): 214–237.

Pew Research Center. 2013. "As Sequester Deadline Looms, Little Support for Cutting Most Programs." Washington, DC, February 22. <http://www.people-press.org/2013/02/22/as-sequester-deadline-looms-little-support-for-cutting-most-programs/> (accessed September 7, 2016).

Piketty, Thomas, and Emmanuel Saez. 2003. "Income Inequality in the United States, 1913–1998." *Quarterly Journal of Economics* 118 (1): 1–39. Tables and figures updated through 2015 in June 2016. <http://eml.berkeley.edu//~saez/TabFig2015prel.xls> (accessed September 7, 2016).

Piketty, Thomas, and Emmanuel Saez. 2007. "How Progressive Is the U.S. Federal Tax System? A Historical and International Perspective." *Journal of Economic Perspectives* 21 (1): 3–24.

Piketty, Thomas, Emmanuel Saez, and Stefanie Stantcheva. 2014. "Optimal Taxation of Top Incomes: A Tale of Three Elasticities." *American Economic Journal: Economic Policy* 6 (1): 230–271.

Plumer, Brad. 2013a. "More and More Americans Are Feeling the Effects of the Sequester." *Washington Post Wonkblog*, May 29. <http://www.washingtonpost.com/blogs/wonkblog/wp/2013/05/29/more-americans-are-feeling-the-effects-of-the-sequester/> (accessed September 7, 2016).

Plumer, Brad. 2013b. "Here's What's in the Budget Deal the Senate's Voting On." *Washington Post Wonkblog*, December 17. <http://www.washingtonpost.com/blogs/wonkblog/wp/2013/12/17/heres-whats-in-the-budget-deal-the-senates-voting-on/> (accessed September 7, 2016).

Pogue, Thomas F. 2007. "The Gross Receipts Tax: A New Approach to Business Taxation?" *National Tax Journal* 60 (4): 799–819.

Pomerleau, Kyle. 2016. "Details and Analysis of the 2016 House Republican Tax Reform Plan." Tax Foundation Fiscal Fact No. 516, Washington, DC, July 5. <http://taxfoundation.org/article/details-and-analysis-2016-house-republican-tax-reform-plan> (accessed September 7, 2016).

Pomerleau, Kyle, and Michael Schuyler. 2015. "Details and Analysis of Senator Ted Cruz's Tax Plan." Tax Foundation Fiscal Fact No. 489, Washington, DC, October. <http://taxfoundation.org/sites/taxfoundation.org/files/docs/TaxFoundation_FF489_0.pdf> (accessed September 7, 2016).

Pomerleau, Kyle, and Michael Schuyler. 2016. "Details and Analysis of Hillary Clinton's Tax Proposals." Tax Foundation Fiscal Fact No. 496, Washington, DC, January 26. <http://taxfoundation.org/sites/taxfoundation.org/files/docs/TaxFoundation -FF496.pdf> (accessed September 7, 2016)

Ponnuru, Ramesh. 2007. "The Full McCain: An Interview." *National Review Online.* <http://www.nationalreview.com/articles/220171/full-mccain/interview> (accessed July 5, 2013).

Poterba, James M. 1990. "Taxation and Housing Markets: Preliminary Evidence on the Effects of Recent Tax Reforms." In *Do Taxes Matter? The Impact of the Tax Reform Act of 1986*, ed. Joel Slemrod, 141–160. Cambridge, MA: MIT Press.

Poterba, James M., and Scott Weisbenner. 2001. "The Distributional Burden of Taxing Estates and Unrealized Capital Gains at Death." In *Rethinking Estate and Gift Taxation*, eds. William G. Gale, James R. Hines Jr., and Joel Slemrod, 422–449. Washington, DC: Brookings Institution Press.

Powell, Edgar. 1894. "An Account of the Proceedings in Suffolk during the Peasants' Rising in 1381." [London: Longmans, Green.] *Transactions of the Royal Historical Society* 8: 203–249.

Prescott, Edward C. 2004. "Why Do Americans Work So Much More Than Europeans?" *Federal Reserve Bank of Minneapolis Quarterly Review* 28 (1): 2–13.

President's Advisory Panel on Federal Tax Reform. 2005. *Simple, Fair, and Pro-Growth: Proposal to Fix America's Tax System*. Washington, DC: Government Printing Office. <http://govinfo.library.unt.edu/taxreformpanel/final-report/> (accessed September 7, 2016).

President's Economic Recovery Advisory Board. 2010. *Report on Tax Reform Options: Simplification, Compliance, and Corporate Taxation*. <http://www.whitehouse.gov/sites/default/files/microsites/PERAB_Tax_Reform_Report_for_final_vote.pdf> (accessed September 7, 2016).

Protess, Ben, and Jessica Silver-Greenberg. 2014. "Credit Suisse Pleads Guilty in Felony Case." *New York Times Dealbook*, May 19. <http://dealbook.nytimes.com/2014/05/19/credit-suisse-set-to-plead-guilty-in-tax-evasion-case/> (accessed September 7, 2016).

Purcell, Patrick. 2009. "Retirement Plan Participation and Contributions: Trends from 1998 to 2006." Congressional Research Service, Washington, DC, January 30. <http://digitalcommons.ilr.cornell.edu/key_workplace/598/> (accessed September 7, 2016).

Rabushka, Alvin. 2015. "Countries or Jurisdictions with a Flat Tax as of March 2015," *Blogspot*, March 20. <http://flattaxes.blogspot.com/2015/03/countries-or-jurisdictions -with-flat_20.html> (accessed September 7, 2016).

Ramey, Valerie. 2015. "Macroeconomic Shocks and Their Propagation." Paper presented at the conference for the forthcoming *Handbook of Macroeconomics*, Vol. 2, eds. John B. Taylor and Harald Uhlig. Conference draft available at <http://www.hoover.org/sites/default/files/ramey-shocks_hom_ramey8april.pdf#overlay-context=events/conference -handbook-macroeconomics-vol-2> (accessed September 7, 2016).

Ramirez, John C. 2012. "Reasonable Compensation Analysis for C Corporations and S Corporations." *Willamette Management Associates Insights* (Spring): 46–52. <http://willamette.com/insights_journal/12/spring_2012_8.pdf> (accessed September 7, 2016).

Rawls, John. 1971. *A Theory of Justice*. Cambridge, MA: Harvard University Press.

Recovery.gov. 2012. "Breakdown of Funding by Category." <http://www.recovery.gov/Transparency/fundingoverview/Pages/fundingbreakdown.aspx> (accessed August 17, 2013).

Redburn, Tom. 2008. "Huckabee's Tax Plan Appeals, but Is It Fair?" *New York Times*, January 6.

Reynolds, Alan. 2011. "Why 70% Tax Rates Won't Work." *The Wall Street Journal*, June 16.

Riera-Crichton, Daniel, Carlos A. Vegh, and Guillermo Vuletin. 2016. "Tax Multipliers: Pitfalls in Measurement and Identification." *Journal of Monetary Economics* 79: 30–48.

Rieschick, Jacqueline. 1997. "GOP Lawmakers Step Up Efforts to Turn Tax Code into 'Road Kill.'" *Tax Notes* 76 (September 29): 1661–1662.

Roberts, Michael L., Peggy A. Hite, and Cassie F. Bradley. 1994. "Understanding Attitudes toward Progressive Taxation." *Public Opinion Quarterly* 58 (2): 165–190.

Roberts, Ryan. 2008. "Why Startups are a Corporation for Venture Capital." *Startuplawyer.com*, July 17. <http://startuplawyer.com/venture-capital/why-the-corporation-is-king-for-getting-venture-capital> (accessed January 25, 2014).

Rodrik, Dani. 1997. *Has Globalization Gone Too Far?* Washington, DC: Institute for International Economics.

Roemer, John E. 1998. *Equality of Opportunity*. Cambridge, MA: Harvard University Press.

Romer, Christina D. 1993. "The Nation in Depression." *Journal of Economic Perspectives* 7 (2): 19–39.

Romer, Christina D. 2011. "What Do We Know About the Effects of Fiscal Policy? Separating Evidence from Ideology." Lecture delivered at Hamilton College, November 7. <http://eml.berkeley.edu//~cromer/Written%20Version%20of%20Effects%20of%20Fiscal%20Policy.pdf> (accessed September 7, 2016).

Romer, Christina D., and David H. Romer. 2010. "The Macroeconomic Effects of Tax Changes: Estimates Based on a New Measure of Fiscal Shocks." *American Economic Review* 100 (3): 763–801.

Romer, Christina D., and David H. Romer. 2014. "The Incentive Effects of Marginal Tax Rates." *American Economic Journal: Economic Policy* 6 (3): 242–281.

Romer, Christina D., and David H. Romer. 2016. "Senator Sanders's Proposed Policies and Economic Growth." Institute for New Economic Thinking, February 25. <https://ineteconomics.org/uploads/general/romer-and-romer-evaluation-of-friedman1.pdf> (accessed September 7, 2016).

Romney, Mitt. 2012. "A Tax Reform to Restore America's Prosperity." *The Wall Street Journal*, February 23. <http://online.wsj.com/article/SB10001424052970203960804577239672484987172.html> (accessed August 8, 2013).

Roper Center on Public Opinion Research. 1993. "Survey Data on Ethics." *Public Perspective* 4 (6): 29–34. <http://ropercenter.uconn.edu/public-perspective/ppscan/46/46029.pdf> (accessed September 7, 2016).

Rosen, Sherwin. 1981. "The Economics of Superstars." *American Economic Review* 71 (5): 845–858.

Rosenbaum, David E., and Richard W. Stevenson. 2001. "G.O.P. Lawmakers and White House Agree on Tax Cut." *New York Times*, May 2.

Rosenberg, Joseph, Leonard E. Burman, James R. Nunns, and Daniel Berger. 2016. "An Analysis of Ted Cruz's Tax Plan." Urban-Brookings Tax Policy Center, February 16. <http://www.taxpolicycenter.org/publications/analysis-ted-cruzs-tax-plan/full> (accessed September 7, 2016).

Rubio, Marco. 2015. "Economic Growth and Family Fairness Tax Reform Plan." <http://www.rubio.senate.gov/public/index.cfm/files/serve/?File_id=2d839ff1-f995-427a-86e9-267365609942> (accessed January 10, 2016).

Ruffing, Kathy, and James R. Horney. 2011. "Economic Downturn and Bush Policies Continue to Drive Large Projected Deficits." Center on Budget and Policy Priorities, May 10. <http://www.cbpp.org/files/5-10-11bud.pdf> (accessed September 7, 2016).

Ryan, Paul D. 2008. *H.R. 6110: Roadmap for America's Future Act of 2008.* Washington, DC: Government Printing Office. <http://www.gpo.gov/fdsys/pkg/BILLS-110hr6110ih/pdf/BILLS-110hr6110ih.pdf> (accessed September 7, 2016).

Ryan, Paul D. 2010. *A Roadmap for America's Future, Version 2.0: A Plan to Solve America's Long-Term Economic and Fiscal Crisis,* January. <https://kaiserhealthnews.files.wordpress.com/2010/11/roadmap2final2.pdf> (accessed September 7, 2016).

Ryan, Paul D. 2011. *The Path to Prosperity: Restoring America's Promise. Fiscal Year 2012 Budget Resolution.* House Committee on the Budget, March. <http://budget.house.gov/uploadedfiles/pathtoprosperityfy2012.pdf> (accessed September 7, 2016).

Ryan, Paul D. 2012. *The Path to Prosperity: A Blueprint for American Renewal. Fiscal Year 2013 Budget Resolution.* House Budget Committee, March 20. <http://budget.house.gov/uploadedfiles/pathtoprosperity2013.pdf> (accessed February 11, 2014).

Ryan, Paul D. 2016. *A Better Way: Our Vision for a Confident America -- Tax.* <http://abetterway.speaker.gov/_assets/pdf/ABetterWay-Tax-PolicyPaper.pdf> (accessed September 17, 2016).

Sabelhaus, John. 1993. "What Is the Distributional Burden of Taxing Consumption?" *National Tax Journal* 46 (3): 331–343.

Sablik, Tim. 2013a. "Taxing the Behemoths." *Federal Reserve Bank of Richmond Econ Focus* (3rd Quarter): 28–30. <http://www.richmondfed.org/publications/research/econ_focus/2013/q3/pdf/feature4.pdf> (accessed September 7, 2016).

Sablik, Tim. 2013b. "Recession of 1981–1982." *Federal Reserve History.* <http://www.federalreservehistory.org/Events/DetailView/44> (accessed September 7, 2016).

Saez, Emmanuel. 2002. "The Desirability of Commodity Taxation Under Non-Linear Income Taxation and Heterogeneous Tastes." *Journal of Public Economics* 83 (2): 217–230.

Saez, Emmanuel. 2006. "Income Concentration in a Historical and International Perspective." In *Public Policy and the Income Distribution,* eds. Alan Auerbach, David Card, and John Quigley, 221–258. New York: Russell Sage Foundation.

Saez, Emmanuel, Joel Slemrod, and Seth Giertz. 2012. "The Elasticity of Taxable Income with Respect to Marginal Tax Rates: A Critical Review." *Journal of Economic Literature* 50 (1): 3–50.

Saez, Emmanuel, and Stefanie Stantcheva. 2016. "Generalized Social Marginal Welfare Weights for Optimal Tax Theory." *American Economic Review* 106 (1): 24–45.

Saez, Emmanuel, and Gabriel Zucman. 2016. "Wealth Inequality in the United States since 1913: Evidence from Capitalized Income Tax Data." *Quarterly Journal of Economics* 131 (2): 519–578.

Safire, William. 1995. "The 25 Percent Solution." *New York Times*, April 20, A19.

Sahm, Claudia R., Matthew D. Shapiro, and Joel Slemrod. 2012. "Check in the Mail or More in the Paycheck: Does the Effectiveness of Fiscal Stimulus Depend on How It Is Delivered?" *American Economic Journal: Economic Policy* 4 (3): 216–250.

Sales Tax Institute. 2015. "State Sales Tax Rates." <http://www.salestaxinstitute.com/resources/rates> (accessed July 21, 2015).

Sammartino, Frank, James R. Nunns, Leonard E. Burman, Jeffrey Rohaly and Joseph Rosenberg. 2016. "An Analysis of Senator Bernie Sanders's Tax Proposals." Urban-Brookings Tax Policy Center, March 4. <http://www.taxpolicycenter.org/publications/analysis-senator-bernie-sanderss-tax-proposals/full> (accessed September 7, 2016).

Sanchirico, Chris William. 2008. "The Tax Advantage to Paying Private Equity Fund Managers with Profit Shares: What Is It? Why Is It Bad?" *University of Chicago Law Review* 75 (3): 1071-1154.

Sandford, Cedric, ed. 1995. *Tax Compliance Costs: Measurement and Policy*. Bath, UK: Fiscal Publications.

Schler, Michael L. 2008. "Taxing Partnership Profits Interests as Compensation Income." *Tax Notes* 119 (May 26): 829.

Schroeder, Peter. 2012. "Hill Poll: Likely Voters Prefer Lower Individual, Business Tax Rates." *The Hill*, February 27. <http://thehill.com/polls/212643-hill-poll-likely-voters-prefer-lower-tax-rates-for-individuals-business> (accessed August 23, 2016).

Schumer, Chuck. 2005. "Elimination of State/Local Tax Deductibility a Dagger to Heart of NYers." *Vote Smart*, October 18. <https://votesmart.org/public-statement/131042/schumer-elimination-of-statelocal-tax-deductibility-a-dagger-to-heart-of-nyers#.VpKlXfkrKM9> (accessed September 7, 2016).

Schuyler, Michael, and William McBride. 2015. "The Economic Effects of the Rubio-Lee Tax Reform Plan." Tax Foundation Fiscal Fact No. 457, March. <http://taxfoundation.org/sites/taxfoundation.org/files/docs/TaxFoundation_FF457_1.pdf> (accessed September 7, 2016).

Schwartz, Nelson D., and Charles Duhigg. 2013. "Apple's Web of Tax Shelters Saved It Billions, Panel Finds." *New York Times*, May 20.

Seligman, Edwin R. A. 1914. *The Income Tax: A Study of the History, Theory, and Income Taxation at Home and Abroad*. 2nd ed. New York: MacMillan.

Seligman, Edwin R. A. 1915. *Essays in Taxation*. 8th ed. London: MacMillian.

Shapiro, Isaac. 2016. "Trump and Cruz Tax-Cut Plans Would Shrink Government to Truman-Era Levels." Center on Budget and Policy Priorities, March 29. <http://www.cbpp.org/sites/default/files/atoms/files/3-29-16tax.pdf> (accessed September 7, 2016).

Shapiro, Matthew D., and Joel Slemrod. 2003a. "Consumer Response to Tax Rebates." *American Economic Review* 93 (1): 381–396.

Shapiro, Matthew D., and Joel Slemrod. 2003b. "Did the 2001 Tax Rebate Stimulate Spending? Evidence from Taxpayer Surveys." In *Tax Policy and the Economy*, vol. 17, ed. James M. Poterba, 83–109. Cambridge, MA: MIT Press.

Shaviro, Daniel N. 2007. "Beyond the Pro-Consumption Tax Consensus." *Stanford Law Review* 60 (3): 745–788.

Shaviro, Daniel N. 2014. *Fixing U.S. International Taxation*. Oxford: Oxford University Press.

Sheppard, Lee. 2008. "News Analysis: Reflections on the Death of Transfer Pricing." *Tax Notes* 120 (September 22): 1112.

Shesgreen, Deirdre. 2013. "IRS: Liberal Groups Got Less Scrutiny than Tea Party." *USA Today*, June 27. <http://www.usatoday.com/story/news/politics/2013/06/27/ways-and-means-irs-werfel-tea-party/2461573/> (accessed September 7, 2016).

Shiller, Robert J. 2014. "Home Buyers Are Optimistic but Not Wild-Eyed." *New York Times*, December 13.

Shulman, Douglas H. 2011. *Written Testimony of Douglas H. Shulman, Commissioner Internal Revenue, Before the House Ways & Means Subcommittee on Oversight Filing Season and FY 2012 Budget Request*, March 31. <http://waysandmeans.house.gov/UploadedFiles/Shulman_IRS_Testimony_Before_Ways_and_Means_-_Filing_Season_and_FY2012_Budget.pdf> (accessed September 7, 2016).

Simons, Henry. 1938. *Personal Income Taxation: The Definition of Income as a Problem of Fiscal Policy*. Chicago: University of Chicago Press.

Slemrod, Joel. 1990. "Optimal Taxation and Optimal Tax Systems." *Journal of Economic Perspectives* 4 (1): 157–178.

Slemrod, Joel. 1992. "What Makes a Nation Prosperous, What Makes It Competitive, and Which Goal Should We Strive For?" *Australian Tax Forum* 9 (4): 373–385.

Slemrod, Joel. 1995. "What Do Cross-Country Studies Teach about Government Involvement, Prosperity, and Economic Growth?" *Brookings Papers on Economic Activity* 2: 373–431.

Slemrod, Joel. 1996a. "High-Income Families and the Tax Changes of the 1980s: The Anatomy of Behavioral Response." In *Empirical Foundations of Household Taxation*, eds. Martin Feldstein and James Poterba, 169–188. Chicago: National Bureau of Economic Research and University of Chicago Press.

Slemrod, Joel. 1996b. "Which Is the Simplest Tax System of Them All? " In *The Economic Effects of Fundamental Tax Reform*, eds. Henry Aaron and William Gale, 355–391. Washington, DC: The Brookings Institution.

Slemrod, Joel. 1997. "Measuring Taxpayer Burden and Attitudes for Large Corporations: 1996 and 1992 Survey Results." Office of Tax Policy Research Working Paper 97–1, University of Michigan, Ann Arbor.

Slemrod, Joel. 2004. "Testimony on Income Tax Compliance Costs. Submitted to the Committee on Ways and Means, Subcommittee on Oversight." Hearing on Tax Simplification, Washington, DC, June 15.

Slemrod, Joel. 2006. "The Role of Misperceptions in Support for Regressive Tax Reform." *National Tax Journal* 59 (1): 57–75.

Slemrod, Joel. 2011a. "Does a VAT Promote Exports?" In *The VAT Reader: What a Federal Consumption Tax Would Mean for America*, 186–191. Washington, DC: Tax Analysts.

Slemrod, Joel. 2011b. "How I Learned to Stop Worrying and Love the VAT." *Milken Institute Review*, First Quarter (January): 16–25.

Slemrod, Joel, and Katherine Blauvelt. 2006. "Why Tax Reform Is So Hard." *Milken Institute Review* 8 (1): 16–27.

Slemrod, Joel, and Marsha Blumenthal. 1996. "The Income Tax Compliance Cost of Big Business." *Public Finance Quarterly* 24 (4): 411–438.

Slemrod, Joel, and Wojciech Kopczuk. 2003. "Dying to Save Taxes: Evidence from Estate-Tax Returns on the Death Elasticity." *Review of Economics and Statistics* 85 (2): 256–265.

Smith, Adam. 1937. *The Wealth of Nations*. New York: Random House. (Originally published 1776).

Smith, James. 2008. "That Elusive Elasticity and the Ubiquitous Bias: Is Panel Data a Panacea?" *Journal of Macroeconomics* 30 (2): 760–779.

Smith, Peter. 1991. "Lessons from the British Poll Tax Disaster." *National Tax Journal* 44 (4), part 2: 421–436.

Sørensen, Peter Birch. 2005. "Dual Income Taxation: Why and How?" *FinanzArchiv/Public Finance Analysis* 61 (4): 559–586.

South China Morning Post. 2014. "China, Hong Kong Committed to Global Alliance to End Banking Secrecy." October 30. <http://www.scmp.com/news/china/article/1628574/china-hong-kong-committed-global-alliance-end-banking-secrecy> (accessed September 7, 2016).

State of California Franchise Tax Board. 2006. *ReadyReturn Pilot Tax Year 2004 Study Results*. <https://www.ftb.ca.gov/readyreturn/ty04rrfinalreport.pdf> (accessed September 7, 2016).

State of California Franchise Tax Board. 2014a. *ReadyReturn Toolkit–2013 Filing Season*. <https://www.ftb.ca.gov/aboutFTB/tool_kits/ReadyReturn/2014_Tool_Kit.pdf> (accessed June 30, 2015).

State of California Franchise Tax Board. 2014b. *ReadyReturn No Longer Available*. <https://www.ftb.ca.gov/aboutFTB/Public_Service_Bulletins/2014/37_12232014.shtml> (accessed September 7, 2016)

State of California Franchise Tax Board. 2015. *CalFile Features*. <https://www.ftb.ca.gov/online/Calfile/new_features.shtml?wtsvl=feat1> (accessed September 7, 2016).

Statistics Canada. 2015. "Dwelling Characteristics and Household Equipment, by Province." <http://www.statcan.gc.ca/tables-tableaux/sum-som/l01/cst01/famil133a-eng.htm> (accessed September 7, 2016).

Stein, Ben. 2006. "In Class Warfare, Guess Which Class Is Winning?" *New York Times*, November 26.

Stein, Herbert. 1998. *What I Think: Essays on Economics, Politics, and Life*. Washington, DC: American Enterprise Press.

Steinhauer, Jennifer. 2013. "Divided House Passes Tax Deal in End to Latest Fiscal Standoff." *New York Times*, January 1.

Steinhauer, Jennifer. 2015. "John Boehner, House Speaker, Will Resign from Congress." *New York Times*, September 25.

Stern, Ken. 2013. *With Charity for All*. New York: Doubleday.

Steuerle, C. Eugene. 1986. *Who Should Pay for Collecting Taxes? Financing the IRS.* Washington, DC: American Enterprise Institute.

Steuerle, C. Eugene. 1992. *The Tax Decade: How Taxes Came to Dominate the Public Agenda.* Washington, DC: Urban Institute Press.

Stevenson, Richard W. 2001. "Down Into the Fray." *New York Times*, January 27.

Stevenson, Richard W. 2003. "Bush Signs Tax Cut Bill, Dismissing All Criticism." *New York Times*, May 29.

Strumpf, Dan. 2014. "U.S. Public Companies Rise Again." *The Wall Street Journal*, February 5. <http://www.wsj.com/articles/SB10001424052702304851104579363272107177430> (accessed June 22, 2015).

Suárez Serrato, Juan Carlos, and Owen Zidar. 2016. "Who Benefits from State Corporate Tax Cuts? A Local Labor Markets Approach with Heterogeneous Firms." *American Economic Review* 106 (9): 2582–2624.

Sullivan, Martin. 1996. "What Rate for the Flat Tax?" *Tax Notes* 70 (January 29): 490.

Sullivan, Martin. 2011a. *Testimony Before the Committee on Ways and Means Hearing on the Current Federal Income Tax and the Need for Reform*. <http://www.taxanalysts.com/taxcom/taxblog.nsf/Permalink/UBEN-8DBM72?OpenDocument> (accessed January 7, 2014).

Sullivan, Martin. 2011b. "Economic Analysis: Apple's High Effective Tax Rate Obscures Foreign Tax Benefits." *Tax Notes* 132 (August 1): 459.

Sullivan, Martin. 2013. "Behind GAO's 12.6 Percent Effective Corporate Tax Rate." *Tax Notes* 140 (July 15): 197–200.

Summers, Lawrence H. 2014. "U.S. Economic Prospects: Secular Stagnation, Hysteresis, and the Zero Lower Bound." *Business Economics* (Cleveland, Ohio) 49 (2): 65–73.

Summers, Lawrence H. 2015. "The Fed Looks Set to Make a Dangerous Mistake." *Financial Times*, August 23.

Summers, Lawrence H. 2016. "The Age of Secular Stagnation: What It Is and What to Do About It." *Foreign Affairs* (March/April): 2–9.

Szilagyi, John A. 1990. "Where Have All the Dependents Gone?" In *Internal Revenue Service Trend Analyses and Related Statistics—1990 Update*. Publication 1500 (August). Washington, DC: Internal Revenue Service.

Tait, Alan A. 1988. *Value Added Tax: International Practice and Problems*. Washington, DC: International Monetary Fund.

Tankersley, Jim, and Jeff Guo. 2016. "There Is Math, There Is Fantasy Math, and Then There's Donald Trump's Economic Math." *Washington Post Wonkblog*, April 4. <https://www.washingtonpost.com/news/wonk/wp/2016/04/04/there-is-math-there-is

-fantasy-math-and-then-theres-donald-trumps-economic-math/> (accessed September 7, 2016).

Tanzi, Vito. 1995. *Taxation in an Integrating World*. Washington, DC: Brookings Institution Press.

Tanzi, Vito. 2011. *Governments versus Markets: The Changing Economic Role of the State*. Cambridge: Cambridge University Press.

Tax Foundation. 2012. "Sales Tax Treatment of Groceries, Candy, and Soda as of January 1, 2012," February 16. <http://taxfoundation.org/article/sales-tax-treatment-groceries -candy-and-soda-january-1-2012> (accessed September 7, 2016).

Tax Justice Network. 2014. "OECD's Automatic Information Exchange Standard: A Watershed Moment for Fighting Offshore Tax Evasion?" *International Tax Review*. <http://www.internationaltaxreview.com/pdfs/TJN2014_OECD-AIE-Report.pdf> (accessed September 7, 2016).

Tax-News.com. 2015. "The Common Reporting Standard: Automatic Information Exchange Goes Global." *Tax-News Global Tax News*, September 25. <http://www.tax -news.com/features/The_Common_Reporting_Standard_Automatic_Information _Exchange_Goes_Global__573079.html> (accessed September 7, 2016).

Thaler, Richard H., and Shlomo Benartzi. 2004. "Save More Tomorrow™: Using Behavior Economics to Increase Employee Saving." *Journal of Political Economy* 112 (1): S164–S187.

Thorndike, Joseph. 2002. "Historical Perspective: Promoting Honesty by Releasing Corporate Tax Returns." *Tax Notes* 96 (July 15): 324–325.

Thorndike, Joseph. 2005. "Historical Perspective: What You Don't Know Can Hurt You." *Tax Notes* 106 (April 21): 429.

Toder, Eric, James R. Nunns, and Joseph Rosenberg. 2012. "Implications of Different Bases for a VAT." Urban-Brookings Tax Policy Center, February 14. <http://www .taxpolicycenter.org/UploadedPDF/412501-Implications-of-Different-Bases-for-a-VAT .pdf> (accessed September 7, 2016).

Toder, Eric, and Alan D. Viard. 2014. "Major Surgery Needed: A Call for Structural Reform of the US Corporate Income Tax." Urban-Brookings Tax Policy Center, April 3. <http://www.taxpolicycenter.org/publications/major-surgery-needed-call-structural -reform-us-corporate-income-tax/full> (accessed September 7, 2016).

Toder, Eric, Roberton Williams, Joseph Rosenberg, Samuel Brown, Elaine Maag, Jim Nunns, and Spencer Smith. 2012. "Tax Proposals in the 2013 Budget." Urban-Brookings Tax Policy Center. http://tpcprod.urban.org/taxtopics/upload/2013-Budget-Analysis -FINAL-3.pdf. (accessed September 7, 2016).

Torgler, Benno. 2007. *Tax Compliance and Tax Morale: A Theoretical and Empirical Analysis*. Cheltenham, UK: Edward Elgar Publishing.

Treasury Inspector General for Tax Administration (TIGTA). 2012. *Further Efforts Are Needed to Ensure the Internal Revenue Service Prisoner File Is Accurate and Complete*. Reference No. 2013–40–011, Washington, DC, December 18. <http://www.treasury.gov/tigta/ auditreports/2013reports/201340011fr.pdf> (accessed September 7, 2016).

Treasury Inspector General for Tax Administration (TIGTA). 2013. *Trends in Compliance Activities through Fiscal Year 2012*. Reference No. 2013–30–078, Washington, DC, August

23. <http://www.treasury.gov/tigta/auditreports/2013reports/201330078fr.pdf> (accessed September 7, 2016).

Treasury Inspector General for Tax Administration (TIGTA). 2014a. *Prisoner Tax Refund Fraud: Delays Continue in Completing Agreements to Share Information with Prisons, and Reports to Congress Are Not Timely or Complete.* Reference No. 2014–40–091, Washington, DC, September 26. <http://www.treasury.gov/tigta/auditreports/2014reports/201440091fr.pdf> (accessed September 7, 2016).

Treasury Inspector General for Tax Administration (TIGTA). 2014b. *Trends in Compliance Activities through Fiscal Year 2013.* Reference No. 2014–30–062, Washington, DC, September 12. <http://www.treasury.gov/tigta/auditreports/2014reports/201430062fr.pdf> (accessed September 7, 2016)

Treasury Inspector General for Tax Administration (TIGTA). 2015. *Interim Results of the 2015 Filing Season.* Reference No. 2015–40–032, Washington, DC, March 31. <http://www.treasury.gov/tigta/auditreports/2015reports/201540032fr.pdf> (accessed September 7, 2016).

Tritch, Teresa. 1998. "Six Mistakes Even the Tax Pros Make." *Money* 27 (March): 104–106.

Turk, Alex, Maryamm Muzikir, Marsha Blumenthal, and Laura Kalambokidis. 2007. "Charitable Contributions in a Voluntary Compliance Income Tax System: Itemized Deductions versus Matching Subsidies." In *The IRS Research Bulletin: Proceedings of the 2007 IRS Research Conference,* eds. James Dalton and Martha Gangi, 51–74. Washington, DC: U.S. Internal Revenue Service. <http://www.irs.gov/file_source/pub/irs-soi/07resconf.pdf> (accessed September 7, 2016).

Urban-Brookings Tax Policy Center. 2006a. "Table T06-0306—Current-Law Distribution of Federal Taxes by Economic Income Percentiles," November 30. <http://www.taxpolicycenter.org/numbers/Content/Excel/T06-0306.xls> (accessed September 7, 2016).

Urban-Brookings Tax Policy Center. 2006b. "Table T06-0306—Current-Law Distribution of Federal Taxes By Cash Income Percentiles," November 30. <http://www.taxpolicycenter.org/numbers/Content/Excel/T06-0304.xls> (accessed September 7, 2016).

Urban-Brookings Tax Policy Center. 2007. "Table T07-0086: Number of Tax Units by Tax Bracket, 2006–2007," February 14. <http://www.taxpolicycenter.org/numbers/Content/PDF/T07-0086.pdf> (accessed September 7, 2016).

Urban-Brookings Tax Policy Center. 2010. "Table T10-0252: Bowles-Simpson Deficit Commission, 'Chairmen's Mark' Option 1: The Zero Plan Variant Retaining the Child Tax Credit and Earned Income Tax Credit, Baseline: Current Policy, Distribution of Federal Tax Change by Cash Income Percentile, 2015," November 18. <http://www.taxpolicycenter.org/numbers/Content/Excel/T10-0252.xls> (accessed September 7, 2016).

Urban-Brookings Tax Policy Center. 2012a. "Taxable Estate Tax Returns as a Percentage of Adult Deaths, Selected Years of Death, 1934–2011" November 30. <http://www.taxpolicycenter.org/taxfacts/content/pdf/deaths.pdf> (accessed September 7, 2016).

Urban-Brookings Tax Policy Center. 2012b. "The Romney Plan" (Updated March 1). <http://www.taxpolicycenter.org/taxtopics/romney-plan.cfm> (accessed July 1, 2012).

Urban-Brookings Tax Policy Center. 2012c. "Table T12-0273: Options to Repeal or Limit Itemized Deductions, Impact on Tax Revenue (billions of current dollars), 2013–2022." October 17. <http://taxpolicycenter.org/numbers/displayatab.cfm?Docid=3590 &DocTypeID=5> (accessed September 7, 2016).

Urban-Brookings Tax Policy Center. 2012d. "Capital Gains and Taxes Paid on Capital Gains," November 20. <http://www.taxpolicycenter.org/taxfacts/Content/PDF/ source_historical_cg.pdf> (accessed September 7, 2016).

Urban-Brookings Tax Policy Center. 2013. "Table T13-0239—Distribution of Federal Payroll and Income Taxes by Expanded Cash Income Level, 2014," September 9. <http:// www.taxpolicycenter.org/numbers/Content/Excel/T13-0239.xls> (accessed September 7, 2016).

Urban-Brookings Tax Policy Center. 2015a. "T15-0039-Baseline Distribution of Income and Federal Taxes, All Tax Units, by Expanded Cash Income Percentile, 2015," June 30. <http://www.taxpolicycenter.org/numbers/displayatab.cfm?Docid=4213&DocTypeID =2> (accessed September 7, 2016).

Urban-Brookings Tax Policy Center. 2015b. "T15-0049-Effective Federal Tax Rates, All Tax Units, by Expanded Cash Income Percentile, 2015, Baseline Current Law," June 23. <http://www.taxpolicycenter.org/numbers/displayatab.cfm?Docid=4223&DocTypeID =2> (accessed September 7, 2016).

Urban-Brookings Tax Policy Center. 2015c. "T15-0059-Share of Federal Taxes, All Tax Units, by Expanded Cash Income Percentile, 2015, Baseline: Current Law," June 23. <http://www.taxpolicycenter.org/numbers/displayatab.cfm?Docid=4233&DocTypeID =2> (accessed September 7, 2016).

Urban-Brookings Tax Policy Center. 2015d. "Brief Description of the Tax Model." <http:// www.taxpolicycenter.org/resources/brief-description-tax-model> (accessed September 17, 2016).

Urban-Brookings Tax Policy Center. 2015e. "Major Candidate Tax Proposals." <http:// apps.urban.org/features/tpccandidate/> (accessed December 14, 2015).

Urban-Brookings Tax Policy Center. 2015f. "AMT Preference Items 2002, 2004–2012," March 18. <http://www.taxpolicycenter.org/taxfacts/Content/Excel/amt_preference .xls> (accessed September 7, 2016).

Urban-Brookings Tax Policy Center. 2015g. "Table T15-0018—Aggregate AMT Projections, 2014–2025," June 23. <http://www.taxpolicycenter.org/numbers/Content/Excel/ T15-0018.xls> (accessed September 7, 2016).

U.S. Bureau of Economic Analysis. 2015. *National Income and Product Accounts of the United States.* <http://bea.gov/national/index.htm> (accessed August 9, 2015).

U.S. Bureau of Labor Statistics. 2015. Bureau of Labor Statistics Home Page. <http:// www.bls.gov> (accessed June 18, 2015).

U.S. Bureau of Labor Statistics. 2016. *Labor Force Statistics from the Current Population Survey.* <http://www.bls.gov/cps/lfcharacteristics.htm> (accessed August 24, 2016).

U.S. Census Bureau. 1992. *Measuring the Effect of Benefits and Taxes on Income and Poverty: 1992.* Current Population Reports, Series P60, No. 186RD, September. <http://www .census.gov/hhes/www/poverty/publications/p60-186rd.pdf> (accessed January 23, 2013).

U.S. Census Bureau. 2014. *Historical Income Tables: Households* . <http://www.census.gov/ hhes/www/income/data/historical/household/> (accessed July 16, 2015.)

U.S. Census Bureau. 2015a. *Housing Vacancies and Homeownership (CPS/HVS) Annual Statistics 2014* . <http://www.census.gov/housing/hvs/data/ann14ind.html> (accessed September 7, 2016).

U.S. Census Bureau. 2015b. *Annual Estimates of the Resident Population by Sex, Age, Race, and Hispanic Origin for the United States and States: April 1, 2010 to July 1, 2014: 2014 Population Estimates,* June. <http://factfinder.census.gov/faces/tableservices/jsf/ pages/productview.xhtml?pid=PEP_2014_PEPASR6H&prodType=table> (accessed September 7, 2016).

U.S. Congress. 1913. *Congressional Record.* 63d Cong., 1st sess., 1Vol. 50, pt. 3840.

U.S. Congress, Senate. 1995. *Freedom and Fairness Restoration Act of 1995.* 104th Cong., 1st sess., S. Doc. 1050.

U.S. Department of the Treasury. 1984. *Tax Reform for Fairness, Simplicity and Economic Growth.* Washington, DC: Government Printing Office.

U.S. Department of the Treasury. 1992. *Report of the Department of Treasury on Integration of the Individual and Corporate Tax Systems.* Washington, DC: Government Printing Office. <https://www.treasury.gov/resource-center/tax-policy/Documents/Report -Integration-1992.pdf> (accessed September 7, 2016).

U.S. Department of the Treasury. 2003. *General Explanations of the Administration's Fiscal Year 2004 Revenue Proposals,* February. <https://www.treasury.gov/resource-center/tax-policy/Documents/General-Explanations-FY2004.pdf> (accessed September 7, 2016).

U.S. Department of the Treasury. 2011. *Investing in U.S. Competitiveness: The Benefits of Enhancing the Research and Experimentation (R&E) Tax Credit,* March 25. <https:// www.treasury.gov/resource-center/tax-policy/Documents/Report-Investing-in-US -Competitiveness-2011.pdf> (accessed September 7, 2016).

U.S. Department of the Treasury. 2012. *The President's Framework for Business Tax Reform: A Joint Report by The White House and the Department of the Treasury.* Washington, DC, February. <https://www.treasury.gov/resource-center/tax-policy/tax-analysis/ Documents/OTA-Report-Business-Tax-Reform-2012.pdf> (accessed September 7, 2016).

U.S. Department of the Treasury, Internal Revenue Service. 2015. *Internal Revenue Code, Section 213(f).* <https://www.law.cornell.edu/uscode/text/26/213> (accessed December 20, 2015).

U.S. Department of the Treasury, Office of Tax Analysis. 1996. "'New' Armey-Shelby Flat Tax Would Still Lose Money, Treasury Finds." *Tax Notes* 70, January 22: 451–461.

U.S. House of Representatives, Committee on the Budget. 2015. *Fiscal Year 2016 Budget.* <http://budget.house.gov/fy2016/> (accessed September 7, 2016).

U.S. House of Representatives, Committee on Ethics. 2013. *The House Gift Rule.* <http:// ethics.house.gov/gifts/house-gift-rule> (accessed July 24, 2013).

U.S. House of Representatives, Committee on Ways and Means. 2013. *Committee Members.* <http://waysandmeans.house.gov/about/members.htm> (accessed July 24, 2013).

U.S. Senate Committee on Finance. 2012. *Summary of the Middle Class Tax Relief and Job Creation Act of 2012,* February 16. <http://www.finance.senate.gov/newsroom/

chairman/release/?id=c42a8c8a-52ad-44af-86b2-4695aaff5378> (accessed September 7, 2016).

U.S. Social Security Administration. 2015. *Benefits Planner: Maximum Taxable Earnings (1937–2015).* <http://www.socialsecurity.gov/planners/maxtax.htm> (accessed June 24, 2015).

Varian, Hal. 1980. "Redistributive Taxation as Social Insurance." *Journal of Public Economics* 14 (1): 49–68.

Varian, Hal. 2001. "Economic Scene: In the Debate over Tax Policy, the Power of Luck Shouldn't be Overlooked." *New York Times*, May 3, C2.

Ventry, Dennis. 2011. "Americans Don't Hate Taxes, They Hate Paying Taxes." *University of British Columbia Law Review* 44 (3): 835–889.

Viard, Alan. 2008. "The Taxation of Carried Interest: Understanding the Issues." *National Tax Journal* 61 (3): 445–460.

Vickrey, William. 1977. "Design of Taxes to Minimize Evasion." Paper presented at a conference on Tax Losses in Turkey and Preventive Measures, Istanbul, October. Economic and Social Studies Conference Board, English Supplement, pp. 27–37.

vos Savant, Marilyn. 1994. "Ask Marilyn." *Newsday Parade Magazine.* April 10, 12.

von Schanz, Georg. 1896. "Der Einkommensbegriff und die Einkommensteuergesetze." *Finanz-Archiv* 13: 1–87.

Warren, Alvin C. 1996. "How Much Capital Income Taxed under an Income Tax Is Exempt under a Cash Flow Tax?" *New York University Tax Law Review* 52 (Fall): 1–16.

Weisbach, David A. 2000. "Ironing Out the Flat Tax." *Stanford Law Review* 52 (3): 599–664.

Weisman, Jonathan. 2013a. "Senate Passes Legislation to Allow Taxes on Affluent to Rise." *New York Times*, January 1.

Weisman, Jonathan. 2013b. "Stories of Struggle and Creativity as Sequestration Cuts Hit Home." *New York Times*, May 5.

Weisman, Jonathan. 2013c. "I.R.S. Spent $4.1 Million on Conference, Audit Finds." *New York Times*, June 4.

Weisman, Jonathan. 2013d. "Documents Show Liberals in I.R.S. Dragnet." *New York Times*, June 24.

Weisman, Jonathan. 2014. "House and Senate Negotiators Agree on Spending Bill." *New York Times*, January 13.

Weisman, Jonathan, and Ashley Parker. 2013. "Republicans Back Down, Ending Crisis Over Shutdown and Debt Limit." *New York Times*, October 16.

Weisman, Jonathan, and Ashley Parker. 2014. "House Approves Higher Debt Limit Without Condition." *New York Times*, February 11.

Wessel, David. 2010. "Channeling Milton Friedman." *The Wall Street Journal*, October 28.

White House, Office of the Press Secretary. 2010. *Financial Crisis Responsibility Fee,* January 14. <https://www.whitehouse.gov/sites/default/files/financial_responsibility_fee_fact_sheet.pdf> (accessed September 7, 2016).

Whitney, Craig R. 1990. "London's Tax Riot Is Called the Work of a Violent Minority." *New York Times*, April 2, 11.

The Who. 1972. "Going Mobile (vocal performance)." By Pete Townshend. Recorded May 1971, with Keith Moon and Jon Entwistle. On *Who's Next*, Decca, MCA, Track, Polydor.

Williams, Roberton. 2013. "Taxing Millionaires: Obama's Buffett Rule." Tax Policy Center *TaxVox Blog*, April 11 <http://taxvox.taxpolicycenter.org/2013/04/11/taxing -millionaires-obamas-buffett-rule/> (accessed January 2, 2014).

Williams, Roberton, and Lydia Austin. 2015. "Income Tax Issues: How Do Phaseouts of Tax Provisions Affect Taxpayers?" Urban-Brookings Tax Policy Center, March 4. <http:// www.taxpolicycenter.org/briefing-book/background/issues/phaseouts.cfm> (accessed June 23, 2015).

Wilson, Daniel J. 2012. "Fiscal Spending Jobs Multipliers: Evidence from the 2009 American Recovery and Reinvestment Act." *American Economic Journal: Economic Policy* 4 (3): 251–282.

Wilson, Janette, and Pearson Liddell. 2010. "Sales of Capital Assets Reported on Individual Tax Returns, 2007." *IRS Statistics of Income Bulletin*. 29 (3): 75–104.

Wilson, John. 1999. "Theories of Tax Competition." *National Tax Journal* 52 (2): 269–304.

Witte, John F. 1985. *The Politics and Development of the Federal Income Tax.* Madison: University of Wisconsin Press.

Wood, Robert J. 2014. "10 Facts About FATCA, America's Manifest Destiny Law Changing Banking Worldwide." *Forbes* 19 (August 19). <http://www.forbes.com/sites/ robertwood/2014/08/19/ten-facts-about-fatca-americas-manifest-destiny-law -changing-banking-worldwide/#1aa92ef21961> (accessed April 17, 2016).

World Bank. 2015. *World Development Indicators.* <http://data.worldbank.org/data -catalog/world-development-indicators> (accessed July 28, 2015).

Yagan, Danny. 2015. "Capital Tax Reform and the Real Economy: The Effects of the 2003 Dividend Tax Cut." *American Economic Review* 105 (12): 3531–3563.

Yellen, Janet L. 2015. "Inflation Dynamics and Monetary Policy." Speech delivered at the University of Massachusetts, Amherst, September 24. <http://www.federalreserve.gov/ newsevents/speech/yellen20150924a.pdf> (accessed September 7, 2016).

Yitzhaki, Shlomo. 1974. "A Note on 'Income Tax Evasion: A Theoretical Analysis.'" *Journal of Public Economics* 3 (2): 201–202.

Zodrow, George. 2010. "Capital Mobility and Tax Competition." *National Tax Journal* 63 (4), part 2: 865–902.

Zucman, Gabriel. 2014. "Taxing Across Borders: Tracing Personal Wealth and Corporate Profits." *Journal of Economic Perspectives* 28 (4): 121–148.

Zucman, Gabriel. 2015. *The Hidden Wealth of Nations: The Scourge of Tax Havens.* Chicago: University of Chicago Press.

Zwick, Eric, and James Mahon. 2017. "Tax Policy and Heterogeneous Investment Behavior." *American Economic Review* 107 (1): 217–248.

Index

Ability to consume, 28–30
Ability-to-pay principle
  benefit principle and, 90–94, 430n21,
    437n90
  complexity issues and, 237–240
  consumption tax alternatives and, 349,
    356, 370
  degree of sacrifice and, 94–95
  enforceability and, 237–240
  fairness and, 90–95, 136, 138–139, 237,
    239–240, 316, 323, 327–330, 349, 356, 370
  reform and, 316–317, 323, 327, 329–330
  tax progressivity and, 349
Administrative costs, 94, 230, 234, 364,
    467n41, 468n56
Adverse selection, 322, 324
Aetna, 266
Aging population, 2, 69, 164–168
Alesina, Alberto, 189, 443n84
Alternative minimum tax (AMT)
  adjusted gross income (AGI) and, 80–81
  budget implications of, 74
  business income and, 56
  complexity issues and, 246–247
  corporate, 64–65, 451n62
  Economic Growth and Tax Relief
    Reconciliation Act (EGTRRA) and,
    76–77, 80–81
  exemptions and, 56, 74–75, 425n70
  George W. Bush and, 77
  inflation and, 56, 74, 78, 81
  Internal Revenue Service (IRS) and,
    64–65, 74
  Jobs and Growth Tax Relief
    Reconciliation Act (JGTRRA) and,
    76–77
  Obama and, 77–78
  patches for, 76–77, 81

personal, 56–57, 74–75
reform and, 394–400
Romney and, 78
small businesses and, 399
tax treatment of, 56–57, 425n71
Altig, David, 385–386
American Opportunity Tax Credit, 59,
    73–74, 78, 81, 83, 214–215
American Recovery and Reinvestment
    Act (ARRA), 72–74, 78, 81, 154, 427n102
Americans for Tax Reform (ATR), 458n22
American Taxpayer Relief Act (ATRA), 3,
    67, 69, 80–82, 246, 426n82
Anarchy, State and Utopia (Nozick), 93
Apple, Inc., 41, 250, 258, 265, 453n100
Armey, Richard, 355
Armey-Shelby flat tax, 378–379,
    466nn36,38, 468n62
Armour, Philip, 431n32
Arm's length transfer pricing, 261, 267
Au, Joey, 441n60
Audits
  discriminant index formula (DIF) and,
    275
  enforceability and, 234, 253, 255–256,
    275–278, 281–286
  IRS and, 7–8, 216, 234, 253, 255–256,
    275–278, 281–286, 332, 352, 364, 452n91,
    456n160, 460n48
  reduction of, 282–283
Auerbach, Alan, 167, 385
Average tax rate
  complexity issues and, 284
  economic prosperity and, 181, 227
  fairness and, 89–90, 109, 120–127, 131,
    139, 433nn47,49, 436n75
  reform and, 290–292, 456n1
  treatment of, 54–55, 424n67